FINANCIAL MANAGEMENT IN NONPROFIT ORGANIZATIONS

SECOND EDITION

RICHARD F. WACHT, Ph.D

1991

Georgia State University
Business Press
College of Business Administration
Atlanta, Georgia

Library of Congress Cataloging-in-Publication Data

Wacht, Richard F.
    Financial management in nonprofit organizations.

    Includes bibliographical references and index.
    ISBN 0-88406-214-7
    1. Corporations, Nonprofit—Finance. I. Title.
HG4027.65.W33   1991
658.15—dc 20   90-4446
                                                                                CIP

Georgia State University Business Press
College of Business Administration
University Plaza
Atlanta, Georgia 30303-3093

94 93 92 91   5 4 3 2

Georgia State University, a unit of the University System of Georgia, is an
equal opportunity/affirmative action employer.

Printed in the United States of America.

Cover design by Patton H. McGinley, Jr.

This book
is dedicated to
three very special ladies,
Linda, JoAnn, and Margie

Contents

Preface

The first edition of *Financial Management in Nonprofit Organizations* was the first financial management text written specifically for those interested in the finance function of nonprofit organizations. It was literally a pioneering effort; the first to argue and present formal proof that for-profit firms and nonprofit organizations are inherently different and, hence, must operate with different sets of financial management decision rules developed within different theoretical frameworks. This second edition builds on the foundation laid by its predecessor. The new text introduces refinements to both the theory and practice of financial management in the nonprofit context, but it retains the basic framework and organization that gained acceptance for the first edition.

The following excerpt, taken from the preface of the first edition, explains why a text devoted exclusively to nonprofit organization is necessary: "The theoretical foundation on which this book is based has developed at a painfully slow pace since its beginnings in the post World War II years. Most of the earlier literature appeared in the area of welfare economics and addressed the resource-allocation problems at the federal government level. The growth of the nonprofit sector of the economy (and the health care industry in particular), beginning in the late 1960s and continuing through the 1970s, brought about a change in emphasis, however, away from welfare economics and toward management decisions in organizations in which the profit motive is absent. Nevertheless, most of the new literature at that time was concerned with transferring extant theory and decision techniques from the for-profit context to nonprofit organizations. Consequently, very little of it broke new theoretical ground.

"Those who chose the 'transfer of technology' route to improving management decisions in the nonprofit context were most likely motivated by the fact that the technology they were working with was (and is) excellent. The justification for applying tools that work well in a business setting to the problems facing what easily can be termed quasi-business organizations, superficially at least, is compelling. But in the final analysis, the transfer of technology in this instance has the effect of redefining the nonprofit organization to fit the requirements of the for-profit financial management theory. And that clearly is improper by any standard."

Organization of the Book

Parts I and II of this book enable the reader to distinguish between a profit-seeking business firm and a nonprofit organization in terms of corporate goals, management structure, accounting systems, and financial requirements. This material also provides a definition of the nonprofit organization that justifies the use of the theory presented therein.

The rest of the book is devoted to explaining how to apply financial management decision rules. Some of these decision rules are similar to those used in the for-profit context, but most are not. And most of those that are not were developed and tested with the assistance of finance practitioners who could not find the help they needed from referencing standard financial management textbooks or consulting with businesspeople.

Again, an excerpt from the first edition's preface is appropriate to explain the need for a financial decision guide for nonprofits only:

"The approach used to gain insight into how the finance function of a nonprofit organization is supposed to work and to formulate financial decision rules was simply to go to the source. Experience proved that most nonprofit organizations face particular financial problems that become perennial issues with which management must constantly deal. In each case the financial officer defined the problems facing him or her in terms that almost invariably suggested that the solution he or she required did not fit the profit or wealth-maximizing framework used in business situations. Instead, the outcome the nonprofit practitioner looked for in decision making was avoidance of current or future financial crises while providing sufficient financial resources to accomplish the organization's basic mission. In almost every situation, the traditional (i.e., the for-profit) approach did not provide a satisfactory solution, as judged by the practitioner. And this was because the result of the transfer of technology was directed toward wealth maximization rather than the avoidance of insolvency or illiquidity — the basic financial management problems facing nonprofit organizations."

Changes in the Second Edition

A survey of the readers of the first edition suggested that the text be directed more toward the smaller nonprofit organizations — those whose annual budgets were in the tens and hundreds of thousands of dollars.

This was done. And at the same time, the examples presented in the text were revised where possible by using actual data provided by smaller nonprofit organizations, however, the names of the organizations were changed to provide anonymity. Almost every chapter in Parts II through V was tailored to this requirement.

Chapter 19 is new. It deals with managing financial distress in the nonprofit organizations. Its approach is that of curing the problem and not merely treating the symptoms.

Using the Book

This is a multilevel text suitable for use as a primary or supplementary text in a college or university undergraduate or graduate classroom or in a program of continuing education for the managers who work in the nonprofit context. It also can be useful as a reference book for academicians, consultants, researchers, or practitioners.

The book stresses the basics of financial management in the nonprofit context. Consequently, it contains a blend of equal parts of institutional and descriptive material and practical applications of financial management theory. Both are presented within a setting of the realities of the finance function in the nonprofit organization.

Based on the readers' comments, the textbook flavor of the first edition was retained, but upgraded to include computer assists and graded end-of-chapter materials. These reader assists include bibliographies, review questions, and problem sets and solutions. Also, a new study guide is available to provide added practice on problems and key review questions. An end-of chapter bibliography of suggested further reading assignments provides the student with an alternative source of information that will either extend or enrich the text material. The use of these outside readings is strongly encouraged.

Each chapter also contains a set of questions based on the material presented in that chapter. The questions are relatively brief and concentrate mainly on general principles and definitions. The purpose of the questions is to enable the students to determine on their own how well they understand the material they have just read.

Finally, where appropriate, end-of-chapter problems are included to give the student the opportunity to use the tools and techniques present in the chapter assignments. The problems are simple, yet challenging, and represent extensions to the examples and illustrations included in the text.

Acknowledgments

I received much assistance from many quarters in preparing both editions of this book. Not all of my debts to others can be adequately acknowledged here, but the principal ones, at least, must be enumerated.

The text could not have developed as quickly as it did had it not been for the encouragement and assistance on the initial drafts of certain chapters by Professor Charles A. D'Ambrosio, University of Washington. Dr. Bruce D. Fielitz, Atlanta Capital Corporation, and Professors David A. Walker, Georgetown University, and Rodney L. Roenfeldt, University of South Carolina, provided constructive critical reviews of parts of the manuscript in various stages of completion. I am grateful to these gentlemen for their assistance.

My thanks goes to Dr. Clayton B. Doss, Georgia State University, for his involving me in many research projects relating to the real world of nonprofit organizations. Many of the insights I gained concerning the subject matter contained in most of the nineteen chapters of this book were obtained as a result of his kind offices.

Special thanks goes to Samanta B. Thapa, Hung-Gay Fung, and Laura Weston, for their assistance in preparing, previewing, and reviewing parts of the first edition text, questions, and problems. The excellent assistance of Bonnie I.T. Stringfield, CPA, in the preparation of the second edition, is likewise acknowledged. She prepared and computerized most of the end-of-chapter questions and problems and did a yeoman's service in developing the materials for the study guide. I also acknowledge a debt of thanks to the staff of Georgia State University Business Press, especially R. Cary Bynum, director; Margaret F. Stanley, editing and production manager; and Edith Kilgo, assistant editor; for their assistance in transforming the manuscript into the bound volume.

While I am indeed grateful to all those just named, I must bear final responsibility for the quality of the product. I am thus culpable for all errors of whatever sort that may have crept into my work. I hope these are few and that they will find a forgiving readership.

PART I

INTRODUCTION

The introduction to financial management in nonprofit organizations consists of three topics, each of which is presented and discussed in the first three chapters of this book. The first chapter examines the role of the financial manager in the nonprofit context and how this role differs from that filled by the financial manager in the for-profit context. The second chapter examines the operational and legal characteristics of nonprofit organizations in order to emphasize those aspects of their operations that impact directly on the financial manager's areas of interest and concern. Finally, chapter 3 presents the basic theoretical framework within which the financial management decision tools and techniques presented in this book have been developed. Together these three chapters provide the foundation on which the entire book rests. The material they contain obviously is important and thus warrants careful study.

1

The Role of the Financial Manager

This book defines and describes the role of the financial officer of a nonprofit organization. This role is based on a financial management theory applicable only to nongovernment, nonhospital organizations that operate without the profit motive. The role is described in terms of a set of financial decision rules that are based on the nonprofit financial management theory and are consonant with the legal and operational environment in which the nonprofit organization functions.

The justification for a finance theory applicable only to nonprofit organizations is presented in the first section of this chapter. The job of the financial manager is described in general terms in the second section, and the third section outlines the organization of the book.

FINANCIAL MANAGEMENT IN NONPROFIT CONTEXTS

The modern theory of financial management of the profit-seeking nonfinancial corporation was created and underwent rapid development during the 1960s. Today there exists a highly refined and thoroughly tested set of normative decision rules that are widely used to guide the analyses and decisions of financial managers in the for-profit context. Most theoreticians, as well as many practitioners, continue to assume that this theory of financial management can be transferred more or less intact to the nonprofit context. Readily apparent differences in the financial aspects of the nonprofit organization versus the profit-seeking corporation often are mitigated by the theorists by modifying the applicable decision rules rather than by altering the underlying theory.

Unfortunately, this approach to developing financial decision rules for

3

nonprofit organizations results in a hit-and-miss mixture of approaches characterized by selectively successful applications in one group of organizations (e.g., schools or museums) and failure in application in other groups. The apologists for the transfer-of-technology approach attribute the uneven success of the theory in application to the fact that managers of nonprofit organizations are faced with decision making in a multigoal framework. Thus, failures are most often attributed to the complexity of the goal structure or the misstatement of the goals facing the decision maker rather than from any inherent weakness in the theoretical structure itself.

The approach taken in this book supports the alternative conclusion; that is, *the for-profit finance theory does not fit the nonprofit organization and hence cannot be transferred thereto with good effect.* Several obvious and compelling reasons support this conclusion.

First, the for-profit finance theory specifies the firm's goal as the maximization of shareholder (owner) wealth, or the maximization of the *market value* of the firm's outstanding securities. This goal cannot be pursued by managers of legally constituted nonprofit organizations because they are not privately-owned entities. To qualify for and retain its nonprofit status, an organization must not permit related individuals to benefit economically from their association with it. Further, since no economic benefits attach to ownership (equity) claims of nonprofit entities, their monetary values must at all times be equal to zero dollars and therefore cannot be maximized.

Second, if society were to be designated as the true owner of all nonprofit organizations, as some theorists argue, benefits would be measured in terms of the market values of the goods and services that these entities provide. But these market values are not generally measureable because (1) volunteer services and external subsidies prevent measurement of the cost of the services, and (2) many such goods and services are provided either free or at below the (real economic) cost to society. Market values are thus both unobservable and subject to serious errors in estimation when viewed from either the cost or sales-price perspective.

Finally, if estimating methodologies could be refined sufficiently to overcome the measurement problem, another major problem in transferring the theory still exists, particularly in those organizations that sell their products of services at prices below their market values. Recognize that society is first *a consumer* of the nonprofit organization's products and services. If we allow that it is also the sole owner of the organization, it follows that society's wealth (utility) remains unchanged whether the organization sells its product or service above, at, or below cost. This is because, in these pricing policy matters, the owners' loss is the consumers' gain, and *vice versa*. Since the owners *are* the consumers under this assumption, no actual transfer of wealth occurs when the cost-price relationship of goods or services is changed.

For-profit finance theory focuses strictly on owner's wealth, and thus is incapable of dealing with societal wealth as an objective. Further, a nonprofit organization that bases its operations on for-profit decision rules could easily advance societal wealth while becoming bankrupt. This is because society will accept increased utility as its share from the entity's operations, but creditors demand cash.

Clearly, the improvement of financial-management practice in the nonprofit context depends on discarding the for-profit finance theory—at least in part—and applying instead a theoretical structure capable of guiding its financial decision making. The need for a book dealing exclusively with financial management in nonprofit contexts is thus clearly established.

THE ROLE OF THE FINANCIAL MANAGER

To many individuals, the terms *finance* and *accounting* are synonymous. Such is not the case, however. Accounting is the language used to describe the results of economic activity. Accounting is concerned with measuring and disclosing the results of the processes that governments, businesses, and nonprofit organizations use to convert existing resources into consumable goods and services or to effect the transfer of those resources intact to another organization, individual, or group. Accounting is therefore more concerned with the *historical* performance of an entity than with its future prospects.

Finance, however, is concerned with managing the resources of an economic entity for the purpose of influencing the *future* outcome of its operations. Specifically, the financial manager of a nonprofit organization normally plays the major role in (1) planning and measuring the organization's need for funds, (2) raising the necessary funds, (3) and making certain that the funds acquired are properly employed.

Occasionally, the financial manager may be called on to take part in solving special, nonrecurring problems, such as those arising from the creation of a new organization or the dissolution of an operating entity. While these are not generally the sole responsibility of the financial officer, they certainly have significant financial implications to which he or she must attend. In these instances financial managers generally are called upon to place value on assets being considered for purchase, estimate future cash flows associated with both individual projects and total operations, evaluate the impact of prospective new investments and programs on the organization's operations, and choose among alternative uses of money on hand.

Measuring the Need for Funds

Because the financial manager is constantly involved in the long-range planning of the organization, he or she must acquire a broad, overall view of its operations. The most vital concerns of the office are with the plans for expansion, replacement of certain assets, and other similar activities that will create a need for unusually large amounts of cash. On the basis of such plans, along with production, cost, and revenue estimates, the financial manager must attempt to measure the flow of cash into and out of the organization over the near future, not only for the continuation of current operations but also in light of the new projects that management may be considering for the future.

We shall see that the financial manager's main concern is with the financial and operating cash flows, both in and out of the enterprise. This is true both on a project basis and for the organization as a whole. If the value of the expected cash inflows for a project or an entity exceeds the value of the cash required to achieve those inflows, the financial manager will approve the plan or plans. Otherwise he or she must formulate alternative financial plans capable of achieving that desirable result.

In developing the plans, the financial manager expects to make the best of an uncertain world, because—as all experienced managers know—an organization's plans will be upset to some degree by forces over which those in charge have little or no control. For example, a fire that damages the building that houses an organization's operations will result in cash-flow patterns that are quite different from those originally forecast. Even with adequate insurance coverage, operations will either cease or be temporarily curtailed. Similarly, the death of a key employee will cause unexpected changes in operations. To accommodate such financial uncertainties, sufficient flexibility is built into budgets and financing arrangements to avoid jeopardizing the solvency of the organization.

When planning has been completed and implementation begins, the financial manager must ensure that actual cash inflows and outflows are balanced and operations are proceeding according to plans. In other words, the operations must be *controlled*.

Controlling the organization's funds involves the creation of a system of reports in which actual expenditures and cash inflows are compared with planned performance. Unusual variations call for an immediate investigation into their causes and adjustments to either the performance or the plan. Likewise, small but persistent variations call for timely action prior to their evolving into more serious problems.

It should be readily apparent that measuring needs for funds not only is an important but also an unavoidably continuous function of the financial manager. Being a continuous function, it is clearly interrelated with the second finance function—acquiring funds—in terms of defining how much money is needed and when it will be required. And it is also clearly and closely related to the third function—using funds effectively—in that a considerable amount of financial analysis and planning should be done before deciding whether to purchase additional long-lived assets or to reserve cash surpluses for future contingencies, for example.

The decision to invest in long-lived, or fixed, assets creates a need to measure and reassess the flow of funds throughout the organization. This is because fixed-asset acquisitions usually set off chain reactions within the entity that will change its basic operating characteristics, and hence its cash flows. Remember, in almost all organizations funds are limited, so a decision to allocate funds to, say, higher salaries and fringe benefits means fewer dollars are available for, say, equipment and supplies. Measuring the need for funds against those available or forthcoming will help the financial manager monitor the flow of all funds within the organization.

Acquiring Funds

If an organization's expected cash outflow exceeds its expected inflow, and its bank balance is too small to absorb the difference, the financial manager must acquire additional funds in order to finance planned operations. The process of obtaining those funds is similar to that of obtaining office supplies or personnel services: management must first seek a supplier in the marketplace and then negotiate terms that are acceptable to both parties.

The markets for lendable and donated funds are competitive. Funds are available from many alternative sources, and they are sought for many competing uses. Lenders and borrowers both base their financing decisions on risk and return considerations. Submarkets for funds exist and are delineated by the terms under which funds are loaned, donated, or invested, including the length of time for which these funds are made available to governments, businesses, individuals, and nonprofit organizations.

The problem encountered by those who need funds is one of finding the set of terms that best suits their individual needs. The terms under which funds are acquired include cost, length of commitment, repayment, and nonfinancial conditions. For example, the lowest-cost sources of funds are typically fixed-repayment commitments. As one might expect, these fixed payments increase the risk of creating future financial problems for the organization; but lower-risk sources of funds—from a grant or donor, for example—are likely to be much more expensive if the terms of the gift place restrictions on the organization's operations and the organization must spend time and money to "court" the donor. In other words, there needs to be a balance between cost and risk in the search for the best source of funds in a given situation.

Another type of balance is that which exists between expected availability of funds and the expected financial condition of the organization. For example, a school that plans to receive a large amount of cash from a major alumni fund-raising campaign in six months should probably not borrow long-term funds now. This is because long-term debt ordinarily is more expensive than short-term debt, and the expected future financial condition of the school (assuming the fund-raising campaign is successful) may not require any debt at all.

The financial manager balances the various sources of funds in terms of risk and expected return as well as in terms of cash surpluses and deficiencies. Moreover, even though acquiring funds is usually episodic, it has continuing effects on cash flows and, thus, on financial planning and control. Borrowing money, for example, necessitates planning for cash outflows for interest and principal payments over the life of the loan. It also raises the problem of the influence of outstanding debt on the ability of the organization to acquire additional funds on favorable terms.

The process of acquiring funds thus is very closely related to the other two important finance functions: measuring the need for funds and using funds. Funds acquisition is in no way of secondary importance to the successful management of a nonprofit organization. On the contrary, because fund raising is episodic and has long-lasting effects, decisions regarding funds acquisition are among the most important decisions in which financial managers are involved.

Using Funds

The financial manager must see to it that the funds generated through the normal operations of the organization and acquired from outside sources are put to use wisely and economically. This function also could be labeled "asset management" since each asset held by a nonprofit organization—from cash in the bank to the bricks and mortar of the building—represents an investment from which management may properly expect the organization and its clientele group to benefit. Each use for funds must be productive in a goal-achievement sense, because each source of funds has a cost associated with it; there is no such thing as "free" money. The financial manager will constantly monitor cash balances and invest even temporarily idle cash; keep a close check on slow accounts and pledges receivable and tighten up credit standards and collection policies when necessary; watch for a build-up of excess inventories and continuously review purchasing policies; and monitor appropriate statistics to make certain that fixed assets (buildings, machinery, office fixtures, vehicles, and so on) are being utilized as effectively and economically as possible.

The decision to invest in fixed assets involves the use of specialized financial tools and techniques. The financial manager must balance expected cash inflows against expected costs. Cash flow, the cost of funds, the timing of the investment, and the available alternatives must all be considered before the final course of action can be determined. Once the decision has been made and the funds acquired, the cash flows associated with the investment become an integral part of the financial manager's ongoing system for planning and control. And that brings the discussion of finance functions through a full circle and back to the beginning once more.

ORGANIZATION OF THE BOOK

The chapter sequence chosen for this book presents a natural progression of material from the theoretical and institutional background to decision making in the several key areas in which the financial manager holds primary responsibility. Part I outlines the basic legal and operational characteristics of nonprofit organizations and examines the theoretical framework within which the finance function can be defined and decision rules developed.

Part II presents the essentials of accounting in nonprofit organizations and the ways in which accounting data are applied directly in financial analysis, planning, and control. Part I and the four chapters that comprise Part II contain concepts and financial management tools that are used extensively throughout the remainder of the book.

Working-capital management and decisions are the central topics of Part III. Each of the four chapters contains institutional material relevant to one of the several components of working capital; however, the focus remains on financial management and decision making in that area of the organization's operations that requires the daily attention of the finance officer.

Resource-allocation decisions are discussed in Part IV, first as they have traditionally been handled in the nonprofit context, and then as they ought to be handled, according to the best current thinking on the topic. These chapters depart from addressing the problems and the decision rules solely from the perspective of the financial manager. Instead, resource-allocation decisions are discussed in terms of achieving both the financial and nonfinancial goals of the nonprofit organization.

Finally, Part V considers the management of long-term sources of externally obtained funds. The first two chapters discuss relevant institutional material along with decision rules in the areas of debt financing and leasing, the third chapter examines the relationship between resource-allocation decisions and financing decisions, and the final chapter addresses the problem of financial distress in the nonprofit context.

Perhaps the best way to gain full benefit from the material present in this book is to read each chapter in sequence. Without question, the assimilation of the subject matter contained in Parts I and II is an absolute prerequisite to obtaining a complete understanding and appreciation of the material in any of the subsequent chapters. Understanding both the financial management theory and the principles of accounting designed specifically for nonprofit organizations will illuminate all of the subject matter with which this text will deal.

SUMMARY

The financial managers of nonprofit organizations perform three basic functions as they work to influence the future outcomes of the operations of their respective entities. These are (1) measuring the need for funds, (2) raising the necessary funds, and (3) making certain that the funds acquired are properly employed. The three functions are, of course, interrelated and often are performed simultaneously, especially during periods of organizational expansion.

The functions are also identical to those performed by financial managers in profit-seeking businesses. However, because nonprofit organizations are fundamentally different from profit-seeking firms in terms of the objectives each pursues, management methods cannot be transferred between them with good effect. Consequently, a new set of analytical and decision techniques must be employed to improve financial-management practice in the nonprofit context. This is the principal task of this book.

FURTHER READING

An overview of the nonprofit organization can be obtained by examining selected chapters in:

Anthony, Robert N., *Management Control in Nonprofit Organizations*. 4th ed. Homewood, Ill.: Irwin, 1988.

Special insights into the comparison of nonprofit and for-profit entities are contained in:

Copeland, Thomas E., and Keith V. Smith. "An Overview of Nonprofit Organizations." *Journal of Economics and Business* (February 1978): 147-154.

QUESTIONS

1. List three reasons why for-profit financial management theory cannot be transferred intact to the nonprofit context.

2. Distinguish between the terms *finance* and *accounting*.

3. What are the three financial management functions? Describe each one briefly.

4. Describe the ways in which cash-flow estimates are used in measuring the need for funds.

5. What are the two types of balance a financial manager must seek in acquiring funds?

6. Why is the funds-acquisition function of relatively greater importance in the nonprofit context compared with the for-profit context?

7. Why is the funds-utilization function sometimes called asset management?

2

Operational and Legal Characteristics of Nonprofit Organizations

This chapter serves as a bridge between the generalized description of the finance function presented in chapter 1 and the discussion presented in the remaining chapters of this book dealing with a financial management theory of the nonprofit organization and the decision tools and techniques prescribed therein. Its tasks are to (1) precisely define the nature of nonprofit organizations, (2) explore certain relevant characteristics of these entities, especially as they relate to their finance functions and the legal forms under which they may be organized, and (3) describe how they may achieve tax-exempt status under federal and state laws.

NONPROFIT DEFINED

The term *nonprofit*, when applied to organizational entities, conveys different meanings to different people. For example, nonprofit may mean *charitable, tax-exempt, publicly owned,* or *service-oriented* to some individuals. It may also suggest *fund-raising drives, volunteer workers, free goods or services,* or a *prohibition against "making money" from operations.* As to the types of activities that nonprofit organizations carry out, most would say *health care* first, and then in some order, *charitable, educational, religious, and cultural.* These popular notions concerning nonprofit organizations, while accurate to a great extent, tend to obscure the real nature of their objectives and operations. Nonprofit organizations were originally so named probably because their operations were guided largely by motives other than monetary gain, or "profit." In general, however, this nomenclature has tended to create significant misconceptions concerning their operations among outsiders and, surprisingly, even among their own managers, especially those appointed or elected to their governing bodies.

For example, many board members are reluctant to permit an organization to do much better than break even financially. They consider that the title *nonprofit* is a legally imposed prohibition against realizing operating cash surpluses. Nothing could be further from the truth, however. In fact, generating cash surpluses may be the only way a particular entity can survive and expand its ability to serve its clientele group.

While it is certainly true that the principal objectives of nonprofit organizations are other than financial, the much coveted surplus of receipts over expenditures (or "profits") plays an important, if not essential, facilitating role in achieving most organizations' charitable, educational, religious, or other nonfinancial goals. An organization must be financially solvent and maintain adequate liquidity in order to continue to operate; hence, it should, to whatever extent its governing board chooses, support itself out of operating cash surpluses. In this sense, nonprofit organizations are in fact profit-oriented.

This statement is in no way intended to diminish the importance of an organization's principal service or societal objectives or even to suggest that the financial goals of liquidity and solvency should take precedence over them under normal circumstances. However, when operating profits are a principal factor in (or even contribute in a minor way to) an organization's economic survival, they must occupy a prominent position within its hierarchy of goals. Since few if any organizations have access to unlimited resources, the rationale for rejecting the literal interpretation of the term *nonprofit* is clearly established.

The definition of a nonprofit organization that will best serve the purpose of a financial management text is as follows: *A legally constituted, nongovernmental, nonhospital organization that has been granted an exemption from the payment of federal and state income taxes and that actively seeks to contribute to the public welfare as its principal objective.* Each element of this definition deserves comment.

First, the term "legally constituted" suggests that the organization has legal status and hence a definite set of objectives and legally imposed financial and operating constraints that serve as guides to its operations.

The principles of financial management can be developed more rigorously for those organizations that have assumed a formal-type of organizational structure and operate within a known legal framework than for those informal entities that operate on an *ad hoc* basis, lacking clear direction and purpose.

Second, this definition excludes governmental units and hospitals because they are special cases insofar as nonprofit organizations are concerned. Both possess unique financial characteristics that prevent them from fitting into the general financial management theory developed in this text. For example, both government and hospital accounting practices differ materially from those of other nonprofit organizations. Further, the taxing power of governmental bodies and the third-party reimbursement system characteristic of hospital operations produce unique revenue streams, the financial analyses of which are not subject to generalization in the nonprofit context. Finally, hospitals are more appropriately classified as regulated firms than as nonprofit organizations because they operate under rate and capital expansion regulations. Notwithstanding their elimination from specific consideration here, financial officers of governmental bodies and hospitals will find many parts of this book useful to aid decision making in those aspects of their operations that are similar to those of other nonprofit entities.

Third, official recognition by the Internal Revenue Service (IRS) and state income tax agencies of an organization's tax-exempt status imparts a degree of homogeneity to this basically diverse group of entities. This is because the analysis of sources and uses of funds is a principal screening device used by the IRS in granting or denying the exemption from the payment of income taxes. It also frees the development of decision rules from the complicating effects of income taxes and tax-related cash flows.

Finally, and perhaps somewhat redundantly, to be included within this definition the organization must meet the test of promoting public welfare, with public defined either broadly, as in the case of the International Red Cross, or more narrowly, as in the case of a neighborhood homeowners association. No organization can be granted tax-exempt status by the IRS unless it is involved in promoting public welfare. Further, an organization that is operated to benefit financially any individual or group of individuals will be denied tax-exempt status. Those entities clearly should employ decision rules that will produce maximum profits or ownership wealth after taxes, rather than follow decision rules in which profits are not the principal concern of management.

Exhibit 2-1 lists a number of classes of organization to which the IRS will grant a tax-exempt status upon submission of proper application.

Exhibit 2-1: **Partial list of nonprofit organizations**

Agricultural and horticultural organizations

Amateur sports organizations

Benevolent life insurance and mutual insurance companies

Business leagues

Cemetery companies

Chambers of commerce

Charitable organizations

Child and animal welfare organizations

Churches, religious, and apostolic organizations

Civic leagues

Cooperative hospital and educational services

Corporations organized under acts of Congress

Employee associations and labor unions

Federal and state chartered credit unions

Fraternal and beneficiary societies

Group legal services

Literary, scientific, and research organizations

Mutual or cooperative irrigation, telephone, crop, and farmers' associations

Schools, colleges, universities, and other educational institutions

Social and recreation clubs

Social welfare organizations

Teachers' retirement fund associations

Title-holding corporations for exempt organizations

War veterans organizations

Source: *Internal Revenue Service, "How to Apply for and Retain Status for Your Organization," Publication 557 (Washington, D.C., Government Printing Office, 1980), 75.*

While this list is not exhaustive, it is sufficiently extensive to justify the existence of a general financial management theory of nonprofit organizations and related decision rules that exclude governmental bodies and hospitals.

CHARACTERISTICS OF NONPROFIT ORGANIZATIONS

Nonprofit organizations are dichotomous in several dimensions, each of which distinguishes this group from for-profit businesses in both theory and practice. These dimensions include (1) the nature of the organization's operations, (2) the organizational form, and (3) the goal and management structure.

Nature of Operations

Nonprofit organizations can be classified into two groups according to the nature of their operations. The first group is composed of *nontrading* organizations that do not sell their products or services to their clientele. Examples of this class of organization include charitable foundations, churches, libraries, civic clubs, museums, and other cultural organizations that do not charge admission to the public.

The second group, the *trading* organizations, operate as businesses in carrying on trade on a more or less continuous basis. The revenues from their business activities sustain the organization's operations and often provide cash surpluses that are used to further their primary (societal) objectives. Examples of this group are schools, colleges, credit unions, cooperatives, cemetery companies, and certain research organizations, such as the RAND Corporation.

Examples of both types of organization operating in the pure form are fairly common, but organizations in which both forms coexist are probably more numerous. For example, most museums and art galleries do not charge admission fees, but most operate museum gift shops established expressly to earn an excess of revenues over cash expenditures. Further, both state-supported and private universities operate dormitories, cafeterias, bookstores, and other similar auxiliary operations that contribute cash surpluses to the educational and research activities of the institution.

The trading and nontrading activities in such organizations should be, and usually are, accorded separate treatment in terms of organizational structure, management responsibility, operating objectives, and accounting systems. And, as will be discussed later in this chapter, all or a part of the profits earned by the trading activities of some nonprofit organizations may be taxed at corporate income tax rates under certain conditions. Clearly, financial decision making will differ between the two classifications of operation. In some cases, the decision rules will be identical with those used by the financial manager of a profit-seeking business; in other cases a new set of decision rules will apply.

Organizational Forms

Nonprofit entities may choose between two forms of organizational structure: the nonprofit corporation and the unincorporated association. An organization may become eligible for tax-exempt status within the provisions of the United States Internal Revenue Code under either organizational form; however, each offers certain unique advantages.

Corporations. The corporate form is usually chosen by organizations that plan to operate some type of business activity or to own real property, since this form facilitates acquiring title to property, borrowing money, and, in general, engaging in trade. The apparent permanency of a corporation and its status as a legal entity underlie this characteristic. Corporations also provide limited liability to their members for any of the organization's actions; that is, a corporation can be sued, but its members cannot be held individually or jointly liable for the actions of the corporation.

Forming a Corporation. The basic procedures and requirements for forming a corporation are specified by the relevant statutes or codes adopted by the state in which the organization wishes to incorporate. Some states have statutes dealing specifically with nonprofit corporations, while others merely include references to nonprofit corporations within their general corporate codes.

Procedures. The procedures for incorporation are fairly standard, and they will generally include the following steps:

1. Drafting articles of incorporation
2. Filing the articles with the appropriate state officers and paying a filing fee
3. Submitting annual reports, along with an associated fee
4. Drafting bylaws
5. Holding an organizational meeting to elect directors and officers and adopt the bylaws
6. Holding an annual meeting of the members

Requirements. Since nonprofit corporations are *nonstock* corporations having no ownership claims, the state of incorporation generally does not impose a minimum capital requirement as a precondition to incorporation. The basic requirements are generally a minimum number of incorporators (usually one), a minimum number of directors (usually three), a minimum number of officers (usually three), and appointment of a registered agent. The duties of a registered agent are to (1) ensure that the corporation can readily be served any legal process, notice, summons, or complaint and (2) provide a permanent address for the corporation for the convenience of the state of incorporation.

Most state laws do not require nonprofit corporations to have members. Thus, the officers and directors can exercise effective control over the corporation and act as a self-perpetuating governing body. In membership corporations, members may be granted or denied voting rights or they may be divided into classes, only some of which have voting rights. When a nonprofit corporation has members, the state laws usually require it to hold an annual meeting, the time and place of which must be reported to the appropriate state office.

Unincorporated Associations. Some organizers may find that the formalities imposed by corporate statutes in forming a new organization and subsequently operating it are too troublesome to bother with and that the principal advantage of the corporate form—limited liability—is relatively unimportant to them. In such cases, the organizers may choose to form an unincorporated association. This organizational form is particularly suited for groups brought together to fulfill a limited or transitory purpose, although such associations are often conceived as permanent organizations.

The unincorporated association normally cannot hold or receive property and cannot sue or be sued. Its individual members, however, can be sued and are liable for the debts of the organization.

The association should be formed by the adoption of articles of association and/or a set of bylaws and by the election of officers. The articles or bylaws should be carefully drafted and should closely resemble the combined articles of incorporation and bylaws of a nonprofit corporation. This is because the application for tax-exempt status by either type of organization is based largely upon information contained in the organization's articles and bylaws, as discussed later in this chapter.

Other Types of Organization. Two other types of organization occasionally are formed as nonprofit entities: "sister" organizations, and charitable trusts. The sister organizations are either corporations or unincorporated associations, and the trust, which is merely a collection of assets, is generally administered by a nonprofit corporation created specifically for that purpose.

Sister Organizations. The sister-organization form came into being as a result of the restrictions imposed by the Internal Revenue Code on the legislative activities of certain tax-exempt organizations. In order to protect their tax-exempt status but yet act to influence the outcome of legislation related to their principal objectives, many nonprofit organizations have formed spin-off, or "sister," organizations that are also tax-exempt but are unable to receive tax deductible contributions to support their activities aimed at influencing legislation.

The two organizations must be truly separate, even to the extent that the sister organization cannot be subsidized by the principal organization. The organization may share personnel and freely exchange information, however, and therein lies the rationale for creating such an arrangement.

Charitable Trusts. A charitable trust is a collection of financial assets or real property administered by a trustee for charitable purposes in accordance with the instructions issued by the grantor. Applicable state laws specify the procedures necessary to form the trust and govern its administration. In some cases, the trustee is an individual, but in most cases it is a nonprofit corporation that the grantor has directed should be established to handle the assets and make the distributions to the beneficiaries of the trust.

A charitable trust is not tax-exempt unless it is classified as a *public charity* or a trust that operates exclusively to support a public charity organization. Public charities are organizations having a sufficiently broad base of financial support to be considered as being truly publicly dependent. When a charitable trust cannot achieve tax-exempt status, it is subject to a 2 percent excise tax on its investment income.

A significant reason for creating a charitable trust to benefit an exempt, nonprofit organization is to remove investment income from the exempt organization's records and thus enable it to continue to operate as a tax-exempt charitable organization, rather than as a private foundation. As will be explained in detail later, a charitable organization enjoys several benefits not allowed to foundations under the current tax laws; thus the combination of the two organizational forms extends its ability to attract larger amounts of money from several sources with a minimum of tax liability. (The tax implications of selecting organizational forms are covered in the next section of this chapter.)

GOAL AND MANAGEMENT STRUCTURE

Most nonprofit organizations operate with a dual-management structure because their survival depends upon the simultaneous achievement of two distinct sets of goals. First, an organization's reason for existence rests upon what may be called its *professional* goals or objectives. For example, a library exists to encourage individuals to read; to extend their knowledge; and to keep current in local, national, and world events. It also may serve as a research facility, a place of entertainment, and often as a center of community cultural activity.

Similarly, a symphony orchestra exists for cultural and entertainment purposes, and a historical society is formed to discover and preserve the history and architecture of a given area. All of these activities require a certain expertise on the part of management, even to the extent of requiring the services of a trained professional to manage certain aspects of the organization's activities: a librarian for the library; a conductor, an arranger, and a music librarian for the symphony; and a historic preservationist for the historical society.

Second, a nonprofit organization must articulate a set of *financial* goals that will facilitate the achievement of its professional goals. Without proper financial planning and control to ensure that cash is available to support the organization's planned activities, even the most worthy charitable, educational, religious, or other such purposes will fail or remain underachieved. In this sense, the financial management objective of the nonprofit organization parallels that of the profit-seeking business—both types of organization must remain financially solvent through time in order to achieve their respective long-range goals. But since nonprofit organizations do not seek principally to maximize profits or owner's wealth, as do the for-profit business firms, the financial goal recommended for use by all nonprofit entities is *cost minimization*, subject to the absolute constraint of *maintaining organizational liquidity and solvency over time*. At the risk of stating the obvious, financial goal achievement is made more certain by the presence of a competent financial manager within the organization's management structure.

As mentioned earlier, the two sets of goals should be pursued simultaneously and with equal vigor; that is, one cannot be given hierarchical priority over the other as a matter of policy. While they may at times appear to be in conflict with one another, the two goal sets are actually highly complementary. An organization will find fund raising easier when it can point to a record of "professional" success coupled with exhibited financial responsibility. But when an organization overextends itself financially to achieve professional goals that may have been even slightly beyond its reach, it may be suspected of possessing poor management or of tolerating operational inefficiencies. Such suspicions, of course, will usually result in the loss of donor support, continued financial problems, and a downward revision of the level of professional goal achievement. Management must therefore balance its attention toward achieving both goals by examining the financial implications of all professional decisions prior to their implementation. A professionally well-conceived program that is poorly financed will produce the same result as well-financed but professionally poorly conceived program. Both will usually waste precious resources and end in professional failure, and donors will be unable to distinguish the root cause.

Professionals and Professional Goals

The key personnel in most nonprofit organizations are the professionals or those with special technical competence—teachers, artists, craftspeople, ministers, researchers, and so forth. In general, these professionals are motivated in their work to achieve standards of performance established by their training or education, and they look to their professional peers for approbation. For the most part, professionals acquire management skills by way of on-the-job experience, rather than through formal management training. And even those most skilled in management techniques prefer to work only part-time on management activities and to direct most of their efforts toward work in their professional areas. Although leadership positions in nonprofit organizations usually require equal measures of management skills and professional competencies, such positions generally are occupied by professionals whose management experience and skills are inadequate in comparison with the demands of their jobs.

In broad terms, professional goals established for nonprofit organizations usually are stated in terms of *maximum quantity* of output of the *highest possible quality*. This goal set, which is consistent with the preceding characterization of the professional manager, explains in part why conflict often develops between financial managers and professional managers; that is, professionals place primary emphasis on professional goals and are generally quite reluctant to place spending limits on goal achievement.

For example, a museum curator's professional success is gauged in part by the *size* and *quality* of the collection he or she oversees (or even by the quality of the museum's security systems). Thus, financial considerations may be set aside, and alternative uses of funds may be ignored when a valuable (and high-priced) museum-quality item is placed on the market, even though the item may have limited local appeal. In fact, most museums and art galleries own many more items than they are able to display at one time. While it is true that items making up their so-called permanent collections are rotated between storage and display to maintain visitor interest, some museums justify expansion of their physical plant based on their extensive collections in storage.

For example, the museum and art collections of the High Museum of Art in Atlanta, Georgia, outgrew the space available to display them many years ago. Because the queue is so long, some have not been seen for years even though the rotation schedule has been fairly rapid. But this problem did not diminish management's enthusiasm for adding to those collections. The larger the collections became, the more inadequate the building appeared to be. In 1982 the major fund-raising campaign for the High Museum of Art used this circular rationalization of institutional growth and financial investment as its theme in order to expand the size of its physical facilities. The achievement of the quality and quantity goals of the professional manager appeared as the dominant objective in this instance.

Another such example concerns the financial plight of the D'Oyly Carte Opera Company of England, the organization that was primarily responsible for the continued popularity of Gilbert and Sullivan's comic operas. In 1980 the company found itself close to bankruptcy as a result of professional decisions to perform Gilbert and Sullivan operas anywhere in the world where they would be appreciated. However, the United Kingdom touring companies, in the face of rising costs, continued the tradition begun during World War I of playing in English towns too small to permit the performances to break even financially. And, in spite of its frugality in maintaining its costumes and property, the company ended its long and artistically successful life in 1982 because of a lack of funds with which to continue its presentations. While one can admire the decision to take Gilbert and Sullivan to the people in rural England, that decision permanently destroyed a valuable and venerable institution because of a lack of attention to the financial implications of continuing an established tradition.

Financial Goals

Just as a professional manager must gain an appreciation of the financial and managerial aspects of operating a nonprofit organization, a financial manager must first become acquainted with the professional aspects of the organization before he or she can serve the best interests of that entity. The financial goals of cost minimization, liquidity, and solvency can easily be accomplished by saying no to every request to spend money. However, that response will result in a total absence of progress toward professional goal achievement, which is, after all, the basis for the organization's existence.

But neither should the financial manager say yes to every request for funds. Unless the initial cash outlay for a project, along with its related explicit and implicit future financial commitments, can be met without reallocating resources from another project of equal or higher professional priority, the financial manager should recommend against adopting the new project. The same holds for funds requested for the expansion of extant programs or to cover inflation-driven budget increases. Unless these cash outflows can be financed with incremental new funds or funds allocated from lower priority expenditures, the financial goals of liquidity and solvency cannot be achieved and financial crisis will inevitably result. The analytical and decision methods the financial manager must use to prevent such crises form the subject matter of this book and are dealt with in subsequent chapters. It is enough for now to suggest the importance of coordinating an organization's professional and financial goals for the good of the organization and its clientele group.

QUALIFYING FOR TAX-EXEMPT STATUS

Regardless of the organizational form chosen for a nonprofit entity, the application for an exemption from federal income taxes should be considered an integral and essential part of of the organizing process.[1] The first step in the application process is to determine the section of the 1954 Internal Revenue Code under which the organization is classified. Exhibit 2-2 contains a list of types of organizations that may qualify for exempt status according to IRS regulations along with each organization's application form number, annual tax return requirement, and charitable contribution status.

Most nonprofit organizations will seek exemption under Section 501(c)(3) or Section 501(c)(4) of the Internal Revenue Code, since these two sections provide the greatest benefits to the organization and its

(text continued on page 25)

---

1. The material presented in this section is based on IRS publication, "How to Apply for and Retain Exempt Status for Your Organization," Publication 557, February 1980.

Exhibit 2-2: Tax Return and Contribution Reference Chart for Nonprofit Organizations.

Section of 1954 Code	Description of organization	General nature of activities	Application form no.	Annual return required to be filed	Contributions allowable
501(c)(1)	Corporations organized under Act of Congress (including federal credit unions)	Instrumentalities of the United States	No form	None	Yes, if made for exclusively public purposes
501(c)(2)	Title holding corporation for exempt organization	Holding title to property of an exempt organization	1024	990[1]	No[2]
501(c)(3)	Religious, educational, charitable, scientific, literary, testing for public safety, to foster certain national or international amateur sports competition, or prevention of cruelty to children or animals organizations	Activities of nature implied by description of class of organization	1023	990 or 990-PF[1]	Generally, yes
501(c)(4)	Civic leagues, social welfare organizations, and local associations of employees	Promotion of community welfare; Charitable, educational or recreational	1024	990[1]	Generally, no[2,3]
501(c)(5)	Labor, agricultural, and horticultural organizations	Educational or instructive, the purpose being to improve conditions of work, and to improve products and efficiency	1024	990[1]	No[2]
501(c)(6)	Business leagues, chambers of commerce, real estate boards, etc.	Improvement of business conditions of one or more lines of business	1024	990[1]	No[2]
501(c)(7)	Social and recreation clubs	Pleasure, recreation, social activities	1024	990[1]	No[2]
501(c)(8)	Fraternal beneficiary societies and associations	Lodge providing for payment of life, sickness, accident or other benefits to members	1024	990[1]	Yes, if used for Sec. 501(c)(3) purposes
501(c)(9)	Voluntary employees' beneficiary associations (including federal employees' voluntary beneficiary associations formerly covered by section 501(c)(10)	Providing for payment of life, sickness, accident or other benefits to members	1024	990[1]	No[2]

Section	Description	Details	Application form	Annual return	Deductibility of contributions
501(c)(10)	Domestic fraternal societies and associations	Lodge devoting its net earnings to charitable, fraternal, and other specified purposes. No life, sickness, or accident benefits to members	1024	990[1]	Yes, if used for Sec. 501(c)(3) purposes
501(c)(11)	Teachers' retirement fund associations	Teachers' association for payment of retirement benefits	No form	990[1]	No[2]
501(c)(12)	Benevolent life insurance associations, mutual ditch or irrigation companies, mutual or cooperative telephone companies, etc.	Activities of a mutually beneficial nature similar to those implied by the description of class of organization	1024	990[1]	No[2]
501(c)(13)	Cemetery companies	Burials and incidental activities	1024	990[1]	Generally, yes
501(c)(14)	State chartered credit unions, mutual reserve funds	Loans to members. Exemption as to building and loan associations and cooperative banks repealed by Revenue Act of 1951, affecting all years after 1951	No form	990[1]	No[2]
501(c)(15)	Mutual insurance companies or associations	Providing insurance to members substantially at cost	1024	990[1]	No[2]
501(c)(16)	Cooperative organizations to finance crop operations	Financing crop operations in conjunction with activities of a marketing or purchasing association	No form	990[1]	No[2]
501(c)(17)	Supplemental unemployment benefit trusts	Provides for payment of supplemental unemployment compensation benefits	1024	990[1]	No[2]
501(c)(18)	Employee funded pension trust (created before June 25, 1959)	Payment of benefits under a pension plan funded by employees	No form	990[1]	No[2]
501(c)(19)	Post or organization of war veterans	Activities implied by nature of organization	1024	990[1]	Yes
501(c)(20)	Group legal services plan organizations	Legal services provided exclusively to employees	1024	990[1]	No[4]
501(c)(21)	Black lung benefit trusts	Funded by coal mine operators to satisfy their liability for disability or death due to black lung diseases	No form	990-BL	No[5]
501(d)	Religious and apostolic associations	Regular business activities. Communal religious community	No form	1065	No[2]

Exhibit 2-2 (continued)

Section of 1954 Code	Description of organization	General nature of activities	Application form no.	Annual return required to be filed	Contributions allowable
501(e)	Cooperative hospital service organizations	Performs cooperative services for hospitals	1023	990[1]	Yes
501(f)	Cooperative service organizations of operating educational organizations	Performs collective investment services for educational organizations	1023	990[1]	Yes
521(a)	Farmers' cooperative associations	Cooperative marketing and purchasing for agricultural producers	1028	990-C	No

[1] For exceptions to the filing requirement, see Part I, Chapter 2 and the instructions for Forms 990 and 990—AR.

[2] An organization exempt under a Subsection of Code Sec. 501 other than (c)(3), may establish a charitable fund, contributions to which are deductible. Such a fund must itself meet the requirements of section 501(c)(3) and the related notice requirements of section 508(a).

[3] Contributions to volunteer fire companies and similar organizations are deductible, but only if made for exclusively public purposes.

[4] Deductible as a business expense.

[5] Deductible as a business expense to the extent allowed by section 192 of the Code.

Source: Internal Revenue Service, "How to Apply for and Retain Exempt Status for Your Organization," IRS Publication 557, February 1980, 75.

(text continued from page 21)

benefactors. Thus, this discussion will concentrate on these organization types. Section 501(c)(3) and Section 501(c)(4) organizations are defined by the Internal Revenue Code as follows:

> Section 501(c)(3): Corporations, and any community chest, fund, or foundation, organized and operated exclusively for religious, charitable, scientific, testing for public safety, literary, or educational purposes . . . no part of the net earnings of which inures to the benefit of any private shareholder or individual, no substantial part of the activities of which is carrying on propaganda, or otherwise attempting to influence legislation . . . and which does not participate in, or intervene in (including the publishing or distributing of statements), any political campaign on behalf of any candidate for public office.
>
> Section 501(c)(4): Civic leagues or organizations not organized for profit but operated exclusively for the promotion of social welfare . . . and the net earnings of which are devoted exclusively to charitable, educational, or recreational purposes.

The major distinction between 501(c)(3) and 501(c)(4) organizations concerns the tax deductibility of contributions received. The income of a Section 501(c)(3) organization is exempt from federal income tax, and contributions to the organization are deductible by the donor for federal income, estate, and gift tax purposes (up to a certain percentage of a donor's adjusted gross income). The income of a Section 501(c)(4) organization is also exempt from federal income tax, but an individual who contributes to the organization directly may not claim the contribution as a tax deductible item on his or her return. Exceptions to this rule include contributions to a charitable fund established by this type of organization and contributions to a volunteer fire department made exclusively for public purposes.

Section 501(c)(3) Organizations

The preferred status for all nonprofit organizations is clearly that accorded under Section 501(c)(3), since that status places the organization in a more favorable position to attract contributions of money or other property from individuals and businesses. To qualify for this special tax status, however, the organization must meet certain requirements of the tax code. Briefly:

1. The entity must be organized and operated exclusively for religious, charitable, scientific, testing for public safety, literary, or educational purposes.

2. No "substantial" part of its activities may consist of carrying on propaganda campaigns or otherwise attempting to influence legislation. Alternatively, in lieu of this indefinite guideline, a Section 501(c)(3)

organization may elect the application of a specific ceiling on lobbying expenditures under an elective provision created by the Tax Reform Act of 1976.[2]

3. It may not participate in or intervene in to *any extent* (including the publishing or distribution of statements) any political campaign on behalf of any candidate for public office.

4. No part of the net earnings of the organization may inure to the benefit of any private shareholder or individual.

Each of these restrictions must be dealt with expressly in the organization's governing instrument—the articles of incorporation or the articles of association. In addition, the organization will not qualify for Section 501(c)(3) status if its governing instrument permits it to engage in activities that are nonreligious, noncharitable, nonscientific, and so forth, even though it does not in fact engage in these other activities. Thus, great care must be taken in drafting the articles of incorporation (or association) to ensure the exempt status is not denied because of what is essentially a drafting error or oversight.

Exempt and Nonexempt Income. A nonprofit organization generally will receive income or revenue from one or more of four possible sources: (1) contributions (including membership fees, gifts, and grants); (2) net income from trade or business activities; (3) investment income; and (4) tax revenues levied for the benefit of the organization. Contributions and tax revenues are tax-exempt under all circumstances for a 501(c)(3) organization, but business income and investment income may be taxed under certain circumstances.

Trade or Business Income. An exempt organization is not precluded from engaging in a trade or business substantially related to the exercise or performance of its primary (societal) purposes. The relationship between the business activity and the purpose must be other than merely providing income with which to carry out that purpose, however. For example, a gunsmith in Colonial Williamsburg employs the methods and tools of the colonial period to manufacture black powder, muzzle-loading rifles and handguns. Barrels are hand-bored on machines operated with "apprentice" power, and locks, triggers, and other hardware are handmade. The gunsmith accepts orders for these expensive hand-tooled and custom-made weapons. The business of selling the guns is related to the purpose of historic preservation and the maintenance of what may be termed a "living" museum, where visitors may observe colonial life firsthand and, in some cases, become apprenticed to the

2. Ibid., 56–58. The limits are 20 percent of exempt purpose expenditures of $500,000 or less; 15 percent on the next $500,000; 10 percent on all exempt-purpose expenditures on the next $500,000 and 5 percent on all exempt-purpose expenditures in excess of $1.5 million, up to a maximum of $1 million per year.

craftsmen to learn these antique skills. Thus, the income from the business is tax-exempt since it is related to the primary purpose of the organization.

However, if the gunsmith added a line of modern weapons and ammunition to his stock-in-trade, income from the sale of those items would be treated as *unrelated business income* by the IRS and would be subject to federal income tax calculated at the prevailing corporate income tax rates. The fact that the gunsmith engages in an unrelated business will not affect the organization's exempt status or cause the application for Section 501(c)(3) status to be denied. But if the primary purpose of the organization is considered to be the operation of an unrelated trade or business, it will not qualify as a tax-exempt organization even if all the profits from such a trade or business are expended in furtherance of its primary societal purposes. The distinction between what constitutes a related and an unrelated trade or business thus may be critical to the financial health of the organization.

Investment Income. An exempt, nonprofit organization will not be subject to a tax on investment income unless the IRS rules that it is a *private foundation* rather than a public charity. Every organization that qualifies for tax exemption under Section 501(c)(3) is presumed by the IRS to be a private foundation unless the organization falls into one of the excluded categories *and* notifies the IRS of that fact. Basically, a private foundation is a Section 501(c)(3) organization that is not thought to have a sufficiently broad base of public support to be considered a *public* organization, in the literal sense of the word. Private foundations are often funded by a single source, such as a family or a company, or draw limited financial or membership support from the communities they are intended to serve. The Internal Revenue Code and accompanying regulations contain various tests for determining whether or not an organization is a private foundation.

When an organization is classified as a private foundation, its investment income is subject to a 2 percent excise tax. In addition, foundations are subject to several operating restrictions, violations of which give rise to other excise taxes and penalties against the organization or its managers.

Besides the imposition of the tax on investment income, private foundations are disadvantaged in two other ways: (1) contributions by individuals or businesses to most private foundations are deductible for federal tax purposes to a more limited extent than are contributions to a publicly supported organization; and (2) foundations normally experience greater difficulty in attracting grants from other private foundations because of certain IRS regulations. Thus, the Section 501(c)(3) organization should prefer to exercise considerable care to ensure that it will avoid classification as a private foundation.

Legislative and Political Activity. The IRS closely guards against the use of a tax-exempt status to promote legislative and political purposes.

Restrictions against political activities are simply stated: a Section 501(c)(3) organization *may not to any extent* participate in or intervene in, directly or indirectly, any political campaign on behalf of or in opposition to any candidate for public office. As to legislative activities, a Section 501(c)(3) organization, unless it elects to comply with lobbying expenditure ceilings specified in the tax code, is subject to the restriction that no *substantial* part of its activities may consist of influencing, or attempting to influence, legislation. The impact of this restriction is quite complex; however, it deserves some elaboration.

"Influencing" legislation is defined in the tax code as either *direct* lobbying or *grass-roots* lobbying. Direct lobbying is dealing with members and employees of a legislative body or any other government official involved in the formulation of legislation. Grass-roots lobbying is attempting to influence the public for the purpose of influencing legislation by publicly advocating adoption or rejection of specific legislative proposals or by urging the public to contact legislators about legislation pending before a legislative body. The term legislation includes action by Congress, state legislature, local council, or similar governing body, or by the public in a referendum, initiative, constitutional amendment, or similar procedure. Administrative actions by a governmental agency to implement legislation are excluded from the definition of legislation. Thus, in the area of zoning, for example, a historic preservation organization seeking enforcement of zoning regulations by opposing exceptions or variances necessary to carry out its preservation activities is not violating the restriction on legislative activities. However, if the organization advocates changing the zoning law itself, it may be denied Section 501(c)(3) tax-exempt status, if such activities are substantial.

Section 501(c)(3) organizations are permitted to carry out certain legislative and political activities without endangering their exempt status. These activities include:

1. Furnishing a representative to testify as an expert witness on pending legislation in its area of interest, when so requested by a legislative committee.

2. Engaging in self-defense lobbying for or against legislation that would affect the organization's existence, powers, tax-exempt status, or the tax deductibility of contributions it receives.

3. Engaging in litigation to accomplish its purposes.

4. Engaging in nonpartisan, independent, and objective analysis, study, or research, even though the result of that effort will support or oppose pending legislation and provided such research is conducted for the purpose of informing or educating the public. The reports of any research conducted must be distributed to persons interested in both sides of the issue under study.

5. Finally, engaging in legislative activities to an insubstantial extent, the definition of which is not apparent in either the code or in court cases.

Distribution of Earnings. A final restriction imposed upon a Section 501(c)(3) organization is that no part of its net earnings may inure to the benefit of any private shareholder or individual. The organization will meet this requirement first by including a provision in its articles of incorporation or association stating that if the organization ceases its operations, any assets remaining after payment of all outstanding obligations will be distributed to other Section 501(c)(3) organizations. Second, the organization's articles must specify that the organization will not distribute cash or other assets to its officers, members, or related individuals in the form of dividends or preferential benefits. This restriction does not, however, prevent the payment of a reasonable allowance to an individual for services rendered to or expenses incurred on behalf of the organization, including salaries of reasonable amounts to officers and employees.

Section 501(c)(4) Organizations

A nonprofit organization granted exempt status under Section 501(c)(4) of the Internal Revenue Code may engage to a substantial extent in legislative activities with impunity, but it may not participate, directly or indirectly, in the campaigns of candidates for public office. As mentioned earlier, contributions to this type of organization are not deductible by the donor for federal income tax purposes.

If engaging in legislative activities is important to carrying out an organization's basic purposes, the group should first consider whether electing to comply with the lobbying expenditure ceilings specified in the tax code would give it sufficient scope for such activities. If not, it should consider establishing both a 501(c)(3) organization and a 501(c)(4) sister organization. In this way, the tax deductibility of contributions may be preserved, insofar as they are used for the group's nonlegislative activities.

Application Procedures

Even though an organization meets all of the requirements for exemption as either a Section 501(c)(3) organization or a 501(c)(4) organization, it is not automatically exempt from tax. In order to be recognized as tax-exempt by the IRS, the organization must file an IRS Application for Recognition of Exemption [*using IRS Form 1023 for a Section 501(c)(3) organization and IRS Form 1024 for a Section 501(c)(4) organization*]. The exemption, if granted, will be effective as of the date when the organization was formed, provided, in the case of a Section 501(c)(3) organization, that the application was filed within 15 months of the date of formation. As part of its application for recognition of exempt status under Section 501(c)(3), an organization that also intends to qualify as a public charity must so inform the IRS and obtain a ruling to that effect. Failure to do so will result in the organization's classification as a private foundation, as mentioned earlier.

An organization's exempt status remains in effect as long as there are no substantial changes in its character, purposes, or methods of operation. Any change in form—even a merger with another tax-exempt organization—will require the organization to resubmit its application for recognition of exempt status.

Finally, most exempt organizations are obligated to file an annual information return, as noted in Exhibit 2-2. Those organizations with annual gross receipts of less than $10,000, or churches and their related organizations, state institutions, and several other types of organizations are excepted from this requirement. But private foundations and organizations subject to tax on income from unrelated business activities are required to file returns regardless of the size of their incomes or their characteristics.

A NOTE ON TAXES

As mentioned earlier in this chapter, nonprofit organizations must pay income taxes on unrelated business income whenever the gross amount of that income totals $1,000 or more in any tax year. The net income after allowance for all normal expenses of conducting the business, including depreciation on plant and equipment, is taxed at the prevailing corporate income tax rates, regardless of the organizational form employed by the entity. Nonprofit organizations are permitted to claim all tax credits permitted to profit-seeking businesses under the current tax code.

Net operating losses from unrelated business activities can be carried back or carried forward to offset taxes already paid in a prior tax year or those that will be paid on such income in a subsequent tax year. These rules are essentially the same as those for profit-seeking businesses; that is, losses may be carried back three years and forward five years.

Certain types of income are *not* considered unrelated business income, even though they are clearly unrelated to the principal purpose of the exempt organization. The types of income excluded are dividends, interest, annuities, royalties, rents, income from research, lending securities, and gains and losses from the disposition of property.

A unique tax provision applicable only to nonprofit organizations concerns unrelated business income received from *debt-financed property*. Debt-financed property is defined as any property held to produce income (including real estate, tangible personal property, and corporate stock) that was purchased totally or in part with borrowed funds. Property used substantially for an organization's exempt purposes (85 percent or more) is not considered as debt-financed property for tax purposes. Property not debt financed is also excluded from the definition, and the rental income from such property is exempt from taxes.

The amount of taxable income from debt-financed property is calculated by multiplying the net income by the *debt/basis percentage*—a ratio of the average debt principal owed on the purchase of the property during the tax year to its purchase price. For example, suppose an exempt organization purchased an office building for $500,000, using $300,000 of borrowed funds and $200,000 of surplus cash. Gross rental income for the current tax year equaled $60,000, and allowable deductions totaled $10,000. The debt/basis percentage is ($300,000/$500,000 =) 60 percent. The net rental of ($60,000 - $10,000 =) $50,000 times 60 percent, or $30,000, is the taxable, unrelated business income from the debt-financed property. Again, if the property is not debt-financed, none of the rental income is taxable as unrelated business income.

SUMMARY

This chapter began with a definition of the term *nonprofit organization* that contained three basic elements. First, the entity is defined as being a *legally constituted organization*, thus requiring it to have a proper management structure, a recognizable legal form, and a means of carrying out its objectives.

Second, the organization's objectives are defined as being concerned with the *public welfare*. This element distinguishes the nonprofit organization from the for-profit business. Finally, the entity is required to possess one or another form of *tax-exempt status* as granted by the IRS. This element clarifies the nature of its cash flows with regard to both sources and disposition of funds.

Within this definition, nonprofit organizations are found to be a fairly diverse group with respect to organizational forms, modes of operation, and specific principal objectives. Points of commonality include the presence of a dual-management structure, containing both "professional" and "business" managers; a dual-goal structure containing both a societal goal set and a financial goal set; and a recognition of the financial advantages of obtaining and retaining a tax-exempt status. The definition and the subsequent discussion of the characteristics of nonprofit organizations provide an essential background to the development of a financial management theory and the many decision rules that are necessary to improved financial management practice in nonprofit contexts.

FURTHER READING

Three IRS publications are relevant to the material contained in this chapter:

"How to Apply for and Retain Exempt Status for Your Organization," IRS Publication 557, February 1980.

"Tax Information for Private Foundations and Foundation Managers," IRS Publication 578, November 1978.

"Tax on Unrelated Business Income of Exempt Organizations," IRS Publication 598, June 1979.

A summary of the tax laws and legal implications of organizational form are found in:

Singer, Barbara. *Nonprofit Organizations, Operations Handbook for Directors and Administrators.* Willmette, Ill.: Callaghan & Company, 1987.

QUESTIONS

1. Discuss the definition of nonprofit organization in terms of the requirements of a financial management textbook.

2. List all of the nonprofit organizations that you have personally had contact with.

3. Distinguish between trading and nontrading organizations.

4. What is the principal advantage of the corporate form of organization? What are its principal disadvantages?

5. What are sister organizations? Charitable trusts?

6. What is the financial management goal recommended for use by nonprofit organizations?

7. Explain why neither the financial goal nor the professional goal should be given priority over the other.

8. Distinguish between the Section 501(c)(3) and Section 501(c)(4) organization. Which is the preferred status and why?

9. What is unrelated business income?

10. What types of income of tax-exempt, nonprofit organizations are subject to federal income taxes?

11. Define direct and grass-roots lobbying.

12. What legislative and political activities are permitted by the tax code to Section 501(c)(3) organizations?

3

Theoretical Framework

This chapter examines a theoretical framework that defines the financial manager's area of responsibility in the nonprofit organization and presents a set of techniques that will assist management in financial planning, control, and decision making.

The discussion begins with a brief examination of what a normative management theory is and why it is a prerequisite to the development of sound, practical decision techniques. Next, the theoretical structure that is employed throughout the remainder of this book is presented and explained.

THE ROLE OF THEORY IN MANAGEMENT

A theory is useful in explaining either (1) how something works or (2) how it should work. The former type of theory is called a *positive*, or descriptive, theory, and the latter type is known as a *normative*, or decision, theory.

Positive Theory

Microeconomists, who deal with economics of the business firm, have concentrated primarily on developing positive models and theories. The traditional emphasis in the microeconomic theory of the firm is on the relationship between profits and the volume of output, given a fixed capital base and the use of profit maximization as the goal of the firm. The purpose of this type of theory is to come as close as possible to duplicating the way in which the firm operates in order to either explain or predict its behavior under alternative sets of circumstances.

Government planners, policymakers, and legislators are the principal "consumers" of microeconomic theory as they attempt to measure the impact of new legislation, proposed changes in policy, and new economic developments on the private sector of the economy. Business managers, however, do not find the economic theory of the firm particularly useful because it offers little in the way of direction for management decisions. While the theory may quite accurately predict, say, the new condition of a firm after a period of growth, it offers no insight into what management should do to achieve that growth or how the firm's assets and capital should be structured to keep it from experiencing financial difficulties during the period. This is the role of normative theory.

Normative Theory

Normative theory is concerned with creating a carefully arranged and systematic program of action for attaining some objective. Its main purpose is to give direction to those responsible for achieving the objective adopted by the organization's governing board. Unlike the positive economic theory of the firm, normative theory may ignore the way in which the firm actually is operated in certain areas and prescribe alternative methods that are more effective or efficient in goal attainment. Thus, the development of positive theory need not precede the development of normative theory, although such precedence often is helpful to the normative theorist.

The benefits that management derives from the existence of normative theory are, first, the theory provides a frame of reference for all managerial activities. It thus helps to effectively organize people and activities and to focus their efforts toward a single purpose. Second, the theory helps to define the environment's impact on organizational activities so that management can either function more effectively within that environment or work to alter the environment in appropriate ways. Third, it helps management determine what information is needed to support the decision-making process. Finally, the existence of a sound theory simply improves managerial decisions and the overall performance of the organization. It also improves the chances of realizing continued improvement in those areas over time.

FINANCE THEORY FOR NONPROFIT ORGANIZATIONS

Both the microeconomic and the financial management theories of the firm are designed to address the theoretical and operational aspects of the *entire* business firm, given a *single* goal or objective which the firm is assumed to be working to achieve. But, as mentioned in chapters 1 and 2, the nonprofit organization is distinguished from the profit-seeking business by the fact that the nonprofit entity operates to achieve a *multiple goal set* rather than a single goal. Consequently, the *financial management* theory of the nonprofit organization is formulated as a *partial*, rather than a complete, theory.

More specifically, the complete theory of the nonprofit organization may be thought of as compromising two (or more) partial theories. In its simplest form, one part covers the *professional*, utility-denominated aspects of the organization's operations, and the other part deals with the *financial*, or dollar-denominated, decisions faced by the entity.[1] Since this is a financial management book, primary emphasis will be placed on financial management theory and decisions. However, in those areas in which professional and financial management decisions overlap, attention will be given to both areas.

The theoretical structure that is best suited to the purposes of this book is summarized in the three elements that constitute normative theory at the level of the firm in both its partial and complete forms: (1) a goal or goals capable of being attained; (2) a systematic and correct basis for measuring goal achievement; and (3) a clear understanding of how managerial decisions affect goal achievement.

Goals of Nonprofit Organizations

As stated earlier, the dual organizational structure of nonprofit organizations imposes a multiple goal decision framework on their managements. The advantages to the organization of retaining the tax-exempt status make it imperative that the professional goals establish the initial criterion for asset selection and that professional managers be given primary responsibility for operations or the delivery of societal benefits to the organization's clientele. Financial management's input is also needed to guide decision making, but only as it is useful to maintain

---

1. Other partial theories may also coexist within the framework of a complete theory. For example, the functional areas of marketing, production, and risk management may contribute partial theories to the overall operation of the nonprofit organization.

liquidity and solvency and to formulate budget constraints in asset selection decisions.

The professionals should be free to choose any operational goal that their training and experience suggest is appropriate for guiding overall operations. And the specific professional goal selected in any given situation need not be expressed in financial terms because that dimension of the decision process is supplied by the financial goal. For example, the professional goal for a private school may be expressed as serving the greatest number of academically qualified students in its district or offering the highest quality of education to those students. A library may express its goal in terms of the total number of volumes in its collection, and a local historical preservation society may seek to preserve and protect the architecture of historical significance in its community. None of these goals is expressed in terms of dollars. And if they are pursued with singleminded purpose, all have the potential of creating serious financial problems for those organizations because they ignore budgeting matters. The financial management goal therefore *must* be introduced into the decision process to ensure that the organization economizes in its use of scarce resources and survives through time as a "going concern."

Given the nature of the professional goal that a nonprofit organization may elect to pursue, the goal that the financial manager should pursue is *cost minimization, subject to an absolute liquidity and solvency constraint*. Again, this goal is not intended to be the goal that guides the overall operation of the entity. Rather, it is the financial goal for the partial theory, and as such, it should be used as the sole guide to decision making only in those areas in which the financial manager has primary or exclusive responsibility. Those areas include fund raising, debt management, investment portfolio management, budgeting, financial analysis and control, and the management of working capital assets (i.e., cash, investments, receivables, and inventories).

The dual-management structure and dual-goal set in nonprofit organizations do not present serious obstacles to managerial decision making, but they do make the process somewhat cumbersome. Fortunately, when the professional goal is perceived as the dominant operating goal of the organization, the financial goal and finance function take on a supporting role. The nature of that role is simply the maintenance of the organization's budgeting integrity, decision by decision. Hence, if the professional manager pursues a utility maximizing goal, the organization itself will seek to maximize utility, subject to a budget constraint specified by the financial manager.

Measuring Goal Achievement

The basis for measuring financial management goal achievement for the nonprofit organization is identical to that employed in the for-profit finance theory; that is, *cash flow.*

Origin of Cash Flows. Cash flows are the inevitable results of all of the activities carried on by the nonprofit organization (i.e., production, sales, distribution, financing, and administration). Whenever cash is received or is paid out for expenses or is paid directly to the beneficiaries of its operations, the organization generates cash flows.

Global, or overall, cash flows are most frequently measured, reported, and analyzed by and for management, as well as for interested outsiders. These cash flows are also the traditional targets management uses for implementing financial controls. However, the exposition and application of the theory should not be directed toward controlling global cash flows. Instead, the theory should be aimed at individual decisions involving the acquisition and management of each of the organization's assets and liabilities and the production of goods or services for its beneficiaries. This is because the global cash flows reported in the organization's financial statements summarize the results of operations; they are the end points, in other words. Proper decision techniques must be designed to affect the *origins* of cash flows rather than their end points. Thus when correct decision rules are applied to the acquisition and management of assets and liabilities and to the production of services, global cash flows should be in balance over time (assuming certainty). That is, the organization should be operating at a minimum cost level with adequate provision for immediate liquidity and long-run solvency.

Financial Management Decisions

Financial management decisions can be classified into two groups: resource allocation decisions and financing decisions. Although achievement of global cash-flow balance requires the integration of those decision areas, a clearer exposition of the theory results from discussing them separately.

Resource-allocation Decisions. The resource allocation process in nonprofit organizations begins when the professional manager designs a program, selects a project, or chooses a real asset that will help the organization achieve its exempt purpose. All professionally acceptable projects must go through a financial analysis before the final accept-reject decision can be made. At this point, the application of the financial management theory enters the decision process.

The criterion by which the financial manager should judge each new investment proposal is *financial viability* or the ability of the project to operate as initially conceived throughout its expected economic life without (1) consuming an excess of resources over that amount made available to it and (2) creating a state of illiquidity or insolvency within the organization.[2] The analysis should deal exclusively with incremental cash flows, and the concept of present value (as discussed in chapter 12) should be employed to achieve intertemporal comparability of these cash flows. The financial viability criterion in this instance becomes an operational statement of the multiperiod budget constraint faced by the decision makers with respect to a specific project or asset being analyzed.

Special refinements to the financial analysis of investments, such as the explicit recognition of asset risk and the measurement of capital costs, are unnecessary in the nonprofit context. They are important to the professional manager's analysis, however.

Asset Risk. Asset risk is the risk inherent in the production of utility to the clientele group, who, you may recall, are both the owners and customers of the nonprofit organization. Asset risk may be measured by the variability likely to occur in the perceived value of the benefits provided to society by the organization. Asset risk is therefore borne by the organization's *beneficiaries* and not by the organization itself. Hence, it is irrelevant to the financial manager of the nonprofit organization, except in decisions involving the purchase and management of financial assets (such as stocks and bonds). Further, the risk of greater variability in benefits generally will not have a direct impact on the organization's professional goal. Its only direct impact will be on the organization's professional reputation.

Asset risk may affect cash flows (and hence liquidity and solvency) indirectly, however, by making fund raising more difficult or by causing the organization to spend larger than anticipated amounts of money in attempting to compensate for a lack of quality or quantity of goods or services produced. But this type of problem can be handled by the financial manager as an uncertainty in operations rather than as asset risk.

Discount Rate Used in Present Value Calculations. The professional manager may use a discount rate equal to the relevant cost of social capital in his or her analyses of new investment projects. The use of this rate facilitates professional goal achievement by focusing on societal wealth maximization. But since the financial management goal in resource-allocation decisions in the nonprofit organization is financial viability rather than wealth or profit maximization, the appropriate discount rate to use in testing for financial viability is the rate of return the organization will earn on its surplus cash.

2. In resource-allocation decisions, the minimum cost objective is assumed to have been achieved when the professional manager uses a theoretically tractable allocational decision criterion. Hence, the financial manager concentrates solely on the liquidity and solvency aspects of the capital-investment decision. The least-cost assumption is not critical to either the financial analysis or to the project's actual financial viability.

From a purely financial (budget constraint) perspective, the rationale for using the short-term investment rate is simply that adjustments to a nonprofit organization's liquidity position are generally made by buying or selling securities for the account of the organization's unrestricted investment fund. In those instances in which the organization must borrow on a short-term basis to balance its cash flows, the interest cost in excess of the rate earned on short-term investments is treated as an additional operating cash outflow that must be covered by the project's total cash resources.

Thus, by discounting a project's or asset's future cash flows at the short-term investment rate (the opportunity cost of funds), the organization's total assets will grow by an amount equal to the total of outside funds utilized by the project plus the return that would have been earned on any surplus cash the organization decided to commit to the project. And when the project breaks even financially on a present-value basis, the organization's total cash resources will grow at the same rate they would have if the project had not been undertaken, leaving the organization's liquidity position unchanged at the end of the planning period.

Financing Decisions. Financing decisions—acquiring short-and long-term capital in the form of debt, leases, or donated funds—are guided by the financial management goal. But, as implied by the discussion of resource-allocation decisions, the financial cash flows (i.e., interest, principal, and lease payments) are included in the analyses that precede the decision to acquire new assets or to begin new programs of service.

Financing decisions involving the choice among alternative long-term sources of funds to be used to finance new investments are made on the basis of cost minimization. Future cash outlays for debt service, lease payments, or donor relations are compared for the given dollar amount of financing required, for example. Similarly, the costs of various short-term credit sources are compared to discover which is the least costly.

Once this task is accomplished for any given financing episode, the cash receipts from the chosen financing alternative and the cash outflows required for its service (e.g., lease and mortgage payments) are integrated with the cash flows associated with the project or asset that the new funds will be used to acquire. Then the financial manager will test the project or asset, given the least costly source of financing, for financial viability. If the project is viable, financing costs can be met without creating a liquidity crisis. If the project is not financially viable (with the least costly source of funds), then the fault lies with either the project's or the asset's acquisition cost or operating expenditures, and not with the method of financing.

This two-stage decision process ensures that (1) the organization will operate with the lowest financing costs and (2) the method of financing will not create global cash-flow imbalances over time. The integration of financing and spending decisions also simplifies the decision process by permitting the analysis to focus on the basic elements that create cash flows rather than on trying to balance global cash flows after the spending decision has been made.

Compatibility of Professional and Financial Decisions. To make this theory work, the professional and financial functions must be sufficiently independent of one another to permit essentially unimpaired progress toward goal achievement for each. In those areas in which responsibility for decisions is shared (or where goals come into conflict), decision rules must be formulated in such a way as to produce consonant results. The only area in which decision responsibility is shared is in the resource-allocation process.

The professional manager of a nonprofit organization is ultimately responsible for resource allocation and may employ orthodox welfare economic theory as a guide to these decisions. He or she may define the organization's utility function and use any acceptable decision or measurement techniques to help in choosing among alternative investment opportunities. For example, the professional manager may employ cost-benefit analysis, in which monetary and monetized nonmonetary costs and benefits are discounted at an appropriate social discount rate and then compared. Or the manager may use multi-attribute decision techniques to rank projects or to make accept-reject decisions.

The successful achievement of the organization's professional goal obviously is affected by the choice of technique and decision criterion, but that choice does not affect the financial analysis of the project or asset or the recommendation that the financial manager will offer. If a professionally acceptable project does not pass the test for financial viability, the professional manager nevertheless may choose to implement it. In so doing, however, he or she is placing the organization in financial jeopardy, which in turn will at least hinder the organization in successfully pursuing its professional goals. Thus, failure to *fully* achieve either the professional or the financial goal in resource-allocation decisions will eventually produce a negative impact on *both* the professional and financial health of the organization.

SUMMARY

The theory presented in this chapter is a normative, or decision, theory of the nonprofit organization. It is also a partial theory, dealing only with financial, or dollar-denominated, decisions facing the entity. Its objective is to permit the organization to minimize costs and achieve immediate liquidity and long-run solvency. It also facilitates achievement of the organization's professional goal set.

The theory translates into decision rules by dealing exclusively with the cash flows that are related to individual assets and liabilities and the production of services for the beneficiaries of the organization. The two basic types of decisions facing the financial manager are in resource allocation and in financing. Financing decisions are based on the cost-minimization goal, and when integrated with resource-allocation decisions, aid in maintaining a balance in global cash flows, thus ensuring adequate liquidity and long-run solvency for the organization.

The following set of statements serves as the foundation of the theory presented in this chapter and the decision rules contained in the remaining chapters of this book:

1. Nonprofit organizations are characterized by their dual-management structures, composed of professional managers and financial managers.

2. The role of the professional manager is to guide the overall operation of the nonprofit organization.

3. The role of the finance function is to facilitate the achievement of the organization's professional goals.

4. The professional manager's goals are generally utility denominated, the precise expressions of which vary among nonprofit organizations.

5. The goal of the financial manager of any nonprofit organization is cost minimization, subject to a budget constraint (i.e., maintaining adequate liquidity and long-run solvency for the organization).

6. The goal and the decision rules employed by the financial manager are unaffected by the goal(s) chosen by the professional manager or the decision techniques the professional manager elects to employ.

FURTHER READING

Jacobs' classic article dealing with the theories of nonprofit hospitals provides certain insights into professional goals and the formulation of theories and models:

Jacobs, Philip. "A Survey of Economic Models of Hospitals." *Inquiry* (June 1974): 83-97.

Complete presentation of the for-profit financial management theory is contained in, but scattered throughout, most principles of financial management texts. The following text is recommended reading:

Brigham, Eugene, F. *Fundamentals of Financial Management*. Rev. ed. New York: Wiley. 1983.

QUESTIONS

1. Define the following terms:
   a. normative theory
   b. positive theory
   c. partial theory

2. What financial management goal is used in the partial normative financial theory of the nonprofit organization? Why was that goal selected?

3. What is the nature of the professional manager's goal set?

4. By what criterion is progress toward financial goal achievement measured?

5. Explain why the financial manager's role in resource-allocation decisions is described as defining the budget constraint?

6. What is meant by financial viability?

7. Defend the selection of the short-term investment rate as the proper discount rate for financial management decisions.

8. Why is asset risk irrelevant to the financial manager in all decisions except those involving financial assets?

9. What is the principal criterion used in financing decisions?

10. Why must financing and spending decisions be integrated?

11. Are professional and financial goals conflicting or consonant? Explain.

PART II

BASIC TOOLS OF FINANCIAL MANAGEMENT

The basic tools of financial management of nonprofit organizations are the accounting data and the techniques needed to transform those data into information useful for short-term financial planning and control. Accordingly, the four chapters that comprise this part of the text (1) describe the special type of accounting systems used by nonprofit organizations, (2) explain how the accounting data can be interpreted to reveal the nature of an entity's cash flows and assess its financial position, and (3) show how to employ that information to plan and control the financial aspects of the organization in the short run.

4

The Generation
of Accounting Data
in Nonprofit Organizations

This chapter and the next examine the nature of accounting data, the unique way in which the nonprofit entity prepares and presents them, and the limitations on their use in financial decision making and financial statement analysis in the nonprofit context.

NATURE OF ACCOUNTING DATA

Financial decision making requires a broad array of data, including much that is nonfinancial—economic, social, political, and legal information, for example. However, the most important quantitative data used by decision makers in a nonprofit organization are the financial data presented in its financial accounting reports—its balance sheet, statement of revenues, expenditures, and changes in fund balance, and sources and uses of funds statement.

The importance of the information contained in those statements can be measured by the frequency of their use both by insiders and by interested outside parties. Creditors, trustees, donors, and others spend considerable time reading and analyzing the financial statements of organizations in which they are interested, and they generally require that management provide them with timely reports on both an interim and an annual (audited) basis.

The reasons for the popularity of the statements are simple. First, the statements are objective—they report the results of actual historical events. Second, they present quantitative data that can be measured, compared, and manipulated arithmetically. Finally, they are expressed in dollars—a common denominator familiar to everyone and especially convenient for comparison with data on other similar organizations or with the organization's own historical financial record. In short, financial accounting data, expressed in dollars and presented in the financial statements, provide the basic ingredient—the raw material—for financial decision making of every kind.

Accounting data are sometimes spuriously precise—not nearly so accurate as their presence in formal financial statements makes them appear. But the efforts of the accounting profession over many years have made most of today's financial accounting data, if generated in conformity with generally accepted accounting principles (GAAP), sufficiently reliable to be useful in financial statement analysis and decision making.

However, accounting data cannot be used intelligently in these ways unless the interested observer or decision maker thoroughly understands the processes through which financial statements are developed and presented. The required level of accounting understanding sometimes transcends the "working knowledge of accounting principles for profit-seeking business enterprise" with which the reader is presumably already equipped. Hence the discussion that follows.

THE PURPOSE OF ACCOUNTING

The basic purpose of accounting stated in the broadest context is to translate the economic activities of business enterprise (including nonprofit organizations) into quantitative terms, using the standard monetary unit—the dollar—as the common unit of measure. The accounting process is governed by a more or less formal set of rules called GAAP, (generally accepted accounting principles). These principles must be applied on a basis consistent with those used in the preceding year, and they are the rules to which public accounting firms refer when certifying the statements of business enterprises whose accounts they have audited.

Differences Between For-profit and Nonprofit Accounting

Although similar in many respects to *business* financial accounting, accounting for nonprofit organizations developed distinctly different characteristics because of the unique nature of the nonprofit entity. Specifically, business enterprise is organized to earn profits, but the ultimate aim of a nonprofit entity is to acquire and allocate resources to fulfill some socially desirable need of the community or its members. This difference in basic purpose has caused the accounting profession to develop a specialized approach to financial accounting for nonprofit organizations. This approach, presented in considerable detail in the following chapter, builds on the fundamental accounting rules developed in response to the needs of business enterprise; however, readily discernible differences exist between the two sets of rules governing the recording and classification of the data, and hence between the forms in which the results of the activities of for-profit and nonprofit entities are presented.

Operational- Versus Dollar-Accountability

The fact that business enterprise is organized and operated solely to earn profits mandates that the forms in which the results of its economic activities are reported reflect *operational-accountability*, or the extent to which and the efficiency with which the profit objective has been achieved. This requirement is easily accommodated within the extant for-profit accounting framework, because the expenses incurred and revenues produced during each accounting period can be directly associated with the level of economic activity that has taken place within the firm during that period. The residual of revenues and expenses— profit or loss—is thus clearly indentifiable as being a function of the firm's central economic activity. Further, since each transaction involved in the profit-producing process is expressed in dollars, the efficiency of the firm's operations is easily measured by relating dollars of cash flow, dollars invested in assets, and dollar claims against income and assets among one another in various combinations. Hence, the form in which the data are presented keeps those responsible for management decisions *operationally accountable* to the firm's owners and creditors, as well as to other interested parties.

In contrast, nonprofit organizations do not always realize revenues as a direct result of their central economic activities. Nonprofit hospitals are the notable exception to this rule; the bulk of their revenues is realized from the sale of health-care services at (more or less) market-determined prices. Nonprofit organizations, such as churches, museums, and charitable organizations, do not set prices on their goods and services or, for that matter, collect much revenue from the beneficiaries to which their activities are principally directed. In some cases, the products or services are provided without charge or at nominal cost to their "customers." Moreover, their operating costs are often understated, principally because (and to the extent that) they rely on volunteer services and donated materials. Hence, providing for *operational-accountability* in the accounting system and statements is impossible for those nonprofit organizations that conduct activities that are nor recorded in the accounting statements.

The absence of both the profit motive and a direct cash-flow return from the nonprofit organization's central economic activity causes the accounting emphasis to be placed on the stewardship or fiduciary role of management. That is, at all times the organization must be able to fully account for the funds it has received and expended in pursuing its basic objectives. For that reason, the accounting systems designed for nonprofit organizations produce financial statements that reveal the entity's activities in terms of *dollar-accountability*, rather than in operational terms. Each dollar of cash inflow and outflow must be traceable through the organization in order to demonstrate the integrity of both management and the organization to all interested parties.

Constancy of Purpose

The accounting rules for both types of organizations are still being developed by the accounting profession in response to changing economic and social circumstances. For example, accountants are now concerned with such problems as how to deal with inflation in a systematic way and how to place a monetary value on the work forces of both business enterprise and especially of the nonprofit organization (the problem of valuing "human capital").

But in spite of continual changes in the body of GAAP, the basic purpose of accounting remains constant. That purpose, detailed in *Accounting Research Study No. 1*,[1] may be summarized as follows:

1. To measure the value of the resources held by the accounting entity

2. To present the value of the claims against and the interests held in those resources

3. To reflect all changes in the values of resources, claims, and interests from one period to the next

4. To express those values in monetary terms

This purpose is carried out in accordance with accounting rules that govern the *recording, measurement*, and *presentation* of the data. Those rules are classified as accounting *principles* and *conventions* (also called *postulates* or *assumptions*). In addition, since the activities of all accounting entities are subject to a wide variety of influences, the rules allow for the exercise of personal judgment in the application of the principles and conventions.

---

1. Maurice Moonitz, "The Basic Postulate of Accounting," *Accounting Research Study No. 1* (New York: American Institute of Certified Public Accountants, 1961).

RECORDING THE DATA

The procedures for recording accounting data are governed by the principle of double-entry bookkeeping, a system based on the duality of every accounting transaction. For example, if an organization is extended credit by one of its suppliers for the purpose of procuring office supplies, it acquires an asset (inventory) in exchange for a claim (accounts payable) against the entity. Moreover, the asset and the claim or liability are recorded as equal in value.

Dollar-accountability accounting systems emphasize *cash* inflows and outflows. The inflows are called *revenues* or *receipts* and the outflows are called *expenditures*. (In contrast, operational-accountability statements label outflows as expenses, which may or may not result in a *cash* outflow during the period.) The basic accounting equation that governs the recording of transactions in these systems is

Assets + Expenditures = Liabilities + Receipts + Fund balance

The more familiar accounting equation used by business enterprise includes neither expenditures nor revenues, and the term *owners' equity*, is used in place of *fund balance*. The reason for the expansion of the accounting equation to include expenditures and revenues is, again, simply to account for all cash inflows and outflows, regardless of their particular sources.

Under the double-entry accounting system, all transactions are recorded and classified under one of the five general headings that comprise the nonprofit accounting equation, and then the counterbalancing accounting entry is appropriately classified and recorded. In general, an increase in any element in either side of the equation will be counterbalanced by either (1) an increase in an element in the opposite side, (2) a decrease in another element in the same side, or (3) some combination of increases and decreases in the other elements in both sides of the equation. In any case, the net dollar changes in both sides of the equation will be equal, thus maintaining the equation's balance.

For example, suppose St. John's Lutheran Church acquired a new organ costing $100,000. The church paid $30,000 in cash from its organ fund; received $10,000 in donations; and borrowed $60,000 from its bank on a 10-year note. The individual transactions that fully account for the relevant cash flows and changes in the balance sheet are as follows:

1. Borrowing:
   Increase cash by $60,000   (assets)
   Increase liability by $60,000   (liabilities)
2. Donations:
   Increase cash by $10,000   (assets)
   Receive revenues of $10,000   (revenues)

3. Purchase of organ:
   Increased fixed assets by $100,000   (assets)
   Decrease cash by $100,000   (assets)

The net change in the church's asset accounts is ($60,000 + $10,000 + $100,000 − $100,000 =) $70,000, thus increasing the left side of the accounting equation by that amount. The total of liability increases and revenues is ($60,000 + $10,000 =) $70,000, making the increase in the right side of the equation equal to that of the left side.

The "business" activities of the nonprofit organization are recorded in this manner continually in the form of *journal entries* that describe and define in dollar amounts each separate accounting transaction. The recorded transactions are based on *source documents*, such as invoices, employee time cards, cash register tapes, and so forth. The journal entries contain specific references to the source documents in order to produce an "audit trail" that facilitates verification of dollar amounts and transaction legality.

Periodically the journal entries are collected and summarized in several *ledgers*, which are books that contain the accounting transactions that individually affect each of the entity's asset, liability, fund balance, and revenue and expenditure accounts. For example, all journal entries involving the *cash account* are transferred, say, daily to the *cash ledger* and those that involve the payment of utility bills are recorded in the *utility expense ledger*. The account representing the summary of all the ledgers is called the *preclosing trial balance* into which all individual revenue and expenditure accounts are closed at the end of each accounting period. The net debit (cash inflow) or credit (cash outflow) balance in that account—reflecting net cash gain or loss for the period—is then closed into the *fund balance account*.

To illustrate this process in a simple context, suppose that the Perkins Housing Authority reported the following information:

1. Beginning balances:
   Cash $ 15,000
   Rents receivable   32,000
   Accounts payable   29,000
   Fund balance   18,000
2. Rent charges to the tenants recorded for
   the period amounted to $ 175,000
3. Rent payments received totaled $ 198,000
4. Purchases of material, supplies, and labor
   on account totaled $ 110,000
5. Salaries paid during the period were $ 63,000
6. Accounts payable paid were $ 122,000

These financial transactions are recorded initially in a journal and then transferred to the ledgers, which are represented by the T-accounts that follow. The numbers in parentheses in T-accounts correspond to the preceding transactions, and the letters correspond to the entries in the preclosing trial balance (Exhibit 4-1) and the financial statements (Exhibits 4-2 and 4-3).

Cash	
(1) $ 15,000	(5) $ 63,000
(3) 198,000	(6) 122,000
$213,000	$185,000
(A) $ 28,000	

Rents Receivable	
(1) $ 32,000	(3) $198,000
(2) 175,000	
$207,000	
(B) $ 9,000	

Accounts Payable	
(6) $122,000	(1) $ 29,000
	(4) 110,000
	$139,000
	$ 17,000 (C)

Fund Balance	
	(1) $ 18,000 (D)

Revenue	
	(2) $175,000 (F)

Expenditures	
(4) $110,000	
(5) 63,000	
(F) $173,000	

The financial data contained in the T-account "ledgers" are then summarized in the preclosing trial balance presented in Exhibit 4-1. This step proves the mathematical accuracy of the recording process and serves as a basis for preparing the financial statements.

After thus closing the ledgers to the trial balance at the end of an accounting period, the balances of all the asset, liability, and fund balance accounts and all the accumulated revenues and expenditures are transferred to what may be termed the grand summaries—the *financial statements*. The statement of revenues and expenditures and the balance sheet for the Perkins Housing Authority are presented in Exhibits 4-2 and 4-3, respectively. In producing such summaries, the accountant must follow established rules that govern the assembly and appropriate display of data collected.

OBJECTIVES OF ACCOUNTING STANDARDS

The preparation of financial statements from accounting data is

---

Exhibit 4-1: Preclosing Trial Balance for the Perkins Housing Authority

	Debit	Credit
A. Cash	$ 28,000	
B. Rents receivable	9,000	
C. Accounts payable		$ 17,000
D. Fund balance		18,000
E. Revenue		175,000
F. Expenditures	173,000	
	$210,000	$210,000

Exhibit 4-2: **Statement of Revenues and Expenditures for the Perkins Housing Authority**

E. Revenues	$175,000
F. Expenditures	173,000
G. Excess of revenues over expenditures	$ 2,000 (to fund balance)

---

governed by rules called accounting standards, which include conventions and GAAP. The purpose of the rules is to endow the financial statements and the information they contain with attributes intended to maximize their usefulness to those who must base decisions on them.

Desirable Attributes

Accounting data in the form of financial statements are used by different people for different purposes. Thus the statements should be clear, complete, comprehensive, and of general purpose. Trade creditors, prospective donors and employees, and managers must be readily able to satisfy their needs for financial information from a single set of statements produced by the organization's accounts. Moreover, the information should be relevant to each; that is, the statements should provide needed data directly and conveniently.

The financial statements should also be objective; that is, free from any influence of concerned individuals or interests. They should be subject to verification through audit and completely reliable. Otherwise their usefulness for financial decision making will be greatly reduced.

A given organization's current financial statements should possess historical (i.e., *intertemporal*) comparability with its statements as of earlier dates. They also should be comparable, both currently and historically, with statement data generated for other similar entities. Such comparability ensures that differences in financial results arise from differences in circumstance, not merely from differences in accounting methods.

Finally, the "current" data should indeed be timely, since the further

---

Exhibit 4-3: **Balance Sheet for the Perkins Housing Authority**

A.	Cash	$ 28,000	C.	Accounts payable	$ 17,000
B.	Rents receivable	9,000	D. & G.	Fund balance	20,000
	Total assets	$ 37,000		Total liabilities and fund balance	$ 37,000

financial information is removed in time from the events that produced it, the less useful it is to those who wish to rely on it in making financial decisions. The statements should be prepared and distributed to all potential users as soon as possible after the end of the accounting period.

Conventions

The desirable attributes enumerated above will not characterize an organization's financial statements unless structure and uniformity are introduced into the process of generating and manipulating the accounting information on which they are based. Accounting *conventions* provide the needed structure and uniformity and are, indeed, the underlying tenets of accounting. Some of the more important of those conventions relate to entity, accounting periods, continuity, conservatism, consistency, and full disclosure.

Entity. Accounting theory assumes that the results of only one major accounting entity should be shown in one set of financial statements. That is the convention of entity. There are a few traditional exceptions, usually involving a group of related organizations engaged in the same type of business operation but legally separate. The majority of such cases involve for-profit corporations, and such statements are referred to as *consolidated.* A primary reason for preparing consolidated statements is that the combined data are more meaningful to users than would be the data presented separately from each of the related entities. As will be seen in the next chapter, nonprofit organizations may also present consolidated statements composed of several "funds" maintained separately by a single organization. These funds and their separate accounting treatment are created because of legal restrictions placed on the use of cash donated to the organization by outside donors.

Accounting Periods. The desirable attributes of timeliness and comparability, which require that accounting data be prepared and presented at frequent and more or less standard intervals, lead to the convention of reporting by accounting period. While comprehensive reports are generally prepared only at annual intervals, more frequent intervals (e.g., quarterly or semiannual) are used for interim reporting.

This convention permits a fiscal year to be defined as a twelve-month period other than a calendar year. For example, a symphony orchestra may elect to end its business year on September 30, a date that corresponds to the close of its summer program and the start of its fall concert and major fund-raising season. A professional association may elect to end its fiscal year at the end of the month in which its annual convention is held. In this way the new officers can assume their positions during the convention and report on the organization's progress at the end of their terms of office (during the next convention).

Continuity. Although financial statements are prepared only periodically, the operations of nonprofit organizations go on continuously. The convention of continuity assumes that those operations will also go on indefinitely; consequently the costs of long-lived assets may properly be carried on the books of the entity over the many accounting periods that constitute their useful lives, without regard to their current market or liquidation values. Similarly the current (due within one year) portions of long-term liabilities are shown in statements as short-term liabilities, to separate the effect of short-term debts on the liquidity of the organization from the effect of long-term debts on its solvency.

Conservatism. The convention of conservatism is based on the proposition that, given the risks and uncertainties inherent in managing the affairs of both business and nonprofit entities, it is better to err on the side of caution in estimating the outcomes of future events. In conformity with that convention, accountants do not record revenue until it is realized but take account of a loss as soon as it can reasonably be foreseen. The valuation of inventories at "the lower of cost or market" is a corollary of the convention, stating that the value of inventories may never exceed cost but that any reduction in their current market value below that cost must immediately be recognized.

At times the convention of conservatism conflicts with that of consistency, in that gains and losses are not handled in the same manner. In all such cases the convention of conservatism takes precedence, to achieve the desirable attribute of objectivity.

Consistency. The convention of consistency requires that both the presentation of accounting data in financial statements and the underlying methods of generating them be consistent over time to preserve the desirable attribute of intertemporal statement comparability. When a material change is made in any of the accounting principles employed, the fact of the change, its effect, and the reason for making it must be fully and immediately disclosed. There is also an underlying, though sometimes rebuttable, presumption that any change in accounting principles employed is always in the direction of generating better accounting data, providing for fairer presentation of the data, or permitting fuller disclosure.

Full Disclosure. Full disclosure does not mean that the whole mass of accounting data generated by the organization's accountants during the year should be included in its annual (audited) financial statements. It means that sufficient information should be presented in such a way as to avoid misleading anyone using the statements. In other words, not only accountants but also—and especially—financial managers, as well as actual and potential donors and creditors, regulatory agencies, and all others interested in a particular organization, should be able to derive conclusions significant to their own interest from an inspection of the organization's financial statements.

Generally Accepted Accounting Principles (GAAP)

Accounting standards and conventions establish the framework in which the generation and presentation of accounting data occur. So-called GAAP are established within that framework and provide answers to such questions as: How are assets to be properly valued? When are liabilities to be shown as having been incurred? How should the accounting recognition of revenues, expenses, and "profits" and "losses" be timed? What formats for the presentation of financial statements are most appropriate?

The principles are not embodied in any authoritative written code, containing mutually exclusive methods or procedures for dealing with accounting data. They exist mostly in the minds of accountants, as "received doctrine" they have come to know during their years of training for and practice of professional accountancy. Changes in the GAAP are communicated to practitioners largely through professional publications. For example, in 1978 the Accounting Standards Division of the American Institute of Certified Public Accountants (AICPA) issued *Statement of Position 78-10*, titled "Accounting Principles and Reporting Practices for Certain Nonprofit Organizations." Its purpose is to recommend GAAP for nonprofit organizations not covered in existing guides. In 1981 the AICPA issued an audit and accounting guide, *Audits of Certain Nonprofit Organizations*. And in 1988, it issued guidelines on depreciation of fixed assets of nonprofit organizations.

In addition to GAAP, which provide the basis for all accounting standards, other sets of principles exist that are relevant to particular kinds of nonprofit organizations. Examples of these include: accounting for colleges and universities, National Association of College and University Business Officers, *College and University Business Administration*, 3rd. ed. (Washington, D.C.: NACUBO, 1974); accounting for hospitals, American Hospital Association, *Chart of Accounts for Hospitals* (Chicago: American Hospital Association, 1976); accounting for voluntary health and welfare organizations, National Health Council, National Assembly of National Voluntary Health and Social Welfare Organizations, Inc., and United Way of America, *Standards of Accounting and Financial Reporting for Voluntary Health and Welfare Organizations* (New York: National Health Council, et al., 1975).

The generally accepted principles are seldom dogmatic. For example, they often go only so far as to state equally satisfactory alternative methods of recording accounting transactions. This, of course, strongly implies that the starting point for any type of analysis of the financial statements should be an investigation, if one is possible, of the principles underlying the data presented. The analyst should not take such data at full face value. Instead, he or she must "go behind" them to ascertain whether any data adjustments are required to conform the statements to the particular needs and interests being served. Sometimes the analyst will have an adequate supply of facts immediately at hand to make such an investigation; at other times such facts will not be available. At those other times, the analyst will be able to do no more than acknowledge and accept the possible existence of *accounting risk* in the resulting analysis.

Accounting risk is defined as the inherent risk that conclusions derived from financial statement analysis may be faulty because of the existence of alternative accounting principles and possible variations in *personal judgments* about the application of those alternatives. It raises the possibility that differing interpretations may be given to the same body of data because of a variation in personal judgment or because different GAAP have been used to generate and present it.

For example, a nonprofit organization usually records *pledges receivable* as an asset and an item of revenue in the year they are expected to be received. However, since no contractual obligation is created by the donors when they pledge cash contributions to an organization, the realizable value of those pledges is open to question. Accounting risk is therefore present to the extent that management either overvalues or undervalues pledges receivable by a significant amount on the organization's books.

The analyst cannot avoid accounting risk; he or she can only attempt to minimize it by becoming as completely knowledgeable as possible about which alternatives management has used in a given situation, and then by keeping that information constantly in mind as he or she proceeds with the analysis of the data.

Bases of Accounting

Profit-seeking business organizations almost always maintain their accounting records on an *accrual basis*. This means that in addition to recording business transactions resulting from and in the receipt and disbursement of *cash*, businesses also record the transactions that result from and in the creation of *financial assets* and *claims*—accounts receivable and accounts payable, for example. Nonprofit organizations, especially the smaller ones, generally employ either the *cash basis* or *modified cash basis* of accounting instead. The cash basis of accounting requires that the organization recognize only those transactions in which cash is involved, either as a receipt or disbursement, at the time the transaction actually occurs. Unpaid bills owed by or to the organization remain unrecorded until cash settlement of the bills is accomplished. The modified cash basis of accounting possesses characteristics of both the accrual and cash bases, but it more closely resembles the cash basis.

Accrual Accounting. The accrual basis of accounting requires the organization to recognize and record both income and expenses at the time the organization and a second party (i.e., a client, donor, customer, supplier, or lender) agree to exchange cash for some specific purpose. The exchange of cash may be immediate, as in a cash purchase of goods or services, or the two parties may agree to delay the exchange of cash, as in the extension of short-term credit or the creation of a pledge to donate cash at a specified later date. Thus a nonprofit organization that maintains material amounts of unpaid bills or uncollected revenues at the beginning or end of an accounting period should use the accrual basis of accounting in order to present an accurate and fair representation of its financial position to both management and interested outside parties.

Accrual basis reporting is also necessary if an organization's management wishes to measure the cost or the profitability of a product or service. Material amounts of costs or substantial amounts of revenues that remain unrecorded because they are represented in unpaid bills or uncollected fees under the cash basis of accounting obviously cannot be ignored in the measurement of product costs and profits.

Accrual accounting is also more useful than other bases when an organization constantly, or even occasionally, faces severe liquidity problems. In such cases, the amounts of both accrued revenues and expenditures become critical factors in short-term financial planning and liquidity management, and therefore must appear on the organization's current financial statements.

Finally, among the GAAP established for both commercial and nonprofit organizations is the one that requires the use of the accrual basis of accounting. Thus organizations that employ certified public accountants (CPAs) as auditors must either maintain their accounting records on the accrual basis or else adjust their statements at the end of the accounting period to reflect this basis. Otherwise, as described later in this chapter, the auditor cannot render an unqualified or "clean" opinion of the organization's operations and financial position, even though that organization's financial and operational activities were completely aboveboard in all respects.

Cash Basis. The principal advantage to the use of cash basis accounting is its simplicity; transactions are recorded only when cash has been received or paid out. A checkbook is generally the only accounting record needed by an organization that elects to use this basis, and when financial statements are required, the financial officer merely transcribes and summarizes the transactions from the check stubs.

Since a checkbook can be an adequate substitute for a formal set of accounting journals and ledgers (provided that the check stubs are large enough to accommodate a complete description of each transaction), an individual with no bookkeeping or accounting training could easily and competently keep the records of a small- or medium-sized organization on the cash basis.

Many larger nonprofit organizations, including some that employ trained accounting and bookkeeping personnel, elect to use the cash basis of accounting because it is simpler. The cash flows of these organizations, however, are usually such that the financial and operational results reported under the accrual and cash bases are not materially different from each other. For example, cash receipts recorded in the current period arising from activities that took place in prior periods may be roughly equal from one year to the next for organizations of this type. Bills for goods and services also may be paid promptly. Thus under the cash basis of accounting, net cash flows balance out from year to year, only a small amount of liabilities is carried forward into succeeding periods, and the omission from the books of unrealized revenues presents a conservative yet realistic picture of the financial position of an organization such as this. And this satisfactory result may be accomplished at considerable cash savings for accounting and bookkeeping services because of the simplicity of the cash basis as compared with accrual basis accounting.

Finally, it is a relatively simple matter to adjust the financial statements prepared on the cash basis to the accrual basis. Moreover, an organization's monthly or quarterly statements may be prepared on the cash basis, with accrual basis adjustments being made only at fiscal year end. In this way, an organization can realize the benefits of operating under the cash basis yet achieve compliance with GAAP for purposes of year-end audit by a CPA.

The adjustments to the cash basis statements are based on two sets of data that may be recorded on worksheets, rather than as formal entries into the organization's accounting records. These data are merely the dollars owed to and owed by the organization at the ends of the previous and current fiscal years. These amounts are classified under the appropriate headings, netted out against each other, and added or deducted from the cash basis figures to produce the accrual figures. An example will help clarify this process.

The cash basis investment income from Cornwell College totaled $30,000 in 1988. Accrued interest payable to the college from bank certificates of deposit, as routinely reported to the IRS by the bank, was $2,500 and $2,900 for years 1987 and 1988, respectively.

Since the check for $2,500 of interest was received in 1988 but was earned in 1987, that amount should be *deducted* from 1988's investment income. And since the 1988 interest of $2,900 will not be received in cash until 1989, that amount must be *added* to the college's 1988 investment income. Thus,

Cash basis investment income, 1988		$ 30,000
Adjustments		
deduct 1987 interest income	−$ 2,500	
add 1988 interest income	+ 2,900	
Net interest income	+	400
Accrual basis investment income, 1988		$ 30,400

All other such items are handled in the same manner, and the adjusted figures are employed in the place of those presented in the cash basis financial statements.

Modified Cash Basis. The modified cash basis of accounting, sometimes called the modified accrual basis, is a kind of compromise between cash and accrual accounting. In general, on this basis, all unpaid bills will be recorded on the accrual basis but revenues will be maintained on the cash basis. In some instances, accounts and pledges receivable will be recorded as accrued items as they are created. In other cases liabilities will be accrued, but not revenues; however, the actual system that will be used will depend largely on the requirements of the individual organization.

As in the case of cash basis accounting, organizations that adopt the modified cash basis need not maintain an elaborate set of accounting records. Check stubs are satisfactory source documents from which to develop the cash basis accounting data. Then, at the end of the accounting period, the bookkeeper will assemble and record the amounts owed or owing in those categories that are to be accounted for on the accrual basis. Adjustments identical to that illustrated earlier are all that are required to complete the modified cash basis financial statements.

PRESENTING THE DATA

The efforts of the accountant in creating and recording the data that measure and present the results of the economic activities of the nonprofit organization culminate in the periodic preparation of financial statements. Accounting standards, conventions, and GAAP govern the process leading to statement preparation and also the form and content of the statements summarizing the organization's activities for an accounting period. The following sections deal with each of the three basic financial statements generally produced and used by nonprofit organizations: (1) balance sheet, (2) statement of support, revenue, expenses, and changes in fund balance, and (3) statement of cash flows. In some cases nonprofit organizations will prepare a separate statement of changes in fund balance, and a statement of functional expenses.

The statement titles listed here are those given to the statements prepared on the accrual basis. Cash basis balance sheets are titled "Statements of Assets and Liabilities Resulting from Cash Transactions," and cash basis statements of revenues, expenses, and changes in fund balances are titled, "Statements of Receipts and Expenditures." These titles are used to emphasize the *cash* aspect of the statements. The statements illustrated here are prepared on the accrual basis of accounting.

Keep in mind that the formats of the financial statements vary considerably from one organization to another, and depend largely on the unique informational requirements imposed by their managers. Those that follow should be typical of many statements that will be encountered in the nonprofit context and, failing that objective, are sufficiently general to enable the reader to understand the content and purpose of each basic statement.

Balance Sheet

The balance sheet is the principal financial statement among the three that are generally prepared. It lists the assets, liabilities, and fund balances of a nonprofit organization as of a certain date. Except for cash and such claims to cash as accounts receivable and investments in securities, the assets listed in the balance sheet both support the organization's activities and will eventually be "consumed" by them, either within one accounting period (current assets), or over time (noncurrent assets).

Liabilities are sums owed to creditors. Their values as shown in the balance sheet are fixed as to amount and maturity either by contract, as in the case of notes or bonds payable, or by customary trade practice, as in the case of accounts payable.

The fund balances, which are roughly equivalent to the equity capital (stockholders' equity or partnership or proprietor's capital) in for-profit accounting statements, represent the aggregate net accounting or "book" value of the organization. Unlike stockholders' equity, the fund balance does not represent residual *ownership* claims, since nonprofit organizations normally do not have stockholders, as used in the corporate sense of the term. Instead, the fund balance comprises the receipt of donated funds—gifts, grants, and bequests, for example—and the excess of receipts over expenditures recorded over time.

Exhibit 4-4 illustrates a common form of balance sheet. The columnar format separating the balance sheet accounts into several "funds" is peculiar to the accounting concept called *fund accounting*, which methodology is widely used by nonprofit organizations. In fund accounting, the assets, liabilities, and fund balances are segregated into categories according to restrictions placed on the use of donated and borrowed funds. Each category is accounted for and reported as a more or less separate entity, principally for dollar-accountability purposes. The following chapter deals with this concept in greater detail.

The arrangement of the assets, liabilities, and fund balances on the balance sheet is the same as that used in for-profit accounting; that is, items are listed in descending order of liquidity for assets and ascending order of maturity for liabilities and equity. Among the assets, for example, the most liquid asset, cash, is listed first, followed by the less liquid current assets and then by the more permanent fixed assets. And among the liabilities, the debts with the shortest maturities are shown first, followed by long-term debt, and finally by fund balances.

Exhibit 4-4: **Conway City Library, Balance Sheet, December 31, 1988**

| | Current funds | | Building and equipment fund | Endowment fund | Totals |
	Unrestricted	Restricted			
Assets					
Current assets:					
Cash	$ 2,280	$ 360	$ 310	$ 430	$ 3,380
Short-term securities	5,000	8,000	2,000	8,300	23,300
Pledges receivable (net)	13,880		3,360	6,590	23,830
Fines receivable (net)	60				60
Grants receivable		10,860	56,800		67,660
Supplies	190		640		830
Total current assets	$ 21,410	$ 19,220	$ 63,110	$ 15,320	$ 119,060
Investments (at market)		9,300	168,000	32,680	209,980
Land, buildings, and equipment, net of depreciation			593,600		593,600
Total assets	$ 21,410	$ 28,520	$ 824,710	$ 48,000	$ 922,640
Liabilities and Fund Balances					
Current liabilities:					
Accounts payable	$ 3,870	$ 1,000			$ 4,870
Accrued expenses	1,900				1,900
Current portion of mortgage			$ 62,500		62,500
Total current liabilities	$ 5,770	$ 1,000	$ 62,500		$ 69,270
Mortgage payable			375,000		375,000
Total liabilities	$ 5,770	$ 1,000	$ 437,500		$ 444,270
Fund balances:					
Unrestricted	$ 15,640				$ 15,640
Restricted:					
Purchase of books		$ 3,860			3,860
Children's programs		13,660			13,660
Purchase of fixed assets		7,000	$ 56,800		63,800
Invested in fixed assets			330,410		330,410
Endowment funds		3,000		$ 48,000	51,000
Total fund balances	$ 15,640	$ 27,520	$ 387,210	$ 48,000	$ 478,370
Total liabilities and fund balances	$ 21,410	$ 28,520	$ 824,710	$ 48,000	$ 922,640

The practice of showing assets at the top (or on the left side) of the balance sheet and liabilities and equity accounts at the bottom (or on the right) is an application of the *accounting equation*:

$$\text{Assets} = \text{Liabilities} + \text{Fund balance}$$

The balance sheet and the accounting equation on which it is based reflect the proposition that, at any given time, the assets of a business are equal in value to the total funds used to acquire them.

Statement of Support, Revenues, and Expenses

The statement of support, revenues, expenses, and changes in fund balances is similar to the income statement used by for-profit firms; however, since nonprofit accounting is oriented toward dollar-accountability rather than toward operational-accountability, the statement emphasizes cash inflows and outflows and not profits or losses. This statement is also called the *Statement of Activity* and the *Operating Statement*.

The statement of support, revenues, expenses, and changes in fund balances is really a statement of activity expressed in dollar terms. The columnar form is appropriate in that it reveals in considerable detail the activities of each major fund. The section at the bottom of the statement shows the aggregate residual effects of these activities on the organization's individual fund balances, along with any interfund transfers that may have taken place during the period. A fairly typical statement of support revenues, expenses, and changes in fund balances is shown in Exhibit 4-5.

Statement of Cash Flows

The statement of cash flows (sometimes called the sources and uses of funds statement or, more colloquially, the "where-got, where-gone" statement) shows the changes in the kinds and amounts of all sources of funds during a given period and details the uses to which the funds were put. It takes up where the statement of revenues, expenses, and changes in fund balances leaves off in that it also encompasses dollar increases and decreases in the organization's assets and liabilities. The data presented in this statement begin with a listing of the excess of revenues over expenses and then account for all balance sheet changes that have taken place between balance sheet dates. The information it conveys is useful in analyzing the full impact of the organization's activities in terms of both cash inflows from external sources and allocations and reallocations of funds to and among its assets. Exhibit 4-6 presents an example of this important financial statement. A discussion of interpretation of the data presented in this and in the other financial statements is presented in chapter 6.

Statement of Functional Expenses

The statement of functional expenses, illustrated in Exhibit 4-7, presents a detailed analysis of the "expenses" section of the statement of support, revenue, expenses, and changes in fund balances. This analysis examines the organization's expenses by type of expense for each of its *programs* and *support areas*. In Exhibit 4-7, the detail is shown for Conway City Library's two primary services (circulation department and

Exhibit 4-5: **Conway City Library, Statement of Support, Revenues, Expenses, and Changes in Fund Balances, Year Ended December 31, 1988**

	Current funds		Building and equipment fund	Endowment fund	Totals
	Unrestricted	Restricted			
Public Support and Revenues					
Public Support					
Contributions	$ 70,380	$ 3,200	$ 4,000	$ 10,900	$ 88,480
Grants		20,500			20,500
Donated services	5,000		1,000		6,000
Total public support	$ 75,380	$ 23,700	$ 5,000	$ 10,900	$ 114,980
Revenue					
Media rental	1,810				1,810
Investment income	300	1,190	19,320	4,340	25,150
Other	980				980
Total revenue	$ 3,090	$ 1,190	$ 19,320	$ 4,340	$ 27,940
Total support and revenue	$ 78,470	$ 24,890	$ 24,320	$ 15,240	$ 142,920
Expenses					
Program	$ 55,910	$ 15,360			$ 71,270
General administration	6,700	1,060	$ 9,000	$ 680	17,440
Operation and maintenance of building			22,220		22,220
Fund raising	7,300				7,300
Interest expense			35,000		35,000
Total expenses	$ 69,910	$ 16,420	$ 66,220	$ 680	$ 153,230
Excess of revenues and other additions over expenses	$ 8,560	$ 8,470	$ (41,900)	$ 14,560	$ (10,310)
Fund balance beginning of year	12,080	19,050	424,110	33,440	488,680
Interfund transfers	(5,000)		5,000		
Fund balance end of year	$ 15,640	$ 27,520	$ 387,210	$ 48,000	$ 478,370

audio and video programs) and its two support areas (administration and fund raising). This statement is considered a supplementary schedule for most nonprofit organizations, but is mandated for voluntary health and welfare agencies. A discussion of the interpretation of the data presented in this and in the other financial statements is presented in chapter 6.

AUDITED AND UNAUDITED STATEMENTS

The examination by independent CPAs of the records of a nonprofit organization's operating and financial transactions during an accounting period, leading to the independent auditors' certification of the financial statements, is the best assurance available to interested individuals of the reliability of the data the statements contain. The user of these data must always remember, though, that at all times and in all situations the financial statements of an organization are primarily the representations of its management. The CPA's task is to review the accounting records and systems, to make such tests and checks of them as he or she deems

Exhibit 4–6: **Conway City Library, Statement of Cash Flows, Year Ended December 31, 1988**

	Current funds		Building and equipment fund	Endowment fund	Totals
	Unrestricted	Restricted			
Cash flow provided by:					
Excess of support and revenues over expenses	$ 8,560	$ 8,470	$ (41,900)	$ 14,560	$ (10,310)
Add: Depreciation			75,800		75,800
Unrealized (gains) and losses on securities		(610)	(4,200)	(980)	(5,790)
Cash flow provided by operations	$ 8,560	$ 7,860	$ 29,700	$ 13,580	$ 59,700
Sales of long-term securities		8,000	52,000		60,000
Total sources of cash flow	$ 8,560	$ 15,860	$ 81,700	$ 13,580	$ 119,700
Cash flow used for:					
Purchase of equipment			$ 6,250		$ 6,250
Reduction in long-term debt			27,500		27,500
Purchase of long-term securities				$ 16,800	16,800
Interfund transfers	$ 5,000		(5,000)		
Total uses of cash flow	$ 5,000	$ 0	$ 28,750	$ 16,800	$ 50,550
Increase (decrease) in net working capital	$ 3,560	$ 15,860	$ 52,950	$ (3,220)	$ 69,150
Changes in net working capital:					
Increases (decreases) in current assets:					
Cash	$ 1,310		$ (1,980)	$ (4,720)	$ (5,390)
Short-term securities	5,000	$ 5,000	(2,000)	6,000	14,000
Receivables	(1,760)	10,860	60,160	(4,500)	64,760
Supplies	10		100		110
Increases (decreases) in current liabilities:					
Accounts payable	(560)		(2,910)		(3,470)
Accruals	(440)		(420)		(860)
Increase (decrease) in net working capital	$ 3,560	$ 15,860	$ 52,950	$ (3,220)	$ 69,150

appropriate, and finally to state in writing (subject to such qualifications as may be necessary) whether in his or her opinion the organization's financial statements have been prepared in conformity with GAAP and fairly present its financial condition on the date of the statements.

The Accountant's Certificate

The purpose of an independent CPA's audit of a nonprofit organization's records is to enable a CPA to express an opinion on the

Exhibit 4-7. **Conway City Library, Statement of Functional Expenses, Year Ended December 31, 1988**

	Program Services		Support Services		
	Circul-ation	A.V. Program	Admin.	Fund Raising	Total Expenses
Salaries and benefits	$16,500	$ 4,620	$14,010	$3,000	$38,130
Supplies	1,250	2,450	1,740	3,000	8,440
Telephone	500	500	800	100	1,900
Postage	1,110	240	360	700	2,410
Publications	38,940	3,860	220		43,020
Occupancy	15,600	3,380	3,240		22,220
Interest			35,000		35,000
Other	970	330	310	500	2,110
Total expense	$74,870	$15,380	$55,680	$7,300	$153,230

validity of the financial statements; the form and nature of that opinion should be carefully considered by those who use the financial statements. The CPA's opinion, sometimes called the auditor's certificate (or report), accompanies the financial statements. The independent outside auditor may suggest and probably has suggested to management how, in his or her judgment, financial statements should be prepared. But the CPA can only suggest; the final decision must always be made by management. To evaluate the statements properly, therefore, interested outside parties should be fully aware of the nature of the CPA-client relationship.

The suggestions of the CPA to management will be based on a thorough analysis of the financial records in the light of GAAP. The opinion rendered will indicate whether or not the financial statements, as finally prepared, reflect a proper application of those principles. It will set out any reservations the CPA might properly express about the adequacy of the examination and the extent, if any, to which he or she differs with management about the way statement data are presented. Any such auditor's reservations should be considered by those reviewing the financial statements, who must decide for themselves, in view of all other considerations, whether the reservations are sufficiently material to reflect on the reliability of the statements.

An unqualified opinion by a reputable CPA firm is regarded by some financial statement analysts as better evidence of the reliability of the financial statements than a detailed outline of the steps taken in the examination of the statements. Competent, experienced CPAs can obtain a "feel" of statement accuracy from first-hand observation of and familiarity with an organization, while the outside analyst would have to be an expert accountant to determine whether the detailed auditing procedures undertaken were sufficient to establish the accuracy of the statements. Accordingly, each analyst should learn the meaning of the various forms of accountants' certificates and attempt to determine the relative competence of the CPA firms whose opinions accompany the financial statements.

Scope of the CPA's Examination

In their examination of a nonprofit organization's books, CPAs seldom make a complete audit of every transaction that has occurred during an accounting period. They base their opinions on a number of more or less standard tests and checks and on their general observations of the organization's accounting methods and systems. Thus in reviewing an audit report, the statement analyst should be careful to read all comments made by the CPA, particularly those outlining the nature and scope of the methods used to verify the statements. From those comments the analyst may draw conclusions as to whether the existence, ownership, and correct valuation of every asset have been reasonably established, the inclusion of all liabilities has been ensured, and the operating results have been satisfactorily verified. Unless the opinion states that a particular procedure has been omitted, the financial statement analyst is generally justified in assuming that reasonable and appropriate tests have been made of the items appearing in statements.

Types of Opinions

If, after all tests deemed necessary and appropriate have been made, a CPA feels that an organization's statements fairly present its current operating results and financial position, he or she will issue an unqualified, or "clean," opinion stating that fair presentation has been achieved. From a financial statement user's point of view, that is the best kind of opinion to have attached to any set of statements being analyzed.

The implication of a clean opinion for a set of financial statements is that, in the CPA's professional judgment, all items appearing in the statement are not only correctly valued but are also properly classified. That is a very important implication for the observer to understand and keep in mind; it would be a grave mistake to think that CPAs carrying out audits are concerned only with the accuracy of dollar amounts.

For example, in the case of the current asset section of a balance sheet, a CPA's clean opinion may be interpreted as follows:

1. The CPA has made such tests of the items included in current assets as, according to professional judgment, are deemed necessary.

2. On the basis of those tests, the CPA in effect asserts that there is a high probability that the current asset section contains cash in the amount stated and all asset items that can reasonably be expected to be converted into cash by the organization's normal operations.

3. The conversion of current assets into cash will occur within the normal operating cycle of the organization or at least within one year of the balance sheet date.

On the other hand, if the CPA feels that the statements are not fair representations of the organization's financial position, he or she will give a negative opinion (deny certification), stating in writing all the reasons for doing so. Occurrences of that kind are rare, however; management seldom wishes its organization's audited financial statements to bear a negative opinion. Typically, then, the client will follow the CPA's suggestions for improving accounting methods and statement adequacy so that fair presentation is achieved.

More frequently the CPA will for some reason not perform all the accounting tests deemed necessary for a clean opinion. He or she will then issue a qualified opinion, identifying the areas left untested. Perhaps the valuation of pledges receivable could not be tested, for example. If that value is a significant piece of information for statement purposes, the CPA will state that the test was not performed and therefore he or she cannot say with assurance that the value is fairly presented.

Unaudited Statements

Most large nonprofit organizations ordinarily prepare interim, unaudited statements for internal management purposes and to accompany fund-raising campaign literature sent to corporate donors because they contain more recent information than the latest available set of audited statements.

However honest and well-intentioned management may be, the strong possibility always exists that it will lean toward the optimistic side in preparing its financial statements for use by outside agencies or donors. The old generalization that a man's possessions are worth more to him than to anyone else is applicable here. An independent, outside verification of account values is needed to obtain an objective viewpoint.

There is even greater danger that unaudited statements may be misleading and misrepresentative through lack of knowledge of accepted accounting principles and procedures or lack of appreciation of the importance of observing those principles and procedures closely in preparing statements. Without intending to mislead, management may allow fixed-asset expenditures to be improperly capitalized, some accrued expenses to be overlooked in figuring earnings or stating liabilities, and the cost-or-market rule to be improperly applied in valuing investment securities.

The interested outside analyst confronted with unaudited statements should, if possible, review them carefully with management to determine whether proper accounting procedures were followed in preparing them. In studying the statements, the analyst should remain aware of possible unconscious or unintentional misrepresentations. In addition, unaudited statements used for external purposes should always be signed ("attested to") by an officer of the organization to establish responsibility for the representations contained in them. For obvious reasons audited statements are always preferable to unaudited ones for purposes of financial statement analysis.

SUMMARY

The principal differences between for-profit and nonprofit accounting systems are based on the difference in the basic purpose for which the accounting entities were formed. For-profit businesses are guided by the profit motive, thus giving their accounting systems the task of revealing management's operational-accountability. Nonprofit organizations are guided by motives other than profit. The stewardship function performed by managers in the nonprofit context imposes dollar-accountability standards on their accounting systems.

This difference in purpose produces differences in the ways in which accounting data are recorded, measured, and presented by businesses and nonprofit entities. These differences, although significant from the user's point of view, are not so great as to require the development of a separate accounting discipline for the nonprofit context. Many of the GAAP used in for-profit accounting have been transferred intact to the nonprofit context. Others have been transferred with only minor modification. The most striking difference in the two accounting systems is revealed in the presentation of the accounting statements, where both the form and the content of the nonprofit statements differ in obvious and material ways.

Finally, the role of the CPA in performing an audit of the nonprofit organization's operational and financial transactions is for all practical purposes identical in scope and purpose to that performed for business enterprise.

FURTHER READING

Robert J. Freeman, et al. *Government and Nonprofit Accounting*. 3rd ed. Englewood Cliffs, N.J.: Prentice-Hall, 1988.

Malvern J. Gross, Jr., and William Warshauer, *Financial and Accounting Guide for Nonprofit Organizations*. rev. ed. New York: Wiley: 1983.

Emerson O. Henke, *Accounting for Nonprofit Organizations*. 3rd ed. Boston: Kent, 1983.

QUESTIONS

1. What three features of financial statements make them useful to the managers of nonprofit organizations and other analysts?

2. What is the basic purpose of accounting in its broadest context?

3. Discuss the differences in the purposes of accounting between for-profit and nonprofit systems.

4. State the accounting equation for a nonprofit organization. How does it relate to the purpose of dollar-accountability?

5. Describe the accounting process, beginning with how the data are recorded and ending with the forms of presentation.

6. List the six accounting conventions discussed in the chapter and briefly summarize the importance of each to the task of the analyst.

7. Compare and contrast the accrual, cash, and modified cash bases of accounting.

8. Must an organization use the accrual method if it wishes to obtain a clean opinion from its auditor? Explain.

9. What is the principal feature of fund accounting?

10. What factors govern the order in which assets and liabilities appear on the balance sheet?

11. How is the dollar-accountability purpose reflected in the statement of support, revenues, expenditures, and changes in fund balances? What additional information does the statement of cash flows provide?

12. Why should a user of financial statements prefer a set of audited statements to an unaudited set?

13. What are the three types of auditor's opinions? What is the information conveyed to the statement analyst by each?

PROBLEMS

1. The Alta Public Broadcasting System reported the following financial information:

    (1) Beginning balances:

Cash	$ 8,500
Accounts and pledges receivable	10,400
Fixed assets	90,600

Accounts payable	12,500
Mortgage payable	50,000
Fund balance	47,000

(2) Public support = $155,000 (all in pledges)
(3) Total operating revenues = $121,400 ($50,100 received in cash)
(4) Collection of accounts and pledges receivable = $221,900
(5) Wages and salaries paid = $93,000
(6) Programming materials purchased on account = $150,300
(7) Payments on account = $141,100
(8) Cash purchase of fixed assets = $30,000
(9) Cash payment on mortgage = $2,500

a. Record the financial transactions in T-account form.
b. Prepare a preclosing trial balance.
c. Prepare a balance sheet and statement of support, revenues, expenditures, and changes in fund balance.

2. The Rosebud Academy maintains its accounts on the cash basis. Its tuition revenues for the current year were reported at $659,375. Uncollected tuition payments at the beginning of the year totaled $83,336, and by year-end that figure fell to $59,870. Restate tuition revenues on the accrual basis.

5

Principles of
Fund Accounting

The preceding chapter introduced the concept of fund accounting and established the rationale for its application to and widespread use in the nonprofit context. The purpose of this chapter is to present in somewhat greater detail the more important principles and procedures of fund accounting systems. This chapter will also examine some of the limitations of accounting data that often obscure real asset and cash flow values and thus create serious data problems for decision makers and others interested in the operations of nonprofit organizations.

FUND ACCOUNTING DEFINED

Fund accounting is a system of maintaining the financial records of a nonprofit organization that, for accounting purposes only, segregates its assets, liabilities, equities, revenues, and expenditures into several separate entities. The entities, which are called *funds*, are identified with either the sources from which the organization has acquired its resources or the purposes for which the resources are to be expended, or both.

Each fund is constituted as a self-balancing accounting unit, with separate sets of accounting records that are summarized into separate sets of financial statements. No theoretical limits to the number of funds that may be created within an organization exist, but practical limits certainly do exist. Resources that have similar restrictions placed on them, or assets that are held for common purposes, usually are grouped together in a single fund in order to reduce the dimensions of the organization's accounting and reporting requirements.

Fund accounting is unique to nonprofit organizations and government entities and their agencies; however, material differences exist in the application of the principles and procedures of fund accounting as they are applied to certain nonprofit and governmental classifications. Those interested in a specific classification of nonprofit organization should, of course, become thoroughly acquainted with fund accounting principles and procedures applicable to that particular organizational classification.[1] But present purposes are best served in this chapter by presenting an overview of fund accounting principles in order to promote a general understanding of the most important facets of nonprofit accounting.

THE CREATION OF FUNDS FOR ACCOUNTING PURPOSES

Most funds are created as a result of a restriction placed by a donor or a grantor on the purpose for which certain resources are to be *used* by the organization. Occasionally, a fund is created in order to recognize the *source* of the contribution, rather than as a result of a restriction on the disposition of assets. In any event, the *restriction*, rather than either the specific source or use of the resources, is the basis on which the separate funds are created.

The restrictions underlying fund creations may be either externally or internally imposed. External restrictions may be imposed by the contributor or result from the nature of the contribution itself. For example, if the Greenville PTA is given $5,000 to be used only in connection with an educational program on drug abuse, the $5,000 must be accounted for separately to ensure that the donor's wishes are carried out. If the Monroe Baptist Church solicits contributions from its members specifically to purchase a new organ, all cash received during the campaign must be segregated and reported on as a separate entity and may be used only for the purpose for which it was received—to purchase an organ.

Internal restrictions on the uses of resources are generally imposed by the organization's governing board, principally as matters of convenience. Funds thus created are termed "board-designated funds," and they result in the accounting segregation of certain assets that management has decided to use for some specified purposes. For example, Metro Family Services, Inc., partitions its general operating fund into several separate *program* funds, such as Drug Abuse, Children's Services, and Care for the Elderly, in order to better account for the resources allocated to each program.

A set of financial statements illustrating the use of multiple board-designated funds is presented in Exhibit 5-1. The financial statements show that most of the organization's activities are concerned with the Drug Abuse program, which is currently operating at a deficit of $15,400.

---

1. For this purpose, see Robert J. Freeman, et al. *Government and Nonprofit Accounting* (Englewood Cliffs, N.J.: Prentice-Hall, 1988).

Exhibit 5-1: **Illustration of How a General Operating Fund is Divided into Several Board-Designated Funds**

METRO FAMILY SERVICES, INC.
BALANCE SHEET
General Operating Fund

	Drug abuse	Children's services	Care for the elderly	General fund totals
Assets				
Cash	$ 9,800	$ 6,300	$ 2,200	$ 18,300
Grants receivable	75,300	0	0	75,300
Inventories	2,200	500	600	3,300
Total assets	$ 87,300	$ 6,800	$ 2,800	$ 96,900
Liabilities and Fund Balances				
Accounts payable	$ 3,900	$ 600	$ 1,100	$ 5,600
Accrued expenses	2,300	7,500	200	10,000
Total liabilities	$ 6,200	$ 8,100	$ 1,300	$ 15,600
Fund balances	81,100	(1,300)	1,500	81,300
Totals	$ 87,300	$ 6,800	$ 2,800	$ 96,900

Statement of Revenues, Support, Expenditures, and Changes in Fund Balances--General Fund

	Drug abuse	Children's service	Care for the elderly	General fund totals
Revenue	$ 20,000	6,000	$ 0	$ 26,000
Support:				
County appropriations	$ 73,000	$ 60,600	$ 50,100	$ 183,700
Gifts	3,300	300	10,300	13,900
Grants	100,500	0	0	100,500
Total support	$ 176,800	$ 60,900	$ 60,400	$298,100
Revenue and support	$ 196,800	$ 66,900	$ 60,400	$324,100
Expenditures				
Personnel services	$ 128,700	$ 42,300	$ 10,800	$ 181,800
Supplies	63,400	20,800	48,200	132,400
Consultants	20,100	0	0	20,100
Total expenditures	$ 212,200	$ 63,100	$ 59,000	$ 334,300
Excess (deficiency) of revenue over expenditures	$ (15,400)	$ 3,800	$ 1,400	$ (10,200)
Fund balance, beginning of year	$ 96,500	$ (5,100)	$ 1,400	$ 92,800
Fund balance, end of year	81,100	(1,300)	2,800	82,600

The Children's Services program has a negative fund balance of $1,300, indicating that it previously sustained operating deficits. Its present operations are providing an adequate margin of safety, however.

The division of the General Operating Fund into the three program funds permits management to exercise better control over operations and facilitates financial planning. The information relating to the operations and financial condition of the individual programs would be difficult to obtain if the data were consolidated, as in the General Fund Totals column in Exhibit 5-1. By creating three board-designated funds, the organization's management can, for example, react to ensure that the Drug Abuse program's operations are better controlled in the future.

Restrictions associated with board-designated funds carry no legal authority. The organization's management can reallocate resources out of and among such funds with impunity and even reconsolidate the funds at any time. However, donor-restricted funds are *legally* restricted to the uses expressed or implied in the donor's instructions. Before it can divert the resources held by these funds from their original purposes, management must either obtain the approval of the donors themselves (or their heirs) or appeal to the court having jurisdiction in such matters for relief from the donor-imposed restrictions.

FUND CATEGORIES

An organization that receives many restricted contributions and grants and operates a number of different programs, each of which may attract a devoted "following" of donors, may be tempted to account for and report on all of the funds in great detail. Such an organization faces the practical problems of overburdening itself with a complex accounting system and burdening interested outside parties with having to read and understand a set of overly complex financial statements. Obviously, the more complicated the accounting system, the more costly it will be to maintain, other things being equal. And unnecessarily high administrative costs reduce the organization's capacity to accomplish its basic societal objectives. The organization must therefore balance the need for detailed accounting data, on the one hand, against the costs involved in their generation and the confusion that such detail will create for the nonexpert user, on the other hand.

Thus, while keeping separate records on a very large number of funds is possible — especially with the help of a computer — practical considerations favor reducing the number of funds actually maintained to the minimum required to provide full dollar-accountability and convey a true financial picture of the organization to those interested in its operations. This is generally accomplished by grouping several funds on the basis of similar types of donor restriction or for the purpose of achieving operational convenience, as in the case of "program" accounting. While many fund designations are both possible and frequently employed, most organizations limit the number of funds they maintain to four basic funds, and perhaps only one or two more either on a permanent or temporary basis. The four funds most frequently used by nonprofit organizations for reporting purposes include current unrestricted fund, current restricted fund, endowment fund, and fixed asset fund.

Current Unrestricted Fund

The general activities of a nonprofit organization are accounted for within the *current unrestricted fund*. This fund, also frequently titled "General Fund," "Operating Fund," or "Unrestricted Fund," contains no restricted assets and is used to record and report on those primary activities for which the organization was founded. All contributions, grants, and other revenue sources that carry no donor restrictions are received by this fund, and all expenditures for unrestricted current operations are made from the cash account maintained for use by this fund.

Board-designated funds are usually created as subcategories of the current unrestricted fund. In most cases, as mentioned earlier, the governing board will segregate unrestricted funds in order to improve its financial and operating controls over the several programs for which it is responsible. Formerly, nonprofit organizations followed the practice of separating board-designated funds from the current unrestricted fund for accounting and reporting purposes. This practice has the unfortunate result of expanding the year-end financial reports of such organizations beyond reasonable size and, as a consequence, tends to diminish rather than enhance the reader's comprehension of an organization's operating results and financial position.

More recently, the accounting profession has announced, through several publications of the American Institute of Certified Public Accountants (AICPA) that relate to specific categories of nonprofit organizations, that for reporting purposes board-designated funds normally should be combined and included with unrestricted funds. Thus, while board-designated funds may continue to proliferate within accounting systems, their use should be restricted to providing internal management with the detailed information it needs to improve the efficiency and effectiveness of the organization's operations.

Current Restricted Fund

Most nonprofit organizations operate several programs that reasonably may be considered integral parts of their central social or economic activities. For example, a private, nonprofit educational institution may offer several courses of study within its overall curriculum. Frequently, a donor will single out a specific program to which he or she will contribute—the music or athletic program, for example. The contributions designated for current expenditures in particular areas within the organization's normal operations will be classified and recorded within the *current restricted fund*.

The current restricted funds are usually relatively small in amount and normally will be spent within the year the contributions are received or certainly by the end of the following year. Thus, the aggregate of these funds is more appropriately summarized in the financial statements under a support or asset category designated simply as "current restricted contributions," rather than reported in detail as a separate fund at year-end.

Endowment Fund

The *endowment fund* is used to account for the receipt, investment, and disposition of resources donated to a nonprofit organization when such gifts are made with the stipulation that only the income earned from the investment of the donated assets may be spent. Only those gifts that bear legal restrictions which the board ordinarily cannot alter are placed in this fund. Endowment gifts may be either restricted or unrestricted as to the ultimate disposition of income earned, and they may be designated as either *term* or *perpetual* endowment gifts.

The principal amount of the term endowment gift must remain invested for the period specified by the donor. At the expiration of that term, the principal amount can become either unrestricted as to possible use or, in rare instances, returned to the donor or the donor's estate. In either case the nonprofit organization benefits from the investment income during the entire term of the gift.

The principal amount of the perpetual endowment gifts, however, ordinarily must remain intact in the endowment fund in perpetuity. Income from such gifts is available as earned for expenditure or reinvestment. Donor stipulations can be relaxed or altered when circumstances change over time, as mentioned earlier, but only with the permission of the donor or through relief granted by a court. A full discussion of endowment funds and their management is presented in chapter 9.

Fixed Asset Fund

The last of the most frequently used fund categories, the *fixed asset fund*, is used to account for the organization's investment in fixed assets—land, building, furniture, equipment, and other long-lived, real assets. This fund, also frequently titled "Land, Building and Equipment Fund" or "Plant Fund," may also include unexpended restricted building fund contributions and certain liabilities, such as accounts payable or a mortgage, that are associated with the acquisition and maintenance of the organization's fixed assets.

The fixed asset fund is a board-designated fund that owes its overwhelming popularity as a separate accounting entity more to tradition than to good accounting practice. Hospital accounting principles, for example, require fixed assets to be reported in the unrestricted fund and not in a separate "plant" fund. Although a 1978 AICPA statement regarding nonprofit accounting indicated that either approach to fixed asset accounting is acceptable, the current trend in accounting practice favors consolidating the fixed asset fund with the current unrestricted fund. The reason for this trend is simple: The separate accounting treatment of fixed assets often presents a confusing picture to those accustomed to reviewing the financial statements of profit-seeking business enterprises. The predominant practice among nonprofit organizations of creating a separate fund for fixed assets carries with it the implications that these assets are not essential and integral parts of the organization's daily activities and that the responsibility for repayment of principal and interest on their associated liabilities is likewise remote from current operations.

While these implications clearly are false, the use of separate fixed asset funds by most nonprofit organizations is fact. And that fact suggests the importance to those responsible for the proper use and interpretation of accounting data generated by nonprofit organizations of acquiring a thorough knowledge of fund accounting. A discussion of the interpretation in fund accounting financial statements is presented in chapter 6.

Other Fund Categories

The rationale, both real and apparent, for the creation of new funds or "subfunds" presents itself to managers of nonprofit organizations with alarming frequency. For example, colleges and universities often will report on resources held in *Loan and Scholarship* funds and *Retirement of Indebtedness* funds. Governmental regulations, contracts associated with grants from public and private sources, restricted and unrestricted contributions, and the need to estimate the cost of programs provide sufficient opportunity to expand the number of funds beyond reasonable limits. Thus, while managers must at all times maintain dollar accountability relative to each source and use of cash employed by a nonprofit organization, they must also attempt to develop and present to others as clear a financial picture of the organization and its activities as is possible. Consequently, many nonprofit organizations that continue to use the fund accounting concept in recording financial data are dropping the fund accounting format for reporting purposes. Instead, they present consolidated financial statements in which line captions and notes to the financial statements disclose pertinent information relative to restricted and other unrestricted funds. This approach gives appropriate recognition to the undisputable fact that a nonprofit organization is indeed an *entity* and not a group of separate entities called "funds."

The consolidated balance sheet of the Jefferson County Historical Society presented in Exhibit 5-2 illustrates the way in which this approach can be employed. Note that the consolidated balance sheet bears a fairly close resemblance to the more familiar financial statement format presented by for-profit business enterprise. This is accomplished by combining the restricted and unrestricted pledges receivable, as indicated by note 1, and consolidating the endowment fund into one line, as indicated by note 2. Additionally, the fixed asset fund with its mortgage is brought into the consolidated balance sheet, and the fund balances—

Exhibit 5-2: **Jefferson County Historical Society, Consolidated Balance Sheet, December 31, 1988.**

Assets

Cash		$ 1,380
Pledges receivable (see note 1)		18,940
Inventories:		
Gift items	$ 640	
Publications	15,760	16,400
Other current assets		50
Current assets		$ 36,770
Investments (at market)		
Unrestricted funds	$ 6,740	
Endowment fund (see note 2)	83,320	90,060
Fixed assets, less depreciation of $6,000		135,000
Total assets		$ 261,830

Liabilities and Fund Balances

Accounts payable		$ 3,550
Current portion of mortgage		7,300
Current liabilities		$ 10,850
Mortgage, 9%, due 2000		75,000
Total liabilities		$ 85,850
Fund balances:		
Unrestricted fund	$ 8,590	
Fixed asset fund, net	74,440	
Unrestricted investment fund	8,940	
Endowment fund	84,010	175,980
Total liabilities and fund balances		$ 261,830

Notes to balance sheet:

1. Unrestricted pledges receivable total $8,900; building fund, $500; and endowment fund, $9,540.

2. Cary Bynum Scholarship fund, $80,000; Josh Pfoutkiss Memorial Garden fund, $3,320.

four of them—are recorded and totaled in the equities section. When properly prepared, the consolidated statements and their accompanying footnotes contain sufficient information to restructure the accounts into the fund accounting format. Thus, both formats contain and present to the reader the same basic financial data.

Presentation and Analysis of Fund Accounting Results

Those organizations that do not consolidate their balance sheets or operating statements face communication problems with the users of accounting data. The financial statement formats presented in the preceding chapter clearly indicate that the presentation of the accounting data for nonprofit organizations is accomplished in a multidimensional framework. The balance sheet, for example, must present the organization's assets, liabilities, and fund balances in terms of both the fund entities and the nature of the restrictions imposed thereon. The statement of support, revenues, expenses, and changes in fund balances must also present its account listing in a similar manner. As mentioned earlier, capturing and presenting these data in a set of financial statements often will make them appear confusing and overly complex, especially to the outside analyst.

Exhibit 5-3 presents graphically the three-dimensional character of the statement of support, revenues, expenses, and changes in fund balances. The front face of the cube presents the data as they appear in the functional expense statement, while the top face separates the funds or programs into their restricted and unrestricted components, as presented in the operating statement. By changing the account names on the outside of the cube to the accounts contained in the balance sheet, we can represent the three-dimensional character of that statement as well. If the analyst approaches the task of examining the fund accounting financial statements of a nonprofit organization with the knowledge that most funds will contain the third dimension of restricted versus unrestricted resources, his or her task of understanding what has transpired during the operating period will be made easier.

SPECIAL FUND ACCOUNTING TREATMENT

Four areas of a nonprofit organization's operations require special accounting treatment as a result of either the uniqueness of these areas to the nonprofit context or the organization's tax-exempt status. The four areas include interfund transfers, accounting for fixed assets, accounting for investments, and accounting for contributions and pledges.

The discussion that follows touches on most of the principles unique to nonprofit accounting. While coverage of these principles must

Exhibit 5-3: **Three-dimensional Character of Fund Accounting Financial Statements**

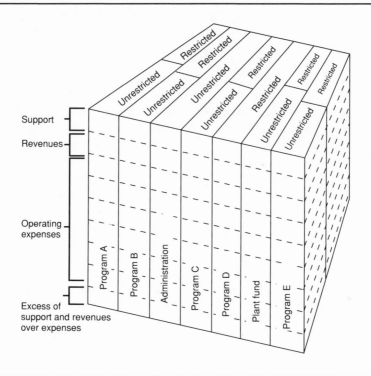

necessarily be brief, their importance to a thorough understanding of the nature of the data on which decision making depends should not be underestimated.

Interfund Transfers

Interfund transfers, as the name suggests, are simply transfers of assets—usually cash—from one fund to another. The governing board of a nonprofit organization has the right to transfer assets between unrestricted funds at any time for any legitimate purpose. It *must* transfer assets from restricted funds to other funds when such transfers are required in order to comply with donor restrictions placed on the management and disposition of assets donated to the organization. A few examples will help clarify this point.

The Jefferson County Historical Society's consolidated balance sheet (Exhibit 5-2) lists four funds in its fund balance section: the Unrestricted Fund, the Fixed Asset Fund, the Unrestricted Investment Fund, and the Endowment Fund. The Unrestricted Investment Fund is a board-designated fund established several years ago when the society's board of trustees transferred $10,000 of surplus cash from the Unrestricted Fund to the newly created fund. The cash was immediately invested in short-term securities. The principal amount transferred to the fund and the income earned from the investment of the cash was earmarked for discretionary use by the society's president at the direction of the board. Periodically, as the need arose, cash has been transferred from the Unrestricted Investment Fund to either the Unrestricted or the Fixed Asset Fund, or to both. Exhibit 5-4 shows the statement of changes in fund balances for the Unrestricted Investment Fund and Unrestricted Fund, illustrating a cash transfer of $2,000 to the Unrestricted Fund to pay for some unbudgeted administrative travel expenses.

Note that the Unrestricted Fund received $6,500 of cash as the result of two transfers during 1988. The second was a transfer of $4,500 of accumulated income from the restricted Endowment Fund and was made in compliance with the terms of a restricted contribution. The restriction states that income from the donated principal amount of $60,000 was to be used to support the society's publication activities in the area of historic preservation. Since the activities involved in publishing that material are central to the society's overall objectives, the expenditure belongs in the Unrestricted Fund, rather than in the Endowment Fund. Thus the interfund transfer of accumulated investment income is the appropriate accounting procedure because it establishes accountability for both the use of restricted cash and the placement of an expenditure in its proper classification.

Interfund transfers are properly shown in the financial statements as changes in the fund balances apart from support, revenues, and expenditures. Transfers should not be shown as support, revenue, or expendi-

---

Exhibit 5-4: **Jefferson County Historical Society, Statements of Changes in Fund Balance, for the Year Ended December 31, 1988.**

Unrestricted Fund

Fund balance, beginning of year	$ 5,400
Excess of (deficit in) contributions and revenues over expenses	(3,310)
Transfer from Unrestricted Investment Fund	2,000
Transfer from Endowment Fund, Sarah Kreps Preservation Fund	4,500
Fund balance, end of year	$ 8,590

Unrestricted Investment Fund

Fund balance, beginning of year	$ 9,750
Excess of (deficit in) contributions and revenues over expenses	1,190
Transfers to Unrestricted Fund	(2,000)
Fund balance, end of year	$ 8,940

ture items because these latter classifications of accounts are to be used to record only operating or financial transactions affecting the organization as a whole. Since interfund transfers are merely internal accounting adjustments and do not represent actual organizational cash inflows or outflows, they should be recorded in such a way as to leave unaffected the excess of revenues over expenditures — the nonprofit organization's equivalent to "net income."

Interfund Borrowings

Governing boards may also authorize interfund borrowings in order to maintain adequate liquidity in a given fund or perhaps even ensure its immediate solvency. These transactions are similar to interfund transfers in that cash is removed from one fund and placed in another; however, instead of recording the transfers in the Statements of Changes in Fund Balance, interfund borrowings are listed only on the balance sheets of the funds involved. The loan appears as an asset, called "due from other funds," on the lending fund's balance sheet, and as a liability, called "due to other funds," on the borrowing fund's balance sheet.

The treatment of an interfund loan is illustrated in Exhibit 5-5. In this example, the Unrestricted Fund of the Jefferson County Historical Society borrowed $13,460 from the Endowment Fund to help pay for the printing expenses of a new historic-preservation publication. While donor restricted contributions held in the Endowment Fund are considered by many to be unavailable for internal transfer to other funds, even on a temporary basis, such loans actually may help preserve

---

Exhibit 5-5: **Jefferson County Historical Society, Balance Sheets, Unrestricted Fund and Endowment Fund, December 31, 1988.**

Assets	Unrestricted fund	Endowment fund
Cash	$ 250	$ 190
Due from other funds	0	13,460
Inventories:		
Gift items	640	0
Publications	15,760	0
Other assets	8,950	70,360
Total assets	$ 25,600	$ 84,010
Liabilities and Fund Balances		
Accounts payable	$ 3,550	$ 0
Due to other funds	13,460	0
Fund balance	8,590	84,010
Total liabilities and fund balance	$ 25,600	$ 84,010

an organization's resources rather than diminish them. (For a discussion of how endowment fund loans may be justified, see chapter 9.) The loan will be repaid from the revenue to be received from the sale of the publication, which is listed at cost under "Inventories" in the asset section of the Unrestricted Fund.

Accounting for Fixed Assets

While a 1988 pronouncement of the AICPA requires nonprofit organizations to depreciate most types of fixed assets, the traditional approach to accounting for fixed assets has been to create a Fixed Asset Fund, record the costs of fixed assets in the fund as they are acquired, and then do nothing more until the assets are disposed of or replaced. Somewhat surprisingly, sound justification exists to support the use of the traditional approach.

The fact that the accounting systems of nonprofit organizations emphasize dollar-accountability, rather than operational-accountability, means that such organizations have no compelling need to record the values of fixed assets and then depreciate those values over the assets' useful lives in the way business firms do. The procedure of matching revenues and costs in each accounting period simply is of little interest to the management of nontrading, nonprofit organizations (i.e., those organizations that do not sell products or services). Hence, the process of reducing current net revenues by the amount of annual depreciation charges, which are *noncash* expenses based on the assets' *original* cost, provides almost no useful information regarding operations to either the management of nontrading organizations or to other interested parties. Further, book values of fixed assets rarely equate with their market values. Consequently, the use of depreciation does not improve the fairness with which the entity's assets are stated.

This position is clearly at odds with that taken both by the 1988 AICPA ruling and with regard to accounting for fixed assets in the for-profit context. The accounting objective of operational-accountability in the for-profit context requires that the cost of fixed assets be allocated to the firm's operations in each period over the assets' useful lives. Thus, those who analyze or review the financial statements of nonprofit organizations must be aware that the fixed asset accounting practices followed by the particular organizations in which they are interested are often quite different from those followed by profit-seeking businesses and may also differ materially from those employed by other nonprofit organizations.

Two approaches to recording fixed assets are commonly used by nonprofit organizations for assets that are exempt from depreciation or by organizations that choose not to depreciate their assets: the immediate write-off method and the capitalization method. Neither method requires that the assets be depreciated over their expected useful lives. However, trading organizations that are interested in measuring the costs of their products or services, and nontrading organizations that elect to follow the 1988 depreciation ruling or otherwise find it useful to claim depreciation as an expense in justifying requests for appropriations or in grant applications, *must* use the capitalization method.

Immediate Write-off Method. Small nonprofit organizations, especially those using the cash basis of accounting and those that are primarily concerned with raising enough cash each year to cover their operating expenses will generally use the *immediate write-off method* to account for their fixed assets. This approach is the simpler of the two commonly used methods. Expenditures for fixed assets are treated as any other expenditure category; that is, the costs of fixed assets are recorded as expense items on the statement of support, revenues, expenses and changes in Fund Balance, but those costs are not recorded in the organization's Balance Sheet. No accounting distinction is made between the purchase of, say, a $100,000 building and a 25-center eraser under this method.

Two principal disadvantages are associated with the use of the immediate write-off method. First, an organization's total assets and fund balance are significantly understated in the financial statements as a consequence of "expensing" capital outlays. An interested observer therefore has no way of knowing, short of acquiring information through other means, the nature of the unlisted, fixed assets owned by the organization and the implied contributions those unlisted assets are making to its overall operations.

The second disadvantage is that the immediate write-off method is not recognized as a generally accepted accounting principle (GAAP). Financial statements thus prepared could not receive an unqualified opinion by the certified public accountant (CPA) responsible for performing an audit of the organization's accounting records.

Capitalization Method. The *capitalization method* of accounting for fixed assets involves recording the fixed asset at its original cost (or estimated market value, if the fixed asset is donated) on the balance sheet, and then continuing to account for that asset over its entire life (or until the asset is disposed of) through any one of three "appropriate" means: (1) using depreciation based on original or capitalized costs; (2) carrying the asset on the books at its original or capitalized cost; and (3) writing down the asset periodically to reflect its actual market or operational value.

Using Depreciation. An organization may depreciate the cost of the assets over their expected useful lives. This method is consonant with GAAP and must be used by organizations that are required to present audited financial statements and want a "clean" auditor's opinion on those statements.

In general, trading nonprofit organizations, those using the accrual basis of accounting, and those having reasons for matching period revenues and costs or measuring costs of goods produced or services rendered should capitalize and depreciate their fixed asset purchases. And while GAAP requires these organizations to *depreciate* their capitalized assets over time, they may elect to use either of the remaining two approaches to account for their fixed assets subsequent to the period in which they have been acquired. Neither of these approaches is in conformance with GAAP, but they are nonetheless superior to the immediate write-off method in most cases.

Carrying the Asset at Cost. First, the organization may choose simply not to depreciate the asset but merely to carry it in the balance sheet at its original cost. Land is never depreciated and should therefore be accounted for in this way. However, buildings reasonably may be handled this way because they often *appreciate*, rather than *depreciate*, in value. This is especially true of historic properties, such as cathedrals and mansions, as well as for works of art. Thus the value of these assets, as periodically revealed in the organization's balance sheet, will represent a more realistic estimate of their worth than would their depreciated value, yet the figure would remain a conservative estimate of true market value. This approach also has the advantage of being as simple to use as the immediate write-off method, yet it reveals the ownership of fixed assets at reasonable accounting values.

Direct Write-down. The second approach—direct write-down—is generally used in accounting for machinery and equipment, which tend to deteriorate (and hence lose some part of their value) with use. The asset is written down, usually at irregular intervals at the direction of management, either by simultaneously reducing the carrying value of the asset and the fund balance by the appropriate amount or by recording the write-down as an expense in the statement of support, revenues, expenses, and changes in fund balance. The direct write-down, when expensed rather than charged directly against the fund balance, is very similar to depreciation. In fact, this approach may be deemed consonant with GAAP if the amount and timing of the write-down are based on rational criteria and are not merely the results of arbitrary determinations.

Comparison of the Basic Approaches. The immediate write-off and capitalization approaches to fixed asset accounting produce strikingly different results in the financial statements of a nonprofit organization, as illustrated in Exhibits 5-6 and 5-7. The statement of support, revenues, expenses, and changes in fund balance and the balance sheets of the Madison YMCA were prepared using both approaches under the assumptions that in January 1987 the organization purchased at a cost of $35,000 the building it formerly leased and that it will (under the capitalization method) depreciate it over ten years at $3,500 per year.

Note that in Exhibit 5-6 the immediate write-off method produced a current operating deficit of $26,570 in 1987 because the entire cost of the building was "expensed" in that year. In 1988, however, the same method showed an excess of revenues over expenses of $11,230, or $3,500 more than did the capitalization method. This illustrates how the annual depreciation charges affect the operating results of an organization. The two methods also show dramatic differences in their respective fund balances and total assets in each year, as shown by a comparison of the data in Exhibit 5-6. These differences will persist over the entire depreciable life of the building—in this instance, ten years—at which time both sets of financial statements will become identical, provided, of course, that the YMCA does not acquire any more fixed assets during that period.

Accounting for Investments

The technical aspects of accounting for investments are complicated by the philosophical issues that have arisen recently regarding the definitions of *principal amount* and *investment income*, especially as they apply to restricted investment accounts and endowment funds. These interesting issues are discussed in detail in chapter 9; however, the present chapter deals only with the few basic accounting principles that govern the recording and presentation of investment values and income in the financial records of nonprofit organizations.

Exhibit 5-6: **Madison YMCA, Alternative Consolidated Statements of Support, Revenues, Expenses, and Changes in Fund Balance (condensed), for the Years Ended December 31.**

	Immediate write-off method		Capitalization method	
	1987	1988	1987	1988
Total support & revenues	$ 46,870	$ 52,300	$ 46,870	$ 52,300
Expenses:				
Other than depreciation and fixed assets	38,440	41,070	38,440	41,070
Fixed asset purchases	35,000			
Depreciation			3,500	3,500
Total expenses	$ 73,440	$ 41,070	$ 41,940	$ 44,570
Excess of revenues over expenses	$ (26,570)	$ 11,230	$ 4,930	$ 7,730
Fund balance, beginning of year	$ 91,730	$ 65,160	$ 91,730	$ 96,660
Fund balance, end of year	$ 65,160	$ 76,390	$ 96,660	$ 104,390

Exhibit 5-7: **Madison YMCA, Alternative Consolidated Balance Sheets (condensed), December 31.**

	Immediate write-off method		Capitalization method	
	1987	*1988*	*1987*	*1988*
Current assets	$ 12,540	$ 14,900	$ 12,540	$ 14,900
Investments (at cost)	80,460	84,980	80,460	84,980
Other assets		2,000		2,000
Fixed assets			35,000	35,000
Less accumulated depreciation			(3,500)	(7,000)
Net fixed assets			$ 31,500	$ 28,000
Total assets	$ 93,000	$ 101,880	$ 124,500	$ 129,880
Total liabilities	$ 27,840	$ 25,490	$ 27,840	$ 25,490
Fund balance	65,160	76,390	96,660	104,390
Total liabilities and fund balance	$ 93,000	$ 101,880	$ 124,500	$ 129,880

Investments made by an organization in financial assets—common stocks, preferred stocks, bonds, notes, commercial paper, and so forth—usually are reported on the balance sheet at cost. When received as gifts, these assets usually are listed at their market values as reported in the *Wall Street Journal,* or in other similar sources of financial information, on the date of the gift, provided such values are in fact reported in the financial news. When no active market exists for a particular security, it will be recorded on the books of the organization at an appraised value. As a permissible alternative, investment assets may be reported at their *current* market or appraised values, provided that this basis is used for all investments held in all of the organization's funds.

The treatment of investment income is not so simply stated as that of recording investment values. This is because investment income can be and is in fact defined in several ways, the relevant definition for any given situation being dependent on state law and/or on the way in which management perceives the role of the fund in which the asset is being held. For present purposes, however, investment income is defined as the total of interest and dividends received, plus the capital gains (or losses) that are realized, either at the time the investment is sold or matures (when the investment is carried at cost) or on a current basis (when the investment is carried at market). This definition may be at variance with the laws of certain states under certain circumstances, or it may be inappropriate for a particular organization, even where the definition is consonant with state law. It is in agreement, however, with the conclusions reached by Ford Foundation Advisory Committee on Endowment Management.[2]

2. *Managing Educational Endowments* (New York: The Ford Foundation, 1969).

Under this definition, all investment income that is unrestricted as to use is recorded in the unrestricted fund as a revenue item, regardless of whether or not the principal amount that generated the income is held in a restricted fund or in the endowment. Such income may not be recorded in the fund in which it is earned and then transferred to other funds; however, transfers of principal amounts may be treated only as interfund transfers and not as a source of revenue.

Similarly, donor-restricted investment income is recorded as revenue in the fund in which it will be spent and, when expended, is recorded as an expense or expenditure in that same account. Thus, the treatment of investment income is accorded consistent treatment under fund accounting procedures; that is, revenues are generally recorded in the fund from which they will be paid out.

The manner of presentation of investment income in the statement of support, revenues, expenses, and changes in fund balance is illustrated in Exhibit 5-8. The Madison YMCA's Endowment Fund produced a total income of $2,680 in 1988, of which $850 was restricted to use for scholarships for college-age members and the remainder, $1,830, was unrestricted as to use. These amounts were thus properly recorded in the Scholarship and the Current Unrestricted Funds, respectively; the unused investment income of $350 was returned to the Endowment Fund for reinvestment. In subsequent periods, that $350 may be returned to the Scholarship Fund as an interfund transfer. The $350 should not be subsequently returned as a revenue item, since it has already been accounted for in that form during the current year. Nor should it be transferred to an unrestricted fund, for obvious reasons.

Exhibit 5-8: **Madison YMCA, Statement of Support, Revenues, Expenses, and Changes in Fund Balances (condensed), for the Year Ended December 31, 1988.**

	Current un-restricted fund	Scholar-ship fund	Endow-ment fund	Total all funds
Support & Revenues				
Other than investment	$ 45,620	$ 0	$ 4,000	$ 49,620
Interest and dividends	1,420	660		2,080
Realized capital gains	410	190		600
Total investment income	$ 1,830	$ 850	$ 0	2,680
Total support & revenues	$ 47,450	$ 850	$ 4,000	$ 52,300
Expenses	44,070	500		44,570
Excess of support & revenues over expenses	$ 3,380	$ 350	$ 4,000	$ 7,730
Fund balances, beginning of year	27,600	0	69,060	96,660
Transfer of excess restricted income to endowment fund		(350)	350	
Fund balance, end of year	$ 30,980	$ 0	$ 73,410	$ 104,390

Accounting For Contributions and Pledges

As a general rule, unrestricted cash contributions should be recorded in the Current Unrestricted Fund as revenue items at the time they are received. Restricted cash contributions (including contributions of financial assets) should be recorded as revenue items in the fund designated or implied by the nature of the donors' restrictions. For example, a cash donation to a building fund must be placed in the Fixed Asset Fund, and a contribution of a number of shares of common stock, the income from which may be used only for scholarships, should be recorded as revenue in either the Scholarship Fund or the Endowment Fund. Certain exceptions to this general rule exist that complicate the recording and reporting process.

Current Restricted Contributions. The first of these exceptions involves the treatment of current restricted contributions; that is, those contributions designated for use in meeting some specific current expense items of the organization. Current thinking in the accounting profession supports the proposition that such gifts are not "earned" until the money is spent to accomplish the purpose for which the gift was intended. Until that time, the organization is liable for the amount of the gift. Thus, an acceptable alternative to recording the gift as revenue in the Restricted Current Fund is to record the gift as a *deferred contribution* in the *liability* section of the balance sheet. When the gift is spent in accordance with the donor's intentions, the amount spent is recorded as both a revenue item and an expense item in the statement of support, revenues, expenditures, and changes in fund balance of the fund in which the expenditure is made.

For example, suppose a private school received a $10,000 gift to be used to supplement teachers' salaries. Since salaries are a current fund expense item, the gift should be recorded as revenue in that fund after the school officials decide how the money will be distributed among the faculty and the salary supplements are paid. If the school officials pay the supplements in monthly installments over ten months, the initial gift of $10,000 will appear in the current fund balance sheet at the beginning of the ten-month period as a *deferred contribution* (a liability), and the *cash* account will increase by $10,000. At the end of the first month, $1,000 will be transferred from the *deferred contribution* account to the current fund *revenue* account, and the cash account will fall by $1,000 in order to pay the expense item, *teacher salary supplements.* This set of transactions will be repeated each month until the amount of the gift is paid out in accordance with the donor's wishes. While this approach is cumbersome from a bookkeeping standpoint, it has the advantage of clearly segregating the restricted gift from the fund's other assets. From a dollar-accountability perspective, the approach therefore has much to commend its use, especially for gifts whose impacts will extend beyond a single accounting period.

Grants. Similar treatment is accorded to grants awarded for specific projects. These amounts should also be accounted for on an "as-earned" basis, with amounts received in advance of their expenditure treated as *deferred grant income.* Conversely, if expenditures are made in advance of the receipt of payment by the grantor, these should be recorded as an expense, and an account receivable, *grant fund receivable*, should be created to reflect the grantor's obligation.

Bequests. Bequests represent a class of gift that is often accorded exceptional accounting treatment. The organization should recognize the bequest as income and record it as an asset at the time it (1) receives official notification that the bequest has been made and properly documented and (2) *is certain of the dollar amount of the bequest.* When the cash or other asset is received—and this may be many years after the bequest was first recorded on the organization's books—the asset, "Bequest," is reduced (or canceled if only one bequest is involved) and the amount of cash received is recorded in the cash account. If the bequest is restricted, it should be accounted for in the proper restricted fund in accordance with the appropriate procedure outlined earlier.

Pledges. A pledge is a promise by a donor to contribute a specified dollar sum to an organization either in a lump sum at some future date or in periodic payments over some specified period. The popularity of making contributions by way of pledging has grown among donors in recent years (and, consequently, also among recipients) owing partially at least to the relatively high interest rates available from investment to short-term securities. Donors are reluctant to make immediate, lump-sum donations of large amounts of cash, especially when they know or feel that the organization to which they are contributing will not spend the entire amount at once but will spend the cash more or less evenly over the current accounting period. They feel that they can be more generous by deferring payment in order to keep their funds fully employed in the interim, although the logic supporting such a proposition is probably more apparent than real.

Most nonprofit organizations will record pledges as assets in their balance sheets when the pledges are made, and many will also create a reserve or allowance for uncollectible pledges. Pledges receivable will generally be recorded as both a current and a noncurrent asset, with pledges due within one year making up the current asset category, "Pledges receivable," and the longer term pledges making up in part the noncurrent asset category, "Deferred revenue." Few organizations will record pledges payable more than two or three years in the future, on the theory that the more distant the date on which the pledge is scheduled to be received, the more likely it will become uncollectible.

Pledges should be recorded as support items in the year they are expected to be received or in the year in which the donors intend that they be used. Pledges that extend beyond the current accounting period should therefore be recorded as deferred support in the balance sheet. Exhibit 5-9 illustrates balance sheet treatment of pledges, including a three-year pledge to the Madison YMCA from a longtime benefactor, payable in annual installments of $1,000 each, beginning on June 30, 1989. Since $1,000 of the total pledge is due in six months, it is recorded among the pledges listed as current assets. The $2,000 balance payable over the next two years is listed as a noncurrent asset, "Deferred revenue (pledges)."

The allowance for uncollectible pledges, listed as $1,600 in Exhibit 5-9, is created in order to reflect the realizable value of the pledges. Historical experience generally will determine the proper size of the allowance, but adjustments for changes in economic conditions or the circumstances of the donors should be made as necessary. Again, the purpose of the allowance account is to reduce the gross amount of the pledges receivable to the amount that will likely be received during the current accounting period. If a high probability exists that *all* of the pledges receivable will be collected on a timely basis, the organization need not establish an allowance for uncollectible pledges. In most cases the need for such an allowance is readily apparent.

LIMITATIONS OF ACCOUNTING INFORMATION

The preceding discussion has been devoted to detailing the ways in which accounting data ought to be recorded on the nonprofit organization's books and reported to interested individuals. The magnitude of the overall accounting problem should be apparent from the discussion. But another aspect of the problem confronting the users of accounting data also deserves attention. The purpose of this section is

---

Exhibit 5-9: **Madison YMCA, Balance Sheet (condensed), December 31, 1988.**

Cash	$	760
Membership dues receivable		2,990
Pledges receivable (net of a $1,600		
allowance for uncollectible pledges)		11,000
Supply inventories		150
Current assets	$	14,900
Deferred revenue (pledges)		2,000
Other assets		112,980
Total assets	$	129,880
Total liabilities	$	25,490
Fund balance		104,390
Total liabilities and fund balance	$	129,880

to dispel any illusions of absolute precision that may be attributed to accounting information (and hence financial statement data) by examining several important limitations of such information. These include the use of the dollar as the common unit of measure, the extent to which accountants' personal judgments enter into the data-generation process, constraints imposed by the accounting period convention, and the possibility that false information may creep into an organization's accounting records.

The Dollar as Common Unit of Measure

One of the most important limitations of accounting information arises from the use of the dollar as the basic unit of measure in recording information and preparing financial statements. The need for a common unit of measure is obvious enough; an organization must be able to know and compare the values of its various stocks of assets, sources of funds, and operating cash flows, and for those purposes some common denominator of value is essential. For performing that function, moreover, the nation's standard monetary unit—the dollar—is the only practical choice. But the immense convenience afforded by its use is subject to a significant disadvantage: the value—the purchasing power— of the dollar has been far from constant; in fact, it has been falling consistently (that is, prices have been steadily rising). This development has seriously compounded the problem of distinguishing properly between accounting asset values (historical costs) and current market values. (A second, less serious problem stems from a rather widespread but false impression that asset values listed on financial statements represent market values.)

Varying Purchasing Power of the Dollar. All of us know about the changes in price levels (downward, or deflationary, and upward, or inflationary) caused by changes in the quantity and hence the value of money. Nonprofit organizations, like the rest of us, are adversely affected by price-level inflation: they find the prices they pay for everything— supplies, utilities, equipment, and the price of labor (wages)—constantly increasing. They naturally do what they can to offset cost increases by trying to increase their cash flows; and what they can do, besides attempting in all ways to increase their efficiency (productivity), is to increase the prices of any goods and services they may ordinarily offer for sale and try in all ways to increase the amount of contributions of cash and services from all available sources.

The effects of a long period of steadily rising prices permeate the accounting records of all organizations. At best, inflation seriously distorts the accounting values contained in the records, and at worst, it completely destroys their usefulness (until adjusted for price changes) for any intertemporal comparison. The problem is greatest in the areas of fixed assets, increases in fund balances, and long-term capital. Specific examples in each of these categories will illustrate this point.

Fixed Assets. Any organization that began purchasing fixed assets—buildings and equipment—in periods when asset prices were lower and has continued to acquire such assets over the years will find that its fixed asset account contains a mixture of dollar values, which vary with the different times when the assets were acquired. Suppose that the City of Greenwood extended its sewer and water lines by fourteen miles to the north in 1980 at a cost of $1 million. Five years later, in 1985, it expanded its sewer and water services to the south in a manner identical in all respects with the northside expansion except that the construction costs increased to $1.5 million. A strict, nominal dollar cost comparison between the two sewer and water line extensions would indicate that the new addition is half again as large as the old one; but that is obviously not true, since the two are by definition identical. The greatly increased cost of the new sewer and water lines results solely from an increased price level—a decreased value of the dollar, accounting's "standard" unit of measure.

Similarly, whatever the amount in dollars of the nonprofit organization's current cash holdings, each dollar of cash held has a different smaller value than any dollar expended for fixed assets had at the time those assets were acquired.

Fund Balances and Price Inflation. Inflation has a double-edged effect on cash surpluses generated from normal operations. First, unless an organization's cash reserves grow at a rate at least as high as the inflation rate, the organization will be left with progressively less purchasing power, either to reinvest in real assets or to distribute to its beneficiaries in accordance with its basic objectives. Second, because of steadily rising costs (inflated values) of new fixed assets, an organization's depreciation allowance also rises steadily. Thus two entities whose sets of fixed assets are identical—except that they were acquired at different times and at different costs—will report different operating surpluses (and fund balances) solely as the result of differences in the timing of fixed asset acquisitions.

For example, suppose that the 1988 sewer and water revenues and operating costs for the two extensions just discussed were reported separately, as in Exhibit 5-9. The depreciation for each extension is charged at 10 percent of asset costs, or $100,000 for the northside extension and $150,000 for the southside extension. Since revenues and operating expenses are identical for both extensions, both report revenues before depreciation of $175,000. But, as Exhibit 5-10 shows, the 1985 incremental investment in the southside extension of $1.5 million returned an operating surplus of only $25,000, or $50,000 less than the 1980 northside sewer and water extension with its investment of $1.0

Exhibit 5-10: **Comparison of Changes in Fund Balance Produced by the Northside and Southside Sewer and Water Extensions**

	Northside	Southside
Sewer and water billings	$ 368,000	$ 368,000
Expenses:		
Other than depreciation	193,000	193,000
Depreciation	100,000	150,000
Total expenses	$ 293,000	$ 343,000
Excess of revenues over expenses	$ 75,000	$ 25,000

million. This inflation-induced reduction in surplus prevents direct comparison of the two operations. The different dollar amounts the city has invested in identical sets of fixed assets lead to different allowances for depreciation, different amounts of surplus, and the apparent paradox that a larger dollar investment in fixed assets yields a smaller net dollar return.

It is possible, though not always easy, to restore interasset comparability by restating historical balance-sheet and income-statement information in current-dollar terms. Accounting theorists have spent much time and effort developing the methodology for such restatements, but the process is not widely used for analytical or decision purposes.

Long-term Capital Accounts. The value of long-term capital accounts—long-term debt and fund balances—is stated on the balance sheet simply as the number of dollars invested whenever capital funds were acquired. Capital accounts thus resemble fixed-asset accounts in that stated dollar amounts really represent some mixture of dollars of various values (purchasing powers). Since the price level has been rising more or less steadily since the late 1930s, a nonprofit organization founded in 1950 will have recorded on its books an initial infusion of capital (fund balance in terms of the value of the dollar at that time); and any subsequent increases in fund balances will have been taken into its accounts at the steadily declining annual dollar values prevailing for the years 1950 to date, say 1988. If it were to suffer an operating loss in 1989, the nominal amount of that loss would be subtracted from the organization's fund balance in terms of dollars of lesser "real" value than any of those "accumulated" there. In current dollar terms, any long-established organization's capital accounts, like its fixed-asset accounts, will always tend to be undervalued.

Accounting Values and Market Values. The word *value* has many shades of meaning when applied to real or financial assets. The committee on terminology of the AICPA has given the following definition of value for accounting purposes in the institute's *Accounting Research Bulletin No. 9*:

"Value: As used in accounts signifies the amount at which an item is stated, in accordance with the accounting rules or principles relating to that item. Generally book or balance sheet values (using the word *value* in this sense) represent cost to the accounting unit or some modification thereof; but sometimes they are determined in other ways, as for instance on the basis of market values or cost of replacement, in which case the basis should be indicated in financial statements."

The value of any item given on the balance sheet of a nonprofit organization must be in terms of dollars, but that value is assigned with the accounting rule judged by the accountant to be most appropriate for that particular item under the circumstances. Accounting value is therefore hardly a definitive concept. Moreover, it may bear little relation to other definitions of value in common use.

To illustrate, a building owned by a nonprofit organization may have many different types of values, depending on the point of view used in establishing its value. For example, the building has an accounting value based on historical cost—its original cost, less depreciation to date, plus any capitalized expenditures made to increase its usefulness. It has a market value—the price it would currently bring if sold—and an assessed value for local property tax purposes. The building also has a replacement value—the cost of reproducing it if it were destroyed by fire, for example. This might, but need not, equal its current market value.

Use of Accounting Judgment

The personal judgments exercised by accountants in generating accounting information that is ultimately transformed into an organization's financial statements should always be taken into account in analyzing such statements. Although the accounting procedures employed in statement preparations are subject to the standards and conventions defining GAAP, accountants have considerable latitude in selecting from among them the particular ones they consider applicable under various sets of circumstances. and their asset-valuation and cash "production" implications will differ from those of others that might have been chosen. A few illustrations may make this point clearer.

Valuation of Noncash Contributions. Accountants are free to use any of several alternative methods for estimating the values of volunteer services and other noncash contributions received by nonprofit organizations. In valuing volunteer services, for example, they may establish individual hourly rates for comparable types of employment in the area and simultaneously record the sum of the hours worked times the "rate of pay" for each class of employee as revenue and expense items in the statement of support, revenues, expenses, and changes in fund balance. Alternatively, accountants may elect to value the services of volunteers "loaned" to organizations by local businesses at the rates of compensation these individuals receive from their places of employment. Finally, since support and expenses recorded in connection with volunteer services are always equal, accountants may choose not to record those values at all.

Considerable latitude is also granted by the accounting rules in valuing contributions of real assets, especially secondhand equipment and securities that are not listed or actively traded on an organized exchange or "over the counter." Valuation by professional appraisal is recommended, but in the final analysis accountants are responsible for exercising their judgment in selecting the proper value to be reported on the organizations' books.

Allowances for Bad Debts. Accountants' judgments may also differ with regard to estimating allowances for doubtful accounts and uncollectible pledges, the valuation reserves applied against accounts, and pledges receivable. The GAAP prescribe historical collection rates as the basis for estimating future bad debt losses and uncollectible pledges. But specific methods of calculating historical collection patterns are permissible under varying economic conditions. Collection rates for accounts and pledges receivable used to establish "appropriate" allowances for doubtful accounts and uncollectible pledges may not always be historical, therefore; they may reflect accountants' expectations about future economic conditions and a change in the characteristics of the donors. Net revenue level, accounts-receivable, and pledges-receivable values will naturally differ according to whether past or expected future collection rates are employed.

Depreciation of Fixed Assets. In the absence of specific laws and regulations to the contrary, accounting principles permit accountants to use either *constant* or one of several *accelerated* rates of depreciation on fixed assets. The accountants' exercise of their choice among acceptable methods of depreciation obviously affects both changes in fund balances and the balance sheet values of depreciable fixed assets.

In addition to permitting the exercise of accounting judgment in the selection of depreciation methods, accounting principles further allow (1) the use of values other than original cost in calculating periodic depreciation charges and (2) discretion in the choice of time period (asset life) over which an asset's depreciable value is to be recovered.

The Accounting Period

The so-called accounting period convention, requiring the preparation and presentation of financial statements at frequent and more or less standard intervals, may sometimes limit the usefulness of accounting data for financial statement analysis.

For example, the standard reporting period for audited statements is twelve months (not necessarily a calendar year, however; a fiscal year may be used). When an organization's operating cycle is shorter than one year, or coincides at least roughly with a period of such length, a twelve-month reporting basis yields generally satisfactory results. Some organizations, however, are involved in long-term projects, such as restoration of historical sites, scientific research, and cultural development, that have operating cycles longer than twelve months. For them, therefore, specialized accounting and reporting methods and techniques might properly be used.

Because they use specialized methods and techniques, however, the financial statements of these organizations are different and will appear "strange" to financial statement analysts unaccustomed to dealing with them. Strange they are, and only by acquiring a full understanding of their unusual characteristics can the analyst hope to interpret them correctly.

Statement Dates. A nonprofit organization is free to select the beginning and ending points of its twelve-month accounting period, subject only to: (1) the practical consideration that its published reports reflect as favorably as possible on its financial condition; and (2) the accounting convention of consistency, which requires that the data represented in the statements be free from such inconsistencies as might be introduced in an organization that is subject to seasonal influences, for instance, by changing accounting periods when reporting dates.

The general constraints do not really bear on the problem of statement comparability between otherwise similar organizations that happen to have accounting periods ending on different dates. Nor do they at all address the problem of calculating norms or averages for all similarly constituted organizations with which individual data may be compared, since they leave open the possibility that the individual organization may not be using common accounting periods and statement dates.

False Statements

When an analyst receives a set of audited financial statements for review, he or she may generally assume that they provide a true picture of the organization's current financial position and the financial results of its most recent operations. Sometimes—though fortunately, rarely—such an assumption may prove to be unwarranted. In a few instances, an organization's accounting records may have been doctored, either to conceal embezzlement or to delineate a more favorable financial condition than its management has actually been able to achieve.

The analyst cannot usually detect the presence of false or intentionally misleading data. The assumption of reliability for an organization's financial statements rests on the analyst's belief in the integrity of its management and in the expertise of the outside accountants who audited the books. The analyst need not suspect fraud every time a questionable statement item catches his or her eye. But neither should the analyst forget that embezzlers and other swindlers do exist and operate within the nonprofit context, albeit in small numbers, or that basically honest business managers and administrators, under the pressure of circumstances, sometimes feel compelled to practice financial deception.

Nevertheless, financial statement analysis is not detective work. Neither, for that matter, are the careful audits of financial records performed periodically by independent CPAs. Such audits are not conducted on the premise that they are expected to uncover fraud; sometimes they do, but unexpectedly. And proper financial statement analysis proceeds from a similar premise: fraud is not what the financial statement analyst is looking for; it is, in fact, what he or she is least likely to find.

SUMMARY

This chapter has provided a brief overview of the principles of fund accounting—the accounting system developed for and used by most nonprofit organizations. Fund accounting methodology segregates the organization's assets, liabilities, equities, revenues, and expenditures into several separate entities called funds. The principles governing the recording, measurement, and reporting of the accounting data are often quite different from those employed in accounting in the for-profit context. Hence, they should be clearly understood by managers of nonprofit organizations and by those other individuals interested in the operations of these organizations.

In addition to the principles of fund accounting, the chapter reviewed some important limitations of accounting data for the purpose of placing the information contained in the financial statements in a proper perspective. From the user's point of view, the use of the dollar as the common unit of measure has decided advantages and disadvantages in intertemporal and interorganizational comparisons. The latitude given to accountants in making personal judgments concerning accounting values also diminishes the user's capacity to draw unqualified conclusions from the data presented.

Of major significance to the financial manager is the fact that all financial decisions are based on accounting data. The source of accounting data and the form in which they are presented influence the decision process; thus, the importance of developing a familiarity with accounting principles is paramount.

FURTHER READING

The following publications of the AICPA prescribe accounting principles and procedures appropriate to specific types of nonprofit organizations:

Audits of Colleges and Universities. New York: AICPA, 1973.

Audits of Voluntary Health and Welfare Organizations. New York: AICPA, 1974.

Hospital Audit Guide. New York: AICPA, 1972.

Industry Audit Guide on Audits of State and Local Government Units. New York: AICPA, 1975.

Excellent fund accounting texts:

Gross, Malvern J. Jr., and Stephen F. Jablonsky. *Financial Accounting Guide for Nonprofit Organizations.* Rev. ed. New York: Wiley, 1983.

Freeman, Robert J., et al. *Governmental & Nonprofit Accounting.* 3rd ed. Englewood Cliffs, N.J.: Prentice-Hall, 1988.

QUESTIONS

1. Define fund accounting.

2. What are the criteria by which funds are created?

3. Contrast the effects of internally versus externally imposed restrictions on the use of resources.

4. What limits the number of funds an organization may create?

5. List and discuss the nature of the four most frequently used fund classifications.

6. Why is the usual fund accounting statement format being abandoned in favor of consolidated statements by many organizations?

7. What is meant by interfund transfers? What specific purposes do they serve?

8. How does the nonprofit emphasis on dollar-accountability affect the way in which fixed assets are handled by accountants?

9. What are the advantages and disadvantages of the immediate write-off method of accounting for fixed assets?

10. Describe the capitalization method of accounting for fixed assets. What three approaches are included under this method? Which is the best approach? Explain.

11. Describe the proper accounting treatment for handling investment income from
   a. a restricted fund for an unrestricted purpose.
   b. an unrestricted fund for an unrestricted purpose.
   c. a restricted fund for a restricted purpose.

12. Describe the proper method of accounting for a restricted gift that will be spent gradually over a three-year period.

13. What is the proper method for estimating the size of the reserve for uncollectible pledges?

14. Discuss the advantages and disadvantages of using the dollar as the common unit of measure in accounting.

15. How does inflation affect the balance-sheet values of fixed assets, fund balances, and long-term capital accounts?

16. Explain the difference between accounting and market values. Are they ever the same? If so, when?

17. How does accounting judgment affect accounting values?

18. Is there any way to guard against false statements in the accounting records of a nonprofit organization?

PROBLEMS

1. The Three Square Agency receives donations and an annual appropriation from the United Way to prepare and deliver three meals each day to a list of qualified elderly persons. The agency decided to purchase with cash a delivery truck specially designed to enable the personnel to deliver the food at the proper serving temperatures. The cost of the truck is $25,500 and has a useful life of five years. The agency currently rents an ordinary van for its deliveries.

The following *forecasts* were prepared by the Three Square Agency:

	1989	1990
Expected public support	$ 125,000	$ 137,500
Expenditures (other than depreciation and fixed asset purchases)	116,700	132,700

The agency's balance sheet for year-end 1988 is presented below:

The Three Square Agency
Consolidated Balance Sheet
December 3, 1988

Assets		Liabilities and Fund Balance	
Cash	$ 39,800	Total liabilities	$ 48,900
Other current assets	22,300	Fund balance	13,200
Total	$ 62,100	Total	$ 62,100

a.Prepare a set of financial statements for both 1989 and 1990 comparing the results of the agency's operations under the following conditions:

(1) The agency uses the immediate write-off method of accounting for the new truck.

(2) The agency capitalizes the cost of the truck and depreciates it in the amount of $5,100 per year.

Assume other current assets and total liabilities remain constant over the period.

b. Comment on the differences each method produces in the agency's operation and financial position.

c. Which method should the agency use to account for the new truck? Why?

6

Financial Analysis
of Nonprofit Organizations

The purposes of this chapter are to explore the nature of the cash flows of typical nonprofit organizations and to show how and why these cash flows form the basis for proper financial analyses of financial position and operations.

THE FLOW OF CASH

Nonprofit accounting systems are useful only to the extent that the data they generate are put to proper use by management and interested outside parties—creditors, donors, and public regulatory officials, for example. When properly used, the data can reveal much about the financial aspects of an organization's operations. But before the tools and techniques of financial analysis can be applied to these data, the analyst must understand the fundamental characteristics of the flow of cash into and through the nonprofit organization.

The cash flow of a profit-seeking business firm has often been depicted as circular flow—without a beginning or end—and is characterized as capital, or funds, *circulating* throughout the business. The business begins its operations with cash, converts the cash into assets, and through normal business operations, reconverts those assets back into cash. For example, when a manufacturing firm buys raw materials that it processes into finished goods, it converts *cash* into the asset known as *inventory*. The inventory, when sold on open account to one of the firm's customers, is converted into another asset called *accounts receivable*. And when the receivable is collected, it is reconverted into *cash*, thereby completing one cash cycle that, because of the ongoing nature of business, appears as a continuous flow of cash through the operating assets of a business firm.

The element that maintains the circular flow of cash and governs the rate at which it circulates in the for-profit firm is *sales*. So long as an effective demand continues to exist for a firm's product or service, the asset conversion process will continue to be (at least potentially) profitable, and the circular flow of cash will be maintained by the firm's operations. As sales increase, the circular flow will become more rapid, in the sense that a larger number of dollars will circulate through the business during each period. This increase in the rate of flow will usually also require the firm to maintain a higher volume of inventories, receivables, and cash to support the higher rate of cash flow. If sales decline or cease, the rate of cash flow will likewise slow down or come to a standstill. The firm's assets will continue to exist, but the rate at which the conversion process takes place will match the decline in sales activity.

A schematic representation of the flow of cash through a manufacturing firm is presented in Exhibit 6-1. The boxes in the diagram represent the firm's assets, liabilities, and equity, while the interconnecting pipes represent the paths through which the conversion process transforms cash (or credit) into operating assets and back into cash again. The diagram is thus a graphic representation of the three basic accounting statements: the *balance sheet* items are shown as boxes, and the *income statement* and *funds-flow statement* are represented by the interconnecting pipes.

The diagram makes it possible to visually trace the paths of various dollars held by a business firm as they circulate in response to management's operating and financial decisions. For example, a firm may raise cash by borrowing on a long-term basis and use that cash to purchase fixed assets. Ultimate repayment of the debt thus incurred will come from cash flows provided by future profitable operations. The impact of these decisions can be analyzed on a conceptual level by referring to the diagram in Exhibit 6-1; however, the precise impact in dollar terms must come from an analysis of the basic accounting statements.

In addition to providing the analyst with a picture of business cash flow, the diagram also demonstrates that the cash-flow cycle is self-contained and self-perpetuating. That is, so long as the firm remains profitable, its production and selling activities will automatically regenerate the cash-flow cycle in the long run. Cash spent on fixed assets, raw materials, work-in-process, and selling expenses will be returned to

Exhibit 6-1: **Cash Flow of a Manufacturing Firm**

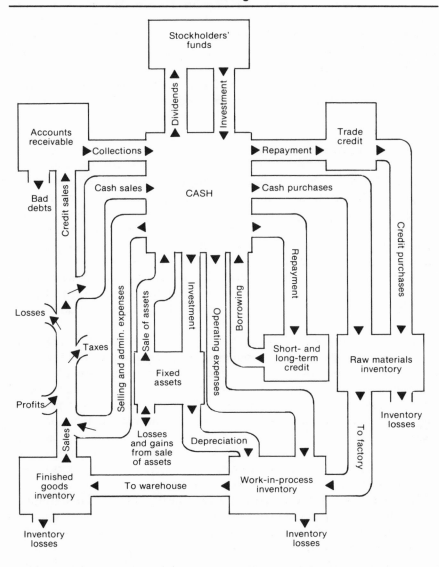

the cash account by way of accounts-receivable collections and cash sales on a more or less continuous basis. Consequently, profitable operations will generally permit the firm to achieve the desirable objectives of liquidity, solvency, and growth. In other words, in the profit-seeking business, doing something well permits the firm to continue doing it.

The trading nonprofit organization is quite similar to the profit-seeking business firm in many respects. Perhaps most importantly, the cash flows of these two types of organizations are almost identical in character. The cash flows of both are circular and self-perpetuating to a large extent, and their rates of cash flow are governed by the rates of sale of their products or services. The cash flows of nontrading nonprofit organizations are quite different from those of the profit-seeking business, mainly because nontrading organizations receive no operating revenues, and hence, their cash-flow cycle is neither circular nor self-perpetuating. These similarities and differences in cash-flow characteristics and their causes are detailed in the following sections.

Trading Nonprofit Organizations

Trading nonprofit organizations were defined in chapter 2 as nonprofit organizations whose main economic activities involve the production and/or the purchase of goods and services for resale to their clientele. The key word in this definition is, of course, *resale*; the process of selling goods or services on account or for cash distinguishes the trading organization from other nonprofit entities.

Like those of profit-seeking businesses, the trading organization's cash flows are circular. To illustrate the nature of the circular flow of cash, consider a private, nonprofit preparatory school, Ramey Academy.

Nonprofit Educational Institution. Ramey Academy began its operations two years ago in a building formerly used as a public high school. The school was closed as the result of a consolidation of the city and county school systems, and Ramey Academy purchased the property from the city government. The academy financed the purchase through a mortgage loan secured from a local savings and loan association. The academy's governing board adopted the policy of setting tuition rates high enough to achieve financial self-sufficiency in its operations. Donations were to be used for scholarships for qualified students whose parents were financially unable to pay full tuition.

The cash flows for the academy are graphically portrayed in Exhibit 6-2. The cash-flow diagram is composed of a series of boxes and interconnecting pipes similar to those presented in Exhibit 6-1. Again, the boxes represent the organization's *balance sheet* accounts (exclusive of the fund balance), and the pipes depict the paths through which cash flows between and among the balance-sheet items. That is, they represent the accounts normally found in the organization's *statement of support, revenues, expenses, and changes in fund balances* and its cash-flow statement. Thus, the cash-flow diagram in Exhibit 6-2 is a graphic summary of the organization's three basic financial statements.

The circle at the bottom of the diagram labeled "educational process" represents the point where the academy's clientele exchanges cash for services, and this is the element that maintains the circular flow of cash and determines its rate of flow through the organization; that is, the

Exhibit 6-2: **Cash Flow of A Private Educational Institution**

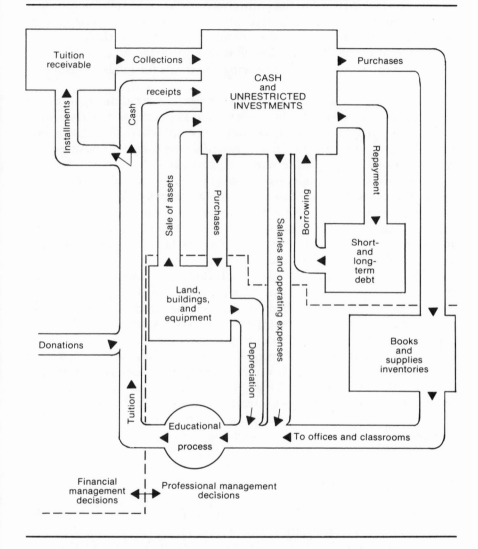

greater the number of students engaged in the educational process, the higher will be the resultant rate of cash flow.

By tracing the flow of cash through the boxes and pipes in Exhibit 6-2 with careful attention to the *timing* of all the cash flows, one may gain an appreciation of the dynamic nature of the operation of this trading organization. Note, for example, that tuition payments will be largely episodic, as will the purchase of books and many items of supplies. However, operating expenses and debt repayment will be more or less continuous throughout the academic year. The balance between cash inflows and outflows therefore must be maintained in two dimensions:

total dollar *amount* and the *timing* of receipts and payments. More will be said about this later, but the point that must be understood at the onset is that the financial manager of any nonprofit entity must become thoroughly familiar with the nature and characteristics of the organization's cash flows. Without such knowledge he or she will be hampered in analyzing and measuring the needs for funds to sustain its operations.

The most significant feature of the cash flows of a trading organization is their potential to sustain the organization's operations over time, even in the event that outside financial support is withdrawn. This fact makes the trading nonprofit organization resemble the for-profit business and causes it to be unique in the nonprofit context.

Finally, the dashed line in Exhibit 6-2 separates the cash flow into two areas of responsibility: professional management decisions and financial management decisions. The academy's professional manager (the head master) bears full responsibility for the educational process and hence must decide on the basic needs for physical facilities, personnel, and educational material. The financial manager, by contrast, must control, manage, and account for all of the cash flows and ensure that adequate funds are always available to pay the academy's bills as they come due.

The placement of the dashed line through the cash flow pipes suggests the points of interface between the two areas of responsibility. Decisions regarding tuition, asset management, and operating expenditures require input from both professional and financial management, but the ultimate authority for all decisions rests with "line" management (in this instance, the educators). Thus the financial manager may only recommend, say, that the organization refrain from hiring personnel based on a concern for solvency or liquidity, but he or she cannot prevent professional management from so doing.

Nontrading Organizations

In contrast to the cash flows of both the for-profit business and the trading nonprofit organization, the cash flows of a nontrading nonprofit organization cannot be characterized as being circular. Instead, the cash-flow cycle is better described as a *linear* flow, because the operations of this type of organization do not directly convert assets or services purchased with cash back into cash at the end of the cycle. Two examples may help illustrate the linear nature of these cash flows.

Private Charitable Foundation. The Warren Foundation is a nonprofit organization founded to lend financial support to individuals, groups, and organizations engaged in activities that are intended to better the quality of community life in Warren County, Georgia. The Warren Foundation was initially funded with a bequest of $2 million from the late Axel Warren, resident of the county and former state senator from the

Warren County district. The foundation currently continues to receive donations from various individuals and business firms located throughout the state. The donations are placed in the endowment fund, and according to the foundation's charter, grants must be paid out of the endowment income only.

The foundation awards cash grants mainly to civic and community-sponsored organizations, based on information supplied by the prospective grantee on the foundation's standard grant application forms. The Board of Trustees approves those grants that it feels have genuine merit. Grant funds are disbursed through the trust department of a local bank that also manages the endowment fund.

The cash flow of the Warren Foundation is graphically portrayed in Exhibit 6-3. Note that flow of cash through the Warren Foundation is linear, rather than circular. The sources of funds, besides the occasional reinvestment of surplus endowment income, are donations and bequests; the uses of funds are taxes on investment income, grants, and operating expenses. The cash disbursed as taxes, grants, or expenses is never recovered: it simply passes out of the control of the organization. Again, the dashed line separates the trustees' functions from those of the foundation's financial manager (the bank).

Although the good works supported by the foundation tend to encourage its donor clientele to continue their annual contributions, the flow of cash cannot be considered circular. Since the foundation and its donors do not exchange goods or services for cash, the foundation is in reality an intermediary between the donors and the grantees. Thus, the linear cash-flow characterization is appropriate.

Museum. The Holt Museum's operations are partially supported by both its endowment income and a continuing annual appropriation from the city in which it is located. The balance of its operating funds and all of its capital requirements are provided by donations solicited during its annual fund-raising campaign.

The museum purchased the building in which its collections are housed with the proceeds of a thirty-year mortgage loan. It employs a full-time staff of personnel for administration, security, and maintenance. The professional staff consists of a curator and two specialists. One specialist is responsible for the art collection and the other has charge of the museum's remaining collections.

Nature of the Cash Flow. Cash flows into and through the Holt Museum are illustrated in Exhibit 6-4. Although this diagram is considerably more complex than that depicting the Warren Foundation's cash flows (Exhibit 6-3), the principles underlying the two cash flows are the same; cash inflows from donations are received and then simply pass through the organization. Some of the cash is invested, but most is used

(text continued on page 112)

Exhibit 6-3: **Cash Flow of a Charitable Foundation**

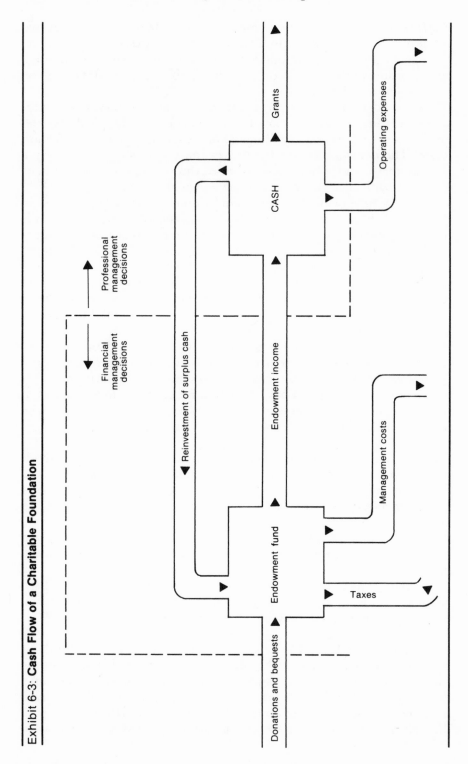

Exhibit 6-4: **Cash Flow of a Museum**

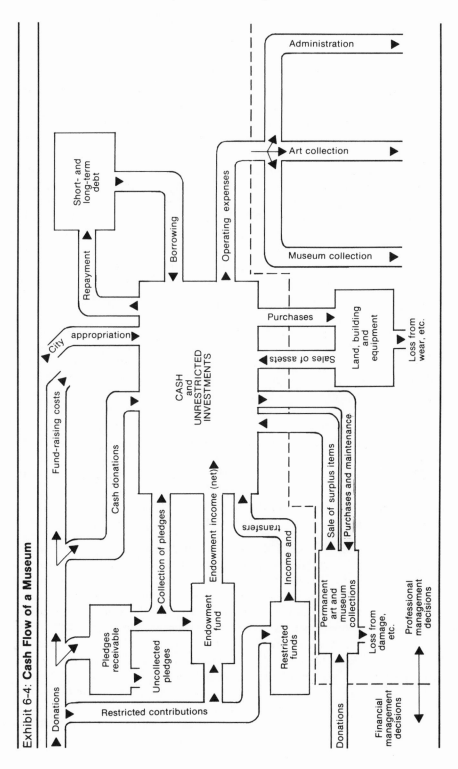

(text continued from page 109)

to purchase permanent assets (where it will remain for long periods) or is consumed by operations (i.e., paid out for salaries and wages, supplies, utilities, and so forth).

Again, the cash flow is linear in that the museum's central economic activities do not generate operating revenues or returns from investments in art or historical treasures that may be used to offset operating expenses or generate "profits" (excess of revenues over expenditures). While it is certainly true that the funds expended, for example, to improve the museum's permanent collection may result in its receiving more cash from donors or a more generous appropriation from the city, the fact remains that the museum does not *sell* a product or service in the classic sense. Hence pricing decisions are never at issue. Further it is not clear which comes first, the improvement in the collection or the promise of added donations that enable the collection to expand. In any event, and whatever the true motives of individual and corporate donors, the cash flows of nontrading nonprofit organizations are better characterized as linear than circular for financial management purposes.

In terms of the operational and theoretical considerations presented in chapters 2 and 3, the quality and quantity of the museum's collection, exhibits, and other activities fall in the professional manager's domain, while the financial manager is concerned with maintaining a proper balance in the organization's cash flows. The dashed line in Exhibit 6-4 separates professional and financial decision areas. In this case, it clearly separates the funds-gathering from the funds-spending activities and makes obvious the delineation between decisions regarding liquidity and solvency and decisions regarding the museum's operations. This adds further justification to the position that financial management decisions are better served by recognizing the linear nature of the cash flows of nontrading organizations, since the cash flows in the financial manager's area of responsibility are clearly linear.

Rate of Cash Flow. The rate of cash flow through nontrading organizations is not governed by the effective demand for a specific product or service offered for sale at a set price, as is the case in trading organizations. Rather, its maximum level is determined in the long run by the rate at which cash is made available from the sum of unrestricted donations, appropriations, and investment income. To survive financially, a nontrading organization must obviously keep its spending rate at a level equal to or less than that of its cash inflows. In the short run, an organization may accelerate its spending rate by borrowing funds or selling some of its assets, but continued reliance on these sources of funds will eventually cause the organization to become insolvent. The rate of spending is thus constrained by the limited resources made available by individuals, businesses, governments, and others, who are otherwise unconnected with the organization's operations.

Cash-Flow Imbalances

If at the end of the fiscal year, the cash inflow of an organization balanced its cash outflow exactly, the job of the financial manager would be greatly simplified. Unfortunately, this does not often happen. What is more, most nonprofit organizations experience periods during a year when their cash outflows may exceed their inflows by amounts sufficient to prevent the financial managers from meeting the organizations' regular financial obligations as they come due, unless steps are taken to secure additional funds. Those imbalances may result from external causes over which management has little or no control, or they may be the result of changes made in an organization's operations or policies.

Since the financial manager bears the responsibility of providing sufficient funds to pay the bills on a timely basis, he or she must correct such imbalances by pumping additional cash into the organization's cash account. Alternatively, in situations when the imbalance lies in the other direction—when too much cash has become available—the financial manager must make sure the excess cash (but no more or no less) is removed from the flow and put to some productive use.

Outside Influences on Cash Flows. What Exhibits 6-2 through 6-4 fail to show explicitly are the complexities added to the cash flows by seasonal, cyclical, and inflationary factors. These factors tend to alter the patterns of cash flow that are considered "normal," as reflected in the organization's historical records. When these changes occur, the financial manager may have to recommend that appropriate allowances be made in the organization's operations to compensate for externally induced cash shortages.

Seasonal Fluctuations. Wide variations in the cash flows of trading organizations occur because of seasonal swings that affect their sales. A farmers' cooperative buying organization is an extreme example of this cash-flow pattern. The co-op purchases seeds, fertilizer, and so forth, for resale to the farmers and then assists them in selling their crops at harvest time. The planting and harvesting seasons will thus produce large fluctuations in the cooperative's cash outflows and inflows, respectively. Nontrading organizations may also experience seasonal variations in their cash flows. For example, churches generally find that their collection baskets are heaviest at Easter and Christmas and lightest during the summer.

Another type of seasonal pattern that affects most organizations is that associated with operating expenditures. Heating and cooling expenses are the most obvious examples, but other seasonal patterns also exist. Summer vacations often will create staffing problems that many organizations solve by hiring part-time or temporary help. Not only is this practice expensive in itself, since vacationing employees continue to draw their pay while they are away, but it may create extraordinary expenses if temporary help is inefficient in performing its assigned duties.

Cyclical Fluctuations. The cash *outflows* of most nonprofit organizations tend to be resistant to the alternate waves of expansion and contraction of economic activity during what is called a *business cycle*. This is because most such organizations face unflagging demands for their services; hence, for organizations such as schools, museums, service organizations, fraternal and social clubs, and housing authorities, even a relatively severe economic recession will fail to prevent their conducting "business as usual." The steady pace at which they continue to provide their particular services is matched by the equally steady rate of spending for salaries and wages, supply purchases, maintenance, and so forth.

The pattern of cash *inflows* is quite another story, however. In most instances, general economic contractions produce pronounced declines in the cash inflows of nonprofit organizations, especially those nontrading organizations that are dependent upon contributions from the general public for their operating requirements. Dues-collecting organizations— trade associations, for example—also register declines in their cash inflows during recessions, but in relatively small proportions as compared with say, charitable organizations. When the economy recovers and the expansion phase of the business cycle begins, the cash inflows for such organizations become easier to obtain and larger in volume as a consequence.

Cyclically vulnerable organizations have three choices during the contraction phase of the business cycle. They may either (1) cut back on their principal activities, (2) draw upon previously established cash reserves to maintain a constant rate of operations, or (3) supplement their reduced cash inflows by borrowing from a financial institution (or from another creditor or related organization). Such organizations obviously must adopt a plan to enable them to survive bad times.

Labor unions present an example of nontrading nonprofit organizations that are cyclically vulnerable in the extreme. For example, some labor unions pay supplemental benefits to members who are laid off during recessionary periods. This increases their normal cash outflows in bad times. Further, many unions (but not all of them) follow the policy of not collecting dues from their unemployed members; thus, their cash inflows fall while their cash outflows increase. The net cash drain is generally paid out of a special fund built up during the industry's (and the union's) better times. If the recession is prolonged, the fund may be depleted and the benefits may cease unless the union decides to borrow to maintain its membership unemployment benefits.

Another type of cyclical influence on nonprofit organizations is exemplified by the recent taxpayers' revolt in the United States. Tax income-dependent organizations (such as research facilities in colleges and universities, certain organizations involved in the performing arts and humanities, and historic preservation groups) generally face cycles in which funding from federal government sources becomes plentiful and then scarce as administrations and legislative attitudes undergo change. Budget cuts at the federal level often mean similar reductions in state and local funding as well, since many federal programs require the grantee to obtain matching funds. The effects of this type of cycle are similar to those previously described. But additionally, the tax income-dependent organizations will respond by increasing their lobbying activities, either directly or through their sister organizations established under section 501(c)(4) of the tax code.

Price Inflation. Another externally induced cause of cash-flow imbalances is price inflation. Recent high rates of inflation have caused severe cash-flow problems for nonprofit organizations that formerly enjoyed rather comfortable annual cash surpluses and maintained relatively large, unrestricted investment funds. Many of these organizations, as well as some not so financially secure entities, find they are unable to maintain their prior year's levels of services or production without drawing down cash reserves, borrowing, or increasing their fund-raising activities. Supplies, operating expenses, interest, and capital equipment costs continue to increase dramatically, thereby increasing the total rate of cash outflow for all nonprofit organizations.

Unfortunately, nontrading organizations cannot pass on their own cost increases to their clientele in the form of higher prices because nontrading organizations do not sell their products or services. Instead, they must rely on their donors and investment managers to increase the rate of cash inflows to match their new, higher rates of cash outflows. In a real sense, therefore, price inflation also creates upward pressures on the cost of charity to donors. While trading organizations can and often do adjust the prices of their goods and services to offset cost inflation, they, too, must often escalate their fund-raising activities in order to break even.

The choices facing the nonprofit organization in a period of rising prices are limited to (1) reducing their outputs of goods or services, (2) increasing prices to paying customers, (3) extending their fund-raising efforts to extreme limits, or (4) facing insolvency. Borrowing to overcome the effects of inflation is not always an acceptable alternative because borrowed funds must be repaid. Unless future cash inflows from other sources promise to be large enough to repay principal plus interest *and* take care of any future cost increases, borrowing to pay price-inflation operating costs will simply postpone the financial failure of the organization. In short, a *permanent* and satisfactory cure for the effects of price inflation for the nontrading nonprofit organization lies only in successfully convincing donors to increase their charitable contributions at rates sufficient to offset the rate at which their operating costs are increasing. If the real incomes of their donors have fallen during the inflationary period, the nontrading organization will face very difficult operating and financial choices as their cash-flow imbalances become severe.

The data in Exhibit 6-5 illustrate one instance of how inflation affects the cash flows of a nontrading organization. The Catskill Training Center works with handicapped persons in the Catskill area. It trains indigent, newly handicapped adults to care for themselves and their

---

Exhibit 6-5: **Effects of Price Inflation on the Statement of Support, Revenues, Expenses, and Changes in Fund Balance of a Nontrading Organization**

**Catskill Training Center, Incorporated
Statement of Support, Revenues, Expenses,
and Changes in Fund Balances
Years Ending December 31, 1987 and 1988**

	1987	Inflation rate	1988
Support and Revenues			
Donations	$ 332,000	3%	$ 341,200
Investment income	13,000	10	14,300
Total	$ 345,000	3%	$ 355,500
Expenditures			
Personnel services	$ 203,000	9%	$ 221,300
Automobile expenses	18,300	30	23,800
Utilities	19,800	25	24,800
Supplies and materials	52,600	15	60,500
Total	$ 293,700	12%	$ 330,400
Excess of revenues over expenditures	$ 51,300		$ 25,100
Interfund transfers			
Debt retirement	$ (23,800)		$ (23,800)
Plant fund	(10,500)	17%	(12,300)
Total	$ (34,300)	4%	$ (36,100)
To fund balance	$ 17,000		$ (11,000)
Fund balance, beginning of year	$ 100,000		$ 117,000
Fund balance, end of year	117,000		106,000

---

dependent children by adapting to and sometimes overcoming their physical handicaps. Its operations are supported mainly from voluntary donations.

The center trained essentially the same number and types of clients in both 1987 and 1988, and it employed the same staff under almost identical conditions in each of the two years. Thus the only differences in the organization's operations, and hence its cash flows, were inflation induced. The middle column in Exhibit 6-5 presents the rates of inflation experienced by the center during 1988. Personnel salary increases averaged 9 percent over 1987, for example, while automobile and utility expenses increased by 30 percent and 25 percent, respectively, largely as a result of an increase in its auto insurance premium and a rate increase granted to the power company by the Public Utility Commission.

In addition to its operating expenditures, the center is obligated to pay $23,800 per year to retire a mortgage on the building that housed its operations, and the director continued to purchase new equipment the center needed to meet its clients' needs. As a result of price inflation alone, the center's net cash flow changed from a positive $17,000 in 1987 to a negative $11,000 in 1988. If the center had not had adequate cash reserves during 1988, it could not have purchased additional fixed assets (represented by "Plant Fund"), costing more than $1,800 (the difference between the center's operating surplus and its debt service requirements).

Internal Influences on Cash Flows. Almost every operating and financial decision that a manager makes will directly or indirectly affect an organization's cash flows. Hiring additional personnel, for example, obviously will increase cash outlays for wages and employee benefits. In addition, that decision also may affect the organization's cash outlays for the supplies and equipment needed to support the activities of the new employees. A secretary will need a desk, a chair, a typewriter, pencils, paper, and other materials in order to be productive. Moreover, if the new employees' duties relate to production or sales (in a trading organization), management should expect to see changes in the patterns or volume of operating revenues as a result of that decision. Thus the addition of one new employee has the potential to permanently alter the total cash flows of a nonprofit organization in obvious as well as not so obvious ways.

The most dramatic changes in the cash flows of a nonprofit entity will result from decisions to add new programs or to increase the capacity of extant programs to deliver greater volumes of services to its clientele. These actions often will result in large dollar expenditures for capital equipment, the creation of new employment opportunities, and perhaps the addition of long-term debt to the organization's capital structure, among other things. But even minor operational changes, such as shifting purchases of typing paper to a supplier who is willing to extend more liberal credit terms, can have an important impact on the financial health of the organization.

Consequently, both professional and financial managers always must measure the effects of organizational or operational changes on an organization's cash-flow patterns prior to implementing such changes. They must also keep close watch over the actual effects these decisions have on cash flows subsequent to their implementation. Discussions of approaches to short- and long-term financial planning are reserved for later chapters; however, the following section of this chapter outlines the principles and presents the basic tools useful both in planning future operations and in the financial analysis of past operations.

OVERVIEW OF FINANCIAL ANALYSIS

Each of the cash-flow diagrams presented in Exhibits 6-2 through 6-4 provides a framework for constructing a system by which the flow of cash through the interconnecting pipes and the accumulation of cash flows in the various asset boxes can be monitored by the organization's management. Each of the paths that an organization's dollars take as they circulate through its operations represents one step in the overall asset conversion process. Since managerial decisions affect both the rate of cash flow through each pipe and the volume of cash held (or invested) in each box, a system of financial analysis should capture relevant information regarding the organization's asset management and conversion processes.

For example, in Exhibit 6-4 the pipe labeled collection of pledges that connects the boxes labeled *pledges receivable* and *cash and unrestricted investments* is the path through which receivables are converted into cash. By monitoring this cash-flow path, management can appraise the quality of its decisions that relate to receivables management. When management determines that the rate of flow through that pipe is, say, either slow in absolute terms or has fallen off from previous periods, it might conclude that it has neglected that area of its responsibility. Then, on the basis of past experience and the conditions prevailing within the organization's environment, management can begin to take action designed to correct that condition. The same procedure can be used in monitoring the flow of cash through each pipe of the system.

TOOLS OF FINANCIAL ANALYSIS

The two tools of financial analysis that are particularly well suited to the task of monitoring operational cash flows are the analysis of financial ratios and the interpretation of the data presented in the cash flow statements. Each is discussed separately in the following sections.

Analysis of Financial Ratios

A more or less standard set of ratios has been developed for use by managers of profit-seeking business firms. They have as their primary objectives the measurement of liquidity, solvency, and profitability. Liquidity and solvency are expressed in terms of the degree of protection accorded to the firm's creditors by the ease and rapidity with which assets may be converted into cash, the size of the cash inflows relative to fixed costs, or the size of the owner's investment relative to that of the creditors. Profitability is generally measured in terms of either efficiency in the use of assets or the efficiency of converting sales into profits.

The successful use of standard ratios is made possible primarily by two characteristics of profit-seeking businesses. First, all businesses emphasize profits as their primary operating objective, and profits are measured and reported by accountants in essentially the same way for all types of firms: (1) large and small businesses; (2) corporations, partnerships, and proprietorships; and (3) retailers, wholesalers, manufacturers, and service firms. Second, both cash receipts and cash expenditures are fairly closely related to the level of economic activity carried on by the for-profit business firm. Hence, among for-profit firms, similar patterns of cash flows and similar sets of assets exist for the purpose of achieving an identical goal, thereby permitting the use of standard ratios for purposes of monitoring those cash flows.

By contrast, nonprofit organizations exist for a number of widely divergent purposes, none of which is expressed in terms of profitability, as used in the strictest sense of the word. A nonprofit organization nevertheless may engage in some activities that are intended to generate a positive net cash flow, or profits. This cash is then placed at the disposal of the organization to be used to further its primary objectives of service. These ancillary activities therefore are conducted not so much for profit as for raising cash to be used in service to its clientele.

The cash-flow patterns of nonprofit organizations are often different from one another, as is the nature of their assets. This is evident in the comparison of the three cash-flow diagrams presented in Exhibits 6-2, 6-3, and 6-4. Finally, the level of economic activity of a nonprofit organization may not be closely related to or even directly produce its cash *inflows*. This is especially true of the cash inflows of nontrading nonprofit organizations. Consequently, the development and use of a standard set of uniform ratios for nonprofit organizations simply is not possible. This does not mean, however, that ratios are not valuable tools for monitoring cash inflows. It simply means that the management of each nonprofit organization must develop its own set of ratios or adapt existing sets of ratios employed by similar organizations to assist it in analyzing the organization's operations and financial position.

Since the use of standard ratios is not recommended for the analysis of nonprofit organizations, a generalized approach to the use of ratios by a financial manager is all that can be prescribed here. To assist in illustrating how a financial analysis might be conducted, the financial statements of The Hobbs Museum of Art and History, presented in Exhibits 6-6, 6-7 and 6-8, are examined in the following sections. The cash-flow diagram of a museum presented in Exhibit 6-4 will be referenced often in this discussion, since it provides an excellent frame of reference for the analysis.

Illustrative Analysis: The Hobbs Museum. The Hobbs Museum, the subject of the following illustrative analysis, is classified as a nonprofit corporation, organized under the laws of Michigan, and operating with a

(text continued on page 125)

Exhibit 6-6: Balance Sheet of a Nonprofit Organization

THE HOBBS MUSEUM OF ART AND HISTORY
Balance Sheet
June 30, 1989 (with comparative totals for 1988)

| | Current Fund | | Collections | | | | Total | Prior Year |
	Unrestricted	Restricted	Art	Museum	Plant Fund	Endowment	All Funds	Total
Assets								
Current assets:								
Cash	$15,300	$2,200	$0	$0	$0	$0	$17,500	$23,700
Accounts & pledges receivable (net) (Note 1)	68,700	7,600	35,800	52,100	0	0	164,200	125,400
Investments (Note 2)	23,500	1,200	0	0	0	1,400	26,100	3,300
Inventories	66,700	0	0	0	0	0	66,700	59,900
Prepaid expenses	14,000	0	0	0	0	0	14,000	12,400
Other current assets	3,500	0	0	0	0	0	3,500	3,400
Total current assets	$191,700	$11,000	$35,800	$52,100	$0	$1,400	$292,000	$228,100
Fixed assets:								
Land	0	0	0	0	89,900	0	89,900	89,900
Plant & equipment	0	0	0	0	267,600	0	267,600	267,600
Less accum. depreciation	0	0	0	0	75,400	0	75,400	57,600
Net plant & equipment (Note 3)	$0	$0	$0	$0	$192,200	$0	$192,200	$210,000
Art collection (Note 4)	0	0	589,900	0	0	0	589,900	555,400
Museum collection (Note 4)	0	0	0	667,800	0	0	667,800	598,900
Investments (Note 2)	115,500	133,500	0	0	0	778,900	1,027,900	1,098,000
Total fixed assets	$115,500	$133,500	$589,900	$667,800	$282,100	$778,900	$2,567,700	$2,552,200
Total assets	$307,200	$144,500	$625,700	$719,900	$282,100	$780,300	$2,859,700	$2,780,300

Liabilities & Fund Balance

Current liabilities:								
Accounts payable	$38,900	$0	$0	$0	$0	$0	$38,900	$34,400
Accrued expenses	17,700	0	0	0	7,500	0	25,200	13,400
Deferred revenue-current portion (Note 5)	7,700	3,400	2,000	0	0	0	13,100	6,800
Current portion of mortgage (Note 8)	0	0	0	0	12,300	0	12,300	12,300
Total current liabilities	$64,300	$3,400	$2,000	$0	$19,800	$0	$89,500	$66,900
Long-term liabilities:								
Deferred revenue (Note 5)	125,700	3,400	6,000	0	0	0	135,100	148,000
Mortgage payable (Note 8)	0	0	0	0	99,600	0	99,600	111,900
Total Long-term liabilities	$125,700	$3,400	$6,000	$0	$99,600	$0	$234,700	$259,900
Fund balances:								
Current unrestricted	$117,200	$0	$0	$0	$0	$0	117,200	115,400
Current restricted	0	137,700	0	0	0	0	137,700	123,600
Art collection	0	0	617,700	0	0	0	617,700	609,900
Museum collection	0	0	0	719,900	0	0	719,900	700,900
Plant	0	0	0	0	162,700	0	162,700	175,700
Endowment	0	0	0	0	0	780,300	780,300	728,000
Total fund balances	$117,200	$137,700	$617,700	$719,900	$162,700	$780,300	$2,535,500	$2,453,500
Total liabilities & fund balance	$307,200	$144,500	$625,700	$719,900	$282,100	$780,300	$2,859,700	$2,780,300

Note: For notes 1 through 8, see Exhibit 6–9.

Exhibit 6-7: Statement of Support, Revenue, Expenses and Changes in Fund Balances of a Nonprofit Organization

THE HOBBS MUSEUM OF ART AND HISTORY
Statement of Support, Revenue, Expenses and Changes in Fund Balances
Fiscal year ended June 30, 1989 (with comparative totals for 1988)

| | Current Fund | | | Collections | | | Total | Prior Year |
	Unrestricted	Restricted	Art	Museum	Plant Fund	Endowment	All Funds	Total
Support:								
Government appropriations	$74,300	$0	$0	$0	$0	$0	$74,300	$74,300
Gifts and grants (Note 4)	89,000	10,300	54,500	77,800	0	0	231,600	202,200
Memberships	9,800	0	0	0			9,800	8,700
Total support	$173,100	$10,300	$54,500	$77,800	$0	$0	$315,700	$285,200
Revenues:								
Admissions	57,600	0	0	0	0	0	57,600	59,800
Investment income	54,400	74,400	0	0	0	0	128,800	112,900
Net realized investment gains (losses)	22,200	12,100	0	0	0	0	34,300	(1,600)
Revenues, gift shop	250,700	0	0	0	0	0	250,700	267,800
Total revenues	$384,900	$86,500	$0	$0	$0	$0	$471,400	$438,900
Total support & revenues (Note 6)	$558,000	$96,800	$54,500	$77,800	$0	$0	$787,100	$724,100
Expenses:								
Program:								
Curatorial & conservation	$137,700	$58,700	$0	$0	$33,800	0	$230,200	$189,700
Education	24,400	2,200	0	0	0	0	26,600	23,300
Accession for collections net of deaccessions (Note 4)	13,700	28,700	50,700	48,900	0	0	142,000	43,200
Support services:								
Administration	110,300	0	0	0	10,200	0	120,500	112,200
Fund raising	45,500	0	0	0	0	0	45,500	40,900
Gift shop costs & expenses	170,500	0	0	0	5,400	0	175,900	174,100
Total expenses	$502,100	$89,600	$50,700	$48,900	$49,400	$0	$740,700	$583,400
Excess (deficit) of support & revenue over expenses	$55,900	$7,200	$3,800	$28,900	($49,400)	$0	$46,400	$140,700

Capital Additions:							
Gifts and grants (Note 5)	0	0	0	0	0	33,600	33,600	12,600
Net investment income	0	0	0	0	0	1,400	1,400	800
Net realized investment gains (losses)	0	0	0	0	0	600	600	(300)
Total capital additions	$0	$0	$0	$0	$0	$35,600	$35,600	$13,100
Excess (deficit) of support & revenue over expenses after capital additions	$55,900	$7,200	$3,800	$28,900	($49,400)	$35,600	$82,000	$153,800
Beginning fund balance	136,500	140,500	567,400	634,500	172,100	802,500	2,453,500	2,299,700
Add (less) transfers (Note 7)	(75,200)	(10,000)	46,500	56,500	40,000	(57,800)	0	0
Ending fund balances	$117,200	$137,700	$617,700	$719,900	$162,700	$780,300	$2,535,500	$2,453,500

For notes 1 through 8, see Exhibit 6–9.

Exhibit 6-8: Statement of Functional Expenses of a Nonprofit Organization

THE HOBBS MUSEUM OF ART AND HISTORY
Statement of Functional Expenses
Fiscal year ended June 30, 1989 (with comparative totals for 1988)

	Program Services				Support Service		Total Expenses	
	Curatorial & conservation	Education	Museum & Art accession	Gift shop	Administration	Fund raising	1989	1988
Salaries & wages	$110,400	$5,600	$68,900	$18,700	$67,700		$271,300	$200,200
Employee benefits	12,300	500	6,200	1,700	6,100	0	26,800	18,000
Payroll taxes	5,000	300	3,500	1,000	3,400	0	13,200	10,000
Total personnel expenses	$127,700	$6,400	$78,600	$21,400	$77,200	$0	$311,300	$228,200
Auto expense	4,900			2,200	3,800		10,900	8,900
Awards & grants		17,300					17,300	16,400
Contract services	16,000		10,700		6,600	45,500	81,000	77,000
Cost of merchandise				131,900			131,900	132,900
Dues & fees	3,500	100	3,400		1,700		8,700	6,000
Equipment rental	10,700				3,000		13,700	10,800
Interest expense	6,500			1,000	1,400		8,900	10,000
Occupancy	14,500			3,200	5,000		22,700	18,900
Postage & shipping	4,400	400	9,800	7,800	1,200		23,600	20,100
Printing & publications	8,900	1,500		2,500	800		13,700	10,900
Supplies	2,200	200	1,600	1,300	7,600		12,900	9,800
Telephone	4,600	700	4,500	1,200	1,800		12,800	10,900
Travel & entertainment	13,100		33,400		5,800		52,300	22,300
Other expenses	400				800		1,200	300
Total expenses before depreciation	$217,400	$26,600	$142,000	$174,700	$116,700	$45,500	$722,900	$583,400
Depreciation of fixed assets	12,800	0	0	1,200	3,800	0	17,800	
Total expenses	$230,200	$26,600	$142,000	$175,900	$120,500	$45,500	$740,700	$583,400

(text continued from page 119)

section 501(c)(3) exemption under the IRS Tax Code. About 10 percent of its annual budget is financed from an appropriation from the city of Lakewood. Its activities include the operation of a museum and art gallery, an educational program that supports local youth pursuing higher education degrees in the arts, and a gift shop.

The museum's accounting system is fairly complex. The relevant financial accounting data taken from the museum's 1989 annual report is presented in Exhibits 6–6, 6–7, 6–8.

By definition, *financial* analysis of a nonprofit organization is confined to the analysis of cash flows within the financial manager's area of responsibility (for example, above the dashed line in Exhibit 6–4). The cash flows included within that area determine the degree of liquidity possessed by the organization and reveal its position vis-à-vis financial solvency. Occasionally, as in the case of the Hobbs Museum of Art and History, a nontrading, nonprofit organization will carry on some amount of trading activities, in this case, operating a museum gift shop. The total cash flows of this type of activity should be included in the financial manager's area of responsibility insofar as financial analysis is concerned, but their analyses should be conducted separately from the organization's cash flows. In this way the contribution of the trading activities to the organization's health and prosperity can be clearly delineated. The analysis of the Hobbs Museum will follow that pattern.

Analysis of Nontrading Activities. The analysis of the nontrading aspects of the Hobbs Museum operations will begin with the pipes and boxes on the left side of Exhibit 6–4 and proceed toward those on the right. The gift shop accounts — the trading portion of the organization — are omitted in this part of the analysis.

Receivables. Data from Exhibits 6–6, 6–7, and 6–8 regarding revenue sources and their corresponding accounts and pledges receivable, are as follows:

			Receivables
Source of Support	Revenue	Year-end	Average
Government appropriations	$ 74,300	$ 13,200	$ 15,700
Grants	32,300	3,000	3,500
Fund raising	199,300	147,000	124,100
Memberships	9,800	1,000	600
Totals	$315,700	$164,200	$143,900

These data can be used to reveal the average rate of cash flow from receivables to cash in each of the categories (e.g., the rate of flow through the *collection of pledges* pipe in the cash-flow diagram.) The

---

Exhibit 6–9: **Notes to the Financial Statements of a Nonprofit Organization**

Notes to the Financial Statements of the Hobbs Museum of Art and History:

Note 1: Accounts and pledges receivable are stated net of the allowance for uncollectible pledges, based on historical experience. The allowance for uncollectible pledges amounted to $5,500 at the end of fiscal year 1989 and $4,100 in 1988. All accounts receivable are considered to be collectible in full. The following amounts were due to the museum as of the end of fiscal years 1988 and 1989:

	1989	1988
Accounts receivable, government	$ 13,200	$ 18,100
Accounts receivable, grants	3,000	6,000
Pledges receivable (net)	147,000	101,200
Accounts receivable, memberships	1,000	100
Totals	$164,200	$125,400

Note 2: Investments are maintained on the balance sheet at cost (net of brokerage fees) at the time of purchase or, in the case of gifts of securities or real estate held in the investment portfolio, at the market value determined on the date of the gift.

Note 3: Net plant and equipment includes equipment, furniture and fixtures, buildings, and capital improvements. Depreciation charges are calculated on a straight-line basis over the estimated useful lives of the respective classes of assets.

Note 4: The value of the art objects maintained in art and museum collections, both purchased and donated, are included in the balance sheet at their respective cost or appraised values. Such values are determined at the time of each acquisition. The values of the objects acquired by gift, which values have been estimated by the museum, are reported as gifts in the Statement of Support, Revenues, Expenses, and Changes in Fund Balances. In 1989 the total values of gifts received by the art collection and the museum collection were $6,500 and $43,200, respectively. No gifts of art objects were received during fiscal year 1988. Grants awarded to the museum for various purposes totaled $32,300 in 1989 and $16,700 in 1988.

Note 5: Deferred revenue comprises the total of gifts, grants, and pledges receivable, the receipt of which was reasonably expected to occur beyond one year from the end of the 1989 fiscal year. The total amounts shown on the Balance Sheet are net of an allowance for uncollectible pledges of $1,300 in 1989 and $1,500 in 1988.

Note 6: A substantial number of unpaid volunteers have made significant contributions of their time to develop the museum's programs. The value of their time is not reflected in these statements because of the difficult measurement problems that are posed in so doing.

Note 7: Interfund transfers were affected from the current fund to the plant fund during fiscal year 1989 to provide for the expenses of operating the plant and for certain capital additions. Other transfers were made from the endowment fund to the art collection to provide for supplemental salaries and expenses for the Artist in Residence program.

Note 8: A mortgage secured by the museum's main building and the land on which it is located is payable in quarterly installments of $5,300 each, including principal and interest. The mortgage carries an interest rate of 8.4 percent per annum. The final payment is due on September 30, 1996.

---

ratio or measure best suited for this purpose is called the *average collection period* or (ACP), and is calculated as follows:

$$\text{Average collection period} = \text{Receivables}/(\text{Revenues}/360 \text{ days})$$

or

$$\text{ACP} = (\text{Receivables}/360 \text{ days})/\text{Revenues}$$

The average collection period for grants is

$$ACP = \$3,000/(32,300/360 \text{ days})$$
$$= \$3,000/\$ 90 \text{ per day})$$
$$= 33 \text{ days}$$

This means that during the 1989 fiscal year, the Hobbs Museum received payment from its grantors on the average of thirty-three days after billing its grant costs. This estimate of the collection period is based on year-end receivables. The ACP, using the average of year-end 1988 and 1989 receivables is

$$ACP = \$3,000/\$49 \text{ per day} = 61 \text{ days}$$

This suggests that the collection of these receivables has become more rapid during the year because the figure, based on the year-end balance, is less than that based on the average of the two years. Alternatively, the relatively short year-end collection period may be the result of very small current billings to the grantors. The correct explanation for the variance between the two figures must be determined by examining both the dates of the billings and their sizes. Management of the receivable is examined in greater detail in Chapter 10.

The collection periods calculated in the same manner for each of the revenue categories are as follows:

	Year-end	*Average*
Government appropriations	64 days	76 days
Grants	33	39
Fund raising	265	224
Memberships	37	22

The collection of funds from donors is the slowest of the cash flows arising from the four sources of support, while cash flows from museum memberships appear to be the quickest.

The standards against which this ratio can be measured are historical performance in each category, and the terms under which the receivables initially were created. For example, suppose that the museum billed grantors under its contracts on terms of, say, net thirty days. This means that each grantor is being asked to pay the entire invoice amount on or before thirty days from the date of the invoice. By fiscal year-end 1989, grantors on the average are only three days past due — a remarkably good record.

However, if the grantors settle their financial obligations to the museum under the terms of the grants only once each quarter, the ACP calculations illustrated here for that group of receivables do not produce valid analytical information since the billing dates may not correspond exactly with the end of the fiscal year. The actual ACP for grants will average out to be forty-five days (one-half of three months) over the period of one year, provided, of course, that the account processing time is very short.

Investment Funds. The Hobbs Museum's balance sheet shows a year-end 1989 investment account balance of $1,054,000, including both the current and long-term investment accounts. The prior year's balances totaled $1,101,300, making the average balance during the 1989 fiscal year equal to $1,077,650. The income from investments shown in Exhibit 6–7 totaled $128,800 in interest and dividends plus $34,300 in net portfolio gains for the year, yielding a return on the average investment account of

$$\text{Percentage return} = (\$128,800 + \$34,300)/\$1,077,650$$
$$= 15.1\%$$

Since the investment income reported in the financial statements includes (in addition to interest and dividends) realized and unrealized gains and losses on securities and income earned on securities purchased and sold between the statement dates, the percentage return on investment permits the outside analyst to draw fairly firm conclusions about the portfolio performance. Nevertheless, this method of calculating investment returns is not a particularly good one. When better, more detailed data are available, the methodology discussed and illustrated in Chapter 9 may be used to develop better performance measures. This method, called the *unit of account* or *share-value* approach, is clearly superior to the rough approximation discussed here.

Fixed Assets. Fixed assets reported by a museum or art gallery on its balance sheet may or may not include the museum pieces or art collections owned by the organization. When they are excluded, the items valued on the balance sheet constitute the "operating" fixed assets, such as buildings, equipment, vehicles, and so forth. Even when the collections are included as balance sheet assets, as is the case with the Hobbs Museum, the total museum fixed assets cannot be considered as an economic "factor of production" in the same sense that a manufacturing firm's assets are used to generate operating revenue. Ratios that relate fixed assets to revenues, "profits," or fund balances, consequently, provide no useful information to the financial manager of the nontrading organization. This position is confirmed by examining Exhibit 6–4. Note that both the museum's collections and its operating fixed assets are located in the professional manager's area of responsibility.

Total Cash Flow. The Hobbs Museum's total cash inflow from its nontrading activities is depicted as all of the cash flowing into the cashbox from all of the connecting pipes in Exhibit 6-4. This total is $536,400 (i.e., total support and revenues less gift shop revenues in Exhibit 6-7.) Cash outflow for 1989, comprising program expenses plus administrative expenses, total $740,700. This amount includes $142,000 in asset purchases for the museum collections, but it does not include debt principal payments. The operating deficit for the nontrading portion of the organization's total operations is total revenue and support minus total operating costs ($740,700 less $142,000 in net accession costs), or $62,300, which is equal to ($62,300/$536,400 =) 11.6 percent of total nontrading revenues. This, figure is a measure of the degree of dependency of the museum on its trading operations for financial survival.

Debt Service. Debt service is defined as the total of interest and principal payments on long-term debt. In Note 8 of the notes to the financial statements, we find that the museum paid a total of ($5,300 × 4 =) $21,200 in principal and interest payments on its mortgage. Of that amount, $8,900 was paid in interest (see Exhibit 6-8) and the remainder, $12,300, went to repay the principal amount of the loan. Since the nontrading operations produced a deficit, total cash flows are inadequate to cover this important cash outflow; however, the organization has a sufficient amount of cash on hand and in investments to pay principal and interest many times over. Further, since the debt is equally the obligation of both the trading and nontrading operations, the total excess of revenues over expenditures listed in Exhibit 6-6 may be used to calculate the coverage of debt service charges.[1] Thus,

Debt service coverage
= Excess of revenues over expenditures/Debt service
= $46,400/$21,200
= 2.2 times

The prior year's debt service coverage equalled ($140,700/$21,200 =) 6.6 times because of uniformly lower expenses.

For a nonprofit organization having fairly stable patterns of both cash inflows and outflows, a coverage ratio of 3 or 4 times is adequate to ensure solvency. A ratio of 2.2 times is an indication that the organization should not add more debt to its capital structure. An organization with highly volatile cash flows may require an extremely large coverage ratio just to borrow modest amounts of cash. Hence the appropriate standard against which to measure the value of this ratio will depend on the operating characteristics of the nonprofit organization.

---

1. When the assets and debt are carried in a consolidated statement format, the ratio takes the following form:

debt service coverage = (excess of revenues over expenditures
+ debt service)/debt service

Coverage of Current Liabilities. So long as the nonprofit organization continues to operate, it will continue to record both current assets and current liabilities on its balance sheet. As one receivable is collected, another will be created to replace it. Similarly, as the organization pays one bill, it will more than likely be in the process of incurring another similar short-term liability. Hence it makes little sense in financial terms to compare amounts owed with amounts owned in the current-assets/ current-liabilities section of the balance sheet, especially when neither will ever be completely liquidated under normal circumstances.

What makes more financial sense is to compare the accounts payable and accruals against cash and marketable securities (investments listed as current assets in the current unrestricted fund). The current liability coverage is measured by the ratio of current liabilities to cash plus investments, and it tells the analyst what portion of current liabilities can be repaid out of cash and near-cash reserve in case cash inflows cease for a time.

The only current liabilities that the museum should use in this ratio are *accounts payable* and *accrued expenses. Deferred revenues* and the *current portion of the mortgage* are of no immediate concern unless the organization fails completely.[2] Thus, for Hobbs Museum:

$$
\begin{aligned}
\text{Current liabilities coverage} &= \text{(Cash + Current unrestricted} \\
&\quad \text{investments/Payables and accruals} \\
&= \$38,800/\$56,600 \\
&= 0.7 \text{ times}
\end{aligned}
$$

If the museum purchases all of its supplies and materials on invoice of net thirty days, the coverage ratio of 0.7 times means that the organization could not immediately pay for all that it has purchased out of its cash and investment portfolio. In fact, if an emergency arose that required a cash payment in excess of $56,600, the organization would find itself in a situation that would require management to make difficult choices regarding which assets to liquidate.

Analysis of Trading Activities. The trading activities of the Hobbs Museum produce cash flows similar to those presented in Exhibit 6–1. They are circular and produce profits (excess of revenues over expenses). The major differences between the two cash flows are that only one type of inventory is maintained by the museum (i.e., finished goods) and

---

2. The current ratio (current assets/current liabilities), a most popular ratio in the for-profit context, is inappropriate for use by nontrading nonprofit organizations. This is because their receivables are not collectible as legal obligations of the debtor, and their inventories can seldom bring market prices as high as their book values. The numerator in that ratio thus simply would not represent even a reasonable approximation to liquidating value.

stockholder funds are omitted in the analysis of nonprofit organizations. The following ratios are basic to the financial analysis of the museum's gift shop operation.

Receivables. Note 1 to the financial statements (Exhibit 6–9) implies that the gift shop operates on a cash basis. Hence, it has no receivables. In organizations that do sell on credit, the trading receivables are analyzed using the same ratio presented earlier.

ACP = Receivables/(Revenues/360)

In this case, however, revenues used in the ratio should be related to *credit sales* only.

Inventories. The cash flow through inventories is measured by the relationship of cost of sales to average or year-end inventories. That ratio is called the *inventory turnover*, and it reveals how efficiently inventories are being used in supporting sales.

The museum's gift shop activities hold inventories totaling $66,700, as shown in Exhibit 6–6. Exhibit 6–8 shows that cost of merchandise was $131,900 for 1989.[3] Inventory turnover at year-end 1989 is therefore:

Inventory turnover = Cost of merchandise/Inventory
= $131,900/$66,700
= 2.0 times

The year-end gift shop inventory was sold twice during 1989, or used in operations once every six months. This low turnover of merchandise suggests two points that the museum's management might consider. First, the gift shop has purchased too many items that its visitors will not buy, either because they are too expensive or of poor quality or appeal. Second, the gift shop has purchased good items in excessively large quantities relative to the volume of sales. Either situation creates a condition of illiquidity for the gift shop and the museum.

Trade Credit. The prompt payment of trade creditors (accounts payable) is a sign of financial strength. The length of time that trade credit remains unpaid can be determined by calculating the average daily purchases in accounts payable.

Days purchases unpaid = Accounts payable/Purchases/360 days)

---

3. The actual figure for cost of sales, which was not published in the annual financial statement, would have been the better figure to use in this ratio.

Under the assumption that accounts payable and accruals presented in the museum's balance sheet include only the trade credit arising from auxiliary activities, the days purchases unpaid for 1989 is

Days purchases unpaid = $56,600/($131,900/360)
                      = $56,600/$366 per day
                      = 154 days

This indicates that, given the assumptions, the organization is paying its trade creditors, on the average, about 154 days after the purchases are recorded (that is, after the receipt of the merchandise).

The standard against which this ratio should be compared is the trade credit terms extended to the organization by its suppliers. If terms of purchase are, say, net thirty days, the organization is "riding" its trade creditors for about two months beyond the net period. Chances are good that the low inventory turnover has created a cash-flow crisis for the gift shop.

Revenue and Expenses. An organization's revenues and expenses can be analyzed most easily by preparing a *common-size statement of revenues and expenses* in which all statement items are expressed in terms of percentages of total revenues. The data in Exhibits 6–7 and 6–8 are reduced to common size in Exhibit 6–10.

The common-size figures clearly indicate that the operating expenses of the gift shop consume only (52.6 percent + 27.2 percent =) 73.5 percent of each revenue dollar, leaving 20.2 percent as a contribution to the organization's (nontrading) programs. Of course, the more detail that is available for analysis in this manner, the better and more penetrating the conclusions can become.

Exhibit 6-10: Common Size Statement of a Nonprofit Organization

---

THE HOBBS MUSEUM OF ART AND HISTORY
Common-Size Statement of Revenues and Expenses
Gift Shop
Fiscal Year 1989

	Dollar amounts	*Common size*
Revenues	$250,700	100.0%
Cost of merchandise	131,900	52.6
Gross profit	$118,800	47.4%
Personnel expenses	24,100	9.6
Depreciation	1,200	0.5
Other expenses	42,800	17.1
Total expenses	$68,100	27.2%
Excess of revenues over expenses	$50,700	20.2%

In terms of the cash-flow diagram (Exhibit 6–1), the ratio of cost of merchandise to sales revenue (52.6 percent) is the cost per dollar of sales that leaves the *finished goods inventory* box as sales; total expenses (27.2 percent) is the cost per dollar of sales flowing through the pipe labeled *selling and administrative expenses*; and the excess of revenues over expenses (20.2 percent) is the amount entering the circular flow as *profits*. Revenues (100.0 percent) is the amount captured by the museum gift shop as *cash sales* in its operation. These data suggest that the trading activities are profitable to the extent that the gift shop's profits are twice as large as the expenses or the museum's education program (see Exhibit 6–8).

Uses of the Ratios. The ratios discussed in the preceding sections are most, but not all, of the more commonly used financial ratios. The financial officer of a nonprofit organization will find that he or she will employ all of those ratios and perhaps even others at one time or another in financial statement analysis. However, the proper application of ratio analysis requires much more than the production of a series of relationships according to specific formulas. The analyst must first be thoroughly acquainted with all of the organization's operations before he or she can interpret the meaning and significance of any of the figures computed from the formulas. As mentioned earlier, the analyst must be familiar with the organization's terms of sales, customers, product or service mix, and collection policies before he or she can determine whether a collection period of, say, sixty-five days is too long or too short, for example. Knowledge of operations is equally as important in the proper interpretation of all of the ratios.

The analyst may also wish to modify the ratios to suit the specific requirements of the organization being analyzed. The coverage of current liabilities ratio, for example, may include other accounts besides those listed in the formula. In analyzing an organization with outstanding short-term notes payable, the financial analyst may include that balance-sheet amount in the denominator of the ratio, since the notes may be coming due shortly. The analyst may also add a portion of receivables in the numerator of that ratio, particularly if those receivables are immediately and unquestionably collectible.

When called upon to analyze a unique set of cash flows of a nonprofit organization, an analyst may be forced to create entirely new ratios. A safe rule in developing relationships between accounts presented in the financial statements is to compare sets of only those cash flow (pipes) or cash accumulations (boxes) that are touching one another or are closely interconnected in the cash-flow diagrams. For example, a ratio of *operating expenses* to *pledges receivable* in Exhibit 6–4 is an illogical relationship. The rate of flow of the operating expenses should not bear any consistent relationship to the amount of the receivables outstanding. But it is clear that total revenues (comprising the inflows to the cash account) should be related in a consistent manner to the *operating expense* flow, since all of those *cash* flows touch the cash box and hence govern the changes in cash and unrestricted investments. Similarly, the cash flows labeled *donations* and *fund-raising costs* are related since their rates logically should move together if fund-raising efforts are efficient and effective. But fund-raising costs and short-term debt are unrelated, and hence any ratio containing only those two items would constitute an illogical relationship.

Finally, most analysts feel that industry average ratios are essential aids in the financial analysis of any economic entity because they provide a benchmark, or standard, against which measured actual performance can be compared. Many nonprofit organizations, through what may be called "trade associations," prepare detailed balance-sheet and operating ratios. Hospitals and other organizations operating in the health care field, opera companies, museums, colleges and universities, and others publish aggregate financial data and statistics to aid in the analysis of individual organizations.

But the problem in using ratios from these sources (or preparing ratios for similar organizations) is that no two nonprofit organizations are exactly the same. In fact, most are truly unique in major aspects. Variations in assets, method of operation, capital structure, and accounting methods can lead to significant differences in the ratios. For example, most museums now depreciate their fixed assets, while some others may use the direct write-down method. Many museums are beginning to include the values of their collections in their balance sheets, as well, while others do not. These differences in fixed-asset accounting will distort the industry figures, thus making them all but useless for comparative analysis of museums using either method. Further, the variability in the quality and scope of products and services, geographic location, professional objectives, donor clientele, and most other conditions under which nonprofit organizations operate lessen comparability even among similarly situated organizations. Marked differences between one entity's ratios and the industry averages would therefore prove nothing. And comparability with industry ratios may not turn out to be desirable operating objective. In many situations, however, the analyst may find that the industry comparisons are useful starting points for ratio analysis. But using them for anything beyond a beginning may not be in management's best interest.

Statement of Changes in Financial Position

The statement of changes in financial position (also called the *funds-flow statement*, *cash flow statement* or *sources and uses of funds statement*) is generally considered one of the most important and useful tools of statement analysis. The statement is essentially an explanation of changes that have taken place in the financial position of a nonprofit organization over a given period as a result of its activities. It is used primarily by analysts to examine an organization's historical operations and explain how external influences and internal management decisions and policies have changed the organization's financial position since the previous balance-sheet date. The statement can also be used in conjunction with budgets and financial statement projections to detail the changes expected in the financial position of an organization over the forecasted budget period.

Analysts increasingly rely on this statement for information on an organization's financial history because it is a near perfect summary of both changes in financial position and results of operations. The analyst readily can determine, for example, why an excess of revenues over expenses of, say, $4,000 shown on the statement of revenues, support, and expenditures has not resulted in an increase of the same amount in the organization's cash balance. The statement clearly contradicts the widely held notion that "profits" and other cash receipts will always improve the organization's cash balance at the bank. In reality, however, total funds acquired by an organization from all sources during a specific period (including those provided by operations) rarely, if ever, wind up at year-end increasing only the organization's cash balance. The funds generated from those sources are constantly being redistributed by normal activities among the entity's various assets and liabilities. The sources and uses of funds statement picks up where the statement of revenues, support, and expenditures leaves off in tracing the flow of funds into and among the accounts in the balance sheet.

Dimensions of Funds Flow. The maximum amount of useful information can be obtained from the sources and uses of funds statement by recognizing that it is reporting simultaneously on two dimension of the organization's cash flows. First, it permits the analyst to address management's skill in handling the organization's major sources and uses of funds. And second, when used with certain other tools of statement analysis, it provides insight into the way in which management allocated the organization's cash flows between permanent and temporary sources and uses of funds. The Hobbs Museum's statement of changes in financial position for 1989, present in Exhibit 6–11, illustrates these analytical dimensions of the statement.

Major Sources and Uses of Funds. Most analysts begin their examinations of the sources and uses of funds statement by taking note of the largest dollar amounts recorded therein. During 1989 the museum's major funds sources were from the *excess of revenue and support over expenses, capital items*, and *net proceeds from sale of long-term investments*. These three sources accounted for $152,100, or 85 percent of the total sources of funds. The largest of the uses of funds by far is the $103,400 used to purchase items for the museum and art collections.

Of major concern in this listing of accounts is the sale of long-term securities. This loss of investment securities from the portfolio serves to emphasize the dependence of the organization on donor and grant income, and it strongly suggests the importance of maintaining excellence of management in that area.

Unfortunately, the statement also reveals an apparent weakness in the management of accounts and pledges receivable and inventories, as suggested by the *increase in current assets* of $70,100. This shows the precise impact on the rather long collection periods calculated earlier.

Permanent Versus Temporary Sources and Uses. The second dimension of the organization's cash flows that is revealed in the sources and uses of funds statement is the balance of flows relating to its permanent and temporary sources and uses of funds. The importance of this dimension arises from the proposition that permanent used of funds (such as purchasing fixed assets and repaying debt) should be financed with long-term sources of funds (such as the excess of support and revenues over expenditures and long-term debt). Temporary assets, such as temporary increases in receivables and inventories, may safely be financed with short-term sources. The statement of changes in financial position, supplemented by certain other financial data, provides a method of examining how an organization finances its operations and whether or not it has balanced its permanent funds uses with permanent sources of funds.

The Hobbs Museum's statement of changes in financial position present in Exhibit 6–11, along with the supplementary data presented in Exhibit 6–12, will be used to illustrate this method. The assumptions relating to the organization's operating and environmental standards are not necessarily realistic but are presented for illustrative purposes only. The target ratios are assumed to be those selected by management to guide its decision relating to the assets and liabilities involved.

Permanent Versus Temporary Sources of Funds. Permanent *sources* of funds are defined as funds from the excess of revenue and support over expenses after capital additions, depreciation, additions to intermediate and long-term debt, direct credits to fund balance, interfund transfers, growth-induced changes in short-term liabilities, and reductions in surplus amounts of assets. All other sources of funds are classified as *temporary*.

Of the sources of funds in the total of all funds column shown in Exhibit 6–11, the following should be considered permanent by definition:

Excess of revenue and support after capital additions	$ 82,000
Depreciation of fixed assets	17,800

Exhibit 6-11: **Statement of Changes in Financial Position of a Nonprofit Organization**

THE HOBBS MUSEUM OF ART AND HISTORY
Statement of Changes in Financial Position
Fiscal year ended June 30, 1989

| | Expendable Funds | | | | Nonexpendable Funds | | Total |
	Current unrestricted	Collection Art	Collection Museum	Plant fund	Current restricted	Endowment	all funds
Resources provided:							
Excess of revenue and support over expenses before capital additions	$55,900	$3,800	$28,900	($49,400)	$7,200	$0	$46,400
Capital additions:							
Gifts and grants	0	0	0	0	0	33,600	33,600
Net investment income	0	0	0	0	0	1,400	1,400
Net realized investment gains	0	0	0	0	0	600	600
Excess of revenue and support over expenses after capital additions	$55,900	$3,800	$28,900	($49,400)	$7,200	$35,600	$82,000
Depreciation of fixed assets	0	0	0	17,800	0	0	17,800
Increase in current liabilities	18,500	0	0	3,900	200	0	22,600
Increase in long-term deferred revenue	(15,300)	1,600	0	0	800	0	(12,900)
Net proceeds from sale of long-term investments	44,800	0	0	0	3,300	22,000	70,100
Total resources provided	$103,900	$5,400	$28,900	($27,700)	$11,500	$57,600	$179,600
Resources used:							
Reduction in mortgage	$0	$0	$0	$12,300	$0	$0	$12,300
Net accessions for collections	0	34,500	68,900	0	0	0	103,400
Increase in current assets	33,400	18,900	16,500	0	1,500	(200)	70,100
Total resources used	$33,400	$53,400	$85,400	$12,300	$1,500	($200)	$185,800
Interfund transfers	(75,200)	46,500	56,500	40,000	(10,000)	(57,800)	0
Increase (decrease) in cash	($4,700)	($1,500)	$0	$0	$0	$0	($6,200)

Net proceeds from sale of long-term investments	70,100
Cash	6,200
Total	$176,100

Funds from the excess of revenue and support over expenses after capital additions and the depreciation of fixed assets clearly fall within the definition of permanent sources. The net proceeds from the sale of long-term investments is considered a reduction in surplus assets. Finally, the decrease in cash of $6,200 is considered a permanent decrease since the organization's ending cash balance, as shown on the balance sheet in Exhibit 6-6, remained above the minimum balance of $15,000.

The only sources of funds not included in this list are *increase in current liabilities* and *increase in long-term deferred revenue*. According to Exhibit 6-12, days purchases unpaid at year-end 1989 was 106. The target ratio, however, is 30 days—the assumed credit period offered by the museum's suppliers. Thus, the organization is utilizing (106 days – 30 days =) 76 days of purchases as a temporary source of funds. Since the average daily purchases, as calculated earlier, totaled $366, 76 days of purchases equal ($366 × 76 =) $27,816. The increase in payables listed in the balance sheet was ($38,900 – $34,400 =) $4,500; therefore, the division of payables between temporary and permanent sources is as follows:

Increase in payables	$ 4,500
Less temporary sources of funds	27,816
Equals permanent sources of funds	(23,316)

Exhibit 6-12: **Supplementary Financial Data for the Hobbs Museum of Art and History**

---

1. Collection period (year-end):

A. Government, 1989 actual	64 days
Target	60 days
B. Gifts and grants, 1989 actual	233 days
Target	180 days
C. Memberships, 1989 actual	26 days
Target	45 days
Combined, 1989 actual	187 days
Target	146 days

2. Year-end inventory turnover, 1989   2 times per year
   Target inventory turnover   4 times per year

3. Days purchases unpaid, 1989   106 days
   Credit terms of purchase   net 30 days

4. Minimum cash balance is assumed to be $15,000

Increase in accounts payable may be considered permanent sources of funds to the extent that such increases are the results of increases in the organization's economic activity. That is, if the organization purchases greater amounts of supplies to support a higher level of services to its clientele, accounts payable will increase *permanently* to a higher level as a consequence. In this case, however, all of the increase was the result of delays in payment to suppliers. The negative amount shown as the permanent source of funds indicates the extent of the reduction in accounts payable needed to eliminate this temporary source of funds.

Exhibit 6–11 also lists long-term deferred revenue as a *negative* source of funds in the total column. A negative source of funds is, of course, actually a *use of funds*. Because deferred revenues are donations due in cash at some date beyond one year after the date of the balance sheet, the decrease in this account represents a drop in the future support from donors; hence, it is a *permanent* use of funds.

Its position in the "resources provided" section of the statement of changes in financial position is a matter of choice, usually dictated by the format used in prior years. Note, however, that deferred revenues are recorded as sources of funds in both the art and current restricted funds.

In summary, sources of funds equal $179,600 plus the $12,900 in negative deferred revenues, or $192,500. Of this total, $27,861 were temporary (and thus had to be repaid quickly), and $164,639 were from permanent sources that either required no repayment or could be repaid over a number of years.

Permanent Versus Temporary Uses of Funds. Permanent *uses* of funds are defined as purchases of fixed assets (including additions to the collections), repayments of any liability, operating losses, direct charges against fund balances, increases in restricted long-term investments, and growth-induced changes in assets. All other uses of funds are considered *temporary*.

The Hobbs Museum's permanent uses of funds include the following items from Exhibit 6–11:

Deferred revenues (a negative source)	$ 12,900
Reduction in mortgage	12,300
Net accessions for collections	103,400
Increase in current assets	70,100
Total uses	$198,700

The first three items in this list are by definition permanent uses of funds. The increase in current assets must be analyzed further prior to classification.

As shown in the balance sheet, all current asset categories (except for cash) increased during 1989. Investments, since they are short-term, are a *temporary* use of funds. And lacking better information, we will assume that the increases in prepaid expenses and other current assets were growth-induced and therefore are *permanent* uses. The remaining two accounts — *receivables* and *inventory* — must be separated into their component parts in the same way the *accounts payable* account was analyzed. According to item number 1 in Exhibit 6–12, the museum's overall collection period should be reduced from the year-end 1989 level of 187 days to the target level of 146 days. This is a reduction of 41 days in total. The majority of the needed reduction is in the receivables due from grantors and donor (53 days).

Note 1 to the financial statements (Exhibit 6–9) shows that government receivables fell by $4,900. Since the 1989 collection period for government support is still above the target, this reduction in receivables is a *permanent source* of funds. This is because the amount of past-due government receivables has been reduced.

In contrast, the accounts receivable due from gifts and grants grew by ($150,000 – $107,200 =) $42,800 in 1989. The average daily support from gifts and grants during the year was $231,600/360 =) $643.33. Consequently, the growth in this group of receivables represents ($42,800/$643.33 per day =) 66.5 days. Since the receivables growth represents 66.5 days of the total of 233 days, the collection period for gifts and grants without the growth in receivables would have been (233 days – 66.5 days =) 166.5 days, which is 13.5 days *below* the target of 180 days shown in Exhibit 6–12. Therefore, the growth in this group of receivables is both temporary and permanent.

$$\text{Temporary} = 53.0 \text{ days} \times \$643.33 \text{ per day} = \$34,100$$
$$\text{Permanent} = \underline{13.5 \text{ days}} \times \$643.33 \text{ per day} = \underline{8,700}$$
$$\text{Totals} \qquad 66.5 \text{ days} \qquad\qquad\qquad\qquad \$42,800$$

Finally, since the collection period for memberships is nineteen days *below* the target at the end of 1989, the $900 growth in membership receivables shown in note 1 to the financial statements is temporary. Thus, the separation of the increase in accounts receivable into temporary and permanent uses is as follows:

Class	Temporary	Permanent	Total
Government	($ 4,900)		($ 4,900)
Gifts and grants	34,100	$ 8,700	42,800
Memberships	900		900
Totals	$30,100	$ 8,700	$38,800

Inventory, according to Exhibit 6–12, must be reduced by an amount that would permit it to "turn" four times per year instead of twice, as was the case at year-end 1989. Cost of merchandise from Exhibit 6–8 was $131,900. The formula for calculating inventory turnover (ITO) is

$$ITO = Cost of merchandise/Inventory$$

Since the target runover ratio is four times per year,

$$4 = \$131,900/Target\ inventory$$
$$Target\ inventory = \$131,900/4$$
$$= \$32,975$$

Actual merchandise inventory at year-end 1989 equaled $66,700 or $33,725 greater than the target level defined by a turnover of four times per year; hence, the entire $6,800 increase in merchandise inventory listed on the balance sheet is a *temporary* use of funds.

Thus, of the total of $185,800 in uses of funds, the reduction in the mortgage of $12,300, the addition of $103,400 to the collections, $9,600 of new accounts receivable, and the total of $1,700 in prepaid expenses and other current liabilities are considered permanent. The increase in long-term deferred revenue of $12,900 must also be listed among these permanent uses of funds. The remaining amounts ($29,200 in receivables, $6,800 in inventories, and $22,800 in short-term investments) are temporary uses of funds. When temporary and permanent sources and uses of funds are compared, the following relationship exists:

Class	Temporary	Permanent	Total
Uses of funds	$58,800	$139,900	$198,700
Sources of funds	27,861	164,639	192,500
Decrease in cash			$ 6,200

Interpretation of the Data. The critical relationship is that of the temporary sources versus the temporary uses of funds. So long as the temporary uses of funds equal or exceed the temporary sources, the organization's cash flows are in balance. This is because the organization's solvency is not threatened by having an excess of permanent financing. But when temporary sources exceed temporary uses of funds, a cash-flow imbalance is created. The organization has invested short-term funds in permanent assets. These assets will not be fully converted into cash within one year, but the short-term funds will have to be repaid almost immediately, thereby posing a serious threat to the organization's liquidity and solvency.

The Hobbs Museum has a surplus of $30,939 of temporary uses over temporary sources. The organization therefore can recover cash from those temporary uses of funds (investments, accounts receivable, and inventory) in a relatively short time in order to repay its overdue accounts payable, the only temporary source of funds the organization is currently using. This demonstrates that the museum held sufficient liquidity to support its operations.

In cases in which the funds flows are out of balance (that is, where temporary sources exceed temporary uses of funds) the amount of the deficit is equal to the amount of permanent financing the organization will need to forestall a potential liquidity crisis that may develop if short-term creditors press for immediate payment of their claims.

SUMMARY

The complexities of both the patterns of cash flows into and through the nonprofit organization and the accounting system used to account for those cash flows present significant challenges to those charged with analyzing the financial statements of such entities. The task of the analyst is made simpler when he or she has a thorough understanding of the basic characteristics of the cash flows of the organization being analyzed and understands the internal and external influences that affect the size and timing of the flows.

For the most part, the analytical approach to assessing the financial position of the nonprofit organization is decidedly different from that generally prescribed for use in the for-profit context. The reason for this difference is the fact that the cash flows of most nonprofit organizations are either partially or completely linear, whereas those of profit-seeking businesses are always circular. This basic difference causes certain standard ratios to become meaningless when applied to the financial data of churches, museums, social clubs, and the like.

In spite of the differences in the specific applications of the tools of financial analysis between the for-profit and nonprofit contexts, the basic framework for statement analysis is the same. Ratios, common-size statements, and the analysis of funds flows remain as the essential elements in the process of measuring the results of the entity's operations and its financial health. The illustrative analysis of the Hobbs Museum of Art and History is clear evidence of that fact.

The use of financial ratios to analyze the flow of funds into and through trading and nontrading operations revealed both similarities and differences between the application of this analytical method to nonprofit and for-profit entities. The illustration also strongly suggested that the analyst must be imaginative in his or her approach to selecting ratios and defining their meanings.

Finally, the analysis of the statement of changes in financial position, while difficult to perform, provides valuable information regarding the balance of the funds flow of the organization between temporary sources and uses of funds. The degree of liquidity possessed by the organization and questions regarding the solvency of the organization are clearly presented by the analysis.

FURTHER READING

These standard texts dealing with financial statement analysis of for-profit businesses provide insights that will prove valuable in planning and executing the analysis of the financial statements of nonprofit organizations:

Helfert, Erich A. *Techniques of Financial Analysis*. 6th ed. Homewood, Ill.: Irwin, 1986.

Kreps, Clifton H., Jr., and Richard F. Wacht. *Analyzing Financial Statements*. 5th ed. Washington, D.C.: The American Banker's Association, 1978.

Lev, Baruch. *Financial Statement Analysis: A New Approach*. Englewood Cliffs, N. J.: Prentice-Hall, 1977.

QUESTIONS

1. What causes the cash flows of a profit-seeking business and a trading nonprofit organization to be circular?

2. If a nontrading organization attributes its success in fund raising to its success in achieving its professional objectives, should its cash flows be treated as circular? Explain.

3. List several organizations whose cash flows are both circular and linear.

4. What are some of the outside influences that affect an organization's cash flows?

5. List the kinds of cycles that can affect the cash flows of nonprofit organizations.

6. Explain why price inflation has been the bane of most nonprofit organizations. Which type of organization suffers most from the effects of inflation? Why?

7. Illustrate the effects of the operation of a new day-care facility on the cash flow of the church that is sponsoring it.

8. What is the relationship between the cash flow diagram presented as Exhibits 6-1 through 6-4 and the financial statements of the entities they represent?

9. Can a standard set of ratios similar to those used by business firms be developed and used by nonprofit organizations? Explain.

10. Why is it important to perform separate analyses of the trading and nontrading activities of a given organization?

11. Write the formulas for calculating the following ratios:
   a. Average collection period
   b. Debt service coverage
   c. Current liability coverage
   d. Inventory turnover
   e. Days purchases unpaid

12. Why is the current ratio (current assets divided by current liabilities) not appropriate for analyzing the current position of a nontrading organization?

13. What special precautions must be taken by an analyst in examining accounts receivable and pledges receivable? Inventories?

14. What are the appropriate standards for comparing the calculated values of the ratios listed in question 11?

15. Discuss the two dimensions of an organization's cash flow revealed in the analysis of the statement of changes in financial position.

16. List the definitionally permanent sources and uses of funds.

17. Explain how the permanent and temporary portions of accounts receivable are calculated when they appear as a use of funds.

18. Why is the distinction between permanent and temporary funds important in financial analysis?

PROBLEMS

1. Prepare a cash-flow diagram, similar to that presented in Exhibit 6-4, for a nonprofit symphony orchestra. Be sure to draw the line separating the financial manager's and the professional manager's areas of responsibility.

2. The Virginia State Historical Association published and distributed several of its own books. It extended credit to book shops on sixty-day terms. Total book sales for 1989 were $63,400, of which $5,080 was on a cash basis. Year-end accounts receivable totaled $10,044. Calculate the association's year-end ACP.

3. The Mayfield Nursing Home's excess of revenues over operating expenditures equaled $13,800 last year. Two years ago the organization borrowed $18,000 at 10 percent to pay for reroofing its building. The note called for the payment of interest-only for three years, after which the note was to retired at a rate of $6,000 per year plus interest on the outstanding balance. If the excess of support and revenues over operating expenses remains constant over the next four years, what will be the home's debt-service coverage in each year?

4. The Madison YMCA's financial statements for the year ended December 31, 1983, are presented below:

MADISON YMCA
Statement of Support, Revenues, Expenditures,
and Changes in Fund Balances
Year Ended December 31, 1989

	Current unrestricted fund	Scholarship fund	Endowment fund
Support and Revenues			
Membership dues	$ 18,920	$ 0	$ 0
Donations	26,700	0	4,000
Investment income	1,830	850	0
Total	$ 47,450	$ 850	$ 4,000
Expenditures			
Administration	$ 18,470	$ 0	$ 0
Debt service	2,100	0	0
Supplies and materials	2,200	0	0
Programs	21,300	500	0
Total	$ 44,070	$ 500	$ 0
Excess of revenues over expenditures	$ 3,380	$ 350	$ 4,000
Fund balances, beginning of year	78,150	6,290	12,200
Interfund transfers	0	(350)	350
Fund balances, end of year	$ 81,530	$ 6,290	$ 16,570

MADISON YMCA
Balance Sheet
December 31, 1989

	Current unrestricted fund	Scholarship fund	Endowment fund
Assets			
Cash	$ 760	$ 0	$ 0
Membership dues receivable	2,990	0	0
Pledges receivable (net)	9,000	0	2,000
Supply inventories	150	0	0
Deferred revenues (pledges)	500	0	1,500
Investments (at cost)	0	6,290	13,070
Fixed assets	93,620	0	0
Total assets	$ 107,020	$ 6,290	$ 16,570

Liabilities and Fund Balances

Accounts payable	$ 640	$ 0	$ 0
Mortgage payable (7.5%)	24,850	0	0
Total liabilities	$ 25,490	$ 0	$ 0
Fund balances			
Current fund	$ 81,530	$ 0	$ 0
Scholarship fund	0	6,290	0
Endowment fund	0	0	16,570
Total liabilities and fund balances	$ 107,020	$ 6,290	$ 16,570

a. Calculate the following ratios for the Current Unrestricted Fund:
   (1) Average collection period for both dues and pledges.
   (2) Total cash flow.
   (3) Debt service coverage.
   (4) Coverage of current liabilities.
   (5) Days purchases unpaid.
b. Comment on the calculated values of each of the ratios.

5. Prepare a statement of changes in financial position using the financial statements presented in problem 4 and the 1988 balance sheet that follows.

MADISON YMCA
Consolidated Balance Sheet
December 31, 1988

Assets

Cash	$ 1,080
Membership dues receivable	2,100
Pledges receivable	7,000
Supply inventories	180
Deferred revenues (pledges)	3,500
Investments (at cost)	15,860
Fixed assets	92,560
Total assets	$ 122,280

Liabilities and Fund Balance

Accounts payable	$ 550
Mortgage payable (7.5%)	25,070
Total liabilities	$ 25,620
Fund balance	96,660
Total liabilities and fund balance	$ 122,280

6. Using the solutions obtained for problems 4 and 5 and the supplementary financial data presented below, determine whether the Madison YMCA has balanced its permanent sources and uses of funds.

MADISON YMCA
Supplementary Financial Data for 1989

Target collection period—Dues	= 30 days
Current pledges	= 30 days
Credit terms of purchases	= 30 days
Minimum cash balance	= $500
Target level of supply inventory	= $150

7

Short-term Financial Planning and Control

This chapter discusses short-term planning and budgeting in the nonprofit context. The first part of the chapter will focus on budgets in general and then specifically on cash budgets. The discussion concludes with a brief examination of financial forecasting.

Financial planning may be defined as a forward-looking appraisal of the financial aspects of an established operational program, leading to decisions regarding the most effective course of action to be taken over a future period. Financial planning encompasses both the operating plan and its translation into terms of the funds needed to carry out the plan. It touches on the acquisition of these funds, control of their expenditure, and the appraisal of the results of the expenditures.

Implicit in that definition of financial planning are the two principal components of the job of the financial manager as he or she measures an organization's needs for funds: (1) long-term planning, which involves identifying both the professional and financial objectives of the organization and forecasting the conditions that will affect those objectives, and (2) short-term planning and budgeting, which include planning cash flows in the short run, controlling them, and appraising the results.

Although it is difficult to separate the various elements of financial planning and to examine them in isolation from one another, it is helpful to concentrate on the development and use of budgets in financial planning as the key element in measuring needs for funds. Financial planning should, of course, precede and control the formulation of a budget, since a good budget is the result of good planning. In the final analysis, however, the budget is the expression in financial terms of the plan of operations designed to achieve the financial and professional objectives of the nonprofit organization.

149

NATURE OF BUDGETS IN THE PLANNING PROCESS

All economic units—whether they are individuals, households, nonprofit organizations, businesses, or governments—engage in financial planning and, to a large extent, carry on their economic activities within a budgetary framework. Those budgets may be voluminous, formal documents, such as those produced by the federal government and the several states, or they may simply be the mental notes of a housewife as she attempts to stretch her husband's pay check to cover the cost of new carpets and drapes for the living room. Regardless of what they look like—or whether they even exist in written form—budgets are essential tools of successful financial management and an integral part of the process of financial planning.

Much more is involved in the budget and the budgeting process than simply the production of a document or an organized approach to forecasting cash flows, however. After the organization's professional goals and objectives have been clearly defined and the long-range forecast of the economic environment has been made, there remain four steps that are necessary to define the budgeting process fully. They are, in their order of performance:

1. Preparing the approved budget to be used as an operating plan for the relevant period

2. Comparing actual results with the budget forecast at regular intervals

3. Analyzing the variances of actual from budgeted performance

4. Deciding on what, if any, corrective action needs to be taken to eliminate the cause of the variance (including, of course, changing the budget)

These four steps are the essence of financial planning and control for nonprofit organizations and profit-seeking firms alike. Differences in form, degrees of formality, and procedures may exist, but the nature and purpose of the budgeting process remain constant.

Preparing the Budget

As suggested earlier, all economic units operate within a budgetary framework. The budget may be only a seat-of-the-pants forecast, it may be an elaborate system of planning and control, or it may fall somewhere in between those two extremes. But if it is less than a *formal* budgeting system, the entity runs a real risk of making costly mistakes that an adequate budgeting system could help it avoid. This is especially true in the nonprofit context.

Each nonprofit organization must develop a budget system that will meet its individual needs. No one given system is suitable for all organizations because no two systems will operate exactly the same way or have executives who have achieved the same levels of competence or sophistication with regard to planning and control methods. However, all soundly conceived budget systems share certain features that are described here.

Types of Budgets. Budgets may be classified according to their flexibility as planning and control devices. The two main types are the fixed budget (sometimes referred to as an appropriation budget) and the flexible budget. A fixed budget is one that is established for a definite period in advance and is not subject to change or alteration during the budget period (except by supplementary appropriations). This type of budget is most characteristic of governmental bodies and nontrading nonprofit organizations. But it is also used by trading organizations that can forecast the demand for their products or services—and, hence, the cost of operating their facilities to meet such demand—over the budget period with a high degree of accuracy (e.g., within a 5 percent range).

The flexible budget, in contrast, is especially suited for those organizations in which operating costs are variable at different levels of activity or that encounter difficulties in accurately forecasting the demand for their products or services. For example, a trade association that represents an industry that has come under close public scrutiny will probably increase its lobbying activities at both the federal and state levels. The association must place itself in a position to react quickly to any legislation that may affect its membership. Its lobbying activities may remain almost dormant for some period and then become very intense subsequent to a pivotal event that makes national headlines. Consequently, it will experience significant variations in its operating costs at more or less irregular periods. Similarly, a neighborhood health clinic, whose patient load is unpredictable in large measure, may operate at full capacity during the flu season and be left with an empty waiting room the following month. The flexible budget makes allowance for such variations from the initial estimates by providing for constant revisions in the estimates of related revenues, expenses, and cash flows. Thus an organization having those characteristics can still achieve good control over its expenditures and plan its operations satisfactorily on a short-term basis by establishing a flexible budget system.

In practice many nonprofit organizations use a combination budget system that comprises both fixed budgets and flexible budgets. The combinations are, of course, unlimited. For example, fixed budgets are commonly applied to such areas as public relations, fund raising, research, data processing, and capital expenditures, while the actual production of goods or the provision of services is controlled under a flexible budget arrangement.

Budgeting Period. The length of the budgeting period is a matter of choice, based on the needs of the organization. Thus, the answer to the question of how long a budgeting period must be is simply "long enough to provide for effective planning."

The typical operating budget covers a period of one year, with a monthly breakdown within the period. In some instances, budgets are made continuous by extending the budget by one month as each month of actual operations comes to a close. For example, near the end of January 1989, the budget for January 1990 is prepared and appended to the budget for the eleven-month interim. In this way, a twelve-month budget is always available. The major advantage of this method is that it reduces the time consumed by the annual budgeting session that usually brings a halt to all other activities within the organization while executives dig out the data needed for revenue forecasts, wage and salary information, utilities costs, and so forth.

In other words, the monthly update permits management to make budgeting and its associated data-gathering processes a routine part of normal operations. Also, organizations that borrow money are usually required to produce projections of operations as part of their loan applications. Having a continuous twelve-month forecast is a decided advantage, especially when the need for funds is unexpected and urgent.

Finally, under a yearly budgeting cycle, in which only one budget is prepared each year, the formal budgeting period averages only six months. Thus, for the last six months of the period, the planning horizon becomes very short, and the organization runs the risk of failing to take into account important events that may lie just beyond the period covered by the budget. Under continuous budgeting, however, the organization always has a twelve-month advance notice of known loan repayments, temporary cash deficits and surpluses, insurance due dates, and so forth.

Some budgets are by their nature made on a long-term basis. Capital improvements budgets are one example. Such budgets include additions to and renovations of equipment, machinery, buildings, and other fixed facilities. Individual construction projects may take several years to complete before operations can begin; therefore, the budget period must be extended to cover the entire building phase, at least, in order to ensure that the funds for the periodic construction payments are available at the proper times. The important point to remember is, as with all other aspects of budgeting, that the budget period must be matched with the needs of the individual organization.

Budgeting Procedure. Although budgeting procedures vary greatly among nonprofit organizations, the typical procedure calls for the organization's departments and subdivisions to prepare individual departmental budgets. The financial manager, who is usually assigned the responsibility of coordinating the budget process, will supply the department heads with certain information on which they will base their estimates. This information will include a statement of the overall professional objectives, general operating policies applicable to the various departments, departmental goals, and relevant statistical and accounting data covering past results. Once they are prepared, the department budgets are brought together to form the preliminary budget, which is subsequently reviewed by top management before they submit it to the governing board for final approval.

The form and content of the preliminary budget, again, should be designed to meet the needs of the individual organization. Some require detailed budgets, some do not, and others require the detail but do not really need it, or vice versa.

Trading Organizations. The maximum detail required for a budget for a typical trading nonprofit organization will probably include the following sections:

1. *Revenues and Support.* This section details revenues expected from sales, approved grants, and all fund-raising activities.

2. *Cost of sales.* Included here are budgets for labor, materials, and overhead items required to produce the goods and services offered for sale.

3. *Administrative expenditures.* Wages and salaries of personnel engaged in administrative tasks (such as clerical and fund raising), and expenditures for utilities, selling, research, insurance, and other similar items are included in this section.

4. *Financial transactions.* Details of debt repayment, borrowing, interest income and expense, and interfund transfers appear in this section.

5. *Capital expenditures.* Departmental requests for new capital improvements are compiled and presented here.

Nontrading Organizations. Nontrading organizations often will budget in a slightly different format. Instead of preparing departmental budgets, they may budget according to specific *operational goals* or *programs* established by the organization's professional management. This approach has the advantage of permitting management to evaluate the revenues and costs associated with each goal or program prior to committing the organization's resources to the entire plan as initially conceived. Budgeting by individual goals or programs has the further advantage of providing excellent feedback for evaluation purposes and, when coupled with a program accounting system, provides the nonprofit organization with an excellent control device with which to monitor its activities.

Budgetary Control. The finished master budgets, which include the revenue and expense budgets by department or program, the capital budget, and the cash budget, can be thought of as the first step of budgetary control. Once the master budgets have been approved and the budget period starts, management must begin at once to exert strong efforts to reach the projected goals and to review these efforts as time goes by.

If properly prepared, budgets are forecasts of reasonably attainable operational results. Achieving the operating results as projected is the responsibility of the managers who prepared the departmental or program budgets; consequently, these same managers can be called upon to give an accounting of the activities over which they have jurisdiction, if actual performance is different from their forecasts. Once the budget variance is discovered, the last two steps of budgetary control can then be taken in order; that is, analyzing the causes of the variance, and taking the appropriate course of action to correct the situation.

When the actual results of operations are reasonably close to expectations, there exists a strong presumption that all is well. But there should also exist that extra effort to attempt to improve performance so that a favorable variance (actual performance that exceeds expectations) will be achieved in the next period. On the other hand, an unfavorable variance (a falling short of expectations) always justifies a search for causes followed by a fixing of responsibility. More will be said about budgetary control later.

ILLUSTRATIVE BUDGET SYSTEM

Because budgets and budgeting systems vary significantly in both form and manner of preparation among nonprofit organizations, generalizations covering all phases of data preparation and recording are difficult at best and may be dangerously misleading at worst. Consequently, the only way to safely approach the topic in specific terms is through a fairly complex illustration that will serve as a model suggestive of what a budget system is supposed to *do* for an organization (rather than of what it should *look like*). The Circle Retirement Center's flexible budget system will be used to illustrate the preparation and use of the revenue and expense budget and the cash budget. The discussion of the capital budget is presented in chapters 14 and 15.

The Circle Retirement Center is a nonprofit organization formed to construct and manage a retirement community for elderly couples and individuals in good health who can afford to maintain their standards of living over time at approximately a middle-class level. Housing arrangements include both cottages and apartment houses that are rented to the residents on a monthly basis. The rent is subsidized to a limited extent through contributions received as the result of an annual fund-raising campaign conducted locally. Other facilities in the center include a clubhouse, outdoor recreation and gardening areas, a swimming pool, and a restaurant and gift shop. The residents are charged an initiation fee, and their monthly rentals entitle them to the use of all of the facilities; however, guests are charged for swimming and for recreation equipment rental. The restaurant and gift shop are operated on a cash basis. Transportation is provided to a nearby city on a regularly scheduled basis to enable the residents to shop for groceries and all other personal requirements.

Revenue, Support, and Expense Budget

The revenue, support, and expense budget, as the name implies, lists all of the organization's revenues, support, and expenses, usually by item and most often by department, program, or function. The purpose of this budget is, first, to *plan the organization's economic activities* for the next period and express the plans in purely financial terms. Second, the budget is used to *test the plans* to see if they are financially workable, given the total resources available at the start of the period. Third, if the plan does not fit the organization's resources, the budget can be used to *formulate and test alternative plans* for their efficacy. Finally, once the budget is given final approval, it becomes the primary *financial control device* for the organization's operations over the budget period. Each of these purposes is examined in the following illustration.

Planning. In making the estimates required to prepare the revenue, support, and expense budget, the executives of the Circle Retirement Center simultaneously are making plans for the future budget period. Some of the decisions that must be made are:
1. Should rent be increased?
2. By how much should salaries and wages be increased next year?
3. Should an assistant recreation director be hired?
4. Will more housing units be needed?
5. How much will equipment replacement costs be next year?
6. Should new programs be undertaken, and if so, how much money will be required to support them?

The budget worksheet presented in Exhibit 7-1 illustrates one way in which the plans and tentative decisions regarding next year's operations can be recorded initially. The worksheet represents the first draft of the budget and contains (for purposes of reference) the current year's budget figures, estimated results of the operations for the current year (since the budget is prepared prior to the end of the fiscal year), tentatively budgeted amounts for the new year, and a set of explanations covering changes in mode of operation where applicable.

(text continued on page 158)

Exhibit 7-1: Budget Worksheet Used in Preparing a Revenue, Support, and Expense Budget

CIRCLE RETIREMENT CENTER
Budget Worksheet—Revenues, Support, and Expenses from Operations
Fiscal Year 1990 (in thousands)

	1989 budget	1989 estimated actual	1990 preliminary budget	Planning notation
Revenues and Support				
Rentals	$ 90.0	$ 81.9	$ 92.7	3% increase over 1989 budget in rental charges, higher occupancy rate
Initiation fees	4.5	6.6	4.5	Lower turnover of residents
Guest fees	2.0	1.9	2.0	No change from 1989 budget
Contributions	65.5	68.3	60.0	Economic downturn expected
Restaurant and gift shop	244.4	209.3	250.0	Increase in food and beverage prices
Other	3.3	1.4	1.4	Downward trend in recent years
Total revenues	$409.7	$369.4	$410.6	
Expenses				
Housing and grounds:				
Salaries and wages	$ 42.1	$ 40.3	$ 46.3	10% increase over 1989 budget for raises
Supplies and materials	11.8	10.1	11.8	No change from 1989 budget
Contractual services	9.4	9.8	9.8	No change from 1989 actual
Total	$ 63.3	$ 60.2	$ 67.9	
Clubhouse:				
Salaries and wages	$ 28.9	$ 27.7	$ 20.0	Laid-off, part-time help; 10% increase in wages
Recreational supplies	6.8	6.0	5.0	Reduced programs
Maintenance	10.2	9.3	10.2	No change from 1989 budget
Total	$ 45.9	$ 43.0	$ 35.2	

				Assumptions (1990 budget)
Swimming pool:				
Salaries and wages	$ 6.2	$ 6.1	$ 6.2	
Maintenance and supplies	2.0	2.2	2.0	
Total	$ 8.2	$ 8.3	$ 8.2	No change from 1989 budget
Restaurant and gift shop:				
Food and beverages	$ 58.7	$ 67.3	$ 70.0	Increase in food cost
Gift shop purchases	33.6	38.1	40.0	Higher cost
Salaries and wages — restaur.	37.0	35.0	40.3	10% raises over 1989 budget
Salaries — gift shop	16.5	16.0	18.1	10% raises over 1989 budget
Bartender	13.2	13.2	13.2	No change
Maintenance and supplies	8.5	8.7	9.0	6% inflation over 1989 budget
Total	$167.5	$178.3	$190.6	
General administrative:				
Salaries and wages	$ 55.5	$ 58.0	$ 61.1	10% raises over 1989 budget
Fund raising	10.0	12.0	18.0	Recession will increase effort
Administrative expenses	16.3	16.0	18.0	10% inflation over 1989 budget
Taxes and insurance	43.0	43.0	48.0	Increase in insurance cost
Total	$124.8	$129.0	$145.1	
Total expenses	$409.7	$418.8	$447.0	
Excess (deficit) of revenues over expenses	$ 0	$ (49.4)	$ (36.4)	

(text continued from page 155)

The data indicate that Circle Retirement Center entered the 1989 fiscal year with a planned balanced budget, but circumstances conspired to create a deficit of almost $50,000 for the year. The operating deficit appears directly attributable to the operation of the restaurant and gift shop, although rental income fell short of budget by $8,100.

Testing the Budget Plans. The preliminary budget figures for 1990 also produce an operating deficit, given the facts that (1) 1990 is expected to be a recessionary year, which could have an unfavorable effect on contributions and restaurant sales; (2) management wishes to grant a 10 percent pay increase to its employees; and (3) the rental charges will go up by 3 percent in 1990, with a higher occupancy rate predicted. Since 1989 will probably turn out to be a deficit year for operations, management obviously should not *plan* for another deficit year. Instead it must modify its plans to ensure at least a break-even year for 1990, or preferably, a surplus year to compensate for 1989 operating losses.

Replanning 1990's Operations. In order to achieve a balanced budget, the management of the Circle Retirement Center faces the following choices:
1. Reduce the quality or number of programs to cut costs
2. Raise food and gift shop prices
3. Raise rents
4. Raise salaries by a smaller percentage
5. Attempt to increase contributions
6. Become more efficient in its operations
7. Increase occupancy rate

By choosing one of the first three alternatives, management may find that total operating revenues will fall because its residents may object to these courses of action and begin to individually relocate in other retirement centers. Consequently, alternatives 4 through 7 appear to be the better choices. Under the assumption that Circle's rents are currently low in absolute terms, management may use the data contained in Exhibit 7-1 to determine how much of a rent increase will be required to produce a balanced budget.

Since the deficit is predicted to be $36,400, total revenues must increase by that amount. This, of course, means that rents would have to increase by almost 41 percent over the 1989 budget base to accomplish that result. Although some rent increase is possible and probably even is in order at this time, the alternative of providing the entire amount by way of rental increases is obviously out of the question.

Another choice is to raise salaries and wages by a smaller percentage than management is now considering. Total salaries and wages subject to increase (that is, all but the swimming pool personnel and the bartender) equal $185,800 in the 1990 budget. This is 110 percent of the base salary for 1989; thus, the amount of salary increase is ($185,800 − $168,900 =)

$16,900. The amount that could be saved by limiting raises is therefore insufficient to fully meet the total cash requirement, and the need to maintain excellent employee relations also tends to mitigate against this alternative.

These two tests are indicative of the way in which the organization will approach the task of adjusting *operating plans* in order to obtain a desired relationship between planned revenues and expenses. Note that operating plans are being adjusted. Revenues and expenses are the results of operations; thus they cannot be adjusted without also changing the size or quality of the operation itself. Exhibit 7-2 presents Circle Retirement Center's final revenue and expense budget prepared on a quarterly basis and reduced to summary form. The center's management decided to balance the budget by tightening up on building and grounds and administrative expenses.

Since the center is located in the mountains of western North Carolina, the change in seasons causes the residents to move their recreation activities indoors during the winter and outdoors during the summer. This creates a slight seasonality in the organization's clubhouse- and swimming-pool-expense patterns, as shown in Exhibit 7-2. The changes in season also affect revenues received from guest fees, and because of menu changes, restaurant revenues and expenses also develop seasonal patterns.

By contrast, rentals and initiation fee revenues do not change from quarter to quarter and, except for fund-raising expenses incurred during the first quarter of the year, neither do general and administrative expenses. While these latter cash flows will not in fact be equal in each quarter, their variable portions will be small relative to total quarterly cash inflows and outflows in these categories. This is because cash flows for items such as rentals and general and administrative expenses are mostly contractual and thus do not vary with changes in season. Nevertheless, these revenue and expense items must be watched as carefully as items that do vary from period to period within the organization's fiscal year to ensure that adequate funds are available at all times. In other words, the final budget forms the basis of a system of fiscal control.

Budgetary Control. The method of reporting and control selected by the Circle Retirement Center's management is illustrated in Exhibit 7-3. The figure shows the results of the first quarter's operations under the column headed "Actual," and compares those figures with the amounts budgeted by management in Exhibit 7-2. The variance column shows the difference between the budgeted figures and the results of operations. "Unfavorable" variances, shown in parentheses, indicate either an underrealization of revenues (in rentals, for example) or an overspending in an expense category (in housing and grounds). "Favorable" variances are those achieved by overrealization of revenues or underspending in an expense category. The column headed

(text continued on page 162)

Exhibit 7-2. **Quarterly and Expense Budget**

CIRCLE RETIREMENT CENTER
Quarterly Revenue and Expense Budget—FY 1990

	First quarter	Second quarter	Third quarter	Fourth quarter	Totals
Revenues and Support:					
Rentals	$ 23,175	$ 23,175	$ 23,175	$ 23,175	$ 92,700
Initiation fees	1,125	1,125	1,125	1,125	4,500
Guest fees	250	1,000	650	100	2,000
Contributions	42,000	9,000	6,000	3,000	60,000
Restaurant & gift shop	65,000	56,500	60,000	68,500	250,000
Other	350	350	350	350	1,400
Total revenues	$131,900	$ 91,150	$ 91,300	$ 96,250	$410,600
Expenses:					
Housing and grounds	$ 11,000	$ 14,200	$ 14,900	$ 11,800	$ 51,900
Club house	10,000	6,300	7,400	11,500	35,200
Swimming pool	700	3,600	3,200	700	8,200
Restaurant and gift shop	49,600	43,200	45,700	52,100	190,600
General and administration	44,675	26,675	26,675	26,675	124,700
Total expenses	$115,975	$ 93,975	$ 97,875	$102,775	$410,600

Exhibit 7-3. **Budgetary Control Report**

CIRCLE RETIREMENT CENTER
Quarterly Budget Report
Three Months ended March 31, 1990

	First quarter budget	First quarter actual	Variance favorable (unfavorable)	Unexpended budget
Revenues and Support				
Rentals	$ 23,175	$ 21,900	$(1,275)	$ 70,800
Initiation fees	1,125	1,375	250	3,125
Guest fees	250	221	(29)	1,779
Contributions	42,000	46,050	4,050	13,950
Restaurant and gift shop	65,000	61,883	(3,117)	188,117
Other	350	291	(59)	1,109
Total revenues	$131,900	$131,720	$ (180)	$278,880
Expenses				
Housing and grounds	$ 11,000	$ 13,660	$(2,660)	$ 38,240
Club house	10,000	9,870	130	25,330
Swimming pool	700	652	48	7,548
Restaurant and gift shop	49,600	48,003	1,597	142,597
General and administrative	44,675	45,877	(1,202)	78,823
Total expenses	$115,975	$118,062	$(2,087)	$292,538

(text continued from page 159)

"Unexpended Budget" presents the differences between the first quarter's actual results and the annual budgeted amount for each budget item (the annual budget figures are found in the last column of Exhibit 7-2).

The terms *favorable* and *unfavorable* variances, as used in budgetary control reports, occasionally may be misleading. For example, consider the revenue and expense items from the restaurant and gift shop operations, as shown in Exhibit 7-3. Actual revenues fell below budget by $3,117—an unfavorable variance—while actual expenses were $1,597 below budget—a favorable variance. In this case, however, the reduction in expenses under the budgeted amount was not so favorable after all. When the data are carefully analyzed, the following revenue-expense relationships become evident:

	Budget		Actual		Variance
Restaurant and gift shop revenues	$ 65,000	–	$ 61,883	=	$ (3,117)
Restaurant and gift shop expense	49,600	–	48,003	=	1,597
Percentage of expense to revenue	76.3%		77.6%	=	(1.3%)

This analysis clearly indicates that expenses did not fall in exact proportion to the decline in revenues; hence, the restaurant operation is slightly out of control, and, more to the point, the "favorable" expense variance is really not as favorable as it should have been.

Further examination of the data in Exhibit 7-3 points to several interesting but as yet tentative conclusions. Additional detailed examination is required to either confirm or alter whatever conclusions the analyst may form from these data; however, the budget report provides an excellent starting point for this analysis.

First, the center's occupancy rate is below expectations, according to the variances in rentals, guest fees, and restaurant revenues. Second, the two areas in which management decided to tighten its belt—housing and grounds and general administrative expenses—showed significant unfavorable variances, thus indicating a failure on the part of management to carry out its plans. Finally, a total unfavorable variance of ($180 + $2,087 =) $2,267 exists at the end of the first quarter, and unless the center can increase revenues or cut expenses by at least that amount by the end of the fiscal year, the center will face an operating deficit for 1990.

These three observations suggest that management is not doing as well as it might in controlling the center's operations; however, as mentioned earlier, such a conclusion may be unwarranted and must certainly be subject to verification by other means. For example, the data suggest that residential occupancy rates are below those forecasted. Further investigation may indeed confirm that this is true; however, the inquiry may also show that several residential units remained unoccupied while they underwent necessary major repairs or extensive redecoration. Thus, instead of concluding that management is failing to properly perform its duties, the center's governing board may conclude that management's decisions to preserve the value of the property are sound. And in spite of the "unfavorable" variances presented in the control report, the board may approve management's performance as entirely satisfactory.

Cash Budget

The cash budget, as its name implies, summarizes the estimated cash inflows and disbursements of an organization over the budget period. It also shows the resultant cash position, generally on a monthly basis, as the budget period develops. It is the formal presentation of the expected flow of cash into and through the organization as discussed and illustrated in chapter 6. The cash budget is an extremely important tool of financial management because its principal purpose is to predict if, when, and by how much the organization's cash resources will likely either be in excess of estimated requirements or become insufficient to cover the checks it must write during the budget period. Once those predictions have been made, the financial administrator can begin to plan how best to utilize existing and anticipated cash resources (including funds secured from outside as necessary) to finance the operations and growth and maintain a satisfactory cash position.

The organization with an established budget system will experience little difficulty in preparing a cash budget, since most of the information required for its preparation is contained in the departmental operating budgets. The financial administrator, in approaching the task of preparing the cash budget, must first decide on the period it will cover. The general considerations involved in selecting a budget period were discussed earlier in this chapter, but it should be pointed out that the cash budget period is largely dependent on the stability of the organization's principal economic activities. If its activities are stable and can be scheduled at a more or less constant rate throughout the year, the period can be set quite long, even beyond the usual one-year limit. If, however, its activities are subject to erratic movement or are dependent on requests for service from its clientele which cannot be accurately forecast, the period of the cash budget must be shortened.

Normally, the cash budget is prepared separately for each month of the budget period. If the organization's cash position is tight, it is usually necessary to prepare separate forecasts on a weekly basis. It is also advisable to prepare a continuous budget and keep the planning horizon far enough removed from the present to avoid as many surprises as possible.

Data Requirement. The first step in preparing the cash budget is the preparation of the departmental operating budgets. To the information that these budgets contain are added the details of probable borrowing and the repayment of outstanding loans, cash flows associated with fund-raising activities, and other such transactions that are independent of the organization's operational flow of cash. It goes without saying that a failure to assemble careful and accurate estimates of transactions of any sort will likely cause the cash budget to contain inaccuracies of significant magnitudes and produce misleading direction to the financial manager in terms of the organization's short-term financial planning. If, for example, the Circle Retirement Center's building foreman in preparing his budget carelessly overlooked the installation of fire resistant doors in the apartment units, as ordered by the county fire marshall, the cash budget will obviously predict a greater cash surplus (or a smaller cash deficit) than will probably exist during the budget period. Borrowing may become necessary, which will increase the unexpected cash outflow by the amount of the interest payment. Most important, however, the financial administrator will have received an unpleasant surprise, and that is exactly what the budgeting process is designed to prevent. Therefore, the reliability and usefulness of the cash budget is highly dependent on the accuracy of the estimates and the care with which *all* budgets are prepared.

When forecasts are known to be merely best guesses, as, for example, in periods characterized by uncertainties regarding price inflation or when an organization adopts a unique new program of service for its clients, the financial manager should be prepared for the worst, even though he or she may hope for the best. In such instances, more than one cash budget should be prepared so that management knows in advance the likely outcome of the worst combination of future events. Appropriate action can therefore be planned well ahead of an event everyone hopes will not occur.

For example, if the cash budget prepared under a pessimistic set of assumptions reveals that the organization's future cash deficit will exceed its borrowing capacity, management will certainly want to protect the organization against insolvency under such circumstances. This will involve arranging for additional financing or adopting a more conservative operating plan for the period. Thus, although accuracy in forecasting is always desirable, it is nevertheless possible to develop good plans under conditions of uncertainty.

Preparing the Cash Budget. The process involved in the preparation of the cash budget is perhaps easier to comprehend in the context of an illustration. Therefore, the Circle Retirement Center example will be continued in this section. The data contained in Exhibits 7-1, 7-2, and 7-3 will provide the raw material out of which a monthly cash budget will be constructed.

The financial officer of the Circle Retirement Center developed the organization's cash budget for the twelve months ending December 31, 1990. The budget, shown in Exhibit 7-4, is a compendium of the departmental operating budgets, the financial transactions (those required contractually, as well as those tentatively planned for), and the capital expenditure plans for the coming year. None of the plans have as yet received the final approval of the organization's governing board; hence the cash budget at this stage is still only a planning device.

The data in lines 1 through 7 of the cash budget were derived from Exhibit 7-2. Monthly data were estimated from the previous year's operating results. The organization does not wish to raise rents or fees, but revenues from the restaurant and gift shop were adjusted upward to account for increases expected in the cost of both food and merchandise purchased for resale.

The entries in lines 8 and 9 were estimated by the financial officer. Investment income (line 8) is the amount each month that the organization is likely to realize from the investment of its surplus cash. The peak month for investment income is February, when the greatest cash inflows from contributions are to be received. The amounts then taper off until September, when the financial officer has in the past liquidated all of the organization's temporary investments.

Proceeds from the sale of property (line 9) consist of sales of household goods left behind by former tenants or the families of deceased residents of the center. Forecasts of these cash flows are completely unpredictable, of course, but past experience indicates that they average about $200 per month.

The data in lines 12 through 20 were derived from Exhibits 7-1 and 7-2. Instead of listing the expenditures by department, however, they are grouped by function (i.e., salaries and wages, supplies, and so forth). This format is used because the center's disbursements are accounted for by function and their accumulation on a monthly basis is easier when actual results are compared with the budget figures. Again, the monthly estimates were based on prior years' experience.

The data in lines 21 through 23 are nonoperating cash flows that do not appear elsewhere. New construction (line 21) represents tentative plans to add a new apartment building, with construction to begin in November. The total cost of the building is estimated to be $150,000, and the date of completion is June 1991.

The organization borrowed $315,000 five years ago to finance twenty residential cottages. Debt service of $7,850 per quarter is required under the terms of the mortgage. The payments, due at the end of March, June, September, and December, are shown in line 22 of the cash budget.

The center's capital budget contains two items (other than the new construction): $4,000 to replace the air conditioner in the clubhouse, and $11,000 for a van to be used for the residents' transportation needs. The costs of these two items appear in February and August, respectively, in line 23, but since these are discretionary expenditures, the figures can be removed if funds are inadequate to support the ongoing operations of the center.

Exhibit 7-4: **Cash Budget**

CIRCLE RETIREMENT CENTER
Monthly Cash Budget
Fiscal Year 1990

Item	January	February	March	April	May
Receipts					
From Operations					
1. Rentals	$ 7,725	$ 7,725	$ 7,725	$ 7,725	$ 7,725
2. Initiation fees	375	375	375	375	375
3. Guest fees	90	60	100	250	350
4. Restaurant and gift shop	23,000	20,000	22,000	20,000	18,500
5. Other	120	110	120	120	115
6. Total operating receipts	$31,310	$28,270	$30,320	$28,470	$27,065
From other sources:					
7. Contributions	6,000	30,000	6,000	4,000	3,000
8. Investment income	0	260	210	200	150
9. Sale of property	200	200	200	200	200
10. Total nonoperating receipts	$ 6,200	$30,460	$ 6,410	$ 4,400	$ 3,350
11. Total receipts	$37,510	$58,730	$36,730	$32,870	$30,415
Disbursements					
For operations:					
12. Salaries and wages	$11,525	$11,525	$11,525	$11,525	$11,525
13. Supplies	2,300	2,300	2,300	2,300	2,300
14. Maintenance	850	850	850	850	850
15. Merchandise for sale	2,800	2,850	2,880	2,900	2,950
16. Food and beverages	5,900	5,700	5,800	5,700	5,500
17. Contractual services	800	800	800	800	800
18. Administrative expenses	13,500	1,500	1,500	1,500	1,500
19. Taxes and insurance				18,000	
20. Total disbursements for operations	$37,675	$25,525	$25,655	$43,575	$25,425
For other purposes:					
21. New construction					
22. Repayment of long-term debt			7,850		
23. Purchase of fixed assets		4,000			
24. Total other disbursements	$ 0	$ 4,000	$ 7,850	$ 0	$ 0
25. Total disbursements	$37,675	$29,525	$33,505	$43,575	$25,425
26. Net receipts (disbursements)	$ (165)	$29,205	$ 3,225	(10,705)	$ 4,990
Financial transactions					
27. Beginning cash balance	5,500	5,335	4,540	4,765	4,060
28. Cash available	$ 5,335	$34,540	$ 7,765	$(5,940)	$ 9,050
29. Sale (purchase) of securities		(30,000)	(3,000)	10,000	(5,000)
30. Short-term borrowing (repayment)					
31. Ending cash balance	$ 5,335	$ 4,540	$ 4,765	$ 4,060	$ 4,050

The data in lines 27 through 31 reveal the transactions that the financial officer will likely engage in during each month of the coming year as a result of the pattern of cash flows produced by the center's planned operations and other activities. In line 27 for the month of January, the financial officer has recorded the organization's beginning

June	July	August	September	October	November	December	Total
$ 7,725	$ 7,725	$ 7,725	$ 7,725	$ 7,725	$ 7,725	$ 7,725	$ 92,700
375	375	375	375	375	375	375	4,500
400	450	150	50	40	40	20	2,000
18,000	18,000	20,000	22,000	23,500	26,000	19,000	250,000
115	115	115	120	120	115	115	1,400
$26,615	$26,665	$28,365	$30,270	$31,760	$34,255	$27,235	$350,600
2,000	2,000	2,000	2,000	1,000	1,000	1,000	60,000
100	75	50	25	0	0	0	1,070
200	200	200	200	200	200	200	2,400
$ 2,300	$ 2,275	$ 2,250	$ 2,225	$ 1,200	$ 1,200	$ 1,200	$ 63,470
$28,915	$28,940	$30,615	$32,495	$32,960	$35,455	$28,435	$414,070
$13,075	$13,075	$13,075	$13,075	$11,525	$11,525	$11,525	$144,500
2,300	2,300	2,300	2,300	2,300	2,300	2,500	27,800
850	850	850	850	850	850	850	10,200
3,000	3,100	3,000	3,100	3,200	3,620	6,600	40,000
5,400	5,400	5,800	6,000	6,200	6,800	5,800	70,000
800	800	840	840	840	840	840	9,800
1,500	1,500	1,500	1,500	1,500	1,500	1,500	30,000
						30,000	48,000
$26,925	$27,025	$27,365	$27,665	$26,415	$27,435	$59,615	$380,300
					10,000	25,000	35,000
7,850			7,850			7,850	31,400
		11,000					15,000
$ 7,850	$ 0	$11,000	$ 7,850	$ 0	$10,000	$32,850	$ 81,400
$34,775	$27,025	$38,365	$35,515	$26,415	$37,435	$92,465	$461,700
$(5,860)	$ 1,915	$(7,750)	$(3,020)	$ 6,545	$(1,980)	(64,030)	$(47,630)
4,050	4,190	4,105	4,355	4,335	4,880	4,900	5,500
$(1,810)	$ 6,105	$(3,645)	$ 1,335	$10,880	$ 2,900	$(59,130)	$(42,130)
6,000	(2,000)	8,000	3,000	(6,000)	2,000	17,000	
						47,000	47,000
$ 4,190	$ 4,105	$ 4,355	$ 4,335	$ 4,880	$ 4,900	$ 4,870	$ 4,870

cash balance of $5,500. January's net receipts (line 26), a negative $165, are added algebraically to the beginning balance, giving available cash of $5,335 in line 28. Since the financial officer has no plans to either buy or sell securities or to borrow additional funds, the available cash is also the organization's ending cash balance (line 31).

The center's governing board has approved the practice of maintaining a minimum cash balance of between $4,000 and $6,000, and the financial officer prefers to keep demand deposits as close as practical to the $4,000 figure. Thus in February, as the proceeds from the annual fund-raising drive are received (line 7), the financial officer plans to use them to purchase short-term marketable securities (line 29). An additional $3,000 will be invested in March, but in April, $10,000 of those securities will be liquidated to help pay an $18,000 insurance premium due in that month (line 19). The remaining entries in line 29 clearly indicate that the financial officer intends to keep surplus cash fully invested.

The only short-term borrowing (line 30) required during the year will occur in December, mainly as the result of the payments for new construction and property taxes. During December a total of $17,000 of investments will be liquidated, and the center will borrow $47,000 from its bank. While repayment of the loan is not shown on the budget, the financial officer will no doubt wish to obtain permanent financing for the new apartment building in the form of long-term debt.

A final observation is necessary to complete the analysis of the cash-budget data. The entries in the last column indicate the center will receive a total of $414,070 during the year (line 11), disburse $461,700 (line 25), and run a cash deficit of $47,630 (line 26) at the year-end. Discretionary expenditures for new construction and purchase of fixed assets (lines 21 and 23) total $50,000; hence normal operating cash flows appear to be in balance. The organization's governing body must decide whether 1991's contributions will be used to cover the funds committed to capital expenditures during 1990.

Limitations of Cash Budgets. The Circle Retirement Center example clearly illustrates why and how a cash budget may be indispensable when it comes to planning for borrowing, repayment of debt, and the efficient utilization of excess (idle) cash balances. But this tool, as indispensable as it may seem, is not without its limitations. First, errors in estimation anywhere along the long line of budgets that must be prepared prior to the cash budget will obviously create inaccuracies in the cash forecast. This means that the cash budget should be reviewed periodically against actual performance so that corrections can be made and plans adjusted accordingly. Budgets are guides for planning and not substitutes for judgment; therefore budgets must be carefully administered after they are prepared.

Second, the time segments covered by the cash budgets may be inappropriate. In the example, the organization planned to invest $30,000 in short-term securities during February, but the budget is unable to indicate when during the month the funds will be available. Will it be early or late February? It is quite possible that the proceeds from the fund-raising drive will not be collected until late in the month, and the center easily could run out of cash altogether by February 10, leaving it without a sufficient bank balance with which to meet mid-month payrolls. Again, in this example, the $47,000 bank loan will not be paid out by the end of the budget period. The bank may wish to have the cash-flow estimates through the month the loan is scheduled for repayment. Thus, the financial officer may find it useful to prepare more than one cash budget, depending on how critical he feels the organization's cash position is. He may prepare a weekly forecast for the next thirty to sixty days, another for one year by month, and yet another long-range forecast for several years. This points up another reason for close administration of the budget.

Other limitations exist, such as the human problems often encountered during an installation of a budget system or during the conversion from one system to another. Budgets are sometimes looked upon as threats to an employee's security or as more paperwork dreamed up by the front office. These may not be financial problems or limitations, but if they are not recognized and solved, they may well be reflected in the degree of accuracy of the various forecasts. Problems may also come downward from the front office, especially when budgeting's several limitations are not fully understood by top management. It is certain that all budgets are going to be wrong. Even when the ending cash balance is exactly as predicted, it will probably be because all of the errors in estimation canceled each other out. Consequently, a top management that demands accuracy above all else is overlooking one of the great advantages of budgeting—being wrong, being able to explain why, and being able to make adjustments if necessary. This places the emphasis on the review process, which is what makes the budget so valuable in the first place.

FINANCIAL FORECASTING

Those managers faced with the task of preparing a budget for the first time quickly discover that budget figures relating to noncontractual revenues and expenses are merely *guesses*. The data, one hopes, will be the results of educated guesses, but the fact remains that they are all someone's guess of the amounts and timing of future cash flows.

Highly refined and complex statistical techniques exist to assist management in making estimates, but almost all of them implicitly assume that the future is a true reflection of the past. Of course, most of the techniques allow for adjustments to compensate for the realities of the present and near-term future outlook, but they each use the past as the common starting point.

Even a partial treatment of statistical methods of forecasting is beyond the scope of this book; however, certain fundamental rules for forecasting operating and financial cash flows are presented here as aids to budgeting for those faced with the task for the first time. As an individual gains experience in preparing budgets and controlling operations with the budget system, his or her forecasting methods will improve and the budget will become both more reliable and less burdensome to prepare.

Using Historical Data

The first rule of forecasting is to start with as much historical data as can conveniently be assembled and used. As is the case with the statistical techniques, less rigorous forecasting methods should be based on historical data and then modified to reflect known or desired changes in the data for the future budget period. Failure to consider the known future changes will result in poor forecasts and at least several unwelcome but perhaps avoidable surprises during the budget period. More important, the likelihood of the occurrence of a financial crisis for the organization is increased with a poor forecast.

Revenue Forecasts

Nontrading nonprofit organizations rely on contributions from members or the general public as their principal source of revenues. Forecasting revenues therefore requires careful considerations of the expected economic climate in the community. Periods characterized by a declining stock market, high unemployment rates, or tight money are periods in which low revenue forecasts are appropriate, for example.

Revenue forecasts for trading organizations should be derived by determining the quantity of each product or the number of units of service likely to be sold in the period, applying to that quantity the price proposed for the product or service, and arriving at the total dollar sales figure. The estimate of the quantity of each product or service likely to be sold should be based on a detailed analysis of the quantities sold over the past three or four years.

Considerations that bear on unit sales are (1) the unit price at which the product or service is to be sold, (2) the amount to be spent on advertising and promotional efforts, and (3) the general economic conditions likely to be encountered. The unit price proposed (having been set with due consideration to the general price level and to competitive and economic conditions) is applied to the quantity estimates to compute the total dollar sales estimate for all products for the period.

The final sales forecast is usually a composite of several forecasts prepared by different methods to ensure that all factors affecting sales have been considered. The usual methods include an econometric, or statistical, forecast, in which past performance is projected into the future through correlation analysis, trend analysis or other statistical approaches; a unit sales forecast; and a dollar sales forecast, prepared by estimating the selling price of the produce or service and relating it to unit sales forecasts. All the forecasts are compared to determine whether they produce a consensus. If they produce divergent results, they must be reconciled, usually be management. If they are in substantial agreement, the results may be recorded on the budget forms.

For example, Exhibit 7-5 contains historical and forecasted revenue and statistical data relating to Circle Retirement Center's restaurant and gift shop operations. The last two columns in the table suggest that a strong positive relationship exists between the center's occupancy rate and the annual percentage changes in sales; that is, the higher the occupancy rates of the rental units, the greater are the restaurant and gift shop sales. Thus, the revenue forecasts must take full account of the expected occupancy rate.

The data presented in Exhibit 7-5 are graphically portrayed in Exhibit 7-6. The three dashed lines in the exhibit are trend lines representing the estimated historical movement of sales, given high, average, and low rental-unit occupancy rates, respectively. When these lines are extended to the 1990 forecast year, they predict revenues within a range of approximately $224,000 and $238,00. Since the occupancy rate is predicted to the highest reached over the last seven years, unit sales will fall at or above the high-occupancy trend line. Further, since menu prices (unit prices) will be raised to cover increased operating costs predicted for 1990 (see Exhibit 7-6), the total revenue figure should be quite high relative to that achieved in the past. Thus the forecasted figure of $250,000 contains input from both unit price and unit sales forecasts within a historical framework.

Collection of Receivables. When the organization extends credit, its credit sales must be analyzed to determine the time lag between sales and

Exhibit 7-5: **Restaurant and Gift Shop Sales for the Circle Retirement Center, 1983–1990 (Dollar Figures in Thousands)**

Year	Restaurant and gift shop sales	Percentage changes from previous year	Rental unit occupancy rate
1983	$172.3	—	90%
1984	189.9	10.2%	93
1985	186.1	(2.0)	88
1986	206.8	11.1	93
1987	204.0	(1.4)	90
1988	224.6	10.1	94
1989	209.3	(6.8)	85
Forecast 1990	250.0	19.4	95

Exhibit 7-6: **Restaurant and Gift Shop Revenues for the Circle Retirement Center, 1983–1990**

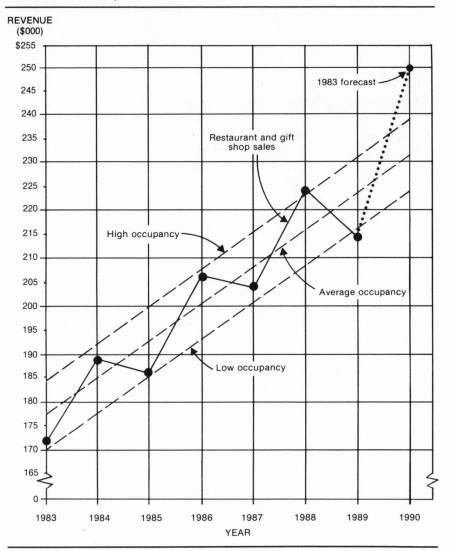

collections. The effect of seasonal variations and general business conditions on collections and on the length of the collection period should particularly be noted. Unless an organization's list of customers changes dramatically from year to year, historical data usually will provide the basis for estimates of the proportion of each month's sales likely to be collected in that month and each month thereafter and how much the organization might expect its collections to change, given the forecast of business conditions over the budget period.

Second, other factors affecting collections must be taken into account.

For example, returns and allowances must be estimated, especially if cash refunds must be made. The amount of cash discounts (if offered as part of the terms of sale) that customers are likely to take should be judged. The effects of any planned changes in either credit policy or collection policy must be estimated. Finally, the bad debts experience must be brought into the picture, along with any expected deviations from historical norms resulting from changes in business conditions or in operating policies.

Other Revenue Sources. Finally, most nonprofit organizations receive cash during the course of their operations from sources other than contributions and the sale of their products or services, usually in relatively small amounts and at more or less regular intervals. Interest income and the sale of assets are two examples of such receipts. When such sources exist, it is necessary to include them in the cash budget. Such receipts generally pose only minor problems in forecasting because they have a minor impact on the overall cash budget. That does not mean, however, that such forecasts can be carelessly made, for even small estimating errors can sometimes lead to major financial problems in the forecast period.

Forecasting Expenditures

The next set of forecasts needed in preparing the cash budget are forecasts of cash expenditures for operations. Their generally close relation to sales (or the level of activity of nontrading organizations) further emphasizes the need for an accurate sales forecast. Operating cash expenses include purchases of materials, payments for direct labor, and all other expenses (further classified as fixed, variable, and semivariable expenses).

Payments on Account. The amounts paid and the timing of payments for raw materials or finished goods purchased for resale or for consumption by the organization itself obviously have a direct relation to the sales volume or the level of activity expected during the budget period. Like the relation between sales and collections, however, this relation is not necessarily precise. It may be upset by a decision to increase or decrease the size of inventories carried or changes in technology or product mix, for example. Therefore, while the *volume* of sales or the level of activity for the forecast period will set the basic purchase requirements, the production schedule and inventory policies adopted will influence the timing and the ultimate quantity of goods purchased.

It is most likely that cash purchases will constitute only a small fraction of cash disbursements in the projected period. However, if some of the organization's products use materials sold cash-and-carry, those cash disbursements must be estimated.

As for accounts payable, there is a time lag between the arrival of materials (and the invoice) and the date when the actual cash payment is made. The length of the time lag is determined jointly by the credit terms extended by the supplier and the organization's policy on the payment of its trade debts. For example, an organization that purchases its goods on credit terms of 1/20, net 30, may pay on the tenth day, the thirtieth day, or any other day after the invoice date it chooses, including a date after the account becomes past due.

Wages for Hourly Workers. Departmental budgets are usually prepared using the hours worked by employees in various job classifications. The conversion to dollars is relatively simple once the hourly rates of pay have been estimated for the budget period. To the estimate of direct wages must be added Social Security taxes, paid holidays, periodic payments into the retirement fund, payments for overtime and vacations, or payments in lieu of vacations.

If management has not prepared an hourly labor budget, the historical relation between materials and direct labor costs (adjusted for relevant expected changes) may be used to forecast this expenditure. The budget preparer must, of course, recognize that purchases of materials relate to the period following their receipt, while wages paid relate to the period preceding their payment. The number of pay days per month (or other budget period) will also influence the size of the cash outflow for hourly labor expenses.

Other Operating Expenses. The remaining disbursements for operating expenses generally can be classified as *fixed expenses*, *variable expenses*, and *semivariable expenses* for purposes of forecasting their timing and magnitudes.

Fixed expenses are those expected to remain constant regardless of the level of economic activity. They include property taxes; insurance; executive compensation; and most dues, fees, and service contracts. Although their level is independent of the level of activity, they cannot be expected to remain constant forever. Property taxes and insurance costs change, especially when new fixed assets are acquired, and executive compensation can be expected to rise from year to year. Thus the same degree of care must be given to estimating payments for fixed costs as is required for all other classes of expense.

Variable expenses are those expected to vary directly with the level of the organization's economic activity. Examples are packaging and shipping costs; certain types of supplies; and certain preprinted production, sales, and administrative forms. A major problem likely to be encountered in forecasting such expenses arises from the changes that occur in their relative prices as the level of activity changes. If, for example, the Circle Retirement Center's food and beverage costs increase by 10 percent at the same time as its new apartment building becomes available for new tenants (who are also new restaurant customers), the effects of those changes on the relation between the two items must be reconciled before an accurate forecast of that expense can be made.

Forecasting problems associated with semivariable expenses arise from two sources. First, the relation between those expenses and the scale of operations may be either direct or indirect and may change at a changing rate. That is because semivariable expenses are in part fixed and in part variable. Second, changes in relative prices have effects on those expenses similar to their effects on the purely variable expenses. Examples of semivariable expenses are indirect labor, plant and equipment maintenance, and utilities.

Pro Forma Financial Statements

In addition to projecting the cash flow of a firm over time by way of the cash budget, the financial officer of a nonprofit organization often will be required to prepare projected or *pro forma* operating statements and balance sheets for selected future dates. Bankers generally request that credit applications be accompanied by such forecasts so that the credit analyst can assess the organization's future financial strength and its ability to service additional debt. And they are also especially useful for internal management in planning and control. They are generally easier to prepare than cash budgets and occasionally may be used as a substitute for that device; however, cash budgets are decidedly superior to pro forma statements insofar as precision and flexibility in planning and control are concerned.

The following method of preparing pro forma statements produces a forecast based on prior years' financial statement relationships and account proportions of the organization. The method is excellent for stable organizations but can easily be adapted for use in dynamic situations.

The Circle Retirement Center's 1990 consolidated statement of support, revenues, and expenditures and balance sheet are projected in the illustration that follows. Historical balance-sheet and support, revenue, and expense data on which the pro forma statements are based are presented in Exhibits 7-7 and 7-8. Note that the relationships among the various accounts are similar for the years 1988 and 1989. The assumption that the basic relationships will remain fixed within certain limits will be adopted in the following illustration.

Pro Forma Statement of Support, Revenues, and Expenses. The first step in preparing a pro forma statement of support, revenues, and expenses is to arrive at an estimate of total revenue and apply the percentages shown in Exhibit 7-8 to the several revenue sources. Alternatively, the individual sources of support and revenues can be estimated and the total figure can be derived from those estimates. The latter approach was

Exhibit 7-7: **Consolidated Balance Sheet and Selected Ratios**

Circle Retirement Center
December 31, 1988 and 1989

	Actual 1988	Actual 1989
Assets		
Cash	$ 4,060	$ 5,500
Pledges receivable	10,400	8,600
Rents receivable	1,380	1,650
Supplies inventories	2,030	2,740
Total current assets	$ 17,870	$ 18,490
Land and buildings	903,420	903,490
Equipment	30,400	27,600
Less accumulated depreciation	(249,000)	(298,500)
Net fixed assets	$ 684,820	$ 632,590
Other assets	2,220	1,110
Total assets	$ 704,910	$ 633,700
Liabilities and Fund Balance		
Notes payable, bank	$ 26,000	$ 0
Accounts payable	6,340	7,210
Other current liabilities	3,640	4,610
Total current liabilities	$ 35,980	$ 11,820
Long-term debt	278,000	268,800
Total liabilities	$ 313,980	$ 280,620
Fund balance	390,930	353,010
Total liabilities and fund balance	$ 704,910	$ 633,630
Selected Ratios		
Pledges receivable to total contributions	16.9%	12.6%
Rents receivable to total rentals	1.9%	2.0%
Inventory to purchases	8.5%	10.7%
Accounts payable to average daily purchases	88 days	96 days

used to develop the forecast in Exhibit 7-9. In practice, the forecast should be adjusted in light of present and expected future conditions.

Again using the comparative common-size data, the forecaster will next analyze past revenue-expense relationships over a relevant period, noting past trends and studying the more recent data to develop a pro forma common-size statement of revenues and expenses for the forecasting period. He or she will also study the dollar figures (not illustrated), noting any apparent stability or trends in those data and, by applying a knowledge of the organization's operations for the period, make appropriate adjustments to the percentages and dollar figures.

Exhibit 7-9 presents the 1990 pro forma statement of support, revenues, and expenses for the Circle Retirement Center. Detailed explanations of how each of the items was estimated are contained in the last column of the statement. This method permits each forecaster to prepare a unique set of statements based on his or her own interpretation of how future conditions will affect the organization's operations.

Exhibit 7-8: **Consolidated Common-size Statement of Support, Revenues, and Expenses**

Circle Retirement Center
Years Ending December 31, 1988 and 1989

	Actual 1988	Actual 1989
Revenues		
Rentals and fees	25.2%	24.5%
Contributions	17.8	18.5
Restaurant and gift shop	56.5	56.6
Other	0.5	0.4
Total revenues	100.0%	100.0%
Expenses		
Housing and grounds	16.6%	16.3%
Clubhouse	11.8	11.6
Swimming pool	2.2	2.2
Restaurant and gift shop	44.4	48.3
General and administrative	31.8	34.9
Nonoperating expense (net)	(1.0)	(.9)
Total expense	105.8%	112.4%
Excess of revenues over expenses	(5.8%)	(12.4%)

Consequently, it is quite likely that three forecasters will produce three quite different forecasts from the same set of data. Hence, careful analysis of the data and intimate knowledge of both the organization and its operating environment are essential to successful application of this forecasting method.

Exhibit 7-9: **Pro Forma Statement of Revenues and Expenses**

Circle Retirement Center
Year Ending December 31, 1990
(in thousands)

Revenues

Rentals and fees	$ 99	10% increase over 1989 in rental charges
Contributions	60	Poor economic outlook
Restaurant and gift shop	250	See Exhibit 7-6
Other	1	No change from 1989
Total revenues	$ 410	

Expenses

Housing and grounds	$ 66	Reduction in personnel (16% of revenues)
Clubhouse	37	Cutback personnel and programs (9% of revenues)
Swimming pool	9	No change from 1989 (2.2% of revenues)
Restaurant and gift shop	197	No change from 1989 (48% of revenues)
General and administrative	131	Cut back to 1989 level (32% of revenues)
Nonoperating expenses (net)	(4)	No change from 1989 (1% of revenues)
Total expenses	$ 436	

Excess of revenues over expenses ($ 26)

Pro Forma Balance Sheet. The 1990 pro forma balance sheet for the Circle Retirement Center is presented in Exhibit 7-10, and the explanations for the estimates contained therein are listed in the right-hand column. The balance sheet is *forced* to balance by omitting the "notes payable bank" account from the current liabilities section of the balance sheet and adding an external balance sheet account to act as a balancing or "plugged" figure. That account is found at the bottom of the balance sheet and is designated "external financing required (excess cash)."

As the explanation for the cash figure states, the minimum cash balance (in this case $4,000) is used to begin the construction of the pro forma balance sheet. All other assets, liabilities, and equity accounts are then estimated, and the two sides of the balance sheet are totaled. If total assets are greater than total liabilities and fund balance, additional (external) financing is required to "force" a balance, and the figure equal to the difference is placed in the external balance sheet account. However, if total assets are less than total liabilities and fund balance, the organization will have a surplus of cash over its minimum balance. In this case the difference in the balance sheet footings is added to the cash balance, again to force the balance sheet to balance. The balancing figure in Exhibit 7-10 is positive on the liability side, indicating that the organization will require $55,750 of external funds to finance its operations as forecast by this method.

Comparing the Pro Forma Statements With the Cash Budget. When the forecast of borrowing needs as derived from the pro forma statements is compared with that obtained by preparing cash budgets (Exhibit 7-4), significant differences are revealed. Some of these differences are:

	Pro forma statements	Cash budget
Ending cash balance	$ 4,000	$ 4,870
Excess of revenues over expenses	(20,000)	1,100
Borrowing required	55,750	47,000

The causes of these differences are quite easy to explain; the two forecasting methods simply use two different sets of assumptions. The assumptions underlying the pro forma method are less defensible than those used in the cash budget method in this instance.

The weaknesses of the pro forma method lie in the assumption that the organization's historical financial positions and operating characteristics as shown in published financial statements are accurate predictors of its future performance. That assumption is obviously weak; however, to the extent that the forecaster can modify the historical relations to reflect management's plans and external influences, the forecasts obtained from the pro forma method will be as reliable as those developed from any other approach.

Exhibit 7-10: **Pro Forma Balance Sheet**

Circle Retirement Center
December 31, 1990

Assets

Cash	$ 4,000	Minimum cash-balance requirement
Pledges receivable	12,000	P.R. to total contributions = 20% (poor economy)
Rents receivable	1,500	R.R. to total rentals and fees = 1.5%
Supplies inventories	2,740	No change from 1989
Fixed assets (net)	635,520	Net increase after depreciation of $3,000
Other assets	1,110	No change from 1989
Total assets	$ 656,870	

Liabilities and Fund Balance

Accounts payable	$ 4,500	60 days purchases (at $75 of purchases per day)
Other current liabilities	4,610	No change from 1989
Long-term debt	259,000	Reduction in principal of $9,800
Fund balance	333,010	Reduction of $20,000 from 1989 fund balance due to operating loss
Total liabilities and fund balance	$ 601,120	
External financing required (excess cash)	$ 55,750	

Using the Forecasts

Financial forecasts in the form of cash budgets and pro forma financial statements are used by managers to gain insights into future operating problems and financial requirements the organization is likely to encounter during the budget period. Specifically, they help management determine the amount and timing of external financing the organization will require, the operational causes of the funds shortages, and the source of repayment the organization will rely on to satisfy the lender's claim.

Management can also use the forecasts to maintain control over operations by comparing at frequent intervals the actual results of operations with the estimates from the forecasts. Those comparisons permit management to determine the causes of deviations from planned operations, appraise the dependability of future projections, and evaluate the organization's success in achieving its professional and financial goals.

But before the forecasts can be put to work as control devices, they must be tested for realism by examining account proportions (that is, reducing the statements to common size), developing sources and uses of funds statements, and computing and analyzing important financial ratios. For nonprofit organizations, historical standards—especially those relating to high and low cycles—provide appropriate bases for comparison. If certain proportions or ratios appear to be unreasonable when compared to the standards, the assumptions underlying the estimates of the accounts should be carefully examined to determine whether they are at least defensible. If not, they should be discarded and replaced by more realistic ones, and the pro forma statements should be revised accordingly.

SUMMARY

The cash budget plays a central role in financial forecasting. Its principal purpose is to determine whether an organization's extant and anticipated cash resources are sufficient to finance its operations, given management's operating strategy. The information contained in the cash budget also forms the basis for developing pro forma statements of support, revenue, and expense and balance sheets. Taken together, these documents constitute the total financial plan for the budget period.

A more direct method of constructing pro forma financial statements was also illustrated in this chapter. This method relies on past percentage relationships and financial ratios for developing estimates of individual balance sheet and revenue and expense accounts. Both forecasting methods are used to evaluate the organization's future performance and financial position, but neither is any more accurate than its underlying assumptions permit it to be.

FURTHER READING

This book reviews the various methods used in business forecasting and their application to problem solving and planning:
Shim, Jae K., and Joel G. Siegel. *Handbook of Financial Analysis, Forecasting, and Modeling*. Englewood Cliffs, N.J.:Prentice Hall, 1988.

QUESTIONS

1. Define financial planning. What are the two principal components of the financial manager's job implicit in that definition?

2. What four steps in the budgeting process remain to be performed after management has defined its goals and assessed the future environmental conditions?

3. Define fixed and flexible budgets. Which is used by most nonprofit organizations?

4. What factors determine the length of the budget period for individual organizations?

5. In what ways do the budgets of trading and nontrading organizations differ?

6. Is it ever appropriate to do nothing about a significant favorable or unfavorable budget variance? Explain.

7. Why is it a good practice to include planning notations in budget worksheets?

8. Why is it necessary to adjust *operating* plans to obtain a more favorable financial plan?

9. Are unfavorable variances always financially unfavorable? Explain.

10. Is it necessary to prepare a cash budget when the operating budget is available for use? Why or why not?

11. Since all projections, predictions, and budgets are merely guesses at what the future holds in store, why should an organization prepare a budget? How can budgetary uncertainty be reduced?

12. Describe the method of financial forecasting based on prior year's financial statement proportions. Is this method more accurate or less accurate than other forecasting methods? Explain.

PROBLEMS

1. The historical pattern of the collection of pledges from the annual fund-raising campaign of the Akron Public Broadcasting System is as follows:

60 percent in the 30 days following the close of the campaign
30 percent in the next 30 days (31-60 days)
8 percent in the next 30 days (61-90 days)
2 percent noncollectible.

On the basis of that information calculate the expected cash receipts from the campaign in each 30-day period, given that donors had pledged to give $263,438 during the campaign.

2. Budgetary data relating to the revenues and expenditures of the printed concert programs of the Bayside Symphony Orchestra are presented below. Calculate the budget variances and the expenditure/revenue ratios. Comment on the overall results of operations in this area.

	Budget	*Actual*
Program sales	$ 980	$ 910
Advertising revenues	6,500	7,250
Total revenues	$ 7,480	$ 8,160
Printing	6,000	5,780
Cost of addendum	0	250
Total expenditures	$ 6,000	$ 6,030
Excess of revenues over expenditures	$ 1,480	$ 2,130

3. The First Baptist Church has budgeted membership tithes as follows:

April	$ 870	August	$ 350
May	420	September	460
June	420	October	500
July	370	November	740
		December	920

Other revenues are expected as follows:

Spring bazaar, May	$ 500
Fall yard sale, October	500
Christmas craft sale, November	350
Revival, September	600

Expenditures for normal operation, including salaries, utilities, supplies, and so forth, are expected to amount to about $510 per month and are expected to remain fairly constant. Other expenditures are:

Painting the church, June	$ 850
Revival, September	450
New tires for the minister's car, May	200

The church's present cash balance is $450.

a. Prepare a summary schedule of cash receipts and disbursements for the nine months April through December.

b. Will the church be required to borrow money during the year? If so, when and how much?

c. You are the chairman of the finance committee. Prepare a set of alternative recommendations describing how the church can get through the period without borrowing any money.

4. The Addison Public Library's cash balance has steadily declined from a high of $2,350 on July 1, the beginning of its fiscal year, to a balance of $1,410 at the end of November. The Board of Trustees decided to prepare a cash budget for the remaining seven months of the year. The following data have been gathered:

a. The annual fund drive will take place in May. A total of $1,900 is expected to be received from donors, a third of which will come in during May and the balance in June. Fund-raising costs will total $40 in May.

b. The county appropriation of $960 is received in three equal installments in September, January, and May. The city appropriation of $500 is usually received in April.

c. Monthly expenditures are constant for the following items.

(1) Telephone = $19
(2) Librarian's salary = $250
(3) Library supplies = $10

d. The electricity bill will amount to $12 per month from December through May and increase to $16 in June.

e. Natural gas for heating is expected to be $40 in December, $45 in January, and then fall steadily to a low of $8 in June.

f. Maintenance costs will be $300 in December and $50 in March.

g. Miscellaneous expenditures are as follows:

December	$ 30
March	20
April	7
June	440

h. The board keeps $100 in its checking account, and the remaining cash is placed in a savings account that earns 5.25%.

Prepare a cash budget for the Addison Public Library for the period December through June. Make whatever recommendations you feel are appropriate.

5. The current financial statements of the Addison Public Library are presented below. Using the statement and the data from problem 4, prepare a set of pro forma financial statements for the library covering the last seven months of its fiscal year. List your assumptions on the statements.

ADDISON PUBLIC LIBRARY
Balance Sheet
November 30, 1989

Assets		Liabilities and Fund Balance	
Cash	$ 1,410	Accounts payable	$ 70
Appropriations receivable		Deferred revenues	
County	640	(appropriations)	1,140
City	500		
Fixed assets (at cost)	33,200	Fund balance	34,540
		Total liabilities and	
Total assets	$ 35,750	fund balance	$ 35,750

ADDISON PUBLIC LIBRARY
Statement of Support, Revenues, Expenditures, and Changes in Fund Balance
July 1 through November 30, 1989

Support and Revenues	
Donations	$ 1,100
Appropriations	320
Total support and revenues	$ 1,420
Expenditures	
Utilities	230
Salaries	1,250
Other operating expenditures	880
Total expenditures	$ 2,360
Excess (deficit) of support and revenues over expenditures	$ (940)
Fund balance July 1, 1989	$ 35,480
Fund balance November 30, 1989	$ 34,540

6. The following financial data relate to the Food Service Fund of Beezely College. Prepare a set of pro forma financial statements based on the previous year's financial statement relationships and account proportions. Revenues are expected to increase to $52,650 in fiscal year 1989–90, and the debt owed to the college's General Fund must be repaid as quickly as possible.

BEEZELY COLLEGE
Food Service Fund
Balance Sheet
June 30, 1989

Assets			Liabilities and Fund Balance		
Cash	$	750	Accounts payable	$	2,080
Accounts receivable		6,530	Due to general fund		5,200
Inventories		2,110	Term loan for purchase		
Total current assets	$	9,390	of equipment		2,600
Equipment		22,170	Total liabilities	$	9,880
Less depreciation		5,880	Fund balance		15,800
Equipment (net)	$	16,290	Total liabilities and		
Total assets	$	25,680	fund balance	$	25,680

BEEZELY COLLEGE
Food Service Fund
Statement of Revenues, Expenditures,
and Changes in Fund Balance
Year ended June 30, 1989

Revenues from operations	$	46,800
Expenditures:		
Food		14,350
Salaries and wages—food service		21,090
Salaries—administration		9,230
Service contracts		880
Debt service		520
Miscellaneous		110
Total expenditures	$	46,180
Excess of revenues over expenditures	$	620
Transfer to general fund	$	1,550
Fund balance, beginning of year		16,730
Fund balance, end of year	$	15,800

PART III
WORKING CAPITAL MANAGEMENT

Working capital management in nonprofit organizations, particularly the larger ones, is a daily task. It consumes most of the attention, time, and energy of the financial manager, who must each day review the organization's cash position, the status of debts owed to and owed by the entity, and the extent to which productive resources are adequate or inadequate in supply to carry out the organization's normal activities. Occasionally, long-range policy decisions are required in the areas of credit, collections, inventory control, and cash management that require lengthy and intensive study, the importance of which equals or exceeds those involving the purchase of long-lived assets and the raising of large sums of money.

The techniques, tools, and analytical decision methods helpful in managing working capital are presented in the following four chapters. Cash management and endowment policy and management are examined in the first two chapters. Decisions involving receivables and inventories constitute the central topics of the third chapter, and the management of short-term credit is examined in the final chapter of this part of the book. While the material presented in these chapters is most useful in managing the larger nonprofit organizations, managers and others involved in the operations of smaller entities will gain useful insights into how to avoid the many problems whose root causes lie in improper working capital management.

8

Management of Cash and Short-term Securities

This chapter discusses the principles of cash management and the investment of excess cash balances in short-term, marketable securities (and other similar investment media). The attention devoted to this area of financial management has intensified in recent years among nonprofit organizations, mainly as the result of (1) the rather persistent fluctuations in interest rates and in continuing increase in the general price levels of goods and services of all kinds, and (2) the increased competition among nonprofit organizations for individual and corporate charitable contributions. These factors have combined to force nonprofit organizations to manage all of their assets more efficiently, and most particularly, their cash resources.

Those organizations that for the first time attempt to improve their cash-management practices generally are rewarded with almost immediate success. This is at least partially because of recent changes in the operating characteristics and regulatory structures of financial institutions and markets in the United States. These changes have made a wider range of investment opportunities accessible to both large and small investors. As a consequence, the trend in both for-profit business and nonprofit organizations of all sizes has been toward reducing idle cash balances and investing those funds in interest-earning assets and deposits. The relatively high interest rates accessible to today's investors, regardless of how modest are their surplus cash resources, have improved profits of business firms, provided additional sources of disposable revenues for nonprofit organizations, and helped to ameliorate the erosion of the purchasing power of the dollar caused by inflation in both contexts.

While it is a relatively simple matter to "skim the cream" from the top of an organization's cash balances for the purpose of earning a few extra dollars of interest, the achievement of *true* efficiency in cash management is not so simple as it may appear at first. Consequently, this chapter develops a conceptual framework for cash management and discusses several tools and techniques that will enable management to safely invest surplus cash without impairing the organization's immediate liquidity or solvency.

MOTIVES FOR HOLDING CASH

John Maynard Keynes, the famous British economist, identified three motives that both individuals and business organizations have for holding cash in the form of currency and demand deposit balances: the *transactions motive*, the *precautionary motive*, and the *speculative motive*.[1] A brief examination of each of these motives will provide the proper perspective for and an excellent starting point in the discussion of cash and cash management.

Transactions Motive

The transactions motive for holding cash, in the present context, refers to the need for the nonprofit organization to maintain adequate cash balances to facilitate its routine cash payments to its vendors, employees, creditors, and (where appropriate) clientele. Such balances are necessary because cash inflows and outflows from normal activities are rarely, if ever, perfectly synchronized. A few examples will help to illustrate why cash balances are indispensable.

The lack of coincidence between cash receipts and disbursements in trading nonprofit organizations often is the direct result of the differences in the timing of transactions necessary to affect the sale of their goods or services. Inventory must be purchased in advance of both the production and sale of a product; therefore, in most cases, suppliers must be paid before the organization's customers are required to make payment and sometimes even before the goods are sold. In those instances in which the organization purchases on credit and sells on a cash-and-carry basis, cash will ordinarily flow in both before and after the date on which the invoice is paid.

For nontrading nonprofit organizations, cash inflows are generally episodic and are received in relatively large amounts from, say, an annual fund-raising campaign or a public or private grant. Cash outflows for wages and salaries, supplies, rent, and other operating requirements are generally stable over time. Obviously, cash inflows must be reserved in part in the form of cash balances to meet regularly recurring obligations.

The amount of cash an organization must hold to satisfy its transactions requirements is largely dependent on the level and nature of

---

1. John Maynard Keynes, *The General Theory of Employment, Interest, and Money* (New York: Harcourt Brace Javonovich, 1936), 195-196.

its central economic activity, although the relationship is by no means precisely measurable. Cash inflows and outflows (and net differences) resulting from an organization's usual transactions tend to increase in direct proportion to the level of sales, production, or service output. Other cash flows, however, such as transactions into and out of investment media, purchases of machinery and equipment, or the repayment of short-term credit extensions, tend to be somewhat more intermittent. The net effect of these types of transactions is also somewhat less predictable, but they would tend to increase over time with relatively large increases in the size of the organization or its level of activity.

Precautionary Motive

The precautionary motive supposes the need to maintain sufficient cash (either on hand or in a readily accessible form) to act as a cushion (or buffer) against unexpected events. Even though management attempts constantly to forecast the organization's cash needs through the cash-budgeting process, budgeting inaccuracies will always occur and require the attention of management. Such inaccuracies may result from a sudden snowstorm that delays mail delivery or keeps customers at home, an increase in utility rates, or the loss of the support of a favorite donor — to mention but a few possibilities. Such events may seriously interrupt even the best-laid financial plans and thus may temporarily destroy the effectiveness of even the best cash budgets. That is why organizations find that they often need to maintain larger cash balances than are required to support normal day-to-day transactions.

The amount of cash an organization must hold to provide for both routine and unpredictable cash needs depends on (1) its willingness to risk running short of cash, (2) the degree of predictability of its cash flows, and (3) its available reserve borrowing power. An organization wishing to absolutely minimize risk would tend to hold very large cash balances in order to meet all of its transaction demands and most of its precautionary demands for funds. In addition, it would maintain good banking relationships as a second line of defense against cash shortages. Thus it would seek to gain maximum protection against almost every contingent cash need.

In contrast, an organization willing to assume some risk for the sake of higher returns would tend to have almost all of its resources—including most of its borrowing power—invested in earning assets. Management's hope, under those circumstances, would clearly be that no sudden and unexpected demand for additional funds would materialize. If returns from the earning assets materialize as planned, the organization probably would ultimately enjoy increased "profits," cash balances, and reserve borrowing power; if the expected returns did not materialize, however, and if some unexpected and urgent need for cash arises instead, the organization might suddenly cease to exist.

The amount of income an organization is willing to forgo by holding precautionary cash balances will determine the upper limit to its investment in cash. Although some consistently overinvest or underinvest in cash, most organizations tend to follow a middle course; they maintain some excess cash balances for precautionary purposes while keeping their bank lines of credit open through prompt repayment of borrowings, so that credit will be available if needed to meet unexpected demands for additional cash.

Speculative Motive

Speculative balances are held to provide an organization with sufficient liquidity to take advantage of unexpected profitable opportunities that may suddenly appear (and just as suddenly disappear if not utilized immediately). In its original (Keynesian) context, the speculative motive related to holding cash balances in order to take advantage of anticipated changes in interest rates and, hence, security prices.

Most nonprofit organizations do not hold cash balances as a speculation against interest rate changes. In an analogous sense, however, an organization may sometimes consider it desirable to hold some reserve cash for the purpose of being able to seize on unexpected profitable opportunities. For example, a symphony orchestra may be given the opportunity to sign a touring soloist of national reputation for a concert because of an unexpected cancellation in the artist's schedule. The symphony may be required to post a cash advance to secure the date. The frequency with which an organization may be confronted with that type or similar opportunities will, of course, dictate the size of the cash balance it will choose to hold for such speculative purposes.

The three motives for holding cash balances—transactions, precautionary, and speculative—form a basis for the following discussion of the nature and size of a nonprofit organization's investment in cash. Since the cash budget and cash budgeting have been examined previously (in chapter 7), this discussion will begin by examining ways to improve the efficiency of cash management through the application of well-known decision techniques. That elusive quantity known as the *minimum cash balance* is then examined, and the discussion is concluded with a description of the various income-earning avenues of investment for temporarily surplus cash balances.

MANAGING CASH FLOWS

Cash budgeting is often regarded as a largely passive management tool; that is, the data provided in the cash budget are often the end products of the planning process. Thus, all that remains to be done by management after preparing the cash budget is simply to measure the size of the cash balance through time with the aid of this tool. Subsequent action is taken (1) to supply funds during periods of cash deficit, and (2) to invest potentially idle funds during periods of cash surplus.

Management may, however, choose to take a more active part in the cash-planning and decision process. To produce superior results insofar as cash management is concerned, the responsible manager must do all he or she can to minimize the periodic cash deficits and maximize the periodic cash surpluses revealed by the cash budget. Several cash collection and disbursement-control techniques are available to increase the immediate availability of cash balances in the nonprofit organization.

Cash-Collection Methods

On one side of the cash management coin is cash collection. If an organization can speed the collection of cash from customers and/or donors, it can increase interest income from investments or reduce the cost of borrowed funds by prompt or advance repayment of loans. Two methods of accelerating the conversion of receivables into spendable cash balances are *concentration banking* and *lockbox systems*.

While these methods are useful only for those organizations that receive cash (from either sales receipts or donations) from many sources disbursed over large geographic areas, the rationale underlying these techniques is useful for cash-management programs of even small, locally oriented organizations.

Concentration Banking. Concentration banking is a method of accelerating funds flows from accounts and pledges receivable by establishing multiple centers for the collection of customer or donor payments, instead of the usual single collection center located at the organization's headquarters. The objective is to shorten the period between the time the payment on accounts is mailed to the organization and the time when the funds become available for spending.[2]

The selection of the collection centers is based on geographic areas served and the volume of billing in various market areas. In some cases, only one collection center may be required; in others, a network of collection centers is established to provide the most rapid collection of funds.

Each collection center is also a billing center for the customers or donors located in the area served by the center. Payments are also received at the center instead of at the organization's headquarters. Payments received at a collection center are immediately deposited in a

---

2. Normally, a commercial bank retains the right to permit a depositor to withdraw funds only after the checks deposited to the account have been collected through the banking system's check clearing process. This usually takes two days (or less) after the funds have been deposited or presented for collection.

local bank. When collected, they are immediately transferred from the local bank to a *concentration bank*—the commercial bank with which the organization has its major deposit accounts.

A *daily wire transfer* is used to move the collected funds (in excess of those required as compensating balances at the local banks). Wire transfers are made through the central bank—the Federal Reserve System—and the funds so moved become immediately available to the organization at its concentration bank.

The use of wire transfers moves funds faster than the more conventional *depository transfer check* arrangement, under which checks are drawn on the local bank for deposit in the concentration bank. The funds represented by transfer checks do not become immediately available at the concentration bank, since the checks must first be collected (sent back to the local bank through the usual Federal Reserve collection channels).

A system of decentralized billings and collections has advantages over a centralized system. First, mailing time in both directions may be significantly reduced. Because the collection center bills customers or donors in its area, the bills or pledge reminders are received by the payor earlier than if the bills were mailed from the home office. In turn, when the remittances are mailed to the organization, the mailing time to the nearest collection center is shorter than that to the head office. Second, the time required to collect a check after its receipt from a customer is likewise reduced, since payments deposited with the collection center's local bank are usually drawn on banks in that general area.

For trading nonprofit organizations whose customers are distributed over wide geographic areas and for nontrading organizations whose fund-raising activities are regional or national in scope, concentration banking may speed up the collection process by as much as three days. Thus, if average daily remittances are large, a substantial volume of funds may be released from cash balances for investment purposes. However, the costs of maintaining a concentration banking collection system are high, even for many large profit-seeking businesses; therefore, careful attention to cash flows is important in deciding whether or not the system can profitably be used by a nonprofit organization. For example, the local banks employed in the collection process will have to be paid for the services they render, and management will have to spend a greater portion of its time making certain that the new funds made available are profitably employed. Obviously, the returns from investing the newly available funds must be greater than the increased cost of operating the more elaborate cash-collection system. The following example illustrates the decision process.

Suppose the Tennessee Sheriff's Association is considering setting up a concentration banking system in connection with its annual statewide telethon conducted in support of the Sheriff's Boys Ranch. In past years, the association billed from its main office located in Memphis, a city at the extreme western border of Tennessee. Clerical personnel made daily deposits in a local bank of pledges received from those who called their local television stations during the telethon. Many donors also sent their contributions to the television stations, whose personnel would forward the cash and checks to the association's Memphis office.

Donors making pledges by telephone during the telethon were told that they would receive a notice by mail reminding them of the amount they pledged and giving them the address to which they should send their checks or money orders. Initial reminders were sent two weeks after the telethon, and two follow-up notices were mailed in one-month intervals to delinquent accounts. Average mailing time between Memphis and the donors was estimated to be two and one-half days each way, and the time required to collect checks was estimated to average two and one-fourth days.

In planning for this year's telethon, the association's management contacted several members of its board of directors living in Nashville and Knoxville. They were asked to estimate the costs of setting up regional billing and collecting centers for their respective areas and maintaining them for ninety days after the telethon. The plan was to divide the state into three areas—East, Central, and West—in order to speed up the billing and collection of cash from pledges. The association's headquarters would bill and collect for the western third of the state, while the new offices—in Nashville and Knoxville to be staffed with paid part-time help—would cover the central and eastern thirds. A study showed that under the new arrangement mailing time would probably be reduced by one day (one-half day each way), and check-collection time could be cut by another full day to one and one-fourth days. The plan called for daily wire transfers from the Nashville and Knoxville banks to the association's principal bank of deposit in Memphis.

The association's Nashville and Knoxville directors persuaded banks in their areas to offer free check-collecting and deposit services for the ninety-day period. Wire transfers—2 per working day or 114 in total—would cost the association $7.00 each, or $798. The two new offices would be located in space donated by the directors and staffed by two part-time employees in each office, for a total of four new part-time employees. During the period, each employee would work an average of four hours per day for fifty-seven days, and receive $4.00 per hour. Total additional expenses (that is, in excess of the continuing Memphis office expense) for personnel are, therefore, $3,648, and the total cost of the concentration banking system is ($3,648 + $798 =) $4,446.

The association's fund-raising goal is $4.3 million for this year's telethon. Since mailing and check-clearing time is expected to be reduced by two days, the association's investment income should increase by two days' interest income on the $4.3 million to be received. Assuming that the relevant interest rate will be 8 percent, the concentration banking system will produce cash benefits of ($4.3 million

× .08 × 2/365 =) $1,885. Unfortunately, the costs exceed the benefits by $2,561 in this instance; thus the Tennessee Sheriff's Association should continue its central billing system.

Worth noting here is that all commercial banks may not be willing to offer free check-collecting and deposit services to nonprofit organizations. Service charges vary among banks; however, the rates presented in Exhibit 8-1 may be considered typical of those of many large banks. The figures in the volume column are estimates of the items that the sheriff's association might experience, and the figures indicate that the bank service charges can easily increase the cost of the concentration system far beyond the benefits available from the faster collection of the pledges receivable.

Lockbox System. A lockbox is an arrangement in which a nonprofit organization permits its bank to intercept checks mailed to it in order to speed the check-collection process. Office practice in organizations that bill and collect cash from customers and donors vary greatly; however, the typical procedure involves the following steps:

1. Pick up mail from a post office or receive carrier-delivered mail
2. Sort and distribute mail
3. Open customer or donor receipts and remove contents
4. Examine and encode checks
5. Separate checks from correspondence
6. Prepare deposit slip
7. Make deposit in local bank
8. Post payments to accounts

Steps 1 through 7 in the procedure take a significant amount of time, especially if the organization's offices are located at considerable distances from either the local post office or the bank or both. The use of a

---

Exhibit 8-1: Bank Service Charges for the Tennessee Sheriff's Association's Knoxville Account

Banking service performed	Unit cost	Volume	Amount
Deposits processed	$ .380	57	$ 21.66
Items deposited	.035	86,500	3,027.50
Wire transfers	2.500	57	142.50
Statements prepared	4.000	3	12.00
Total charges			$ 3,203.66

Average daily collected balances: $980
  Earnings credit @ 10% per annum
  Number of days account was active: 90

Earnings credit (980 × .10 × 90/365)			$ 24.16
Total service charges payable			$ 3,179.50

lockbox arrangement transfers all of the first seven steps to a commercial bank, thus speeding up the collection of checks through the banking system and increasing the availability of cash to the organization. A lockbox arrangement may be used in conjunction with centralized or decentralized billing or with regional or centralized collection systems. Its sole purpose is to enable the organization to initiate the check-collection process earlier than would otherwise be possible.

Setting up the system begins with renting local post office boxes. Regional banks (or the organization's local bank) are authorized to pick up customer or donor remittances mailed to the boxes. The organization may continue to bill centrally, but payors are instructed to mail their payments to their nearest local box, where the regional bank receives them and deposits them to the organization's account.

The participating bank or banks regularly send the organization both deposit slips and lists of payments received, along with any other correspondence that may have accompanied the payments. The organization using a lockbox system never needs to process checks from customers itself but has all the information it needs to post and maintain its accounts and pledges receivable on a current basis.

Using a lockbox system gets customer or donor checks deposited sooner; consequently, collected balances become available more quickly than if the checks were processed by the organization's own personnel prior to deposit. But maintaining the system is expensive in absolute terms since the organization must pay one or several regional banks to provide the services usually performed by its own personnel (that is, the services listed as steps 1 through 7 above). The banks generally charge a flat fee for their part and may also expect the organization to maintain adequate compensating balances. The decision to use the lockbox system must be made in relative terms, however; if the system generates additional funds that yield more income than the system costs, not using it would be expensive, as pointed out earlier in the Tennessee Sheriff's Association example. The decision criterion and the method of analysis are thus almost identical to the concentration banking decision.

Other Methods. Several other methods of accelerating cash inflows may be employed. The first of these, and perhaps the most obvious, is to increase the proportion of cash customers and donors associated with the organization. But this, too, involves a trade-off: most organizations find that sales and contributions are greater in absolute dollar amounts when customers are permitted to purchase on credit from trading organizations, and donors are allowed to take several months to honor their pledges. By insisting on cash payments, the organization may find its total revenues are smaller than they might be otherwise. At the same time, however, by conducting its affairs on a cash basis, the organization will avoid the administrative expenses involved in maintaining and collecting accounts and pledges receivable. The net effect of the choice between operating on a cash or credit basis must be analyzed carefully before either is adopted as policy by the organization. (This topic is examined in greater depth in the discussion of receivables management in chapter 10.)

Second, organizations that frequently or even occasionally receive large remittances from donors or customers give special attention to their handling. In some cases, management personnel will visit the donor or client to pick up the check or else request the remittor to wire the funds or use special delivery postal service. In this way, the organization can more quickly convert the remittances into spendable funds.

The third method, appropriate to national organizations or those that are organized in autonomous or semiautonomous divisions, involves consolidating several bank accounts that are currently serving the needs of the organization's several cash-collecting and/or disbursing units. For example, a YMCA operating several facilities in a large urban area may be able to establish central accounts payable and payroll operations, enabling each facility to operate without its individual bank account and releasing cash that can then be invested or put to other uses.

Fourth, an organization can accelerate cash inflows from accounts and pledges receivable simply by sending the bills and reminders as quickly as possible. For example, a trading organization that normally mails its bills two weeks after orders are delivered to customers can speed up cash collection by two weeks simply by including the invoices with the orders as they are shipped. Similarly, pledges that are payable in two or more installments can be received more rapidly by making the first installment *due immediately* on receipt of the reminder, with the balance due in four-week (twenty-eight-day) rather than one-month (thirty- or thirty-one-day) intervals. This practice will reduce the time required to collect the pledges by more than two weeks in most cases, depending, of course, on how quickly the first reminders are sent to the donors.

Finally, the organization can bypass the problem almost entirely by entering into an arrangement with a national or local bank credit card company that would enable the organization's customers and donors to settle their accounts with their Visa, MasterCard, American Express, Diners Club, or other credit cards. More will said about this method in chapter 10.

Control of Disbursements

In addition to techniques for accelerating collections, effective control of disbursements can also result in larger excess cash balances. Whereas the underlying objective of collections is to minimize delays in converting cash receipts into usable funds, the objective for disbursements is to maximize delays in making cash payments without damaging the organization's credit standing.

The timing of payments is important to obtain maximum use of cash. If the organization is purchasing materials on terms of 2/10, net 30 (that is, the organization receives a 2 percent discount if payment is made within ten days and must pay within thirty days, in any event), it should schedule its payments to suppliers on the tenth day after the date of invoice. Thus, by delaying payment until the last day, the organization will have the use of its funds for the maximum period and yet will not lose its cash discounts.

Another way to increase cash availability is by utilizing *bank float* as fully as is practical. Bank float is the difference between the total dollar amount of checks written on a bank account and the balance shown in that account on the *bank's* books. That difference arises because of the time it takes for the check, once it is written, to reach the payee and then return to the organization's bank through the normal check-clearing systems.

When the check is written to a local business that maintains its account at the bank on which the check is written, the float may be as short as one day. If the payee is located at a considerable distance from the paying organization, however, the float may run for a week or longer. While the check remains uncollected, the funds on deposit remain unused and unproductive to the organization (but not to the bank, of course).

The organization may put those idle funds to work simply by investing the bank float in some suitable short-term investment medium. That is, it can write a check equal to the size of the float and deposit it in, say, a savings account where it will earn interest. While the organization is "playing the float" in this manner, its own account records will show a *negative* cash balance, but because checks outstanding have not been collected from its bank account, the bank's records will show a *positive* (or a zero) balance in the organization's account.

The major disadvantages to the organization of playing the float are, first, the organization may occasionally overestimate the size of the float and develop negative balances at the bank. Since negative bank balances, or *overdrafts*, are illegal in most states, the organization may run the risk of having a check returned to a supplier for insufficient funds, incur an extra service charge at the bank, or both.

Second, banks prefer that their customers keep large, rather than small, balances in their accounts and will accord preferential treatment to those customers who maintain large balances and are never overdrawn. Thus, those organizations that receive a significant amount of free services from their bankers may be well-advised not to play the float. In this way they may avoid the imposition of bank service charges and higher interest costs on borrowed funds from a not-so-friendly banker.

Finally, playing the float is both time-consuming and plain hard work. The manager responsible for the organization's cash position must constantly be ready to shift funds in and out of earning assets, continually analyze the organization's receipts and disbursements, and monitor the costs of his or her activities against the returns from investing the float.

The Minimum Cash Balance

The ability of an organization to minimize its investment in cash balances depends on both its transaction needs and the efficiency with which it manages its cash account. Although minimum cash needs may change over time, management can determine what they are and how they are changing by carefully evaluating the collection and disbursement patterns of the organization. The cash budget discussed in chapter 7 provides the best estimates of these patterns and hence of minimum cash needs. Management may also improve the efficiency of cash management by using such techniques as concentration banking and lockbox systems; however, certain institutional constraints limit the ability of the organization to reduce cash holdings below certain levels, even when the cash budget indicates that the organization may safely do so. The most important of these constraints is the necessity to maintain *compensating balances* with the organization's bank. Other constraints include provisions of loan agreements with creditors that specify a minimum cash balance requirement and self-imposed restrictions that govern cash management practice.

Many business firms and nonprofit organizations establish their minimum balance requirements at the levels suggested by the account officer at their principal bank of deposit. The size of the compensating balance that an account officer may require is related to the profitability of the deposit account to the bank. Many banks determine account profitability by calculating the size of the average collected balance and subtracting the percentage of the deposit that must be held as a legally required reserve. The difference represents lendable funds from which the bank can generate income. Gross account profitability is then determined by applying some current earnings rate to the amount of lendable funds supplied by the account. The cost of servicing the account is then subtracted from the gross profit figure.

Most banks have a schedule of costs per item for certain transactions, such as funds transfers and check processing. The account is analyzed for a typical month during which all transactions are multiplied by the per item cost and totaled. If the total cost is less than the total income from the account, the account is profitable. Otherwise, it is not; the minimum level of balances that will be deemed commensurate with the services provided by the bank is the level at which the bank at least breaks even. Exhibit 8-2 presents a typical account analysis form used by a commercial bank to measure customer account profitability. The analysis of the Piedmont Cattlemen's Association indicates that the account is profitable, and the association is maintaining an average surplus deposit of $5,610.

Because banks differ in their earnings rates as well as in their costs and methods of calculating account profitability, the determination of compensating balances for a given level of activity will vary from bank to bank. Also, if a bank is extending credit to an organization, it may require larger balances than those that would be commensurate only with the organization's deposit and payments activity.

CASH MANAGEMENT MODELS

At least theoretically, and disregarding compensating balance requirements, the optimum size of an organization's cash balance should be very close to zero since management should play the float in order to

---

Exhibit 8-2: **Commercial Bank Account Analysis Form**

FIRST AMERICAN BANK
Account Analysis

Customer: Piedmont Cattlemen's Association

Account Number: 18 0163 3

Period Covered: 08-10-89 through 09-11-89

Average ledger balance	$ 36,370
Less: average funds in collection process	4,430
Average collected balance	31,940
Less required reserves @ 12%	3,830
Average available balance to support account activity	$ 28,110 (AAB)

Service	Number of items	Charge per item	Total charge	Average available balance required*
Deposits posted	18	$ 6.00	$ 108	$ 1,350
Deposited items	2,808	.48	1,348	16,850
Checks paid	118	.78	92	1,150
Bank wires	4	12.00	48	600
Collections				
Lock box				
Accounts reconcilement				
Safekeeping	6	24.00	144	1,800
Credit investigations	4	12.00	48	600
Other statement rendered	1	12.00	12	150
Total balances required to support account activity				$ 22,500 (TBR)
Excess (deficit) of available balance (AAB) – (TBR)				$ 5,610

* *Earning credit @ 8% per annum is used to calculate required balances.*

keep cash in its nonearning asset form to an absolute minimum. As bills come due (or are in danger of becoming too far past due, under appropriate cash disbursement controls), the organization will depend on cash receipts from sales, donations, interest income, dividends, conversion of assets, or borrowing to provide the cash necessary to keep its bank balances from becoming negative.

But as mentioned earlier, this kind of constant attention to cash management may be inconvenient at the least or costly at the extreme. Thus, most households, business firms, and nonprofit organizations hold various amounts of cash in demand deposit accounts to facilitate normal cash transactions, while implicitly or explicitly recognizing the trade-off between the costs and benefits of holding cash in its nonearning form. This trade-off is amenable to fairly precise measurement with the aid of any of several analytical cash-management models, two of which are particularly appropriate for use by nonprofit organizations.

The first of these models, proposed by William Baumol in 1952, may be used by nontrading nonprofit organizations whose operations are financed largely from donations or periodic appropriations.[3] The second model, referred to as the Miller-Orr Model, is appropriate for those nonprofit organizations whose cash inflows and outflows are unpredictable in both size and timing.[4] Both models divide the available cash into (1) a transactions (demand deposit) balance and (2) a portfolio of short-term marketable securities, and both present a set of rules for liquidating the securities when cash becomes short and for reinvesting cash when a surplus accumulates. Finally, both models are designed to balance the various costs associated with cash management.

The Baumol Model

The Baumol cash-management model may be employed by nontrading nonprofit organizations whose cash balances behave in a sawtooth manner, such as that illustrated in Exhibit 8-3. If the organization conducts an annual fund-raising campaign, receives regular appropriations (e.g., monthly or quarterly) from a parent or government organization, or receives grant funds periodically, its cash balance will increase sharply at times 0, 1, 2, 3, and so forth. The organization's operating expenditures will occur continuously at a fairly constant rate over time; permanent employees will be paid at regular intervals; utility bills, insurance premiums, and payments on account for supplies will come due and be paid at predictable intervals; and services performed for

---

3. W. J. Baumol, "The Transaction Demand for Cash: An Inventory Theoretic Approach," *Quarterly Journal of Economics* (November 1952): 545-556.

4. M. H. Miller and D. Orr, "A Model of the Demand for Money by Firms," *Quarterly Journal of Finance* (August 1966): 413-435.

Exhibit 8-3: **Cash Balances of a Nonprofit Organization Over Time**

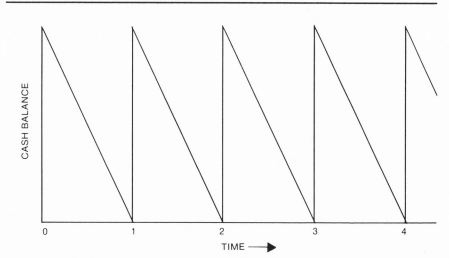

its client group will have to be supported financially on a year-round basis. Consequently, cash balances will fall at a more or less constant rate between the dates on which cash inflows occur, thus producing a sawtooth pattern of cash balances over time.

By contrast, the cash balances of *trading* organizations do not follow a sawtooth pattern. Their cash inflows are most often continuous, rather than intermittent, as are their cash outflows. The pattern of cash balances of these organizations will therefore differ from that assumed by the Baumol model, thereby making its application inappropriate for managing the balances of trading entities.

Since the cash outflows of the nontrading nonprofit organization are fairly predictable in amount and timing, and cash inflows are measurable after the fact, the Baumol model permits the nonprofit nontrading organization to adopt an optimal cash-management policy under the assumption that cash flows are known with certainty. The application of the model reduces the cash-management problem to the determination of three variables:

1. The amount of cash to be invested out of each large periodic cash inflow
2. The portion of the periodic cash inflow to be retained in cash
3. The amount of securities to be sold at regular intervals to satisfy cash requirements between cash inflow dates

Exhibit 8-4 illustrates the nature of the decision variables and the resulting cash flows and security transactions, and the cash balances for a typical application of the Baumol cash-management model. The upper

Exhibit 8-4: **Securities Transactions Required to Produce the Maximum Net Returns Using the Baumol Model**

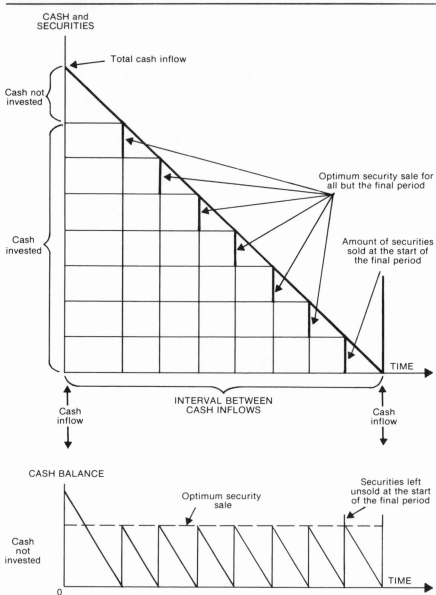

portion of the figure shows how the total cash inflow at the start of the period is distributed between *cash not invested* and *cash invested in short-term marketable securities*. As the cash balance, shown in the lower portion of the figure, reaches zero, an optimal amount of securities is sold to build up the organization's cash balance. The process is repeated until the amount remaining in securities is sufficient for more than one but less than two optimal security transactions, at which time the remaining securities are liquidated. Note that the first and last periods are longer than those in between, and the rate of cash expenditures per period is constant.

To calculate the optimum beginning cash balance (cash not invested) and the optimum security transaction, the following data are required:

1. The fixed and variable costs of security transactions
2. The interest rate at which surplus cash will be invested
3. The total amount of cash inflow expected (or received) initially

The interest rate must have the same time dimension as the planning period; that is, if the interval between cash inflows is one month, the interest rate must be expressed as one-twelfth of the annual percentage rate. The application of the Baumol model is best described by way of an example.

New House, a juvenile drug rehabilitation facility, is currently being sponsored by the Catholic Bishops Fund in Atlanta, Georgia. New House is due to receive its annual appropriation of $81,000 in one lump sum on July 1 of this year. Since the facility currently is operating at capacity and is maintaining a waiting list of clients, its expenditure rate is expected to be fairly constant throughout the fiscal year.

The administrator of New House expects short-term interest rates to hold fairly constant at about 10 percent per annum. He generally purchases short-term securities through a local brokerage house that selects the securities that New House will hold in its portfolio and manages the portfolio in accordance with the organization's general requirements. No management fees are charged by the broker, but investment and liquidation fees are set at $50 per transaction (purchase or liquidation) plus 0.5 percent of the dollar amount involved.

Optimum Security Sale. The optimum amount of the security sales during the period is calculated as follows:

optimum security sale =

$$\sqrt{\frac{2 \times \text{fixed cost of security sale} \times \text{initial cash inflow}}{\text{interest rate at which cash is invested}}}$$

$$= \sqrt{\frac{2 \times \$50 \times \$81,000}{.10}}$$

$$= \sqrt{\frac{\$8,100,000}{.10}}$$

$$= \sqrt{\$81,000,000}$$

optimum security sale = $\underline{\$9,000}$

Thus, the financial manager should plan to arrange for the sale of $9,000 of securities each time the organization's operating cash balance reaches zero.

Optimum Beginning Cash Balance. The optimum beginning cash balance (cash not invested out of the initial cash inflow) is calculated using the following formula:

optimum beginning cash balance = optimum security sale +

initial cash inflow $\times \left(\dfrac{2 \times \text{variable cost of security transaction}}{\text{interest rate at which cash is invested}} \right)$

$$= \$9,000 + \$81,000 \times \left(\frac{2 \times .005}{.10} \right)$$

$$= \$9,000 + \$81,000 \times \left(\frac{(.01)}{.10} \right)$$

$$= \$9,000 + \$8,100$$

optimum beginning cash balance = $\underline{\$17,100}$

When New House receives the appropriation check from the Catholic Bishops Fund, the financial manager should deposit $17,100 in its checking account and invest the balance in marketable securities.

Cash-Management Decision Rules. The application of the Baumol cash-management model produces the decision rules just outlined. The rules may be restated in more specific terms as follows:
   1. New House should deposit $17,100 of the $81,000 appropriation in its checking account and send the balance of ($81,000 – $17,100 =) $63,900 to its broker with instructions for investment.

Since New House's average daily spending rate will be ($81,000/365 days =) $222, the initial cash balance will last for about 77 days. The cash provided from the optimum security sale will last for ($9,000/$222 per day =) 40 days, approximately. Therefore,

2. New House should instruct its broker to be prepared to liquidate $9,000 of securities in 77 days and another $9,000 every 40 days thereafter.

Finally, since the amount initially invested ($63,900) will last for seven 40-day periods with $900 left over (i.e., $63,900/$9,000 per period = 7 periods),

3. the organization should instruct its broker to liquidate the balance remaining in the portfolio at the start of the last period, when $9,900 remains in the portfolio.

Exhibit 8-5 presents the costs and benefits from investing and liquidating securities in accordance with the decision rules just outlined along with those of two other sets of arbitrarily selected decision rules. Under alternative A, New House would hold $9,000 as its beginning cash balance and liquidate $9,000 in each period thereafter. Under alternative B, the organization would hold $6,750 in cash and sell a like amount of securities at the end of each month during the year. The net interest income, using the Baumol model, produces a higher interest income and lower brokerage costs than either of the other alternatives.

The net income from the cash management efforts is assumed to accumulate during the planning period. This cash flow may therefore be used as a precautionary cash balance until the end of the period and then may be added to the subsequent year's appropriation in calculating the optimal beginning cash balance and security sales.

The Miller-Orr Model

The Miller-Orr cash-management model uses the *control limit* approach to guiding the actions of the cash manager in determining the size and timing of transfers between the investment account and the organization's cash balance. As mentioned earlier, this model is designed for use by businesses and nonprofit organizations whose cash inflows and expenditures are largely unpredictable in both size and timing. The cash balances of such entities behave through time as if they were governed by a random process and may appear as illustrated in Exhibit 8-6.

Exhibit 8-5: Net Returns From Three Cash-Management Decision Rules

Decision rules	Interest income*	Number of transactions	Brokerage Fees Fixed	Brokerage Fees Variable	Brokerage fees Net income
Baumol model	$ 3,509	9	$ 450.00	$ 684.00	$ 2,375.00
Alternative A	3,200	9	450.00	720.00	2,030.00
Alternative B	3,403	12	600.00	742.50	2,060.50

* *Based on simple interest earned on unliquidated portfolio balances in each period.*

Exhibit 8-6: **Cash Balance Typical of Many Trading Nonprofit Organizations Over Time**

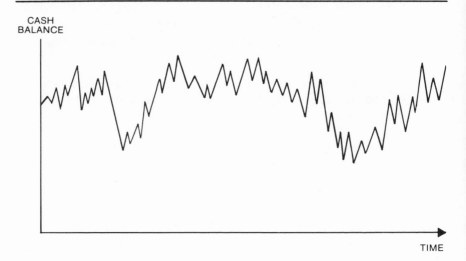

CASH
BALANCE

TIME

More precisely, the Miller-Orr model, in its most widely used form, assumes that the cash balance is equally likely to increase or decrease by the end of the next period (usually a day or week). The model employs two decision rules that are related to the *upper* and *lower control limits,* or maximum and minimum cash balances allowable. The decision rules are:

1. When the cash balance equals or exceeds the upper control limit, the cash manager must purchase securities in an amount sufficient to reduce the cash balance to a specified amount, called the *return point.*

2. When the cash balance equals or falls below the lower control limit, the cash manager must sell securities in an amount sufficient to increase the cash balance to the return point.

The model defines the upper control limit and the return point mathematically so as to minimize the sum of the transaction costs (costs of buying and selling securities) plus the opportunity cost of keeping cash in its nonearning form. The lower control limit is established at a level selected by the organization's management, either at some minimum level selected on the basis of transactions needs or by compensating balance requirements, for example. The implementation of the model will cause cash balances to behave in a manner similar to that illustrated in Exhibit 8-7. The cash balance in the exhibit triggers decision rule number 2 at points A and C, and triggers decision rule number 1 at point B.

The return point is determined mathematically by solving the following equation:

return point =

$$\frac{3 \times \text{fixed transactions cost} \times \text{variance of daily cash balance}}{4 \times \text{interest rate earned on cash invested}}$$

As in the Baumol model, the interest rate is expressed in the same time dimension as the planning period. The variance of the daily cash balance is a statistical measure of dispersion about the mean value of the cash balance, as observed over some reasonably long period. It is represented by the symbol, σ^2, and is calculated by (1) calculating the mean, or average, of the observed daily cash balances $(\bar{x})$, (2) subtracting the mean value $(\bar{x})$ from each observed cash balance (x). (3) squaring the differences thus calculated $(\bar{x}-x)^2$ (4) adding the squared differences, and (5) dividing by the number of observations minus 1 $(n-1)$. In equation form the variance is

$$\sigma^2 = \frac{\Sigma\, (\bar{x} - x)^2}{(n - 1)}$$

Exhibit 8-7: Cash Balances and Securities Transactions Prescribed by the Miller-Orr Cash-Management Model

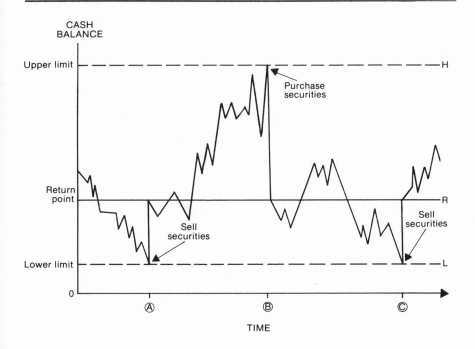

The upper control limit is calculated simply as three times the return point minus two times the lower control limit for the case in which cash inflows and outflows are equally likely to occur in the next period. An example will help clarify this approach to cash management.

The Auxiliary Services Division of a large private university was operated on a semiautonomous basis. It was required to operate on a financially self-sufficient basis, including providing its own capital equipment for replacement and expansion. The university charged it a rental fee for the space it occupied in the various dormitories and other buildings throughout the campus and took a small percentage of gross revenues as well.

The Auxiliary Services Division operated the campus book stores, several cafeterias in the residence halls, the main university dining room, the faculty club, vending machines, and a catering service. The division manager noted that its cash balance followed a random pattern and decided to use the Miller-Orr model to manage the division's cash and investment portfolio decisions.

By using data from the division's bank statements over the past year, the manager was able to compute the variance of the cash balance. He also asked the university's treasurer to assist him in managing his portfolio of investment securities. The treasurer agreed to help but told him that the division would have to pay the brokerage fees incurred on all transactions. After a thorough analysis of the situation, the manager developed the following data for use in obtaining a Miller-Orr solution:

Fixed cost of security transactions	= $ 100
Variance of the cash balance	= $ 9.0 million
Interest rate at which cash is invested	= 8 percent
Minimum cash balance requirement, or lower control limit	= $ 1,500

By substituting these values into the Miller-Orr equations, the manager calculated the return point, R, and the upper control limit, H, as follows:

$$R = \sqrt[3]{\frac{3 \times \$100 \times \$9,000,000}{4 \times .08}} + \$1,500$$

$$= \sqrt[3]{\frac{\$2,700,000,000}{.32}} + \$1,500$$

$$= \sqrt[3]{\$8,437,500,000} + \$1,500$$

$$R = \$2,036 + \$1,500 = \underline{\underline{\$3,536}}$$

$$H = (3 \times R) - (2 \times L)$$

$$H = (3 \times \$3,536) - (2 \times \$1,500)$$

$$= \$10,608 - \$3,000$$

$$H = \underline{\underline{\$7,608}}$$

Given the solution values, the manager of the Auxiliary Services Division of the university should employ the following decision rules:

1. When the cash balance reaches the upper control limit, H, he should purchase ($7,608 - $3,536 =) $4,072 of securities.

2. When the cash balance reaches the lower control limit, L, he should sell ($3,536 - $1,500 =) $2,036 of securities.

Applying Cash Management Models

Decision models of the type illustrated in this section are imperfect in certain respects. For example, neither model considers the fact that an organization may be able to borrow to meet its temporary cash needs and that the cost of borrowing may be less than the combined transactions cost and opportunity cost of selling securities. Further, the models employ very restrictive assumptions regarding the organization's cash-flow patterns in order to define the decision rules in specific operational terms. The Baumol model assumes a constant spending rate with no receipts during the planning period, and the Miller-Orr model does not allow for the possibility that the organization can delay payments on account for a day or two until it receives additional cash receipts. To the extent that these underlying assumptions concerning the patterns of cash flows do not correspond perfectly to the actual cash-flow patterns of the organization, the solutions produced by these models will be defective.

Some of the data needed to solve the equations may be difficult to obtain or estimate accurately. Spending rates for the Baumol model and cash account variance for the Miller-Orr model are two obvious examples of hard-to-estimate data. If these estimates are faulty, the models obviously will produce defective decision rules. Finally, because smaller nonprofit organizations will likely place their surplus cash in savings deposits of financial institutions, rather than maintain their own investment portfolios, their transactions costs will be zero, thus preventing the models from producing any solution values at all.

In spite of these problems, decision models provide useful insights into the relevant variables that must be considered in any cash-management program. And to the extent that their assumptions are realistic in the case of a particular nonprofit organization, the models may be used as a guide to, but not a substitute for, intelligent decision making.

SHORT-TERM INVESTMENT MEDIA

The preceding sections of this chapter contain frequent reference to *short-term securities* and *portfolios of marketable securities*. It is now appropriate to examine the nature and types of short-term investment media in which a nonprofit organization may invest its temporarily idle cash balances.

Basic Characteristics of Short-term Investment Media

The basic characteristics of short-term investment media may be classified under four general headings: default risk, interest rate risk, marketability, and expected investment yield. The securities available for purchase differ according to these characteristics and therefore must be examined by the nonprofit organization in light of its investment requirements at the time of the planned purchase.

Default Risk. Default risk refers to the potential inability of a borrower to comply with the initially agreed-on schedule of interest payments and the repayment of principal at maturity. With few exceptions, all marketable securities are subject to some degree of default risk. The exceptions are those securities issued by the federal government, which are backed by the full taxing powers of the government as well as its power to print money. Other governmental issuers of marketable securities—states and municipalities—do not possess the power to print money, although they too have the power to tax; consequently, even the most credit-worthy of these state and local government issuers cannot without qualification promise to pay interest and repay the principal in strict accordance with the schedule originally agreed upon.

In determining the default risk applicable to a given nongovernmental security, the following three factors are paramount: (1) the systematic risk of the issuing firm, which is common to all firms engaged in similar operations; (2) the singular risk of the issuing firm, which arises from the nature of its operations and management policies, as compared with those of other concerns in the same industry; and (3) the maturity of the particular security under examination.

Organizationally, the management structures of most nonprofit organizations do not include personnel or departments with sufficient time or expertise to properly assess the inherent default risk of all available short-term marketable securities. In all likelihood, their investment decisions will rely heavily on the analyses prepared by brokerage firms, professional investment advisors, and the scores of publications devoted to analyzing publicly traded securities.

Interest Rate Risk. Interest rate risk refers to the relationship between the price of an interest-bearing security and changes in the general level of interest rates. This relationship is inverse (i.e., securities prices fall as market interest rates rise, and *vice versa*); however, the magnitude of the change in price for a given change in interest rates varies with the time to maturity. The prices of long-term bonds are far more sensitive to changes in interest rates than are those of short-term securities.

From the investing organization's point of view, maintaining at least the original market value of the investment portfolio at all times is generally an important consideration. The portfolio composed primarily of *long-term* securities could quickly decline in market value as a result of an upward shift in the level of interest rates. Moreover, this loss in dollar terms would be substantially greater for long-term securities than for those maturing within one year. Consequently, short-term securities are generally chosen as the more suitable investment medium for temporarily idle cash balances.

Marketability. Marketability refers to the ease with which a security may be converted into cash. Securities that are regularly traded either on an organized securities exchange or "over the counter" tend to sell closer to their most recently quoted market price than do securities that are seldom traded. For example, U.S. Treasury bonds or bonds issued by major corporations have wide appeal among security buyers; hence, the risk associated with the marketability of these securities is negligible. However, if an investor holds securities that have few potential buyers, the prices at which these securities can be sold, *ceteris paribus*, will be lower than those of frequently traded securities.

The marketability of most short-term securities is generally excellent. Investors, therefore, may safely ignore the marketability risk in a portfolio of short-term securities. And even in those rare instances in which a security cannot be readily sold in the market, the maturity is close enough at hand to diminish any hardship the holder may have to endure while waiting for its ultimate redemption. Hence, the most frequently held marketable securities are short-term, or money market instruments.

Expected Interest Yield. The returns from investments in short-term securities are generally lower than those available from securities having longer maturities. This difference results from the higher default and interest rate risks inherent in the long-term securities. In general, however, the yield differential is not an important consideration. As previously stated, nonprofit organizations maintain marketable security portfolios for the purpose of profitably employing cash that has been reserved for certain known future cash outflows (or, less frequently, to use in case of emergencies). Thus, safety of the principal is of primary concern, and yield considerations are secondary. Consequently, marketable securities portfolios held by most organizations are composed almost exclusively of short-term securities.

Short-term Securities

Several classes of short-term securities are widely recognized as excellent media for temporary investment. Exhibit 8-8 summarizes the basic characteristics of the principal types of these securities. Each type listed in the exhibit is described in further detail in the following sections.

Eurodollar Deposits. Eurodollars represent deposits denominated in dollars but held in European banks. Similarly, Asian dollars are deposit accounts denominated in dollars held in Asian banks. Actually, Eurodollars are not traded in the United States' money market. However, due to major advances in transatlantic communications, multinationals, other large domestic corporations, and other investors that engage in international transactions frequently sell Eurodollars (i.e., deposit dollars abroad) as a sound alternative to purchasing domestic money market instruments.

The primary reason that investors may prefer to hold their excess cash in Eurodollar deposits is because most foreign banks are not subject to *legal maxima* on interest payable on deposits. Consequently, investors that have idle dollars but do not wish to exchange those dollars for other currencies in order to purchase foreign money market instruments may enter the Eurodollar market in an attempt to receive a higher rate of interest than might otherwise be paid on domestic money market instruments. The average maturity of Eurodollar deposits is one month. However, as mentioned in Exhibit 8-8, the range of maturities varies from what is essentially an overnight deposit to those of one or two years' duration. Finally, since the minimum investment amount is $1 million, the small investors are excluded from this particular investment opportunity.

Commercial Paper. For the nonprofit organization looking for a slightly higher yield on its investment in domestic securities, commercial paper represents an attractive alternative to short maturity Treasury obligations (discussed later on). Commercial paper consists of short-term, unsecured promissory notes issued by finance companies and certain financially strong industrial firms. The instruments are sold either directly to the investor or through dealers. Large sales finance companies, such as General Motors Acceptance Corporation and Commercial Credit Corporation, sell their paper directly to investors; however, most industrial companies and smaller finance companies issue their paper through dealers.

Rates on commercial paper are somewhat higher than those on Treasury bills of the same maturity. Usually, commercial paper is sold on a discount basis, with maturities running from four to six months. Within this range, a wide selection of maturities is available to the investor; in fact the large direct-issuing finance companies will tailor maturities to the buyer's specifications. Most commercial paper purchased is held to maturity because no active secondary market exists for it. However, direct sellers of commercial paper will often repurchase their paper upon request.

Bankers' Acceptances. Bankers' acceptances are the major instruments used in financing international trade. They are used by domestic firms to finance both exports and imports. The risk inherent in the individual instrument of this type does not reflect the creditworthiness of the drawer of the acceptance but rather that of the bank that has accepted the draft. They are traded in an over-the-counter market by a few principal dealers.

Like Treasury bills, bankers' acceptances are sold on a discount basis. The quality of these securities is such that they typically pay a slightly higher rate of interest than Treasury bills. Bankers' acceptances generally have maturities of less than 180 days, with the average maturity being 90 days.

Certificates of Deposit. In early 1961 American commercial banks began to issue negotiable time certificates of deposit (CDs) as evidence of time deposits placed with the issuing bank. The certificates are basically receipts representing interest-bearing time deposits, and they are fully negotiable (salable after issuance). Negotiable CDs offer yields that vary with conditions in the money market, the maturity of the certificates, and the size and financial reputation of the issuing bank. The large New York City banks offer CDs with maturities of from less than 90 days up to one year. Denominations of $1 million and up are common, but banks outside New York City sometimes offer denominations as small as $25,000, and sometimes even smaller denominations are issued. Many corporate financial administrators prefer the certificates of the larger banks because of their somewhat greater marketability. Consequently, rates obtainable on the CDs of smaller banks run about 0.25 percent higher than those paid by the larger banks located in national and regional financial centers.

A good secondary market has developed for the CDs of the large banks, making them readily marketable. Consequently, the market prices of

(text continued on page 218)

Exhibit 8-8: Summary of the Basic Characteristics of Short-term Investment Media

Investment security	Characteristics	Usual minimum denomination	Normal maturity	Earning's computation basis	Usual source of purchase
Eurodollar deposits	A time deposit, denominated in dollars, placed in a European bank. Low risk and highly liquid.	$1 million	1 day or more	Interest on a 365-day basis	European bank
Commercial paper	Unsecured, interest-bearing notes of large corporations. Very safe but sometimes lack liquidity.	$25,000	3 to 270 days	Discounted on a 360-day basis	Issuing corporation, commercial bank, or security dealer
Bankers' acceptances	Time drafts drawn by shipper of goods on large banks and on which accepting bank substitutes its credit by "acceptance." Low risk, and highly liquid in New York market.	Varies, based on the value of the goods; generally $25,000	30 to 270 days	Discounted on a 360-day basis	Commercial bank or dealer
Certificates of deposit (CDs)	Large denomination ($100,000 and over) are negotiable instruments, evidencing time deposits in a commercial bank. Low risk. CDs of major banks are highly liquid. Small denominations CDs are also low risk but lack liquidity.	$100,000 for large denominations, $100 for others	New, 30 days; outstanding issues, 1 day	Interest on a 360-day basis	Commercial bank or dealer
Federal agency issues	Bonds, notes, and debentures issued by six major federal agencies. Riskless and highly liquid.	$1,000 but most are $10,000	6 months to 25 years	Discounted or interest-bearing on a 360-day basis, paid semiannually	Commercial bank or dealer

Treasury bills	U.S. government obligations maturing within one year. Riskless and highly liquid. New 3-6 month issues sold weekly; 9-12 month issues sold monthly.	$10,000	3 months to 1 year	Discounted on a 360-day basis	Federal Reserve bank, commercial banks, dealers and brokers
Treasury notes and bonds	U.S. government obligations with initial maturities of one year or longer. Riskless and highly liquid.	$1,000, but most are $10,000	1 to 30 years	Interest on a 365-day basis, paid semiannually	Federal Reserve bank, commercial bank, dealer or broker
Money market funds	Mutual fund holding a portfolio of money market securities. Low risk and usually highly liquid.	$1,000	Demand	Daily investment income paid on new shares or used to increase share values	Fund office
Repurchase agreements	Short-term purchase of any money market security from a dealer who agrees to repurchase at the same price plus interest at a specified later date. Riskless but lacks liquidity.	$100,000	1 to 29 days, and sometimes longer	Interest on a 360-day basis	Commercial bank or dealer

(text continued from page 215)
outstanding CDs fluctuate as their yields follow market rates of interest, putting them in almost the same class with commercial paper.

Federal Agency Issues. Apart from Treasury bills, notes, and bonds, all of which are unconditionally guaranteed (for payment of principal and interest) by the federal government, certain federal agencies sell bonds that are also guaranteed by the government. The principal agencies issuing such securities are Federal Land Banks, Federal Home Loan Banks, the Federal National Mortgage Association, the Federal Intermediate Credit Bank, and the Banks for Cooperatives. To compensate the investor for what appears to be (but is not, really) a slight additional investment risk, United States agency bonds yield a higher return than direct Treasury issues. The agency issues generally have good marketability since they are sold in the secondary market through the same dealers who sell Treasury issues.

New issues of Federal agency bonds are generally of interest to investors seeking temporary investments only when the money will not be needed for several years. As the issues come nearer to maturity, however, agency bonds become more suitable for short-term investment of temporarily idle cash balances.

Treasury Securities. The most widely used outlets for temporarily excess balances are U.S. Treasury securities. Their strong appeal to investors lies in their safety of principal, broad marketability, and wide range of maturities. The principal types of Treasury securities are bills, notes, and bonds.

Treasury bills are issued each week and mature in ninety-one days; issues of six-, nine-, and twelve-month bills are also outstanding. All bills are sold at auction and bid prices are stated in the form of a discount from face value. Thus, the yield on a Treasury bill is determined by this spread between purchase price and face (maturity) value. Large dollar amounts of bills are always outstanding, so an investor need not be concerned about the availability of suitable issues at any time. Further, transaction costs of purchasing and selling Treasury bills in the secondary market are small, making the instruments doubly attractive for temporary (short-term) investment.

The federal government also issues Treasury notes, having maturities of from one to seven years, and Treasury bonds, with maturities of more than seven years. Notes and bonds would not ordinarily be of interest to the nonprofit organization at the time of their initial offering; however, with the passage of time, they enter the short-term category and take on the general characteristics of Treasury bills. When their remaining life is short, they usually sell on a yield basis comparable with other short-term government securities. And as with the Treasury bill, the market for notes and bonds is well developed and active.

Money Market Mutual Funds and Accounts. Many investors wishing to profit from investing their idle cash balances may lack the time or expertise to maintain a properly balanced, marketable security portfolio. The existence of money market mutual funds or money market deposits of commercial banks and savings and loan associations allow such investors to indirectly invest in money market instruments, thereby achieving excellent portfolio balance and results with only a minimal amount of management time. Basically the only decisions the investor must consider are the amounts that should be invested in and withdrawn from the mutual fund or account and the timing of these transactions.

Money market funds were established to enable small investors to gain access to that portion of the short-term securities market in which interest rates are not regulated. Since these are funds managed by professionals, the use of these funds by investors with limited resources (or, as previously stated, those investors who lack the time and/or expertise to manage their own portfolios) enables them to earn additional profits from the investment of what might otherwise be idle or underemployed cash balances.

Most of these money market funds are open-end funds; that is, the managing investment company stands ready to redeem shares at or near their asset values at all times. Typically, the fund manager will extract an annual fee of about 0.5 percent of the average asset value per year for services rendered. In addition, there are usually no "load" charges levied by the fund for either share purchases or redemptions. This means the managing investment company will offer to sell and redeem shares at current asset values.[5] Furthermore, money may be added or removed from an account at almost any time. Dividends are usually declared daily and paid monthly. Finally, some funds have arrangements with a cooperating bank that permit an investor to conveniently redeem shares by writing a check on an account established at that bank by the fund's management. The bank is reimbursed by transferring funds (redeeming shares) from the fund's bank balance when the check clears. Thus the cash invested in the fund continues to earn interest until the check is cleared by the cooperating bank.

Money market accounts of banks and savings and loan associations operate in a fashion similar to that of the mutual funds. Money deposited in these accounts, however, is loaned out to bank customers. Minimum balance requirements and restrictions on the number of withdrawals per period also are common features of these accounts. Their yields generally will be slightly lower than those of the mutual funds because of the reserve requirements imposed on deposits of financial institutions by their respective regulatory agencies.

---

5. A few money market mutual funds designated as "load funds" offer shares through brokers or other selling organizations. These firms add a percentage charge (or "load") to the net asset values of the shares for sales, redemptions, or both sales and redemptions.

Repurchase Agreements. Another alternative for the investment of temporarily idle funds is a repurchase agreement with a government securities dealer. Under such an agreement, the investor purchases Treasury obligations from the dealer, who in turn agrees to repurchase the securities at a set price on a specified date. The length of the agreement is set by the needs of the investor. Repurchase agreements give investors a great deal of flexibility with respect to maturity and still yield a respectable return on funds invested. The rates on repurchase agreements are related to the open-market rates on Treasury bills and to the customer loan rates on loans to government security dealers by commercial banks.

SUMMARY

The three universal motives for holding cash in the form of currency and bank demand deposits are the transactions motive, the precautionary motive, and the speculative motive. The demand for cash to satisfy all three is tempered by the availability of short-term, highly marketable investment media that for practical purposes are close substitutes for cash. Nevertheless, the amount of cash that an organization must hold to maintain adequate liquidity depends on (1) its willingness to risk running short of cash, (2) the degree of predictability of its cash flows, and (3) its available reserve borrowing power.

In managing the cash account of a nonprofit organization, the financial manager should attempt to accelerate collections and control disbursements so that cash remains with the organization as long as is practical. Collections can be accelerated by means of concentration banking and lockboxes. Effective control of disbursements through careful timing of payments and the use of bank float can also result in a larger volume of available cash balances.

The decision to invest temporarily idle cash balances can be guided by the application of one of several cash management models. The two models discussed in the chapter were the Baumol model, recommended for use by nontrading organizations, and the Miller-Orr model, suggested for use by trading organizations. Both models separate total available cash resources into operating cash balances and investable surplus. The final section of the chapter describes the several types of short-term investment media suitable for purchase with temporarily idle cash balances.

FURTHER READING

These articles describe the development and derivation of cash-management models presented in this chapter:

Baumol, W. J. "The Transactions Demand for Cash: An Inventory Theoretic Approach." *Quarterly Journal of Economics* (November 1952): 545-556.

Miller, M. H., and Daniel Orr. "A Model of the Demand for Money by Firms." *Quarterly Journal of Economics* (August 1966): 413-435.

QUESTIONS

1. Why have financial managers begun to devote more attention to cash management in recent years?

2. List and discuss the three principal motives for holding cash in the form of currency and demand deposit balances.

3. How does the interpretation of the speculative motive for holding cash differ today from its original statement by Keynes?

4. Define concentration banking and lockbox systems. What kinds of nonprofit organizations will find these cash collection methods most useful?

5. Distinguish between a wire transfer and a depository transfer check as means of moving cash balances.

6. What other methods of accelerating cash inflows are available for use by nonprofit organizations?

7. Discuss the use of bank float as a means of controlling cash outflows.

8. What two ways may an organization use to define its minimum cash balance requirement?

9. Briefly outline the essential features of the Baumol cash-management model.

10. Why is the Baumol model particularly applicable to the cash-management problem in nontrading organizations?

11. State the decision rules of the Baumol model in general terms.

12. Briefly outline the essential features of the Miller-Orr cash-management model.

13. State the Miller-Orr decision rules.

14. What are the limitations of the two cash-management models presented in the chapter?

15. Discuss the four basic characteristics of short-term investment media.

16. What are the differences between Treasury bills, notes, and bonds?

17. Why are Treasury bills the most attractive security form used in cash management?

18. Describe the features of money market mutual funds.

19. Define repurchase agreement.

PROBLEMS

1. The Christian Search is a nationwide religious organization that reaches its members by way of local radio broadcasts. Its members and friends are asked to make contributions by mail. At present, the organization receives the contributions an average of five days after they are mailed, and funds are deposited a day later, after processing. Average daily deposits total approximately $43,500.

The financial manager of Christian Search is considering a concentration banking proposal involving four banks that would reduce combined mailing and processing time to three days and save the organization $620 per month in administrative costs. The plan calls for Christian Search to keep a $15,000 compensating balance in each of the four banks and pay the lead bank a fee of $18,000 per year.

    a. By how much will the plan increase the organization's cash balances?
    b. What rate of return must Christian Search earn from investing its cash balance increase to make the plan worthwhile?

2. The Dominion Ballet Company conducts two semiannual fund-raising campaigns in conjunction with its productions. The company's cash needs are fairly constant throughout the year, and it invests its surplus cash in a pooled investment account managed by a local bank. The investment is expected to yield about 10 percent per annum over the next six months. The bank charges each investor $15 per withdrawal plus 0.25 percent of the amount withdrawn from the account.

The company's recent campaign and performance netted the organization $165,800, which it plans to invest in the pooled investment account.

    a. Using the Baumol model, calculate the optimum amount of periodic withdrawal from the account during each of the next six months.
    b. Calculate the optimum beginning cash balance.
    c. State the cash-management decision rules specific to this application.
    d. Calculate the net return from the cash-management process.

3. Calculate the variance of the following observed daily cash balances:

Day	Cash balance
1	$ 1,380
2	1,250
3	2,100
4	1,640
5	1,000
6	1,990

4. Given the following values, apply the Miller-Orr model in constructing a control system for managing cash balances:

Fixed transaction costs	$ 52
Variance of daily cash balances	$ 722,500
Interest rate	12%
Lower control limit	$ 1,000

State the decision rules specific to this application.

9

Endowment Policy
and Management

*Those nonprofit organizations that are fortunate enough to be endowed
quickly learn how important the cash flows from these funds can be to
their financial well-being. This fact supports the placement of a chapter
on endowment policy and management in the working capital section of
this text. We will see that managing an endowment fund should be an
integral part of the nonprofit organization's overall financial strategy.*

The provision for adequate liquidity and the maintenance of solvency
in many nonprofit organizations are heavily dependent upon the cash
flows provided by their endowments. Professional activities consume
current revenues, and short-term and long-term debt must be repaid on
schedule if the organization is to survive and continue to serve its
clientele group. When other sources of revenues fail or their collections
are delayed, the organization's endowment funds must be used to meet
these current expenses and maturing obligations.

Further, the long-term professional goals of many nontrading
organizations often include the expansion and enrichment of their
product or service lines. Increasing either the quantity or the quality of
their lines generally also increases their cash expenditures without also
directly increasing their cash revenues; hence, the nontrading
organization generally will look to its endowment fund to supplement
cash inflows from its other revenue sources in order to support its
planned growth.

Finally, because the endowment fund may in fact support a portion of
the organization's current operations, cash management principles
become relevant to endowment policy and practice; that is, a sufficient
amount of liquidity must be maintained in the endowment fund to ensure
that cash will be available in the proper amounts and at the appropriate
times to meet current expenditures. Thus, although endowment

management is often, but erroneously, considered as a separate financial management function involving only the task of managing a portfolio of long-term investment assets, it does in fact involve important short-term considerations that are quite closely related to the organization's current operational cash flows.

Since an adequate treatment of investment decisions and portfolio management techniques is sufficiently extensive to fill an entire textbook, those topics will not be covered here. Instead, this chapter will briefly re-examine the definitional and legal characteristics of the endowment and its management and discuss several critical areas of endowment policy.

ENDOWMENT FUNDS

As explained in chapter 5, endowment funds are used in a legal-accounting sense to account for resources obtained from *outside* donors or grantors who have placed restrictions on the use of either the principal amounts of their gifts and grants or the income earned on those principal amounts. Board-designated funds are not generally included within this group of funds for accounting purposes, but for financial management purposes, the endowment of a nonprofit organization is defined here is *the total of the investment-type funds it holds*. This definition is purposefully broader than the legal-accounting definition of endowments. The reason for adopting so broad a definition is simply to facilitate the integration of operational and investment cash flows (and hence, short-term liquidity) with long-term asset planning by the endowed organization.

Legal Aspects of Endowment Management

Endowment funds are created in a legal sense when an outside donor or grantor transfers cash, securities, or real property to the control of a nonprofit organization under a contractual agreement that (1) requires the organization to maintain the principal in perpetuity and invest it to produce income, (2) stipulates that the principal and/or accumulated income must be used only for a specified purpose, or (3) grants the use of the income earned on the principal for a limited period, after which the principal amount reverts to the donor or to the donor's heirs or estate. Board-designated funds carry no such legal restrictions and are not legally classified as endowments since they may be liquidated at any time by appropriate board action.

Accountability. Because of the many different purposes for which endowment funds may be created and maintained, each endowment gift or grant must be established as a separate accounting entity. That is, the principal amounts of each restricted fund must be readily identifiable, the income earned during each accounting period must be identified with the fund that produced it, and the ultimate expenditure of such income must be easily traceable. In the absence of adequate records, the donor may appeal to the courts to reclaim his or her gift, plus interest, on the basis that the organization failed to live up to the terms and conditions of the gift or grant.

While the record-keeping obviously must be done on an individual fund basis, the organization is permitted to "pool" the assets of the various funds, including board-designated funds, for investment purposes. This allows the fund manager to employ more effective investment practices in managing the endowment's resources. For example, pooling assets permits the organization to obtain the higher yields usually available only from investment media requiring large minimum investments. It also tends to reduce brokerage and other transaction costs to relatively small percentages of both fund income and total fund assets. When assets are pooled, the participating funds share in total income, after expenses, in proportion to the average principal amount available for investment during each accounting period. In most cases, the income distributed may be used for immediate expenditure or reinvested to provide for greater future earning power of the endowment.

Legal Definitions of Endowment Income. Until the late 1960s, the general consensus among fund managers and legal counsel to nonprofit organizations held that endowment *income* consisted only of interest, dividends, and rents. Gains and losses on endowment fund assets were considered adjustments to the original principal of the endowment and hence could not be used for current expenditures in those cases in which the principal amount of the fund was restricted. This consensus was based on *trust law* which seeks to simultaneously protect the interests of both the income beneficiary of a trust and the remainderman by separating "cash" income from capital gains; income from the trust assets are distributed to the beneficiary, and capital gains (and losses) remain in the trust as permanent adjustments to the principal. When the trust expires, usually on the death of the beneficiary or on the occurrence of some other event (e.g., completion of college by the beneficiary), the individual who establishes the trust (or his or her heirs, if the individual is deceased) receives the liquidation value of the trust assets. The rationale for the separation of income from capital is thus obvious, insofar as trust law and trust management are concerned.

In 1969 the Ford Foundation's Advisory Committee on Endowment Management offered a counterargument to this traditional view by stating that endowments are subject not to *trust* law but, rather, to *corporate law*. Under corporate law, cash income and gains in capital values are considered equivalent forms of income, and both may be used for current expenditures.[1] The distinction between trusts and endowments that places endowments more logically under corporate law is the removal, in most cases, of the antagonistic interest of the residual owner of the trust. The emphasis in endowment management is thus placed on the short- and long-run spending needs of the organization and not on the residual value of the endowment at some future time. The organization itself should be permitted to determine how best to allocate total income between current spending and reinvestment for future needs.

The Prudent Man Rule. The Prudent Man Rule, stated by Justice Samuel Putnam in 1830, is often used to support the traditional position that capital gains should be treated as principal rather than income.[2] This rule, however, is equally supportive of the position taken by the Ford Foundation. The Prudent Man Rule reads in part:

> All that can be required of a trustee is that he shall conduct himself faithfully and exercise sound discretion. He is to observe how men of prudence, discretion and intelligence manage their own affairs, not in regard to speculation, but in regard to the permanent disposition of their funds.

Today's "prudent men" may be observed following what is referred to as the *Total Return Concept* in the management of their own investment portfolios, as well as in the portfolios they manage professionally for profit-seeking businesses and nonprofit organizations. In following this concept, prudent men do not make a distinction between cash income and capital gains, but instead seek high *total returns* from their investment activities. Moreover, when their objective is the accumulation of wealth for a specific purpose, these men do not hesitate to spend a part or all of the original principal amount to accomplish their goals. Thus, the prudent man rule is completely consonant with the conclusions and recommendations of the Ford Foundation's Advisory Committee in advancing the Total Return Concept in the management of endowments for nonprofit organizations.

Donor Restrictions. In spite of the general acceptance of the Total Return Concept among fund managers and its adoption by the legislatures of several states and by many governing boards, donor restrictions still take

---

1. The Ford Foundation Advisory Committee on Endowment Management, *Managing Educational Endowments* (New York: The Ford Foundation, 1969), and William L. Cary and Craig B. Bright, *The Law and the Lore of Endowment Funds* (New York: The Ford Foundation, 1969).

2. *Harvard College vs. Amory*, 26 Mass. 446, 461 (1830).

almost absolute legal precedence in determining how the individual endowments will be managed. In those instances in which a donor insists on restricting current spending to cash income only or else requires management to invest the principal in high-grade corporate bonds, that portion of the total endowment will be managed under the traditional (trust law) approach, notwithstanding the overall investment policy of the organization.

Fortunately, donor restrictions are often avoidable by negotiating favorable terms with the donor at the time the gift is offered, and they may be amended subsequent to the gift's acceptance by the organization. In order to maintain the maximum degree of flexibility in allocating available resources among competing alternative uses, management should attempt to avoid new donor restrictions that tend to interdict its investment policies. Management should also attempt to amend extant restrictions either by direct negotiation with the donors or through application of state laws favorable to the employment of the Total Return Concept. Even for those organizations whose governing boards prefer to follow the traditional approach in defining endowment income, removal of donor restrictions is a sound procedure. Once they are removed, the organization automatically places itself in a more flexible position in managing its own affairs, whether or not it ever chooses to take advantage of that position.

ENDOWMENT POLICY

Three critical areas of endowment policy require careful consideration by the governing board of an endowed organization:

1. Defining the specific objectives the endowment fund must achieve for the organization
2. Deciding whether or not to use a professional investment manager to manage the endowment fund
3. Adopting a policy regarding the use of the endowment principal

The policy statements that evolve from the discussion of the issues at the board level will differ among nonprofit organizations, of course. But several general principles that underlie sound financial management practice will tend to lend considerable uniformity to the final statement of policy in the three critical areas.

Endowment Objectives

As pointed out earlier, many endowed organizations rely to a greater or lesser extent on the income from their endowment funds to meet a portion of their current expenditures. Further, as their total cash outlays for operations increase (as a result of expansion, from the effects of cost inflation, or both), the endowment fund manager is usually put under pressure to increase the endowment income to maintain the organization in a solvent, if not liquid, financial position. In such a situation, the endowment manager may be forced to turn to investments that offer high current (or cash) yields and turn away from investments that offer comparable or usually higher yields from a combination of current cash income and capital growth. Specifically, an overemphasis on cash income from investments usually results in a portfolio containing a high proportion of bonds and equity securities that offer little prospect of increase in the total market value of the portfolio.

Without internal growth in the portfolio itself, an organization's growth and solvency may be threatened; its steadily rising need for cash income will eventually exceed the endowment's ability to generate current cash income. When that happens, the endowment will have to be increased from external sources—gifts and grants—and that is becoming an increasingly difficult and expensive task. The endowment problem thus involves the choice between allocating investment income between current and future expenditures of the organization.

High Investment Income. Under the Total Return Concept of endowment fund management, the organization is free to direct the fund manager to maximize the *amount* of investment profit over time and ignore, for accountability purposes, the *form* in which the profits are earned. The timing of cash profits may also be relegated to a lower priority in selecting portfolio assets, since realized capital gains accumulated in the portfolio may be used for current expenditures or reinvested as the governing board sees fit.

Further, the endowment fund manager is free from the burden of dealing with income taxes on investment income, since tax-exempt foundations alone are taxed on their net investment income (including capital gains), and then at a flat rate of only 2 percent. Charitable organizations pay no taxes at all on investment income, except for that earned on corporate stock purchased on margin (that is, purchased with borrowed funds). Consequently, a dollar of interest or dividends earned is equally as valuable to the endowment fund as a dollar of capital gains realized on a security transaction. Thus, the first objective of the endowment is *to produce the highest possible total return on the available resources* commensurate with the risk the governing board is willing to assume in the investment program.

Allocation of Investment Income. The second objective of the endowment involves the allocation of the income between current spending and reinvestment for future spending needs. In essence, the endowment fund is required to meet two conflicting objectives: First, *to help maintain the organization's current level of services to its clientele*, and second, *to provide for growth in the quantity and quality of its services.* Two basic approaches have been suggested to achieve a balance between these two objectives.

Fixed Rate of Return Approach. The first, called the fixed rate of return approach, begins with the selection of a "spending rate" by the organization's governing board. The spending rate is defined as a percentage of the endowment portfolio's average total assets over a given period (at market value over a year, for example) that will be used to support current expenditures. Any investment income received in excess of this fixed spending rate is reinvested in the endowment fund. The amount of income reinvested retains its identity as income (rather than becoming a part of the endowment principal), however, and may be used later for current expenditures under the Total Return Concept.

Setting the spending rate is a difficult conceptual task. Most governing boards either select the spending rate arbitrarily, or derive the rate by calculating the dollar amount that will balance the organization's budget and then dividing that amount by the portfolio value. Many organizations that employ the Total Return Concept, however, set the spending rate equal to the rate of return the endowment would normally earn if the manager followed an investment policy that concentrated exclusively on interest and divided income. The remaining income, mainly from capital appreciation of the portfolio's assets, is reinvested as earned. Exhibit 9-1 illustrates this method.

As the data in the table show, the traditional approach to endowment management (i.e., investment in bonds having high coupon yields) promised in 1986 to produce a long-run average return of 7 percent. By contrast, management felt that the Total Return Concept would produce an average return of 12 percent per year from a balanced investment portfolio of stocks, bonds, and some real assets. Thus, the spending rate was set at 7 percent and the residual income would be reinvested as earned.

In those years in which the actual return from the endowment fund fell below the spending rate (that is, in 1987 and 1988), a portion of the previous years' reinvested income was withdrawn to make up the difference. Over time, given accurate estimates of rates of return, the growth and current spending objectives will be achieved under this method, and more important, the organization will be able to budget a certain amount of income to be used for current expenditures. Current spending thus need not be curtailed because of a poor portfolio earnings performance in any given year, and portfolio growth needed to support future spending is also given due consideration in portfolio and asset planning. In other words, the portfolio manager is free to take short-run losses to increase investment earnings in the long run without significantly affecting either the organization's current budgetary needs or its planned future financial requirements.

Exhibit 9-1: Division of Endowment Income Under the Fixed Rate of Return Approach (Dollar Figures In Thousands)

	1986	1987	1988	1989
Average portfolio value	$ 2,500.0 (100.0%)	$ 2,620.0 (100.0%)	$ 2,606.9 (100.0%)	$ 2,554.7 (100.0%)
Income (dividends, interest, and realized gains)	295.0 (11.8%)	170.3 (6.5%)	130.3 (5.0%)	459.8 (18.0%)
For current expenditures, at 7% spending rate	175.0 (7.0%)	183.4 (7.0%)	182.5 (7.0%)	178.8 (7.0%)
Income reinvested (liquidated)	120.0 (4.8%)	(13.1) (0.5%)	(52.2) (2.0%)	281.0 (11.0%)
Ending portfolio value	$ 2,620.0	$ 2,606.9	$ 2,554.7	$ 2,835.7

Inflation Protection Approach. While the fixed rate of return approach places primary emphasis on current spending, the inflation protection approach emphasizes the maintenance of the purchasing power of the endowment portfolio. In this approach, an appropriate inflation rate is used to determine the level of income reinvestment required to protect the portfolio against the loss of purchasing power, and the residual income is used for current spending. In those years in which the inflation rate exceeds the portfolio's rate of return, the entire amount of the endowment income is reinvested, thus sacrificing current spending in favor of future spending.

Most organizations employing the inflation protection approach use the U.S. Department of Labor's consumer price index (CPI) as the appropriate inflation rate; however, the use of that index is generally inappropriate for nonprofit organizations. This is because the major cost element in the budgets of nonprofit entities is personnel, and personnel salary and benefits increases for individual organizations have historically tended to be either well above or well below the CPI in each period.

Since the inflation protection approach is designed to protect the purchasing power of the endowment, and the endowment is used to purchase personnel services for the most part, the appropriate inflation index is obviously closer to the expected average annual wage and salary increase for the organization's own employees than it is to the CPI.

Exhibit 9-2 illustrates how this method is applied. The income rates are those used in Exhibit 9-1, and the inflation index was set at 7.5 percent, the governing board's target for its employee annual salary and wage increases for the period. Note that in 1987 and 1988 no endowment income was available for current spending, but the 1989 portfolio value was almost a half million dollars greater under this approach than it would have been under the fixed rate of return approach.

When the two approaches are compared (recognizing, of course, the unique but realistic set of assumptions from which the data in Exhibits 9-1 and 9-2 were derived), the significant disadvantages of each become evident. On the one hand, the fixed rate of return approach produced only a 13.4 percent gain in portfolio value over the four-year period, while the inflation protection approach produced a 29.2 percent portfolio gain overall. Portfolio income under the latter approach also was higher in each of the last three years. On the other hand, total current spending for the four-year period was $296,600 less under the inflation-protection approach, and zero dollars were spent out of a total income of $317,800 in the period 1987–1988. Moreover, this policy could have placed a severe financial strain on current operations in those two years.

The comparison of these two diametrically opposed approaches to dividing portfolio income between current and future spending suggests the wisdom of avoiding inflexible policies that could impair the organization's operations in either the current period (by withholding

Exhibit 9-2: Division of Endowment Income Under the Inflation Protection Approach (Dollar Figures in Thousands)

	1986	1987	1988	1989
Average portfolio value	$ 2,500.0 (100.0%)	$ 2,687.5 (100.0%)	$ 2,862.2 (100.0%)	$ 3,005.3 (100.0%)
Income (dividends, interest, and realized gains)	295.0 (11.8%)	174.7 (6.5%)	143.1 (5.0%)	541.0 (18.0%)
For current expenditures, (residual)	107.5 (4.3%)	0 (0.0%)	0 (0.0%)	315.6 (10.5%)
Income reinvested (at 7.5%) to protect the purchasing power of the portfolio	187.5 (7.5%)	174.7 (6.5%)	143.1 (5.0%)	225.4 (7.5%)
Ending portfolio value	$ 2,687.5	$ 2,862.2	$ 3,005.3	$ 3,230.7

needed cash) or in the future (by excessive current spending). Obviously, the organization must survive the current period in order to fully benefit from larger future income. Just as obviously, price inflation will cause the organization's future expenditures to be higher than its current spending, given a constant level of operations. A better approach must combine the best features of both approaches to ensure that a realistic division of endowment income is achieved.

Flexible Approach. Chapter 7 discussed *cash budgeting*, in which the organization's operating cash inflows and outflows were forecasted for a twelve-month period. The residual values in the cash budget, when positive, are available for investment purposes, and when negative, signal a need for additional cash. To carry out its operating plans when the budget discloses a need for additional cash, the unendowed organization will have to acquire the funds externally. But the endowed organization may call upon the endowment to cover cash-flow deficits at the times they occur.

A flexible approach to the division of endowment income is based on three forecasts: (1) a cash-flow forecast, such as that provided by the cash budget; (2) an endowment income forecast; and (3) a long-term capital and program expansion forecast. The three forecasts are combined in a planning context to ensure that the organization's current and long-term operating requirements are met in a reasonable and coordinated manner. The long-run aspects of this problem are discussed fully in chapters 14 and 18. At this point, however, the flexible approach to dividing endowment income will be illustrated for a single year.

Public broadcasting radio station WGKB has an annual operating budget of $288,000 funded from a number of sources, including donations; federal, state, and local grants; cable-TV revenues; and its endowment. Grants from local business, industry, and individuals are the primary source of revenue for the organization and are the most uncertain as well, in terms of both timing and amount. These grant revenues are solicited by the station's marketing department by offering specific programs—opera, jazz, lectures, and so forth—to local patrons who underwrite the costs of the programs. The patrons are recognized as the grantors at the beginning and end of each program segment they have sponsored.

The station prepared a monthly cash budget for 1990, a summary of which is presented in the upper portion of Exhibit 9-3. The cash budget indicates that WGKB will incur an operating deficit of $36,800 for the year and experience adverse cash flows from February through September. The center portion of the table shows that the endowment maturities and income will total $168,200 for the year, and the bottom portion of the table indicates how the cash flows from the endowment will be used to maintain WGKB's operations on a current basis.

In this example, WGKB's endowment income is expected to total

Exhibit 9-3: Division of Endowment Income Under the Flexible Approach

RADIO STATION WGKB
Cash and Endowment Income Budget, 1990

[In thousands of dollars]	Jan.	Feb.	March	April	May	June	July	Aug.	Sept.	Oct.	Nov.	Dec.	Total
Operating cash flows:													
Total cash receipts	$ 26.7	$ 23.0	$ 20.2	$ 16.3	$ 18.5	$ 19.3	$ 18.0	$ 18.7	$ 20.0	$ 28.5	$ 30.0	$ 36.0	$ 275.2
Total cash Expenditures	22.0	22.5	22.8	23.5	23.0	24.2	24.8	25.0	25.0	24.7	24.9	25.6	288.0
Net cash flow	$ 4.7	$ 0.5	$ (2.6)	$ (7.2)	$ (4.5)	$ (4.9)	$ (6.8)	$ (6.3)	$ (5.0)	$ 3.8	$ 5.1	$ 10.4	$ (12.8)
Less:													
Debt service	2.0	2.0	2.0	2.0	2.0	2.0	2.0	2.0	2.0	2.0	2.0	2.0	24.0
Cash surplus (deficit)	$ 2.7	$ (1.5)	$ (4.6)	$ (9.2)	$ (6.5)	$ (6.9)	$ (8.8)	$ (8.3)	$ (7.0)	$ 1.8	$ 3.1	$ 8.4	$ (36.8)
Endowment cash flows:													
Cash income	0.6	1.3	3.3	6.0	0.7	8.3	1.0	3.6	9.8	1.1	3.3	6.7	45.7
Capital gains (losses)	0	10.0	0	0.2	1.3	0	0	0	0	0	0	0.2	11.7
Return of principal	0	90.0	0	1.8	9.0	0	0	0	0	0	0	10.0	110.8
Total	$ 0.6	$ 101.3	$ 3.3	$ 8.0	$ 11.0	$ 8.3	$ 1.0	$ 3.6	$ 9.8	$ 1.1	$ 3.3	$ 16.9	$ 168.2
Net cash surplus (deficit)	$ 3.3	$ 99.8	$ (1.3)	$ (1.2)	$ 4.5	$ 1.4	$ (7.8)	$ (4.7)	$ 2.8	$ 2.9	$ 6.4	$ 25.3	$ 146.4
Cash available for reinvestment	$ 3.3	$ 99.8			$ 4.5	$ 1.4			$ 2.8	$ 2.9	$ 6.4	$ 25.3	$ 146.4
Additional cash requirements			$ 1.3	$ 1.2			$ 7.8	$ 4.7					$ 15.0
Cumulative reinvestment (liquidation)	$ 3.3	$ 103.1	$ 101.8	$ 100.6	$ 105.1	$ 106.5	$ 98.7	$ 94.0	$ 96.8	$ 99.7	$ 106.1	$ 131.4	$ 131.4

($45,700 + $11,700 =) $57,400 for the year, while the cash operating deficit is expected to be $36,800. Thus, a total of ($57,400 – $36,800 =) $20,600 of income will be reinvested to help maintain the purchasing power of the endowment fund. The plan presented as Exhibit 9-3 also provides the investment manager with sufficient data to enable him or her to schedule maturities of short-term securities, preplan liquidation of investments, and hold sufficient liquidity in the portfolio to meet monthly cash deficits as they occur.

The major disadvantage to using the flexible approach is that the operations manager may quickly get used to relying on the endowment income to provide his or her cash needs, thus reducing the organization's incentives to control its operating costs. However, given that an organization employs excellent managers who are able to conceptualize operations in both the short and long run, the flexible approach is superior to other approaches that impose inflexible rules governing the distribution of endowment income.

Provision for Liquidity. The third objective that the endowment fund should attempt to achieve for the endowed nonprofit organization is to provide *sufficient liquidity to satisfy the organization's precautionary and speculative demands for cash.* (See chapter 8 for a discussion of the Keynesian motives for holding cash and short-term marketable securities.) The occasion of financial adversity and the sudden appearance of "profitable" or otherwise beneficial opportunities require that an organization have immediate access to spendable cash resources. The endowment policy should therefore include appropriate provision for liquidity to (1) absorb the initial shock of a sudden decline in revenues or an acceleration of cash outflows, and (2) enable management to take advantage of sudden and fleeting opportunities that promise to greatly benefit the organization or its clientele. The means of providing for adequate liquidity for these purposes involve creating a *liquidity reserve* and a *defensive reserve* within the endowment portfolio, and maintaining adequate *reserve borrowing power* within the organization itself.

Liquidity Reserve. The liquidity reserve can be created by investing a portion of the endowment's assets in short-term, highly marketable securities. The size of the reserve can usually be rather modest relative to the total market value of the portfolio since it is not necessarily designed to meet *all* emergency cash needs. Rather, it should merely be large enough to buy time for the portfolio manager while he or she conducts an orderly and inexpensive liquidation of some of the endowment's less liquid assets. In other words, the liquidity reserve is simply the first line of defense an organization will use in an emergency. Its secondary lines of defense for this purpose are the defensive reserve and its ability to borrow on a short-term basis.

Defensive Reserve. The purpose of the defensive reserve is to carry the organization through an adverse economic period without serious disruption of its programs. But while the reserve remains unused (or is being replenished after such an adverse period), the rate of return on the resources allocated to the reserve should be as high as practical. Thus, the assets held in the defensive reserve should be invested in high-quality, fixed-income securities, having maturities spanning a three- to five-year period. The reason for selecting these assets is to balance the requirements of adequate "second-line" liquidity against the need for high income for the organization's programs.

The size of the defensive reserve may be determined by analyzing the cash flows of the organization during adverse economic periods in its recent history. Management should not, however, become overly enthusiastic in allocating endowment resources to this reserve, since a large liquidity reserve will tend to reduce investment income without adding significantly to the organization's safety.

Reserve Borrowing Power. When an organization has depleted its liquidity reserve in an emergency situation, and the portfolio manager faces market conditions that limit his or her ability to liquidate other defensive investment securities without foregoing high yields or incurring sizeable capital losses in the process, the organization often will seek short-term loans from its commercial bank. The borrowed funds will be employed until such time as the emergency situation has eased or has been reversed or the securities markets have become more favorable to the liquidation of the portfolio assets. Repayment of the loans generally comes from the sale of securities out of the portfolio or improved cash inflows to the organization.

The presence of reserve borrowing power in a nonprofit organization is ensured by (1) prompt repayment of previously borrowed amounts, (2) the existence and clear evidence of continuing donor support, (3) clear evidence of excellence of management within the organization, (4) a plentiful supply of high-quality investment securities that the organization legally may offer as collateral for bank loans, and (5) maintenance of excellent relationships with the organization's principal bank of deposit. Further discussion on short-term borrowing and banker relations is presented in chapter 11.

The Investment Manager

The first recommendation enumerated in the report of the Ford Foundation's Advisory Committee on Endowment Management reads as follows: 1. "Trustees [of nonprofit organizations] should not themselves attempt to manage their endowment portfolios. The decision-making responsibility should be clearly and fully delegated to an able professional portfolio manager with a capable group of fellow professionals around him."[3]

That report also places considerable emphasis on freeing the investment manager from rigid rules regarding the types of securities that may be acquired, the mix of cash income *versus* capital gains that the endowment should produce, and the manner in which the manager should invest the endowment's resources. In short, the investment committee's function, according to the advisory committee's report, is to establish overall policy, hire a professional manager to make the investment decisions, and evaluate the portfolio's performance on a regular basis.

The basis for these recommendations is simply that professional portfolio management is a complex and time-consuming activity. The members of governing boards of nonprofit organizations are generally employed on a full-time basis in their own businesses and professions and, hence, rarely have sufficient time to devote to portfolio management, even assuming they are professionally competent to do so. In most cases, therefore, the professional portfolio manager will be able to increase annual endowment income by an amount that will exceed his or her compensation.

While the governing board can delegate its authority to make investment decisions to a professional portfolio manager, it cannot delegate its fiduciary responsibility to the organization or those who endowed it. The board remains completely responsible for the safety of the endowment principal and for achieving satisfactory returns on its employment. Some boards are therefore understandably reluctant to turn over complete control of a sizeable amount of money to "outsiders."

One method of maintaining control over the endowment assets while still delegating decision-making authority to an investment manager is by adopting the "Harvard System" of portfolio management. Under this system the investment manager, who is given decision-making authority in portfolio matters, sends immediate notices of all transactions to one or more board members. The board can then veto and require immediate reversal of any transaction about which it has serious reservations. The Harvard System has been employed by a number of organizations, including Harvard University, but the veto has apparently never been exercised by any of the governing boards operating under the system.

Selecting the Portfolio Manager. The prospective portfolio manager obviously should possess the proper credentials. Professional designations earned by individuals, such as CFA (chartered financial analyst) or CFP (certified financial planner), are indicative of adequate preparation and background knowledge in the investment area; however, they do not in themselves guarantee that the individual possesses complete competence or will provide excellent results for the organization. By contrast, the professional designation of CPA (certified

---

3. Ford Foundation, *op. cit.*, p. 9.

public accountant) suggests that the individual has adequate knowledge in the field of accounting, but it does not suggest that he or she has any knowledge of investment management.

Beyond the basic educational or professional credentials, the individual or investment firm being considered should have a demonstrated history of successful investment management for individuals, endowments, and/or pension funds of a size comparable to the organization's own portfolio. The prospective manager or firm should also possess an unimpeachable reputation for honesty and fair dealing. Once the candidate has demonstrated that he or she possesses these desirable characteristics, the organization may begin to determine whether the prospective financial manager's investment philosophy and approach are congruent with the needs and desires of the organization.

Those organizations with large endowments (i.e., several millions of dollars) often may benefit from dividing the portfolio among several investment managers. Since the approaches used by investment managers may differ appreciably, a portfolio that is diversified among managers may in the long run yield higher returns both as a result of the diversification of approaches and from the creation of a sense of competition among the managers themselves. Alternatively, such diversification of approaches may result in the endowment's assets being invested in a market portfolio of assets, which returns are more inexpensively obtained by investing in a so-called index mutual fund (a fund that, for example, holds stocks that constitute the Dow Jones industrial average). Thus, careful selection of managers is even more difficult when the portfolio is to be divided.

Measuring Investment Results. Once the investment manager has been selected, the governing board must continually monitor the portfolio's performance to be certain the manager is achieving the desired results regarding the portfolio's liquidity and defensive reserves, special (e.g., legal and donor) requirements, and especially the rate of return on investment. The simplest, most direct, and perhaps best method of measuring the returns on the endowment portfolio is on a unit of account or share value basis.

Under this method of measuring investment performance, the portfolio is divided into shares having an arbitrarily determined initial value of, say, $10 (or some other small amount). The number of shares is determined on the date this method is initiated by dividing the initial share value into the market value of the portfolio as of the close of business on that date. Subsequent transactions—additions, withdrawals, reinvestment of cash income, and so forth—are accounted for on a per share basis at the share value calculated at the close of business on the date on which each individual transaction takes place. The following example will illustrate the method.

Suppose that the market value of the Morrin Chamber Orchestra's endowment totaled $658,000 on June 1, 1989. The endowment itself comprised three separate funds: Fund A, a board-designated fund earmarked for the construction of a concert hall, and having a market value of $251,000; Fund B, a bequest to be held in perpetuity, the income from which was unrestricted, and having a market value of $191,000; and Fund C, a visiting artist fund, the income from which is used to pay the fees charged by visiting musicians and conductors, and having a market value of $216,000.[4] The governing board set the initial share value at $10.

Transactions for June and July 1989 were as follows:

June 4: The board received a $60,000 contribution for addition to Fund C.

June 29: The board transferred the surplus revenues earned from the Holiday Concert Series totaling $11,000 to Fund A.

July 10: The board paid $3,000 to a visiting soloist out of Fund C.

July 31: The board transferred $6,000 of reinvested earnings from Fund B to the general fund to pay for instrument repairs.

Exhibit 9-4 illustrates the way in which the market value of the endowment portfolio is translated into share values during the two-month period. The market value of the portfolio may be determined daily by the investment manager, who will usually have ready access to market quotations for stocks, bonds, and other financial assets. The changes in the market value of the Morrin Chamber Orchestra's investment portfolio on each of the above dates are as follows:

June 4: Increased by $9,000 from 6-1-89
June 29: Decreased by $1,000 from 6-4-89
July 10: Decreased by $2,000 from 6-29-89
July 31: Increased by $26,000 from 7-10-89

The first line in Exhibit 9-4 shows the initial value of the shares and the portfolio, and the subsequent lines illustrate the combined effects of (1) the changes in the portfolio's market value and (2) the changes brought about by the four transactions that occurred during the two-month period. The figures in columns (2) through (4) are used to calculate the changes in the share value as a result of investment income (or loss), and columns (6) through (9) show the impact each transaction had on the value of the portfolio.

Of particular interest to the governing board are the figures contained in column (5) and column (9). Column (5) indicates that the investment manager has increased the value of each share by $0.4539 (or by over 4.5

---

4. Under the strict legal-accounting definition of endowment funds, Fund A, the board-designated fund, cannot be counted as a part of the endowment. It must instead be accounted for as a restricted fund separate from both the current fund and the endowment fund. However, the board may elect to *pool* the resources held in Funds A, B, and C for investment purposes, thereby opening the way for a combined accounting and reporting treatment of the three funds.

Exhibit 9-4: Worksheet for Calculating Share Values for a Pooled Investment Fund

MORRIN CHAMBER ORCHESTRA

Calculation of Share Values of the Pooled Investment Fund
June–July 1989

(1) Date	(2) Shares outstanding prior to transaction	(3) Dollar change in the portfolio	(4) Market value prior to transaction [ending market value + (3)]	(5) Share value (4) ÷ (2)	(6) Transaction Data Value (given)	(7) Transaction Data No. shares (6) ÷ (5)	(8) Shares outstanding after transaction (2) + (7)	(9) Market value after transaction (4) + (6)
Jun 1	0	0	0	$ 10.0000	0	0	$ 65,800.0*	$ 658,000*
Jun 4	$ 65,800.0	$ 9,000	$ 667,000	10.1368	$ 60,000	5,919.0	71,719.0	727,000†
Jun 29	71,719.0	(1,000)	726,000	10.1228	11,000	1,086.7	72,805.7	737,000
Jul 10	72,805.7	(2,000)	735,000	10.0954	(3,000)	(297.2)	72,508.5	732,000
Jul 31	72,508.5	26,000	758,000	10.4539	(6,000)	(573.9)	71,934.6	752,000

* The board set the initial share value at $10.00, thus creating 65,800 shares having a combined value equal to the market value of the portfolio (i.e., $658,000).

† Rounded to nearest $1,000.

percent) in the two months ending July 31, 1989. The annualized rate of return is therefore (4.539 percent × 12/2) =) 27.2 percent. This figure is readily comparable with published annual rates of leading mutual funds, market averages, and other endowment funds to determine how well the investment manager is performing in a relative sense. For example, Exhibit 9-5 presents the approximate yields for several types of securities on June 10, 1979, August 7, 1983, and July 5, 1989. The differences in the yields on these dates provide an interesting intertemporal comparison of returns from money and capital market investments. The data in Exhibit 9-5 also show that the endowment earnings of 27.2 percent compare favorably with current investment yields.

Exhibit 9-5: **Yields on Selected Investment Securities on June 10, 1979, August 7, 1983, and July 5, 1989**

	Approximate Yields (Annualized)		
Security	*June 10, 1979*	*August 7, 1983*	*July 5, 1989*
U.S. Treasury bills	4.8%	15.6%	7.96%
U.S. Treasury notes	6.8	15.2	8.09
U.S. Treasury bonds	7.6	14.1	8.07
Prime commercial paper	5.5	16.5	9.3
Negotiable certificates of deposit			
with U.S. banks	6.0	17.2	9.3
Money market mutual funds	5.1	16.8	9.2
Eurodollars	6.1	19.3	9.2
Corporate bonds (Aaa)	8.2	15.3	9.0
Municipal bonds (Aaa)	5.7	12.5	6.6
Dividend yields, Dow Jones			
30 industrial stocks	na	5.9	3.7
20 transportation stocks	na	3.4	1.5
15 utility stocks	na	9.7	7.2

The data in column (9) of Exhibit 9-4 show the overall growth (or decline) in the endowment. These figures, of course, are influenced by both investment income and the financial transactions initiated by the board and the organization's donors. The total size of the endowment is, of course, an important statistic for financial planning and control purposes.

Of equal importance to the figures in column (9) are the values of the individual funds contained within the total portfolio. Their beginning and ending values are summarized in Exhibit 9-6. The share values and shares per transaction contained in Exhibit 9-4 are used to calculate the ending values in Exhibit 9-6.

Exhibit 9-6: **Market Values of Individual Funds in a Pooled Investment Fund**

Fund	June 1, 1989			July 31, 1989		
	Share value	No. of shares	Market value	Share value	No. of shares	Market value
A	$ 10.0000	25,100.00	$ 251,000	$ 10.4539	26,186.7	$ 273,760
B	10.0000	19,100.00	191,000	10.4539	18,526.1	193,670
C	10.0000	21,600.0	216,000	10.4539	27,221.8	284,570
Portfolio	$ 10.0000	65,800.0	$ 658,000	$ 10.4539	71,934.6	$ 752,000

Spending the Endowment Principal

The final policy area deals with the expendability of the endowment principal. While it is clear that legal restrictions will prohibit the governing board of a nonprofit organization from using the *entire* endowment principal for current or capital expenditures, it should be equally clear from the preceding discussion that the liquidity and defensive reserves must be considered expendable during a crisis. These funds are essential to maintain the organization as a "going concern" while management adjusts its operations to fit the expected future patterns of cash flows when the crisis ends. It is unthinkable to permit the organization's current operating fund to fall into bankruptcy while the principal amount of the endowment remains intact.

In the absence of a crisis, however, a trading organization may consider spending a part of the endowment principal without actually diminishing its market value. This can be accomplished by treating the endowment fund as a *lending institution* to which the organization itself may apply for credit. When an investment manager is given decision-making authority over investments, he or she may conduct arms-length transactions with the organization by extending credit to it for soundly conceived purposes, especially when repayment of principal plus interest is highly likely.

For example, an organization may apply to its own endowment manager for a loan to finance the construction of a new building, having already arranged permanent financing with, say, a mortgage lender. Such a construction loan is considered practically riskless in most cases. If the new facility is expected to pay for itself out of net operating revenues over time, the endowment manager may even negotiate permanent financing out of the endowment at a rate that is simultaneously lower than that offered by a commercial lender and equal to or higher than the portfolio could earn on assets with a comparable risk. Under these circumstances, such an arrangement is both profitable and completely rational for both the organization and the endowment manager.

Moreover, if the organization defaults on the loan, the endowment really does not suffer a financial loss greater than it otherwise would have. That is, if the organization borrowed from a commercial lender and could not repay principal and interest, the endowment's liquidity and defensive reserves would have been liquidated and paid out to the lender to save the organization from bankruptcy. Thus, little difference exists between the endowment's taking a loss as the lender or as the guarantor of the loan.

This assumes, of course, that the organization is, in fact, sufficiently creditworthy to be granted the loan in the first place and that the endowment manager is free to turn down the organization's loan application without fear of reprisal. Finally, to make this policy completely workable, the agreements between the organization and its donors should permit this type of credit arrangement.

SUMMARY

The emphasis in chapters 7 and 8 was placed on financial planning and control in a single-period context. The tools presented in those chapters were designed to provide financial flexibility and safety to the ongoing operations of the nonprofit organization. The present chapter has continued that emphasis by introducing the Total Return Concept of endowment management, among other things. Implicit in this discussion is the central role of the endowment: to assist in the accomplishment of the organization's basic goals and objectives.

This role can be properly carried out only when the goals of the endowment manager are totally consonant with those of the operations management. The formation of endowment policy and the election of an investment manager are critical decisions that face the organization's governing board. Such decisions can best be made by individuals who are familiar with the daily financial and operating requirements of the organization and yet are comfortable in dealing with the long-run issues that are essential to its survival and growth.

FURTHER READING

Two important publications dealing with the legal and managerial aspects of endowments are:

The Ford Foundation Advisory Committee on Endowment Management. *Managing Educational Endowment*. New York: The Ford Foundation, 1969.

Cary, William L., and Craig B. Bright. *The Law and the Lore of Endowment Funds*. New York: The Ford Foundation, 1969.

A valuable resource for aiding governing boards in evaluating their endowment performance is:

Williamson, J. Peter. *Performance Measurements and Investment Objectives for Educational Endowment Funds*. New York: The Common Fund, 1972.

QUESTIONS

1. How do the cash management principles examined in chapter 8 apply to endowment management?

2. What is the legal-accounting definition of an endowment? Why is the financial management definition somewhat broader?

3. What are the advantages of pooling all investment-type funds for investment purposes?

4. Contrast the treatment of endowment income under trust and corporate law.

5. What is the Prudent Man Rule? Does it support the traditional concept or the Total Return Concept of defining investment income? Explain.

6. List the three critical policy areas of endowment management.

7. Explain the fixed rate of return approach to allocating investment income. How may the spending rate be set?

8. Explain the inflation protection approach to allocating investment income. How may the inflation rate be selected?

9. In the flexible approach to allocating investment income, what three forecasts are used?

10. Why must the endowment manager establish a provision for liquidity? What are the three elements that make up the overall liquidity position?

11. How may an organization maintain an adequate reserve borrowing power?

12. Should the governing board of a nonprofit organization manage the endowment or hire a professional portfolio manager? Why?

13. What are the desirable qualities of a portfolio manager?

14. Describe the unit of account method of measuring returns on the endowment.

15. What are the advantages to an organization borrowing from its own endowment for short- and long-term purposes?

PROBLEMS

1. The investment returns earned by Crandock Academy's portfolio manager for the past three years were 12.8, 15.6, and 9.4 percent, respectively. The average market value of the portfolio in the first year was $630,000. Calculate the ending portfolio value, and the amounts spent and reinvested under the following approaches:
   a. Fixed rate of return, using a spending rate of 10 percent
   b. The inflation protection approach, using an inflation rate of 8.5 percent

2. On January 1, the market value of your organization's portfolio was $300,000, with a share value of $100. Dividend and interest income for January totaled $3,750, and the market value of the portfolio securities increased by $900 at month end. Calculate the portfolio market value, the number of shares, and the share value on January 31.

3. On January 31, your organization received a donation of 50 shares of common stock, quoted on the New York Stock Exchange on that date at $23.50 per share. You added the stock to the portfolio described in problem 2. Recalculate the portfolio's market, number of shares, and share value.

4. The endowment portfolio of the Southport City Zoo consisted of four funds having a combined market value on January 1 of $3,278,800. The market values of the individual funds are as follows:

Fund A	$ 1,873,300
Fund B	405,500
Fund C	927,600
Fund D	72,400

The financial officer of the city zoo decided to pool the funds for investment purposes and assigned a $25 share value to the portfolio. The following transactions were recorded during the first quarter of the current year:

Date	Transaction	Portfolio income between transactions
1-10	Donation to Fund A, $32,700	$ 6,300
1-22	Interfund transfer from Fund B, $6,900	5,800
2-03	Interfund transfer from Fund A, $100,000	10,900
2-12	Donation to Fund B, $75,000	(2,800)
2-20	Interfund transfer to Fund D, $10,000	8,600
3-08	Interfund transfer from Fund A, $208,000	10,500
3-16	Donation to Fund B, $25,000	15,500
3-31	Interfund transfer from Fund C, $8,200	(3,300)

a. Calculate the share values, number of shares, and portfolio market values after each transaction. Round share values to the nearest one-tenth of a cent, round number of shares to the nearest one-tenth of a share, and round portfolio values to the nearest $100.

b. Calculate the share values, number of shares, and market values for each fund on January 1 and March 31.

10

Management of Receivables and Inventory

This chapter deals with the important issue of measuring the rate of return on the investment in working capital assets — both receivables and inventories. In addition, it examines several areas of financial decision making involving each of these assets and discusses methods useful in measuring the effectiveness of an organization's receivables and inventory management programs.

The appearance of receivables and inventories on the balance sheet of a nonprofit organization implies that the organization is somehow better off with these assets than it would be without them. In other words, management elected to invest cash into, or otherwise acquire, receivables and inventories in the hope of either facilitating the achievement of its professional objectives, realizing a positive financial return on the investment, or both. If this were not the case, the ownership of these assets would cause the organization to incur at least an opportunity cost, and at the most, a measurable net cash expense related to their management. Thus, before a nonprofit organization acquires either receivables or inventories, management should ascertain whether or not the organization is likely to realize a "return on its investment" from both a professional and financial perspective.

RECEIVABLES MANAGEMENT

Nonprofit organizations may hold two basic types of receivables: (1) *accounts receivable* that arise from the extension of open-account credit to an organization's customers in the normal course of doing business and (2) *pledges receivable* that usually arise from the organization's formal fund-raising activities. Trading nonprofit organizations often will hold both types, but nontrading organizations obviously will acquire and hold only *pledges* receivable.

As illustrated and discussed in chapter 6, accounts receivable are created when a trading organization sells a product or service to a customer on an open account (a form of credit arrangement in which no formal document evidencing indebtedness is executed). This type of receivable is therefore the result of either the conversion of one asset form (inventory) into another (receivables) or the conversion of a cost of producing a service into the asset, accounts receivable. In either case, accounts receivable represent an actual investment of cash on the part of the organization, the ultimate recovery of which is critical to the completion of the cash-flow cycle and hence to the maintenance of the organization's financial health.

In contrast, pledges receivable simply happen as a result of the organization's efforts to raise money and are operationally unrelated to its central economic activities. Further, pledges receivable do not represent a cash investment by the organization, and the claims they represent are not legally enforceable. Nevertheless, their ultimate collection, or conversion into cash, is just as critical a process to the financial health of the organization as is the collection of accounts receivable. Consequently, both types of receivables must be properly managed to prevent the occurrence of unfavorable cash-flow imbalances.

Rationale for Holding Receivables

Profit-seeking business firms extend open-account credit to their customers because the offer of credit provides a competitive advantage to their products and services, thereby increasing their sales and hence the firm's profits. Where credit is an integral part of the sales program of a given industry, competition will require that firms at least match each other's credit terms. The logic behind that view is that firms selling on credit are, in effect, offering the customer a package consisting of two parts: (1) the goods they manufacture or distribute and (2) purchase financing for a limited period. While credit is only one of several factors that may influence sales volume, a firm that adopts a conservative credit policy when its competitors extend credit liberally may find that such a policy has a dampening effect on its sales.

A similar rationale underlies the extension of trade credit by trading nonprofit organizations. But instead of seeking to increase profits, such organizations offer credit terms to their customers merely to operate at or near full capacity. This is because most nonprofit organizations wish to maximize the *quantity* of output (goods or services), and they seek profits (excess of revenues over expenditures) only as a secondary or tertiary organizational goal. Competition or customary practice in an "industry" often will influence the credit policies of individual nonprofit organizations but, again, not for the same reasons as they do in the for-profit context.

The rationale for the creation of pledges receivable is different from that underlying accounts receivable. It is also quite simple: First, given a choice between making charitable contributions in one lump sum or spreading their giving over a number of periods, most donors will choose the latter method. Second, since many potential donors have limited amounts of surplus cash at any given time, they are likely to be more generous to charitable causes if they have the opportunity to budget periodic payments or are allowed to take the time to conduct an orderly and relatively inexpensive liquidation of earning assets. Hence, by carrying pledges receivable, a nonprofit organization will normally raise more than it otherwise could and will improve donor relations at the same time.

The important point here is that the nonprofit organization receives tangible benefits from investing in or acquiring both types of receivables. They are therefore important "earning" assets; however, the "investment" in these assets cannot be made without incurring certain associated costs, which costs must be controlled through appropriate management techniques.

The costs of carrying accounts receivable include the out-of-pocket expenses incurred in maintaining the accounting records, preparing invoices, effecting collections, and the like, plus the cost of the funds invested in the receivables. The costs of carrying *pledges* receivable *do not* include the cost of funds, since this type of receivable does not represent an actual investment on the part of the organization. The cost of funds may be expressed in terms of either interest income forgone (an opportunity cost), as a consequence of having to carry the receivables or as a direct interest cost to the organization, when it must borrow short-term funds in order to carry the receivables. These costs and the management techniques designed to control them are discussed in the following sections.

Management of Accounts Receivable

As mentioned earlier, only *trading* nonprofit organizations will be concerned with having to manage *accounts* receivable arising from commercial transactions with their customers. Those organizations that elect to extend trade credit will have to establish policies governing financial decisions in four areas: (1) establishing credit terms, (2) gathering credit information, (3) granting credit, and (4) collecting receivables.

Establishing Credit Terms. While the customary practices followed by similar organizations or business firms frequently dictate the nature of the credit terms offered, the nonprofit organization can design and use its own credit terms. Thus credit terms can be a dynamic instrument in an organization's overall sales effort and a positive factor in enhancing professional goal achievement and increasing the cash flows, or "return," on the investment in accounts receivable.

In setting specific credit terms, management must take full account of the organization's professional objectives as well as those of its credit policies as they relate to sales and the resultant investment in accounts receivable. The credit terms must, of course, be consonant with the economic situation of the organization's clientele or customers in order not to exclude them from receiving the benefits from its products or services.[1] In financial terms, however, the relevant policy variables are the length of credit period and the size of the cash discount offered. Together, they play a large role in determining the average collection period and, hence, the size of the investment in receivables. Moreover, they also affect the general quality of the organization's accounts receivable and, hence, its own credit quality as viewed by banks and other creditors.

Credit Period. The credit period established as a part of the organization's trade credit terms is offered as an inducement to the potential customer to make a purchase or to make it easier for the clientele to purchase the goods or services being offered for sale. The terms of credit are generally published in the seller's trade advertising copy, brochures, pamphlets, and catalogs, and always appear on the invoice accompanying the goods or services when delivered. The credit period is expressed by the notation *net 30 days* if the seller expects payment within 30 days of the date of the invoice, or *net 90 days* if the purchaser is given three months to pay, for example. Other credit periods are expressed in terms such as *net 10 EOM* meaning the seller must pay within 10 days after the end of the month in which the invoice is dated.

When management establishes a credit period for the first time or selects a credit period different from that offered by similar organizations, it should recognize the obvious trade-off inherent in that decision. On one hand, too short a credit period will not encourage prospective buyers or clients to enter the market or to choose the seller's products or services over those of the competition. Sales and service potential is therefore diminished. On the other hand, an excessively long credit period will not only tie up the organization's cash flow in

---

1. A trade-off between professional and financial goal achievement is possible in managing receivables. The decision involves a choice between social benefits and costs and financial costs and profits. A discussion of such issues is presented in chapter 13. The present discussion, however, deals only with financial implications of receivables management.

receivables for longer periods, but will also tend to increase its incidence of bad-debt losses. While the cost of lost sales, the opportunity cost of lower cash balances, and the cost of bad debts to be incurred in the future cannot be estimated with total accuracy, management must nevertheless carefully consider these factors in setting the credit period for the sale of its products and services and must do so by using a sound approach to the credit-period decision. The following section illustrates a procedure that is simple yet effective.

Lengthening the Credit Period. When an organization changes its credit policy by lengthening the credit period, it usually does so primarily in order to increase its sales. But the changes in policy also generally will produce an increase in the excess of revenues over expenditures (or net operating income). Speaking strictly in financial terms, some of the revenue from the expected increase in sales may be offset by the added costs associated with the more liberal credit policy. Also, some of the new customers affected by the organization's more liberal credit terms are likely to possess a lower credit rating on the average than its present customers. Consequently, the organization may experience increases in both its collection costs and bad-debt losses. However, such a result will not necessarily follow a change in credit terms, especially if the organization does not lengthen its credit period excessively.

In addition to those possible benefits and costs of offering more liberal credit terms to its customers, the organization must consider the costs involved in increasing its investment in receivables as a result of the higher levels of sales and the longer average collection period that will almost certainly come about. Obviously, funds allocated to support the increase in receivables cannot be utilized elsewhere within the organization. And in order for the investment in receivables to be worthwhile, the return they earn must be commensurate with that realized from other available investment opportunities.

To illustrate how management can determine the profitability of general liberalization of credit terms, consider the case of the Glory House Publishers, Inc., a nonprofit publisher of religious books used by a certain religious denomination in its Sunday School classes. The organization publishes an entire interrelated series of religious instruction materials covering preschool to adult class levels. Forecasts for the current year estimate that sales will be ten thousand units at a selling price of $500 per unit. A unit is defined as an entire series of materials, consisting of materials at five levels of instruction and containing sufficient quantities for an average class size of ten persons at each level. Individual churches may purchase one or more units or minimum quantities of selected materials, but Glory House schedules production and records sales in unit terms.

The organization's current credit terms of sale are net 30 days, but management is considering lengthening the credit period to 60 days.

This change in policy is expected to increase sales by 20% to 12,000 units, with most of the new sales coming from small, less financially sound churches.

The average total cost per unit (fixed plus variable costs) at the current level of production is approximately $450 and the per unit variable costs are currently $400. The organization anticipates that the change in credit policy will increase the average collection period from the current level of 35 days to 65 days and increase collection costs from $30,000 to $40,000 annually. Bad-debt losses are expected to increase from 1 percent to 1.5 percent of sales because most of the new sales will be to less creditworthy organizations. Finally, Glory House expects to finance the growth in its receivables by selling securities out of its unrestricted investment account, which is currently yielding a net return of 10 percent per year.

At the projected sales level, the unit sales and total manufacturing costs are:

Current unit sales × average total cost per unit: 10,000 × $450 = $4,500,000

Increased unit sales × variable cost per unit: 2,000 × $400 =   800,000

Total sales and manufacturing costs: 12,000 units $5,300,000

Thus the average total manufacturing cost at the expected sales level is $5,3000,000 per twelve thousand units, or $442 per unit. The reduction in unit cost results from spreading the fixed costs (e.g., the cost of making the printing plates, supervisor salaries, and overhead) over a greater number of units sold.

If all other expenses are assumed to remain unchanged (except for collection and bad-debt costs), management can compare the expected net operating income under each credit policy by constructing a set of pro forma statements of revenue and expense. As shown in Exhibit 10-1, Glory House can expect its net operating income to increase by ($570,000 – $420,000 =) $150,000 per year.

Exhibit 10-1: **Credit Policy Income Analysis for Glory House Publications, Inc., Using Pro Forma Statements of Revenue and Expense**

	Present policy (Net 30 days)	New policy (Net 60 days)		Change
Sales (units)	10,000	12,000	+	2,000
Sales (dollars)	$ 5,000,000	$ 6,000,000	+$	1,000,000
Manufacturing costs	4,500,000	5,300,000	+	800,000
Operating income	$ 500,000	$ 700,000	+$	200,000
Collection costs	30,000	40,000	+	10,000
Bad debt losses	50,000	90,000	+	40,000
Net operating income (exclusive of other general expenses)	$ 420,000	$ 570,000	+$	150,000

In order to realize this additional income, the organization must "invest" a certain amount of additional cash into its accounts receivable. The amount of that investment can be determined as follows:

1. Under the new credit terms, Glory House's customers will take 30 additional days to pay their bills:

Collection period under the new policy	=	65 days
Previous collection period	=	35 days
Increase in collection period	=	30 days

2. Since new customers will switch their business from other suppliers to Glory House because of their extended credit terms, average daily sales will increase. The amount that will be invested in receivables is calculated at the cost of sales.

Forecasted level of sales (at cost) = $ 5,300,000
Average daily sales at cost = $5,300,000/365 days = $ 14,521 per day

3. By combining the lengthening of the collection period with the increase in average daily sales, Glory House can calculate the resultant total increase in its accounts receivable:

Increase in investment in receivables	=	Average daily sales × Increase in collection period
	=	$ 14,521 per day × 30 days
	=	$ 435,630

In other words, in order to increase its net operating income by $150,000 per year from increased sales, Glory House will have to sell $435,630 in securities out of its unrestricted investment fund in order to finance the expected increase in accounts receivable. Since the organization will no longer earn interest income of 10 percent on those securities, its net investment income will fall by $43,563. However, its excess of revenues over expenditures will increase by a net amount of ($150,000 – $43,563 =) $106,437 per year. Stated alternatively, Glory House is giving up a 10 percent return on its investment in short-term securities in order to realize a ($150,000/$436,630 =) 34.4 percent return on an alternative investment in receivables. The organization can well afford to be more liberal in its extension of credit and should adopt the 60-day terms.

Cash Discounts. Cash discounts are usually offered by an organization principally to speed up its receivables collections and thereby reduce its average investment in receivables. The question to be answered in deciding whether or not cash discounts should be offered is whether the funds "freed up" by reducing the level of receivables can be used to earn a return that is larger than the cost of the discount.

To illustrate, suppose that Glory House adopts the net 60-day terms and wishes to determine whether it should also offer a 2 percent cash discount for payment within 10 days of the date of the invoice. Management estimates that about half of the organization's customers (in terms of dollar volume of sales) would take advantage of such a discount of it were available. If this forecast is correct, Glory House's pro forma average collection period can be calculated by taking a weighted average of collection periods:

50 percent of customers pay in 65 days: 65 days × .5 = 32.5 days

45 percent of customers pay in 10 days: 10 days × .5 = <u> 5.0 days</u>

New collection period = 37.5 days

Since half of the organization's customers will take the 2 percent discount, the cost of the cash discount will be $6,000,000 × 0.5 × 0.02, or $60,000. Since the average collection period will be reduced from 65 days to 37.5 days, the average investment in receivables is:

$$\text{Accounts receivable} = \frac{\text{Sales}}{360 \text{ days}} \times \text{Collection period}$$

$$= \frac{6.0 \text{ million}}{360 \text{ days}} \times 37.5 \text{ days}$$

$$= \underline{\underline{\$625,000}}$$

Thus, receivables will fall by ($986,300 − $625,000 =) $361,300. If the cash thus made available for other uses can be invested to earn the desired minimum rate of return of 10 percent (the yield on the organization's unrestricted fund), the additional revenue will be ($361,300 × .10 =) $36,130 per year. That figure is ($60,000 − $36,130 =) $23,870 less than the cost of the cash discount, making the addition of the 2 percent discount to the organization's credit terms appear to be undesirable. If, however, the same or nearly the same result could be obtained by a 1 percent cash discount, Glory House could profit by the more liberal credit terms.

Gathering Credit Information. Customer credit evaluation is the most important aspect of any accounts receivable management program.

Without an adequate assessment of the likelihood of prompt payment, no amount of attention to the terms of credit will produce the desired collection period or the optimum investment in receivables. However, two considerations—cost and time—limit the extent of the search for credit information on which customer evaluation must necessarily be based. For some customers, especially small ones, the cost of collecting comprehensive credit information may exceed the profitability of the account. Thus, nonprofit organizations often are forced to make decisions based on limited information. Besides the dollar costs of information collection, management must also consider how much time it can justifiably spend on new customer credit analysis. For example, a sale to a prospective customer may be lost if the shipment of goods on order is delayed by a lengthy credit investigation.

The various sources of information available to assist management in deciding whether (and how much) credit should be granted to a particular account are discussed in the following pages; however, since the customers of most trading nonprofit organizations are either individuals or other nonprofit organizations, these traditional sources of information tend to be of limited value for decision purposes. Nevertheless, some information is generally better than none at all.

Financial Statements. The prospective business customer's latest available set of financial statements is a very useful source of credit information. Such statements are most readily obtained from the customer himself, since most business and nonprofit organizations expect to provide their current statements to suppliers. In general, firms in sound financial position are happy to demonstrate that fact.

Credit Ratings and Reports. While financial statements provide the nonprofit organization with an excellent source of information about a customer, there can be significant time delays in receiving the information. Consequently, an organization may find that it has lost an order (and possibly a customer) in the process of obtaining the "best" information available. This will be particularly true if prompt delivery is of major importance to the customer. Because of the impracticality of direct investigation, especially where small orders are involved, organizations selling on credit may rely a great deal on their commercial banks, of course, but they may also use the services provided by mercantile agencies or credit bureaus for their credit information.

Perhaps the best-known source of this type is Dun & Bradstreet, Inc., which provides two services of primary importance to the organization seeking information about its *business* customers: its *Reference Book* and written credit reports. The *Reference Book*, containing the names of over three million business establishments, is issued six times a year to Dun & Bradstreet subscribers. Through a key system of letters and symbols, information is provided concerning the line of business, the company's estimated net worth, and Dun & Bradstreet's opinion of the creditworthiness of the firm.

In addition to its rating service, Dun & Bradstreet provides credit reports on request on individual business firms. These include a brief history of the business, biographies of the owners or chief officers, a description of the method of operation, a simple balance sheet, and results of a trade check of suppliers. This last information is of great interest to the organization requesting the report. It summarizes suppliers' recent payment experience with the company and indicates whether its payments to suppliers are discounted (paid in advance), prompt (paid more or less on time), or past due (generally paid well after the due date).

A source of information concerning the payment habits of individuals are the national credit bureaus, such as Equifax, Inc., who have owned or affiliated credit bureaus. Ordinarily, a supplier seeking credit information on a potential customer located in another city will ask his or her bank to request the desired data from either the credit bureau or a local bank in every state and most major cities. Credit inquiries to Equifax facilitates the gathering of credit over considerable distances.

Commercial Banks. Most commercial banks of at least moderate size have credit departments that perform credit investigations for their customers. Generally, the banks will access the credit files maintained by the national credit bureaus. Ordinarily, a supplier seeking credit information on a potential customer located in another city will ask his or her bank to request the desired data from either the credit bureau or a local bank in the prospective buyer's area. Such requests are usually made only when the amount of credit to be extended is substantial. But bank credit information is especially useful because it usually includes the level of bank balances maintained and data relating to extensions of bank credit.

Other Sources. Mercantile agencies, credit bureaus, and commercial banks are the most commonly used sources of credit information; but insights into a customer's ability and willingness to pay may be gathered from a number of other sources. Personal contact with the customer often can provide management with accurate impressions of the way in which customers conduct their businesses. Information obtained from personal visits by the manager are particularly useful in this regard, and such visits may also prompt customers not to be delinquent.

The organization's own credit-gathering experience yields the best information on its present and former customers and clients. In a real sense, each credit extension is a means of "buying" information about a particular customer's payment habits. Thus, a customer's cumulative payment history is suggestive of the payments pattern to be expected from him or her in the future, assuming, of course, that no dramatic changes take place that alter his or her financial position. Thus, trading organizations should always maintain complete records on the payment histories of their customers.

Credit-Granting Decision. After all the readily available credit information concerning a potential credit customer has been assembled, it must be analyzed to determine the customer's creditworthiness. When an applicant's credit standing is either far above or far below established credit standards, creditworthiness (or its absence) is easy to determine. The difficult decision relates to customers who are marginally creditworthy at best. In those cases in which "profits" are an important consideration, managers must attempt to balance potential profitability against potential loss from default. Experienced managers can often make such judgments intuitively, but the use of certain techniques of analysis will provide explicit information on which sound judgment can be based. Even when an organization's objectives do not include earning an excess of revenues over costs, management still must make sound credit decisions.

Using Profit as a Criterion. Assume, for example, that Glory House has just received a credit request involving an order for one unit of educational materials from a newly formed church in a distant city. Its experience in dealing with new churches suggests that one of two equally likely outcomes will occur. First, if the church fails in its primary mission, Glory House will be unable to collect any of the amount due. It will consequently lose an amount equal to the *variable cost* of the merchandise shipped to the church—in this example, $400 per unit sold at an invoice price of $500.[2] Alternatively, if the church succeeds, Glory House will receive orders for one or more additional units during the year, depending on how quickly the church's membership grows. Each unit sold will contribute $100 toward coverage of fixed costs and "profits." The structure of the decision facing Glory House may be summarized in a payoff matrix, illustrated in Exhibit 10-2.

Parts A and C of the matrix show that if Glory House refuses to extend credit, it will neither gain nor lose regardless of what happens to the church. If the organization does extend credit and the church pays its bill, as in part B of the matrix, the payoff from the sale of one unit will be $100 in "profits." Conversely, should credit be granted and the church fail, Glory House will lose $400 (the variable cost of one unit), as shown in Part D of Exhibit 10-2.

Before making the credit decision, management must analyze the church's financial position to determine how long it is likely to continue in its mission and estimate the likelihood of its maintaining the account

---

2. Variable costs are used as the value of the merchandise shipped to customers, and hence the *investment* in receivables, since this is the amount of *cash* spent on producing the product. Fixed costs will continue to be incurred, regardless of the level of sales. Thus, the difference between selling price and variable costs is the item's contribution to fixed-cost coverage and to the excess of revenues over total costs.

Exhibit 10-2: **Payoff Matrix for Glory House Publishers Credit Decision**

	Refuse Credit		Grant Credit	
Church pays	A. Incurs cost of	$ 0	B. Incurs cost of	$ 400
	Receives in cash	$ 0	Receives in cash	$ 500
	Net gain (loss)	$ 0	Net gain (loss)	$ 100
Church fails	C. Incurs cost of	$ 0	D. Incurs cost of	$ 400
	Receives in cash	$ 0	Receives in cash	$ 0
	Net gain (loss)	$ 0	Net gain (loss)	($ 400)

on a current basis. If the church expects to purchase five units (or $2,500) of educational materials per year from Glory House, and the maximum credit amount is $500, the most Glory House can lose at one time is the $400 cost of one unit. However, if the church keeps its account current for one year, Glory House stands to realize a net return over variable costs of (five units × $100 =) $500.

If, during the second year of its life, the church fails to pay its account, Glory House would lose its investment in the last order shipped, or $400, as shown in part D of the payoff matrix. But since the first year's total gain from the relationship with the church was $500, the overall gain after the $400 loss amounts to $100. Thus, the longer the church continues to succeed, the more profitable the relationship will be, provided, of course, that the account is maintained on a current or almost current basis over the period.

The decision rule should be clear: Since a trading nonprofit organization cannot carry out its societal mission without selling its goods or services, it should extend credit to customers whenever it is reasonably certain of recovering its investment in that relationship *over time*. Note that the recovery of the investment may take several months or even in excess of a year.

Selling Products or Services at or Below Cost. If an organization's budget requires it to realize even a very small portion of its total revenues from the sale of its goods or services in order to remain solvent, the credit decisions become just as important as when receivables collections are the organization's sole source of funds. In such cases management, for goal achievement purposes, may price the organization's products or services below the costs of production and distribution, but it must extend credit wisely and then fully collect *all* the receivables it creates in the process. To do otherwise is to invite serious financial difficulties for the organization.

Since organizations that price their products at or below cost cannot cover bad-debt expenses with "profits," the objective of receivables management becomes the minimization or elimination of bad debts. If bad debts are inevitable because of the economic status of the organization's clients or customers, the cost of bad debts must be taken into account in the organization's pricing decision.

For example, suppose that Health Care Rental, a nonprofit organization specializing in renting hospital and health care equipment to the medically indigent, prepared its annual budget calling for total revenues of $300,000, of which $100,000 is to be realized from the rental of wheelchairs and hospital beds. Its customers are handicapped and elderly persons whose Medicare and Medicaid coverage will pay for the rental charges. About 10 percent of the customers will become bad debts, however. Average rental charges total $100 per unit from renting the 1,000 units currently owned by the organization.

Since 10 percent of the rentals will eventually prove to be uncollectible, cash collections on account will be equal to total charges less 10 percent, or

Total charges = 1,000 units × $100	=	$ 100,000
Less uncollectible rentals ($100,000 × .10)	=	10,000
Cash collections		$ 90,000

If the organization must collect $100,000 from its rental operations, it must price its rentals high enough to compensate for bad-debt losses. The break-even unit price (BEUP) that will achieve the desired results can be calculated as follows:

$$\text{BEUP} = \frac{\text{Desired cash collections}}{\text{Expected rental volume } (1 - \text{Bad-debt percentage})}$$

In the present example,

$$\text{BEUP} = \frac{\$100,000}{1,000 \text{ units } (1 - .10)}$$

$$= \frac{\$100,000}{1,000 \text{ units} \times .90}$$

$$= \frac{\$100,000}{900 \text{ units}}$$

$$\text{BEUP} = \$ 111.11$$

In other words, if the organization rents all 1,000 units at an average rental charge of $111.11 per unit, it will bill a total of (1,000 units × $111.11 =) 111,111. Then 10 percent, or $11,111, will be uncollectible, leaving $100,000 in cash receipts for the year.

Collecting Receivables. The final step in managing credit extensions is the collection of receivables. Customers who pay promptly—and generally most customers will—require little or no collection effort. Some customers will at least be slow in paying, while a small percentage of all accounts will prove to be ultimately uncollectible in full. The objective of collection policies is to speed up slow-paying accounts and reduce the percentage of bad debts, without affecting the value of the organization's objectives to its clientele or reducing the inherent profitability in such accounts (where profitability is the relevant criterion).

Speeding up slow-paying accounts requires care and patience. When an organization feels it must collect the debt owed to it, the key concern is how far past due an account should be allowed to go before stringent collection procedures are initiated. Unfortunately, there is no simple solution. For example, if the collection policy is too lenient, customers with a natural tendency toward slow payment may become even slower to settle their accounts, and the incidence of bad debts is likely to increase. Overly aggressive collection efforts, however, may offend good customers who inadvertently may have failed to make payments when due, thereby causing a loss of sales (and profits) and goodwill.

Generally speaking, most customers are strongly motivated toward prompt payment because they are well aware that continued slow payment is quickly noted in all quarters, both by credit extenders—suppliers and banks—and by credit-reporting agencies. Thus, in most cases, a politely worded "reminder" letter is sufficient to bring a temporarily delinquent account to current status. But if the first letter brings no response, additional letters of more serious tone may be sent. Next may come a telephone call. If none of those evokes an appropriate response, the organizations, as a last resort, may have to take legal action against the delinquent customer.

Legal Action. Regarding legal action, if the manager knows that a customer is having serious financial difficulty, the threat of legal action may have little effect on his ability to pay but could speed up his decision to seek legal relief from his financial distress. When a firm declares bankruptcy and the action proceeds to the firm's liquidation, suppliers may find that there is little left to satisfy their claims after legal and administrative expenses and secured creditors are paid. Thus, a nonprofit organization may find that legal action against a delinquent customer is simply too expensive a course of action to take. A more thorough credit investigation may be more costly at the onset of a relationship with a new customer, but it may be less expensive in the final analysis.

Collection Agencies. Many nonprofit organizations use commercial collection agencies to collect their past-due accounts. While specific arrangements can be tailored to meet most special requirements an organization may wish to impose, the operations of most agencies are fairly standard.

Collection agencies prefer to receive past-due accounts as soon as possible after they become delinquent or are classified as such by the organization's internal policies. This is because the likelihood of ultimate collection of the account diminishes as the account ages. Communication between the agency and the debtor generally will clearly reveal that the agency is "in charge" of the collection process and that payments must be mailed or brought to the agency's offices.

Collection agencies normally will retain a percentage of total collections they effect. The percentage rate is seldom fixed but instead is negotiated based on the age of the accounts to be collected, the socioeconomic profile of the typical debtor, the nature of product or service sold by the organization, and so forth. Since the agency is a profit-seeking business, the rate it will offer and attempt to secure will be relatively high—25 percent to 35 percent in most cases. In other cases, when the debtors are inclined to leave town or the likelihood of full payment is extremely small, for example, the rate may be as high as 50 percent to 75 percent. In such cases, the returns to the agency are small and its collection expenses are relatively high. If the agency is at all successful, the organization stands to receive 50 percent to 25 percent of a portion of its receivables it otherwise would have written off completely.

Thus, the cash returns, rather than the percentage rates, should govern the decision of whether or not to employ a collection agency. For example, an organization probably will not be able to set up an in-house collection department and realize cash inflows (net of cash expenditures) equal to those that an agency might produce for it. Thus, the arrangement with a commercial collection agency is generally beneficial to the organization with a large dollar volume of uncollectible accounts.

Management of Pledges Receivable

As mentioned earlier, pledges receivable arise out of an organization's normal fund-raising activities. They therefore do not represent a true investment on the part of the recipient organization. But by carrying pledges receivable, the organization incurs two types of cost: (1) the administrative costs required to account for and collect the pledges and (2) an opportunity cost arising from the delay in the receipt of cash thus pledged.

First, the organization that is willing to let its donors delay their donations for a period, or spread them over a number of months or even several years, must obviously record the pledges, organize them so that they can readily be accounted for, and send out timely reminders or payment notices to those who have pledged cash donations. The cash receipts must then be matched with the donors' records, deposited in a bank account, and accounted for in the organization's books. Even when fully staffed with volunteer help, the organization will incur the cost of paper, envelopes, and postage. And in those cases in which the donors have changed their minds about honoring their pledges, the organization will have to spend additional money, time, and effort in ascertaining that fact before it will write off those pledges to the *allowance for uncollectible pledges* account. Since pledges are not generally considered as legal debts of the donor, the organization can do little else besides send gentle and perhaps poignant reminders when pledges become past due.

Second, since cash can earn interest when invested in earning assets, any delay in collecting the cash from donors will cause the organization to incur an opportunity cost equal to the lost interest income on the amount of the donation. For example, if a donor promises to give an organization $1,000 at the end of three months, the organization is giving up the interest it could have earned on the donation if it were made immediately in cash. At, say, 5.5 percent (from a passbook savings account), the opportunity cost equals ($1,000 × .055 × 3/12) $13.75. If the organization can earn a 10 percent interest return on its investments, the opportunity cost increases to ($1,000 × .10 × 3/12) $25.00. Theoretically, the donor receives the interest income that the recipient organization "gives up" under a pledge of cash arrangement and hence can be more generous in his or her giving as a consequence. However, considerable doubt exists that the opportunity cost to the organization is equal to or less than the enhanced generosity of the donors who pledge cash gifts at future times.

Thus, while permitting donors to make pledges instead of immediate cash gifts may make an organization's fund-raising efforts appear easier and more productive, the recognition of administrative and opportunity costs suggests the existence of a trade-off of costs against benefits. Unfortunately, opportunity costs are subject to errors of estimation, and the implied benefits of enhanced giving are difficult to measure in dollar terms. The decision to accept pledges in lieu of cash gifts therefore must be based largely on subjective criteria.

Many nonprofit organizations accept pledges only for relatively large amounts (e.g., $1,000 and more). They consider the administrative and collection costs simply too high to justify the acceptance of pledges of smaller sums. Other organizations accept pledges only from businesses, citing the better collection experience as the principal justification for this policy. Still other organizations accept pledges only after all efforts to obtain a cash gift from a donor have been exhausted. Finally, those organizations that solicit funds over the telephone receive most, if not all, of their donations in the form of pledges. Collection experience varies. As compared with other types of campaigns, however, the administrative and collection costs per dollar of contributions received are very high.

While that should not be interpreted as a blanket condemnation of telephone solicitations, their overall effectiveness vis-à-vis other methods has not been clearly demonstrated.

Shifting the Costs of Carrying Receivables

The costs of holding, administering, and collecting accounts receivable and pledges receivable of *individuals* can be, and usually are, high. The nonprofit organization may be able to shift a large portion of these costs to bank or credit card companies by entering into contracts with them that enable individual consumers (and donors) to pay for products or services (and make cash gifts) using local bank or nationally distributed credit cards.

The credit card contracts generally require the merchant (in this case, the nonprofit organization) to pay a percentage of total charges to the credit card company to cover the credit and collection costs shifted to them. This fee—usually 2 percent to 5 percent of charges—is discounted (deducted) when the charge tickets are processed by the credit card company's paying agent. In some cases, however, the company will waive the fee for nonprofit organizations, hoping to cover their incremental expenses by collecting finance charges from the credit card holder.

Unfortunately, not all consumers are credit card holders, and some that are prefer not to use their cards in all instances. Thus, nonprofit organizations that enter into agreements with credit card companies may still have to carry receivables and incur their associated administration and collection costs. But to the extent that customers or donors use their credit cards, the organization's opportunity and real costs of carrying receivables will be lower, especially if the credit card company waives the customary merchant fee.

Those trading organizations that carry *business* receivables may also be able to shift a portion of their costs to a third party. Business firms that specialize in purchasing accounts receivable or acting as collection agents for other businesses and nonprofit organizations may be found, especially in urban areas. These firms, most often known as *finance companies*, operate in a manner similar to that of the credit card companies; that is, they generally purchase the receivables at a discount and collect the amounts due for their own accounts. They usually bear the burden of all administrative expenses, including bad debts, leaving their clients free from the bother of even accounting for the receivables. In most cases, however, the finance companies reserve the right to reject any accounts that they feel will not be collectible.

In some cases the finance company will take the accounts on a "best effort" basis. That is, instead of purchasing them from the organization, the finance company will attempt to collect them for the organization's account, billing it either on a flat rate or on a percentage basis. The organization must collect or charge off those accounts that the finance company fails to collect after giving its best effort to the task.

Still other arrangements are common. For example, the finance company may purchase the receivables *with recourse*. In this case, the organization agrees to repurchase any accounts that the finance company is unable to collect. And as mentioned earlier, the arrangement with the finance company may permit it to select only the best accounts, leaving the greater credit risks for the organization to collect on its own.

In most cases the organizations will request that the collection agencies not reveal their role in the collection process. When such requests are made and honored, the customers and donors are never aware that their accounts have been sold by the organization. The finance company will ask that checks be made payable to the organization and the remittance be mailed to it at a post office box address. The organization permits the finance company to endorse the checks and deposit them to its own account. The organization notifies and "bills" the finance company as new receivables are created by sending it copies of the customers' invoices. The finance company in turn sends the organization a check in the amount of the invoices, less the discount, of course, after receiving the invoices.

The cost of this service is quite high, generally in excess of 20 percent of the receivables discounted. However, the finance company's charges may be less than the total cost incurred by the organization to administer and collect the receivables for its own account. Further, under a purchase arrangement, the discounted receivables are converted into cash immediately, thus enabling the organization to put its cash to work without having to wait until its customers pay their bills. Thus, in deciding whether or not to discount its business accounts receivable, a nonprofit organization must compare the cost of the discount with the expected savings in administrative and collection costs, plus the reduction in opportunity costs of having immediate access to cash.

For example, suppose Chester College is considering selling the pledges it will solicit during its annual fund-raising campaign to an agency that agreed to accept all pledges without recourse; that is, it agreed to bear the loss of all pledges that turned out to be uncollectible. The agency contract called for the purchase of the pledges at 90 percent of their face value plus a flat fee of $10,500 to cover the administrative costs of transferring the school's donor records to its computer.

The school expects to receive a total of $340,000 in pledges during the campaign. Past experience indicates that uncollectible pledges will likely equal 2 percent of total pledges, and the school's accounting office estimated that half of the pledges would be collected in two months, with the remainder taking an average of four additional months to collect. Total cost of collecting the pledges last year was $7,200, but inflation has increased the school's total budget by 10 percent since then. Finally, the college invested its surplus cash in a portfolio of assets having a current annual yield of 12 percent. The outlook for the next six months suggested that the portfolio yield would be stable at existing levels.

The agency contract includes two costs:

10 percent discount ($340,000 × .10)	=	$ 34,000
Flat fee	=	10,500
Total cost of selling pledges	=	$ 44,500

The savings that the college will realize include:

Avoidance of uncollectible pledges ($340,000 × .02)	=	$ 6,800
Collection costs	=	7,200
Inflation effects on collections ($7,200 × .10)	=	720
Total savings	=	$ 14,720

In addition, the college will receive the cash immediately, rather than having to wait until the pledges are collected. Thus, another benefit of the contract is the interest income that the college will earn from an early receipt of the cash. The college will receive 90 percent of the pledges, less the fee of $10,500, or $295,500. Half of that amount will be received two months earlier than would otherwise be the case, and the other half will be received six months earlier. Thus, given a 12 percent annual return expected on invested cash:

Interest earned on cash received 6 months early: $147,750 × .12 × 2/12 =	$	2,955
Interest earned on cash received 2 months early: $147,750 × .12 × 6/12 =	$	8,865
Increase in interest income	=	$ 11,820

Total cash benefits promised under the contract with the agency are ($14,720 + $11,805 =) $26, 525, an amount that is $17,975 less than the total cost of selling the pledges. In this case, Chester College will be better off collecting the pledges itself rather than entering into the proposed agency contract.

EVALUATING RECEIVABLES MANAGEMENT

The basic purpose of credit extension by trading nonprofit organizations is to increase sales and thus achieve its professional goal of increasing the quantity of goods or services sold. In strict financial terms, however, credit terms of sale should not be so restrictive that sales to potentially profitable accounts are jeopardized. Conversely, terms should not be so liberal that collection costs and bad-debt losses exceed potential gains in profitability. Putting the professional aspects of the matter aside for the moment, the organization should strive to operate in such a manner that the gains from any incremental sales induced by credit extension more than offset all the costs of credit extension, including bad-debt losses. Very often, however, receivables managers are judged solely by the percentage of bad debts to sales. The use of that criterion alone makes as little sense as judging the financial success of the organization by examining its costs and ignoring its sales (or vice versa).

It is difficult to evaluate receivables management on almost any basis, especially in the nonprofit context. One of the major problems is that of not being able to measure all of the relevant dollar costs, not to mention the professional costs of lost sales. Many of the dollar costs, such as bad-debt losses, may easily be obtained through the accounting system. However, major measurement problems present themselves when management attempts to identify the costs of rejecting potentially profitable accounts that did not meet its credit standards. These so-called opportunity costs are invisible in the sense that they do not appear on the financial statements, but they do place a kind of ceiling on future sales and income.

Another problem is that many of the methods for evaluating the financial management of accounts receivable tend to measure two things at once: the efficiency of the credit-granting process and the efficiency of the collection process. For instance, if an organization shows a higher level of accounts receivable in relation to sales (a lower receivables turnover) in one period than in previous ones, how can management assign a cause to this event? Are the credit standards too lenient, or has there been some laxity in collection? What is needed are performance measures that, when viewed collectively, produce some reasonably objective judgment about the efficiency with which the organization is managing its receivables.

The turnover of accounts receivable is one measure of the effectiveness of credit policy. It is computed, of course, by dividing annual credit sales by average (or year-end) volume of receivables. Its purpose is to measure the liquidity of the receivables. An annual turnover rate of six means that, on the average, the organization collects its receivables six times each year or every two months. If the turnover rate is four, the collection period is a month longer (three months instead of two). High turnover rates for receivables may indicate that restrictive credit extension policies are screening out slow-paying customers. This may be good if the collection costs are higher than the profit these customers are generating; but if the customers are profitable, the high turnover rates may signal a poor credit-granting policy. In contrast, low turnover rates may indicate that the organization is either pursuing lenient credit terms or is lax in its collection efforts. Again, the low rates may be interpreted as either a good or bad sign, depending on the facts underlying the creation and implementation of the receivables policy.

A more refined measure that may be used in conjunction with accounts receivable turnover rates is an "aging" of the accounts receivable. A typical aging schedule might appear as shown in Exhibit 10-3. By aging

Exhibit 10-3: **Aging Schedule of Accounts Receivable**

Period outstanding	Amount outstanding	Percent
30 days or less	$ 3,200,000	66.66%
31-60 days	800,000	16.66
61-90 days	600,000	12.25
Over 90 days	200,000	4.43
Total receivables	$ 4,800,000	100.00%

the receivables, or measuring the dollar amounts that have been outstanding for periods spaced at regular intervals, management may be able to detect any developing trend toward a slower rate of receivables collections. In this sense, aging of the accounts receivable can provide a kind of early warning device useful in predicting a deterioration in receivables quality and an increase in the probability of large bad-debt losses. Provided general economic conditions have not changed significantly, any noticeable increase in the percentage of "old" receivables may be the result of either an easing of credit standards or shortcomings in collection procedures, or both. While management may not be able to pinpoint the problem on the basis of the aging analysis alone, the analysis will at least indicate where to begin looking for the answers it must have before appropriate corrective actions can be initiated.

INVENTORY MANAGEMENT

Many trading nonprofit organizations maintain inventories of various products. For example, most colleges and universities hold inventories of food, paper supplies, books, and gift items; farmers' cooperatives hold seeds, implements, fertilizer, and tractor parts in inventory; and research organizations maintain supplies of computer paper and cards, chemicals, paper, animals, and so forth. For these and similar organizations, inventory management is an important function. Other types of inventories, such as the permanent collections of museums and art galleries, are classified as *fixed assets* and are under the direct control of professional managers, rather than financial managers. The decision rules discussed in chapters 13-15 and 17-18 apply to the management of those kinds of assets.

The goal of inventory management for organizations that purchase products for resale or distribution to their clientele is to *minimize the costs associated with the investment* in that group of assets. At the same time, the organization must maintain a sufficient quantity of merchandise on hand to ensure that its customers' and clients' needs can reasonably be satisfied under fluctuating, or uncertain, demand and supply conditions.

The most widely used approach to solving the cost minimization problem employs the concept of an economic order quantity (EOQ) that enables management to determine the optimum inventory level for a given item over a specified period. The precise definition of inventory costs is essential to the proper application of the methodology prescribed by the EOQ approach.

Inventory Costs

Inventory costs may be classified into two categories: *acquisition costs* and *carrying costs*. *Acquisition costs* are those cash expenses, excluding the purchase price of the inventory, necessary to effect delivery of inventory items to the purchasing organization. When inventories are purchased from outside sources, the purchaser incurs order costs, which include the costs of preparing and processing requisitions, purchase orders, and other kinds of administrative paperwork.

Acquisition costs per order are generally independent of the size of the order. For example, the cost of the paperwork sent to a supplier to order one unit is the same as that required to order fifty units. Larger orders, however, will mean that the organization will have to "acquire" inventory less frequently and, hence, over time reduce its total acquisition costs.

The other category of inventory costs are the expenses associated with physically maintaining the inventory. These are called *carrying costs* and, in contrast to acquisition costs, tend to increase in proportion to the size of the inventories being maintained.

One component of the cost of maintaining inventory is an internal transfer related to the cost of obtaining the funds for investment in inventories. That cost may be set equal to the total value of the inventory multiplied by either the interest rate the organization pays for short-term credit or an opportunity cost measured by the rate of return which can be expected on an alternative investment opportunity with the same degree of risk. As in the case of accounts receivable, if funds are not invested in inventories, they can be invested in short-term securities from which the organization can expect to receive a return on its investment. Therefore, whether it uses external or internal sources of funds, the organization incurs an "interest charge" in connection with maintaining inventories.

In addition to interest costs, the maintenance of inventory almost always involves *storage costs*, which are incurred by either leasing or owning warehousing space. Warehouse ownership gives rise to such items as heat and light, janitorial service, warehouse labor, depreciation, and taxes. While such costs are fixed in the short run, increases in the inventory level may increase the costs if the organization outgrows its existing facilities.

Other costs, which tend to vary more immediately with changes in the inventory level, include insurance premiums, taxes, and the costs of deterioration and obsolescence. Insurance premiums are usually tied to the value of the inventory; in many locales, the value of the inventories on hand is often included in the assessed valuation of its property for local tax levies.

The two other costs—obsolescence and deterioration—are often important factors in the determination of the size of inventories some organizations carry. A museum gift shop, for example, may find that some of its stock is continually subject to obsolescence because of the rapid changes in tastes and the seasonal nature of the demand for its products. King Tut souvenirs sold at record levels during the exhibit's tour of the United States in 1979 and 1980; however, the demand for items has since all but disappeared. Since the risk of inventory obsolescence generally increases with the passage of time, the more inventory on hand, the greater the risk the owner incurs. Thus, the presence of such a potential cost encourages low inventories for some operations of that type.

Deterioration represents another kind of potential inventory loss, the exact nature and timing of which varies greatly from product to product. In the case of food, it may be rapid and irreversible, while in the case of durable goods it is a slow but often repairable process. Whatever its nature, deterioration gives rise to higher costs or lower profits because the items involved must be either scrapped, reworked, or sold at a loss. In such circumstances, too, inventories subject to rapid or irreparable kinds of deterioration are best kept at minimum levels.

Economic Order Quantity (EOQ) Approach

As indicated in the preceding section, certain costs will increase as the level of inventory increases, whereas others will remain fairly constant in dollar amounts in the short run. If all of the relevant costs increased as the level of inventory increased, the best policy would be to carry no inventories. Conversely, if unit costs decreased as the level of inventory increased, then the organization could maintain as much inventory as it deemed appropriate to keep it from running out (that is, to prevent *stock-outs*). Since neither is the case, management must consider a number of different levels of inventory for a particular item and select that level which yields the lowest total cost.

The EOQ approach to inventory management helps the organization to accomplish that goal. Its most effective form is called the order-quantity-reorder-point system of inventory control. This particular inventory control system begins with the specification of three parameters for a given inventory item: (1) reorder point, defined as a specified level of inventory at which additional units must be ordered to prevent stock-outs; (2) order quantity; and (3) minimum inventory that must be maintained.

Reorder Point. To illustrate this system, assume that the director of the city zoo decides to maintain a minimum inventory of 20 bushels of grain to supplement the diets of several types of grazing animals. Suppose also that the director generally purchases the grain in lots of 60 bushels that are delivered at one time. In order to determine the point at which an additional supply of grain must be ordered, two factors must be estimated: (1) the length of time required for the farmer to deliver a replacement order, and (2) the rate at which the animals consume the grain. Assume that two days are required for delivery to the city zoo and that the usage rate is 240 bushels per month. The reorder point may be determined using the following equation:

Reorder point = Minimum inventory level + (Delivery time × Usage rate)

The reorder point and the minimum inventory level are expressed in *units* of inventory. The delivery time and usage rate are expressed in the same units of time; that is, they both must be stated as days, weeks, or months. In the present example, since delivery time is expressed in days, the usage rate must be translated from 240 bushels per *month* to the equivalent rate of 8 bushels per *day*.

The inventory data, when inserted into the reorder point equation, indicate that the

Reorder point	=	20 bushels + (2 days × 8 bushels per day)
	=	20 bushels + 16 bushels
	=	36 bushels

Thus, the director should place an order for 60 bushels when the inventory level reaches the reorder point of 36 bushels in stock. If all goes as expected (if the animals actually consume 240 bushels of grain per month and if the replacement order is received two days after the order is placed), the level of inventory will take on the saw-toothed pattern as illustrated in Exhibit 10-4.

Exhibit 10-4: **Inventory Pattern for the City Zoo Under the EOQ Approach**

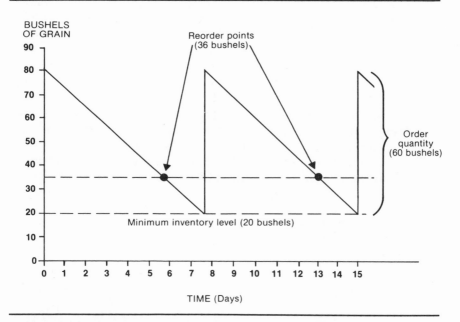

While the application of the system is simple in concept, it can only be effective if management can accurately estimate the proper size of the order quantity and its minimum inventory requirement. The definitions of those two important parameters are covered in the following sections. Worth noting at this point, however, is that the reorder point is independent of the *order quantity* but dependent on the *minimum inventory level.* That is, the reorder point will remain at 36 bushels in the example regardless of how many bushels the city zoo orders at one time. But if the minimum inventory level changes, so too will the reorder point.

EOQ. The order size that results in the lowest cost per period is known as the *EOQ,* and is the amount of material management should purchase for inventory replacement per period if it wishes to have the optimum inventory level with respect to total costs, as defined here. The function of the EOQ in this approach to inventory management is to minimize total inventory costs. This is accomplished by finding the particular order size that produces the lowest sum of acquisition plus order costs. The following relationships between order size and inventory costs prescribe the methodology involved in finding the correct order size—the EOQ:

1. Acquisition costs *fall* as order size *increases.*
2. Carrying costs *increase* as order size *increases.*

Typically, as the order quantity for a particular inventory item is increased, acquisition costs tend to decrease at a faster rate than inventory carrying costs increase. Consequently, the total inventory cost per period falls as the order size becomes larger. At some point, however, acquisition costs will decrease at a slower rate than the rate of increase in carrying costs. At that point, total inventory cost reaches a minimum and then begins to rise as order size increases further. The order size that results in the lowest cost per period is known as the *economic order quantity* and represents the amount of material that management should purchase for inventory replacement per period if it wishes to optimize its inventory level with respect to total costs, as defined here.

The simplest, most direct way of determining the EOQ for a particular item of inventory is by solving the EOQ formula. The formula is

$$EOQ = \sqrt{\frac{(2 \times \text{acquisition cost per order} \times \text{usage rate}) + \text{fixed acquisition costs}}{\text{carrying cost per unit}}}$$

The usage rate and the carrying cost per unit must be expressed in identical units of time (weeks, months, years), and the carrying cost must be expressed as a dollar amount per unit of inventory. The following example will illustrate the application of EOQ model both graphically and numerically.

Illustration. Suppose the grain that the city zoo purchases costs $4.00 per bushel delivered to the zoo. The order cost consists of an annual bookkeeping charge of $1.90 plus $1.79 per order including postage, order forms, and check processing. The director has estimated that the carrying costs of the grain total about $1.03 per bushel per year, defined in terms of the opportunity cost of lost interest income on the cash invested in inventory, handling, and insurance. Finally, as mentioned earlier, the animals consume about 240 bushels of grain each month. Since the usage rate and the carrying costs must be expressed in the same time frame, the annual rate of consumption will be used in the calculation: that is (12 × 240 =) 2,880 bushels.

The optimum order size can be calculated by substituting these data in the EOQ formula:

$$EOQ = \sqrt{\frac{(2 \times \$1.79 \times 2,880 \text{ bushels}) + \$1.90}{\$1.03 \text{ per bushel}}}$$

$$= \sqrt{\frac{\$10,312.3}{\$1.03 \text{ per bushel}}}$$

$$= 100 \text{ bushels}$$

This amount is 40 bushels more than the quantity the director is currently ordering, and each order represents about a 12.5-day supply of grain, based on the consumption rate of 240 bushels per month. The graph in Exhibit 10-5 shows the relationship between inventory costs and order size for this example. The EOQ is read on the horizontal axis at the point at which total inventory costs are at a minimum. The data presented in Exhibit 10-6, from which the graph was drawn, clearly indicate that total annual inventory costs are minimized when the order size is equal to the EOQ. In this case, the director can save only ($139.32 – 125.02 =) $14.30 per year by increasing his customary order size from 60 to 100 bushels; however, the concept and the model are clearly valuable tools for managers who are responsible for inventory control.

Exhibit 10-5: **Relationship Between Inventory Costs and Order Size**

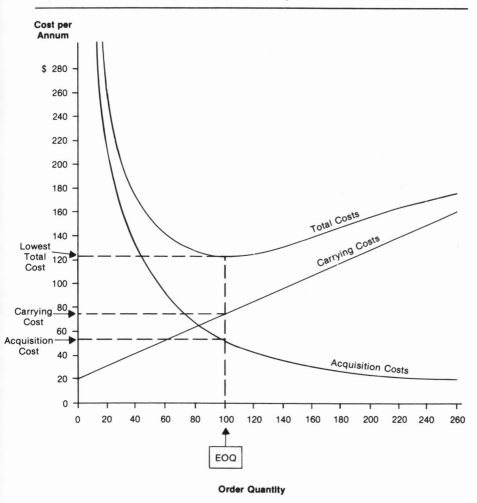

Order Quantity

Exhibit 10-6: Inventory Cost Analysis for the City Zoo

(1)	(2)	(3)	(4)	(5)	(6)	(7)
Annual usage rate	Order quantity	Orders per year (1)/(2)	Average inventory* [(2)/2] + 20	Carrying costs (4) × $ 1.03	Acquisition costs [(3) × $ 1.79] + $ 1.90	Total cost (5) + (6)
2,880 bu	20 bu	144	30	$ 30.90	$ 259.66	$ 290.56
2,880	40	72	40	41.20	130.78	171.98
2,880	60	48	50	51.50	87.82	139.32
2,880	80	36	60	61.80	66.34	128.14
2,880	100	29	70	72.10	53.81	125.91
2,880	120	24	80	82.40	44.86	127.26
2,880	180	16	110	113.30	30.54	143.84
2,880	240	12	140	144.20	23.38	167.58

* Includes minimum inventory level of 20 bushels.

Minimum Inventory Level. As previously indicated, in order to construct an operational inventory control system, management must estimate the minimum inventory level, or safety stock. The size of the safety stock carried for a given item is determined by the variability in demand for the item and the risk management is willing to take of running out of inventory and thus interrupting operations or losing sales. All other things being equal, the smaller the safety stock an organization maintains for a given inventory item, the greater are its chances of stock-outs.

While an organization may substantially reduce the number of delayed orders and related costs incurred from stock-outs by increasing its safety stock, the relationship between the size of inventory and the reduction of stock-outs is not linear; that is, if an organization whose sales are not subject to wide seasonal swings can satisfy 50 percent of its customer orders by carrying a safety stock of 10 percent of expected annual sales, it does not necessarily follow that it can satisfy 100 percent of its demands by increasing the safety stock to 20 percent. The experience of many inventory managers indicates that the relationship between delayed orders as a result of stock-outs and safety stock is similar to that shown in Exhibit 10-7. The graph indicates that an organization may achieve a

Exhibit 10-7: Relationship Between Percentage of Delayed Orders and Safety Stock for a Hypothetical Organization

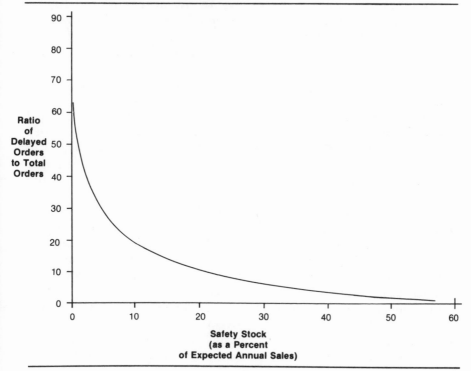

large reduction in delayed orders as it increases its safety stock from, say 10 percent to 20 percent of sales; however, a corresponding improvement is not obtained if the safety stock is increased to 30 percent. Thus, management cannot eliminate stock-outs completely, unless it is willing to commit a prohibitively large amount of funds to inventory.

In practice, most managers attempt to define some "tolerable" level of stock-outs for an inventory item, based on how critical inventory shortages are to their professional objectives or the needs of their clientele. For example, the educational needs of students attending a university may prompt the manager of the bookstore to overstock such items as hand-held calculators and calculator batteries. Similarly, a city recreation department cannot afford to run short of baseballs during the Little League baseball season, but the concession stands may find a bubblegum stock-out tolerable, so long as it does not happen too frequently.

EVALUATING INVENTORY MANAGEMENT

There is no single measure that can be used to test the overall effectiveness with which inventory is being managed. As in the case of accounts receivable, the organization must rely on a number of measures in order to properly evaluate this area of managerial concern.

One of those measures is the turnover of inventory as measured by the ratio of the cost of goods sold to average inventory. The inventory turnover indicates in general whether inventory is too high or too low relative to sales or consumption (measured at cost). When the turnover is unusually low, the suggestion is that there may be obsolete, or at least slow-moving, stock on hand. An unusually high turnover may reveal inefficiencies in more than one dimension. For example, efforts to maintain especially high turnover of paper supplies in an educational institution may result in periodic interruptions of or changes in planned classroom activities because of stock-outs. This suggests inefficiencies in managing inventories. By the same token, a high turnover of paper supplies and frequent stock-outs may be the result of waste and inefficiencies *in the classroom*. Thus, the ratio itself does not automatically produce a "good" or "bad" rating for the inventory manager. Rather, it signals the need to evaluate policies that govern both purchasing and using the inventory. Finally, it should be emphasized that current inventory turnover figures are significant only when compared with some target rate peculiar to that organization alone and established through past experience and short-range planning.

Efficient inventory management also depends on how well the physical requirements of the inventory items are being met. Management must establish mechanisms and systems to prevent rapid and unnecessary deterioration of the inventory and to eliminate the dangers from fire and theft to whatever extent it deems appropriate. Although adequate insurance coverage helps, it is not the entire answer, since an organization that is unable to fill a customer's order (even though it may be insured) inconveniences that customer at the least and certainly decreases the effectiveness of the organization's programs.

SUMMARY

Not all nonprofit organizations hold receivables and inventories. But those that do must recognize their critical roles in both professional and financial goal achievement. Many trading organizations list accounts receivable in their balance sheets as a result of their decisions to extend credit to their customers or clientele. These organizations are faced with the need to establish policies governing credit terms offered, the conduct of credit investigations, credit extension decisions, and collections. The financial implications of these policy decisions may have significant impacts on the organization's cash flows and the excess of its revenues over expenditures.

Decision rules to guide the management of accounts receivable include those governing the length of the credit period, using cash discounts as an incentive for prompt payment, and granting credit. The decision rules are based on financial criteria, but their professional implications are clearly relevant in all cases.

Many nontrading organizations elect to accept pledges in lieu of cash donations during their fund-raising campaigns. As a result, they must establish accounting and collection systems for this type of receivable. Pledges receivable are quite different from accounts receivable; thus, their management requires a different approach.

Organizations that carry receivables of either kind may be able to shift the responsibility for their management to a third party—a credit card company, finance company, or collection agency, for example. This decision also has professional and financial implications that require careful analysis.

The management of inventories centers on the proper measurement of inventory costs and their use in the EOQ model. In addition to the optimum order size, which will result in minimizing total inventory costs, the organization must establish the size of the safety stock of inventory and the timing of purchases to prevent or minimize stock-outs.

Evaluation of both receivables and inventory management is an important aspect of working capital management. Its performance is hampered by the fact that customary measures, such as ratios, tend to measure two things at once. Careful consideration of cash flows and policy requirements is required to develop a true evaluation of management in these areas.

FURTHER READING

Excellent in-depth coverage of the analytical aspects of receivable and inventory management may be found in the following books:

Mehta, Dileep R. *Working Capital Management*. Englewood Cliffs, N.J.: Prentice-Hall, 1974.

Smith, Keith V. *Guide to Working Capital Management*. New York: McGraw-Hill, 1979.

A standard text on the practical and institutional aspects of credit management is:

Beckman, Theodore M, and R. S. Foster. *Credit and Collections: Management and Theory*. 8th ed. New York: McGraw-Hill, 1969.

QUESTIONS

1. What two types of receivables may a nonprofit organization hold?

2. Discuss the rationale underlying the creation of accounts receivable by trading organizations.

3. List the four areas in which policies are required in managing accounts receivable.

4. What is meant by the expression, net 10 EOM?

5. What does an organization hope to achieve by lengthening its credit period?

6. What criterion does the financial manager use in analyzing proposed changes in an organization's credit terms?

7. Describe the changes in sales, accounts receivable, and operating costs that are likely to result from a liberalization of credit terms?

8. What are cash discounts? Why do organizations offer cash discounts as a part of their credit terms?

9. List some of the sources of credit information an organization may find useful in evaluating a customer's ability to pay?

10. Describe the method of break-even pricing used when an organization must recover the full cost of goods sold.

11. In what ways do pledges receivable differ from accounts receivable?

12. Discuss the collection arrangements an organization may make with a:
   a. credit card company
   b. collection agency
   c. finance company

13. What is the appropriate criterion to use when analyzing the arrangement proposed by one of the three organizations mentioned in the preceding question?

14. Describe the various methods of evaluating receivables management, and discuss their shortcomings.

15. What is EOQ? What is the formula used for its calculation?

16. List the relevant costs used in constructing an inventory management system.

17. Define the following items:
   a. reorder point
   b. stock-out
   c. safety stock
   d. usage rate
   e. opportunity cost

18. Describe the relationship between:
   a. Carrying costs and acquisition costs
   b. Safety stock and the ratio of delayed orders to total orders

19. How may inventory management be evaluated?

PROBLEMS

1. The Beaver Valley Farmers Cooperative currently extends its members 30-day terms on all purchases other than seeds and fertilizer, which are billed at harvest. Management feels that more liberal credit terms will increase membership. It is therefore considering extending credit for 90 days and expects to increase sales from the current level of $986,000 to $1,185,000 as a result of the more liberal credit terms. The cooperative follows the policy of adding a 10 percent mark-up over cost on all merchandise to cover administrative expenses.

The organization has never incurred any bad debts, but it expects to lose about 0.5% of sales to bad debts under the new credit terms. Administrative expenses are currently $85,000 per year, and they are expected to remain constant except for the bad-debt losses. The organization has invested all of its excess revenues over expenditures in an unrestricted fund earmarked for expansion of its facilities. The fund is expected to earn 12% during the coming year.

a. Calculate the increase in "profits" expected under the new credit terms.

b. If the collection period increases by 65 days, calculate the increase in the investment of receivables (at cost).

c. If the co-op is going to sell securities to finance the increase in receivables, should it liberalize its credit terms?

2. The Alevar Retirement Center has offered a cash discount of 1% to its residents who pay their rent ten days in advance. The center's management estimates that because Social Security and pension checks generally arrive on the first of the month, the occupants of only 20 to 25 of the center's 150 units will take advantage of the discount. Each unit rents for $125 per month. The center is currently repaying a bank loan on which it is paying 15 percent interest. Has the center's management made a wise decision regarding the cash discount?

3. A home nursing organization wishes to maintain its operating revenues at $350,000. It expects to render 35,000 hours of care next year, for which it will bill its clients. Past experience places bad debt at close to 18% of total charges. What hourly rate should the organization charge to reach the target revenue figure?

4. The Acme Collection Agency offered to assist the home nursing organization described in problem 3 by purchasing all of its accounts receivable without recourse at 85% of face value, and charge an annual adminstrative fee or $12,300. The organization would be able to save $6,300 in administrative costs per year under the arrangement and will receive payment from the agency about 45 days sooner than it would if it handled its own collections. The organization invests its surplus cash at 10%. Should it accept the offer made by the Acme Agency?

5. The Key, Incorporated trains high school dropouts and other unskilled youth in secretarial skills. The organization is located in the center of a large city and has the capability to provide training to over 500 individuals at one time in the areas of typing, shorthand, filing, telephone courtesy, and so forth.

The Key purchases typing paper for $5 per package through a special arrangement with the city's purchasing department. The department fills each order and delivers the paper at a charge of $3 plus an annual administrative fee of $25 to cover the cost of billing the organization. The Key's administrator estimates carrying costs to be 8 percent per year of the average inventory value — the rate at which she is currently investing the organization's surplus cash balances.

The typing classes consume about 22 packages of paper each month, and the administration uses about 1 additional package per month. The administrator prefers to keep a minimum of 3 packages on hand at all times.

a. Using the EOQ model, calculate the optimum order quantity.

b. If the city takes three days to process each order prior to delivery, what is Key's reorder point?

6. The North Philadelphia Lions Club meets once each month for lunch. Each member is charged $6.50 for the meal and $5 for dues. The secretary mails the bills monthly to the 88 members. Luncheon attendance averages 70 members per month, so the average monthly bill per member is $10.17. The club spends about $25 per month to prepare and mail the bills. If the club invests its surplus cash at 10% per year, how often should the secretary bill the membership? (Hint: Use the EOQ formula and let the billing costs = acquisition costs, the average monthly bill × interest rate = carrying costs, and 12 × the membership = usage rate. Your answer will be the "optimum billing quantity per annum." This figure divided by the number of members will tell you how many bills each member should receive each year.) Prove your answer in tabular form.

11

Short-term Financing

Trade credit and bank credit are the two most readily available and frequently used sources of short-term financing employed by nonprofit organizations. This chapter will discuss the principal characteristics of these credit forms and the proper management of the current liabilities that result when an organization finances its current funds needs with one or both of these forms of short-term financing.

TRADE CREDIT

In American business practice, buyers are not generally required to pay cash on delivery for the goods and services they order. Instead, the sellers invoice, or bill, the buyers on delivery, as mentioned in the preceding chapter, according to the terms of the particular trade or line of business in which they are engaged. That is, sellers extend credit to buyers, and this extension of credit provides a temporary source of funds to the buyer in the form of accounts or notes payable. Because suppliers (sellers) are generally more liberal in extending credit than banks are, trade credit has become the most important source of short-term business funds in terms of the dollar volume of credit supplied. Among nonprofit organizations, trade credit has taken on an even greater significance than is true in the for-profit context. This is because many financial institutions do not know how to extend credit to organizations whose accounting methods and cash-flow characteristics are mysteriously different from those of firms with whom they are accustomed to dealing. Consequently, when a nonprofit organization experiences a temporary shortage of cash, it often has little choice other than to rely on trade credit for its immediate operating needs.

This is not to say that using trade credit is necessarily a proper approach to financing a nonprofit organization's short-term needs; it is merely a statement of fact that the financial manager must face. *Proper* approaches to the management of current debt — obligations due within one year — are discussed later in this chapter.

Forms of Trade Credit

While there are many forms of trade credit extension in more or less common use by business firms, only two forms are in general use in the nonprofit context: (1) the *open account*, which is by far the most common, and (2) the *promissory note*.

Open-Account Credit. Open-account credit is ordinarily extended after the seller conducts an investigation of the buyer's credit standing and reputation, unless, of course, the seller is already well-acquainted with the buyer's reputation. The open account derives its name from the fact that the buyer does not sign a formal debt instrument evidencing the amount he owes the seller as would be the case if the organization purchasing the merchandise applied for and obtained bank credit. The only evidence the seller has that credit has been extended is the buyer's purchase order, a copy of the invoice showing that merchandise was shipped, and an entry in the seller's accounts receivable ledger. It is indicative of the extent to which a credit economy has developed in this country that, when most trade credit is arranged, this is all that is done and all that is required to be done to establish legal evidence of indebtedness.

Promissory Notes. In some situations, however, a promissory note may be used in the transaction. A promissory note is a written promise by one person to another to pay on demand or at a fixed or determinable future time a certain sum of money to order or bearer. The promissory note is generally an interest-bearing instrument. Buyers are required to sign such notes most often in cases where their open accounts have become delinquent and the seller wishes to obtain a formal acknowledgment of the debt, a definite maturity date, and, at times, a return in the form of interest on the funds thus committed for an extended period. Promissory notes appear on the seller's balance sheet as "notes receivable" and on the buyer's balance sheet as "notes payable," of course.

Terms of Sale and Trade Credit

Promissory notes are used rather sparingly in American commercial transactions; therefore, the more relevant terms of trade credit are those pertaining to open accounts. Three aspects of this form of credit warrant discussion: (1) the maximum period that can elapse before payment of the net invoice price is required; (2) the size of the cash discount, if any, from the net invoice price which is given for making cash payment within a specified period; and (3) the period within which payment must be made if the cash discount is to be allowed.

Types of Discount. It is important to distinguish a cash discount, offered for prompt payment of an open account, from both a quantity discount and a functional discount. A *quantity discount*—generally expressed as a percentage reduction from list price—is given for purchasing certain minimum amounts of a particular item. *Functional* (sometimes called *trade*) *discounts* are differential discounts given different types of customers—a wholesaler, for example, may be given a larger discount than a retailer, and, in some cases, any nonconsumer may be entitled to a discount from the suggested retail price.

Terms of Sale and Terms of Credit. Terms of sale and terms of credit, which vary from industry to industry, are specified on each invoice and may be categorized according to both the net period within which payment is expected and the terms of the cash discount allowed.

CBD and COD. "Cash before delivery" (CBD) and "cash on delivery" (COD) are two common terms of sale. Under CBD, a buyer must pay for the goods before the supplier will ship them. When a supplier imposes these terms, the credit manager either knows nothing at all about the buyer's creditworthiness or, more frequently, knows too much about the customer's unreliability in managing his or her business affairs. In the latter circumstance, to eliminate the risk of nonpayment completely, the supplier may even wait for the customer's check to clear the bank before shipping the order. Under COD, the supplier will ship the goods ordered, but the buyer must pay for them before taking possession. The only risk involved with COD is that the customer may refuse the shipment and the seller will have to pay the cost of shipping the merchandise in both directions. Transactions completed under either CBD or COD terms are considered cash transactions because suppliers are required to extend no credit at all.

Net Terms, No Cash Discount. When net terms are quoted, the supplier specifies the period permitted for payment in full. For example, "net 30" means that the amount of the net invoice must be paid in full within thirty days. If the seller bills on a monthly basis, the invoice may stipulate such terms as "net 15 EOM," meaning that all goods shipped before the end of the month must be paid for in full by the fifteenth of the following month. Sometimes, "bill-to-bill" terms are specified; that is, the bill for a previous delivery is collected at the time a new delivery is made.

Cash Discounts. In addition to extending credit on net terms, suppliers may offer a cash discount for payment more prompt than the net terms require. The terms "2/10, net 30," for example, indicate that the buyer is offered a 2 percent discount for payment within ten days of the date of the invoice. If this discount is not taken, the full amount is due within thirty days. When the buyer is far removed from the seller, or the method of shipping the goods is slow, terms may be "2/10, net 30 AOG" (arrival of goods). That arrangement affords the buyer the opportunity to inspect the goods before paying for them. More important, it provides all buyers with an equal opportunity to earn the cash discount, regardless of their distance from the point of shipment or the transit time required for the goods to reach them. In general, cash discounts average close to 2 percent of the invoice amount, but may be set as high as 10 percent. The discount periods are usually fairly short—ten to twenty days in most cases.

Rationale for Trade Credit Terms

The variations in trade credit terms described above have a rationale. First, the length of the period for which credit is granted is related to the nature of the commodity sold. High-style items or perishable merchandise are generally sold on fairly short credit terms because the supplier may not be willing to bear the risk of obsolescence or spoilage. Second, the estimated degree of credit risk is generally reflected in the terms of sale. Retail shops in the apparel trades are characterized by a somewhat high rate of failure, for example. This may explain the rather large cash discounts usually allowed such retailers—the size of the discount reflects suppliers' desires to be paid as quickly as possible. Third, the nature and extent of competition among suppliers is expressed in credit terms as well as in prices and services. When a product is new, or if a supplier is soliciting business from a new account, granting more liberal credit terms than are customary may be one way of generating additional sales.

Fourth, a supplier short of working capital may offer rather large cash discounts to his customers to induce them to settle their accounts quickly. In this way, the supplier reduces the time it takes to collect his outstanding accounts receivable and thus reduces his total working capital requirements. A thinly capitalized supplier (and thus a high-risk borrower) may find that the cost of offering large cash discounts is less than the costs of borrowing or raising additional cash by other means to meet his or her working capital needs.

Finally, the financial strength of the supplier relative to that of his or her customers is also a determinant of credit terms. Although logic might suggest that a financially strong supplier could dictate stringent terms to smaller, more dependent customers, by doing so he or she may succeed only in losing some customers and possibly even putting others out of business. In reality, in many lines of business, smaller companies are carried by their (financially stronger) suppliers.

Trade Credit as a Source of Funds

Since buyers generally do not pay for goods or services until some time after they are received, trade credit is a short-term source of funds. If an organization automatically pays all its bills a certain number of days after the invoice date, trade credit becomes a spontaneous, or a built-in, source of financing that varies with the amount of goods purchased or the frequency of the use of the services by the seller. As the organization increases its rate of purchases, accounts payable increase proportionately, thereby providing some of the funds needed to finance the increase in the organization's activities. Similarly, as activity decreases, purchases, and thus accounts payable, decrease.

Although changes in the size of an organization's accounts payable may not be exactly proportional to changes in the level of its central economic activity because of possible inventory adjustments, there will ordinarily be a strong degree of correspondence between the two. If an organization adheres strictly to the practice of always paying its bills a certain number of days after invoice date, the activity, purchases, and trade credit will move in concert over time. But while such a payment policy increases the predictability of cash flows, it removes trade credit as a *discretionary* source of financing. Instead, it becomes *determinate* insofar as it is dependent on the purchasing plan of the organization.

Although prompt payment of such obligations is generally to be commended, certain advantages may be gained from using trade credit as a discretionary source of short-term financing. To demonstrate the desirability of such a policy, we need only examine the true cost of using trade credit.

Cost of Trade Credit

For purposes of measuring the true cost, or the effective annual rate of interest associated with use of trade credit as a discretionary source of short-term funds, it is necessary to consider the effects of its use both when (1) an organization fails to take its cash discounts but nevertheless pays within the net period and (2) an organization fails to take its discounts and allows its payables to become overdue. These two situations are the only ones that involve an actual cost to the debtor. If no cash discount is offered, then there is no cost for the use of credit during the net period, however long it may be. By the same token, if a discount is available and the buyer takes it, there is also no cost for the use of credit during the discount period. However, if a cash discount is offered and is not taken, there is an explicit and measurable opportunity cost for the use of this credit.

For example, the Bible Baptist Church purchases its printing and mailing services from Pioneer Press on terms of 2/10, net 30. It thus has the option of using the funds (or in essence borrowing the money from the printer) for 20 days after the discount period if it "passes" the discount but pays on the final day of the net period. The church, however, must pay 2 percent for the privilege of using the printer's funds for those extra twenty days. This is equivalent to paying interest at an approximate percentage cost, on an annual basis, calculable using the following equation:[1]

$$R = \frac{C(365)}{D(100 - C)}$$

where

C = The cash discount
D = The number of extra days the church has the use of the printer's funds
R = The approximate percentage cost for the use of these funds

In this example, $C = 2$ percent, $D = 20$; the effective annual interest rate for the church is approximately

$$R = \frac{2\,(365)}{20\,(100 - 2)} = 37.24\%$$

---

1. A more precise measure of the cost, using the same notation as above, is the annual rate, $R^* = \left(1 + \frac{1}{1 - C}\right)^{360/D} - 1$. In this case $R^* = \left(1 + \frac{.02}{.98}\right)^{360/20} - 1$

$$= (1.0204)^{18} - 1$$

$$= 43.8\%.$$

Thus, the Bible Baptist Church case clearly illustrates that passed discounts can transform trade credit from a normally costless source of funds into a very expensive form of short-term financing. Therefore, if bank financing is available, even at relatively high interest rates, say, 18 to 20 percent, the church's financial officer is well advised to borrow from a local bank in sufficient time to take advantage of any cash discounts offered by the printing firm.

Sometimes, organizations that are short of cash and lack reserve (bank) borrowing power may be forced to not only pass up cash discounts but also to postpone payment beyond the net period. This practice is referred to as "stretching" accounts payable or "riding" trade creditors. There are two types of costs incurred by an organization that stretches its accounts payable: (1) the explicit cost of discounts forgone, as outlined above, and (2) the implicit cost of permitting its trade credit rating to deteriorate. If an organization rides its creditors excessively, so that its trade payables become noticeably delinquent, its credit rating among all suppliers with whom it trades will surely suffer. They will view the organization as increasingly risky to sell to and may quickly begin to impose rather strict terms of sale, up to and including COD or CBD.

Proper Use of Trade Credit

As compared with other kinds of short-term credit—bank loans, for example—trade credit is almost automatic. And because it may be much more readily acquired, nonprofit organizations must exercise continuing care to avoid falling into the habit of using trade credit to excess.

Because suppliers regard the extension of trade credit as a part of their overall sales promotion programs, they often extend trade credit to many marginally creditworthy businesses and nonprofit organizations that do not qualify for and consequently cannot obtain credit from other suppliers of short-term funds. It is also quite easy to get into debt through the use of trade credit. An organization needs only to order additional goods or services from its suppliers; and if it is occasionally late in making payment, the sales promotion aspect of trade-credit extension may prompt suppliers to "look the other way," so that the organization's credit reputation may suffer no immediate harm.

Finally, trade credit is exceedingly useful and valuable precisely because nonprofit organizations can usually obtain it when, as, and to the extent that it is needed. For example, a mission serving the homeless men and women of a large northern city must increase its inventories of food and clothing items as the cold weather approaches; trade credit will automatically finance a part of that increase. Then as fund-raising activities increase, say, during the Thanksgiving and Christmas holidays when most people respond more readily to the needs of the beneficiaries of the mission's activities, the organization may use the funds to reduce its higher trade accounts payable.

Thus, an organization's financial officer, while ensuring that the organization benefits from the availability of trade credit in every legitimate way, should always plan for and/or maintain the liquidity required to pay all bills as they come due. Beyond this, considering the extremely high cost of passing discounts, the financial officer should certainly plan to pay all of the organization's trade bills within the discount period. Doing so will have favorable results, not only on the organization's credit reputation among its suppliers but, more importantly, on its current and long-run solvency as well. Because its legitimate needs for funds will always be met by those with whom the organization has been dealing fairly, the longer the list of happy creditors, the easier it will be for the organization to acquire funds when the need arises. In a negative but equally significant sense, following the policy of prompt payment will automatically avoid the possible financial overextension of the organization that could result from its succumbing to the temptation to use trade credit excessively "because it is there."

BANK CREDIT

Short-term, unsecured loans made by banks to profit-seeking business firms are generally regarded as self-liquidating in that the uses to which the borrower puts the funds are ordinarily expected to generate cash flows adequate to repay the loan within one year. Formerly, banks chose to confine their business lending almost exclusively to this short-term, self-liquidating type of loan. While they now engage in a much wider variety of business lending (also by choice), the short-term, self-liquidating loan still meets the specific needs of most business borrowers and thus remains a very important source of business financing.

Unfortunately, because of the linear nature of the cash flows of nontrading nonprofit organizations, the extension of short-term bank credit to these entities cannot be considered as self-liquidating in the same sense as it is for profit-seeking enterprises. As explained earlier in chapter 2, the cash receipts of nontrading organizations are not related directly to or do not arise directly from the organizations' central economic activities. Consequently, banks that extend short-term credit to these organizations must rely mainly on cash flows from their fund-raising activities for ultimate repayment of their loans. Such credit is extended on a *transaction* basis. But loans to trading nonprofit organizations (that is, those whose operating characteristics and cash flows resemble for-profit businesses) can be accommodated on a short-term basis under a *line of credit*, under a *revolving credit agreement*, or on a *transaction basis*. These classifications of bank credit are discussed in the following sections.

Line of Credit

A line of credit is simply an agreement between a commercial bank and a borrowing customer regarding the maximum amount of credit the bank is willing to extend to that customer over a given number of months. Such lines of credit are commonly requested by borrowers on a seasonal basis. By preparing and analyzing a cash budget reflecting his or her organization's operations over some period, the financial officer estimates the patterns of seasonal financing needs and arranges a line of credit with the bank, the upper limit of which equals the (trading) organization's forecasted peak requirements, as shown in its cash budget. Then, as seasonal buildups of inventories, accounts receivable, or both create needs for funds, the organization's financial officer simply signs promissory notes for the amounts required at the time they are required, and the bank credits the organization's account in the proper amounts. Subsequently, the postseasonal shrinkage in working capital needs permits the organization to repay the advances with funds generated from the sale of inventories and the collection of accounts receivable. Colleges and universities that permit their students to spread tuition payments over a portion of the semester or quarter may find it convenient to borrow under such a line of credit, for example.

Seasonal lines of credit usually run for a year at a time but can be renewed periodically. Since the loans extended under such lines are made for the purpose of augmenting permanent working capital temporarily, the lending banks ordinarily require their seasonal line-of-credit borrowers to be completely out of debt to the bank at some time during the year. This annual cleanup period of a month or two is proof to the bank that funds advanced are being used only for seasonal expansion (that is, to provide temporary working capital). From the point of view of the organization's financial officer it also serves as an excellent internal control device that helps keep the organization's working capital position in line. Failure of a seasonal borrower to achieve an annual cleanup of bank debt, moreover, suggests that the organization is using bank funds as *permanent* working capital. While banks are not averse to helping customers finance their needs for permanent working capital, they generally prefer to do so with term loans rather than short-term seasonal loans.(Term loans are discussed in chapter 16.)

Revolving Credit Agreements

A revolving credit agreement is a variant of the line of credit. Its popularity is due to the flexibility it provides to the borrower in using the borrowed funds. As under the seasonal line, the borrower and its bank agree on an upper limit of credit. Within this maximum amount, however, the amount actually borrowed may revolve continuously. That is, the organization may borrow, repay, and then subsequently reborrow, as the need arises, in the amounts appropriate to the firm's shortage or surplus of cash. This can be done also under a seasonal line, of course, but only for the one-year period of the credit arrangement. But revolving lines typically run for more than a year. Many have, in fact, an indefinite length of life—they may extend on and on, so long as (1) the lending bank and the borrowing customer are both happy with the arrangement as originally negotiated, and (2) the borrower remains sufficiently creditworthy to qualify for the maximum amount of the line.

Revolving lines often differ from seasonal lines in yet another way. They are frequently negotiated by the bank as formal commitments to lend, and a commitment fee is charged on any portion of the line that is unused. For example, if a nonprofit organization has a formal revolving credit agreement with its bank for $100,000 and average annual borrowings for a given year total only $40,000, a commitment fee is payable on the $60,000 portion of the line that is unused. That is in addition to the interest charged on the $40,000 portion of the line that is used. If the commitment fee is 0.5 percent, the cost to the borrower of having the bank keep the unused $60,000 available would be $300 for the year. Needless to say, such an arrangement may increase the cost of borrowing significantly, especially when the line of credit is consistently underutilized.

Nonprofit organizations whose operations involve the undertaking of a few large projects each year will find the revolving credit arrangement a very convenient form of financing. For example, a nonprofit publishing house may borrow under a revolving line of credit as its books enter the composition and printing phases of the production process. Funds for repayment are generated from the sale of the published volumes. Or an international disaster-relief agency may use such an arrangement to provide critically needed supplies and materials as quickly as possible after a disaster, using donated funds collected subsequent to a general appeal to repay the amount borrowed under the line. In both of these examples, the revolving credit is the superior arrangement because of the uncertainties regarding the exact timing of the cash needs—authors of books seldom are able to meet their publishers' deadlines, and the timing of natural disasters cannot be predicted or scheduled.

Since revolving credit agreements frequently extend beyond one year, many of them involve the extension of intermediate-term rather than short-term credit. For this reason, further discussion of revolving credit is presented in chapter 16.

Transaction Basis

When an organization borrows only occasionally for specific purposes that may differ from time to time, it will generally negotiate each loan with the bank as a separate transaction. For example, the Westside

Baptist Church applied to its bank for a loan to replace the roof on the pastor's residence and to complete the final phase of the construction of its new education building. When the building is completed, the church will partially repay the bank with the proceeds of a mortgage loan from a life insurance company. The balance of the loan (to finance the new roof) will be repaid over time out of membership tithes. In such cases, the bank will evaluate each request as a separate transaction, with its own cash-flow-for-repayment characteristics, and will either extend credit for one or both purposes, or turn down both requests.

Cost of Bank Credit

Interest rates on bank loans to all of their borrowers are determined through negotiation with the customer. In unsecured lending, the rate charged tends to vary directly with the credit quality, or the creditworthiness, of the borrower. The largest, soundest, profit-seeking businesses, possessing the very highest credit quality, are able to borrow, unsecured, at the *prime rate*. The prime rate is the borrowing rate of interest at which the nation's largest banks lend to their biggest and best short-term business borrowing customers. It is the connecting link between a commercial bank's customer loan rates and short-term, open-market, money rates. The prime rate measures, in effect, the opportunity cost to banks of lending rather than investing in high quality, short-term, open-market instruments. Since the latter are virtually riskless, it follows that prime-rate borrowers must possess credit qualities of the very highest order to qualify for the lowest bank-loan rate.

Just as relatively few business borrowers qualify for the prime rate, few, if any, nonprofit organizations can borrow at that lowest of bank-interest rates. Nevertheless, financial officers must constantly work to raise their organizations' credit quality to the highest possible level and maintain it at that point in order to minimize the costs of acquiring funds. An examination of the concept of credit quality from the lender's point of view will indicate how this can be accomplished.

Concept of Credit Quality. The credit quality of a nonprofit organization that is applying for a loan is revealed to the lending banker through inquiries made of the organization's present and past creditors; through analysis of the organization's financial statements; and by comparisons of the prospective borrower's financial situation (as revealed by its financial statements) with those of other similarly constituted organizations. With respect to short-term borrowers, good credit quality includes the following components indicated by statement analysis and verified through objective means:

1. Good reputation among its creditors, both for prompt payment of trade payables and for fair dealing with suppliers.

2. Satisfactory current financial position, as revealed by an analysis of its financial statements.

3. Satisfactory level of debt, as indicated by its ability to generate adequate cash flows for debt service.

4. Excellence of management of both the business and professional affairs of the organization.

5. Continuing justification for the basic (professional) objectives that the organization originally was created to achieve.

6. Community support in terms of demand for the organization's product or service by its clientele group, successful fund-raising activities, and volunteer services provided to the organization.

In addition to meeting all six criteria of good credit quality, the organization that wishes to be offered the lowest possible interest rate when it borrows from a bank must be able to demonstrate its ability to repay the loan within one year. The source of repayment may be from operations, in the case of a trading organization, or from gifts or grants due to be received in the case of a nontrading organization. Or the ultimate repayment can be made or become the responsibility of a third party—a trustee or other benefactor who is willing to add his or her personal endorsement to the loan, for example, or another affiliated organization, such as the headquarters of a religious group that sponsors the borrower's activities.

Setting the Interest Rate. In setting the interest rate to be charged on a loan to a nonprofit organization, a commercial bank not only looks at the prospective borrower's credit quality but also at the nature of its deposit relationship with the bank. If the borrowing organization maintains balances that are judged to be "commensurate" with its credit requirements, a lower rate may be placed on the loan than otherwise would be justified. That is, in evaluating any loan opportunity, the problem faced by the commercial bank lending officer is that of comparing, and if possible, equating the expected returns available to the bank from making the loan with the risk that the loan will not be repaid at maturity or otherwise handled by the borrower as agreed. The returns available to banks for lending include the direct interest return on the loan, of course, and may also include the indirect benefits realized from the maintenance of satisfactory compensating balances—cash held in the form of demand deposits in the bank—as well as other commensurate advantages thought to accrue to the bank as the result of making the loan. These other commensurate advantages, though real enough in the banker's mind, are not susceptible to quantitative measurement in the same sense as interest rates and balances are, however.

When are a borrower's balances commensurate with its credit requirements? No single answer to that question can be given, and there are many variations. But for most banks, demand deposit accounts of about 20 percent of the outstanding bank loan are considered reasonable. In fact, many banks explicitly or implicitly request a borrowing customer to carry average balances equal to at least 20 percent of the stated line of credit or contemplated maximum borrowings from the bank. Some banks set the figure at 15 percent of the expected high borrowing figure or line of credit, and a few, at 10 percent. Other banks request balances equal to 10 percent of the line when the organization is not borrowing and balances equal to 20 percent when the line is in use. Still other banks—those most desirous of according their customers liberal treatment—consider compensating balances to be average deposit balances for a twelve-month period that are equal to at least 20 percent of average loans during the year. This is usually (but may not be vastly) different from balances equal to 20 percent of maximum loans.

Calculating the Cost of Borrowing. If the minimum level of balances judged to be commensurate is higher than the level an organization normally would keep for operational liquidity purposes, the effect may be to reduce the effective amount of its credit line (or borrowing ability) and to raise its effective cost of credit. To take a simple example, the Washington Community Center's cash budget indicates that its seasonal borrowing requirements will reach a high of $4,750 during a year in which current bank credit terms are 10.5 percent interest and a compensating balance requirement equaling 15 percent of borrowings. The organization's normal needs for operational liquidity (and hence its bank balance) total $500.

The size of the loan the organization requires to meet its peak credit needs may be calculated using the following formula:

$$L = \frac{N - B}{1 - C}$$

where

L = The dollar amount of the loan
N = The organization's peak credit needs (from the cash budget)
B = The organization's operational cash needs
C = The compensating balance requirements

Substituting, we find that

$$L = \frac{\$4,750 - \$500}{1 - 0.15} = \$5,000$$

Thus, the Washington Community Center will have to borrow $5,000 even though it can make effective use of only $4,750. It would also pay interest on the full $5,000. Consequently, from the organization's point of view, the effective interest rate on its usable bank borrowing's will be ($5,000 × .105)/$4,750 = 11.05 percent.

Other Commensurate Advantages. Banks look favorably on loan situations that also generate, or at least have the potential to generate, other advantages to the bank—securing a desirable new customer, obtaining a needed new service that the organization will provide for the bank's community, or accommodating organizations whose executives or principals are likely to make, or may be induced to make, substantial use of the bank's trust-department services. The greater the number of these other commensurate advantages, or the greater the profit potential to the bank from them, the more favorably disposed will the bank be toward honoring legitimate credit requests of the organization.

Borrowing Against Pledges Receivable

The rise in interest rates in 1981 to historically high levels and their frequent fluctuations within brief periods have led to the increased use of a relatively new form of short-term credit. It is specifically designed for nontrading organizations and involves the use of *pledges receivable* as security for short-term borrowing.

The ability of corporations and individuals to gain access to investment media that yield excellent returns, as compared with the cost of short-term credit, has caused corporate financial managers to become more aware of the benefits of conserving and properly managing their firms' cash balances. The obvious benefits available from a sound cash-management program are, first, the corporation's needs for short-term bank credit are reduced, thereby also reducing its total costs, and second, the interest income from the investment of surplus cash increases the firm's net profits. Unfortunately for the nontrading nonprofit organization in search of funds, these factors also are causing corporate donors to become increasingly reluctant to part with their surplus cash balances.

To persuade corporate boards of directors to maintain at least their past levels of cash donations that are so desperately needed by the nonprofit organizations, fund raisers have had to work harder than in the past, thereby escalating fund-raising costs. Fund raisers also have had to face up to the fact that single large cash donations are currently almost impossible to obtain. Instead, most corporations prefer to spread their larger gifts over three-year to five-year periods, and sometimes even longer. Thus, in order to accommodate their corporate donors' needs for investment income while meeting their own cash needs for current operations and capital formation, nonprofit organizations are recording on their balance sheets larger amounts of pledges receivable than ever before. These receivables, while gratefully accepted and acknowledged by the recipient organization, are not equivalent to cash and, hence, cannot be used by them to pay bills or purchase new assets.

Financial managers of nonprofit organizations have long recognized that pledges receivable are valuable assets and for many years offered them to banks as collateral for loans. However, most banks (and most other lenders as well) in years past refused to lend against the security of pledges receivable, mainly because the donor is not legally required to honor his or her pledges in terms of either the dollar amount promised or the timing of the payments. In fact, many lenders formerly were reluctant to assign any value at all to pledges receivable when analyzing the financial statements of nontrading organizations applying for credit. In so doing, they also refused to recognize any means of loan repayment and consequently did not grant many loans to nontrading nonprofit organizations.

Similarity Between Pledges and Accounts Receivable. In recent years, commercial banks have come to recognize the similarity between pledges receivable and *accounts receivable* (i.e., legal obligations to pay) insofar as their cash-flow characteristics are concerned. Both kinds of receivables present risks of default on the part of the donor and debtor, but experience has indicated that each default rate is low. And among those businesses and organizations that manage their receivables well, the default rates are extremely low relative to the total volume of receivables held. As a consequence, the growth in the number and dollar volume of loans extended by banks against the security of pledges receivable has been dramatic in recent years. Along with this growth has come a set of standards for this type of credit extension.

Purpose of Loans Against Pledges. Financing with pledges receivable as collateral is usually arranged for the purpose of meeting current obligations as they come due. In many cases, however, donors pledge gifts in support of capital expenditure projects, thereby making this type of bank credit a form of *construction lending*. That is, the organization uses the proceeds of the loan to pay for capital assets and uses the cash received from the honored pledges to repay the loan when it comes due. Since large construction projects may take several months or even years to complete, the cash flow from more distant pledges is timed perfectly for debt service.

Assessing the Quality of Pledges Offered for Collateral. Not all pledges held by a nonprofit organization will qualify as collateral for bank loans. First, only those pledges due to be collected within one year (or two years at the longest) are considered as sound collateral by lenders. When loans are used for construction purposes, banks will sometimes accept more distant pledges made by financially sound businesses and foundations.

Second, pledges of corporate donors are more readily accepted by lenders than are pledges by individuals. Third, only those pledges evidenced by written agreements are acceptable as security for loans. Thus, from a lender's point of view at least, pledges obtained through telephone solicitation are considered as having very little collateral value. Finally, banks will generally lend up to a maximum of 75 to 80 percent of pledges that qualify as acceptable loan collateral.

Cost of Receivables Financing. The interest cost of borrowing from commercial banks against pledges receivable may range from two to four percentage points above the prime rate. In addition, many banks levy service charges of an additional 1 or 2 percent of the loan as an administrative fee. Because of the sensitive nature of donor relations, most banks simply rely on the organization to make its loan payments as the pledges are collected, rather than request that the donor make his or her payment directly to the bank. The lender will require periodic status reports on the pledges offered as collateral while the loan remains outstanding and will examine new pledges as they are received. In some cases the bank will require the organization to add the new pledges to the collateral list without advancing additional funds. But when the organization is diligent in managing its receivables, the bank will remit the previously agreed-on percentage of the new pledges as they are recorded. The administrative fee thus represents a real cost to the bank in extending this type of loan and is not merely a means of increasing the yield on funds committed.

SUMMARY

Short-term financing refers to those obligations of an organization that mature in one year or less. Short-term credit is most frequently used to finance a temporary or a seasonal expansion of current assets, and the principal sources of such funds are trade credit and bank credit.

Trade credit is by far the most important source of short-term financing for nonprofit organizations. It is a spontaneous source of credit that arises from and varies in amount directly with the level of activity carried on by the organization. It may be either a discretionary or a determinate source of funds, depending on the debtor's policy regarding the timing of payment of its invoices. Finally, trade credit is a costless source of funds, except when the supplier offers a cash discount for prompt payment and the purchaser fails to take advantage of the offer. In that case, trade credit can become the most expensive source of funds available.

Bank credit is available to nonprofit organizations under seasonal and revolving lines of credit and on a transaction basis. As prerequisites to extending credit, banks typically require evidence of ability to repay, an excellent record of financial dealings, and adequate compensating balances. In most cases, nonprofit organizations will arrange unsecured financing with their banks, but in some cases, loans must be collateralized with the pledge of receivables or the endorsement of donors or trustees.

FURTHER READING

This book is recommended for those interested in an extensive inquiry into trade credit terms and costs:

Brosky, John J. *The Implicit Cost of Trade Credit and Theory of Optimal Terms of Sale*. New York: Credit Research Foundation, 1969.

A practical approach to bank lending policy from both a banker's and a bank customer's perspectives is presented in:

Hayes, Douglas A. *Bank Lending Policies: Domestic and International*. Ann Arbor, Mich.: University of Michigan, 1971.

To make certain that borrowing costs are reasonable, the following article is a must:

Conover, C. Todd. "The Case of the Costly Credit Agreement." *Financial Executive* (September 1971): 40-48.

QUESTIONS

1. What is open account credit? How does it differ from extending credit involving the use of a promissory note?

2. Distinguish between cash discounts, quantity discounts, and functional discounts.

3. What do the following abbreviations mean?
   a. COD
   b. CBD
   c. AOG
   d. EOM

4. Discuss some of the factors that help explain differences in trade credit terms offered by different suppliers.

5. Explain how an organization may use trade credit as a discretionary source of funds.

6. When is trade credit a costless source of funds, and when does it carry an explicit cost?

7. List and discuss the major forms of bank credit available to nonprofit organizations.

8. What characteristics distinguish seasonal lines from revolving lines of credit?

9. Describe the qualities that a borrower must possess to be considered highly creditworthy by a commercial bank.

10. How does the compensating balance requirement affect the cost of a bank loan?

11. What are "other commensurate advantages" in banking relationships? How do they affect the cost and availability of bank credit?

12. What types of pledges receivable are considered satisfactory collateral for bank loans?

PROBLEMS

1. The State University Alumni Association purchases printing services on terms of 2/10, net 30. A review of the records reveals that payments are usually made fifteen days after the invoice date. When asked by the auditor why the organization did not take advantage of cash discounts, the secretary-treasurer replied that he invested surplus cash in a money market fund that was yielding 17 percent annually, whereas the discounts were merely 2 percent.

  a. What two mistakes is the secretary-treasurer making?
  b. Calculate the approximate annual percentage cost of passing up the discount and paying fifteen days after the invoice date.
  c. What is the cost of credit if the payment were made on the last day of the credit period?

2. The state Democratic party is undertaking a major fund-raising program consisting of a series of dinners, rallies, theatrical benefits, and dances. The initial stages of the program will require financing of $100,000. Party leaders agree that the organization has only two alternative sources of short-term financing:

  a. Slow down the repayment of its trade credit and lose discounts granted on a 1/10, net 30 basis.
  b. Borrow from a commercial bank at 13 percent.

The bank loan carries with it a compensating balance requirement of $10,000 more than the party's current average bank balances. Which alternative is the less costly?

PART IV

RESOURCE-ALLOCATION DECISIONS

The allocation of resources among competing alternative uses may be the most important decisions that managers of nonprofit organizations must make. These decisions not only establish the basic direction an organization will take in serving its clientele group, but they also profoundly affect its cash flows both immediately and in the long-run. As the chapters in this part of the text will clearly demonstrate, the responsibility for resource-allocation decisions should be shared between an organization's professional and financial managers. Both must provide important input before the final and correct decisions can be made. And both must be aware that neither the professional nor the financial goals of the organization can be ignored in the decision process if the organization is to survive and prosper both financially and professionally.

Chapter 12 begins the discussion of resource-allocation decisions by examining one of the principal tools of long-run financial analysis, the arithmetic of compound interest. Chapter 13 presents and discusses the traditional approaches used in capital investment analysis to ascertain that the professional goals of the nonprofit organization are properly addressed in the decision process. Chapter 14, by contrast, presents a decision model that the financial manager should apply to ensure that the organization's financial goals are achieved. Finally, chapter 15 offers a rather complex methodology that permits the simultaneous consideration of both the professional and the financial goals in resource-allocation decisions.

12

Compound Interest, Present Value, and Financial Decisions

This chapter presents the fundamentals of compound interest in its several forms, all of which are essential to an understanding of the financial decision processes and techniques appropriate for use within the nonprofit context. The concepts of compound value, present value, and annuity are presented in the first section of the chapter. The final sections deal with several common problems in the application of the concept of the time value of money to investment decisions. Liberal use of examples aid in achieving clarity in these discussions and serve as guides in applying those concepts to problems contained in the remainder of the text.

The concept of compound interest—the so-called mathematics of finance—is often a key consideration in financial decision making. It facilitates the comparison of the costs of alternative sources of short- and long-term financing, including the decisions concerning whether to lease assets or to borrow funds to finance their ownership. Decisions involving the prepayment of debt having fixed maturities and the analyses of financial-structure alternatives also rely heavily on the use of the compound interest concept. On the asset side of the balance sheet, compound interest enters into decisions relating to investments in short- and long-term securities and the acquisition of fixed assets. Financial managers obviously must be thoroughly conversant with compound interest and the techniques of its application to decisions in their areas of responsibility, since compound interest is a tool they will employ almost daily in managing the financial affairs of nonprofit organizations.

Compound interest is an important factor in the decisions outlined above because it permits management to compare dollars paid out and received at different times in fund-raising or investment decisions. That kind of comparison is essential because a dollar in hand today does not have the same value as a dollar to be received a year from now. And that is the result of an individual's or an organization's ability to invest dollars in real or financial assets that earn *interest* or a financial return. In the simplest case, if a person has a dollar today, he or she can lend it or invest it at some rate of interest and receive more than a dollar at the end of a year. Interest is, therefore, the price at which money is exchanged for a promise to pay at some future date. And interest is what gives money a *time value* and what causes the timing of cash flows to take on importance in financial decision making.

COMPOUND VALUE

Jackson College plans to invest cash balances totaling $2,000 held in its Unrestricted Investment Fund in a commercial bank time-deposit account that pays 5 percent interest compounded annually. The amount that the account will contain at the end of one year from today—its *compound value*—may be calculated, using a formula that contains the following terms:

P = Principal sum, initial investment, or original deposit
r = Interest rate
I = Dollar amount of interest earned during the period
V = Value of the account at the end of the period

The amount on deposit in the bank account at the end of the period is obviously the sum of the original deposit plus the interest earned, or

$$V = P + I$$

Since the interest earned during the period (I) is equal to the principal sum (P) times the interest rate (r), the product (Pr) can replace I in the equation, and V can be redefined as $V = P + Pr$, or simply as

$$V = P (1 + r) \qquad (12.1)$$

The term $(1 + r)$ in the right side of equation (12.1) is called the compound interest factor (CIF). To find the amount on deposit in Jackson College's account at the end of one year, the original deposit (P) is multiplied by the CIF, $(1 + r)$, as in the equation. Given that $r = 5$ percent, or 0.05,

$$V = \$2,000 (1 + 0.05) = \$2,000 (1.05) = \$2,100$$

Jackson College's bank account will grow from $2,000 to $2,100 in one year.

If Jackson College leaves the $2,000 on deposit for three years, it will have grown to $2,315 at the end of that period. Equation (12.1) can be used to construct Exhibit 12-1, which provides a step-by-step illustration of how the solution to this problem is derived.

Exhibit 12-1: **Compound Interest Calculations**

Year	Principal sum (P)	×	CIF (1 + r)	=	Ending value (V)
1	$ 2,000		1.05		$ 2,100
2	2,100		1.05		2,205
3	2,205		1.05		2,315

An alternative route to the same solution can be found by noting that the amount on deposit in account at the end of the second year, V_2, is calculated as

$$V_2 = P(1 + r)(1 + r) = P(1 + r)^2$$

Therefore

$$\$2,000(1.05)^2 = \$2,000(1.05)(1.05) = \$2,205$$

Similarly, V_3, the balance at the end of the third year, is calculated as

$$V_3 = P(1 + r)(1 + r)(1 + r) = P(1 + r)^3$$

The compound value of the account at the end of any year, n, can be calculated using the general equation

$$V_n = P(1 + r)^n \qquad (12.2)$$

Equation (12.2), although apparently quite simple in its generalized form, can obviously become quite unwieldy when n becomes large and r is expressed in halves, quarters, or eighths of a percent, as is commonly the case in business decisions. Fortunately, however, tables have been constructed for the value of $(1 + r)^n$ for wide ranges of r and n; Exhibit 12-2 is illustrative. The table in Appendix A is a more complete table.[1]

---

[1]The fact that relatively inexpensive hand-held calculators are available that are capable of performing compound interest calculations almost automatically renders these tables practically obsolete; however, the financial manager must thoroughly understand the concepts underlying this financial tool in order to gain maximum benefit from its use. The remaining examples in this chapter will therefore rely for the calculations on the compound-interest factors found in the tables.

Exhibit 12-2: **Compound Value of $1**

Year	1%	2%	2.5%	5%	10%	25%
1	1.0100	1.0200	1.0250	1.0500	1.1000	1.2500
2	1.0201	1.0404	1.0506	1.1025	1.2100	1.5625
3	1.0303	1.0612	1.0769	1.1576	1.3310	1.9531
4	1.0406	1.0824	1.1038	1.2155	1.4641	2.4414
5	1.0510	1.1041	1.1314	1.2763	1.6105	3.0518
10	1.1046	1.2190	1.2801	1.6289	2.5937	9.3132
20	1.2202	1.4859	1.6386	2.6533	6.7275	86.736
50	1.6446	2.6916	3.4371	11.467	117.39	70065.

With the aid of the compound value table, the Jackson College example can be extended to encompass different interest rates over a number of periods and can determine the ending balances (compound values) with little difficulty. For example, Exhibit 12-2 can be used to compute the value of Jackson College's account at the end of the third, fifth, and tenth years. Again assuming that the account earns 5 percent interest, the correct interest factor for year 3 is found in the 5 percent column and the year 3 row. The interest factor is 1.1576, which is also the numerical value of $(1 + 0.05)^3$. In other words, the table eliminates the need to multiply $(1 + 0.05)$ by itself three times. The figure 1.1576 is the CIF at 5 percent at the end of the third year. If we let $CIF_n = (1 + r)^n$, equation (12.2) can be rewritten as $V_n = P(CIF_n)$, where the subscript n stands for the year. Then using the compound interest factor of 1.1576, the compound value of Jackson College's $2,000 deposit at the end of the third year is calculated as follows:

$$V_3 = P(CIF_3) = \$2,000(1.1576) = \$2,315$$

This procedure produces precisely the same figure that was obtained by the long method shown in Exhibit 12-1.

The compound value of the $2,000 for the fifth and tenth years can be found in the same way. The compound interest factors from Exhibit 12-2 are 1.2763 and 1.6289 respectively. Therefore,

$$V_5 = \$2,000 \ (1.2763) = \$2,553$$
$$V_{10} = \$2,000 \ (1.6289) = \$3,258$$

These same answers are obtainable using the more complex and time-consuming procedure outlined in Exhibit 12-1.

PRESENT VALUE

The financial manager often is confronted with a problem that is very similar to the determination of compound value. However, instead of knowing the principal sum, the financial manager knows the ending balance or value and must calculate the principal sum or its *present value*. And finding present value (or *discounting* an amount to be received at some future date) is simply the reverse of finding compound value.

For example, suppose the financial officer of Jackson College has a temporary cash surplus and decides to purchase ten U.S. Treasury bonds due to mature in one year. When the bonds mature, the U.S. government will pay the principal of $1,000 plus interest of $65.75 on each bond. The only other alternative use of the idle funds is to add to its 5 percent bank time-deposit account. The question, therefore, is what maximum amount should the financial officer bid to purchase the securities in the market?

The answer may be obtained by solving for P in equation (12.1). That is, the financial officer wants to know what principal sum invested immediately will yield $1,065.75 at the end of one year at an interest rate of 5 percent. To say it another way, P is the present value of $1,065.75 due at the end of one year discounted at 5 percent. If $V_1 = P(1 + r)$, then

$$P = \frac{V_1}{(1 + r)} = \frac{\$1,065.75}{(1 + 0.05)} = \$1,015$$

If the college is the successful bidder at $1,015 per bond, it will have gotten them at a price that will yield the firm exactly 5 percent on its investment. However, Jackson College could have done equally as well to deposit the same amount at the bank for the one year at 5 percent interest. This is easily proven using the compound interest factors in Exhibit 12-2. The compound value of a time deposit of $1,015 at the end of one year is equal to the amount of the deposit times the CIF for one year at 5 percent. The CIF for 5 percent for one year (from Exhibit 12-2) is 1.0500; thus

$$V_1 = \$1,015(1.0500) = \$1,065.75$$

or the same amount as the bond principal plus interest.

If Jackson College's financial officer desires a better return from the investment in the bonds, he or she obviously should recalculate the bid price using a higher interest rate. If the financial officer selects 25 percent as the required return, he or she would submit a bid price for the bonds of

$852.60 each. It is quite unlikely that Jackson College would be the successful bidder at a price that low (having that high a return) unless, of course, the market rate of interest for short-term government securities was as high or higher than 25 percent.

The problem becomes slightly more complex when several time periods are involved, but equation (12.2) can quite readily be transformed into the present value formula simply by dividing both sides of the equation $(1 + r)^n$ and dropping the subscript n from V_n. The transformation yields

$$\text{Present value} = P = \frac{V}{(1 + r)^n} = V \frac{1}{(1 + r)^n} \qquad (12.3)$$

where the term $1/(1 + r)^n$ is called the present-value factor (PVF).

Tables similar to the compound value table have been constructed for the PVFs for various values of r and n; Exhibit 12-3 is illustrative of such tables. A more complete table is found in Appendix B. (You may wish to calculate the present value of $1,065.75 [due in one year, discounted at 5 percent and 25 percent] using Exhibit 12-3.)

Exhibit 12-3: **Present Value of $1**

Year	1%	2%	2.5%	5%	10%	25%
1	.9901	.9804	.9756	.9524	.9091	.8000
2	.9803	.9612	.9518	.9070	.8265	.6400
3	.9706	.9423	.9286	.8638	.7513	.5120
4	.9610	.9239	.9060	.8227	.6830	.4096
5	.9515	.9057	.8839	.7835	.6209	.3277
10	.9053	.8204	.7812	.6139	.3855	.1074
20	.8195	.6730	.6103	.3769	.1486	.0155
50	.6080	.3715	.2909	.0872	.0085	

To illustrate the use of the table, assume that a wealthy investor, Alvin George, wants to determine the present value of $10,000 due in ten years and discounted at 10 percent. His inquiry may be prompted by a desire on his part to either buy or sell an instrument of indebtedness or a promise to pay. In either case he would need to know its current value (market price) under his particular set of circumstances. If Alvin had access to Exhibit 12-3, he should look down the year column to 10, then across to the 10 percent column to find the PVF of .3855. This figure multiplied by the ending value, or the promise to pay, of $10,000 yields the present value, or the market value, of the instrument. Letting PVF = $[1/1 + r)^n]$ or the table value,

$$P = V(\text{PVF})$$
$$= \$10,000(.3855)$$
$$= \$3,855$$

In other words, assuming that Alvin George requires a minimum of 10 percent return on this particular investment, he should pay no more than $3,855 for the instrument of indebtedness.

ANNUITIES

An annuity is the payment of a fixed amount of money at uniform intervals over some specified period. *Ordinary* annuities are those in which the payments are made at the *end* of each interval. An *annuity due* is one in which the payments are due at the beginning of each interval, as in life insurance premiums. Unless otherwise indicated, this discussion of annuities is confined to ordinary annuities.

Examples of annuities are rent on the use of property and pension payments received by a retiree. Two aspects of the annuity are particularly important in financial decision making: (1) the compound value of an annuity and (2) its present value.

Compound Value of an Annuity

The financial administrator of the Baker Foundation decided to establish a cash reserve that ultimately will be used to pay for the planned expansion of its office space. From his financial forecasts, the financial administrator has determined that the foundation will generate excess cash balances totaling $30,000 per year for the next several years. The financial administrator also feels that the cash reserve will be able to earn at least 10 percent compounded annually. The target date for the completion of the construction is four years away. How much will be available in the cash reserve at that time? Exhibit 12-4 provides a step-by-step illustration of how that particular compound value is calculated arithmetically.

Exhibit 12-4: Compound Value of an Annuity

Cash reserved at the end of year 1	$ 30,000
Interest earned during year 2 (at 10 percent)	3,000
Cash added to the reserve at the end of year 2	30,000
Total reserve at the end of year 2	$ 63,000
Interest earned during year 3	6,300
Cash added to the reserve at the end of year 3	30,000
Total reserve at the end of year 3	$ 99,300
Interest earned during year 4	9,930
Cash added to the reserve at the end of year 4	30,000
Compound value at the end of 4 years	$ 139,230

Since the first $30,000 will not be available for investment until the *end* of the first year, no interest is earned during the initial period. By the end of the second year, the cash reserve has grown to $63,000, of which $3,000 represents interest earned during the second year on the first year's $30,000 investment. At the end of the fourth year, the total cash accumulated is $139,230. A total of $120,000 was added to the reserve by the foundation during the four-year period, and $19,230 is the amount of compound interest earned.

The compound value of the annuity may also be expressed algebraically by the formula

$$A = R \left[\frac{(1 + r)^n - 1}{r} \right]$$
(12.4)

where

A = Compound value of the annuity
R = Periodic payment (cash added)
r = Interest rate
n = Number of periods covered by the annuity

The expression enclosed in brackets in equation (12.4) has been used to construct tables that list the values of the compound sum of an annuity of $1.00 per period for various combinations of n and r. Exhibit 12-5 presents an illustrative set of these values; a more complete set may be found in Appendix C.

Exhibit 12-5: **Compound Value of an Annuity of $1**

Year	1%	2%	2.5%	5%	10%	25%
1	1.0000	1.0000	1.0000	1.0000	1.0000	1.0000
2	2.0100	1.0200	2.0250	2.0500	2.1000	2.2500
3	3.0301	3.0604	3.0756	3.1525	3.3100	3.8125
4	4.0604	4.1216	4.1525	4.3101	4.6410	5.7656
5	5.1010	5.2040	5.2563	5.5256	6.1051	8.2070
10	10.462	10.950	11.203	12.578	15.937	33.253
25	28.243	32.030	34.158	47.727	98.347	1054.8

To find the answer to the Baker Foundation's annuity problem using Exhibit 12-5, the CIF located in the year 4 row and 10 percent column is substituted for the bracketed term in equation (12.4). That compound annuity factor (CAF) is 4.6410, and the compound annuity value of the $30,000 annual investment is:

$$A = R(CAF) = \$30,000 \, (4.6410) = \$139,230$$

The answer is the same as the one derived by the long method illustrated in Exhibit 12-4. If the $139,230 is too small to cover the cost of the foundation's planned expansion program, the financial administrator may attempt to invest more cash, increase the return on investment, or both.

Present Value of an Annuity

Jenny Wagner, a high school senior, won the grand prize in a giveaway contest that offered her the option of selecting either an annuity providing an annual income of $5,000 per year for five years, for a total of $25,000, or an immediate lump sum payment of $20,000. Jenny plans to save the money until she graduates from college, and then use it to travel extensively. Regardless of which option she selects, Jenny will place the money in a savings account paying 5 percent interest, compounded annually. Which alternative should she take under those circumstances?

The decision in this instance may be based on the comparison of the lump sum with the present value of the annuity. If the present value of the annuity turns out to be less than $20,000, she should select the lump sum; if it is greater than $20,000, the annuity should be Jenny's choice.

To aid her in this decision, tables have been constructed using the following formula, which represents the present value of an annuity of R dollars per period, A^*. The symbols r and n continue to represent the interest rate and length of the annuity.

$$A^* = R \left[\frac{1 - \dfrac{1}{(1 + r)^n}}{r} \right] \tag{12.5}$$

The expression in brackets is the present value annuity factor (PAF) from which the tables in Exhibit 12-6 and Appendix D were constructed. The PAF for five years at 5 percent is 4.3295. Therefore,

$$A^* = R(PAF) = \$5,000 \times 4.3295 = \$21,647.50$$

In other words, the present value of five annual payments of $5,000 each is worth more than the immediate lump-sum payment (if deposited in an interest-bearing savings account) offered as an alternative in the giveaway contest. Jenny should therefore take the annual income option.

Suppose, however, that Jenny's uncle, Fred, on hearing of her good

Exhibit 12-6: **Present Value of an Annuity of $1**

Year	1%	2%	2.5%	5%	10%	25%
1	0.9901	0.9804	0.9756	0.9523	0.9091	0.8000
2	1.9704	1.9416	1.9274	1.8594	1.7355	1.4400
3	2.9410	2.8839	2.8560	2.7232	2.4869	1.9520
4	3.9020	3.8077	3.7620	3.5460	3.1699	2.3616
5	4.8534	4.7135	4.6458	4.3295	3.7908	2.6893
10	9.4713	8.9826	8.7521	7.7217	6.1446	3.5705
25	22.0232	19.5235	18.4244	14.0939	9.0770	3.9849

fortune, offered to let her buy a one-fourth interest in his timber harvesting business for $20,000 and guaranteed her a return of 10 percent on her investment. He promised to buy back the share at the end of five years, if she wanted to sell it at that time. Under these circumstances what should Jenny do?

Since the discount rate has jumped from 5 percent to 10 percent, the present value of the annuity must be recalculated using the interest factor from Exhibit 12-6 found in the 10 percent column and the year-5 row. The present value of the stream of payments then becomes

$$A^* = \$5,000(3.7908) = \$18,954.00$$

Under these circumstances, the annual income of $5,000 is less valuable than the lump sum invested at 10 percent. If Uncle Fred's business is sound, Jenny should take the lump sum option and invest in her uncle's business.

Annuities With Unequal Payments

Thus far the discussion has dealt only with annuities with constant, or equal, annual payments. Many financial decisions do involve series of even cash receipts—debt repayment, lease payments, and certain operating costs, for example. But cash receipts from business operations, because they are received from many sources, frequently are received in varying amounts over time. Consequently, it is necessary to develop a method of calculating the present values of uneven annuities, or cash-flow streams of varying amounts.

Suppose Jenny Wagner's uncle had an opportunity to purchase another harvesting operation that holds leases on several tracts of timberland. According to the logging schedule Uncle Fred developed, the profits from the new venture would be $1,500 at the end of the first year; $700 at the end of the second year; and $1,200 at the end of the third year. How much should Uncle Fred pay for the business, assuming the appropriate interest (discount) rate is 5 percent?

The calculations needed to determine the purchase price for the timber operations are shown in Exhibit 12-7. The interest factors in the column headed PVF are taken from the 5 percent column for years 1, 2, and 3 in Exhibit 12-3. When the profits in each year are multiplied by the corresponding interest factor, and the resultant present values are added, the sum is the present value of the investment, or $3,100.06. If the assumptions in the example hold true, Uncle Fred should be willing to pay $3,100.06 for the projected profits from the timber harvesting operations.

Exhibit 12-7: **Present Value Calculations for an Uneven Series of Payments**

Year	Profits	×	PVF	PV
1	$ 1,500		.9524	$ 1,428.60
2	700		.9070	634.90
3	1,200		.8638	1,036.56
	$ 3,400		PV of investment =	$ 3,100.06

Another example will illustrate the same concept under a slightly different set of circumstances in which *even* and *uneven* cash receipts are involved. Suppose a rich uncle died and left you two bonds in his will. One matures in one year and pays $1,030, and the other matures in five years and pays $35 per year in interest with a maturity value of $1,000. Your uncle's will stipulates that you would have to either hold both bonds until they matured or sell both immediately. Assuming you decided to sell, and the appropriate discount rate is 5 percent, how much does your inheritance represent in cash today?

The stream of interest and principal payments from these bonds may be arranged as shown in Exhibit 12-8. The interest factors were obtained from Exhibits 12-3 and 12-6. Note that only one factor is used to calculate the present value of the payments received at the end of years 2, 3, and 4. This factor is calculated from interest factor values in the 5 percent column in Exhibit 12-6 by subtracting the interest factor for year 1 (0.9523) from the interest factor for year 4 (3.5460). The difference, 2.5937, is the present value of an *even* stream of payments of $1 received at the end of years 2, 3, and 4. When it is multiplied by $35, the product represents the present value of the $35 annual interest payments from bond number two for the middle years.

Exhibit 12-8: **Present Value Calculations for an Uneven Series of Payments**

Year	Source of Receipts	Receipts	×	PVF or PAF	=	Present Value
1	Principal plus interest on bond number 1 plus interest on bond number 2	$ 1,065		0.9524		$ 1,014.31
2 3 4	Interest on bond number 2	35 35 35 } $ 35		2.5937		90.78
5	Principal plus interest on bond number 2	1,035		0.7835		810.92
	Total	$ 2,205				$ 1,916.01

The interest factors for years 1 and 5 were taken directly from the 5-percent column in Exhibit 12-3. The sum of the present values in the fifth column of Exhibit 12-8 is, of course, today's cash value of the inheritance left to you by your uncle.

COMPOUNDING PERIODS

Obviously, cash is received by businesses, individuals, and organizations more often than once a year, but this fact presents no great difficulty in applying the present value and compound value concepts to real financial decisions and problems. In fact, the same tables can be used when compounding occurs more than once a year. The only adjustments required to the usual procedure are that the interest rate must be divided by the number of compounding periods *per year* and the "year" column in the tables is interpreted as being the number of compounding periods involved in the problem. For example, if an investment promises a return of $1,000 every six months for five years at a discount rate of 5 percent, the present value can be calculated in four stages:

1. Divide the discount rate by 2 (.05/2 = .025)
2. Determine the number of six-month periods in five years (10)
3. Find the interest factor in Exhibit 12-6 for 10 periods at 2.5 percent (8.7521)
4. Multiply the interest factor by $1,000 ($1,000 × 8.7521 = $8,752.10)

Thus, the present value of $1,000 every six months, discounted at 5 percent compounded semiannually, is $8,752.10.

If the compounding period in this example were set at a year instead of six months, and the investment promised a return of $2,000 at the end of each year instead of $1,000 every six months, the present value of the investment would equal $2,000 × 4.3295, or $8,659.00. This amount is

$93.10 less than the present value of $8,752.10 obtained by compounding every six months. Thus, as the number of compounding periods per year increases, the present value of the investment, or the stream of cash from the investment, likewise increases.

THE POWER OF COMPOUND INTEREST

Cash invested for long periods accumulates to incredibly large amounts even when invested at relatively low rates of interest. For example, if the Algonquian Indians had invested at 6 percent the $24 that legend says they received from the sale of Manhattan Island in New York, and the interest was compounded quarterly, the tribe would have accumulated a total of approximately *$9.6 billion* by this time (about 340 years later). Further, if the tribe had "shopped" for interest rates and compounding periods, it could have done even better. For example, Exhibit 12-9 compares the compound values that the Algonquians would have accumulated under various interest rates and compounding periods. Naturally, the higher the interest rate and the more frequent the compounding, the higher the compound value will be. If the Algonquians had a sharp financial manager, they could have purchased all of New York City's debt when it was experiencing financial difficulties in the 1970s, demanded immediate repayment, reclaimed Manhattan Island, and had money left over. In fact, the Algonquians could have by now accumulated sufficient cash to foreclose on the United States, as Exhibit 12-9 shows.

Exhibit 12-9: **Compound Values of $24 Under Selected Interest Rates and Compounding Periods**

Frequency of compounding	Total no. of periods	Interest rates			
		1%	*3%*	*6%*	*8%*
Annually	330	$707	$ 555,735	$ 9.6 billion	$ 5.5 trillion
Semiannually	660	713	598,577	12.9 billion	9.2 trillion
Quarterly	1,320	716	621,564	14.9 billion	11.9 trillion
Monthly	3,960	718	637,510	16.5 billion	14.3 trillion
Daily	120,532	719	645,406	17.3 billion	15.5 trillion

Another way to test the power of compound interest is to measure the length of time it takes to double a cash investment. A rough rule of thumb for calculating the time required to double an investment is called the "Rule of 72." Under this rule, the relevant interest rate, when divided into 72, yields the time required to double the amount invested at that rate under annual compounding. For example, at 10 percent interest and annual compounding, an investment will double its value in $(72/10 =)$ 7.2 years, using the Rule of 72 in calculating the estimate.

Exhibit 12-10: **Time Required to Double an Investment**

Interest rate	Years to double	
	Annual compounding	Quarterly compounding
1%	69.7	69.4
2	35.0	34.7
4	17.7	17.4
6	11.9	11.6
8	9.0	8.7
10	7.3	7.0
15	5.0	4.8
20	3.8	3.6

Exhibit 12-10 contains the *actual* number of years required to double an investment under both annual and quarterly compounding periods for selected interest rates. The number of years to double were calculated using equation (12.2) and solving for n. One particularly dismal aspect of the figures in the table is the fact that they may also be related to *price inflation*. That is, the double-digit inflation rate of the consumer price index of between 15 and 20 percent in the late 1970s and early 1980s, if it had been sustained, would have doubled the cost of the market basket of goods and services purchased by an average family in less than five years.

Another aspect of these concepts is worth noting: While interest is accumulating in an investment account, price inflation is eroding the purchasing power of the money invested therein. As a rough approximation, therefore, the *real* rate of interest an investment produces is equal to the *nominal* rate being paid on the asset, minus the rate of inflation. For example, suppose the annual cost of attending Harvard University currently is $12,000. A very proud grandfather gives his newborn grandson $48,000 to cover the cost of four years at that institution. If the child's parents invest that sum at 10 percent compounded annually and the cost of attending Harvard grows by 8 percent per year, the college fund will accumulate real interest at only 2 percent per year, since the principal sum plus the first eight percentage points of the total annual earnings will have to be spent for the child's education in eighteen years. If college costs grow by more than 10 percent per year, the child will receive a negative return on the investment, since more money will have to be added to the compound value of the $48,000 gift to enable him to attend Harvard for four years.

SELECTING THE APPROPRIATE INTEREST RATE

As is evident from some of the preceding examples, the appropriate interest rate to be used in any given situation is determined largely by the circumstances involved in the problem. In most cases, the interest rate is established by the next best available investment alternatives or market rates of interest prevailing on similar instruments or investments of similar risk at the time the decision is made. However, to be precise, interest rates are determined through the principal dimensions of location, time, risk, and maturity. Additionally, rates may be influenced by the marketability of the instrument, the size of the principal sum involved, the legality of the arrangement, the tax status of the instrument, and the nature and intentions of the parties involved.

Rates on a specific type of loan, for example, may vary from city to city and country to country; this is the dimension of location. Or the rates on the same type of loan may change from day to day; this is the time dimension. Again, at a specific time and place there usually is a wide range of interest rates, the differences among which vary according to risk, maturity, size of loan, and so forth. In the decision-making process as outlined in this chapter, the financial officer generally accepts as a given the existing set of interest rates he or she finds at the time in the local, national, or regional markets. The final choice then becomes that of selecting the appropriate rate with reference to the *term structure* and *risk structure* of interest rates.

The *term structure* of interest rates arises because actual interest rates vary with the maturity of the instrument or the time horizon prescribed by the problem. This comes about because the returns become more uncertain as maturity lengthens. It is thus inappropriate to discount the cash flows from a twenty-year investment at the rate prevailing on short-term business loans. Similarly, a financial officer would not wish to compare the returns from a riskless but permanent investment in fixed assets with those available from a ninety-day U.S. Treasury bill simply because the maturities of the two investments are quite different and consequently their respective returns are not comparable.

The *risk structure* of interest rates arises because actual interest rates vary with the degree of risk associated with the investment. In general, the greater the risk, the higher the available returns (or associated interest costs). This of course results from the fact that investors and financial administrators will avoid taking risks whenever possible and will seek risky situations only when they are adequately compensated for risk taking by receiving greater than normal returns. In selecting the appropriate interest rate to use in decision making, the financial officer should make allowances for risk differentials between alternative investments by increasing the required rate of return on, or adding a *risk premium* to, the riskier investment. The practice of adding a risk premium to the returns from risky assets is a common one and, indeed, a necessary one, if there is to be a demand for risky assets.

In most instances, as mentioned earlier, the problem itself will prescribe fairly closely the appropriate interest rate to be used in decisions involving compound interest; however, the financial officer must examine each situation carefully to ensure that the alternatives examined are comparable in all of the dimensions that act to determine the levels of interest rates. Also, as discussed more fully in later chapters, the financial officer must be confident that the alternatives facing the organization are both relevant and the best available at that particular time.

For example, consider an organization that is facing the choice of either prepaying a short-term loan or investing that cash until the maturity date of the note. First, the financial officer must determine how much more interest the bank will charge if the loan is paid at maturity instead of immediately. Then, he or she will have to examine the available low-risk investments that will be readily marketable or redeemable on the day the bank loan is due. The risk must be low since the funds must be available on that date to prevent the loan from being in default. After locating the several short-term investment opportunities that meet these criteria, the financial officer must calculate the rate of return on each and use the highest rate for purposes of comparing the two alternative uses of the organization's funds.

The precise form of this decision and other types of financial analyses involving the use of compound interest are presented throughout the remaining chapters of this text. These decision rules and their requisite analytical formats are varied, but the application of the compound interest formulas is a constant in each situation.

SUMMARY

The concepts relating to compound interest permit the financial manager to measure intertemporal cash flows on a comparable basis. This kind of comparison is essential in financial decision making because a dollar in hand today is more valuable than a dollar that will be received at some future date. Decision techniques involving alternative sources of financing and competing investment opportunities universally prescribe the use of compound interest.

The key to the successful application of these concepts is the selection of the appropriate interest rate. This rate must be determined based on the circumstances inherent in the problem to be solved. In general, the interest rate is indicated by the available investment alternatives or the prevailing market rate of interest on similar instruments at the time the decision will be implemented.

QUESTIONS

1. What types of financial decisions involve the use of compound interest?

2. What is the difference between each of the following pairs of concepts?
   a. present value and compound value
   b. present value of a dollar and present value of an annuity
   c. annual compounding and quarterly compounding

3. You calculate the present value of an annuity as $5,000, but your neighbor calculates the present value of the same annuity as $4,800. Who used the higher interest rate in the calculations?

4. Explain or define each of the terms in the generalized form of the compound interest formula,

$$V_n = P(1 + r)^n.$$

5. What do the following abbreviations stand for and explain the meaning of the terms they represent:
   a. CIF
   b. PVF
   c. CAF
   d. PAF

6. Explain how to find the present value of an annuity with unequal annual payments.

7. How does a change in the compounding period affect the rate of return earned on an investment?

8. What is the Rule of 72?

9. How is the approximate real rate of return from an investment calculated?

10. Define the following terms:
    a. term structure of interest rates
    b. risk structure of interest rates
    c. risk premium

11. List and discuss the four principal factors that determine interest rates. What other factors also influence the rates?

PROBLEMS

1. How much will $500 invested today be worth at the end of five years, assuming an interest rate of
   a. 5 percent?
   b. 10 percent?

2. What is the present value of $2,000 to be received at the end of six years, assuming an interest rate of:
   a. 8 percent?
   b. 14 percent?

3. The church council has decided to set up a fund to replace the minister's car on a five-year cycle. The council expects an annual cash surplus of $600 will be available for this purpose and has estimated that if new-car prices hold steady the new car can be purchased five years hence at a cost of $3,800, plus the old car as a trade-in. If the cash can be invested at a rate of 10 percent compounded annually, will sufficient cash be available in five years?

4. The church council in problem 3 learned that the price of autos has been increasing at an annual rate of 7 percent. It also discovered that it could invest its cash at an annual rate of 12 percent compounded quarterly. Will it have sufficient cash at the end of five years to purchase a new car for the minister if it invests $150 each quarter?

5. Given the circumstances presented in problems 3 and 4,
   a. how much should the church council set aside each quarter to purchase the new car in five years?
   b. if the council decided to make a single investment immediately, instead of making quarterly investments, how much cash would it be required to invest to reach its goal?

6. Use the Rule of 72 to calculate the amount of time it would take to double an investment at 16 percent interest compounded annually. Compare this with the actual time, calculated using the appropriate compound interest formula or the interest tables.

7. Calculate the present value of the following cash-flow stream, using a discount rate of 10 percent compounded annually:

Year 1	$ 2,500
Year 2	$ 3,000
Year 3	$ 500

8. At what rate of discount will the present value of the cash flows in problem 7 equal $5,447.50?

13

Traditional Approaches to Resource-Allocation Decisions in Nonprofit Contexts

This chapter provides brief overviews and evaluations of the major approaches seriously recommended for use in the public and nonprofit sectors. Dating from the immediate post-World War II years, some of these approaches have their roots in both welfare and economics, while others are based on for-profit financial management techniques. While each has its strengths, each is also flawed in material ways as applications to financial management decisions in nonprofit organizations.

The theoretical framework on which this book is based emphasizes the dual-management structure as a fundamental characteristic of organizations operating within the nonprofit context. As detailed in chapters 2 and 3, nonprofit organizations are directed by professional managers and assisted by staff executives, such as financial managers. In the critical area of resource-allocation decisions, the professional managers are ultimately responsible for selecting those projects that will best achieve the professional goals of the nonprofit organization. The financial managers, in contrast, specify the budget constraint within which such choices must be made in order to keep their organizations from foundering financially.

This chapter and the two chapters immediately following examine the decision-making processes appropriate to both the professional manager's and the financial manager's areas of responsibility. The present chapter examines the professional decision techniques traditionally applied to allocating resources in the nonprofit (and especially the governmental) context. Chapter 14 describes the resource-allocation decision process from the financial manager's perspective in terms of maintaining organizational liquidity and solvency. Finally, chapter 15 illustrates a technique, called goal programming, that may improve the resource-allocation process when an organization must choose from among a number of alternative capital investment projects under capital rationing.

TECHNIQUES FOR THE PROFESSIONAL MANAGER

The literature dealing with resource-allocation decisions by nonprofit organizations is found mainly in the economic and political science journals. It focuses primarily on *program budgeting* and, more specifically, on the allocational technique called *cost-benefit analysis*. This technique is the one most commonly advocated by welfare economists for use in allocating resources among competing alternative uses in the public sector. Another technique, called *zero-base budgeting*, has been recommended as an appropriate tool for reviewing ongoing programs for the purpose of reallocating resources to achieve greater effectiveness or efficiency in their use. Finally, a few authors have suggested that the *net present value* (NPV) technique, developed for use by profit-seeking businesses in capital investment analysis, is equally applicable for this purpose in the nonprofit context.

These are the so-called traditional approaches to imparting rationality to resource-allocation decisions in nonprofit organizations. Each approach will be examined in turn in the following sections to reveal its nature and purpose and to fully evaluate its usefulness both to an organization's professional management and to its financial manager. As the discussions will reveal, none of the approaches meet the special requirements of the *financial* manager in achieving the goal of maintaining organizational liquidity and solvency; however, they may be of considerable value to the *professional* management of nonprofit organizations when they are properly applied and the results of the applications are properly interpreted.

Program Budgeting and Cost-Benefit Analysis

Program budgeting is not easy to define in simple, straightforward terms because it is more of a conceptual process than a specific analytical decision methodology. As its name implies, its primary focus is on the appraisal of individual *programs*, and its purpose is to help decision makers *identify objectives, design alternative ways to achieve each objective*, and *allocate resources* optimally to accomplish the stated objectives. Program budgeting does not replace the accounting-budgeting system normally used by an organization, but in most cases it can have a dramatic impact on the design of the accounting system because of its unique informational requirements.

Program budgeting is an extremely complex process. More has been written and published on the topic than on any other single issue in the fields of financial management, political science, and welfare economics (the three fields of inquiry under which program budgeting is most often classified). Entire textbooks, monographs, collections of articles from the professional literature, and numerous guides describing "how to" have been published on the topic since the early 1960s, when certain agencies of the federal government began refining the process and sharing their experiences broadly. David Novick, a pioneer in the field, notes that the earliest formulation of the basic features of program budgeting appeared in General Motors Corporation's *Budget and Finance Procedures* (1924).[1] Other early publications include *Efficiency and Economy in Government Through New Budgeting and Accounting Procedures* by David Novick (1953), and *Program Budgeting* by Eugene Elkins (1955).[2] An exhaustive bibliography on program budgeting and related topics, if indeed it could be made exhaustive, would be sufficient in itself to fill a small book.[3]

Obviously, one cannot hope to synthesize that whole body of literature in one section of a single chapter; however, present purposes can be well served by presenting a simple outline of the basic concept of program budgeting so that its relationship to financial management's and professional management's roles in the operation of a nonprofit organization can be made clear.

The Concept of Program Budgeting. Decision making is made easier in both the for-profit and nonprofit contexts when a problem is reduced to its elemental components. Program budgeting is designed to do just that. It provides a specific *structure* for addressing the problem; it delineates the *informational requirements* for the decision process; and it prescribes an *analytic methodology* that produces an indicator that the professional manager can use in both accept-reject decisions and in ranking alternative approaches, programs, and objectives. The structure and informational requirements and the analytic methodology—widely known as *cost-benefit analysis* (CBA)—are examined in the following sections.

Structure. The structure that program budgeting will generally assume in an organization is identical to the organizational form of the programs the nonprofit organization undertakes to achieve its professional objectives or goals. For example, a program structure for a church may be defined in terms of education, missionary activities, visitation, liturgy, building and grounds, and social welfare. A structure

---

1. *Program Budgeting*, ed. David Novick (Cambridge, Mass.: Harvard University Press, 1967), xxi-xxii.

2. David Novick, *Efficiency and Economy in Government Through New Budgeting and Accounting Procedures*, R-254 (Santa Monica: RAND Corp., 1953), and Eugene Elkins, *Program Budgeting* (Morgantown, W. Va.: West Virginia University, 1955).

3. The book edited by Hinrichs and Taylor entitled *Program Budgeting and Benefit-Cost Analysis* (Goodyear, 1969), contains a 40-page bibliography, for example.

that patterns itself after the organization's basic activities is intuitively appealing because programs easily can be perceived as the organization's basic operating units and are generally end-product oriented.

While the annual line-item or departmental budget may tend to obscure the fact that money gets allocated toward goal achievement by way of programs, managers at all levels plan, operate, and control largely on the basis of individual programs. For example, a university's college of business may be organized along departmental lines, but department chairmen must plan individual course offerings to meet the needs of the undergraduate, master's, and doctoral programs. Sufficient resources must also be devoted to achieving research, to continuing education, and to university service objectives. Thus, staffing patterns respond to program, rather than to departmental, requirements.

The concept of program budgeting emphasizes the long-range perspective in which a single year's budget allocation represents the results of specific short-range decisions made within the context of a multiyear plan. The objectives of a nonprofit organization are not really accomplished unless they continue to be achieved year after year. In this sense, a program may never terminate, although in rare instances some may appear to reach completion. For example, assistance for abandoned, neglected, and abused children will always be needed; hence, the foster care program in a community will never end, but its objectives may be accomplished fully every year. Further, a program begun to save a significant historical landmark from destruction may be short-lived, since the goal may be permanently achieved in a matter of a few weeks. But if the goal is expressed in terms of *historic preservation*, rather than saving one structure, the program can be perceived as continuing over time.

Informational Requirements. The end-product orientation of programs permits measurement of results and lends a sense of organizational unity to activities, as the preceding examples indicate. Thus, the organization can evaluate its professional operations on the basis of *inputs* and *end products*. While inputs, or resources, and end products may not be similarly denominated for a given program, the principle of rationality in choosing among alternative courses of action both within and among different programs is well served under the structure provided by program budgeting. The costs of preserving the historic landmark just mentioned can be measured in terms of inputs, such as time and money, but the end product cannot be so easily valued in the same terms. The fact that the structure was saved from destruction is undeniable. In that sense the end result is observable.

The informational requirements implied by the terms "inputs" and "end products" suggest that program budgeting requires the support of an information system that will produce or assist in accumulating the necessary data to measure and forecast the quantities and/or costs of inputs and end products for each program undertaken by an organization. These data are essential to the processes of planning, measuring progress toward goal achievement, and controlling the expenditure of resources allocated to the programs.

Thus program budgeting requires the integration of a formal long-range plan with a single-period (financial) budgeting-accounting system. The long-range plan must include information that will facilitate the preparation of the organization's annual operating budget. In this way, management can be assured that current operations are completely consonant with long-range objectives. Without the underlying support of a program-oriented budget-accounting system, program budgeting will be reduced to an ineffective and abstract exercise.

Steps in Program Budgeting. Done properly, budgeting of any type is a continuous process. It is a continuous function in that the final draft of the budget document will almost always serve as the starting point for the next period's budget. Program budgeting is no exception to this rule. Although it is a long-range planning tool, the organization and its operating environment are subject to dynamic influences that necessitate almost constant revision in plans and methods of operations. For example, price inflation will alter cost-volume relationships, often requiring the organization to modify its service objectives. New technology will create changes in an organization's capital-expenditure plans or even cause it to completely reorganize its production or service facilities. Nevertheless, it is useful to define program budgeting as having a starting point and an end point.

A consensus among authorities on the topic suggests that the following six steps are required to develop a program budget:

1. Define the program's objective in terms of output(s) desired.
Example: Provide temporary shelter for abused or neglected children.

2. Delineate the activities needed to carry out the objectives.
Example: Recruit, investigate, train, and certify foster parents, and provide continuing counseling for foster children, their natural parents, and the foster parents.

3. Determine the nature and levels of resources needed to support the activities.
Example: One social worker should carry a maximum caseload of twenty families. One secretary can support three social workers and one supervisor. Develop a per-diem room-and-board payment structure for foster parents.

4. Develop the budget requirements, given the resources defined in step 3.
Example: Given the number of children expected to be placed in the foster care program; the salary scales for secretaries, social workers,

supervisors, and other personnel; per-diem rates for room and board; and so forth, a line-item budget for the current year and object budgets for future years can be developed.

5. Prepare a *performance* budget by developing a budget for each activity listed in step 2.

Example: One-tenth of a social worker's time is used in foster care training; thus one-tenth of annual salary, including fringe benefits, is allocated to foster parent training plus the cost of training materials, supplies, and transportation.

6. Prepare a *program* budget by grouping the activity budgets by program objectives or outputs defined in step 1.

Steps 1, 2, and 3 generate the data necessary to define the program in *operational* and *physical* terms. Steps 4, 5, and 6 translate those data into financial terms by creating three different types of budgets: Step 4 produces a line-item or objective budget useful for financial management control purposes; step 5 produces a performance budget that can be used to evaluate alternative means of performing activities; and step 6 produces the program budget used in resource-allocation decisions. The decision process itself—cost-benefit analysis—is performed using the program budget as input; hence, program budgeting is not in itself a resource-allocation tool.

Many authorities prefer to treat cost-benefit analysis as an integral part of program budgeting—a seventh step in the preceding outline— claiming that (1) cost-benefit analysis cannot be performed without first creating a program budget, and (2) program budgeting is merely redundant to line-item budgeting unless its data are used in cost-benefit analysis. The logic is compelling.

Cost-Benefit Analysis. Cost-benefit analysis is an economic (as opposed to a financial-management) tool that systematically examines all economic aspects of a program and produces an objective indicator that a decision maker may employ in resource-allocation decisions for nonprofit organizations. It examines the costs required to establish a program and achieve an objective. It requires the monetization of end products, costs, and benefits, and compares program costs and benefits over an extended planning period: hence the name, *cost-benefit analysis*.[4]

---

4. This process is called by a variety of names, including benefit-cost analysis, cost-effectiveness analysis, systems analysis, operations research, and cost-utility analysis. While some authors belabor the point that each of these names refers to a different analytical tool, their similarities in structure, application, and results are so great that a single nomenclature is rendered not at all unreasonable.

The application of cost-benefit analysis basically involves calculating the value of Z using the equation:

$$Z = \sum_{t=1}^{n} B_t(1 + r)^{-t}/[K + \sum_{t=1}^{n} C_t(1 + r)^{-t}]$$

Here B_t *is the expected benefits arising from the program in year t.* The word "benefit" implies the recognition of both cash inflows to the organization and monetary values of noncash returns, generally taken as benefits to society. The term $(1 + r)^{-t}$ is the PVF used to discount future benefits at the relevant interest rate r. The summation (Σ) of these benefits over the planning period to year n produces the present value of future benefits. The process of discounting allows intertemporal comparison of dollar values over the program's entire life, as explained in chapter 12.

The symbol K represents the initial outlay of funds in the current period for the construction of building and/or the acquisition of equipment necessary to the proper functioning of the program. The symbol C_t is the value of cash spent by the organization to operate and maintain the program plus the monetized value of any noncash (societal) "costs" attributable to the program. The annual program costs are discounted at interest rate r and their present value is the summation of these discounted costs to year n. The ratio of the present values of benefits to costs, given as Z in the equation, is the objective indicator of the value of the program to the organization; a ratio equal to or greater than a calculated value of one signals acceptability of the program. The following illustration will help explain the methodology.

Initial Investment. In most instances, the starting point in the application of cost-benefit analysis is that of determining the net investment (K in the equation) required to build, equip, or otherwise place the program in a position to begin operating or producing the expected benefits. Assume that the Humane Society of Rockville is considering the construction of an animal shelter. Purchase of the land and building costs will total $9,800. In addition, the Humane Society will have to purchase food and water dishes for the cages, office equipment, certain veterinary equipment, inventories of pet food, veterinary supplies, and office supplies. Equipment and inventories will require a cash outlay of $5,200. Thus, a total outlay of $15,000 will be required before the animal shelter can be made operational.

Operating and Other Costs. Cash operating costs and nonmonetary costs, represented by C_t in the equation, are estimated for each year of the project's expected life. The amounts may vary from year-to-year. The Humane Society estimates that the shelter's cash-operating costs, including utilities, building maintenance, food, veterinarian services, and so forth, will total about $16,500 per year. Because the Humane Society felt that the proposed structure would probably become inadequate to service the community's needs in about ten years, a ten-year project life was chosen as the planning period. The animal shelter project would be restudied at that time.

Because the animal shelter site borders on a residential area in Rockville and some outdoor dog pens are planned, real estate experts feel that property values in the immediate area will likely fall by a combined total of $40,000 initially; however, the historical rate of increase in value should not be permanently altered by the presence of the shelter. The $40,000 loss in property values represents a *societal cost*, and in the cost-benefit framework must be accounted for as a project cost. Exhibit 13-1 presents the combined investment, operating, and social costs associated with the project.

Exhibit 13-1: **Initial Investment, Operating Costs, and Other Costs Associated With the Animal Shelter Project**

Year	Item	Amount
0	Land and building cost (K)	$ (9,800)*
0	Equipment and inventories (K)	(5,200)
1	Decline of property values (C_t)	(40,000)
1-10	Operating cost (C_t)	(16,500) per year

* Parentheses denote costs or cash expenditures.

Expected Benefits. Expected benefits from the project include actual cash revenues to be realized from the operation of the shelter plus the nonmonetary (societal) benefits the project is likely to generate. The Humane Society expects that about 40 percent of the animals sheltered will be either returned to their owners or adopted. In either case, the shelter will collect a $20 fee from the person claiming or adopting the animal. Another 10 percent of the animals will be suitable for use in medical research, for which the shelter will collect another fee of $5 per animal. Cash receipts from those sources are estimated to total about $6,800 per year.

In addition to the cash benefits, the animal shelter is expected to help control animal population growth and to reduce the incidence of dog bites, damage to domestic and farm animals, the nuisance factor associated with roving packs of dogs, animal litter, and so forth. The monetary value of these admittedly qualitative benefits was estimated by the Humane Society to amount to $21,500 per year over the life of the project. The dollar amount was derived from statistics provided by the Rockville Police Department, regarding complaints and incidents involving stray and uncontrolled animals, and from discussions with veterinarians and others. The monetary benefits are imputed to be received by the community in kind, rather than as an actual cash flow to the Humane Society. Or looked at another way, Rockville's "quality of life" is expected to be enhanced to that extent by the presence of the animal shelter.

The Discount Rate. The project's costs and benefits must be adjusted for intertemporal differences so that all cash flows and nonmonetary costs and benefits are comparably valued. This is done by discounting all costs and benefits to their present values using an appropriate discount rate. (See chapter 12 for an exposition of compound and present values and the techniques of their application.)

Unfortunately, no one rate of discount is uniquely suited for this purpose or may be considered theoretically unambiguous; however, the consensus seems to favor the use of either the rate of interest paid on long-term government securities or some other cost of social capital adjusted for the riskiness of the project or the uncertainty of the future costs and benefits. Justification for the use of the long-term borrowing rate is simply that it represents the marginal cost of long-term funds raised for the purpose of investing in or producing public goods. A risk adjustment is generally called for in order to compensate society by providing a greater return on risky social investments. In this instance the Humane Society decided to use the risk-adjusted interest rate of 15 percent.

Decision Criterion. The decision criterion, Z in the equation, is calculated by discounting project benefits and costs at the appropriate discount rate and calculating the ratio of the present value of benefits to the present value of costs. The present value calculations are presented in Exhibit 13-2.

Exhibit 13-2: Present Values of Costs and Benefits Associated With the Annual Shelter Project

(1) Year (t)	(2) Costs (K + C_t)	(3) Benefits (B_t)	(4) Present Value Factors @ 15%	(5) Present Value of Costs (2) × (4)	(6) Present Value of Benefits (3) × (4)
0	$ (15,000)	0	1.0000	$ (15,000)	0
1	(56,000)	$ 28,300	.8696	(49,132)	$ 24,610
2	(16,500)	28,300	.7561	(12,476)	21,398
3	(16,500)	28,300	.6575	(10,849)	18,607
4	(16,500)	28,300	.5718	(9,435)	16,182
5	(16,500)	28,300	.4972	(8,204)	14,071
6	(16,500)	28,300	.4323	(7,133)	12,234
7	(16,500)	28,300	.3759	(6,202)	10,638
8	(16,500)	28,300	.3269	(5,394)	9,251
9	(16,500)	28,300	.2843	(4,691)	8,046
10	(16,500)	28,300	.2472	(4,079)	6,996
Totals				$ (132,161)	$ 142,033

The values in column (2) in Exhibit 13-2 are the costs found in Exhibit 13-1. The annual benefits in column (3) are the total of the cash receipts of $6,800 plus the $21,500 that represents the monetized value of the projects nonmonetary social benefits. Column (4) contains the present value factors (PVFs) from the table in Appendix B for each year using the 15 percent discount rate. The PVFs are multiplied by the figures in columns (2) and (3), producing the present values of project costs and benefits contained in columns (5) and (6) respectively. The value of Z, given the sums of the present values in columns (5) and (6) in the exhibit, is

$$Z = \frac{\text{Present Value of Benefits}}{\text{Present Value of Costs}} = \frac{\$142,033}{\$132,161} = 1.075$$

Since Z is greater than one, the project is considered acceptable according to the criterion established by cost-benefit analysis.

Evaluation of Program Budgeting. The purpose of program budgeting, as stated previously, is to improve resource-allocation decisions in nonprofit contexts by reducing each problem to its elemental components. The objective implied by the data requirements and analytic methodology is to *maximize societal wealth* by selecting only those projects that promise an excess of (cash plus social) benefits over (cash plus social) costs. A professional manager of a nonprofit organization ought to subscribe to such an objective, because most nonprofit organizations operate with public funds or charitable contributions for the purpose of achieving one or more objectives that benefit at least a small segment of society. Thus, society is clearly better off—wealthier, if you will—because nonprofit organizations exist. And society's wealth will be enhanced if such organizations make only wise professional choices in allocating resources placed at their disposal.

But wise choices are possible only if the data on which the decisions are based are flawless. In the example used to illustrate the application of cost-benefit analysis, the monetized values of the social costs and benefits could hardly be treated as precise values. For example, placing an absolutely accurate dollar value on animal population control or on reducing the incidence of uncontrolled animals roaming the city's streets simply is not possible. The calculated value of Z = 1.075 in the example nevertheless suggests that extreme accuracy has been attained. However, anything in excess of a 7.1 percent error in overestimating benefits or underestimating costs would have resulted in a malallocation of resources for the Humane Society and a net reduction in wealth for society as a whole. Professional managers of nonprofit organizations must therefore exercise considerable caution in applying this tool and in generating data and interpreting the results of cost-benefit analysis.

The true strength of program budgeting for professional managers is its focus on individual programs. Planning, budgeting, accounting, and control systems that are program based promise much clearer statements of objectives, better delineation of alternatives, the probability of better choices, and superior management and control systems.

The primary weakness of program budgeting relates to the purely financial aspects of the process of monetizing nonmonetary costs and benefits. The major aim of the nonprofit organization's *financial* manager is to maintain the organization in a liquid and financially solvent state. However, because cost-benefit analysis does not distinguish between actual cash flows and monetized societal costs and benefits in producing the objective measure, Z, the organization may become both illiquid and insolvent while investing in projects that promise to increase societal wealth (that is, have values of Z greater than one). The Humane Society example illustrates how this can happen.

The total *cash* outlays required to build and operate the animal shelter project are $15,000 for land acquisition, construction, and equipment costs, plus $16,500 per year in cash operating expenses after construction is completed. Cash receipts, however, are expected to total only $6,800 per year, thus leaving the Humane Society with an initial cash deficit of $15,000 and an operating cash deficit of ($16,500 – $6,800 =) $9,700 per year for the next ten years. Thus, while the project is professionally acceptable, based on the cost-benefit criterion, it promises to become a financial liability for the Humane Society. The implication of the cost-benefit technique for the financial manager is thus made clear: once the project has been approved and implemented by professional management, the financial manager must find the means to keep the organization's budget balanced in the face of continued operating-cash deficits. This posture leads to crisis management, and that is simply an unacceptable management philosophy.

Zero-Base Budgeting

Zero-base budgeting is a systematic method of reviewing either all or a selected number of areas of organizational activity for the purpose of *reallocating* resources to improve operational effectiveness and/or efficiency. In contrast to incremental budgeting, which starts with the prior year's budget as a base and allocates *incremental* receipts or appropriations to the organization's activities, zero-base budgeting starts with a base of *zero dollars* for each activity. Under this method, management "takes away" the entire budget of a department or program during the budget planning period and requires the department head or program administrator to rejustify the existence of his or her area's activities from the ground up. After reviewing the budgets for the activities of all zero-base components of the organization, management will reallocate funds in accordance with appropriate criteria.

The results of zero-base budgeting for a particular activity will be a restoration of budget within a range of 0 percent to 100 percent or more of its prior year's budget. For example, management may discover during the review process that a given activity simply is no longer needed or that its usefulness to the organization is so slight in comparison with other activities that it should be discontinued and its entire budget reallocated to other programs. Other activities may suffer budget cuts because their importance has diminished relative to others but has not yet disappeared. And still other activities may receive budget increases commensurate with their respective contributions to organizational goals.

As mentioned earlier, an organization may not subject all of its budgetary units to zero-base review. The creator of zero-base budgeting, Peter A. Pyhrr (pronounced *peer*), stated that its best applications are in "service and support areas of company activity, rather than [in] manufacturing operations proper."[5] Of course, Mr. Pyhrr was referring to the application of this technique to a profit-seeking business, Texas Instruments Incorporated, where the organizational distinction is easily drawn between line and staff functions. Line functions, such as manufacturing and sales, are judged on the basis of profitability and need not be reviewed under a zero-base budget. Staff functions, such as maintenance, accounting, and personnel, for example, are not profit centers; hence their individual value to the firm must be measured by criteria other than profit. And zero-base budgeting was designed to facilitate this measurement.

In nonprofit organizations, and especially in nontrading organizations, a larger proportion of activities is classified as service and support. Thus the scope of zero-base budgeting apparently is to be broader in that context. But to the extent that the value of an activity to the nonprofit entity is measurable more directly, it may be exempted from zero-base review.

Zero-Base and Program Budgeting. A careful review of the literature dealing with program budgeting and zero-base budgeting reveals that only two major differences exist between the two. First, program budgeting deals with *new* programs or activities, while zero-base budgeting deals mainly with ongoing programs. Second, program budgeting is a multiperiod technique while zero-base budgeting has a single-period focus. Both analyze expenditures on a program basis, both use a form of cost-benefit analysis in the decision process, and both are

---

5. Peter Pyhrr, "Zero-base Budgeting," *Harvard Business Review* (November-December 1970): 112.

intended to achieve allocational efficiency or effectiveness in the use of limited resources.

Steps in Zero-Base Budgeting. Once the activities to which zero-base budgeting is to be applied have been identified, the managers responsible for each of them are directed to develop *decision packages*. The decision package is a document that describes a specific activity in such a manner as to permit its evaluation by upper-level management. Specific information required in this step includes: (1) the specific objectives or goals of the activity; (2) the way in which the goals are to be achieved; (3) benefits expected from the activity; (4) alternative ways of achieving the same results; (5) the consequences of not approving the package; and (6) a detailed budgetary request in terms of dollars, numbers of personnel, physical requirements (e.g., office space), and other similar standard measures. An example of a decision package developed for zero-base review in the State of Georgia is presented in Exhibit 13-3.

The decision package is presented in incremental form. First, a minimum level of activity necessary to achieve the specified goals at a minimally acceptable level is developed; this serves as the "base package." Higher levels of goal achievement are then added incrementally to the base package along with information relating to the incremental costs and benefits associated with each higher level.

Since individual decision packages are usually operationally interrelated with one or more other decision packages (that is, the level of funding of one package will cause changes in funding requirements elsewhere), the next step in zero-base budgeting is to *integrate the packages* by forming the activities into identifiable programs. As a first approximation, management will identify the level in each program that represents "business as usual," in terms of last period's operations. Next, the base packages are assembled and adjusted in level to achieve a least-cost profile of the programs operating collectively at their lowest practical levels. Finally, the benefits and costs of the incremental packages are coordinated to achieve balanced operations at incrementally higher levels of activity within the organization. Finally, the effects of new programs and activities on the organization's ongoing operations are considered in a cost-benefit framework.

The final step in the process is to *rank the decision packages* in order of decreasing benefit to the organization. Top priority is granted to those packages funded at levels sufficiently high to (1) satisfy minimum legal or operating requirements or (2) produce significant new benefits to the organization. Lowest priority is given to those packages that are of questionable or marginal benefit to the organization. The cutoff point is actually a budget line that sets the maximum expenditure allowable for the zero-base decision packages. Management's task is to assemble the top-ranked packages into an operationally consonant unit by selecting packages and levels of packages that produce the greatest benefit or goal achievement at the targeted budget level.

(text continued on page 338)

Exhibit 13-3: Decision Package Used for Zero-Base Review in the State of Georgia

(1) Package Name Air Quality Laboratory (1 of 3)	(2) Agency Health	(3) Activity Air Quality Control	(4) Organization Ambient Air	(5) Rank 3

(6) *Statement of Purpose*
Ambient air laboratory analysis must be conducted for identification and evaluation of pollutants by type and by volume. Sample analysis enables engineers to determine effect of control and permits use of an emergency warning system.

(7) *Description of Actions (Operations)*
Use a central lab to conduct all sample testing and analysis: 1 Chemist II, 1 Chemist I, 2 Technicians, and 1 Steno I. This staff could analyze and report on a maximum of 37,300 samples. At 37,300 samples per year, we would only sample the 5 major urban areas of the state (70% of the population). These 5 people are required as a minimum to conduct comprehensive sample analysis of even a few samples on a continuous basis.

(8) *Achievement from Actions*
Ambient air laboratory analysis yields valuable information for management and field engineers to enable them to evaluate effects of the Air Quality Program, identify new or existing pollutants by type and volume, and maintain an emergency warning system.

(9) *Consequences of Not Approving Package*
Field engineers would be forced to rely on their portable testing equipment which does not provide the desired quantitative data (the portable equipment only identifies pollutants by major type, does not measure particle size, and does not provide quantitative chemical analyses to determine the specific chemical compounds in the pollutant), and greatly reduces the effectiveness of the emergency warning system which requires detailed quantitative chemical analyses.

(10) Quantitative Package Measures	FY 1971	FY 1972	FY 1973
Samples analyzed & reported	38,000	55,000	37,300
Cost per sample	$4.21	$4.07	$3.75
Samples per man hour	3.8	3.9	3.7

(11) Resources Required ($ in Thousands)	FY 1971	FY 1972	FY 1973	% FY 73/72
Operational	160	224	140	63%
Grants				
Capital Outlay				
Lease Rentals				
Total	160	224	140	63%
People (Positions)	5	7	5	71%

Manager _____   Prepared By _____   Date _____   Page 1 of ___ 2

(1) Package Name	(2) Agency	(3) Activity	(4) Organization	(5) Rank
Air Quality Laboratory (1 of 3)	Health	Air Quality Control	Ambient Air	3

(12) *Alternatives (Different Levels of Effort) and Cost*

Air Quality Laboratory (2 of 3): $61K*—Analyze 27,700 additional samples (totaling 55,000 samples), which is the current level), thereby determining air quality for 5 additional problem urban areas and 8 other counties chosen on the basis of worst pollution (covering 80% of the population).

Air Quality Laboratory (3 of 3): $45K—Analyze 20,000 additional samples (totaling 75,000 samples), thereby determining air quality for 90% of the population, and leaving only rural areas with little or no pollution problems unsampled.

*(Note: $61K = $61,000)

(13) *Alternatives (Different Ways of Performing the Same Function, Activity, or Operation)*

1. Contract sample analysis work to Georgia Tech—Cost $6 per sample for a total cost of $224K for analyzing 37,300 samples. Emergency warning system would not be as effective due to their time requirement on reporting analysis work done by graduate students.

2. Conduct sample analysis work entirely in regional locations—cost a total of $506K the first year and $385K in subsequent years. Specialized equipment must be purchased in the first year for several locations if central lab is discontinued. Subsequent years would also require lab staffing at several locations at minimum levels which would not fully utilize people.

3. Conduct sample analysis work in central lab for special pollutants only, and set up regional labs to reduce sample mailing costs—cost a total of $305K for analyzing 37,300 samples. Excessive cost would persist due to minimum lab staffing at several locations in addition to the special central lab.

(14) Source of Funds ($ in Thousands)	FY 1971	FY 1972	FY 1973
Federal			
Operational: Other			
State			
Grants: Federal			
State			
Capital and Federal			
Lease State			

(15) Projection of Funds Committed by This Package	FY 1974	FY 1975	FY 1976	FY 1977	FY 1978
Funds					
State					
Total					

Reasons:

Source: *George Minmier and Roger Hermanson, "A Look at Zero-Base Budgeting—The Georgia Experience," Atlanta Economic Review (July-August 1976): 10.*

(text continued from page 335)

Evaluation of Zero-Base Budgeting. Again, the objective of zero-base budgeting is to reallocate all or a part of an organization's resources to achieve professional operational efficiency or effectiveness in goal achievement. This objective is pursued by requiring individual managers in essence, to respond to the following questions regarding their own areas of responsibility.

1. Should your area of responsibility be abolished?
2. If not, can its functions be performed at a lower level of activity and remain as productive as it was last year?
3. If your budget is increased next year, will the incremental costs outweigh the incremental benefits?

Few managers would risk unqualified affirmative responses to any of these inquiries. Thus, while zero-base budgeting purports to be able to justify budget levels for activities and ultimately to achieve allocational efficiency or effectiveness in the use of resources, the process is hampered by its total reliance on subjective data supplied by individuals whose biases are clearly evident and whose motivations are substantially economic at a personal level.

Even if all managers were totally honest in designing their decision packages, another inherent weakness in the technique diminishes its usefulness in many instances; that is, zero-base budgeting is time-consuming. Texas Instruments Incorporated applied the zero-base technique to only "two small divisions" with a total of 100 cost centers, each of which produced from three to ten decision packages.[6] This volume of paperwork—about 450 packages in total—would certainly overwhelm top management in any organization. Obviously, methods of reducing the dimensions of the review and coordination processes are necessary if top management is to carry out its other routine duties during the annual budget review.

Texas Instruments solved the volume problem by consolidating the review and ranking process at several lower-management levels prior to top management's review. In this way top management was able to concentrate on the analysis of truly discretionary packages for their potential values, while merely skimming over the consolidated packages approved at the last management level prior to this review.

Another solution to the volume problem was employed by the State of Georgia. Instead of performing "true" zero-base budgeting, the state instituted an 85-percent-base budgeting system. That is, all decision packages whose funding requirements did not exceed 85 percent of their prior year's budget allocations were automatically approved without review. The rigor of the review intensified as the percentage increased,

---

6. Ibid., 117.

with the highest percentage increase—120 percent or more—requiring then-Governor Jimmy Carter's personal approval.

A third solution offered to reduce the process to manageable proportions is to perform zero-base review on only a few areas of the organization each year. Under this system a review of the entire organization will take as long as five or six years to complete, depending on its size and the complexity of its operations.

Unfortunately, each of these solutions defeats the basic purpose of zero-base budgeting. First, consolidation at lower levels practically guarantees that most of the resources originally allocated to the entity's principal organizational divisions will remain intact. This is because consolidation of decision packages begins at the level of the operating units and passes upward through the chain of command. Thus, resources may be reallocated within major divisions, but they will not likely be reallocated *among* those divisions. The allocations of the new zero-base budget, therefore, are apt to be strikingly similar to those that incremental budgeting would have produced.

Second, 85-percent-base budgeting automatically retains any decision packages, regardless of their intrinsic value to the organization or its goal achievement, so long as their budget requirements are reduced by 15 percent compared with the prior year's allocations. Only the areas of the organization that are able to stand close scrutiny will forward decision packages that require an increase in funding. Thus the group of packages that are potentially worthy of higher funding will be examined while the packages deserving of no more than oblivion are permitted to hide in the nonviolable 85-percent pack. Granted that a 15-percent reduction in the less worthy activities is better than no reduction at all; however, a 100-percent reduction, if desired, is the best outcome. This is also the outcome prescribed by zero-base budgeting, but it cannot be achieved under the 85-percent rule.

Finally, performing zero-base review on a five- or six-year cycle does not permit the organization to achieve an optimal reallocation of resources. This is because the most deserving packages may not come up for review at the time the least deserving packages are identified and receive budget cuts (or *vice versa*). Further, an activity whose importance is diminishing year by year will be able to continue operating at prior years' budgetary levels between zero-base reviews. Similarly, activities whose importance is growing will not receive their proper allocations either because they go unnoticed or because insufficient resources are available for reallocation to those activities.

Clearly, the concept of zero-base budgeting and review has much to commend it as a method of approaching resource-allocation decisions in the nonprofit context. But practical limitations force those who adopt zero-base budgeting for this purpose to employ it in its less powerful and discriminating forms. The results of its application—for most large organizations especially—are hardly distinguishable from those that would result from incremental budgeting.[7]

Net Present Value Method

The net present value (NPV) method of capital expenditure analysis has gained wide acceptance both in the professional finance literature and among finance professionals employed in profit-seeking businesses. The method discounts the cash flows associated with new capital investment proposals, using a relevant rate of interest, in order to take account of the time value of money. The present values of cash inflows and outflows are compared, and projects whose *discounted net cash inflows* are positive are included in the capital budget. Those projects whose discounted net cash flows are negative are rejected from further consideration. The application of this decision tool is intended to result in maximizing stockholder wealth or the market value of the firm.

The Methodology. In algebraic form, a project's NPV is:

NPV = Present value of incremental cast inflows – present value of net investment

$$
= \frac{C_1}{(1 + r)^1} + \frac{C_2}{(1 + r)^2} + \ldots + \frac{C_n}{(1 + r)^n}] - [\frac{I_1}{(1 + r)^1} + \frac{I_2}{(1 + r)^2} + \ldots + \frac{I_m}{(1 + r)^m}]
$$

$$
= \sum_{t=1}^{n} \frac{C_t}{(1 + r)^t} - \sum_{t=1}^{m} \frac{I_t}{(1 + r)^t}.
$$

where C_1, C_2, and so forth, represent the incremental net cash inflows generated by the project; I_1, I_2, and so forth are the incremental cash outlays required to make the project operational; r is the relevant discount rate; n is the project's expected life; and m is the last year in which cash outlays for the project's investment are required.

For example, a boat manufacturer is considering building a new factory-warehouse. Land acquisition, construction, and equipment costs of $1 million will be required, and cash inflows from operations will begin in two years. A ten-year project life is used for planning purposes, and the relevant discount rate is 10 percent. Exhibit 13-4 demonstrates the NPV methodology.

---

7. George Minmier and Roger Hermanson, "A Look at Zero-Base Budgeting—The Georgia Experience," *Atlanta Economic Review* (July-August 1976): 11. The authors report that the zero-base budgeting system installed in Georgia increased the time and effort required for budget preparation, did not improve resource allocation, and was ineffective in coping with changes in the level of funding caused by fluctuations in revenue estimates.

Exhibit 13-4: **Net Present Value (NPV) Calculations for a New Capital Project**

(1)		*(2)*	*(3)*	*(4)*
			Present Value Factors @	Present Value of Cash Flow
Year	Item	Cash Flows	10%	(2) × (3)
0	Land	$ (100,000)	1.000	$ (100,000)
1	Construction and equipment	(900,000)	.909	(818,100)
2		60,000	.862	51,720
3		100,000	.751	75,100
4		200,000	.683	136,600
5		250,000	.621	155,250
	Operating net cash flows			
6		250,000	.564	141,000
7		250,000	.513	128,250
8		250,000	.467	116,750
9		250,000	.424	106,000
10		250,000	.386	96,500
11		250,000	.350	87,500
		Net present value (NPV)	=	$ 176,570

The cash flows for the capital project are listed in column (2). The firm will acquire the land immediately at a cost of $100,000, and construction will be completed in one year. Cash payments for construction and equipment are scheduled at the end of the construction period. Incremental cash inflows from operations (i.e., the total of profits after taxes plus noncash charges against revenue, such as depreciation) will begin in year 2 at $60,000, grow to a $250,000 level in year 5, and level off thereafter.

Column (3) contains the PVFs from Appendix B. The present values of the cash flows expected in each year are calculated by multiplying the cash flows in column (2) by the PVFs in column (3). When these products are totaled algebraically in column (4), the sum is the NPV of the capital project. In this example, it is positive and the proposed factory-warehouse is an acceptable investment for the firm.

The NPV method is useful to *both* the financial and the professional managers of nonprofit organizations in only one type of application: the evaluation of investment projects designed to provide their own financial resources to cover their cash operating costs. The relevant discount rate that the *financial* manager should use for this type of investment analysis is the cost of the funds used to finance the project—either (1) the rate at which the organization must borrow to finance the project, (2) the opportunity rate of interest the organization must forgo on the investment of surplus cash used in the initial investment of the project, or (3) the cost of leasing the equipment associated with the project. The *professional* manager should, however, discount these same cash flows at the social discount rate used in the analysis of the organization's other projects.

Financial and professional managers use different discount rates because each is attempting to achieve a different goal. The financial manager's task of maintaining liquidity and solvency requires that cash flows be discounted at a rate that permits the organization to at least break even over the life of the project on a cash-flow basis. The professional manager is, of course, attempting to allocate resources to achieve what is basically a societal goal; hence a social rate of discount must be used by the professionals. Regardless of the method of financing or the specific professional goal being pursued, the organization will be financially and professionally better off as a result of the investment when the project promises a positive NPV in each analysis.

For example, suppose the Atlanta Lung Association can save $5,000 per year by purchasing a small business computer to handle its accounting, mailing lists, and solicitation follow-up activities. The computer has an expected life of five years and costs $15,000, including the necessary software and a maintenance contract. The association will have to borrow the $15,000 from a local bank at 10 percent to purchase the computer. Since the funds will be borrowed, the borrowing rate should be used to discount the cash flows. The project's NPV is calculated as follows:

$$NPV = [\sum_{t=1}^{5} \$5,000 \ (1 + .10)^{-t}] - \$15,000$$

$$= (\$5,000 \times 3.7908) - \$15,000$$

$$NPV = \$18,954 - \$15,000 = \underline{\underline{\$3,954}}$$

Exhibit 13-5 presents the relevant cash flows that clearly demonstrate that the association will become financially better off as a result of investing in the computer. Column (4) shows that the annual net savings

Exhibit 13-5: Cash Flows Related to a Cost Reduction Investment Project

(1)	(2)	(3)	(4)	(5)	(6)
Year	Cash Savings	Debt Repayment	Net Cash Inflows (2) - (3)	Present Value Factors @ 10%	Present Value of Cash Flows (4) × (5)
1	$ 5,000	$ 3,957*	$ 1,043	.909	$ 948
2	5,000	3,957	1,043	.826	862
3	5,000	3,957	1,043	.751	783
4	5,000	3,957	1,043	.683	713
5	5,000	3,957	1,043	.621	648
Total					$ 3,954

*The $15,000, 10% loan is amortized in five equal annual installments of $3,957 each.

(after repayment of principal and interest on the borrowed funds) is $1,043. The present value of this cash-flow stream, discounted at 10 percent, is, of course, $3,954, the project's NPV.

Similarly, if the association sells securities out of its unrestricted investment account to purchase the computer, the discount rate used for calculating the NPV will be the opportunity rate of interest on the securities sold. If the association gives up securities with a yield to maturity of, say, 10 percent, the project's NPV will be positive. Thus, the annual cash savings generated by the project will more than fully recover the initial $15,000 cash investment plus the interest forgone on the securities. At a 10 percent discount rate, the cash flows will be identical to those shown in Exhibit 13-5.

Alternatively, when a project's NPV is negative, regardless of the financing method an organization elects to use, the project should be rejected on financial grounds. This is because the cash savings will be insufficient to fully service the debt or fully compensate the organization for the loss of interest income on securities sold.

As will be shown in chapter 14, the NPV method as described here is deficient in one material aspect; that is, it ignores the effects of price (cost) inflation on the project's expected cash flows. This problem is explored fully in that chapter.

Finally, if the social discount rate the Atlanta Lung Association uses for analyzing capital investments of this type is, say, 18 percent, the computer project's NPV is

$$NPV = [\sum_{t=1}^{5} \$5,000 \ (1 + .18)^{-t}] - \$15,000$$

$$= (\$5,000 \times 3.127) - \$15,000$$

$$NPV = \$15,635 - \$15,000 = \underline{\$635}$$

Since the project's NPV is positive even at the higher social discount rate, the professional manager should approve the purchase of the computer, or at least permit the project to be ranked among those acceptable alternatives in the organization's current capital budget.

Evaluation of the NPV Method. Although the NPV method has intuitive appeal, especially for those who are familiar with modern financial-management theory, it suffers from several theoretical defects when applied to capital-expenditure problems in the nonprofit context. First, not all worthwhile capital projects proposed for adoption by nonprofit organizations are designed to generate operating cash inflows.

The trustees of a museum may decide to build a new wing to house a permanent art collection, for example. If the museum charges no admission fees, the new wing will not generate any incremental operating revenues and will therefore fail the NPV test as applied by the financial manager. But the trustees may be considering other (nonmonetary) benefits of the project, in which case they should apply *cost-benefit analysis*, rather than use the NPV method.

Second, the selection of an appropriate discount rate is a problem that apparently defies solution. The capital structure, if it can be so named, of a nonprofit organization is typically weighted heavily with funds provided by "society." Thus if management were to select an appropriate discount rate, it would have to estimate the "cost of social capital" and use it as either the discount rate or an element in some weighted average cost of capital peculiar to the organization itself. As mentioned earlier, a theoretically acceptable rate representing the cost of social capital does not appear to exist.

Third, and most damaging of all, the NPV method was designed as a wealth-maximizing decision tool. The objectives of nonprofit organizations, however, do not include wealth maximization since such entities are not permitted to operate for the economic or financial benefit of one or more interested parties. The NPV method prescribes the exclusive use of cash flows in the decision process, while society is often more interested in nonmonetary benefits; hence the method cannot be used to increase even societal wealth.

Finally, the NPV method can properly be used by nonprofit organizations only when all project costs and benefits are true cash flows, as they are in pure cost reduction projects. In these instances, the organization's own wealth (in cash terms) is enhanced when projects having positive NPVs are implemented.

SUMMARY

This chapter has examined three methods traditionally advocated for use in resource-allocation decisions in nonprofit organizations. The first, program-budgeting and cost-benefit analysis, was shown to be a soundly conceived approach to professional management decisions; however, it is deficient as a financial-management tool because its application cannot assure that the organization will achieve financial liquidity and solvency. Beyond that, benefit-cost analysis poses significant data problems to the decision maker in the areas of selecting the appropriate discount rate and monetizing nonmonetary benefits.

The second approach, zero-base budgeting, is designed to reallocate existing resources in order to achieve greater operational effectiveness or efficiency within an organization. It, too, is theoretically tractable, but its practical limitations render it no more formidable in reducing operational inefficiencies than are incremental budgeting techniques. The most serious limitations of zero-base budgeting are the enormity of the task of justifying each separate activity in which the organization engages and the concomitant consumption of time spent in documenting those activities and reviewing the documentation. This problem has produced hybrid forms of zero-base budgeting that lose much of the potential impact of the pure form on resource-allocation decisions.

Finally, the NPV approach, in which discounted cash flows are used in the decision process, also fails as a generally applicable method for resource-allocation decisions in the nonprofit context. Except in those situations in which total costs and total benefits are actually cash flows, the focus of the NPV method is too narrow to justify acceptance or rejection of new investment proposals. When benefits and/or costs are monetized social benefits, benefit-cost analysis is clearly superior to the NPV method.

FURTHER READING

A comprehensive yet completely readable exposition of program budgeting is contained in the following paperback:

Hinrichs, Harley H., and Graeme M. Taylor, eds. *Program Budgeting and Benefit-Cost Analysis.* Pacific Palisades, Calif.: Goodyear, 1969.

An excellent survey article with an extensive bibliography is:

Prest, A. R., and R. Turvey. "Cost-Benefit Analysis: A Survey." *The Economic Journal* (December 1965): 683-735.

A quick and easy summary of the major features of zero-base budgeting is contained in the following article:

Phyrr, Peter. "Zero-base Budgeting." *Harvard Business Review* (November-December 1970): 111-121.

QUESTIONS

1. What are the three traditional approaches applied to resource-allocation decisions in the nonprofit context?

2. What are the three main elements characteristic of the program-budgeting concept?

3. Briefly describe the structure of program budgeting.

4. What are the basic informational requirements of a program-budgeting system?

5. List the six steps in the program-budgeting process.

6. Define the following terms:
   a. cost-benefit analysis
   b. initial investment
   c. discount rate
   d. nonmonetary costs and benefits
   e. benefit-cost ratio

7. Discuss the strengths and weaknesses of program budgeting.

8. Compare and contrast zero-base budgeting and
   a. incremental budgeting
   b. program budgeting

9. List the steps in zero-base budgeting.

10. In what ways may an organization reduce the time it takes to perform the review process required of zero-base budgeting? Why are these solutions generally unsatisfactory?

11. Describe the NPV method of analyzing capital investment projects.

12. Under what circumstances is the NPV method useful in resource-allocation decisions in a nonprofit organization?

13. Why is the NPV method inappropriate as a decision criterion in the nonprofit context?

PROBLEMS

1. The Webber Foundation is considering financing a mobile health-screening clinic that would offer mini health examinations free of charge to the citizens in a three-county metropolitan area. The purchase price of the mobile unit fully equipped is $137,500, and its operating costs, including fuel, maintenance, supplies, and staff personnel, would total $216,000 per year.

The program's sponsor has estimated that the examinations would produce two major benefits. First, early detection of diseases, such as heart disease, cancer, and diabetes, will save the individuals involved the combined total costs of about $75,000 per year in medical costs. Second, the examinations have the potential of saving two lives per year, on the average. Research studies have concluded that the economic value of a human life is equal to the present value of future earnings of the individual over the remaining productive years of his or her life. Statistical analysis places that value at about $160,000 per life for the mobile unit's target population.

The Webber Foundation estimates the current social discount rate to be 16 percent. The sponsor places the life of the mobile unit at five years. Use the cost-benefit decision criterion to determine whether the Webber Foundation should finance the project.

2. The Webber Foundation decides to set up a nonprofit organization to operate the mobile examining unit described in problem 1. Its plan is to fully endow the unit to permit its operation for five years. If the current return on similar endowment funds is 12 percent, how much money should the foundation transfer to the new organization?

3. The financial officer of the new organization created by the Webber Foundation in problem 2 recalculated the operating costs of the mobile unit to include the effects of price inflation on personnel, supply, and maintenance costs. The new operating costs for the next five years are:

Year	Operating costs
1	$ 216,000
2	231,100
3	247,300
4	264,600
5	283,100

The Webber Foundation's one-time grant totaled $800,000, and the financial officer estimated that he could raise about $15,000 per year in donations to help finance the project. The cost of the mobile unit is $137,500, and the rate of return on the endowment is expected to be 12 percent.
   a. What is the project's NPV?
   b. What should the financial officer do?

14

Capital Expenditure Analysis

This chapter examines an analytic approach to the determination of project acceptability on a purely financial basis. The first section briefly reviews the normative theory of resource allocation for nonprofit organizations developed previously in chapter 3. The second section describes a technique designed to assist a nonprofit organization's financial manager in testing the financial viability of incremental capital investment proposals (or new programs that may or may not involve large initial capital outlays).

THEORY OF RESOURCE ALLOCATION IN NONPROFIT CONTEXTS

The dual-management structure that characterizes nonprofit organizations produces two sets of objectives for decision purposes. Both sets of objectives are defined by and are the responsibility of the professional and financial managers, respectively. The *professional* objectives are those that form the basis for the existence of the organization and guide its day-to-day operations. An organization may simultaneously pursue more than one professional goal, and the goals for any one organization may change over time with changing social conditions.

The *financial* objective, which in a normative sense is a constant among all nonprofit organizations, arises from the need for the organization to continue as a going concern through time. The objective termed *financial viability*, when fully realized, ensures that the organization will operate at minimum cost levels and achieve short-run liquidity and long-run solvency. By concentrating on this objective, the financial manager places emphasis on the organization's survival through time and enables it to continue to work toward achieving its professional goals or objectives.

Unfortunately, the achievement of financial viability does not ensure the overall success of the nonprofit organization; it is a necessary condition, but it is not sufficient of itself to guarantee *professional* goal achievement. Resource-allocation decisions in the nonprofit context must therefore involve two determinations: professional acceptance *and* financial viability.

Neither the professional objectives nor the financial goal can be given clear priority. Insufficient attention to attainment of the financial goal will clearly reduce the ability of an organization to achieve its professional goals by creating a climate characterized by constant financial crisis. Conversely, overemphasis on financial security will simply result in a malallocation of resources away from the support of the organization's professional activities and toward "cashness" or building the values of endowment simply for the sake of having larger portfolios of financial assets. Failure to pursue one or the other of these goals will create severe problems for the organization, while successful pursuit of both will ensure the ultimate success of the nonprofit organization in both dimensions.

Decisions Involving a Single Project

When a nonprofit organization is considering only one capital project for implementation during a given budget period, an acceptable resource-allocation decision technique need only produce an accept-reject response. To be acceptable, the project must be both professionally and financially viable; failure to achieve either professional acceptance or financial viability should either disqualify the project from further consideration or cause its sponsor to redesign it so that it meets *all* of the organization's acceptance criteria.

Professional Acceptance. The ultimate criterion for professional acceptance of a capital project is the formal recognition that it meets the minimum standards established within the profession (such as health care, medicine, education), as judged by competent and qualified professional managers or consultants employed by the organization. In some cases, this judgment can be based on a quantitative analysis of fairly explicit sets of standards. Requirements established for accrediting schools and colleges and standards for rating the quality of fire protection provided by volunteer fire departments are two examples of explicit criteria.

In other instances, the project's professional acceptance can be based almost entirely on *qualitative* factors relating to the organization's basic mission. For example, a foundation that supports basic scientific research cannot easily evaluate any given research proposal on other than qualitative factors. Consequently, the foundation's professional management must simply decide whether to fund a particular proposal, and that decision must necessarily be a matter of professional judgment based on experience and knowledge of the subject matter covered by the proposal.

In both cases, the professional decision process can be aided significantly by analyzing the relevant qualitative and quantitative factors within an appropriate framework, such as that provided by cost-benefit analysis or goal programming. The basic objective here is to make certain that the organization attains the highest possible level of professional goal achievement with its available resources.

Financial Acceptance. After a capital project has gained professional approval, it must be tested for financial viability. A financially viable project is one that can be implemented and then operated over its expected life, using either available (unallocated) financial resources or those acquired specifically for that project. Further, the project may generate surplus cash, but it may not consume cash in amounts in excess of the planned allocation over time.

A financially *nonviable* project, if accepted and implemented, either will cause the organization to eventually experience illiquidity or insolvency or will result in the subsequent involuntary reallocation of resources from other ongoing programs in order to keep the new project viable. When resources are reallocated from financially viable projects, those projects frequently become nonviable as a result of the loss of funds. The unfortunate but inevitable result in either case is a diminution of the organization's overall professional effectiveness. That is, the quality of service increases as a result of the addition of a nonviable project, but at the sacrifice of either the quantity or quality of service provided elsewhere within the organization.

TEST FOR FINANCIAL VIABILITY

The test for financial viability may be accomplished on a project by project basis using a model specifically designed for use by nonprofit organizations.[1] Briefly, the model presented here helps the financial manager of a nonprofit organization to achieve financial self-sufficiency

---

1. This section of the chapter is based on Richard F. Wacht, "A Long-Range Financial Planning Technique for Nonprofit Organizations," *Atlanta Economic Review* (September-October 1976): 22-27.

for incremental capital investment projects by coordinating the net cash flows of a planned capital expenditure (or other long-term project that incurs operating deficits) with the cash resources available to the organization for use in implementing new capital projects. The solution of the model is expressed in terms of the (nominal) dollar "target" in cash needed to fully fund the project.

Although the solution is stated in nominal terms, the model employs the concept of the time value of money in equating the present value of future cash expenditures (adjusted for the effects of inflation) with the present value of available cash resources and future cash inflows from operations, cash gifts, pledges, grants, and so forth. The nominal value of total cash receipts is derived from the present value of cash inflows, given the relevant discount rate, and from estimates of the division of receipts among cash on hand, immediate cash gifts, and future collections of cash from various sources.

This particular solution possesses operational merit: First, it facilitates decision making because the time dimension has been eliminated through the use of present values. Second, fund-raising goals, expressed in terms of nominal dollar amounts, are readily communicated between both the administrator and the fund raiser (for example, the college president and the alumni office) and subsequently between the fund raiser and donor or lender.

The Model

The model separates the cash flows associated with a capital expenditure project into three parts. The first part is the initial capital investment required to construct and equip the facility (or simply establish a noncapital-based program) and prepare it for operation. The second part consists of the project's net operating revenues (or deficits), and the third part is the cash that must be raised externally or reallocated from other areas within the organization in order to make the project financially viable. The model uses these cash-flow components as inputs and performs two adjustments on each of them.

The first adjustment relates to the need to consider the effects of *inflation* on future cash flows, and the second relates to the need to achieve *intertemporal comparability* of all future cash flows with existing cash on hand. In other words, all future cash flows, whether they are receipts or expenditures, are inflated whenever necessary to produce an estimate of the actual cash receipts or disbursements that will occur during the project's life. These adjusted cash flows are then reduced to their present values for decision purposes.

The model prescribes decision rules that serve as tests of project financial viability under alternative circumstances. The decision rules employ the present values of the inflated project cash flows as inputs and produce qualitative values useful in the decision process.

The model and its several component parts are described in general terms below. Following that discussion, an illustrative application of the model is presented to demonstrate how the model works. A mathematical version of the model is included in the appendix to this chapter for the purpose of presenting it in its precise form.

The Capital Investment. The capital investment of the project is defined as the cash outlays required to construct the facility, to renovate existing space to make it suitable for the project's operation, to purchase a building or other real property, and/or to purchase the equipment necessary to begin operation. Both the dollar amounts of these cash outlays and their timing must be estimated. In addition, the appropriate inflation rates for construction and equipment costs must be estimated in those cases in which construction or equipment purchases are to be affected in the future.

Inflated Costs. When an organization requests that bids for construction and/or equipment purchases be timed for specified periods in the future, the bidders generally will make implicit allowances for inflation in estimating their costs, thereby guaranteeing their prices to the purchaser through the delivery dates listed in their bids. In such cases the organization's adjustment for inflation is unnecessary unless the organization decides to delay construction or equipment purchases beyond the initial delivery dates.

Alternatively, when an organization decides to shop for equipment after construction is completed, the equipment costs will have to be inflated to more accurately estimate the future cash outlays for the equipment purchases. For example, suppose that a capital project costing $30,000 to construct will take three years to complete. The organization will make payments to the contractor of $10,000 per year at the end of each of the next three years. The contractor's price represents a firm bid. Suppose further that the organization will purchase $12,000 worth of furniture and equipment (valued at today's prices) when the building is completed three years hence. Furniture and equipment prices have been increasing and are expected to continue to increase at an annual compound rate of 10 percent.

In this case, the cash outlays for construction should not be inflated since the contractor's price is firm. However, the actual cash outlay for furniture and equipment is likely to be higher than the $12,000 needed today to ready the building for operation. Given the 10 percent equipment inflation rate, $12,000 worth of furniture and equipment at today's prices will probably cost $12,000 × $(1 + .10)^3$ = $15,972 in three years. Thus, cash-flow estimates for the project's capital investment are:

Year 1	=	$10,000 for construction
Year 2	=	$10,000 for construction
Year 3 $10,000 + $15,972	=	$25,972 for construction and equipment

Finally, suppose the organization must postpone the project for one year. The construction costs will have to be inflated in this instance but only to account for one year's inflation, since the total contract price has already been implicitly adjusted by the contractor to account for cost increases over the construction period. Thus, if the construction inflation rate is 18 percent, the progress payments will increase from $10,000 to $10,000 × $(1 + .18)^1 = \$11,800$ per year, and the equipment costs will total $12,000 × $(1. + .10)^4 = \$17,569$ four years from today.

Present Value of Inflated Costs. The second adjustment called for by the model is the calculation of the present value of these cash outlays. The purpose of this step, of course, is to enable the decision maker to compare on the same basis cash paid out or received at different times.

Since a project's periodic cash flows pass through an organization's general fund and any cash surpluses or deficits are added to or paid out of the unrestricted investment account, the appropriate rate to use in calculating a project's present values is the rate of return on the investment of surplus cash in short-term investment media. This rate represents both an explicit return and an opportunity cost to the nonprofit organization in its liquidity management decisions. Since the purpose of capital expenditure analysis from the financial manager's point of view is to achieve project financial viability by at least breaking even over time in terms of cash flow, the rate of return on the unrestricted investment fund is the logical choice for the discount rate.

In the preceding example, the cash flows for the project when delayed for one year were $11,800 per year for three years to cover construction costs, beginning in year 2, and $17,569 for equipment payable in year 4. Given a discount rate of 9 percent, which is the expected average yield on short-term securities, the present value of the project's capital investment is shown in Exhibit 14-1.

Exhibit 14-1: **Calculation of the Present Value of Capital Investment Outlays**

Year	Cash outlay	PVF @ 9%	Present values
1	0	.9174	0
2	$ 11,800	.8417	$ 9,932.06
3	11,800	.7721	9,110.78
4	29,369	.7084	20,805.00
		Present value =	$ 39,847.84

The figure $39,847.84 in the table is the amount the organization must have on hand today to fully pay for the construction and equipment outlays, given their timing and the fact that the organization can earn 9 percent on any unspent cash balances. In other words, if the organization had $39,847.84 in cash on hand, it could invest that cash at 9 percent, pay out $11,800 at the end of years 2 and 3, pay out $29,369 at the end of year 4, and have no cash left in its investment account. Exhibit 14-2 illustrates this fact by examining the beginning and ending cash balances of the project in each year from the present through year 4.

Exhibit 14-2: **Cash Flow Analysis of a Capital Investment**

(1) Year	(2) Beginning cash balance		(3) Interest earned @ 9%		(4) Cash outlay		(5) Ending cash balance
0	0		0		0		$ 39,847.84
1	$ 39,847.84	+	$ 3,586.32		0	=	43,434.15
2	43,434.15	+	3,909.07	–	$ 11,800.00	=	35,543.22
3	35,543.22	+	3,198.89	–	11,800.00	=	26,942.11
4	26,942.11	+	2,424.79	–	29,369.00	=	(2.10)

Given the beginning balance of $39,847.84, the organization will earn ($39,847.84 × .09 =) $3,586.31 during the first year and spend nothing, leaving a cash balance at the end of year 1 of ($39,847.84 + $3,586.31 =) $43,434.15, as shown in column (5). In year 2 the construction payment of $11,800 will leave the cash balance at year-end at $35,543.22, after adding interest income. The negative balance of $2.10 at the end of year 4 is the result of rounding errors in both the calculation of the present values and in the table itself. The point is well made, nevertheless: the model enables the organization to plan its cash flows to protect its liquidity position and prevent insolvency.

Operating Cash Flows. If the organization has sufficient resources to cover the cash requirements for the *initial* capital investment, it still may not have provided sufficient cash resources to achieve financial viability on a project basis. Once the facility or program is ready to begin its operations, the organization must also provide resources on a continuing basis to operate the project over its planned life, as it was originally designed and approved. Thus, management must also estimate project operating revenues and costs at current price levels, adjust those estimates for increases in price levels, and calculate their present values. This procedure will provide an estimate of the funds required to begin the project *and* operate it over its expected life.

Revenues. Trading organizations often will initiate revenue-generating projects. The revenues may or may not be sufficient to cover all operating and capital costs, but cash flow realized as operating revenues must be included in the project analysis. Estimates should be made for each year of the planning period and should include an adjustment for changes in the volume of goods or services sold. When a project does not generate revenues, this portion of the model can be ignored.

Once the revenue estimates have been made, they must be adjusted for expected changes in the prices at which the organization plans to sell the product or service. For example, many organizations increase their prices to offset all or a portion of the expected increases in the project's operating costs.

Finally, the inflated revenue estimates must be discounted at the relevant interest rate to produce the present value of the project's operating revenues. Exhibit 14-3 provides an example of the calculations required by this part of the model. The sample project illustrated in the table is expected to achieve a growth in volume of 2 percent per year, and selling prices are expected to increase by 5 percent per year. The organization expects to earn a return of 9 percent on its surplus cash and uses that rate to discount the revenues.

Exhibit 14-3: Calculation of the Present Value of Inflated Project Revenues

(1) Year	(2) Operating revenues	(3) Growth CIF @ 2%	(4) Price CIF @ 5%	(5) Inflated operating revenues (2) × (3) × (4)	(6) PVF @ 9%	(7) Present value of operating revenues (5) × (6)
1	0	–	–	0	.9174	0
2	0	–	–	0	.8417	0
3	$ 2,000	1.0000	1.0000	$ 2,000.00	.7722	$ 1,544.40
4	2,000	1.0200	1.0500	2,142.00	.7084	1,517.39
5	2,000	1.0400	1.1025	2,294.08	.6499	1,490.35
6	2,000	1.0612	1.1576	2,456.89	.5963	1,465.04
7	2,000	1.0824	1.2155	2,631.31	.5470	1,439.33

Present value of operating revenues = $ 7,456.51

Column (2) of Exhibit 14-3 contains the revenue estimates of $2,000 per year. The compound interest factors (CIFs) in columns (3) and (4) adjust those dollar amounts for the expected growth in volume and changes in selling prices, respectively. The inflated operating revenues in column (5) are calculated by multiplying the figures in column (2) by those in columns (3) and (4). The present value of the inflated operating revenues over the seven-year planning period is the sum of the figures in column (7), or $7,456.51.

Note that the project is not expected to generate revenues until year 3, presumably after construction has been completed. Thus, the growth in volume and prices will begin in year 4. When calculating present values, however, the discounting process must begin with year 1, whether or not revenues are received at that time.

Operating Costs. Operating costs are defined as cash expenditures exclusive of overhead cost allocations, depreciation, and financing costs. For any given year the project's operating costs may be equal to, less than, or greater than its operating revenues.

The model treats operating costs in exactly the same way as it does the operating revenues; that is, the costs must be adjusted for projected growth and price inflation and then discounted to determine their present value. Suppose the project being examined employs one person at a cost of $15,000 per year and will consume $2,000 worth of supplies each year, both at today's prices. The growth in the production of goods and services will not affect operating costs, but price inflation is expected to increase total annual operating costs by 8 percent per year over the seven-year planning period. As before, the discount rate used by the organization is 9 percent. Exhibit 14-4 illustrates how the operating costs are adjusted, using CIFs and present value factors (PVFs) found in the tables of Appendixes A and B, respectively. (See chapter 12 for a discussion of compound interest.)

In this case, the operating costs are inflated, beginning with year 1, since both salaries and supplies can be expected to move upward as the result of price inflation. Note that the operating cost figure in column (1) of $17,000 per year at today's prices will have grown to $21,414.90 by the time the project begins its operations in year 3, and then will likely grow to almost $30,000 by year 7. This clearly supports the rationale of not stopping with the estimate of capital outlays, but also including operating costs and revenues in the analyses of new programs.

A refinement to the calculations illustrated in Exhibit 14-5 is advisable when the components of operating costs are subject to significantly different inflation rates. For example, if the organization's personnel policies include a provision for a 7 percent salary and wage increase whenever possible, and it has been experiencing a 10 percent annual inflation rate in its supplies purchases, the decision maker should inflate the two components separately at their respective rates prior to adjusting total cost to a present value basis.

Suppose that the operating costs in column (2) of Exhibit 14-4 comprise $14,000 of salaries and $3,000 of supplies each year. Given the

Exhibit 14-4: Calculation of the Present Value of Inflated Project Costs

(1) Year	(2) Operating costs	(3) Price CIF @ 8%	(4) Inflated operating costs (2) × (3)	(5) PVF @ 9%	(6) Present value of operating costs (4) × (5)
1	0	1.0800	0	.9174	0
2	0	1.1664	0	.8417	0
3	$ 17,000	1.2597	$ 21,414.90	.7722	$ 16,536.59
4	17,000	1.3605	23,128.50	.7084	16,384.23
5	17,000	1.4693	24,978.10	.6499	16,233.27
6	17,000	1.5869	26,977.30	.5963	16,086.56
7	17,000	1.7138	29,134.60	.5470	15,936.63
			Present value of operating costs =		$ 81,177.28

inflation rates of 7 percent and 10 percent for salaries and supplies, respectively, Exhibit 14-5 shows how the inflated operating costs are calculated. Note that the figures contained in column (8) of Exhibit 14-5 are different from those in column (4) of Exhibit 4-4. This shows that the decomposition of the operating costs provides an opportunity to achieve greater accuracy in estimating cash flows.

Exhibit 14-5: **Calculation of the Present Value of Decomposed Inflated Project Costs**

---

(1)	(2)	(3)	(4)	(5)	(6)	(7)	(8)
		Price level	Supply	Price level	Inflated salaries	Inflated supply costs	Inflated operating costs
Year	Salaries	CIF @ 7%	costs	CIF @ 10%	(2) × (3)	(4) × (3)	(6) + (7)
1	0	1.0700	0	1.100	0	0	0
2	0	1.1449	0	1.2100	0	0	0
3	$ 14,000	1.2250	$ 3,000	1.3310	$ 17,150	$ 3,993	$ 21,143
4	14,000	1.3108	3,000	1.4641	18,351	4,392	22,743
5	14,000	1.4026	3,000	1.6105	19,636	4,832	24,468
6	14,000	1.5007	3,000	1.7716	21,010	5,315	26,325
7	14,000	1.6058	3,000	1.9487	22,481	5,846	28,327

Net Project Cost. After calculation of the present values of a project's capital investment, revenues, and operating costs, the decision maker can determine the *net project cost* by adding these present values algebraically. The purpose of this calculation is to determine whether the operating revenues are sufficient to fully fund the project, and failing that, how much money (in a present value sense) is needed to achieve project financial viability.

For example, suppose that present values of a project's capital investment, operating revenues, and operating costs have been calculated. The net project costs can be determined as follows:

Present value of capital investment	$ 39,848	(Exhibit 14-1)
Present value of operating costs	81,177	(Exhibit 14-4)
Present value of total cash outlays	$ 121,025	
Less present value of operating revenues	−7,457	(Exhibit 14-3)
Net project cost	$ 113,568	

In this example, the net project cost of $113,568 is the amount of cash needed immediately to fully finance the project. This estimate, of course, assumes that the estimates of cash flows, inflation rates, and the discount rate are accurate.

Financing the Project. Most nonprofit organizations must rely on cash contributions to finance their capital expenditures. A few organizations—notably schools, churches, and many trading organizations—are able to borrow money on an intermediate-term or long-term basis to finance their capital outlays. However, to simplify the present exposition, the assumption of a prohibition against intermediate-term and long-term borrowing will be adopted. (This assumption is relaxed in chapter 18 where an integrated financial management model is presented. That model permits the financial manager to select among available financing alternatives the one that will achieve project financial viability with the least financial risk to the organization.)

Once the net project cost has been determined, the financial manager must balance this net cash outlay with (1) the amount of cash on hand that has been appropriated to support the project and (2) the present value of the cash receipts from gifts and pledges expected to be realized from the organization's fund-raising activities. These two sources of project financing together must equal or exceed the net project cost to achieve financial viability and gain approval for the project from the financial manager.

Determining the Fund-raising Goal. The application of this part of the model to capital investment analysis involves estimating the timing of the cash receipts from the fund-raising efforts to be carried out on behalf of the project and then performing a present value calculation to produce a target fund-raising goal.

For example, suppose that an organization's past fund-raising efforts produced, after fund-raising costs, 50 percent of total contributions in immediate cash gifts, 5 percent as two-year pledges, 15 percent as three-year pledges, and 30 percent as five-year pledges. The pledges are payable by the donor in equal annual installments. Further, the organization has appropriated a total of $30,000 in cash to support a project whose net cost is $113,568.

The first step in calculating the target fund-raising goal is to calculate a weighted-average PVF from the percentages of cash inflows expected from the present until the final pledges are collected. Exhibit 14-6 illustrates this procedure. Columns (2) through (5) contain the proportions of gifts and pledges expected in each of the next five years from the four gift and pledge categories listed earlier. The column totals correspond with the estimates based on historical experience. These annual proportions are summed in column (6) and discounted at the organization's rate of return from its unrestricted investment account (9 percent, in this case). The total of the figures in column (8) is the weighted-average PVF for the fund-raising campaign.

Exhibit 14-6: Calculation of the Weighted-Average Present Value Factor for Contributions

(1)	(2)	(3)	(4)	(5)	(6)	(7)	(8)
		Proportion of total contributions			Annual cash		Weighted
Year	One-time gifts	Two-year pledges	Three-year pledges	Five-year pledges	inflow (2) + (3) + (4) + (5)	PVF @ 9%	present value (6) × (7)
1	.500	.025	.050	.060	.635	.9174	.5825
2		.025	.050	.060	.135	.8417	.1136
3			.050	.060	.110	.7722	.0849
4				.060	.060	.7084	.0425
5				.060	.060	.6499	.0390
Total	.500	.050	.150	.300	1.000		.8625

The campaign goal is calculated by, first, subtracting the cash on hand from the net project cost and then dividing the difference by the weighted-average PVF. In the example, the nominal amount of funds that the organization must raise is:

$$\text{Campaign goal} = (\$113,568 - \$30,000)/.8625$$
$$= \$83,568/.8625$$
$$= \$96,890$$

Interestingly, the fund-raising goal of $96,890 is $13,338 greater than the net project cost, less available cash on hand. That difference represents a cost to the organization of accepting pledges of two-, three-, and five-years' duration. That cost is in fact the total interest lost on the uncollected pledges over the five year period during which the longest pledges remain outstanding.

Endowed Versus Unendowed Organizations. The discussion in chapter 9 pointed out that an endowed organization should view its own endowment fund as a potential source of short-term and intermediate-term credit, provided that the organization can repay the loan principal plus interest at a rate equal to that which the fund would receive from alternative investments (that is, the opportunity cost of the funds borrowed). When available endowment funds are inadequate to meet the organization's financing requirements or the organization is not endowed, temporary operating cash deficits must be covered with funds borrowed from outside sources, usually at a rate higher than that being earned by the endowment. This has special significance in the analysis of new capital projects.

When an organization raises funds for new capital expenditures and meets its quota largely through long-term pledges, projected cash outflows for the project are likely to exceed cash inflows from fund raising by substantial margins in early years, thus creating cash deficits. If cash transactions for the capital investment project are handled through the institution's endowment fund, a cash deficit in any year will be paid out of the endowment fund's liquid assets at a cost to the project equal to the endowment fund's rate of return on investment times the amount of the project's cash deficit in that year. In this case, since the earnings rate and the borrowing cost are identical, the model compensates automatically for the endowment's loss of income as a result of the deficit. Hence no further adjustment is needed.

If, however, the institution has no endowment and must borrow funds from an outside source to cover any cash deficit at a rate higher than it is able to earn on cash surpluses, an adjustment to the calculation of the present value of the net project cost is required. That adjustment is simply the addition of the present value of the incremental interest cost over the rate of return being earned on the endowment fund. For example, suppose a project produces cash deficits of $10,000, $20,000, and $7,000, respectively, during the first three years of its life. The organization is earning 10 percent on its endowment, and it must borrow on a short-term basis at 12 percent. The increase to the net project cost arising from the 2 percentage point incremental interest cost is calculated in Exhibit 14-7.

The project's incremental interest rate is (12 percent −10 percent =) 2 percent. The dollar interest costs for each year are listed in column (3) of

---

Exhibit 14-7: **Calculation of the Present Value of Incremental Interest Costs**

(1)	(2)	(3)	(4)	(5)
		Incremental		Present value of
	Cash	interest cost		interest cost
Year	deficit	.02 × (2)	PVF @ 10%	(3) × (4)
1	$ 10,000	$ 200	.9091	$ 181.82
2	20,000	400	.8264	330.56
3	7,000	140	.7513	105.18
				$ 617.56

---

the table. The discount rate used in the calculation is 10 percent, the return on the endowment fund. The sum of the figures in column (5), $617.56, is the present value of the incremental interest cost, and that figure is added to the net project cost for decision purposes.

Illustrative Calculation

The Maybridge Public Library building, an old wooden structure, burned to the ground. The structure and contents were woefully underinsured, leaving the library with only $13,000 of insurance proceeds to rebuild and restock the library.

After six months and over twenty board meetings, plans for a new building were approved and the cost for furniture, equipment, and the start of a new collection were estimated. Exhibit 14-8 contains the estimates for all of the variables needed to test the project for financial viability. The library board elected to plan for operations over a ten-year period after construction was completed.

The board also decided to finance the new library with the insurance money and a community fund-raising campaign. A survey of the local merchants and industry revealed that most of the money would be raised in the form of pledges spanning periods of from two to four years. The estimates of the distribution of these pledges are also shown in Exhibit 14-8, as variables number 7 through 10.

Finally, the library held an endowment fund of $20,000, the income from which was restricted to use in building the collection of books suitable for children and young adults. The board permitted the library to borrow from the fund at a rate equal to the current return on investment, which was 9 percent.

Capital Investment and Net Operating Costs. Total cash outlays for the library project, including continuing operating costs, can readily be obtained by performing the calculations in a table, such as the one presented in Exhibit 14-9. The present value of the construction costs is

Exhibit 14-8. **Planning Estimates for the Maybridge Public Library Rebuilding Project.**

Data and Sources	Timing	Values
From the architect:		
1. Contract price for construction	Year 1	$30,000
	Year 2	$30,000
2. Cost of furniture, equipment and books	Year 2	$25,000
From the library planning committees:		
3. Planning period		12 years
4. Operating costs, net of revenues	Years 3-12	$2,000
5. Rate of return on the endowment	Years 1-12	9%
6. Cash on hand available for the project	Year 0	$13,000
From the library fund-raising committee:		
7. Maximum amount that reasonably can be raised locally	Years 1-4	$95,000
8. Distribution of fund raising receipts:		
a. One-time, first year gifts	Year 1	23%
b. Two-year pledges	Years 1-2	12%
c. Three-year pledges	Years 1-3	21%
d. Four-year pledges	Years 1-4	44%
From other sources:		
9. Construction inflation rate	Years 1-12	18%
10. Inflation rate for furniture, equipment and books	Years 1-12	8%
11. Operating cost inflation rate	Year 1-12	6%

Exhibit 14-9: **Calculation of the Present Values of Inflated Cash Outflows**

	(1)	*(2)*	*(3)*	*(4)*	*(5)*	*(6)*
						Inflation
			Adjustment for inflation		*Present*	*adjusted*
		Cash			*value*	*present values*
	Year	*outflows*	*Percent*	*CIF*	*factors @ 9%*	*(2) × (4) × (5)*
A.	**Construction costs:**					
	1	$ 30,000	18%	1.000	.917	$ 27,510
	2	30,000	18	1.000	.842	25,260
						$ 52,770
B.	**Costs of furniture, equipment, and books:**					
	2	$ 25,000	8%	1.166	.842	$ 24,544
C.	**Operating costs:**					
	3	$ 2,000	6%	1.191	.772	$ 1,839
	4	2,000	6	1.263	.708	1,788
	5	2,000	6	1.338	.650	1,739
	6	2,000	6	1.419	.596	1,691
	7	2,000	6	1.504	.547	1,645
	8	2,000	6	1.594	.502	1,600
	9	2,000	6	1.690	.460	1,555
	10	2,000	6	1.791	.422	1,512
	11	2,000	6	1.898	.388	1,473
	12	2,000	6	2.012	.356	1,433
	Total					$ 16,275

calculated in part A. Note that the price-level CIF is equal to 1.000 for both years because construction is to begin immediately. If construction were to be delayed, the construction costs would rise because of inflation. Part B shows that the present value of the cost of furniture, equipment, and books is $24,544, and Part C reveals that the present value of the library's net operating costs for ten years is $16,275. The low figure for operating costs is explained by the fact that the library staff is totally volunteer.

These three figures are summed to produce the net project cost:

Net project cost = $52,770 + $24,544 + $16,275 = $93,589

These calculations tell the library board that the library can be built, equipped, staffed, and operated for ten years for an equivalent sum of $93,589 in cash on hand, as of today. Because the board has only $13,000 in cash, it must raise the equivalent of ($93,589 – $13,000 =) $80,589 during the fund-raising campaign. But since most of the money will be pledged rather than collected immediately, the board will have to determine how the timing of these cash inflows will affect the amount of the fund-raising goal.

Fund-raising Goal. Item Number 7 in Exhibit 14-8 indicates that the fund-raising campaign will probably yield a total of $95,000 in contributions from local sources. If all the cash were available immediately, the project would be financially viable. However, because most donations will be in the form of pledges, the contributions must be examined on a present value basis.

Exhibit 14-10 illustrates the calculation of the weighted PVF for contributions. Columns (2) through (5) show the percentages of the total campaign goal that are expected to be received in each year from each pledge category. These percentages are summed in column (6), and then multiplied by the 9 percent PVFs. The sum of the figures in column (8), .8501, is the PVF used to calculate the library's fund-raising goal. Since the library has $13,000 on hand, the goal is:

$$\text{Campaign goal} = (\$93,589 - \$13,000)/.8501$$
$$= \$80,859/.8501$$
$$= \$94,799$$

In other words, the library board will have to raise a total of $94,799 in cash and pledges in the proportions given in column (6) of Exhibit 14-10

Exhibit 14-10: **Calculation of the Weighted Present Value for Contributions**

(1) Year	(2) One-time gifts	(3) Two-year pledges	(4) Three-year pledges	(5) Four-year pledges	(6) Annual cash inflow (2) + (3) (4) + (5)	(7) Present value factors @ 9%	(8) Weighted present value (6) × (7)
1	.23	.06	.07	.11	.47	.9174	.4312
2		.06	.07	.11	.24	.8417	.2020
3			.07	.11	.18	.7722	.1390
4				.11	.11	.7084	.0779
Total	.23	12	.21	.44	1.00		.8501

in order to realize an equivalent of $80,589 of cash in hand. Since this amount of $201 less than the library expects to receive from donations, the plan for rebuilding the library, as it is currently formulated, is financially viable.

Cash-Flow Summary. Exhibit 14-11 presents the cash-flow summary for the project's twelve-year planning period. All dollar figures are nominal amounts (that is, they are inflated, but are not present values). Columns (2) and (3) show the amounts that will be paid out and received, respectively, in each year, and column (7) shows the library's ending cash balance for each year.

The last figure in column (7) should equal zero for any project subject to this type of analysis, but because of rounding errors, it probably will lie in a range of between plus or minus $200, depending on the relative size of the project's cash flows. The ending zero balance arises from the

Exhibit 14-11: **Cash-Flow Summary, Maybridge Public Library**

(1) Year	(2) Inflated cash Outflow*	(3) Receipts from fund raising Campaign†	(4) Net cash flows (3)–(2)	(5) Beginning cash Balance	(6) Interest earned (5) × .09	(7) Ending cash balance (4) + (5) + (6)
1	30,000	44,556	14,556	13,000‡	1,170	28,726
2	59,160	22,752	(36,408)§	28,726	2,585	(5,097)
3	2,382	17,064	14,682	(5,097)	(459)	9,126
4	2,525	10,428	7,903	9,126	821	17,850
5	2,676		(2,676)	17,850	1,606	16,780
6	2,837		(2,837)	16,780	1,510	15,453
7	3,007		(3,007)	15,453	1,391	13,837
8	3,188		(3,188)	13,837	1,245	11,894
9	3,379		(3,379)	11,894	1,070	9,586
10	3,582		(3,582)	9,586	863	6,867
11	3,797		(3,797)	6,867	618	3,688
12	4,024		(4,024)	3,688	332	(4)**

* *From Exhibit 14-9; column (2) × column (4).*
† *From Exhibit 14-10; column (6) × Q.*
‡ *Insurance settlement.*
§ *Figures in parentheses are cash deficits.*
** *This figure does not equal zero because of rounding errors.*

break-even nature of the model; that is, at the minimum, a project is financially viable when the present value of its cash inflows is equal to the present value of its cash outflows. Thus, residual cash balances should equal zero.

In the present illustration, the large cash outlays in year 2 for construction and the purchase of furnishings and books cause the ending cash balance for that year to fall to a *minus* $5,097; that is, the board will have to borrow that amount at the end of the year in order to open the library on schedule. If the board borrows that amount from the library's endowment fund, it will pay interest in the amount of $459 (9 percent times $5,097) to the fund during year 3, as shown in column (6) of Exhibit 14-11.

However, suppose that the board had to borrow the $5,097 at 11 percent interest from a local bank. In this case, the fund-raising goal would have to be calculated using an adjusted net project cost. In solving for the new net cost, the incremental $5,097 occurs in year 3.

Thus, the adjusted net project cost is calculated as follows:

$$\text{Net project cost} = \$52,770 + \$24,544 + \$16,275 + $$
$$(.11 - .09)\$5,097/(1 + .09)^3$$
$$= \$93,589 + \$102/1.295$$
$$= \$93,589 + \$79 = \$93,668$$

The net effect of this calculation is to add the present value of the incremental interest cost (that is, the interest in excess of the 9 percent endowment rate) to the present value of the other cash outflows. If cash balance deficits exist in other years, the present values of the incremental interest charges for each of those years would be added as well. The new value for the fund-raising campaign goal becomes ($93,668 – $13,000)/.8501 = $94,892, an amount that is $93 greater than that initially calculated.

THE DECISION

This model *does not make decisions*; rather, it produces information for the decision maker. When applied to the Maybridge Public Library project, the model produces several relevant pieces of information that the board will find useful in planning and making its decision.

First, and perhaps most important, the model tells the library board that it will have to raise $94,799 (or $94,892 if it must borrow in year 3) to build the facility and operate it for ten years. If, in the board's judgment, this amount is beyond reason insofar as voluntary public support is concerned, the project will have to be either (1) scaled down, (2) abandoned, or (3) financed from other available sources. If the board decides to build a smaller facility, it will have to reestablish all the cash flows and recalculate the fund-raising goal using the new estimates.

Second, the model forces the decision makers to recognize the fact that simply providing the amount of cash necessary just to build the new library is really not sufficient; the building must also be equipped, furnished, and operated in order to fulfill its basic purpose. In the Maybridge illustration, inflated net operating costs totaled $16,275, in terms of present value, and when divided by the weighted PVF of .8501, made up $19,124 of the total fund-raising goal. This amount represents about 20 percent of the total project cost, a percentage too great to overlook.

Third, assuming that the library board adopts the initial plan, the model predicts a project cash-flow deficit of $5,097 at the end of year 2. Knowledge of the timing of cash flows permits the endowment manager to schedule the maturities of fixed-income securities to correspond with projected funding requirements or provides him or her with sufficient advance warning to permit the orderly liquidation of investment securities in advance of cash needs. Such information facilitates portfolio management by permitting the available funds to be more fully invested in higher yielding (longer maturity) investment securities and minimizing the proportion of assets held in liquid form as a defense against uncertainty in cash outflows.

Fourth, the model permits the library board to examine the effects on the amount of financing the project will require, given a delay in implementation of one or more years. Exhibit 14-12 portrays graphically the changes in the fund-raising goal as a result of delaying construction up to the tenth year, using the data given in Exhibit 14-8 as the basis for these results. It is assumed that the library is unendowed and must

Exhibit 14-12: **Net Project Cost of the Mayfield Public Library, Assuming Delays in Project Implementation**

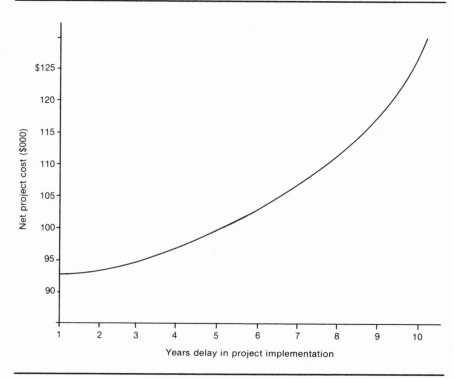

Net project cost ($000)

Years delay in project implementation

borrow funds in cash deficit years (for example, in year 3) at 12 percent interest. Because of the 18 percent annual inflation rate for construction costs, it is not surprising to find that delays in project implementation will increase the fund-raising goal indefinitely at an increasing rate. Thus, the fund-raising goal is at a minimum when the project is begun immediately.

A final benefit realizable from the application of the model is the production of the data useful for controlling both the fund-raising and the project-implementation phases of the capital expenditure program. The cash-flow projection presented in Exhibit 14-11, for example, can serve as a gross check on the project's actual cash inflows and outflows. Variations of actual experience from the forecast levels will serve as signals that the desired results are not being achieved. For example, the failure to reach the desired fund-raising goal or a slowdown of pledge payments in early years, if left unchecked, will probably produce a shortage of funds later on in the project's implementation or operation phases. By replacing forecasted cash flows with actual experience, the library board can perform the necessary computations to determine the extent of change required in the project as a result of the variations—that is, how much must be added to the campaign goal or cut from planned expenditures to reestablish equality between cash inflows and outflows. Of course controls of this type would require a program accounting system in order to be effective.

ANALYSIS OF MULTIPLE PROJECTS

When a nonprofit organization is considering several capital-expenditure projects for more or less concurrent implementation, the financial manager should analyze each separately, rather than combine their cash flows and treat them as a single capital expenditure item. The requirement for separate analyses arises from the fact that most nonprofit organizations operate with limited funds and are often pressured by their constituencies to expand their operations to encompass a wider range of service to the public. In short, nonprofit organizations, like businesses and individuals, must continually face the classic economic problem of too few resources and too many needs. The financial analysis of each project provides management with the data needed to ensure that available resources are not overcommitted.

Decisions Involving Several Projects Under a Budget Constraint

The resource-allocation problem is complex when several professionally acceptable projects are being considered during a given budget period and when the combined net project costs will exceed available resources. In this case, each project offered for serious consideration must be both professionally acceptable and *capable* of being made financially viable. This, of course, is accomplished by using financial resources that have been identified as being available to implement and support new capital projects.

If the organization attempts to implement *all* of the projects, it will, by definition, violate the budget constraint (run short of cash) and face the threat of future illiquidity or insolvency or both. The problem thus becomes that of maximizing professional goal achievement within the budget constraint.

In some cases, an organization's professional manager may present a number of projects of more or less equal professional quality. The selection among those projects under a budget constraint simply involves selecting the combination of projects that yields the largest *quantity* of services while remaining collectively viable. For example, suppose an organization is considering the five projects listed in Exhibit 14-13 but has only $65,000 in resources to commit to expansion of services. In this instance, it should select projects C, D, and E, because this combination of projects will produce 35 units of service at a cost of $65,000. All other

Exhibit 14-13: **Choice of Projects Under a Budget Constraint**

Project	Amount of resources required	Units of service produced
A	$ 28,000	10 units
B	32,000	18
C	20,000	9
D	40,000	20
E	5,000	6

combinations will produce fewer units within the budget constraint. The model described in this chapter thus cannot be used to rank alternative capital projects. The test for financial viability is not designed to reveal which, among several projects, is superior in terms of nonfinancial or professional goal achievement and thus cannot indicate which of the viable projects should be selected when the organization lacks the resources to fund all of its capital expenditure projects. The solution to resource-allocation decisions of this type is approachable in most cases through the *goal-programming* technique. This technique and its application to the special problem of selecting among alternative capital investment projects is presented in chapter 15.

SUMMARY

The model presented in this chapter is designed to provide a financial test of projects that previously have been given the professional manager's stamp of approval. That test is designed to ensure that each new project will be *financially viable*, in that it can be implemented and then operated over some specific planning period without violating the multiperiod budget constraint.

The model adjusts the project's cash flows to account for the likelihood of price and cost inflation during the planning period and then discounts the cash flows to allow the comparison of cash paid out and received at different times. The test of project financial viability involves comparing the present values of cash inflows and outflows; that is, if the adjusted cash outflows are less than the adjusted inflows, the project is viable.

The model can be used to analyze capital expenditures on a project-by-project basis only. When more than one project is being considered by a nonprofit organization, the ranking of viable projects must be done on the basis of professional, rather than financial, criteria. The capital budgeting decision for nonprofit organizations is thus a two-part process that must be closely coordinated between the professional and financial managers.

FURTHER READING

The model presented in this chapter is presented in mathematical form in:

Wacht, Richard F. "A Long-Range Financial Planning Technique for Nonprofit Organizations," *Atlanta Economic Review*, (September-October 1976): 22-27.

QUESTIONS

1. Briefly summarize the major aspects of the theory of resource-allocation decisions in nonprofit contexts.

2. What is financial viability? What is its operational definition?

3. Why must a project be both professionally and financially viable before it can be classified as an acceptable investment?

4. Explain how an organization that is faced with a budget constraint can select among several alternative projects.

5. Explain the rationale underlying the following features of the capital expenditure model presented in this chapter:
   a. inflating the cash inflows and outflows
   b. discounting cash flows
   c. using the rate of return on the investment of surplus cash as the discount rate
   d. adding interest costs to total project cash outflows

6. What specific information does the model provide to the decision maker?

7. Explain how decisions involving multiple projects should be handled.

PROBLEMS*

1. The Burks County Historical Society is considering the purchase and restoration of an old house that it will use for its headquarters. The house can be purchased now for $20,000, and renovations over a one-year period will cost an additional $20,000, payable at the time the work is completed.

   a. How much money must the society have on hand to cover the purchase and restoration, given that it can earn 10 percent on its unrestricted investment fund?

---

*A computer supported model for performing tests of financial viability is included with the study guide materials. This model may be used to reduce the computations required in solving problem 6 in particular.

b. Real estate values in Burks County are growing at a 6 percent annual rate, and construction and repair costs are rising at an 18 percent rate. How much more cash will the society need today to complete the project if it decides to wait one year to purchase the house?

2. The Valley Wells Retirement Center has been approached by a local laundromat operator who has offered to open a coin laundry in the center's recreation building. The terms of the offer require the center to purchase the equipment for $5,500 and to supply the water and electricity. The operator will install the washers and dryers, perform the maintenance on them, and keep the laundry areas clean. The gross revenue will be shared equally between the center and the operators, with each receiving an estimated $4,800 per year. The equipment has an expected life of five years.

The center's operating costs are estimated to be about $1,500 for the first year, but its utility costs have been increasing at an annual rate of 7 percent.

a. If the center uses a 12 percent discount rate in its capital expenditure analyses, what is the present value of the project's operating revenues over the five-year period?

b. Calculate the present value of the project's operating costs.

c. Calculate the net project cost.

d. Should Valley Wells Retirement Center approve the project on a financial basis? Explain.

3. The Central City AME Church has purchased a new church organ for $52,000 installed. Its organ fund contains $16,800, which will be used for the down payment. The organ manufacturer has agreed to let the church pay the balance, plus an 8 percent per year carrying cost, over a four-year period.

Fifty-five members of the church have volunteered to share the financial burden of paying off the new debt by making equal annual contributions to the organ fund.

a. Calculate the weighted-average PVF for the contributions

b. What is total campaign goal that the church members must meet?

c. How much will each member have to contribute each year?

4. The net project cost of a new gym for the Bostwick Junior Academy is $1.56 million. The academy's professional fund raiser expects the following distribution of gifts and pledges:

One-time, first year gifts	28%
Two-year pledges	60%
Three-year pledges	12%

If the academy's rate of return on its endowment is 11 percent, at what amount should the fund raiser place the campaign goal?

5. The Northside YMCA's soccer project has an initial net project cost of $28,700. The cash-flow analysis indicates cash deficits during years 2, 3, and 4 of the project in the following amounts:

Year	Cash deficit
2	$ 6,280
3	4,430
4	1,100

The YMCA will have to borrow to cover the deficits at an annual rate that is three percentage points above the rate it receives on the investment of its surplus cash.

a. What is the net project cost, including the adjustment for the incremental interest costs? Assume a borrowing rate of 15 percent.

b. If the YMCA borrowed from its cash reserves at a rate equal to the reserves's rate of return, would an adjustment to the net project cost be required? Explain.

6. The following data are the planning estimates for the creation of the Mansfield Arts Center, which will house an art gallery, museum, and theater. The Arts Center Foundation, the governing board of the organization, was established as a result of a gift of $2.0 million from a wealthy benefactor. Of that amount $1.5 million was to be used as an endowment to provide operating funds for the Arts Center.

a. From the data provided, determine whether the Arts Center project is financially viable as planned.

b. Construct a cash-flow summary under the assumption that the Arts Center is able to raise the exact sum of money from its fund-raising campaign that is required to permit the project to break even on a cash-flow basis.

c. If the Arts Center can borrow on a short-term basis at 10 percent, what is the present value of the incremental borrowing costs for the project?

d. What should the Arts Center do to make the project financially viable?

Item	Timing	Values
1. Construction costs (firm)	Year 1	$ 500,000
	Year 2	$ 2,200,000
2. Equipment and furnishings	Year 2	$ 630,000
3. Additions to the permanent collection	Years 3-5	$ 150,000
4. Planning period		7 years
5. Operating costs	Years 3-7	$ 95,000
6. Operating revenues	Years 3-7	26,000
7. Rate of return on the endowment	Years 1-7	8%
8. Cash on hand available for capital investment	Year 0	$ 510,000
9. Maximum amount expected from fund raising	Years 1-3	$ 3,000,000

10. Distribution of fund-raising receipts:			
a. One-time, first-year gifts	Year 1		34%
b. Two-year pledges	Years 1-2		48%
c. Three-year pledges	Years 1-3		18%
11. Transfers from the endowment	Years 1-7	$	120,000
12. Construction inflation rate	Years 1-7		18%
13. Inflation rate for equipment and furnishings	Years 1-7		8%
14. Inflation rate for art objects	Years 1-7		15%
15. Inflation rate for operating costs	Years 1-7		7%
16. Annual increase in revenues	Years 1-7		10%
17. Expected growth in the principal amount of the endowment	Years 1-7		8%

Appendix 14-A

MATHEMATICAL FORMULATION OF THE TEST FOR FINANCIAL VIABILITY

PROJECT CASH FLOWS

F = The present value of inflated cash outflows

$$F = PVC_c + PVC_e + PVC_f \qquad (1)$$

PVC_c = The present value of inflated construction costs
PVC_e = The present value of inflated equipment costs
PVC_f = The present value of the net annual shortfall of project revenues under operating costs

Construction Costs

$$PVC = \sum_{t=n}^{m} [C_a(1 + r)^{-t}](1 + i_c)^{n-1} \qquad (2)$$

n = Year in which construction begins
m = Year in which construction is complete
C_a = Progress payment made to contractor in year t
r = Rate of return earned on the organization's unrestricted investment account
i_c = Inflation rate of construction costs

Equipment Costs

$$PVC_e = \sum_{t=n}^{m} [C_{et}(1 + r)^{-t}](1 + i_e)^t \tag{3}$$

     C_{et} = Cash outlays for equipment in year t
     i_e = Inflation rate applicable to equipment costs

Operating Cost and Revenues

$$PVC_f = \sum_{t=j}^{k} [R_t(1 + r)^{-t}(1 + i_r)^t - 0_t(1 + r)^{-t}(1 + i_o)^t] \tag{4}$$

     R_t = Project revenues received in year t
     i_r = Growth rate of project revenues
     0_t = Project operating costs incurred in year t
     i_o = Inflation rate applicable to operating costs

ALLOCATED CASH FLOWS

Donated Funds

     PVQ = The present value of cash on hand allocated to the project plus the receipt of cash gifts and pledges of cash due from the organization's fund-raising activities

$$PVQ = Q[b_g(1 + r)^{-1} + \sum_{t=1}^{2} \frac{b_2}{2} (1 + r)^{-t} + \sum_{t=1}^{3} \frac{b_3}{3} (1 + r)^{-t} + \ldots$$

$$+ \sum_{t=1}^{a} \frac{b_a}{a} (1 + r)^{-t}] + K \tag{5}$$

     Q = The fund-raising goal needed to achieve project financial viability
     b_g = Percentage of the fund-raising goal to be received as onetime gifts in year 1 of the project
     $b_2, b_3, \ldots, b_a$ = Percentages of Q to be received in equal annual installments from pledges of 2, 3, . . ., a year's duration, respectively
     K = Cash on hand allocated to the project

Equation 5 may be reduced to

$$PVQ = Q_z + K \qquad (5a)$$

by setting Q_z equal to the sum of the terms contained within the brackets in that equation.

Borrowed Funds

Assuming that borrowed funds will be repaid in equal annual installments of principal plus interest, the annual installment payment = A.

$$A = D[\frac{r^*}{1 - (1 + r^*)^{-s}}] \qquad (6)$$

D = Principal amount of the loan
r^* = Borrowing rate of interest
s = Maturity of the loan
PVA = Present value of debt service costs

$$PVA = D[\frac{r^*}{1 - (1 + r^*)^{-s}} \cdot \frac{1 - (1 + r)^{-s}}{r}] \qquad (7)$$

When PVC_j is negative (i.e., when project operating revenues exceed project operating costs) or when the organization allocates a portion of its annual net cash surplus of revenues over expenditures to pay the project's debt-service costs, the maximum loan principal, D, may be calculated by setting $PVC_j(-1)$ equal to PVA and solving equation (7) for D:

$$PVA = PFC_j(-1) = D[\frac{r^*}{1 - (1 + r^*)^{-s}} \cdot \frac{1 - (1 + r)^{-s}}{r}] \qquad (7a)$$

$$D = PVC_j(-1)[\frac{1 - (1 + r^*)^{-s}}{r^*} \cdot \frac{r}{1 - (1 + r)^{-s}}] \qquad (8)$$

Similarly,

PVP = The present value of annual allocation of surplus net receipts available for debt service

$$PVP = P_t[\frac{1 - (1 + r)^{-s}}{r}] \qquad (9)$$

P_t = Annual allocation for debt service

$$D = PVP[\frac{1 - (1 + r^*)^{-s}}{r^*} \cdot \frac{r}{1 - (1 + r)^{-s}}] \qquad (10)$$

TESTS FOR FINANCIAL VIABILITY

Donated Funds

A project is considered viable when the value of Q, as calculated in equation (11), is equal to or less than the amount that the organization reasonably can expect to raise during the campaign conducted on behalf of the project.

$$Q = (F - K) \tag{11}$$

Borrowed Funds

A project that produces operating revenues in excess of operating costs is considered financially viable when

$$D \geq PVC_c + PVC_e - K - PVQ. \tag{12}$$

A project that does not produce annual net cash surpluses from operations is considered financially viable when

$$D \geq F - K - PVQ. \tag{13}$$

CASH-FLOW DEFICITS

When a project's cash reserves become negative at the end of any given year, and the organization must borrow at a rate higher than it is able to earn on its unrestricted investment fund, the present value of project cash outflows, F, must be adjusted for the incremental interest costs. The adjusted value, F', as calculated in equation (14), is used in place of that calculated in equation (1).

$$F' = PVC_c + PVC_e + PVC_f + \sum_{t=1}^{k} [r' - r)d_t](1 + r)^{-t}$$

r' = The organization's borrowing rate

d_t = The size of the deficit in the project's cash reserve at the end of the year t

k = The last year in which a deficit occurs

15

Allocating Resources to Achieve Multiple Goals

This chapter is based largely on research published by Richard F. Wacht and David T. Whitford under the title "A Goal Programming Model for Capital Investment Analysis in Nonprofit Hospitals," in Financial Management *(Summer 1976). Although the material presented here is relevant, it is also inherently complex. Moreover, since the technique is directed principally toward professional managers, this chapter may be skimmed by the interested finance student or else omitted without risk of creating a gap in the acquired knowledge of the subject matter.*

As explained in earlier chapters, the nonprofit organization must be perceived as a *social entity* whose central economic activities are directed toward a multiplicity of goals, the most important of which are internally nonfinancial and noneconomic. That is, the organization's central activities do not in most instances provide direct financial or economic benefits to itself. Instead, the organization exists primarily to provide societal benefits or to contribute to the public welfare.

This fact places the responsibility for the nonprofit organization's resource-allocation decisions largely in the professional arena. The financial implications of capital expenditures, presented in chapter 14, are important and should govern the decision in a negative sense; that is, they should prevent the organization from adopting financially nonviable projects. However, the final selection from among alternative financially viable projects is a professional decision; as such, it must be supported by a decision technique capable of dealing with a multiplicity of goals within a budget constraint. One technique uniquely suited to solving problems of this nature is *goal programming*. This chapter describes this technique and illustrates its application to a resource-allocation problem faced by a nonprofit organization.

GOAL PROGRAMMING

Goal programming is a linear mathematical programming technique that permits the decision maker to simultaneously consider several relevant organizational goals while seeking a *satisfactory* solution to a resource-allocation (or other type of) problem. Goal programming cannot select an optimum solution (that is, prescribe a maximizing behavior) because the solution process involves trade-offs among the several goals that management has decided to pursue. Moreover, in defining the problem for application of the technique, management must determine satisfactory ranges of attainment for each of its goals. This computational procedure selects from among all possible realistic solutions the one (or ones) that best fulfills management's requirements. Thus the technique leads to "satisfactory," rather than optimum or maximum, resource-allocation decisions.

The following discussion relies on two illustrative cases to teach both the principles and the proper application of the goal-programming technique to resource-allocation decisions from a professional perspective. The problem formulation and the interpretation of the solution values are emphasized in the discussion, but the computational methodology is purposely ignored. Because calculating the solutions to problems of even small dimension is extremely complex and time-consuming, computer assistance in solving goal-programming programs is for practical reasons considered all but mandatory. But, as will be explained in due course, those nonprofit organizations that do not have access to computer facilities will nevertheless find the material in this chapter of considerable value in designing an approach to resource-allocation decision making.

The key to understanding what goal programming is and how it works is the acquisition of a working knowledge of the basic components of the technique. These components are introduced in the next section and are explained in greater detail in the illustrations that follow.

Components of the Technique

The basic components of the goal-programming technique, as applied to resource-allocation decisions in the nonprofit context, are: (1) capital expenditure projects, (2) organizational goals, (3) environmental constraints, (4) deviational variables, and (5) an objective function. Each of these components is expressed as a mathematical equation in formulating the goal-programming problem; however, simple nonmathematical definitions of these components will provide a better basis for describing the technique.

1. *Capital expenditure projects* are the investment alternatives management is considering. They are the focal points of the resource-

allocation decision process and represent the means by which an organization hopes to achieve its goals.

2. *Organizational goals* are management's expression of the aims or end results of the entity's operations. The goals should be expressed in operational terms so that measurement of their achievement is possible.

3. *Environmental constraints* are legal, physical, financial, and operational conditions that limit management's freedom to choose among alternative strategies or that inhibit the full attainment of one or more goals. They are generally unforgiving limitations that management must abide by in decision making.

4. *Deviational variables* are numeric expressions inherent and unique to the goal-programming technique. Their presence is mandated in order to produce a mathematical solution of the desired form. Their function is to measure the amounts by which a goal is overachieved or underachieved, given the alternative solutions to the allocation problem.

5. *Objective function* is what drives the goal-programming technique and produces a solution. It is an expression of management's willingness to accept overachievement or underachievement of its goals.

When properly formulated, the goal-programming technique searches for that combination of *capital expenditure projects* that enables the organization to operate within the boundaries specified by the *environmental constraints*, while minimizing the sum of the priority-weighted *deviational variables*. The priority weights are specified by management in the *objective function*, and the resultant solution to the resource-allocation problem is that which produces the highest level of *organizational goal* achievement.

A Simple Illustration

A simple and basically nonquantitative illustration may help clarify the way in which the resource-allocation problem is formulated and solved with the aid of the goal-programming technique. Suppose an organization has two *goals*: (1) to serve more clients (quantity); and (2) to serve them better (quality). The organization is currently considering two financially viable projects. Project A will enable the organization to serve more clients but will not affect the quality of the service it provides, and Project B will improve the quality of service but will leave unchanged the number of clients served. Each project will require 100 square feet of space and three new employees to become operational.

The organization faces two *environmental constraints* that prevent it from selecting both projects: (1) the building the organization occupies has only 150 square feet of space available for new projects, and (2) budgetary considerations prevent management from hiring more than four new employees. Finally, management feels that the societal objectives of the organization are better served by enhancing the quality of its services than by increasing the number of clients served. In other words, its *objective function* shows a clear preference for quality over quantity of service. The problem is summarized below:

	Project A	Project B	Constraints
Goal served	Quantity	Quality	Quality is preferred
Space required	100 ft²	100 ft²	150 ft² is available
Staffing	3 employees	3 employees	Limit of 4 employees

The solution to this problem is intuitively obvious. The organization's management cannot accept both projects because of space and budget limitations, but it can select either one or the other without violating either of these constraints. Since Project B promises to improve the quality of service, it is the better choice for implementation in accordance with management's stated goal preference.

But that solution leaves the organization with 50 square feet of unused space and the ability to hire one more employee. Therefore, if Project A can be partially implemented and still increase the number of clients served, management can also approve one-third of that project. That is, it can hire one-third of the number of employees required to fully implement Project A and presumably consume one-third of the project's total space requirements (or 33.3 square feet of the 50 square feet of uncommited space). In this way, the organization's expanded operations will contribute toward both its quantity and quality goals.

The discussion has thus far failed to consider the role of the *deviational variables*. This is primarily because it was unnecessary to do so to find the best solution; however, it is a simple matter to introduce the concept at this point.

This component of the goal-programming technique requires a mathematical expression of the objective function so that the technique can produce a solution that results in a measurable minimization of the deviations away from the desired level of goal achievement. This requirement can be met in the present illustration by assuming that management welcomes overachievement of both of the goals but does not desire their underachievement. Further, management has stated that it values quality enhancement *twice* as highly as it does increases in the quantity of clients served.

Let the symbols Y_1 and Y_2 represent the deviational variables associated with the quantity goal and quality goal, respectively. Since management prefers quality "two-to-one" over quantity of service, the expression of the objective function for this organization is:

$$\text{minimize: } 1Y_1 + 2Y_2$$

The solution value assigned to Y_1 by the goal-programming technique in this case is equal to one minus the percentage of Project A accepted, or

$(1 - .333 =)$ 66.7 percent. Similarly, the value assigned to Y_2 is equal to one minus the percentage of Project B accept, or $(1 - 1.000 =)$ 0 percent. Thus, the value of the objective function, Z, becomes

$$Z = (1 \times .667) + (2 \times 0) = .667$$

which is the minimum value for this problem. If management failed to implement one-third of Project A, the solution value for Project A would have been $(1 - 0\% =)$ 1, producing a value of Z equal to

$$Z = (1 \times 1.00) + (2 \times 0) = 1.00$$

And if management had decided to fully implement Project A and only one-third of Project B, the objective function would have been

$$Z = (1 \times 0) + (2 \times .667) = 1.33$$

since $Y_1 = (1 - 1.0) = 0$, and $Y_2 = (1 - .333) = .667$. The first solution is therefore the best since it does indeed minimize the value of the objective function.

A More Complex Illustration

The preceding illustration was purposely designed so that its solution would be transparent in order to clearly present the way in which the various components of the technique fit together. The next illustration is more complex, is quite realistic, and is formulated and solved both mathematically and intuitively.

The Newton County Humane Society is considering four capital projects, each of which is financially viable when considered separately, given the society's present financial resources. But because the society's available resources total $34,340 and the combined net project cost of the four projects is $43,770, management cannot implement all four of them at present. Moreover, the organization's existing facilities will accommodate expansion of only 1,600 square feet without violating the county's building and land-use codes. The problem is thus partly that of selecting among the four projects the combination that will satisfy the budget and space constraints.

In addition to the physical and financial constraints, the society had also established three basic goals to serve as guides in decision making. The first goal, in terms of the organization's overall priorities, is animal population control; the second is placement of homeless animals with families or individuals who will care for them properly; and the third is disease control among common household pets. The society's board of trustees has stated that half of the organization's efforts should be directed toward achieving the first goal—population control—with only about a 10 percent effort in the area of disease control, since that goal is also shared with the county's health department and the many veterinarians practicing in the area. The remaining 40 percent of the society's activities should be centered on the animal placement goal.

The four projects that the society has under consideration are:

A. Expanding its animal shelter area.
B. Replacing its existing animal rescue vehicle with a larger, better-equipped unit.
C. Creating pet adoption program
D. Establishing a small-animal health-screening clinic.

The society's planning had thus far considered financial viability requirements (in terms of the cash and fund-raising goals), contributions toward goal achievement, and space requirements for each project. The planning data are summarized in Exhibit 15-1.

Exhibit 15-1: **Summary of the Newton County Humane Society's Capital Budget**

	PROJECT				
Project Number	A	B	C	D	
Description	Expansion of animal shelters	Vehicle replace-ment	Pet adoption program	Small animal health screen-ing clinic	Totals
Net project costs	$ 10,770	$ 4,200	$ 8,800	$ 20,000	$ 43,770
Space requirements	800 ft²	0	400 ft²	1,000 ft²	2,200 ft²
Goal achievement percentages					
1 Population control	20%	70%	0%	0%	
2 Animal placement	60	5	80	0	
3 Disease control	20	25	20	100	
Total	100%	100%	100%	100%	

The net project costs for each project, as listed in the exhibit, are the present values of the cash resources needed to make the project financially viable (see chapter 14). The *goal-achievement* percentages listed in Exhibit 15-1 are the estimates made by the society's management regarding the relative contribution each project would make toward the three organizational goals. For example, from a professional perspective management has estimated that 60 percent of the benefits to be realized from project A will be directed toward achieving the animal placement goal. Therefore, implicitly at least, 60 percent of the funds spent on project A—expansion of the animal shelters—represents funds spent on achieving goal 2—the animal placement goal. By similar implication, 20 percent of the cost of project A is to be spent achieving each of the other two goals. Also implicit in these estimates is the assumption that all projects are equally effective in *professional* terms; that is, a dollar channeled to a particular goal through any one project will achieve the same impact as a dollar invested in any other project channeled to that same goal.

Problem Formulation. The problem facing the Newton County Humane Society is expressible in a series of equations and inequalities—mathematical expressions of the relationships contained in Exhibit 15-1. The first set of inequalities are *true* constraints in that they limit project acceptance to no more than one of each of the four projects. Constraints 1 through 4 are written as follows:

$$1.\ X_A \leq 1$$
$$2.\ X_B \leq 1$$
$$3.\ X_C \leq 1$$
$$4.\ X_D \leq 1$$

where the variables X_A, X_B, X_C, and X_D represent the numbers or fractions of projects A through D, respectively, that the goal-programming technique is permitted to accept. Constraint number 1 is read, "X_A must be equal to or less than 1." Its exact interpretation is as follows: The society can use no more than one of project A, but it will settle for some fraction of that project if that is necessary in order to achieve the best solution possible. The goal-programming technique does not recognize negative solutions, but it may produce in a solution a value between zero and one, inclusively, for each of the four projects as a result of the way in which these constraints are written. Implementing fractional portions of the projects is possible only when the projects are divisible, of course. This problem is addressed later in the chapter.

Space Constraint. Constraint number 5 is also a true constraint in that it limits the selection of projects to a combination that can be accommodated within the 1,600 square feet available for expansion. The formulation of constraint 5 uses the data presented in Exhibit 15-1 and is expressed in terms of square feet. It becomes:

$$5.\ 800\ ft^2(X_A)\ +\ 0\ ft^2(X_B)\ +\ 400\ ft^2(X_C)\ +\ 1{,}000\ ft^2\ (X_D)\ \leq\ 1{,}600\ ft^2$$

The space constraint is a mathematical expression that prohibits the allocation of more than 1,600 square feet of space to new projects. For example, if projects A and C are selected and both projects are implemented in full, the numerical value of 1 is substituted for X_A and X_C, and zeros are substituted for the rejected projects X_B and X_D. Thus, the solution to constraint 5 becomes:

$$800\ ft^2(1)\ +\ 0\ ft^2(0)\ +\ 400\ ft^2(1)\ +\ 1{,}000\ ft^2(0)\ \leq\ 1{,}600\ ft^2$$

$$800\ ft^2\ +\ 0\ +\ 400\ ft^2\ +\ 0\ \leq\ 1{,}600\ ft^2$$

$$1{,}200\ ft^2\ \leq\ 1{,}600\ ft^2$$

The space constraint is satisfied in this case since 1,200 square feet is less than the 1,600 square feet available for new projects. If, however, the technique attempted to choose projects A, C, and D, the space constraint would be violated (since 800 ft^2 + 400 ft^2 + 1,000 ft^2 is greater than 1,600 ft^2), and that alternative solution would be rejected automatically by the technique.

Budget Constraint. The budget constraint is expressed in the form of three goal statements. As explained earlier, each project is regarded as professionally acceptable. Further, project costs are considered to be in line with expected professional or societal benefits; thus, the total dollars to be expended are considered to be an acceptable surrogate for goal-achievement in this instance. The next step is therefore to convert the goal-achievement percentages into dollar amounts.

The priorities assigned by the board of trustees to the three organizational goals specify that 50 percent of the available funds should be allocated to the first goal (population control), 40 percent to the second (animal placement), and 10 percent to the third (disease control). Exhibit 15-2 shows the dollar amounts corresponding to these percentages, the sum of which equals the amount of money available for new capital investment.

Exhibit 15-2: **Budget Allocation to Goal Achievement**

Goal	Assigned priority	Budget allocation
1 Population control	50%	$ 17,170
2 Animal placement	40	13,736
3 Disease control	10	3,434
Totals	100%	$ 34,340

Goal-achievement percentages for each project, as listed in Exhibit 15-1, can likewise be converted into dollar amounts, based on funds requirements for each project. For example, project A (expansion of the animal shelter) requires $10,770 to achieve financial viability, and its goal-achievement percentages are 20 percent for goal 1, 60 percent for goal 2, and 20 percent for goal 3. In other words, 20 percent of project A's benefits (and implicitly its fund requirements) arise from achievement of goal 1, and this translates into (.20 × $10,770 =) $2,154 being spent on (and being received as benefits from) pursuing goal 1. Similarly, since 60 percent of the project's total contribution is directed toward goal 2, a total of ($10,770 × .60 =) $6,462 of project costs and benefits is allocated to goal 2. The allocation to goal 3 is the residual 20 percent or $2,154. Exhibit 15-3 presents the imputed goal-achievement allocations for each of the three projects, based on the data contained in Exhibit 15-1.

Exhibit 15-3: Imputed Dollar Benefits of Project Goal Achievement

Project	Goal 1		Goal 2		Goal 3		Net project cost
X_A Shelters	$ 2,154	+	$ 6,462	+	$ 2,154	=	$ 10,770
X_B Vehicles	2,940	+	210	+	1,050	=	4,200
X_C Pet adoption	0	+	7,040	+	1,760	=	8,800
X_D Health clinic	0	+	0	+	20,000	=	20,000
Totals	$ 5,094	+	$ 13,712	+	$ 24,964	=	$ 43,770

The data in Exhibits 15-2 and 15-3 are combined to form the three budget constraint/goal inequalities. They are:

6. $\$2,154X_A + \$2,940X_B \leq \$17,170$

7. $\$6,462X_A + \$210X_B + \$7,040X_C \leq \$13,736$

8. $\$2,154X_A + \$1,050X_B + \$1,760X_C + \$20,000X_D \leq \$3,434$

The values assigned to projects X_A, X_B, X_C, and X_D (to the left of the inequality signs) are taken from Exhibit 15-3. The values to the right of the inequality signs are the allocations of total available funds ($34,430) distributed to each of the three goals as shown in Exhibit 15-2.

Inequality number 6 states that no more than $17,170 (that is, 50 percent of the total budget) may be spent on pursuing goal 1 (population control), and of the four projects, only projects A and B contribute to that goal. If projects A and B are accepted, a total of ($2,154 × 1) + ($2,940 × 1) = $5,094 will be spent on goal 1, leaving $12,076 unspent. These funds will not be reallocated to the other two goals (placement and disease control) unless the inequalities are modified to accomplish this desirable result.

Deviational Variables. Three deviational variables can be added to force the goal-programming technique to allocate funds from higher- to lower-priority goals (but not in the opposite direction). The deviational variables are associated with the three goals and are labeled Y_1^-, Y_2^-, and Y_3^-. The minus sign in the supra position will be explained later. Inequalities 6, 7, and 8 in their modified, final format become equalities with the addition of the deviational variables. They are restated as:

6. $\$2,154X_A + \$2,940X_B + Y_1^- = \$17,170$

7. $\$6,462X_A + \$210X_B + \$7,040X_C - Y_1^- + Y_2^- = \$13,736$

8. $\$2,154X_A + \$1,050X_B + \$1,760X_C + \$20,000X_D - Y_2^- + Y_3^- = \$3,434$

Equation number 6 now states that deviational variable Y_1^- will take on a value equal to the unspent funds originally allocated to goal 1. Equation 7 will add that same amount to its allocation of \$13,736, and deviational variable Y_2^- will take on a value equal to funds not spent on goal 2. The process continues in the same manner through goal 3. In other words, if projects A and B are accepted and fully implemented, the value of equation 6 becomes:

$$(\$2,154 \times 1) + (\$2,940 \times 1) + \$12,076 = \$17,170$$
$$\$17,170 = \$17,170$$

and equation 7 becomes:

$$(\$6,462 \times 1) + (\$210 \times 1) + (\$7,040 \times 0) - \$12,076 + \$19,140 = \$13,736$$
$$\$13,736 = \$13,736$$

The deviational variable, Y_2^-, reallocates \$19,140 to goal 3, and equation 8 becomes:

$$(\$2,154 \times 1) + (\$1,050 \times 1) + (\$1,760 \times 0) + (\$20,000 \times 0) -$$
$$\$19,140 + \$19,370 = \$3,434$$
$$\$3,434 = \$3,434$$

The deviational variable, Y_3^- indicates that a total of \$19,370 remains unallocated as a result of the selection of projects A and B. Other things being equal, this is not a good solution, since project C, if undertaken as well, will provide for additional goal achievement without violating the budget constraint. Again, the highest-ranking goal constraint must be listed first, followed by the others in descending order of priority.

Flexible Constraints. Frequently, an organization faces one or more operating or environmental restrictions that may be violated without serious penalty (and/or without significant reward if the restrictions are completely avoided). This type of constraint is often called a *goal* in the mathematical programming literature; however, in order to distinguish it from the *organizational* goals introduced earlier, these restrictions shall be called *flexible constraints.* The goal-programming treatment of these constraints is similar to that accorded to the final budget constraint/goal inequalities 6, 7, and 8.

To illustrate, assume that the Newton County Humane Society's four projects will affect the recruitment of additional volunteer personnel in different ways. Projects A and C will reduce the need for volunteer personnel by two positions and three positions, respectively, and projects

B and D will increase the need for additional volunteers by six and nine positions, respectively. The society's director has found that the time and effort required to administer the volunteer program increases directly with the number of individuals recruited and maintained in staff positions.

The director told the board of trustees that he would prefer not to add more than five volunteers to the staff, but that he would locate, train, and supervise as many as the new projects required. He cautioned them that the addition of more than five volunteers would reduce his overall effectiveness in administering the society's existing operations, however.

This constraint is expressed in terms of *volunteer positions* and takes the following form:

$$9.\ -2X_A + 6X_B - 3X_C + 9X_D - Y_4^+ + Y_4^- = 5$$

where Y_4^+ is the number of volunteers that would be added in excess of the targeted five positions, should the solution require the addition of more than five volunteers, and Y_4^- is the reduction in the number of volunteers below the target level. The plus sign in the supra position thus indicates overachievement of the target and the minus sign indicates underachievement. The values assigned to the projects correspond to their respective effects on the volunteer program.

Objective Function. The objective in goal programming is to minimize the deviations from the goals (including what have been termed flexible constraints). In formulating the problem, the decision maker is permitted to rank the goals in ordinal sequence; that is, he or she may assign *priority weights* to each goal that is included in the objective function. The priority weights may be thought of as reward or penalty points for underachievement or overachievement of the goals.

For example, deviational variables, Y_1^-, Y_2^-, and Y_3^-, are related to and permit the full utilization of resources in achieving organizational goals 1, 2, and 3, respectively. Their companion variables, Y_1^+, Y_2^+, and Y_3^+, are not included in the problem formulation because of the special structure and use of the negative deviational variables to create a cumulative flow of unallocated resources to lower-priority goals. The priority weights assigned to them are taken from Exhibit 15-2; that is,

$$50Y_1^- + 40Y_2^- + 10Y_3^-$$

These may be thought of as "penalty points" for deviations from goal achievement. That is, the closer the organization comes to achieving its goals, the lower the total penalty points.

The values of the priority weights assigned to the two remaining deviational variables, Y_4^+ and Y_4^-, depend on how strongly the director and trustees feel about the implied cost of administering the volunteer program. If the director is only mildly interested in keeping the number of new volunteers below five, he might assign a low-reward point value (that is, a small negative number) to the underachievement of that constraint. A negative priority weight, of course, will offset a positive value elsewhere in the solution, or else result in a higher negative value to the objective function—a desirable outcome when minimization of the objective function is being sought.

If the director is indifferent to underachieving the personnel constraint, he will assign a zero priority weight to Y_4^-. Or if he is opposed to adding *less than* five new positions, he will assign a positive (a penalty point) value to that deviational variable.

For purposes of obtaining a solution in the present example, assume that the director and trustees prefer to keep the number of new positions below five and are fairly strongly disposed against increasing the number of new positions by an amount greater than five. Hence the priority weights assigned to Y_4^+ and Y_4^- are 5 and -2, respectively. The negative value assigned to underachieving the personnel goal can be thought of as a reward for keeping the number of new volunteers under the target of five.

The objective function for this problem thus becomes:

$$\text{Minimize } 50Y_1^- + 40Y_2^- + 10Y_3^- + 5Y_4^+ - 2Y_4^-$$

Note that this objective function emphasizes the value of achieving the organizational goals over that of achieving the personnel goal, Y_4^+; the director and trustees have given Y_4^+ a priority weight value of only five. This value makes the personnel goal only half as important as the least important of the organizational goals (goal 3).

The problem statement in a logical format is presented in Exhibit 15-4. Each row in the exhibit represents a constraint, and each column contains the value assigned to a project or deviational variable by the constraint. The empty cells in the matrix mean the value assigned by the constraint is zero.

Project Divisibility. Mathematical programming solutions may be either integer or continuous. *Integer* solutions are employed when the projects are not divisible; that is, some fractional part of a project cannot be implemented for technical or other practical reasons. *Continuous* solutions permit acceptance of fractional projects. *Mixed-integer* solutions permit the decision maker to specify which projects are divisible and which are not prior to solving the program.

Exhibit 15-4: Problem Statement for the Newton County Humane Society's Resource Allocation Problem

Constraint number	Project A	Project B	Project C	Project D	Deviation variables					Sign	Values
					1^-	2^-	3^-	4^+	4^-		
1	$1X_A$									$\leq$	1
2		$1X_B$								$\leq$	1
3			$1X_C$							$\leq$	1
4				$1X_D$						$\leq$	1
5	$+800\,\text{ft}^2 X_A$		$+400\,\text{ft}^2 X_C$	$+1{,}000\,\text{ft}^2 X_D$						$\leq$	$1{,}600\,\text{ft}^2$
6	$+\$2{,}154 X_A$	$+\$2{,}940 X_B$	$+7{,}040 X_C$		$+1Y_1^-$					$=$	\$17,170
7	$+6{,}462 X_A$	$+\$210 X_B$	$+\$1{,}760 X_C$	$+\$20{,}000 X_D$	$-Y_1^-$	$+1Y_2^-$				$=$	\$13,736
8	$+\$2{,}154 X_A$	$+1{,}050 X_B$				$-1Y_2^-$	$+1Y_3^-$			$=$	\$ 3,434
9	$-2\ \text{vol.}\ X_A$	$+6\ \text{vol.}\ X_B$	$-3\ \text{vol.}\ X_C$	$+9\ \text{vol.}\ X_D$				$-1Y_4^+$	$+1Y_4^-$	$=$	5 volunteers

Objective function: minimize $\qquad 50Y_1^- + 40Y_2^- + 10Y_3^- + 5Y_4^+ - 2Y_4^-$

In the Newton County Humane Society illustration, project B—vehicle replacement—is not divisible, but the other projects are divisible to a greater or lesser extent. If all divisible projects are *completely* divisible—that is, each project can be implemented on at least a modest scale with an investment as small as one dollar—the problem formulation need not be changed from its present form. However, when some minimum investment is required to implement the project, an integer solution to the problem must be specified. Because of the large number of computations needed to solve integer programming problems of even moderate size, the decision maker who must deal with nondivisible projects should use a computer to determine the best solution to his or her resource-allocation problem.[1] In the humane society illustration, all projects will be treated as if they are completely divisible, in order to simplify the results.

Mathematical Solution. The solution to the resource-allocation problem presented by the Newton County Humane Society was solved with the aid of a computer using the *simplex method.*[2] The percentages of each of the four projects that will minimize the deviations from the goals (including the flexible constraint) are as follows: project A, 100%; project B, 100%; project C, 100%; project D, 40%. If project D were an "all or nothing" alternative, it would have to be dropped from further consideration because of the budget constraint; however, if a 40 percent implementation of that project is practical, the organization's goal achievement will obviously be enhanced by its addition.

In addition to the selection of projects, the solution also includes values for the deviational variables. These values are:

$$Y_1^- = \$12,076$$
$$Y_2^- = \$12,100$$
$$Y_3^- = \$\ 2,570$$
$$Y_4^+ = 0$$
$$Y_4^- = .4 \text{ volunteers}$$

The interpretation of these results is as described earlier: a total of $12,076 ($Y_1^-$) remains unspent on the achievement of goal 1 and is reallocated to goal 2; $12,100 ($Y_2^-$) remains unspent on the achievement of goal 2 and is reallocated to goal 3; and $2,570 ($Y_3^-$) of the total available

---

1. For a discussion of integer programming, see James C. T. Mao, *Quantitative Analysis of Financial Decisions* (Toronto, Ontario: Collier-MacMillan Canada, 1969), 244-257.

2. A complete discussion of linear and goal programming, including the mathematical and graphic solution methods, is presented in James C. T. Mao, *Quantitative Analysis*, chapters 3 and 4.

resources remains unallocated and may be spent for other purposes by the organization. The remaining two deviational variables, Y_4^+ and Y_4^- are related to the personnel constraint. The zero value for Y_4^+ means that the number of new volunteer positions did not exceed the desired level of five, and the 0.4 value for Y_4^- means that the desired level of five new positions was underachieved by 0.4 of one position. In other words, the solution added (5 – 0.4 =) 4.6 new volunteer positions to the organization's staff.

Intuitive Solution. Resource-allocation problems such as that posed by the Newton County Humane Society obviously are difficult to formulate, and solutions to these problems are obtainable only with the assistance of a computer.

In most instances, however, a precise mathematical solution to the goal-programming problem is not required. Proper specification of the problem, although a difficult exercise in itself, often provides sufficient insight into the important dimensions of the problem to allow the decision maker to arrive at the best solution through intuitive means. In other words, the process involved in setting up the problem in the form of goals, constraints, and the objective function very often will make one or more satisfactory solutions readily apparent to the decision makers.

To illustrate, let's again examine constraints 5 through 9, but this time without their respective deviational variables:

$$
\begin{array}{lllll}
5.\ +\ \ \ \ \ 800X_A\ + & & +\ \ \ \ \ 400X_C & +\$\ \ \ 1,000X_D & \leq 1,600\ \text{ft} \\
6.\ +\$\ 2,154X_A\ +\ \$\ 2,940X_B & & & & \leq \$17,170 \\
7.\ +\$\ 6,462X_A\ +\ \$\ \ \ 210X_B & +\$\ 7,040X_C & & & \leq \$13,736\ (\text{plus residual cash}) \\
8.\ +\$\ 2,154X_A\ +\ \$\ 1,050X_B & +\$\ 1,760X_C & +\$\ 20,000X_D & & \leq \$3,434\ (\text{plus residual cash}) \\
9.\ -\ \ \ \ \ \ \ 2X_A\ + & 6X_B & -\ \ \ \ \ 3X_C & +\ \ \ \ \ \ \ 9X_D & \leq 5\ \text{volunteers} \\
\end{array}
$$

Close and careful inspection of these inequalities will reveal several obvious facts. First, constraint 5 clearly shows that the Humane Society cannot implement both project A and project D, because together they consume 1,800 square feet of space. But any combination of two or three projects each that does not contain both A and D can be housed in the society's available space. Second, given that goal 1 is considered by the trustees as the most important goal to achieve, projects A and B must be considered leaders for implementation. And since constraint 6 is not violated when both projects are selected, they both remain in the running.

Third, since goal 2 is the second most important goal, projects A, B, and C appear to be the best combination of projects, and their selection does not violate constraints 5, 6, or 7.

Fourth, if projects A, B, and C are selected, volunteer positions will increase by only one, according to constraint 9 [i.e., $(-2 \times 1) + (6 \times 1) - (3 \times 1) + (9 \times 0) = 1$]. Therefore, the personnel constraint is satisfied.

Finally, since the implementation of projects A, B and C will cost only $23,770 (see Exhibit 15-1), and given the assumption that project D is completely divisible, the remaining $10,570 of the $34,340 available for capital expenditures should be used to partially implement project D.

This intuitive selection will satisfy all constraints, including number 9, and result in the maximum level of goal achievement possible. It is also worthwhile to note that this solution is almost identical with that produced by the computer using the simplex method.

Of course, not all problems will work out this neatly under intuitive analysis; however, the statement of the problem in the goal-programming format and the quantification of the constraints and the priority weights in the objective function will most often reveal to the decision maker the proper direction in which the best solution may be found, if not (as in this example) the best solution itself. The goal-programming technique is therefore a very powerful and useful tool for resource-allocation decisions. Even though the decision maker may not be able to calculate the precise mathematical solution for his or her statement of the organization's resource-allocation problem, the professional aspects of the problem are nevertheless well defined, and resource-allocation decisions are improved by the application of the goal-programming technique up to and including the *intuitive solution*.

SUMMARY

This chapter departs from the discussion of purely financial matters in order to present a way of dealing with both the financial and professional aspects of resource-allocation problems. The decision method discussed here, goal programming, is a linear, mathematical programming technique that permits the decision maker to simultaneously consider multiple organizational goals in selecting among alternative capital-investment projects.

Instead of describing the technical, mathematical procedures necessary to produce a solution in application, the discussion stresses the basics of problem formulation and the way in which intuitive solutions may be obtained for fairly complex resource-allocation problems. The goal-programming technique requires that the problem definition be structured in mathematical terms in the form of constraints that describe the decision environment. The technique also forces the decision maker to express the organizational goals in precise terms and order them according to priority in achievement. Once this task has been accomplished, the solution that produces the best results without violating the rules of the game, as defined by the constraints, often becomes evident to the decision maker. Hence, the framework provided by the technique often will guide decision makers to optimum solutions without their having to actually perform the complex mathematical calculations prescribed by the technique.

The goal-programming model described in this chapter was designed to meet both the financial manager's and the professional manager's requirements in resource-allocation decisions. That is, implementation of the optimum solution will ensure that the organization achieves both professional and financial viability on a project basis.

FURTHER READING

Two approaches to formulating a goal-programming problem are presented in the following articles:

Keown, Arthur J., and John D. Martin. "Capital Budgeting in the Public Sector: A Zero-One Goal Programming Approach." *Financial Management* (Summer 1978): 21-27.

Wacht, Richard F., and David T. Whitford. "A Goal Programming Model for Capital Investment Analysis in Nonprofit Hospitals." *Financial Management* (Summer 1976): 37-47.

The most comprehensive and readable presentation of the mathematical programming techniques is found in the following text:

Mao, James C. T. *Quantitative Analysis of Financial Decisions*. Toronto, Ontario: Collier-MacMillan Canada, 1969, especially chapters 3 and 4.

QUESTIONS

1. Why must the professional manager in a nonprofit organization be charged with the responsibility for resource-allocation decisions?

2. List and define the five components of the goal-programming technique.

3. Explain in general terms how goal programming works and what it is designed to accomplish.

4. Explain the special function of the deviational variables in goal programming.

5. What is meant by the term flexible constraint? How do the flexible constraints differ from the true constraints?

6. Explain why goal achievement is likely to be greater when projects are divisible than when they are not.

7. Describe how an intuitive solution to a goal-programming problem is formulated.

PROBLEMS

1. The Chicago Chamber Orchestra has budgeted $3,500 for purchasing new music arrangements during this quarter. The librarian has received orders for five pieces. The price for each arrangement is as follows:

A	$ 675
B	1,018
C	990
D	776
E	1,148
Total	$ 4,607

Write a programming constraint describing the limitation introduced by the music budget on the orchestra's ability to acquire music.

2. The music librarian of the Chicago Chamber Orchestra asked the director to rank each arrangement listed in problem 1 on a scale of 1 to 5 (with 5 being the best ranking) according to its expected audience appeal. The rankings follow:

$$A - 2$$
$$B - 4$$
$$C - 3$$
$$D - 2$$
$$E - 5$$

    a. If the goal is to buy the largest number of arrangements, which ones should the librarian order?

    b. If the goal is to purchase the music with the greatest audience appeal, which arrangements should the orchestra buy?

    c. Compare the total costs and audience appeal "scores" for each of your solutions. What is your recommendation on the purchase of the arrangements?

3. The Historic Preservation Society of Boston has decided to emphasize two goals during the coming year: (1) oral historic preservation, and (2) historic preservation through photography. The society is considering three projects that will contribute to achieving one or both goals:

Project A is an oral history project in which society members are trained and equipped to interview selected individuals and record their personal recollections of historic interest. The tapes are then reviewed, indexed, and stored for future use.

Project B is the creation of a quarterly magazine in which the preservationists in the Boston area would be given an opportunity to publish the results of their efforts.

Project C involves locating and copying old photographs of people, places, and events of historic significance.

Relevant data pertaining to each project is summarized in the following table.

	Project A	Project B	Project C
Net project cost	$3,366	$5,480	$1,940
Space required	320 ft^2	1,000 ft^2	200 ft^2
Volunteer hours	6,000 hr/yr	500 hr/yr	2,900 hr/yr
Goal achievement levels:			
1. Oral history	90%	50%	10%
2. Visual history	10%	50%	90%

The society has allocated $7,500 of its cash reserves to achieving financial viability for new projects, and it currently has 1,350 square feet of unused space in its headquarters. The society's membership now totals 115, each of whom are available to work for the organization on the average of 4 hours per week. A total of 14,000 volunteer hours per year are required to sustain current operations.

a. Write constraints in the goal-programming format for the budget, space, and volunteer-hour limitations specified in the problem. Use the notation X_A and X_B to represent projects A, B, and C, respectively. Which constraints, if any, do not restrict the society's choice among the projects?

b. Projects A and C are totally divisible, but Project B cannot be divided. Considering only the budget constraint, what choices are possible if all of the $7,500 allocation is to be spent?

c. Now considering only the space constraint, what choices are possible if all the space allocation is to be used?

d. If the society's membership expresses a preference of visual history over oral history, what is the optimum solution to this resource-allocation problem? Given your solution, calculate the amount of surplus budget, unused space, and surplus of volunteer hours.

4. The Boys Club of Toledo is considering three projects designed to contribute toward its two organizational (professional) goals. The projects, goals, and net project costs are presented here:

	Goal contribution		
Project	Goal A	Goal B	Net project cost
1	10%	90%	$ 13,430
2	65%	35%	$ 8,380
3	40%	60%	$ 10,300

a. Calculate the imputed dollar benefits of goal achievement for each project (see Exhibit 15-3).

b. The Boys Club has allocated $25,000 for new projects, and it has assigned a priority of 75 percent to achieving Goal A and 25 percent to achieving Goal B. Use these data and your answer to part *a* to construct two budget constraint/goal inequalities.

c. Transform the inequalities prepared in part *b* to equalities by adding the required deviational variables, Y_a^- and Y_b^-, and specify the objective function using the deviational variables.

d. None of the three projects is divisible. Which of the following solutions do not violate the budget constraints? Select the optimum solution (that is, the one that minimizes the objective function.)

Solution

1. Project 1
2. Project 2
3. Project 3
4. Projects 1 and 2
5. Projects 1 and 3
6. Projects 2 and 3
7. Projects 1, 2, and 3

e. Suppose the director of the Boys Club changed his mind about the priority weights for the two goals. He decided to assign 25 percent of the club's efforts to achieving Goal A and 75 percent to Goal B. How does this affect the optimum solution? (Hint: repeat parts *b* through *d* using the new weights, and list the constraint for Goal B first).

PART V
LONG-TERM FINANCING

The final part of this text deals with managing the capital structure of the nonprofit organization. Because the nonprofit organization has a unique legal status (as compared with for-profit business firms), the only components of the capital structure of a nonprofit organization that must be "managed" are borrowed funds, examined in chapter 16, and leases, the topic of chapter 17.

Since nonprofit organizations are not permitted to have stockholders who may exercise claims against either the organizations' incomes or assets, their financial managers are not required to address such issues as dividend policy, share values, and returns to owners. Consequently, the task of the financial manager of the nonprofit entity is considerably simpler in this regard than that of his or her counterpart in the for-profit context. Balancing this comparative advantage, however, is the fact that the unique characteristics of the finance function of the nonprofit organization require the explicit and complete integration of its long-run investment and financing decisions, while the for-profit finance theory permits their separate consideration. Chapter 18 examines this interesting aspect of the financial manager's area of responsibility and decision analysis.

Finally, the existence of short-term and long-term financial claims against the nonprofit organization brings with it the possibility of financial distress. Chapter 19 outlines an approach to managing resources in periods characterized by the absence of adequate financial resources to continue operations at current levels.

16

Management of Debt Capital

This chapter begins with a discussion of intermediate-term financing in which the nature of the funds requirements, the means of repayment, the formal loan agreement, and the sources of loans are examined. The nature and characteristics of long-term debt are discussed next, followed by several sections dealing with the acquisition and management of debt capital. Finally, the role and functions performed by investment bankers (the principal middlemen in the nation's capital markets) in arranging long-term financing for nonprofit organizations are presented. This material plus that contained in the following two chapters comprises a modern and comprehensive coverage of capital structure management for nonprofit organizations.

Nonprofit organizations often have needs for funds that cannot appropriately be met by short-term borrowing—needs created by an organization's growth to finance its permanent requirements for additional long-lived assets and permanent increases in current assets. For example, a private school located in a growing community may decide to build additional classrooms to accommodate large numbers of students. Also the school will certainly have to maintain larger inventories of paper and other classroom supplies to support the increases in usage rates brought about by increased enrollments. The building and the increase in working capital are considered permanent increases in the school's assets. To the extent that such permanent funds needs cannot be (or are not) met from other permanent funds sources—large gifts and grants, for example—they may be and frequently are met by acquiring permanent *debt capital*; that is, by obtaining funds through intermediate-term and long-term debt.

When financing the acquisition of permanent assets, including growth-induced additions to current assets, the use of long-term debt is preferred to that of short-term debt because of what is known as the *matching principle* of debt financing. The matching principle states that short-term needs ought to be financed with short-term funds and long-term needs ought to be financed with long-term funds. On a personal level, the matching principle means that the average person should never finance a house or a new car with a ninety-day note, since the average person's income over a three-month period is simply not large enough to purchase property priced at several thousands of dollars and cover his or her current living expenses as well.

The same thing is true in the case of the profit-seeking businesses and *trading* nonprofit organizations. The costs of long-lived assets purchased by these entities are recovered out of operating cash flows over a number of years; hence debt repayment, which depends on cash generated from the financially profitable employment of those assets, is normally accomplished over an extended period. In the absence of profits or the excess of cash receipts over cash expenditures, debt repayment may take even longer than it otherwise would.

In *nontrading* organizations, assets do not directly generate operating cash flows. Therefore, unless debt repayment is guaranteed from the organization's endowment fund or by some individual or agency outside the organization, the nontrading organization should normally avoid debt financing altogther.

INTERMEDIATE-TERM CAPITAL

For the purposes of this discussion, intermediate-term debt (generally referred to simply as term debt) is defined to include obligations with initial maturities between one to ten years, while long-term debt has an initial maturity of longer than ten years. This is admittedly an arbitrary classification of debt capital, because some term lenders—notably smaller commercial banks—often are reluctant to extend term credit over periods longer than five to seven years, while other lenders will extend what they call term credit for periods longer than ten years. Regardless of these variations from the ten-year breaking point, these definitions of term and long-term debt will be followed in this chapter in order to avoid complicating the exposition of the principles of debt management.

Intermediate-term loans are a form of permanent capital to the nonprofit organization. The term *permanent* is used in the sense that the funds thus acquired are normally used to purchase fixed assets or to permanently increase the amount of current assets held by the organization. Ultimate repayment of the term loan will not affect the permanency of the assets acquired; hence repayment must be effected by one or another form of long-term funds—either the further addition of debt capital, gifts, and grants or an accumulated surplus of cash receipts over cash expenditures.

Lenders extend term loans to nonprofit organizations for two different reasons. First (and most usual), they extend term credit to finance investment in additional fixed assets and permanent current assets. Such loans are made with the expectation that they will be repaid with funds generated from operations. This kind of term loan is most easily arranged for by those organizations that generate positive cash flows from the sale of goods or services produced from their principal economic activities (such as schools or nonprofit publishing houses) or that have reasonably permanent and certain sources of cash receipts in excess of their current operating needs (such as some churches and professional associations).

Second, lenders sometimes extend term credit to permit organizations to proceed with a program of asset acquisition while a mortgage or a planned sale of an issue of bonds is pending or until a major fund-raising campaign has been completed. Most commonly, such loans are used to finance the initial states of a plant expansion program. As construction progresses, the borrowing organization utilizes the funds to make progress payments to contractors. Then, with construction completed and its total cost known, the intermediate-term loan is repaid from the proceeds of the sale of securities in the capital market, the proceeds of a mortgage, or the fund-raising efforts of the organization. This arrangement economizes on the use of funds, since they are borrowed initially only as needed. Such interim financing is often extremely useful to organizations with high proportions of fixed plant and equipment to total assets—as is the case of rural electric cooperatives, for example. This form of capital is also important for churches, schools, and almost any nonprofit organization that requires a permanent home and elects to purchase, rather than to lease, the facilities needed to support its operations.

Repayment of Term Debt

Scheduled repayment of term loans is usually required by the lender in periodic installments. The payment schedule of a loan is subject to negotiation between the lender and the borrower and is usually geared to the borrower's ability to generate the cash flows needed to service the debt. Typically, this schedule calls for payment at regular intervals, but the payments themselves may be either constant or irregular with respect to dollar amounts. Exhibit 16-1 illustrates repayment schedules for a five-year term loan, given quarterly, semiannual, and annual

Exhibit 16-1: **Size of Payment Required to Amortize a Five-Year, $10,000 Term Loan Under Various Repayment Intervals and Interest Rates**

Payment intervals	Interest rate			
	5%	8%	10%	15%
Quarterly	$ 568.20	$ 611.57	$ 641.47	$ 719.62
Semiannual	1,142.59	1,232.91	1,295.05	1,456.87
Annual	2,309.75	2,504.56	2,637.97	2,983.16

payment dates and several interest rates. The equal periodic payments in the table contain both interest accrued from the previous payment and the principal amount to be retired at the end of the period.

Sometimes the term loan is amortized in equal periodic installments except for the final payment, known as a *balloon* payment, which is larger than any of the others. This arrangement conserves the borrower's cash until final maturity of the loan, at which time the borrower usually liquidates some assets to retire the debt, borrows an amount equal to the balloon payment, or obtains funds from some other source to meet the balloon payment. In almost every instance, however, the source of funds for final retirement of the term loan is planned for at the time the loan is granted, as discussed below.

Formal Loan Agreements

Formal loan agreements between the lender and borrower are written documents, often of extreme complexity. It is therefore very important that the borrower seek legal counsel before entering into such an agreement; however, from a *business* perspective, financial managers of nonprofit organizations should be familiar with three basic elements of the loan agreement that have the potential to dramatically affect the organization's method of operation and future financial arrangements. These three elements are protective covenants, interest costs, and collateral requirements.

Protective Covenants. When a nonprofit organization approaches a lender with a request for a term loan, the financial manager should be aware of the way in which the lender will consider the application for credit, given the inherent risks associated with term lending. Specifically, when a lending institution extends term credit, it provides the borrower with funds for a fairly extended period. During this time the financial condition of the borrower is subject to change; to protect itself from the risks of loan default associated with the occurrence of unfavorable change, the lender may require the borrower to maintain a financial condition over the life of the loan at least as favorable as it was when the loan commitments was initially made. This requirement is specified in various protective, or restrictive, covenants in the loan agreement.

These covenants are tailored to the specific loan situation, of course, but the general classes of covenants, which may be used singly or in some combination to limit the lender's risks, are (1) provisions to prevent the dissipation of assets, especially cash; (2) provisions to prevent the pledge of assets to others; and (3) provisions to assure the lender of continued efficient management of the organization and reliable information about the borrower's affairs.

Covenants Against Asset Dissipation. In most cases, nonprofit organizations will be required to maintain an excess of current assets over current liabilities of some specified minimum amount or proportion while the term loan is outstanding. This requirement ensures the lender that the borrower will not incur an extraordinary amount of short-term debt, thus preventing impairment of its short-term liquidity and solvency.

The more common types of restrictions for nonprofit borrowers involve placing limits on long-term cash commitments. For example, the lender may insert a protective clause in the loan agreement requiring that the organization obtain its written permission before increasing officers' salaries. Also, to prevent the borrower from tying up funds in illiquid investments, the lender may require that the additional capital expenditures be limited in amount during the life of the loan. Such expenditures, for example, may be limited to a fixed, maximum dollar amount each year. More commonly, however, they are limited to the amount of annual depreciation expenses on fixed assets or to some percentage of that figure.

Covenants Against Asset Pledging. The term-lending institution is not interested only in limiting its risk exposure through possible asset dissipation by its borrowing customer. It also wishes to lessen its risk by protecting the priority of its claim against the borrower's assets in case liquidation of the organization is required to recover the loan principal. Consequently, it may request that covenants be included in the loan agreement restricting additional secured borrowing, or sometimes restricting any additional borrowing, at least without its consent. Usually, a borrower is permitted to incur additional debt within reasonable limits for seasonal and short-term purposes, provided the minimum net working capital requirement is maintained. Also, the term loan agreement may contain a *negative pledge clause*, which prevents the borrowing organization from pledging any assets to any other creditors. In parallel fashion, the borrower may in addition be restricted from guaranteeing or endorsing any obligation for any other organization or person.

Information Covenants. Since a term lending institution is making a relatively long-run financial commitment to the term borrower, it is naturally interested in the continuation of the organization's present management and also in being regularly informed of developments within the organization. To achieve these ends, it may request the insertion in the loan agreement of a covenant against management changes without the lender's foreknowledge and consent. It may also require that life insurance policies on the lives of key officers be purchased by the organization, with the lending institution named as beneficiary of the policies. Finally, an almost standard provision of term loan agreements stipulates that the borrower must provide the lender with audited annual financial statements and with interim statements on a semiannual, quarterly, or (in high-risk loans) monthly basis.

Penalty Covenant. Another standard component of most term loan agreements is a covenant that spells out the penalty the borrower must face if it violates any of the other covenants. The penalty covenant generally takes the form of an *acceleration clause*, which states that if the borrower fails to make any required payments when due, or fails to conform to any other provisions of the agreement, the whole loan will immediately become due and payable. An acceleration clause enables a lending institution to step quickly into a deteriorating situation and take whatever action may be necessary to protect its interests. Beyond such an ultimate use, the presence of an acceleration clause or other penalty covenants in the term loan agreement works both to motivate the borrower to conform to the agreement's other provisions and to permit the lender to make forceful suggestions for improving the borrower's financial position whenever they may be required.

Overview of Restrictive Covenants. Although the restrictive and penalty covenants found in term loan agreements may appear to be quite onerous to term borrowers, their apparent harshness is tempered by two considerations. First, the restrictions imposed by the lender generally only make explicit the implicit bounds of good professional and financial management. Certainly any operating entity should maintain adequate working capital and should restrict capital expenditures and other discretionary spending to reasonable amounts in relation to available resources, whether or not it is bound by restrictive covenants to do so. Second, because a term borrower is dealing with only one lender, the borrower is in a position to renegotiate aspects of the term loan agreement that turn out to be particularly burdensome. Since the fortunes of the lender often parallel those of its borrowing customers, it is no more in the lender's best interest than in the borrower's to impose restrictions that hinder the nonprofit organization's ability to operate, grow, and maintain adequate liquidity. Thus the borrower will generally find that the lender will permit it more maneuvering room when unfavorable conditions arise that force it to violate certain covenants, especially when the record shows that the organization has been scrupulous in attempting to operate within all the covenants of the loan agreement.

Interest Costs. Interest rates on term loans are generally higher than rates on short-term loans of similar size. The spread between short-term and intermediate-term financing costs varies both with the size of the loan and with conditions in the money and capital markets. Exhibit 16-2 compares interest rates charged by commercial banks on short-term and intermediate-term loans with long-term bond rates.

Term loan interest rates may be established either as (1) a fixed rate over the whole life of the loan or (2) a variable rate, the level of which depends on that of the *prime rate* (the lowest commercial bank rate at which the largest, most creditworthy, profit-seeking businesses are able to borrow to meet their short-term credit needs). Where the term loan rate follows the prime rate, it is common also for the lender and borrower to agree to include both a floor and a ceiling on the rate charged. For example, the interest rate on a term loan may be set at one percentage point over the prime rate, with the further stipulation that the rate will not fall to more than two percentage points below or rise to more than three percentage points above the current prime rate of interest.

If no provision is contained in the loan agreement for prepayment without penalty, the lender is entitled to interest payments for the full life of the loan, even when the loan is repaid prior to its scheduled maturity. However, most term lending institutions allow the prepayment of loans without penalty, or with only moderate penalties, unless, for example, prepayment is effected with funds acquired from other lenders in order to take advantage of a decline in interest rates.

Collateral Requirements. Term loans are more frequently secured than are short-term (seasonal) loans. The increased use of security in term lending is understandable when the risks inherent in credit extension over a relatively long period are considered. And as previously noted, the average term loan maturity is around five years, with some maturities as long as ten years. Much can happen to a borrower's financial position during that long a period.

To illustrate, the cash receipts of most nonprofit organizations (and hence their net cash flows) are at least marginally sensitive to the general state of the economy. That is, trading organizations often will experience sales declines during recessionary periods. And nontrading organizations often find that their fund-raising activities generally are less expensive and more successful in periods of economic prosperity than during recessions. While economists can sometimes predict with some accuracy how healthy the economy will be during the next twelve months, projections for longer periods become less reliable because they are subject to much greater degrees of uncertainty. To compensate for their inability to predict the future with accuracy, term lenders often will require security for a term loan when they are perfectly willing to lend unsecured at short term to the same borrower.

To a certain extent, the security interest is taken more for its psychological effect than with the expectation that the assets pledged will offer adequate protection in case of loan default. The willingness of an organization to pledge its assets as security for a term loan is viewed by the lending institution as a good indication of the organization's intent to repay the loan in accordance with the terms of the loan agreement.

Revolving Credit as a Term Loan.   Revolving credit is a formal commitment by a lender to lend up to some maximum amount to a borrower during a specified period. The notes evidencing the debt are usually short-term; i.e., from 30 days to one year. However, the borrower may renew the notes and also borrow additional funds up to the specified maximum throughout the duration of the commitment.

Many revolving credit commitments are made for periods of more than a year, with some lasting as long as three to five years. As with a term loan, the interest rate charged under this kind of arrangement is usually higher than the rate at which an organization could borrow from the same lending institution on a short-term basis under a seasonal line of credit. Further, when a lending institution makes a revolving credit commitment, it stipulates that the funds will be available when the borrowing firm wishes to "take them down" (use them). The borrower pays the lender a *commitment fee*, typically amounting to 0.1 percent of loan principal, for this guarantee of funds availability. In theory, at least, this fee compensates the bank for the opportunity cost of not lending funds in the amount of the unused line of credit to another eligible business customer. In some cases, the commitment fee is refunded when and if the borrower uses the full line.

Because most revolving credit agreements have a life of more than one year, they are generally regarded as intermediate-term financing; however, this type of borrowing arrangement has some features of both short-term and term borrowing. The organization borrows only what it needs on a short-term basis; but it does have access to the total amount of the lender's commitment for the duration of the agreement. Revolving credit agreements can be set up so that at the termination of the commitment any amount still owed by the borrower can be converted into a straight-term loan.

Nonprofit organizations with highly seasonal patterns in their operations or those that are experiencing growth in assets will find the revolving credit commitment an excellent financing device. For example, a private school established in a growing community will find it necessary to either limit enrollment or undertake a program of modest expansion in the number of classrooms on a three- or four-year cycle, depending on the community's growth rate. Tuition payments are received largely in advance, giving the school a temporary surplus of funds that may be used for construction purposes. As these expenditures and operating expenses (such as teachers' salaries) consume the cash surplus, the school can begin to use its revolving line of credit, and then effect repayment (partial or full) at the time of the next tuition payment date. Of course, to ensure that the loan is ultimately retired, the capital expansion costs must be included as part of the basic tuition. When such costs are prohibitive, the revolving credit device may still be useful as interim financing prior to a major fund-raising campaign. Even considering the cost of a commitment fee, this type of loan generally is less expensive than other alternative financing plans because it requires the borrower to pay for only the funds it uses, when and as it uses them.

Sources of Term Loans

Nonprofit organizations generally have access to only two sources of term loans, but certain of them may have a third choice. The two most important term lenders are commercial banks and life insurance companies.

Commercial Banks. Commercial banks are by far the most readily accessible source of term credit for nonprofit organizations. There are two reasons why this is true. First, they are experienced term lenders and generally have allocated sufficient amounts of resources to this area of their loan portfolios to honor the requests of a fairly large number of term borrowers. Second, commercial banks are very sensitive to the needs of the communities in which they are located and will therefore be likely to respond favorably to a request for term credit from a nonprofit organization, provided, of course, that the lending officer can be convinced that the loan can be repaid as agreed.

Unfortunately, because lending to nonprofit organizations has not been common practice until recent years (because such organizations were formerly content to "do without" if donated funds were inadequate to meet planned expenditures), many banks are not experienced in dealing with the nonprofit borrower. Fund accounting statements confound them, and many bank officers will presume that a nonprofit organization is simply not allowed to generate a "profit" (a surplus of receipts over expenditures), and thus cannot possibly repay any kind of loan. Hence in dealing with any potential lender, a financial officer of a nonprofit organization must be prepared to educate the inexperienced lending officer in these areas of its operations.

Life Insurance Companies. Life insurance companies compete with commercial banks in extending term credit. However, the nature of the life insurance business makes for some important differences both in loan maturities extended and in interest charges levied on the borrower.

Life insurance companies prefer long-term investments. Their policy liabilities are long-term, and their funds inflows from premiums are steady. Liquidity is therefore not a critical problem and is certainly a minor matter as compared with its importance to commercial banks. Consequently, insurance companies view term loans as but one among a number of investment opportunities; they make them only when the returns are commensurate with the loans' costs, risks, and maturities, and with the prevailing yields on alternative investments. Also, since an insurance company does not benefit from the deposit balances or from other business by its term borrowers, the rates of interest it charges on term loans tend to be higher than commercial bank rates.

Insurance companies often participate with commercial banks in longer term loans. In such cases, the insurance company usually takes the long-maturity part of the loan (that part lasting over five years, say) while the bank keeps the short-maturity part (under five years). In such cases, the borrower signs two promissory notes, one for the short-term maturities payable to the bank and the other for the longer maturities payable to the insurance company. Under such arrangements, the bank generally acts as collecting agent for the life insurance company and services the loan over its entire life.

Other Sources of Term Credit. Nonprofit organizations with religious affiliations may find that the best and lowest cost sources of term loans are the local, regional, or national offices of their particular denominations. In some cases the loans are interest-free or nearly so, and the payment schedules are very favorable.

Private foundations and wealthy individuals are often willing lenders to nonprofit organizations. In fact, former donors who have been as hard pressed by high rates of inflation as have the beneficiaries of their philanthropy, have drastically reduced the sizes and numbers of their contributions but are nevertheless willing to extend term credit on favorable terms to these same organizations.

A significant disadvantage is sometimes associated with these sources of funds, however. Organizations easily can become dependent on this type of financial arrangement and may fail to develop and maintain sound internal financial management practices. As a consequence, when the organization is required to obtain financing from more conventional sources, it may be unable to meet one of the basic criteria of creditworthiness—that is, sound management of its financial affairs.

Finally, several term-lending programs are administered by government agencies. Since these programs are often short-lived, or else their lendable funds grow, shrink, or disappear altogether based on the direction of the political tide, even a partial listing of these programs would quickly become outdated material. The financial officer should therefore keep abreast of changes in these programs through routine perusal of relevant literature.

From the point of view of the borrower, it is important to note that government agency programs have certain common characteristics. First, their emphasis is on intermediate-term loans; neither short-term credit nor long-term equity funds are made available. In addition, the government agencies operating the programs view themselves as "lenders of last resort." In most cases, in order to borrow under one of the programs, an organization must be able to show that it has tried without success to secure credit accommodation from banks or other private sources. This view is taken to keep the agencies out of direct competition with private lenders.

As last-resort lenders, the agencies receive many marginal loan applications, a high proportion of which must be rejected. Loans made are usually extended at a uniform interest rate that is almost always below the market rate for loans in that "risk class." In other words, there is an element of subsidy involved in loans from government agencies. Finally, in almost all cases, only secured loans are made.

LONG-TERM DEBT

Long-term debt is a source of permanent financing for nonprofit organizations, but it also represents a commitment on the part of the borrower to repay the principal amount plus interest, usually in installments, over an extended period. Such borrowing arrangements therefore must be entered into by both borrower and lender with considerable caution and only after the borrowing organization's present and prospective financial conditions have been properly analyzed and assessed.

For most nonprofit organizations, the only form of long-term debt that is available is in the form of a *mortgage loan* from a commercial bank, a savings and loan association, or a mortgage company. But many larger nonprofit entities are able to issue *corporate bonds* to finance their long-term funds needs. These two forms of debt capital have much in common. The major differences between them are (1) bond issues are generally associated with corporate borrowers while mortgage loans are extended to unincorporated entities, and (2) bond issues are divisible into units of generally not less than $1,000 and the units are marketable in most cases, whereas a mortgage is not divisible, but it nevertheless may be marketable. The terms and conditions under which lenders are willing to extend long-term credit under either form are strikingly similar; thus, the following discussion centers on the more complex of the two instruments, the bond. The basic characteristics relating to the management of long-term debt, regardless of its form, are covered in the following sections.

Long-term Corporate Debt Instruments

The bond is the basic corporate long-term debt instrument. It is a long-term promissory note, and it retains this basic character regardless of the varying terms and conditions that may surround its issue. The corporate bond issuer (borrower) promises to repay a certain sum, with interest at a stated rate, at some specified future date. The contractual terms of the borrowing arrangement are stated in the bond indenture. This document may be very lengthy, since it must cover all matters of importance relating to the bond issue. For example, it states the precise form in which the bonds are issued, provides a complete description of the security (if any) to be pledged, and stipulates protective clauses or covenants, such as limitations on the borrowing corporation's total indebtedness and the liquidity position it must maintain. The bond indenture may also outline provisions for early redemption of the bonds (call privileges), sinking fund payments by the borrower, and penalties for nonperformance under the terms of the contract.

The terms of the indenture are enforceable on behalf of the collective interests of the bondholders by the *trustee* for the issue, who is named in the indenture and who is usually a corporate trustee—for example, the trust department of a commercial bank. The trustee's duties include certifying the bond issue from a (legal) contractual point of view, ensuring that the borrowing corporation observes all the terms of the bond indenture, and taking appropriate action on behalf of the bondholders in case of any default. The qualifications required of trustees for corporate bond issues, as well as the limitations imposed on their activities, are stated in the Trust Indenture Act of 1939.

A bond, a long-term promissory note, has a usual maturity of ten years or longer. It may be either secured or unsecured. Secured bonds are backed by a pledge of specific assets that can be used to satisfy creditors' claims in the event of bankruptcy and liquidation. Unsecured bonds carry no such pledge, of course.

Secured and unsecured bonds share a common characteristic: their repayment is anticipated from the corporate borrower's forecasted surplus of cash receipts in excess of expenditures over the expected maturity of the bond issue; repayment does not depend on the amount or composition of the organization's assets. A pledge of specific assets may nevertheless be required when the borrowing organization's expected net cash inflows over the life of the issue are judged to be too variable (risky) to make repayment from operations a virtual certainty.

Mortgage Bonds. Mortgage bondholders have a claim (a lien) on certain or all of the real assets of the borrowing corporation. If the mortgage covers all of the real assets, it is referred to as a *blanket mortgage*. An important provision contained in the indenture of a blanket mortgage is the *after-acquired property clause*, which stipulates that any real property acquired after the sale of the bond issue is to serve as additional security for the issue. From the bondholder's point of view, such a clause decreases the possibility of a decline in the market value of the assets being pledged as security for the bond issue. As the organization grows, other things being equal, the protection of the principal afforded by the pledged assets increases. From the borrower's point of view, however, the clause may hinder future financing because any subsequent bond issues would be forced to accept the position of junior securities (they would be second or third mortgages) having secondary claims to pledged assets.

Because of the possible adverse effects of such a provision on future financing, the borrowing corporation may decide that it is best to redeem the mortgage bonds and replace them with another issue at an early date or else ask the bondholders (through the trustee) for a bond indenture modification that would eliminate the after-acquired property clause. Failing those two approaches, the borrower can resort to several circumventions of the clause in its future financing efforts.

One avenue open to the organization is the leasing mechanism that permits it to use the desired facilities or items of equipment without purchasing them. (Long-term financing through leasing is covered in chapter 17.) Another is the *purchase-money mortgage*, used when new property is acquired with a mortgage attached. This is equivalent to a vendor's lien in law and takes precedence over the after-acquired property clause.

Unsecured Bonds. While the secured bond represents an important class of debt, a nonprofit organization may also issue bonds that carry no specific pledge of assets as security. These are known as *debenture bonds* (or simply debentures), and they represent an unsecured loan. Because debentures are not secured by specific property, their owners, in the event of liquidation, become general creditors of the organization. Although debentures are unsecured, the debenture bondholder is normally protected by the insertion of a clause in the issue's indenture that limits the corporation in subsequently pledging its assets to other creditors. Debenture holders must look exclusively to the issuing corporation's residual cash flow for interest and principal payments; therefore, only well-established organizations whose creditworthiness is beyond doubt are able to issue debentures successfully. Although many nonprofit organizations could easily qualify as unsecured borrowers, lenders prefer to extend long-term credit to nonprofit entities only on a secured basis. This fact, coupled with the fact that almost all long-term borrowing arrangements in the nonprofit context are for the purpose of fixed-asset acquisition, makes the debenture bond somewhat of a rarity in the capital structures of nonprofit organizations.

CASH FLOWS RELATED TO DEBT FINANCING

The use of debt to finance intermediate-term and long-term funds requirements exerts decided influences on the cash flows of the debt-issuing organization over the life of the debt. Those influences are both direct (arising from servicing the debt issue) and indirect (altering the organization's operational and other cash flows).

Direct Influences

Debt service charges are defined as interest payments while the debt is outstanding plus the repayment of principal, either at maturity or on some scheduled basis over the life of the debt. Both interest payments and principal repayments affect residual cash flows in predictable ways. The organization's overall cash-flow patterns therefore should be carefully examined and their consequences accounted for by the organization's financial manager, as explained earlier in chapter 7 in the discussion dealing with budgeting.

From a cash-flow point of view, the financial manager must be aware of the effects of interest payments on the organization's cash position. If possible, he or she should time interest payments to coincide with seasonal cash surpluses (if the organization is subject to seasonal patterns in its cash flows) or with annual fund-raising activities.

Since debt must be repaid, the timing of repayment is of great importance in financial planning. The organization might benefit from a long repayment period with attendant small annual repayment requirements and from the right to make advance repayment without penalty. Lenders, however, usually prefer shorter maturities, sometimes with penalties for advance repayment, since advance repayment reduces the lender's yield on the investment. Such differences must be compromised, of course. The controlling factor is ordinarily the organization's ability to generate cash for interest payments and debt retirement as well as the ability to meet its operational needs for funds. The repayment schedule—the term of the loan—is a function of this cash-generating ability. The interest rate charged—the cost of the debt— is a function (among other things) of its planned maturity or redemption schedule.

Indirect Influences

The way in which debt will affect an organization's operating and other cash flows can be determined by analyzing the restrictive covenants contained in the term loan agreement or bond indenture. For example, most debt contracts will include a provision requiring the borrower to maintain some minimum liquidity position while the loan or bonds issue is outstanding. The requirement may be expressed in terms of maintaining a better than standard set of balance sheet proportions or a minimum amount of residual cash flow for debt service purposes. Either type of requirement necessitates close attention by management to cash balances, receivables collection, inventory control, the use of short-term credit, and the control of operating costs.

Sometimes, bond indentures and loan agreements limit the acquisition of additional funds through the issuance of long-term debt. Such limitations restrict an organization's ability to expand through external financing since additional borrowing is prohibited. This type of restriction is perhaps the most severe of all for an organization that is experiencing substantial growth. A debt issue carrying such restrictions may prove ultimately to be more costly than would an alternative issue that carries a higher interest rate.

ACQUIRING AND MANAGING DEBT

Lenders generally look to one or more of three sources of cash flow that a nonprofit organization will use to service a debt issue. The first and most important of these sources is the excess of cash receipts over expenditures that is expected to arise from the employment of the fixed assets scheduled to be purchased with the proceeds of the bond issue or mortgage loan. For example, if a private, nonprofit school proposes to issue bonds to expand its classroom space, the incremental academic fees and tuition charges received from the increased enrollment should be planned to be sufficient to cover both the incremental operating costs associated with the new classrooms (for example, teachers' salaries, supplies, and utilities) and the debt service charges of the proposed bond issue.

In applying for a loan or preparing formal documentation to present in support of an application for long-term debt, the management of a nonprofit organization must therefore first establish that the new facilities are needed. It must also be able to verify that the facilities will attract new clientele in sufficient numbers to fully utilize the planned capacity, and more important, to generate the cash flows required to keep the project financially viable. (Chapters 14 and 18 deal with the question of financial viability.)

The second of the three sources of cash flows that lenders consider important for debt service is donated funds. Community support is an important factor in assessing a nonprofit organization's overall creditworthiness, especially when the proceeds of the debt issue will purchase fixed assets that will only indirectly generate incremental cash flows. For example, a church may borrow money to build an educational building, but the project may not increase the size of the congregation. In this case, a lender will examine the organization's financial history to assess the degree of success it will achieve both in increasing weekly offerings from the church's membership and in managing periodic fund-raising campaigns.

Lenders look on the nonprofit organization's fund-raising activities as a primary source of debt repayment for nonrevenue-generating projects and as a secondary line of defense against insolvency if and when incremental revenues become insufficient to fully service the debt issued to purchase revenue-generating assets. Thus donated funds are often compared with common stock issues of profit-seeking businesses for purposes of assessing a nonprofit organization's overall creditworthiness.

Finally, the organization's "profits"—that is, its total excess of revenues over expenditures from *existing* operations—(where present) is the third and least important source of cash flows from which debt service charges are paid. As a practical matter, operating surpluses are not a common phenomenon in the nonprofit context; such organizations generally have too few resources relative to their too many opportunities to spend money. Staff professionals—teachers, curators, conductors, and researchers, for example—can always use surplus funds to make up for past budgetary inadequacies. Hence, lenders are often reluctant to place heavy reliance on operating surpluses for debt service purposes. But they do appreciate the fact that the existence of "profits" is clear evidence of sound management practice. And a well-managed organization can be depended on to channel the cash flows arising from incremental revenue and community support into debt service and ultimate retirement of the bond principal as required. The financial manager of a nonprofit organization should keep these facts clearly in mind when preparing for an initial interview with a lender or investment banker.

Measuring the Cost of Debt Capital

The financial managers of most nonprofit organizations shop around for the lowest interest rates for short-term and intermediate-term loans and spend considerable time in analyzing the costs of the alternative long-term financing plans presented by their investment bankers or long-term lenders. While the costs of short-term credit offered by different lenders are easily compared, because most lenders are required by law to state their interest rates as annual percentage rates (APRs), the costs of alternative-term and long-term credit plans are not so easily compared or measured. Because repayment schedules may differ among financing plans, their true interest costs are consequently different from the coupon rate of interest or the nominal rate of interest quoted by the long-term lenders.

The importance of cost measurement to nonprofit organizations should be obvious; the higher the cost of debt capital, the greater and/or the sooner will be the subsequent cash outflows for debt service. As discussed in chapter 12, a *lender* should prefer larger cash inflows in earlier rather than later years in order to increase the rate of return on the invested funds, and a *borrower* should prefer to pay little in earlier years and delay ultimate repayment for as long as possible in order to minimize borrowing costs.

This same concept holds true for nonprofit organizations but for more than merely these financial reasons. High costs of debt capital also reduce the total pool of resources that an organization is able to devote to achieving its professional goals. An organization is better off producing societal benefits in large quantities as quickly as possible and will likely be in a better position to survive and prosper financially if it is able to accomplish good results for its clientele group very quickly. In short, if a nonprofit organization can minimize its cost of debt capital, it will simultaneously become capable of maximizing the present value of societal benefits (in the classic cost-benefit sense).

True Interest Cost. The best method to use in making cost comparisons among alternative intermediate-term and long-term financing plans is called the True Interest Cost (TIC) method. It is widely used by state and local governments in evaluating and awarding competitive bids on new issues of municipal bonds. The formula for computing TIC, when interest is paid annually is

$$C = \sum_{n=1}^{m} \frac{P_n + I_n}{(1 + TIC)^n}$$

where C is the total amount of cash received from the lender or the investment banker as proceeds from the financing plan; $\sum_{n=1}^{m}$ means the sum of cash flows from year $n = 1$ to $n = m$; m is the year in which the debt is repaid in full; P_n is the amount of principal repaid in year n; I_n is the amount of interest paid during year n; and TIC is the True Interest Cost expressed as a rate of interest in decimal form. For example, the TIC of a three-year loan of $9,000 repayable at the rate of $3,000 at the end of each year plus interest at 10 percent on the outstanding balance is

$$\$9,000 = \frac{\$3,000 + .10(\$9,000)}{(1 + TIC)^1} + \frac{\$3,000 + .10(\$6,000)}{(1 + TIC)^2}$$
$$+ \frac{\$3,000 + .10(\$3,000)}{(1 + TIC)^3}$$

$$\$9,000 = \frac{\$3,900}{(1 + TIC)^1} + \frac{\$3,600}{(1 + TIC)^2} + \frac{\$3,300}{(1 + TIC)^3}$$

The value of TIC that will equate the right side of the equation with the left must be determined by trial and error. The calculations can be done on a hand-held calculator with or without the aid of the present value tables discussed and illustrated in chapter 12. Note that the expression $1/(1 + TIC)^1$ is the present value of $1 in one year at an unknown interest rate, TIC, and $1/(1 + TIC)^2$ is the present value of $1 in two years, also at the same TIC percent.

When the value of the TIC is set at 10 percent, the preceding equation may be solved using a hand-held calculator in the following steps:

$$\$9,000 = \frac{\$3,900}{(1.10)^1} + \frac{\$3,600}{(1.10)^2} + \frac{\$3,300}{(1.10)^3}$$

$$\$9,000 = \frac{\$3,900}{1.10} + \frac{\$3,600}{1.21} + \frac{\$3,300}{1.331}$$

$$\$9,000 = \$3,545.45 + \$2,975.21 + \$2,479.34$$

$$\$9,000 = \$9,000$$

In this case, the TIC of the loan is equal to 10 percent, the stated interest rate. This is to be expected since the borrower was given the use of the full amount of the loan principal and paid interest on the outstanding balance. In many loan situations, however, the lender charges certain fees, or loan *closing costs*, that are deducted from the loan principal. In mortgage loans, for example, the borrower must pay for title transfer costs, title search, lawyer's fees, and recording of the deed of trust with a city or county government. Consequently, the borrowing organization receives at closing an amount less than the principal amount on which it must pay interest and which it must ultimately repay. These lender charges cause the TIC of the loan to be greater than the stated interest rate.

Suppose the closing costs of the loan in the preceding example were $225.88, and the lender deducted these costs from the $9,000 loan principal. The borrower thus received ($9,000 – $225.88 =) $8,774.12. To find the TIC of the loan under these circumstances, the analyst must use a trial and error method to arrive at the TIC that will equate the right side of the equation with the loan proceeds of $8,774.12. A short search will turn up the correct TIC—11.5 percent. This is verified below:

$$\$8,774.12 = \frac{\$3,900}{(1 + .115)^1} + \frac{\$3,600}{(1 + .115)^2} + \frac{\$3,300}{(1 + .115)^3}$$

$$\$8,774.12 = \frac{\$3,900}{1.1150} + \frac{\$3,600}{1.2432} + \frac{\$3,300}{1.3862}$$

$$\$8,774.12 = \$3,497.76 + \$2,895.75 + \$2,380.61$$

$$\$8,774.12 = \$8,774.12$$

To illustrate further, the Global Research Corporation, a nonprofit research organization, was extended intermediate-term credit of $80,000 to purchase a computer. Net proceeds from the lender, after certain fees and charges, totaled $77,850. The lender agreed to accept interest-only payments for two years, and then required principal payments of $20,000 per year plus interest on the unpaid balance at the end of each of the next four years. Interest was to be charged at a rate of 12 percent per year. The relevant cash flows, P_n and I_n, are presented in Exhibit 16-2.

Exhibit 16-2: **Term Loan Repayment Schedule for the Global Research Corporation**

(1) Year	(2) Principal payment P_n	(3) Unpaid principal balance (BOY)	(4) Interest payment, I_n (3) × 12%	(5) Annual debt service (2) + (4)
n = 1	0	$ 80,000	$ 9,600	$ 9,600
2	0	80,000	9,600	9,600
3	$ 20,000	80,000	9,600	29,600
4	20,000	60,000	7,200	27,200
5	20,000	40,000	4,800	24,800
6	20,000	20,000	2,400	22,400

The TIC of the Global Research loan is that rate of interest that will equate C (the proceeds of the loan) with the present value of the sum of the annual debt service charges. The appropriate methodology involves a trial-and-error selection of interest rules until the TIC is located. Exhibit 16-3 illustrates one approach, in which 12 percent was selected as the

Exhibit 16-3: **Calculation of TIC by Trial and Error**

(1) Year	(2) Annual debt service *	(3) PVF @ 12%	(4) Present value of debt service (2) × (3)	(5) PVF @ 13%	(6) Present value of debt service (2) × (5)
n = 1	$ 9,600	.89286	$ 8,571	.88496	$ 8,496
2	9,600	.79719	7,653	.78315	7,518
3	29,600	.71178	21,069	.69305	20,514
4	27,200	.63552	17,286	.61332	16,682
5	24,800	.56743	14,072	.54276	13,460
6	22,400	.50663	11,349	.48032	10,759
Totals			$ 80,000		$ 77,429

* From column (5), Exhibit 16-3.

discount rate for the first trial. The present value factors (PVFs) in columns (3) and (5) were taken from the present value tables in the Appendix, but they could have been calculated as just illustrated. Note that the present value of the debt service charges in the first trial [column (4)] is equal to $80,000, the principal amount of the loan. Because Global received less than the principal in cash from the lender, the cost of the loan is higher than 12 percent; thus, the discount rate selected for the second trial was 13 percent. Again, table values were used to determine the present values of the debt service charges.

The present value of the debt service charges in the second trial, column (6), is slightly less than the amount of cash that Global will receive from the lender; hence, the TIC of this term loan is slightly less than 13 percent—about 12.8 percent.

Each alternative financing arrangement involving debt capital should be analyzed using the TIC method, and the one with the lowest TIC should be given serious consideration. However, the covenants and other nonfinancial considerations should also be carefully weighed prior to the final selection of the financing plan. The one selected certainly should be low cost, but it should also be one that the organization will find easy to live with, in terms of timing of repayment, maintenance of working capital position, and so forth.

Debt Refunding

Even though all aspects of a long-term financing arrangement have been carefully planned, a financial manager may want to make certain adjustments in the organization's debt structure long before the bond issue or term loan has reached its final maturity. The purpose of acquiring new debt to replace existing debt—a process known as *refunding*—is most commonly one of the following: (1) to eliminate contractual restrictions that have become burdensome or awkward for the organization to live with; (2) to consolidate several loans or bond issues to simplify their management; (3) to effect a lengthening of debt maturity to improve the organization's cash flows; or (4) to reduce debt service; that is, the cost of carrying debt capital.

Although each of those reasons may be sufficient cause for refunding, the most important by far is cost reduction. The reason is obvious: intermediate-term and long-term interest rates change often enough and in large enough increments to make refunding operations quite attractive at times. Also, a financially weak organization generally occupies a commensurately weak bargaining position in the negotiations for debt capital. As it gains financial strength, however, it may be able to command more favorable rates of interest on borrowed funds.

A simple comparison of two interest rates is hardly justification for undertaking a refunding operation, however. Other costs besides interest expenses are involved. For example, since refunding itself is generally a relatively expensive process, analysis of the question of whether or not to refund debt is similar to an analysis that precedes an investment in a financial asset (such as common stock), where the principal criterion is that of return on investment. The investment in the case of debt includes all additional costs associated with refunding debt; the returns are measured in terms of the reduction of cash outflows as a result of the refunding operation. To illustrate the proper method that should be used to analyze the desirability of refunding, consider the twenty-five-year mortgage on the headquarters of the North Georgia Farmers Cooperative.

The mortgage was obtained five years ago in the amount of $100,000, and carries an interest rate of 12 percent. The monthly payments are $1,053.20, and the unpaid balance currently is $95,651. The terms of the mortgage include a prepayment penalty of 1.75 percent of the unpaid balance.

The management of the cooperative has watched the movement of mortgage rates very carefully and noted their decline to 10 percent. In discussing refunding of the mortgage with several lenders, the organization's financial manager determined that the lowest cost alternative would require payment of closing costs of 3.25 percent of the principal amount of the loan plus $200 for a current land survey. The amount to be borrowed is $95,651, and the term of the new mortgage will be twenty years.

Exhibit 16-4 illustrates the way in which the net investment of the refunding operation is calculated. Cash expenses involved in refunding, as listed in the exhibit, total $4,983. In short, the organization will have to invest, or reduce its available cash by, $4,983 in the refunding operation in order to realize an annual reduction in the cost of servicing its outstanding long-term debt.

Exhibit 16-4: **Calculation of the Net Investment Required by the Refunding Operation**

Retirement of old mortgage	$ 95,651
Prepayment penalty @ 1.75% of balance	1,674
Closing costs of new mortgage @ 3.25% of principal amount	3,109
Land survey	200
Cash outflow needed to refund the mortgage	$ 100,634
Less: proceeds of the new mortgage	95,651
Net investment required by refunding operation	$ 4,983

The amount of the monthly cost reduction to be realized over the subsequent twenty years from that cash investment is shown in Exhibit 16-5. The figures indicate that the cooperative can save $130.15 per

---

Exhibit 16-5: Calculation of Monthly Cash Savings from the Refunding Operation

Monthly payment on the old mortgage	$ 1,053.20
Monthly payment on the new mortgage	923.05
Monthly cash savings	$ 130.15

---

month for twenty years, provided it is willing to immediately invest $4,983 in the refunding operation. The financial manager can test the efficiency of that investment by discounting the savings over twenty years and comparing the present value of the cash savings with the cash investment. The appropriate discount rate to use in this procedure is the rate of interest the organization is earning on its surplus cash balances (that is, its opportunity cost of cash investment). Two reasons suggest that this is the appropriate rate. First, the alternative to investing in the refunding operation is to retain the cash in the unrestricted investment account. Second, the refunding operation is a riskless investment in the sense that once the decision is made, the monthly savings are guaranteed by contract with the new lender, and the amounts and timing of the savings are known with certainty. Thus the organization need not add a risk premium to its cash investment rate.

To simplify the calculations (and get an approximation of the present value of the cash savings), the *annual* cash savings and an annual discounting period may be used in place of the monthly figures. The annual savings from refunding are:

$$\$130.15 \text{ per month} \times 12 \text{ months} = \$1,561.80$$

Given that the cooperative is earning 8 percent on the investment of its surplus cash, the present value of $1,561.80 per year for twenty years, discounted at 8 percent is

$$\$1,561.80 \times 9.8181 = \$15,333.91$$

In other words, for an investment of $4,983, the cooperative can effect a savings of cash worth over $15,000, in present value terms, by refinancing its headquarters building. Again, given the nature of the investment, the investment is risk-free in the sense that the organization can be certain of the permanent reduction in debt service. The refunding operation therefore should be undertaken by the organization.

INVESTMENT BANKING

The efficient functioning of the capital market (the market for intermediate-term and long-term funds) in general, and the primary securities market (the market in which *new* securities are originally sold to investors) in particular, depends to a large extent on the services performed by the investment bankers. The services benefit both the investing public and the corporation, state or local government, nonprofit institution, or agency that undertakes to issue securities. Traditionally, the investment banker acts as a middleman, channeling new liquid savings of individuals and business firms into the purchase of new corporate and government securities, especially bonds. By purchasing new (primary) securities for resale to ultimate (individual and institutional) investors, the investment banker makes new capital funds available for a variety of worthwhile purposes—building schools, factories, churches, offices, hospitals, ships, and planes; acquiring equipment and rolling stock; or financing the increasing permanent working capital needs of growing businesses.

Although the distribution of new securities issues is the principal function of investment bankers, they also do other important work in the capital market. For example, they sometimes handle the distribution of large blocks of already outstanding securities; they act as financial advisers both to securities issuers and to their own investor clients; they "make a market" for security issues they have distributed; and they act as "finders" for direct placements (new securities sold by the issuer directly to an institutional investor through private negotiation). Although the main thrust of their several functions is aimed at servicing the needs of the issuer of new securities, investment bankers must also necessarily represent the interests of the securities purchasers (ultimate investors) to whom they sell the new securities. What is more, they are often, if not usually, called upon to represent both sides simultaneously.

Since the investment banking firm's primary responsibility is to the client who is an issuer of new securities, its efforts are concentrated in planning and distributing (originating) the new issue to raise funds for the issuing organization. Services performed for the investment banking firm's investor clients are, of course, valuable in themselves; in a real sense, however, they merely facilitate its efforts to distribute new security issues.

A successful investment banker must therefore have a large following of both types of clients: investors are needed to buy the issues sponsored by the firm; issuers are needed to supply the stock in trade—new security issues. And the surest way to succeed is by developing a solid reputation for competence, honesty, and integrity in the financial community and among corporations and municipalities that frequently go to the capital market for long-term financing. Nonprofit organizations that hold large endowment funds may be able to benefit from a close association with an investment banker as either an investor or a security issuer.

Originating a New Issue

The security issues that investment bankers purchase and sell to investors are obtained by either private negotiation with issuing corporations or by competitive bidding. Historically, most new issues have been originated through negotiation; however, securities regulations have required that interstate railroad issues and most public utility issues originate by competitive bidding. Also, state and local government agency security issues are almost invariably originated by competitive bidding.

Industrial corporations and private, nonprofit organizations very seldom select investment bankers in this manner, however. The managements of these entities generally feel that their organizations benefit more over time from a continuing relationship with one investment banking firm. Thus, except for the securities of municipalities and corporations in regulated industries, which must be originated through competitive bidding, nearly all industrial securities, and those issued by nonprofit organizations, originate through negotiation.

If an organization contemplating new financing has an established relationship with an investment banker, the organization's financial manager should involve the investment banker in discussions of the new financing at a very early stage. If the organization has not established such a relationship, an investment banker must be chosen. The particular investment banking firm selected will depend on the competence and degree of specialization required to handle the financing successfully. It will also depend on the firm's overall reputation, including (especially) its past record of successfully managed issues for similarly situated fund-seeking organizations.

Not all investment banking firms are equally equipped with the knowledge and expertise needed to advise all nonprofit organizations regarding their long-term financing needs. There are, for example, only a few investment bankers that specialize in the origination and placement of church bonds. Similarly, the special knowledge required to fully analyze and structure a municipal or hospital bond issue is not universally possessed by all investment banking houses. Consequently, the selection of an investment banker by the management of a nonprofit organization must be done with considerable care and an eye toward selecting one from among those firms that can provide the special insights and services required by the organization.

The investment banking firms that can best meet the unique requirements of a particular nonprofit organization—a school, a church, or a museum, for example—are in a strategic position to advise their corporate clients about the type or types of securities to be issued, the size of issue that will be well received by investors, the best maturity for the issue, the protective features that the market will expect, and the nature of the collateral (if any is required) that should be pledged.

Planning the New Issue

Once the issuing organization has decided on the investment banking firm, its financial administrator must be prepared to spend much time answering questions, explaining details of prior and planned financing transactions, and generally assisting in the investment banker's investigation of the organization and its operations. If the investment banking firm has not dealt previously with the organization, it may decide to undertake a brief preliminary investigation, which will generally include an analysis of the organization and its operations based on readily available information. If the preliminary study yields favorable results, and the investment banker believes that further investigation is justified, the issuing organization will be asked to provide assurance that the investment banking firm will be given first priority for underwriting the proposed issue. With this assurance in hand, the firm will begin an intensive, thorough, and far-reaching analysis of the organization and its environment, leading ultimately to a complete financing plan.

The complete investigation is generally broken down into three parts: (1) an engineering study dealing with the organization's existing physical facilities and the proposed plant expansion, if one is planned; (2) a financial and accounting analysis; and (3) a legal analysis. The three reports are then combined and summarized into a final report prepared by the investment banking firm's buying department. The final report generally will include all or most of the following items: an appraisal of the issuer's credit standing; a financial rating of the proposed securities issue; the organization's standing in terms of other similar organizations; a summary of all engineering, accounting, and legal findings of consequence; and, finally, an opinion of the investment banking firm's buying department concerning the desirability of purchasing the proposed issue. This report is used by the investment banking house in its decision to recommend either for or against advising its client corporation to proceed with the securities issue.

By the time the final report has been prepared, and if the report supports the decision to proceed, most of the details of planning the issue of necessity will have already been completed. The investigation will have indicated the type of security most suitable to the issuer's situation, along with the issue's optimum size, maturity, and other terms. The investigation will have also produced most, if not all, of the data required by state and federal laws governing the public sale of newly issued corporate securities and the *prospectus*, a report designed to apprise potential investors of all of the relevant factors related to the proposed security issue.

Exhibit 16-6 presents the public announcement printed on the cover of a prospectus for a recent tax-exempt bond issue offered by Emory University in Atlanta, Georgia. The bonds were issued through and under the authority of a state agency, the Private Colleges and Universities Facilities Authority, which assumes limited liability for the payment of principal and interest on the bonds and thereby lends the issue its tax-exempt status. Exhibits 16-7 and 16-8 present the table of contents of the prospectus and a summary statement, respectively. Several features of the prospectus are worthy of comment.

First, two independent bond-rating agencies, Moody's and Standard and Poor's, have rated the bond issue, as indicated in the upper-right corner of Exhibit 16-6. Since the bond issue has a relatively short maturity (three years), Moody's rated the issue MIG 1, which stands for Moody's Investment Grade 1. This is the highest rating given under the MIG class, the lowest being MIG 6. Standard and Poor's rated the issue as AA-, which is a high, but not the highest, rating. It is nevertheless an investment-quality bond issue and, based on these ratings, may be purchased for the portfolios of organizations that are prohibited from holding risky securities.

Second, the table of contents of the prospectus presented in Exhibit 16-7 lists those areas on which the investment banker—The Robinson-Humphrey Company, Incorporated, in this case—concentrated in its investigation and analysis of Emory University, the state bond issuing authority, and the project for which the bonds were issued.

Finally, Exhibit 16-8 provides an overview of the major provisions of the bond issue. It indicates that the bonds are being issued by the Private Colleges and Universities Facilities Authority. The authority will lend the proceeds of the bond issue to Emory University which will in turn repay the loan out of its anticipated surplus of revenues over expenses over a three-year period. The authority will use these payments to retire the bond issue.

Pricing the Issue. The final question remaining to be settled between the investment banker and the issuer is the price at which the issue will be sold. The price emerges from a process of head-to-head bargaining between the investment banker and the issuer. The investment banker's compensation lies in the spread between the price the issuer receives from the investment banker for the new securities and the price the investment banker receives from their sale to the investors who purchase the securities for their portfolios. The issuing organization would naturally like the highest price possible for its securities, while the investment bankers must price the securities so they will be easy to sell in the market. Thus, the final price is usually determined only after considerable discussion, and is generally influenced largely by the current market prices of similar securities.

(text continued on page 428)

Exhibit 16-6: **Public Announcement of a Securities Issue from a Prospectus, for a University Bond Issue**

NEW ISSUE

Ratings:
Moody's: MIG 1
Standard & Poor's: AA –
(See "Ratings" herein)

In the opinion of Bond Counsel, interest on the Bonds is exempt from Federal income taxation and from state income taxation within the State of Georgia under existing rulings, regulations, statutes and court decisions.

$28,000,000

Private Colleges and Universities Facilities Authority (Georgia)

9½% Revenue Bonds (Emory University Project)

Series 1981-A

Dated August 1, 1981   Due August 1, 1984

Interest on the Bonds is payable semiannually on February 1 and August 1 in each year, commencing February 1, 1982. The Bonds are to be issued in coupon form in the denomination of $5,000 each, registrable as to principal only, or in fully registered form in denominations of $5,000 or any multiple thereof, and are interchangeable as provided in the Indenture. Principal of coupon Bonds (unless registered) and interest on coupon Bonds are payable at the principal office of Trust Company Bank, Atlanta, Georgia (the "Trustee") or at the principal office of any paying agent of the Authority or of the University. Principal of fully registered Bonds and of coupon Bonds registered as to principal only is payable only at the above principal office of the Trustee. Interest on fully registered Bonds is payable by check mailed to the registered owner thereof.

The Bonds are subject to redemption prior to maturity as described herein.

Price 100%

(plus accrued interest from August 1, 1981)

The proceeds of the Bonds will be used to pay the costs of constructing student residential housing facilities and a physical education center on land owned by Emory University (the "University") and to pay expenses related to the issuance of the Bonds. The Bonds are limited obligations of the Private Colleges and Universities Facilities Authority (the "Authority") and are payable solely from and secured by money and revenues received from the University pursuant to a Loan Agreement between the University and the Authority.

Neither the State of Georgia nor any political subdivision thereof shall, in any event, be liable for the payment of the principal of or interest on the Bonds, or for the performance of any pledge, mortgage, obligation or agreement of any kind whatsoever that may be undertaken by the Authority, and none of the Bonds or any of the Authority's agreements or obligations shall be construed to constitute a debt or a pledge of the faith and credit of the State of Georgia or any political subdivision thereof within the meaning of any constitutional or statutory provision whatsoever and the Bonds do not directly, indirectly or contingently obligate the State of Georgia or any political subdivision thereof to levy or to pledge any form of taxation whatever therefor or to make any appropriation for the payment thereof.

The Bonds are offered when, as and if issued by the Authority and received by the Underwriters, subject to prior sale and to the approval of legality by Messrs. King & Spalding, Atlanta, Georgia, Bond Counsel, the approval of certain matters for the University by its Counsel, Robert Wiggins, Esq., Atlanta, Georgia, the approval of certain matters for the Authority by its Counsel, Messrs. Alston, Miller & Gaines, Atlanta, Georgia, and the approval of certain legal matters for the Underwriters by their Counsel, Messrs. Haynes & Miller, Washington, D.C. It is expected that the Bonds in definitive form will be available for delivery in New York, New York on or about August 27, 1981.

The Robinson-Humphrey Company, Inc.

August 7, 1981

Exhibit 16-7: Table of Contents from a Prospectus for a University Bond Issue

No dealer, broker, salesman or other person has been authorized to give any information or to make any representations, other than as contained in this Official Statement, and if given or made, such other information or representations must not be relied upon. This Official Statement does not constitute an offer to sell or the solicitation of an offer to buy nor shall there be any sale of the Bonds by any person in any jurisdiction in which it is unlawful for such person to make such offer, solicitation or sale. The information set forth herein is furnished by the Authority and the University and includes information from other sources which the Authority and the University believe to be reliable but is not guaranteed as to its accuracy or completeness by, and is not to be construed as a representation by, the Underwriters. The information and expressions of opinion herein are subject to change without notice and neither the delivery of this Official Statement nor any sale made hereunder shall, under any circumstances, create any implication that there has been no change in the affairs of said Authority or University since the date hereof.

IN CONNECTION WITH THIS OFFERING, THE UNDERWRITERS MAY OVERALLOT OR EFFECT TRANSACTIONS WHICH STABILIZE OR MAINTAIN THE MARKET PRICE OF THE BONDS AT A LEVEL ABOVE THAT WHICH MIGHT OTHERWISE PREVAIL IN THE OPEN MARKET. SUCH STABILIZING, IF COMMENCED, MAY BE DISCONTINUED AT ANY TIME.

TABLE OF CONTENTS

Exhibit 16-8: **Summary Statement from a Prospectus for a University Bond Issue**

SUMMARY STATEMENT

The following summary is subject in all respects to the more complete information set forth in this Official Statement, including the attached Appendices.

Issuer

The Bonds will be issued by the Private Colleges and Universities Facilities Authority (the "Authority"), a public body corporate and politic, organized and existing under the laws of the State of Georgia, having its principal place of business in Atlanta, Georgia.

Purposes of Issue

The proceeds of the Bonds will be used to pay the cost of constructing student residential housing facilities and a physical education center on land owned by Emory University (the "University") and to pay expenses relating to the issuance of the Bonds.

Security

The Bonds will be limited obligations of the Authority payable solely from payments and certain other amounts to be derived by the Authority under a Loan Agreement (the "Agreement") with the University. Pursuant to the Agreement, the University has agreed to make loan payments sufficient, together with other moneys available under the Trust Indenture hereinafter described, to pay the principal of and redemption premium, if any, and the interest on the Bonds as the same become due and payable and certain costs and expenses of administering the trust created by said Indenture. The University's obligation to make loan payments under the Agreement will be a general obligation, payable from any and all unrestricted funds of the University, including revenues, gifts, grants, bequests, endowment funds, trust funds and the proceeds of borrowing legally available therefor.

Loan payments and other amounts due from the University under the Agreement will be pledged to the Trustee under a Trust Indenture between the Authority and the Trustee.

The University

The University is a privately endowed, not-for-profit, institution of higher learning located in Dekalb County, Georgia. The University was founded in 1836 by the Methodist Church and today has become a major national teaching, research and service center with an enrollment of approximately 8,000 students. The University's main campus consists of 570 acres owned by the University.

For the fiscal years ended August 31, 1979 and August 31, 1980, the University had an excess of current funds revenues over expenditures and mandatory transfers of $7,859,000 and $7,995,000, respectively, and net increases in current funds balances of $5,023,000 and $11,502,000, respectively. On August 31, 1980, the University had total fund balances (including unrealized appreciation of securities) of $511,398,000, of which $31,693,000 were "unrestricted current funds". Approximately $145,488,000 of the market value of the University's Endowment Funds at that date were unrestricted. All of the amounts set forth in this paragraph include amounts attributable to the ownership and operation of Emory University Hospital and The Crawford W. Long Memorial Hospital.

Simultaneously herewith, the University is offering through the Authority approximately $12,515,000 in principal amount of revenue bonds which, together with other available funds, will be applied to pay the costs of defeasing certain outstanding debt incurred by the University in respect to The Crawford W. Long Memorial Hospital.

Risk Factors

Certain risks are involved in the purchase of the Bonds. See "CERTAIN RISKS" herein. This Official Statement, including the Appendices hereto, should be read in its entirety.

(text continued from page 424)

Issuing Costs. Besides the periodic interest payable to investors after the initial sale of the securities has been completed, the issuing organization must bear certain costs relating to the issuing process. The first of the issue costs is the investment banker's compensation, which is generally the difference between the price the investment banking firm pays the issuer for the securities and the price at which it sells them to the ultimate investor. In other words, the investment banker literally buys low and sells high, or at least hopes to. The issuing organization must also bear the costs of printing the new securities and preparing the paperwork required by federal and/or state securities regulatory agencies. Finally, the issuing organization is liable to the investment banker for any omissions of material facts or misleading or untrue statements concerning the issue for which the issuer is responsible and must indemnify the firm for any liabilities it incurs as a result.

SUMMARY

The matching principle of debt financing makes a clear case for the use of intermediate-term and long-term debt in financing the acquisition of long-lived assets and the permanent growth of working capital assets. Intermediate-term debt—that which is repayable within one to ten years—is the most frequently used form of permanent debt financing. The arrangements under which nonprofit organizations borrow from term lenders are usually tailor-made to fit the unique requirements of both the borrower and lender. The term loan agreements, although complex, merely make explicit the implicit bounds of good management of the borrowing organization.

Term loans are most often secured by the borrower's real assets and are repaid out of funds generated from operations. A revolving line of credit also provides a form of intermediate-term loan in which the borrower is permitted to use as much or as little of the line as its current credit needs dictate at any one time. Repayment is effected when and as the borrower's operations generate surplus cash. The principal term lenders are life insurance companies and commercial banks.

Long-term debt is defined as debt having an initial maturity of over ten years. The bond is the basic corporate long-term debt instrument. The form in which bonds may be issued are mortgage bonds and debentures, or unsecured bonds. The most important aspects of managing long-term debt from the point of view of the issuer include the selection of an investment banker, plans for meeting the debt service costs, and measurement of the actual cost of raising permanent capital in this way. Occasionally, an organization's financial manager will be called on to analyze the costs of replacing an outstanding bond issue with a newer, lower cost issue, a process known as *refunding*.

One of the most valuable relationships a corporate borrower can form is that with a competent investment banker. The investment banker provides valuable assistance to a prospective bond issuer in planning, underwriting, and marketing the bonds in a public issue, or in locating a lender when the bonds are placed directly.

FURTHER READING

A thorough treatment of the way in which capital markets function is presented in:

Dougall, Herbert E. *Capital Markets and Institutions*. 2nd ed. Englewood Cliffs, N.J.: Prentice-Hall, 1970.

Management of debt capital is dealt with extensively in the following sources:

Donaldson, Gordon. *Corporate Debt Capacity*. Boston: Division of Research, Harvard Business School, 1961.

Bierman, Harold. *Financial Policy Decisions*. New York: Macmillan, 1970. Especially chapters 2 and 12.

An excellent article on bond rating is presented in:

Billington, Robert A. "How Corporate Debt Issues Are Rated." *Financial Executive* (September 1974): 28-37.

Two articles on the topic of bond refunding are worth reading. Note, however, that the tax effects of the process should be ignored by a nonprofit organization:

Bowlin, Oswald D. "The Refunding Decision: Another Special Case in Capital Budgeting." *Journal of Finance* (March 1966): 55-68.

Bierman, Harold. "The Bond Refunding Decision." *Financial Management* (Summer 1972): 22-29.

QUESTIONS

1. Explain the matching principle of debt financing.

2. Distinguish between long-term debt and intermediate-term debt.

3. For what two principal purposes do nonprofit organizations seek term loans?

4. List the sources of repayment generally relied on by term lenders.

5. What purpose is served by the addition of protective convenants to term loan agreements? List the principal categories of these covenants and give examples of each.

6. Define the following terms:
   a. negative pledge clause
   b. acceleration clause
   c. prime rate
   d. revolving credit
   e. commitment fee

7. List the various institutions to which nonprofit organizations may apply for term credit accommodation.

8. What are the major differences between a mortgage loan and a corporate bond?

9. Define the following terms:
   a. bond indenture
   b. call privilege
   c. sinking fund
   d. debenture
   e. trustee
   f. blanket mortgage

10. Describe fully the direct and indirect influences that long-term borrowing exerts on an organization's cash flows.

11. Briefly describe the methodology prescribed for measuring the True Interest Cost of a bond issue.

12. What is meant by bond refunding? Why cannot the refunding decision be based solely on the comparison of the old bond interest rate with the proposed bond interest rate?

13. What is an investment banker? What is the investment banker's role in getting a new bond issue to market?

PROBLEMS

1. The Brightwood Elks Lodge obtained a term loan of $5,840 from the First National Bank to remodel its lodge hall. The repayment schedule required the Elks to pay $1,000 per year for three years and a balloon payment of $4,000 at the end of the fourth year. The payments included principal and interest charges. Calculate the True Interest Cost of the loan.

2. The Pittsburgh Symphony Orchestra issued $12,515,000 of bonds in 1981 to build a new symphony hall. The amounts, rates, and maturities of the bond issue are as follows:

Amount	Coupon rate	Due
$ 1,345,000	8.75%	1982
1,475,000	9.00	1983
1,605,000	9.25	1984
1,755,000	9.40	1985
1,920,000	9.55	1986
2,105,000	9.70	1987
2,310,000	9.85	1988

The interest on the bonds is payable annually and the Pittsburgh Symphony Orchestra received $12,323,000 in proceeds from the investment banker. Calculate the True Interest Cost of the bond issue.

3. The Clairmont Research Foundation is considering refunding its current mortgage in order to lower its debt service requirements. The existing and new mortgage loan data are presented below:

	Existing mortgage	New mortgage
Balance	$38,740	$38,740
Prepayment penalty	1.5% of unpaid balance	2% of unpaid balance
Maturity	10 years	10 years
Closing cost	—	2.75% of principal
Interest rate	16%	12%
Quarterly payment	$1,856.50	$1,676.00

     a. How much will Clairmont Research have to invest in the refunding operation?

     b. Calculate the present value of the quarterly savings, given the relevant interest rate of 8 percent compounded quarterly.

     c. Should the foundation refund the mortgage?

17

Leasing
in Nonprofit Contexts

This chapter provides a frame of reference for analyzing lease arrangements for nonprofit organizations. Various forms of lease arrangements commonly employed by nonprofit organizations are discussed first. Subsequent sections discuss the accounting treatment of leases and the institutions involved in leasing. The chapter's final section presents an approach to making leasing decisions from the lessee's point of view. That section sets forth guidelines for judging whether particular lease arrangements are superior to other available financing alternatives.

Because contributions of large sums of money are becoming increasingly difficult to obtain and the effects of inflation have cut deeply into the purchasing power of contributions and other revenue sources ordinarily used to support their ongoing operations, nonprofit organizations have found that accumulating funds in sufficient amounts to meet their periodic capital investment requirements has become more difficult than ever before. As a consequence, many nonprofit organizations have discovered that leasing assets is a practical (and often the only) alternative to financing the purchase of those assets through other means.

While leasing has been viewed as a relatively modern development, it has actually been used for centuries by farmers as a means of obtaining the temporary use of agricultural lands. Sharecropping, in which the farmer gave a portion of the produce of the land as the lease payment to the landowner, is an example of this type of arrangement. To a landowner who was either unwilling or unable to sell his property or could not profitably employ the land himself, the lease represented a means of generating an income that otherwise could not have been obtained.

Leasing assets other than farmland and other real estate became a common practice only after World War II. The main impetus to the growth of leasing was its flexibility in meeting the needs of companies whose limited access to the usual sources of long-term credit seriously threatened to reduce their rates of growth in the rapidly expanding postwar economy. The lease arrangement often proved to be the only way such firms could obtain the use of capital equipment or facilities. Also, the lease arrangement proved to be of great help to equipment manufacturers in maintaining *their* growth rates during this period.

Largely as a result of those factors, leasing grew rapidly not only in volume but also in scope. At present, the list of assets that can be leased from one source or another is almost inexhaustible; it extends from almost every conceivable type of consumer good to ready-to-use factories. The total sales effort of many manufacturing firms often includes an offer of lease alternatives to customers. This device has proved to be a helpful sales tool, particularly when (1) the useful life of the equipment extends beyond the period for which the customer plans to use it; (2) the price of equipment is high relative to the financial resources of the customer; (3) the user wants to test the equipment before committing to its purchase; or (4) ownership of the equipment carries a high risk of early obsolescence, such as is the case with data processing equipment.

From the customer's point of view, leasing must be considered as a financing device and not as an alternative to merely owning an asset. Because of the contractual nature of the lease obligation and the similarities between a lease contract and a loan agreement, the lease should be considered an alternative to financing the purchase of the asset by borrowing. Both the lease payment and the payment of principal and interest on debt are fixed obligations; the inability to meet either of these payments on schedule can result in serious financial problems for the organization. Consequently, a leasing arrangement should not be entered into without performing as critical an analysis as would be undertaken prior to the decision to borrow funds on an intermediate-term or long-term basis for the purpose of buying the asset. This is an important point to keep in mind for future reference.

FORMS OF LEASE ARRANGEMENTS

In general, a lease is a contractual arrangement in which the owner of an asset (the *lessor*) grants the use of his or her property to another party (the *lessee*) under certain conditions for a specified period. The title to the property remains with the lessor, but the physical possession and control of the property pass to the lessee.

Conditions regulating the use of the property are first negotiated and then spelled out in the written lease contract signed by the lessor and lessee. For example, the period over which the lease remains in effect is subject to negotiation. Some agreements give the lessee the option to continue to lease the property after the initial contractual period. The lessee also may be given the option of purchasing the property either during the lease period, at prices specified in a schedule prepared by the lessor, or at a set price after the initial lease has expired. The terms, conditions, and options included in lease arrangements vary widely from contract to contract; thus the discussion of the major lease forms must necessarily be framed in general terms. Any number of options may be added to the basic forms discussed below, but these will not change a lease's underlying characteristics.

Operating Versus Financial Leases

Leases may be classified as either *operating leases* or *financial leases*. An operating lease is an agreement in which the lessee acquires the use of an asset on a period-to-period basis; that is, the operating lease is cancelable at the option of the lessee upon notice properly given to the lessor. This type of lease may be written, say, on a month-to-month basis and without any specified expiration date. The chief advantage of this arrangement is that the lessee is able to avoid the risks of ownership of the property. However, the operating lease generally is more expensive than the financial lease since the lessee must compensate the owner (lessor) for the risk of having to take possession of the property and subsequently redispose of it through either lease or sale.

By contrast, the financial lease, or *capital lease* as it is usually called, is a contractual arrangement in which the lessee agrees to make a series of payments to the lessor in return for the use of a particular asset. The size of the payments—which may be paid monthly, quarterly, semiannually, or annually—is scaled so as to (1) recover the lessor's investment in the asset, (2) cover the lessor's operating expenses, and (3) return the desired rate of profit on the transaction over the life of the lease.

During the initial term of the financial lease, the contract cannot be canceled except by mutual agreement between both parties. The lessee is therefore committed to continue making the lease payments over the entire period specified in the contract, thereby guaranteeing that the lessor will recover the initial investment in the asset and make a profit (provided, of course, the lessor's operating expenses were accurately estimated). From the point of view of the lessee, the financial lease guarantees uninterrupted use of the asset at a certain cost known in advance. It also provides the lessee with a method of financing the acquisition and subsequent use (but not the ownership) of the asset involved.

It is important to note at this point that the distinction between an operating lease and a financial lease is not based on the *length* of the contract. A financial lease may be entered into for less than a year, while operating leases are often contracted for on a year-to-year basis. Rather, the distinction between the two lease forms exists because of the differences in their respective methods of cancellation.

Sale and Lease-back Versus Direct Leasing. Another way in which leases may be classified rests on the prior ownership of the asset to be leased. If an organization sells an asset it already owns (and may also have physical possession of) to a (leasing) firm that, in turn, leases the asset back to the previous owner, the resulting lease arrangement is known as a *sale and lease-back*. The selling price of the asset is negotiated between the parties involved. The price agreed on may be greater than, equal to, or less than the asset's fair market value, but it generally depends on the initial cash needs and subsequent cash flow of the seller-lessee. The advantage of this kind of transaction to the nonprofit organization that sells and leases back is that it receives cash from the sale of the asset, which may be used for other purposes by the organization, while still retaining the services of the asset for the life of the lease. The for-profit lessor also benefits from its participation in such arrangements. The most important benefits are certain tax advantages in property ownership that are not available to nonprofit organizations because of their tax-exempt status. Consequently the partnership of for-profit and nonprofit interests through lease arrangements often proves beneficial to both in absolute terms.

Financial, rather than operating, lease arrangements are almost always used in sale and lease-back transactions. The use of the device is most common in real estate financing. The usual arrangement is for an institutional investor—for example, a life insurance company—to buy a property from an organization and then lease it back to that same organization. Under the alternative arrangement, known as *direct leasing*, an organization acquires the services of (but not the title to) an asset that it did not previously own. Direct leasing may be arranged through either a builder, a manufacturer, or a financial institution. Banks, finance companies, and independent leasing companies enter into the business of acquiring property for clients requiring certain assets in their operations. Once the financial institution has title to the asset, a direct lease is arranged under the usual conditions. More will be said about this topic in the section dealing with financial institutions involved in leasing.

Leveraged Leases. The leveraged lease is a specialized form of lease that has evolved in connection with the financing of fixed assets, such as supertankers, which require large cash outlays. From the standpoint of the lessee, there is little difference between the leveraged lease and any other financial lease, except that a leveraged lease may be less expensive to the lessee than are other lease forms.

Under a leveraged-lease arrangement, the lessee contracts to make periodic payments over the lease period and, in return, acquires the use of the asset, as is the usual procedure. However, the role of the lessor changes somewhat. While the lessor must own the property involved in a lease agreement, a leveraged-lease acquisition is financed in part by an equity investment and in part by borrowed funds, usually long-term debt. In most cases, the loan to the lessor is secured by a mortgage in the asset as well as by assignment of the lease and/or lease payments. In some cases, the lessee will guarantee (co-sign) the loan.

The lessor, generally a for-profit financial institution, receives significant tax benefits from the leveraged-lease arrangement. As owner of the asset, the lessor is entitled to (1) use the depreciation associated with the asset as a tax-deductible expense and (2) deduct for tax purposes the interest portion of the loan payments as an expense of doing business. These tax-deductible expenses create a favorable pattern of cash flows, with inflows being very heavy in the early years of an asset's life, followed by a period of lower cash inflows because of declining tax benefits. These tax effects, and the relatively small equity investment (normally less than 20 percent of the asset's cost), have the potential to produce an unusually high return on investment for the lessor. In most cases, however, the lessee shares in the lessor's good fortune by receiving more attractive lease terms than those offered by manufacturers or other lessors. Thus, while the nonprofit lessee need not be concerned with the technical aspects of leveraged leases, a knowledge of the profit potential inherent in this device may prove beneficial to the lessee in the negotiation process.

Maintenance of Leased Property. There are three general forms of lease agreements that assign the responsibility for maintaining an asset during the life of the lease: (1) maintenance leases, (2) nonmaintenance leases, and (3) net leases. The *maintenance lease* requires the owner of the property (the lessor) to perform all of the maintenance and repair work necessary to keep the asset in good working order as well as to provide insurance and pay all state and local taxes that may be levied on it. Such an arrangement is often used in leasing technologically complex equipment, such as computers, for which the lessee cannot support (or chooses not to support) a competent maintenance staff.

Nonmaintenance leases place the burden of maintenance, repairs, and other expenses on the lessee, as, for example, in the long-term leasing of land and buildings. The lessor continues to bear the risks of ownership; however, expenses such as insurance premiums and taxes are usually paid for by the lessee under the terms of the contract. In contrast, the *net lease* permits the lessor to escape practically all vestiges of ownership, even to the point where the lessee assumes responsibility for any losses incurred in the disposition of the property after the lease expires. The lessor usually provides the financing and performs only the function of buying and selling the property—all maintenance and other services are provided at the lessee's expense. This lease form is common in fleet leasing of vehicles.

Maturity and Risk. The period for which equipment or buildings are leased is related to both the useful economic life of the asset and the needs of the lessee. For those assets for which rapid technological changes can result in a high rate of obsolescence, the lease contract will be of relatively short duration. Buildings, on the other hand, may be leased for periods of thirty years or longer. The cost of leasing for short periods is usually higher than that of leasing an asset for the greater portion of its economic life. This differential in relative cost is directly related to the degree of potential risk of obsolescence borne by the lessor. When the property is returned to the lessor after the lease contract expires, the leasing company runs the risk of having a large portion of its capital tied up in used equipment that it may not be able to either sell or lease at prices or rentals high enough to assure a profitable return. Thus, to compensate the lessor for assuming this risk, the lessee generally is required to pay a premium in short-term leasing contracts.

Because of the different types of assets that are available for leasing, payment schedules vary widely. In recent years, lessors have emphasized the need to earn profits during the life of the lease instead of relying on the sale of the used equipment to provide the profit margin for the lease arrangement. In addition to merely recouping the initial dollar investment, the lessor will also expect to earn a suitable return on the use of the funds invested in the asset. Thus both pricing and maturity are critical factors in the lessor's contract consideration.

The term, or life, of a lease offered to the lessee by the lessor may also be influenced to some extent by the financial strength and credit responsibility of the lessee; that is, the poorer the credit risk, the shorter the life of the lease, and the sooner the full cost of the asset is recovered. Nevertheless, the significant value of the asset, from the standpoint of the lessor, rests on both its income-producing capabilities and the degree of flexibility the lessor has in being able to lease it consecutively to a number of users, regardless of their respective creditworthiness. Thus, a lessor faced with the alternative of acquiring for purposes of leasing either a parking-lot building or a general-purpose factory building, should prefer the factory building, if both offered roughly the same rate of return. While the lessee of the factory may have no greater chance of business success that the owner of a parking ramp, there is a greater chance of re-leasing the factory than the parking ramp if the original lessor fails to meet the scheduled lease payments. This is because the factory building will appeal to a broader range of potential lessees than will the parking building.

ACCOUNTING TREATMENT OF LEASES

The accounting treatment of leases has undergone considerable change since 1964 when the accounting profession first required that information concerning leased assets be disclosed in either the audited financial statements of the lessee or the footnotes to the statements. Prior to that time leasing was known as an "off balance sheet" method of financing, because leased assets belonged to the lessor, and the obligation to make lease payments for extended periods did not have to appear as a liability on the lessee's balance sheet. Management of an organization could therefore conceal from both its governing board and interested outside parties the fact that it was contractually liable for a series of future lease payments.

The guidelines under which the 1964 disclosure requirements were implemented were vague, however, and consequently were inconsistently applied by the accounting profession. While the accountants and others debated the issues involved in lease disclosure, leasing rapidly gained in popularity as a financing tool. Finally, in 1976 the Financial Accounting Standards Board (FASB) issued Statement Number 13 that standardized the accounting treatment of leases in the financial statements of both lessors and lessees and, more important, required that certain types of leases be capitalized on the (audited) balance sheets of lessees.[1]

Leases that must be capitalized—called *capital leases* in FASB terminology—have contractual terms that include at least *one* of the following conditions:

1. The lessee obtains title to the asset by the end of the lease period.
2. The lessee is given the option to purchase the asset at a bargain price.
3. The term of the lease covers 75 percent or more of the asset's estimated economic life.
4. The present value of the lease payments over the entire term is equal to 90 percent or more of the fair value of the leased asset.

When one or more of these terms are included in the contract, the lessee is said to acquire most of the economic benefits and risks normally

---

1. Financial Accounting Standards Board, *Statement of Financial Accounting Standards No. 13, Accounting for Leases* (Stamford, Conn.: FASB, November 1976).

associated with an *ownership* interest in the asset. This provides the rationale for capitalizing the lease and including it as an asset on the lessee's balance sheet, even though title to the asset remains with the lessor during the terms of the lease.

Capitalized Value of a Lease

The method of calculating the value of a capital lease and recording it on the balance sheet of the lessee is known as *capitalizing* the lease. A more accurate description of the methodology would be to say that the lease *payments* are capitalized by calculating the sum of their present values over the life of the lease. This dollar amount is used by the organization to represent both the book value of the asset being leased and the liability the lessee must reveal on its balance sheet as a result of entering into the lease arrangement.

According to FASB Statement No. 13, the portion of the total lease payment that is capitalized is that which represents the actual *rental* amount agreed on, exclusive of such executory costs as insurance, maintenance, and taxes. This basic amount must be discounted over the life of the lease at a discount rate equal to the lower of (1) the rate of interest the lessee would have to pay a lender if the lessee borrowed to finance the asset, or (2) the lessor's implicit interest rate (if that rate can be determined). An example will help illustrate the methodology.

Suppose the Greensboro Symphony Orchestra wishes to lease a bus that will be used to transport certain of its musicians and their instruments to locations within the state where the symphony has agreed to present educational programs and music demonstrations. The lease agreement calls for lease payments of $7,670 per year, with each payment due at the beginning of each of the next eight years. Taxes, insurance, and maintenance costs must be paid by the lessee. The symphony's incremental borrowing rate is 8 percent.

The lessor purchased the buses it leases for $45,000 each, and the buses normally have only nominal residual values after eight years of use. The lessor's implicit interest rate can be determined by finding the discount rate that equates the sum of the present value of the lease payments with the cost of the bus. Exhibit 17-1 illustrates this procedure.

Since the lease payments are due in advance, the first annual payment of $7,670 is due on or before the lessee takes delivery of the bus (in year zero), and each subsequent payment is due at the end of each of the next seven years. The implicit interest rate is determined by trial and error. First, an arbitrarily selected discount rate is used to calculate the present values of the lease payments. The sum of the present values is then compared with the cost of the asset. If the sum of the present values of the lease payments is greater than the cost of the asset, a higher discount rate is selected and the process is repeated. If the asset's cost is higher than the

Exhibit 17-1: **Calculation of the Lessor's Implicit Interest Rate**

Year	Lease payment	PVF @ 10%*	Present value of lease payments
0	$ 7,670	1.000	$ 7,670
1	7,670	.909	6,972
2	7,670	.826	6,335
3	7,670	.751	5,760
4	7,670	.683	5,239
5	7,670	.621	4,763
6	7,670	.564	4,326
7	7,670	.513	3,935
Total			Cost of the bus = $ 45,000

* *Present value factors are found in Appendix A, Present Value of $1 at the End of n Years.*

present value of the lease payments, a lower discount rate is used in the next trial. The process continues until the present value of the lease payments is equal to the cost of the asset. The discount rate that equates the lease payments with the cost of the asset is the implicit cost of the lease. Exhibit 17-1 shows the results of the final trial for the symphony example. In this case, the implicit interest rate is exactly 10 percent.

Because this interest rate is greater than the symphony's relevant borrowing rate of 8 percent, the 8 percent rate must be used to calculate the capitalized value of the lease. In most instances, the lessee's borrowing rate will be lower than the lessor's implicit interest rate; however, insofar as is practical, the lessee is obligated to attempt to determine the implicit interest rate being charged in the lease and to use that rate when it is below the lessee's relevant incremental borrowing rate.

Given that the Greensboro Symphony Orchestra must use the 8 percent rate to discount the lease payments, the capitalized value of the lease is calculated as follows:

Capitalized value of the lease = lease payment × present value factor representing the present value of $1 per year for 7 years at 8 percent interest

Capitalized value of the lease = $7,670 × 5.206 = $39,930

These calculations reflect the fact that the capitalized value of the lease that will be recorded on the balance sheet does not include the initial lease payment made in advance (year zero). Thus, only the remaining seven payments (in this example) are capitalized. The present value factor, 5.206, is found in Appendix B, Present Value of $1 Per Period for *n* Periods.

Recording the Capital Lease on the Financial Statements

The amount recorded on the lessee's balance sheet is the *lower* of the capitalized value of the lease payments, as calculated above, or the fair value of the leased asset, as measured by the market value of an identical or similar fixed asset. The leased property is listed on the lessee's balance sheet as a fixed asset, with two offsetting entries recorded in the current and long-term liability sections. The present value of the lease payments due within one year is listed among the current liabilities, and the present value of the remaining lease payments is listed under noncurrent liabilities, as illustrated in Exhibit 17-2.

Exhibit 17-2. **Balance Sheet Treatment of Capital Lease Obligations, Greensboro Symphony Orchestra, September 30, 1989**

Current assets		$360,200	Current:	
			Accounts payable	$106,028
Gross fixed assets:				
Land	$20,660		*Obligations under*	
Building	78,420		*capital leases*	*6,972*
Equipment	65,030			
Capital lease	*39,930*	$204,040	Other	3,873
Less accumulated			Total current	
depreciation	$16,800		liabilities	$116,873
Capital lease				
amortization	0	16,800	Noncurrent:	
			Obligations under	
			capital leases	*$ 32,958*
			Mortgage payable	120,431
			Total liabilities	$270,262
Net fixed assets		$187,240	Fund Balances	277,178
Total assets		$547,440	Total liabilities and Fund Balances	$547,440

The leased assets may be segregated, as in Exhibit 17-2, or they may be grouped with assets owned by the organization. When the leased assets are combined with other fixed assets, however, management must disclose the capitalized value of the leased assets and their accumulated amortization in a footnote to the financial statements. (FASB Statement No. 13 also requires similar disclosure for operating leases and noncancelable leases with remaining terms in excess of one year.) Regardless of how the data are presented, a footnote relating to capital leases must disclose the following additional information:

1. Total future lease payments.
2. A schedule of annual lease payments over the next five years.
3. Total sublease rentals to be received.
4. Details of terms of purchase, renewal options, and escalation clauses.

5. Rentals that are contingent on factors other than the passage of time.

6. Details of financial or operating restrictions imposed by the lease agreement.

Amortizing the Capital Lease. Since the lessee's total financial obligation under the lease agreement diminishes over time, as does its remaining right to use the leased property, the balance-sheet treatment of capital leases must reflect these periodic changes in status. In other words, the capitalized value of the leased property must be amortized and the corresponding liability reduced over the term of the lease.

The method selected by an organization to amortize the value of the lease is generally the same method the organization uses to depreciate the fixed assets that it owns. If the Greensboro Symphony Orchestra uses the straight-line method for depreciating its other assets, for example, the annual amortization charge against the capitalized value of the bus would be calculated as follows:

Annual amortization = (Capital value + Initial lease payment)/Lease term
= ($39,930 + $7,670)/8
= $5,950

As shown in Exhibit 17-2, the gross amount of the capital lease is recorded initially on the balance sheet at its capitalized value—$39,930— with no amortization listed until the end of the first year of the lease. At the beginning of year 2, the value of the leased property will be listed as $39,930 – $5,950 = $33,980; at the beginning of year 3, as $33,980 – $5,950 = $28,030; and so forth. The capital lease amortization account will grow in annual increments of $5,950 beginning at the end of year 1.

Reducing the Liability Created by the Lease Agreement. The method prescribed by FASB Statement No. 13 for reducing the liability created by the capital lease arrangement is called the *interest* method. This method divides the lease payments into interest and principal components in the same way that mortgage payments are broken down in the amortization schedules supplied to homeowners by many residential mortgage lenders. The lease obligation contained in the balance sheet is reduced each year by an amount equal to the principal component that remains after deducting the interest component from the annual lease payment. The calculations illustrating the interest method for the bus being leased by the Greensboro Symphony Orchestra are presented in Exhibit 17-3.

The interest rate used to calculate the interest component is the same rate used to capitalize the lease payments—in the present example, 8 percent. Since all payments are made in advance, the entire amount of the first payment (due in year zero or at the time the lease agreement is signed by the lessee) is applied against the initial principal amount of the

Exhibit 17-3: **Calculations Illustrating Interest Method**

(1) Year	(2) Principal owed beginning of year	(3) Interest at 8% (2) × .08	(4) Lease payment	(5) Principal payment (4) − (3)	(6) Principal owed end of year (2) − (5)
0	$ 47,600	0	$ 7,670	$ 7,670	$ 39,930
1	39,930	$ 3,195	7,670	4,475	35,455
2	35,455	2,837	7,670	4,833	30,622
3	30,622	2,450	7,670	5,220	25,402
4	25,402	2,033	7,670	5,637	19,765
5	19,765	1,582	7,670	6,088	13,677
6	13,677	1,095	7,670	6,575	7,102
7	7,102	568	7,670	7,102	0

lease (in this case $39,930 + $7,670 = $47,600 in year zero). The remaining lease payments are composed of amounts representing the principal and interest components as shown in Exhibit 17-3, columns (5) and (3) respectively. The figures in column (6) are recorded on the lessee's balance sheet as the lease liability outstanding at the end of each year of the lease's term.

Recording the Lease Expense. The lease expense for each year in the lease term is calculated as the sum of the annual amortization charge plus that year's interest component of the lease payment. Since the interest expense declines over the life of the lease (because the residual liability under the lease obligation declines), the lease *expense* varies from year to year in spite of the fact that the actual annual *cash payment* the lessee makes to the lessor remains constant over the life of the lease. However, under the interest method, the sum of cash payments over the lease term is always equal to the total lease expense taken over the same period. Exhibit 17-4 calculates the annual (variable) lease expense and compares those figures with the annual cash lease payments.

Exhibit 17-4: **Annual Lease Expense and Lease Payments**

(1) Year	(2) Amortization of capitalized lease (straight-line)	(3) Annual interest expense (from Exhibit 17-3)	(4) Annual lease expense (2) + (3)	(5) Annual lease payment
0	0	0	0	$ 7,670
1	$ 5,950	$ 3,195	$ 9,145	7,670
2	5,950	2,837	8,787	7,670
3	5,950	2,450	8,400	7,670
4	5,950	2,033	7,983	7,670
5	5,950	1,582	7,532	7,670
6	5,950	1,095	7,045	7,670
7	5,950	568	6,518	7,670
8	5,950	0	5,950	7,670
Totals			$ 61,360	$ 69,030

While this procedure is considerably more complex than the former procedure of simply recording the amount of the lease payment as an expense, the underlying reason for the change is compelling. The financial obligations created under lease contracts are very similar to those incurred through borrowing. The prescribed accounting treatment thus makes these two forms of financing the acquisition of fixed assets completely comparable in terms of costs, legal obligation, residual asset values, and "indebtedness." The net effect of this change is to make the analysis of financial statements easier and the results of the analysis more reliable than before.

FINANCIAL INSTITUTIONS INVOLVED IN LEASING

Accompanying the growth in leasing has been the emergence of a new class of professional lessors who act as intermediaries between owners of property and prospective users of it. Professional lessors function to provide a financial service by making equipment or facilities available to their customers without requiring them to make a capital investment. Large, well-capitalized lessors, such as commercial banks or insurance companies, may sometimes furnish out of their own resources the total amount required to purchase the items being leased. In some cases professional lessors merely arrange outside financing for their clients or borrow for their own accounts from any one of several types of lending institutions. Then, as both owner and lessor, the professional lessor assigns rental payments under the lease to the lending institution, thus providing for the retirement of the loan used to finance the purchase of the property.

Independent Leasing Companies

The independent leasing company is the most important class of professional lessor in terms of volume of business. There are three basic types of leasing companies: (1) service leasing companies, (2) finance leasing companies, and (3) lease brokers. While technically each may perform a distinct service, their respective functions may overlap considerably, depending on the customer and the nature of that customer's needs.

Service Leasing Companies. Service leasing companies generally specialize in leasing automobile equipment; office equipment; and, to some extent, industrial equipment. Their fundamental function is to relieve their clients of the burdens and responsibilities of ownership by (1) purchasing new equipment, (2) disposing of worn-out or obsolete equipment, (3) maintaining and repairing leased equipment, (4) providing insurance coverage on equipment being leased, and (5) paying applicable taxes and license fees. Those services may be provided as a package or contracted for separately, depending on the arrangement between the leasing company and its client.

The service leasing company acquires most of its operating capital from financial institutions. It does so by assigning lease revenues as security for its debt. In some cases it may obtain funds by discounting leases; that is, it may sell its right to future rental collections to a lending institution such as a bank. The service leasing company does not usually borrow from or discount leases at the customer's own bank, thus avoiding any impairment of the customer's established line of credit. The leases negotiated by a service leasing company are generally cancelable and, in most cases, are short-term leases.

Finance Leasing Companies. The finance leasing company, in arranging leases for its customers, accommodates firms requiring financial assistance beyond what is afforded by the firm's established lines of credit. A finance leasing company will buy and take title to a piece of equipment or a facility, arrange for delivery of the asset to the customer, and then lease it to the customer. The normal responsibilities of ownership, however, are generally borne by the lessee. Items leased by finance leasing companies include real estate, large automotive fleets, and longer-lived pieces of capital equipment, such as machinery, rail cars, and ships.

The smaller finance leasing companies, whose financial resources tend to be minimal, normally arrange separate underlying financing for each lease transaction. The large, well-capitalized finance leasing companies are able to obtain sufficient funds at relatively low cost from banks and other financial institutions. Thus, the interest they pay (and must recoup in lease rentals) is accordingly lower than that paid by smaller (and less well-capitalized) leasing companies.

Lease Brokers. The lease broker brings together a client wishing to lease a particular type of capital equipment, a manufacturer wanting to sell it for cash, and a financial institution (such as a bank) willing to finance the transaction. The lease broker may at times be called upon to assume the nominal role of a lessor in order to accommodate a bank or a client. In that event, the broker will borrow the money needed to buy the asset to be leased. The lender in such situations generally relies on the equipment as collateral for the loan and looks to the creditworthiness of the lessee for the ultimate repayment of the loan. Under such an arrangement, lease payments usually are made directly to the bank. The broker is compensated by being credited with an excess of rentals over the amounts needed to pay off the loan and meet interest charges.

Commercial Banks

In addition to extending credit to the independent leasing companies, banks are involved in leasing in a variety of ways. A few banks—for the most part the larger ones—engage in direct leasing. Banks engaged in direct leasing are likely to be the "full service" banks that view leasing as primarily a financing mechanism. These institutions offer leasing to their customers as an alternative to borrowing. However, because of restrictions in their charters or because they are sometimes reluctant to create and staff direct leasing departments, most banks are content to rely on financing methods that avoid ownership of leased property.

Commercial banks may participate indirectly in leasing by lending to leasing companies. Conventional lending arrangements, such as term loans, equipment trust notes, and revolving credit lines, are usually employed. Although the leased equipment or facilities generally serve as collateral for the loan, the assignment of the lease payments to the bank is actually the major security for the loan extension.

In some instances, banks and large finance leasing companies execute joint agreements under which the bank negotiates a lease with a client and participates with the leasing company in both the total income and the residual value realized from the sale of the asset after the lease expires. The bank, through a loan to the leasing company, furnishes an agreed-on percentage of the purchase price of the facilities being leased. In addition to putting up the rest of the purchase price, the leasing company supplies administrative services and assumes the burdens, expenses, and responsibilities of property ownership. The leasing company, of course, receives the larger portion of the total returns from the investment while the bank exercises complete control over the lease negotiations.

Insurance Companies

Insurance companies, in playing their traditional role as suppliers of intermediate-term and long-term financing, have for many years played an important role in direct and indirect leasing. Within the bounds of the restrictions many states have placed on the lending activities of insurance companies, the companies engage in leasing in much the same manner as large commercial banks. Their investments in property acquired for direct leasing or the underlying loan to finance leases written by leasing companies are commonly repaid in full by the lease payments. While the kinds of leasing undertaken by insurance companies vary according to the size and the investment policy of the company, insurance companies are most often involved in long-term leasing of high-cost facilities, such as office buildings.

Others

Other lessors with which a corporate lessee may negotiate are educational and religious institutions, foundations, pension funds, and industrial development agencies. While those institutions may be able to offer some special advantage to a corporation in certain cases, the volume of leases they handle comprises only a small part of the total leases written and financed.

THE LEASING DECISION

If an organization wishes to acquire the use of certain properties, it may have no choice but to lease, but in some cases assets required by the operations of nonprofit organizations are available either by purchase or by lease from a number of different sources. Thus, an organization contemplating the acquisition of an asset must decide first, which leasing firm offers the most favorable terms, and second, whether it should lease the asset or borrow the funds and buy it. Note that the alternatives are stated as *lease versus borrow and buy*. As indicated earlier in this chapter, what is being compared are two methods of financing. Whether an organization leases or borrows and buys an asset, it still acquires the services of the asset by creating a fixed repayment obligation that must be serviced over some future period.

Step One: Lease Versus Lease

Not all lease agreements are identical, even for identical pieces of equipment. For example, a manufacturer of office equipment may offer its customers the option of either purchasing or leasing its products. It offers the lease option partly to move additional units, thereby spreading its fixed production costs over a larger volume of output and realizing a higher profit per unit sold and leased as a consequence. The manufacturer, therefore, can—and often does—offer favorable lease terms to its customers in order to gain the extra benefit of higher profits from its manufacturing division. A service lease company may not be able to match the manufacturer's lease terms, since its profits accrue only from rental agreements and the sale of used equipment and not from the original sale of the new equipment.

This example should not be interpreted as a general statement to the effect that the manufacturer's terms are always superior to those of other lessors. That is certainly not the case. In fact, some manufacturers offer to lease their equipment only because their competitors do. But sometimes these manufacturers will price their lease arrangements high enough to encourage their customers to buy rather than lease the equipment. In following this practice, the manufacturers are hoping to avoid the costs of financing the leased equipment and to improve their cash flows from operations while at the same time giving the appearance of meeting the competition.

The nonprofit organization considering a lease option is therefore well advised to shop around, not only for the best available building or equipment, but also for the best available lease terms. The basic features of the lease arrangement were discussed earlier, and these are relevant to making choices among alternative lease contracts. But the financial analysis of the lease-versus-lease decision must obviously deal with the cost of the leases, and the calculation of the costs depends on cash flows.

In most cases, the determination of which one of two alternative lease arrangements is the less expensive is a matter of simply comparing the sizes of the two periodic payments and selecting the lower of the two. For example, if an organization must choose between two maintenance leases for a personal computer, one of which costs $200 per month and the other $210 per month over the same two-year period, the organization should select the lower of the two, other things being equal, of course.

When the terms or the timing of the cash payments differ between or among alternative lease plans, the analysis becomes slightly more complex. The decision rule under these circumstances is to select the lease arrangement with the lowest present value of cash outflows, using the organization's rate of return on its unrestricted investment fund as the discount rate. An example will illustrate the methodology.

Catholic Charities of Savannah, Incorporated, is considering leasing one of two equally suitable properties for its headquarters. The first alternative—2,400 square feet of office space in a building owned and partially occupied by a bank—is being offered under a maintenance lease contract at a cost of $3,000 per month. The lessee is required to sign a three-year lease and pay the cost of partitioning the space into individual offices, supply rooms, work areas, and so forth. The office layout required by Catholic Charities is expected to cost $6,500. Janitorial services, maintenance, and all utilities are provided by the lessor, and those costs are included in the lease payment.

The second alternative is a converted residence of approximately equal size and available under a three-year nonmaintenance lease contract for $1,800 per month. Under the contract, the lessor will pay for insurance and property taxes, but the lessee must maintain the property in good repair and pay all the usual costs, such as utilities, janitorial services, and yard care. In addition, a refundable damage deposit of $3,600 is required.

Exhibit 17-5 contains the cash outlays required under the two alternatives. Note that the second alternative requires the lessee to pay a deposit for its utilities, and both contracts call for advance payments of all lease payments.

To determine which lease contract is the less expensive, the cash flows of each are discounted at 12 percent, the relevant interest rate used by Catholic Charities. Since the leases call for monthly outlays, the

Exhibit 17-5: **Lessee Cash Outlays Under Two Lease Alternatives**

Year		Office building	Converted residence
0	Damage deposit	—	$ 3,600
0	Utilities deposits	—	500
0	Leasehold improvements	$ 6,500	—
0	Initial lease payments	3,000	1,800
1-3	Rental payments	3,000/month	1,800/month
1-3	Operating and maintenance costs	—	1,500/month
3	Recovery of deposit	—	(3,600)

discounting process will use a 1 percent monthly rate over 36 monthly periods. Exhibit 17-6 presents the calculations.

Exhibit 17-6: **Present Value Calculations for Two Lease Alternatives**

Period	Cash outlays		Present value factors @ 12%/12 months	Present values	
	Office building	Converted residence		Office building	Converted residence
0	$ 9,500	$ 5,900	1.000	$ 9,500	$ 5,900
1-35	3,000	3,300	29.409	88,227	97,050
36	0	(3,600)	.699	0	(2,516)
Totals				$ 97,727	$ 100,434

The present value of the net cash outlays required to lease the office building space is ($100,434 – $97,727 =) $2,707 less than that required under the alternative lease contract. Catholic Charities should therefore choose the office building lease, even though the initial cash outlay is higher by ($9,500 – $5,900 =) $3,600 under that alternative.

Step Two: Lease Versus Borrow and Buy

Once the lowest-cost lease has been selected, the question remains as to whether the organization would be better off financially to lease the property or to borrow funds and buy it. The leasing decision thus becomes one of weighing the relative advantages and disadvantages of leasing as compared with debt financing, especially in terms of effects on the lessee's cash flow. Many advantages are claimed for lease financing; some of the claims are valid and some are not. An examination of some of the asserted advantages of leasing will aid in determining to what extent they are in fact supportable.

Shifting Risk of Ownership. If an organization holds title to an asset, it must bear the risk that the asset may become obsolete. Thus, nonprofit organizations such as publishing houses and research institutes that require specialized equipment in their operations (high-priced data processors and technical or scientific equipment, for example) tend to regard a lease as protection against heavy losses that could result from a rapid obsolescence of the equipment. The risk of obsolescence, although difficult to predict ahead of time, may be so great that some organizations regard any additional costs that may accompany the leasing alternative as a necessary form of insurance. Not only may improved designs make present equipment relatively inefficient and expensive to operate, but the present equipment may well become inadequate to meet future operating requirements. Thus management sometimes concludes that it cannot risk the heavy potential loss that the purchase of equipment with a high rate of obsolescence might entail.

Arguments for shifting the risk of ownership to the lessor assume that lessors, as specialists in their fields, are in a better position than are prospective lessees to estimate expected obsolescence accurately. Consequently, the more knowledgeable leasing firm management will include an appropriate factor for obsolescence in its calculations of rental charges. It will not necessarily be an explicit charge; it may, instead, be reflected in appreciably higher payments during the earlier part of the lease or in a shorter lease term so that the lessor recovers his investment as rapidly as possible.

The lessee may benefit from shifting the risk in ownership of an asset through a lease arrangement if the rate of technological change of that asset increases and the equipment becomes obsolete more rapidly than the lessor has anticipated. The lessee may also benefit from the fact that the lessor firm may be able to spread the risk of obsolescence over many lease contracts involving many different types of assets. This situation prevails in the data processing industry, where a particular generation of computers that may be inadequate to serve the needs of one customer are just right for a user with less sophisticated requirements. The risk of sudden obsolescence, which may be too great for an individual lessee to assume, may be safely borne by the lessor through such diversification. The net effect of the spreading of risk is that the charge for obsolescence built into the lease agreement is likely to be small compared with the loss potential inherent in individual, nondiversified ownership.

Avoiding Debt's Restrictive Covenants. As discussed in chapter 15, many bond indentures and term loan agreements contain covenants restricting the actions of the borrower in terms of both operational and financial requirements. To be sure, similar limitations may be found in lease agreements, although, in many cases, they are neither as common nor as restrictive as those contained in bond indentures. For example, the size of the lease payments may be determined in part by the number of hours per day that a piece of leased equipment will be operated, or changes or adjustments in the equipment without the consent of the lessor may be prohibited by the contract. Consequently, organizations that elect to lease to avoid the restrictions that lenders generally impose on borrowing customers may or may not be better off when they acquire the use of the asset under the terms of a lease.

Cost Savings. One of the critical questions facing an organization as it attempts to decide whether to lease or to borrow and buy is whether the total cost of leasing will be greater or less than that of borrowing. As a general rule, the implicit interest rate under leasing is likely to be higher than the rate related to debt financing. Moreover, whereas a term loan or bond issue may be refunded at almost any time prior to maturity in order to lower interest costs or reduce the burden of debt service, leases cannot always be "refunded" (renegotiated). Thus, if interest rates decline, an organization may find itself paying a far higher cost of financing by leasing than it would have paid if it had borrowed and may have no way of lowering this cost until the lease expires.

Whether lease financing or borrowing and buying is favored from a cost standpoint will depend on both the total amounts and the patterns of cash flows associated with each financing alternative. An example will help illustrate the proper method to use when comparing leasing versus borrowing and buying a fixed asset.

The Middletown Ambulance Service (MAS) is a nonprofit organization servicing the City of Middletown and its two general hospitals. Recently, the city council of Fairview, a neighboring city approximately five miles distant, requested MAS to consider serving that community and its general hospital as well. Among the several problems that MAS will face as a result of the expansion of its service area is the need to replace its two-way radio equipment with a system having a greater range. The manufacturer of the communication system used by MAS has offered to take the radios MAS is now using in trade for the new equipment and either to finance the balance through a lease arrangement or to sell the new system outright, without any difference in the maintenance agreement or cost.

If purchased, the two-way radio equipment will cost MAS $25,000 installed, after the trade-in allowance. The ambulance service's bank has offered to finance the purchase with a five-year, 14-percent term loan repayable in equal annual installments of $7,282. The first payment is due one year from the date of the loan. The market value of the equipment after five years is expected to be about $4,000, although the manufacturer cannot guarantee that MAS will be able to recover that amount.

The manufacturer of the radio equipment is willing to lease the equipment to MAS for five years at an annual rental of $6,250 per year, payable in advance. MAS will have to pay a $1,000 installation fee at the time the equipment is delivered and installed and title to the equipment will remain with the manufacturer at the end of the lease term.

The cash flows associated with the two financing methods differ in both timing and magnitude; thus, any comparison of the cash flows must be made on a present value basis to ensure intertemporal cost comparability. Occasionally, the timing of lease-and-loan payments will not coincide. When one set of payments is, say, quarterly and the other is annual, the present values of both shoud be determined using the more frequent compounding period. Exhibit 17-7 presents a comparison of MAS's financing alternatives in which the *net advantage* (that is, the cost savings) to borrowing and buying over leasing is calculated at $1,773, in present value terms.

Exhibit 17-7: **Comparison of Leasing Versus Borrowing and Buying a Fixed Asset**

(1)	(2)	(3)	(4)	(5)	(6)
	Cash outflows		Net advantage to borrowing	Present value factors	Present value advantage to borrowing
Year	Leasing	Term loan	(2) - (3)	@ 9 percent	(4) × (5)
0	$ 7,250*	0	$ 7,250	1.0000	$ 7,250
1	6,250	$ 7,282	(1,032)	.9174	(947)
2	6,250	7,282	(1,032)	.8417	(869)
3	6,250	7,282	(1,032)	.7722	(797)
4	6,250	7,282	(1,032)	.7084	(731)
5	0	3,282**	(3,282)	.6499	(2,133)
Total	$ 32,250	$ 32,410	$ (160)		$ 1,773

---

* Lease payment of $6,250 payable in advance, plus installation cost of $1,000.
** Loan payment of $7,282, less expected salvage value of $4,000.

Columns (2) and (3) in Exhibit 17-7 contain the amounts of cash payments required of MAS under the two financing alternatives. The net advantage to borrowing and buying the radios is found by subtracting the figures in column (3) from those in column (2). Negative figures in column (4) indicate the *disadvantage* to borrowing in those years.

Note that the leasing alternative *appears* to be superior when the two sets of *nominal* dollar cash flows are compared, as in column (4) of Exhibit 17-7. However, when these cash flows are discounted at the rate at which MAS can invest its surplus cash—9 percent—the advantage of borrowing and buying over leasing becomes clear.

The MAS should elect to borrow and buy the radio equipment, in spite of the fact that leasing will save the organization a total of $160 over the five-year period, because the lease arrangement requires the organization to pay out its cash *sooner* than does the term loan agreement. In this example, MAS has the opportunity to invest the initial cash payment of $7,250 required by the lease at 9 percent interest for one year before it must use the cash to make its first loan payment to the bank. This amount will grow to ($7,250 × 1.09 =) $7,902.50 by the end of year 1, thus leaving ($7,902.50 - $1,032 =) $6,870.50 after paying the $1,032 difference between the lease and the loan payments.

By the end of the five-year period, $1,773 of the initial lease payment plus accumulated interest (at 9 percent) will remain unspent and, theoretically at least, be available for other uses within the organization.

Hence, the algebraic sum of the figures in column (6) of Exhibit 17-7 indicates which of the two financing alternatives should be selected. A positive figure, as in this illustration, indicates that ownership is the preferred alternative; a negative present value indicates that leasing is the more advantageous method of financing.

A final consideration involves the treatment of the residual, or salvage, value of the equipment after the five-year period. The analysis presented in Exhibit 17-7 implies that the $4,000 in salvage value is certain to be received in cash in year 5, but the manufacturer could not guarantee that figure. Obviously, the residual economic value of any asset used by an organization for a period is subject to uncertainty, whether it is actually sold at the end of that period or continues in use. On one hand, if the analysis of lease versus borrow and buy ignores the amount that might be received as a salvage value, the results could be biased in favor of leasing. And on the other hand, if the salvage value is overestimated, the results will be biased in favor of debt financing.

Fortunately, in most cases the present value of any residual economic value left at the end of an asset's useful life is so small that it will not influence the decision either way. In those cases in which the salvage value is important, such as the MAS illustration, management should test various *likely* values in the decision process in order to fully assess the implications of the uncertainty relative to the salvage value.

Exhibit 17-8 lists the present values of the net advantage to borrowing in the MAS example for several alternative estimates of the equipment's salvage value. The point of indifference between the alternative financing methods is very close to the point at which the salvage value of the equipment is equal to $1,000. The exact salvage value figure is $1,272, and is calculated as follows: $7,282 - [($1,773 + $2,133)/.6499] = $1,272. The present value of the net advantage for the five-year period is added to the present value of the advantage for year 5. That sum is divided by the present value factor .6499 in order to determine the amount of the cash outflow required under the term loan alternative to make the net advantage equal zero.

While the estimate is imprecise, it nevertheless enables management to subjectively assess the likelihood of the equipment selling for less than

---

Exhibit 17-8: Present Values of Net Advantage to Borrowing Corresponding With Various Estimates of Salvage Value

Estimated salvage value	Present value of net advantage (disadvantage) to borrowing
0	$ (827)
$ 1,000	(177)
2,000	473
3,000	1,123
4,000	1,773
5,000	2,423

a given amount—in this case $1,000. While an equipment manufacturer might be unwilling to guarantee a $4,000 figure for these purposes, he might be willing to "bet his shirt" that the market value of the radio equipment will be above $1,000 five years hence. In such a situation, the analysis clearly favors the borrow-and-buy alternative.

Conserving Cash. Promotional literature distributed by leasing companies still commonly maintains that leasing frees up capital that would otherwise be invested in fixed assets. This is not a completely valid line of reasoning because it treats the investment decision and the financing decision as one. But they are clearly two separate issues. For an organization to begin and continue its operations, it requires the services of a certain mix of assets. Whether it has title to them all is a different matter.

Once the proper mix of assets is determined, questions of how the assets are to be financed remain to be answered. Two possible methods of financing are leasing and borrowing, and the ultimate question is whether lease financing or debt financing is the more expensive method. As in the case of the Middletown Ambulance Service, the cost of leasing can be greater than that of borrowing, though this may not be true in all cases. But the point is that the organization's cash balance will not be affected by the choice of financing methods.

Providing an Additional Source of Financing. Leasing is sometimes viewed as an *additional* source of external financing for an organization in the sense that it enlarges the total pool of capital that it may draw on to finance its long-term needs. In many cases, more capital can be obtained through a combination of leasing and borrowing than is available to it through borrowing alone. One reason for this circumstance is that funds suppliers generally apply less rigid standards to lease arrangements than to loan agreements, thus making lease financing the easier to obtain when similar principal amounts are involved. The typical leasing company management, for example, is less conservative than the management of a typical commercial bank; it is thus willing to accept greater credit risks. Furthermore, because the leasing companies have close contacts with resale and lease-renewal markets, they often are able to recoup at least part of any losses caused by the default of a lessee by either selling the used equipment or working out a re-lease arrangement with another lessee.

Unless advance rental payments are required, leasing offers 100 percent financing with no down payment. While this may not be so important to an organization with adequate cash reserves or untapped borrowing capacity, it can be vital to an expanding organization whose growth is checked by its limited capacity to obtain external long-term financing. As an example, leasing can be of great advantage to an organization that is just getting started. And even well-established organizations may resort to leasing when they have no superior means of financing the acquisition of needed equipment or facilities.

Such organizations may find, from time to time, that when their sources of short-term funds are being fully utilized or when an existing loan agreement restricts further direct borrowing, the lease-financing route is still open. Also, even in situations where conventional financing is available, leasing may be advantageously employed to (1) gain the use of relatively low-valued facilities, while conserving established lines of credit or senior debt capacity for major capital facilities, and (2) avoid the very expensive practice of borrowing relatively small amounts of money under long-term debt arrangements.

The ability of leasing to provide additional sources of financing in the past has rested on the fact that creditors did not recognize the obligatory nature of the lease. However, with the issuance of FASB Statement 13, lenders are more fully informed of the existence of leases in the capital structures of loan applicants, and most have become more fully aware of the implications of a lease obligation on the financial condition of an organizaiton with whom they deal. Since lenders have begun to place restrictions on subsequent leasing in term loan agreements, leasing will probably become somewhat less important as a means of expanding the total pool of funds available to nonprofit organizations. But it will nevertheless remain a very popular financing method, especially for the smaller, less creditworthy organization.

SUMMARY

Nonprofit organizations have come to view leasing as a financially acceptable alternative to financing the purchase of land, buildings, and equipment through other means. Too frequently, however, these organizations choose to lease an asset without examining the costs or other financial and legal implications of the lease arrangement. This chapter has detailed the various forms of lease contracts and the proper approach that the organization's financial manager should use to evaluate the choice between leasing and borrowing to finance an asset's purchase.

Leases can be classified as operating leases or financial leases, based on the rights given to the lessee to cancel the contract; an operating lease can be voided by the lessee, but the capital lease cannot. The use of property may be acquired through direct leasing or under a sale and lease-back arrangement. And the responsibility for maintaining the leased property during the term of the lease is defined in the contract as belonging either to the lessee or lessor.

Prior to 1976, leasing was known as "off balance sheet financing" because neither the contractual obligation nor the leased asset appeared on the lessee's balance sheet. Subsequent to the issuance of FASB

Statement No. 13, however, lessees were required to capitalize lease payments and to include both the capitalized value of the asset and the liability created by the lease contract in their audited financial statements. The effect was to make explicit the debt-like character of lease arrangements and to present a more realistic set of financial statements to those interested in the affairs of a leasing organization.

Many financial institutions are involved either directly or indirectly in leasing property. Consequently, many forms of lease contracts are available, none of which can be termed standard from the point of view of specific terms and overall costs. This fact makes the leasing decision complex, since an organization must first locate the source of lease financing that offers the best terms and then compare those terms with the alternative of borrowing an amount sufficient to purchase the asset. The lease versus borrow-to-purchase decision involves comparing the cash flows of the two alternatives on a present value basis. Qualitative factors, such as restrictive covenants in the two financing methods, also enter into the decision.

FURTHER READING

Most of the current literature dealing with the lease decision is not directly applicable to tax-exempt organizations. This is because lease analysis in the for-profit context includes discussion of tax shields provided by depreciation, interest expense, and lease payments. Consequently, the reader should take care to separate the relevant material from that which is not, insofar as the nonprofit lessee is concerned. The following references provide further insights into leasing:

Gant, Donald R. "A Critical Look at Lease Financing." *Controller* (June 1961).

Miniccuci, Rick. "Rather Try Than Buy? You Can Do It With Leasing." *Administrative Management* (June 1974): 26-27.

Sorrenson, Ivar W., and Ramon E. Johnson. "Equipment Financial Leasing Practices and Costs: An Empirical Study." *Financial Management* (Spring 1977): 33-40.

Vanderwicken, Peter. "The Powerful Logic of the Leasing Boom." *Fortune* (November 1973): 136.

QUESTIONS

1. Explain why leasing must be viewed as a financing device rather than as an alternative to asset ownership.

2. Define the following terms:
   a. operating lease
   b. financial lease
   c. sale and lease-back
   d. direct leasing
   e. leveraged lease

3. Describe the difference among maintenance, nonmaintenance, and net leases.

4. What factors determine the cost of leasing?

5. List the four criteria used to determine whether or not a lease must be capitalized on the audited financial statements of the lessee.

6. How are leases capitalized?

7. What are the four balance sheet accounts that pertain to lease contracts?

8. How are capital leases amortized? How are their offsetting liabilities reduced?

9. List the principal financial institutions involved in leasing.

10. Do all leasing firms perform the same functions for their lessee clients?

11. Name the two parts of the leasing decision.

12. The following list contains some of the advantages claimed for lease financing. Which are valid and which are not? Explain.
   a. shifts the risks of ownership
   b. avoids restrictions generally imposed on borrowers
   c. is less costly
   d. conserves cash
   e. provides an additional source of financing

PROBLEMS

1. Claxton Fine Arts Institute is considering leasing a $35,000 minicomputer from the manufacturer to assist in handling its accounting, payroll, budgeting, and accounts payable. The lease period is five years, and the basic rental amount is $8,255 per year payable in advance, exclusive of the standard maintenance agreement. The institute's management has determined that it could borrow the amount needed to purchase the computer on five-year terms at 12 percent.
   a. What is the implicit cost of the lease? (Hint: start your search at the institute's borrowing rate.)
   b. Calculate the capitalized value of the lease.
   c. Calculate the amounts that the accountant should enter on the

balance sheet as the current and noncurrent obligations under the capital lease.

d. Calculate the balance-sheet value of the capital lease two years hence, net of amortization.

e. Calculate the long-term liability portion of the lease obligation that would appear on the balance sheet three years hence, using the interest method of reducing the lease obligation.

2. The Smithston Volunteer Fire Department is considering alternative lease proposals for acquiring a rescue vehicle.

The first alternative will provide the vehicle fully equipped for annual lease payments of $7,750 for six years. The second alternative requires the fire department to purchase certain pieces of rescue equipment at a cost of $12,000 and requires lease payments of $4,885, also over six years. Both alternatives require payments in advance and provide the fire department with the option to purchase the leased property at the end of six years for $1.00. The relevant interest rate is 10 percent. Which alternative should the fire department choose?

3. The Carlton Youth Offender Rehabilitation Center is a nonprofit organization formed to assist individuals referred to them by the juvenile courts in the state. The center is a voluntary residence center in which the youths are taught a trade, such as woodworking or metalworking, auto repair, and electronic service. After they have been trained, each is placed with a cooperating employer in or near his or her hometown.

The center needs to replace the equipment in its aging and obsolete electronics shop. Its inquiries have turned up three financing alternatives. The first is a 16 percent, $20,000 term loan that provides the full amount needed to purchase the equipment. The loan is payable over five years with quarterly payments of $1,471.67 including principal and interest. The first payment is due in three months.

The second alternative is a lease arrangement from the manufacturer. The lease contract calls for quarterly payments of $1,200 per quarter over five years and requires the center to purchase the equipment at the end of the lease period for $1,500. All lease payments are due in advance.

The third alternative was offered by a service leasing company specializing in electronic equipment. Its terms are $4,400 per year, payable annually over five years. The equipment will be returned to the lessor after five years. Both lease plans call for payments in advance.

The salvage value of the equipment after five years is expected to be about $3,500. While it may be higher than that figure, it is not expected to be much lower.

a. Given a relevant interest rate of 16 percent for the center, which of the leases should be preferred?

b. Using the same discount rate and the better of the two leases, compare the lease and the borrow-and-buy alternatives.

18

Integrating Investment and Financing Decisions

This chapter continues the analysis begun in chapter 14. The model presented there focused on a test of financial viability for incremental capital investments and new programs. This chapter extends that model to encompass the analysis of asset acquisition, financed either completely or in part with debt capital.

The key to maintaining long-run liquidity and solvency in a nonprofit organization is the integration of capital-asset acquisition decisions and permanent-financing decisions. Management's decisions in these two important areas determine the nature, amounts, and timing of an organization's basic, long-term cash flows. As a consequence, the long-run financial health of an organization depends on how well those decisions turn out. For example, when an organization purchases a capital asset (or implements a long-lived, noncapital program), it must also be prepared to pay all of the daily operating and maintenance costs associated with that asset or program over its entire useful life. If expected cash inflows from operations (that is, from the sale of goods and services produced by the capital investment) are inadequate to cover those costs, permanent sources of financing must be planned for, obtained, and properly managed to ensure that the organization itself, as well as each of its ongoing programs, remains financially viable and continues to achieve its established professional goals. Thus, each new long-lived asset, program, and project should be acquired or implemented only after all acquisition, operating, and financing cash flows have been analyzed in an integrated framework.

In operational terms, when a project is tested for financial viability, using the cash-flow model presented in Chapter 14, and it is found to be

461

financially nonviable, the analysis should be expanded to include locating a cash-flow break-even point, given any one or a combination of the following four sources of financing: (1) surplus cash on hand; (2) incremental operating "profits"; (3) donated funds; and (4) intermediate-term or long-term debt. An expanded version of the cash-flow model is designed to support this process.

Two illustrations are used to present this expanded model. The first illustration involves the use of the organization's operating profits as a primary source of funds to be used for debt-service charges. The second illustration is an extension of the first, in which the model's flexibility in financial planning is demonstrated. The final section of this chapter describes the proper approach to integrating total cash flows under capital-lease financing.

"PROFITS" USED FOR DEBT SERVICE

For present purposes, "profits" are defined as the surplus of cash receipts over expenditures realized from the organization's total operations. If an organization's overall operations are capable of consistently generating an annual excess of cash-operating revenues over total cash expenditures and can maintain that position over time, a part or all of that excess cash flow (or profit) can be employed to repay the interest and the principal funds borrowed to implement a new project or program. The question to be answered in such situations is, "What is the maximum amount of debt that the organization can repay out of a forecasted stream of profits?" If the answer shows that this maximum debt amount is greater than the *net project cost* of the proposed capital investment, the project is financially viable. (Net project cost was defined in chapter 14 as the sum of the present values of the yearly inflated cash flows of a particular project.) But if the net project cost is greater than the maximum debt size that can be repaid using only the organization's expected profits, the project is nonviable.

For example, suppose the Norwich Academy is considering borrowing money to install a central air-conditioning unit in its classroom building. At present, the academy's operations are producing an annual cash surplus, and the surplus is expected to continue for several years into the future. In financial terms, the purchase of the air conditioning unit will mean that the academy will have to use its annual cash surplus to (1) repay the borrowed funds, and (2) pay the higher utility bills that will result from operating the air conditioner during the hot months of the school year. If the academy's operating cash surplus over time is large enough to cover both of those cash outflows, the project is financially viable. If, however, the annual surpluses are smaller than the debt-service charges plus the additional utility bills, the project is nonviable as it is proposed.

Extending the Model

The basic model presented in chapter 14 is easily extended to encompass the debt-financing decision. Under the assumption that the nonprofit organization will repay debt principal and interest in equal annual payments, in the amount of A dollars, beginning at the end of the first year of project implementation (i.e., year 1), the amount to be borrowed is equal to the present value of the stream of payments from the first year to the debt's final maturity—from year 1 to year 5. Algebraically, annual debt service, A, is defined as follows:

$$A = D\left[\frac{d}{1 - (1 + d)^{-s}}\right] \qquad (1)$$

where D is the principal amount of the debt, d is the rate of interest charged by the lender, and s is the number of years to final maturity. The term in the brackets is the compound interest formula for calculating the amount required to be paid at the end of each period to repay one dollar of initial debt principal (plus interest charged at d percent). The value can be calculated, with the help of a hand-held calculator, or obtained from a compound interest table.

For example, a loan of $50,000, carrying an interest rate of 9 percent, can be paid off in five years at an annual debt-service charge of

$$A = \$50,000[.09/(1 - .6499)]$$

$$A = \$50,000 \times 0.2571$$

$$A = \$12,854.62$$

The present value of A, discounted at the rate of return the organization is earning from investing its surplus cash, is:

$$PVA = D\left[\frac{d}{1 - (1 + d)^{-s}}\right]\left[\frac{1 - (1 + r)^{-s}}{r}\right] \qquad (2)$$

The term in the second set of brackets in this equation is the compound interest formula for determining the present value of one dollar per period received at the end of each period. The symbol r stands for the rate of return the organization expects to earn from its unrestricted investment fund. (The justification for using this definition of r is presented in chapter 3.) If the debt-service charge of \$12,854.62, calculated in the example just given, is discounted at an interest rate of 8 percent, the present value of debt service is

$$PVA = \$50,000 \times 0.2571 \times \frac{1 - (1 + .08)^{-5}}{.08}$$

$$PVA = \$12,854.62 \times \left[1 - \frac{1}{(1 + .08)^5} \right] / .08$$

$$PVA = \$12,854.62 \times (1 - .6806)/.08$$

$$PVA = \$12,854.62 \times 3.9925$$

$$PVA = \$51,322.07$$

As defined in equation (2), PVA is the present value of total cash *outflows* required to repay principal plus interest of a bond issue or term loan, when repayment is accomplished in equal annual payments. This amount must be equal to or less than the present value of cash *inflows* or *profits* available for debt-service purposes. Thus all that remains to complete the integrated model is to define algebraically the present value of cash inflows, then compare the two figures.

The cash inflows are made up of profits, defined earlier as the excess of cash revenues over cash expenditures from the organization's operations that are available to support a nonrevenue-producing project. The relevant period over which the profits are counted is the number of years to the final maturity of the debt. This period, rather than the project's life, is used because sufficient cash must be available prior to the final maturity to fully service the outstanding debt. Profits generated by the organization beyond the debt-maturity date may be treated as true surplus cash and disposed of in any way management feels is appropriate.

Algebraically, the present value of profits earmarked for debt service, PVR, is defined as:

$$PVR = \sum_{t=1}^{s} R_t (1 + i_R)^t (1 + r)^{-t} \tag{3}$$

where R_t is the annual profit expected in year t, the term $(1+i_R)^{-t}$ is the compound interest factor describing the growth of profits at an annual rate i_R, and the term $(1+r)^{-t}$ is the present value factor used to discount the profits at the interest rate r. The term i_R may be positive, negative, or zero.

For example, suppose an organization expects to have a surplus of revenues over expenditures of $10,000 per year for the next five years. The annual profit is expected to grow after year 1 by 2 percent per year, and the relevant discount rate is 9 percent. The present value of this stream of profits is calculated in Exhibit 18-1. The CIFs at 2 percent and the PVFs at 9 percent in columns (3) and (4), respectively, are found in the compound interest tables. The total of the inflated present values in column (5) is the present value of the profits, PVR. The value of PVR thus calculated is compared with the value of PVA as calculated using equation (2). If PVA is less than or equal to PVR, the project is financially viable. If PVA is greater than PVR, the project is nonviable as it is planned.

Exhibit 18-1: **Calculation of the Present Value of Profits Earmarked for Debt Service**

(1)	(2)	(3)	(4)	(5) Present value of profits
Year	Profits	CIF @ 2%	PVF @ 9%	(2) × (3) × (4)
1	$ 10,000	1.0000	.9174	$ 9,174
2	10,000	1.0200	.8417	8,585
3	10,000	1.0404	.7722	8,034
4	10,000	1.0612	.7084	7,518
5	10,000	1.0824	.6499	7,035
				PVR = $ 40,346

Illustration

To illustrate how the extension to the basic model is applied to situations in which profits are used for debt service, consider the Norwich Academy's plan to install central air conditioning in its classrooms. The project could not be financed with an increase in tuition or other revenues for competitive reasons. But since the academy has been realizing excesses of revenues over operating expenditures for several years and expects those profits to continue and to grow at a compound rate of 3 percent per year, its trustees decided to apply those profits to repay indebtedness. Exhibit 18-2 presents the relevant data required to extend the model.

Exhibit 18-2: **Planning Estimates for the Norwich Academy Air-Conditioning Project**

Item	Timing	Values
1. Net project cost	Year 0	$48,380
2. Planning period		5 years
3. Cash on hand allocated to the project	Year 0	$6,000
4. Expected annual profit allocated to the project	Years 1-5	$9,300
5. Growth rate of profits	Years 1-5	3%
6. Rate of return on investment of surplus cash	Years 1-5	9%
7. Interest rate on borrowed funds	Years 1-5	10%
8. Debt maturity		5 years

The net project cost, item number 1 in Exhibit 18-2, was calculated using the basic model presented in chapter 14. The amount to be borrowed, D in equation (1), is calculated by subtracting cash on hand from the net project cost; hence, $D = \$48,380 - \$6,000 = \$42,380$.

The academy's trustees arranged for a five-year term loan from a local bank, the annual payments for which are calculated using equation (1) and a hand-held calculator:

$$A = \$42,380 \left[\frac{.10}{1 - (1 + .10)^{-5}} \right]$$

$$A = \$42,380 \left(.10 / \left[1 - \frac{1}{(1 + .10)^5} \right] \right)$$

$$A = \$42,380 \left(.10 / \left[1 - \frac{1}{1.61051} \right] \right)$$

$$A = \$42,380 \, (.10/[1 - .6209])$$

$$A = \$42,380 \, (.10/.3791)$$

$$A = \$42,380 \times .2638$$

$$A = \$11,180$$

The same result can be attained by using the compound interest tables, as described later in this chapter.

Present Value of Cash Outflows. The test for financial viability of this financing plan involves calculating the values for *PVA*, using equation (2), and *PVR*, using the approach illustrated in Exhibit 18-1, and then comparing those values. To clearly illustrate the algebra involved in solving equation (2) for the value of *PVA*, given the data presented in Exhibit 18-2, the three components of the right side of the equation are lettered, and their values are calculated sequentially, as might be done with the aid of a hand-held calculator.

$$
\underbrace{PVA \;=\; D}_{(a)} \times \underbrace{\left[\frac{d}{1 - (1 + d)^{-s}}\right]}_{(b)} \times \underbrace{\left[\frac{1 - (1 + r)^{-s}}{r}\right]}_{(c)} \tag{2}
$$

(a) The first component of equation (2), D, is the amount of money that must be borrowed to purchase and operate the air-conditioning system. In this case

D = Present value of project cash outflows minus cash on hand
D = \$48,380 – \$6,000
D = \$42,380

(b) The second component of the equation is the compound interest formula for calculating the amount of the annual debt payment of principal and interest. The value of this component may be calculated algebraically, as shown below, or may be calculated as the reciprocal of the present value of an annuity of one dollar per period for five years at 10 percent. The present value factor found in the tables is 3.7908, and its reciprocal is 1/3.7908 = .2638. Algebraically, the same figure is calculated as follows:

$$
\frac{d}{1 - (1 + d)^{-s}} = .10/[1 - (1 + .10)^{-5}]
$$

$$
= .10/\left[1 - \frac{1}{(1 + .10)^5}\right]
$$

$$
= .10/\left[1 - \frac{1}{1.61051}\right]
$$

$$
= .10/(1 - .6209)
$$

$$
= .10/.3791
$$

$$
= .2638
$$

(c) The third component of equation (2) is the compound interest formula for calculating the present value of the debt payments. The value of this component may be found in the table of present values of an annuity of one dollar. That value at 9 percent for five years is 3.8897. Algebraically,

$$\left[\frac{d}{1 - (1 + d)^{-s}}\right] = [1 - (1 + .09)^{-5}]/.09 \qquad (1)$$

$$= \left[1 - \frac{1}{(1 + .09)^5}\right]/.09$$

$$= \left[1 - \frac{1}{1.53862}\right]/.09$$

$$= .35007/.09$$

$$= \underline{\underline{3.8897}}$$

When the values obtained for each of the three components are substituted into equation (2), the value for PVA can be calculated. Thus

$$PVA = \quad (a) \quad \times \quad (b) \quad \times \quad (c)$$

$$= \$42,380 \times .2638 \times 3.8897$$

$$= \underline{\underline{\$43,486}}$$

Present Value of Profits. Equation (3) defines the present value of expected profits in equation form; however, the best approach to calculating this value is by setting up a table similar to that presented in Exhibit 18-1. The calculations for this example are presented in Exhibit 18-3. The tabular form is preferred since it simplifies the calculations whenever profits vary from year-to-year or grow at varying rates over the relevant period. The values appearing in columns (3) and (4) in the table are found in the compound interest tables. Column (3) values are the future value factors of one dollar at the end of each period, with the growth of the profits beginning in year 2 instead of year 1. This is because the profit forecast for year 1 is the base figure on which the 3-percent

---

Exhibit 18-3: **Present Value of Profits Earmarked for Debt Repayment**

---

(1)	(2)	(3)	(4)	(5)
		Compound	Present	Present value
	Profits	interest	value	of profits
t	(R)	factor @ 3%	factor @ 9%	(2) × (3) × (4)
1	$ 9,300	1.0000	.9174	$ 8,532
2	9,300	1.0300	.8417	8,063
3	9,300	1.0609	.7722	7,619
4	9,300	1.0927	.7084	7,199
5	9,300	1.1255	.6499	6,903
				PVR = $ 38,316

---

growth rate is calculated. Column (4) values are the present value factors of one dollar at the end of each period. The sum of the values in column (5), $38,216 is the present value of the profits earmarked for debt repayment by the academy's trustees.

Test for Financial Viability. Since the present value of the air-conditioning project's cash outflows ($43,486) is greater than the present value of the profit allocated to debt service ($38,316), the project is not financially viable as it is currently planned. The difference in the two figures, $5,170, may be thought of as a shortfall of cash inflows, or it may be defined for planning and decision purposes in several different ways. For example, the financial manager of Norwich Academy could take one or more of the following steps to eliminate the disparity between the cash outflows and inflows:

1. Negotiate a lower price for the air-conditioning system (by $5,170).
2. Ask the alumni to contribute $5,170 toward the project.
3. Negotiate a lower interest rate for the loan.
4. Increase the return on investment of surplus funds.
5. Increase the profits allocated to the project.

While the model provides a clear answer to the question of how much the initial cost of the project must be reduced (or how much additional cash must be raised) to make the project viable, the academy does not know the maximum interest rate it can pay, the minimum return on investment it must earn, or the minimum size of the annual profit it must realize to achieve the desired financial result. But the model can produce these answers with only minor modification to the equations. The following section illustrates the model's flexibility in this regard.

Financial Planning

The financial-planning feature of this extension of the basic model enables the financial manager to examine all of the alternatives open to the organization in replanning a proposed project. The concept is very simple. Equation (2) is set equal to equation (3), and the equality is forced by solving for the variable that the planner wishes to examine. This feature is illustrated in the context of the Norwich Academy problem, in which the borrowing rate, the investment rate, and the operating profits are examined in turn.

Borrowing Rate. Recall that equation (2) was divided into three components in order to facilitate the calculation of the value of *PVA*. The second component of the equation is the compound interest formula for calculating the annual debt payment, given a maturity of five years and a 10-percent interest rate. The numerical value of that component will decline as the borrowing rate is lowered. Hence, to determine the maximum borrowing rate that will permit the project to achieve financial viability (that is, the rate that will equate *PVA* and *PVR*), the financial manager will set equation (2) equal to the value of PVR calculated in Exhibit 18-3 and solve for the second component (component *b*) of equation (2). Thus,

$$PVA = (a) \times (b) \times (c) = PVR$$

$$= \$42,380 \times (b) \times 3.8897 = \$38.216$$

$$\$164,845.486 \times (b) = \$38,216$$

$$(b) = \$38,216/\$164,845.486$$
$$(b) = \underline{\underline{.2318}}$$

The maximum borrowing rate necessary to achieve project financial viability can be found by, first, calculating the reciprocal of component (*b*):

$$1/.2318 = 4.3141$$

Next, that value, or the value nearest to it, is located in the five-year row in the table of present values of an annuity of one dollar. The calculated value of 4.3141 falls between the table values in the 5-percent column (4.3295) and the 6-percent column (4.2124) in the five-year row. Thus, the maximum borrowing rate that the academy can afford to pay on funds borrowed for this project is slightly greater than 5 percent per year. In all probability, the academy's financial manager will not be able to negotiate the borrowing rate downward from 10 percent to 5 percent. Therefore, some other adjustment will be required.

Investment Rate. Since the rate of return on the investment of surplus funds is used in calculating both *PVA* and *PVR*, determining the rate that will permit the project to become financially viable is determined through a trial-and-error method. The method involves recalculating *PVA* and *PVR* using a different value for *r* in each trial. The trials continue until that value for *r* is found that equates *PVA* and *PVR*. If in the initial trial *PVA* is greater than the *PVR*, a higher value for *r* must be used in the next trial calculation.

To illustrate, the first trial will be conducted using $r = 15$ percent. The value for *PVR*, using the approach illustrated earlier in Exhibit 18-3, is $32,831.

The value for *PVA* is calculated using the shortened form of equation (2):

$$PVA = (a) \times (b) \times (c)$$

where the first and second components retain the values originally calculated in solving the equation, and the third component takes on the value given by $r = .15$, and $s = 5$. The value for component (c), found in the present value of an annuity table, is 3.3522, and

$$PVA = \$42,380 \times .2638 \times 3.3522$$
$$= \$37,477$$

Since *PVA* is greater than *PVR* at the discount rate of 15 percent, the academy will have to earn a rate of return *greater* than 15 percent to make the project viable.

Exhibit 18-4 presents the calculated values of *PVA* and *PVR* for selected values of *r*. Obviously, since even a 100 percent annual return fails to equate *PVA* and *PVR*, the academy will be hard-pressed to earn a rate of return high enough in each of the next five years to make the project financially viable. Exhibit 18-4 also clearly indicates that the decision regarding the project is relatively insensitive to the rate of return earned on the organization's cash surplus.

Exhibit 18-4: **Calculated Values of *PVA* and *PVR* for Selected Values of *r***

r	*PVA*	*PVR*	*PVA-PVR*
9%	$ 43,486	$ 38,216	$ 5,270
15	37,477	32,831	4,646
20	33,434	29,218	4,216
50	19,415	16,765	2,650
80	13,235	11,347	1,888
100	10,380	9,240	1,140

Profits. Calculating the minimum annual profit required to achieve project financial viability involves setting PVA equal to PVR and solving for profits, R. In this case, the value of PVA is that value originally calculated using the data contained in Exhibit 18-2 (that is, $PVA = $43,486$). That value is set equal to PVR as redefined in equation (4):

$$PVR = R(CIF^*) \qquad\qquad (4)$$

where CIF^* is a compound interest factor equal to the sum of the products of columns (3) and (4) in Exhibit 18-3. The calculation of CIF^* is illustrated in Exhibit 18-5. The figures in columns (2) and (3) are taken from Exhibit 18-3. When they are multiplied and the resultant products are totaled, the value for CIF^* becomes 4.1092. A different CIF^* will result for different values for i_R and r.

Exhibit 18-5: **Calculation of CIF***

(1) t	(2) CIF @ 3%	(3) PVF @ 9%	(4) CIF* (2) × (3)
1	1.0000	.9174	.9174
2	1.0300	.8417	.8670
3	1.0609	.7722	.8192
4	1.0927	.7084	.7741
5	1.1255	.6499	.7315
			CIF* = 4.1092

When the value for CIF^* is substituted into equation (4) and PVR is set equal to the value for PVA, the equality becomes

$$PVA = PVR$$
$$\$43,486 = R(4.1092)$$

And the minimum annual profit needed to achieve project viability is calculated by solving that equation for R:

$$R = \$43,486/4.1092$$
$$R = \$10,583$$

The minimum level of profits is ($\$10,583 - \$9,300 =$) $\$1,283$ greater than that forecasted by the academy. It is a relatively simple matter to translate that dollar amount into a per-student tuition increase, for example, should the trustees wish to increase profits in that way.

The Decision

Once all of the changes in the financial variables have been tested by way of the expanded model, the financial manager will select the plan or the combination of plans that will achieve project financial viability within realistic parameters. For example, the academy may be able to find a lender who is willing to reduce the borrowing rate to 8.5 percent or 9 percent per year, thus enabling the trustees to hold the increase in tuition to a minimum level.

However, if the interest rate cannot be reduced, and the level of tuition has already risen beyond that which the professional managers perceive as the optimum level, the financial manager will have to recommend rejection of the air-conditioning project. If the academy's professional management decides to go ahead with the project regardless of the recommendation, the financial manager is obligated to point out that the additional $1,000 per year needed to finance the project will have to come from the reduction in costs—and services to the students—elsewhere within the academy's operations.

LEASE FINANCING

The discussion of lease financing in chapter 17 indicated that lease agreements generally obligate an organization to pay a fixed amount each period (month, quarter, or year) in return for obtaining the services of property. Thus, lease payments should be treated as *operating expenses* in the basic model, and not as financial cash flows in the extensions to the model.

The proper approach to testing for financial viability of a capital project in which leasing is a possible financing alternative is, first, to follow the decision technique outlined in chapter 17 for choosing between leasing and borrowing and buying the asset. If the technique indicates that lease financing is the preferred alternative, the lease payments should then be treated as an operating expense in calculating the net project cost in the basic model. If the project turns out to be financially viable, so also is the method of financing (leasing). But if the project is not financially viable according to the testing procedure, and leasing is the preferred financing alternative, the project cannot be made viable by choosing to finance it with borrowed funds; to do so would only make matters worse for the organization in terms of cash flows.

SUMMARY

This chapter is an extension to chapter 14, in which the basic long-range, financial-planning model was presented. The purpose of the discussion in this chapter is to integrate the material presented in chapters 16 and 17, dealing with capital-structure management, with the material dealing with resource-allocation decisions.

The extended financial-planning model facilitates the simultaneous examination of all long-term cash flows, prior to resource-allocation decisions. It may also be employed to test an organization's overall operations for financial viability. This is easily accomplished simply by aggregating net operating cash flows and total financial cash flows and treating them as if they were project cash flows in the application of the model.

The benefits from integrating the resource-allocation decisions and the financing decisions on either an aggregate or project basis are clearly stated in terms of financial-goal achievement. The financial-management goal in the nonprofit context of maintaining organizational liquidity and solvency cannot be achieved without systematic financial planning in a framework that explicitly accounts for the total cash flows of the organization. By implementing only those projects that are financially viable, the organization is ensuring that it will continue in operation in the long-run while serving the best interest of its clientele group.

FURTHER READING

This monograph presents the extended model developed for use by municipal governments:

Wacht, Richard F. *A New Approach to Capital Budgeting for City and County Governments*. 2nd ed. Atlanta: Georgia State University Business Press, 1987.

QUESTIONS

1. What benefits does the nonprofit organization realize from the integration of long-term-financing and capital-asset-acquisition decisions?

2. Explain in general terms how to determine the maximum amount of long-term debt that a stream of profit of a certain size can repay.

3. Define *PVA* and *PVR* in terms of the variables contained in equations (2) and (3), respectively.

4. What is the test for financial viability prescribed by the expanded model?

5. List the options available to management if it wishes to make a financially nonviable project viable.

6. What is the proper approach to testing a project involving base financing for financial viability?

PROBLEMS

1. Calculate the annual debt-service charges for a three-year, $35,000, 12-percent term loan.

2. What is the present value of the debt-service charges in problem 1, given a 15-percent discount rate?

3. The Butler Street YMCA expects its membership dues to generate a surplus of $1,500 over planned expenditures during this year (year 1). It also expects the surplus to continue for the subsequent three-year period (years 2-4), but the amount of surplus is expected to fall by 2 percent per year.

    a. Calculate the amount of profit, or surplus, expected in each year of the four-year period.

    b. If the YMCA earns 8 percent on the investment of surplus cash, what is the present value of those profits?

4. The chairman of the Holy Cross Lutheran Church's budget and finance committee prepared the following planning estimates for financing the construction of a log house to be used by the Boy Scout and Girl Scout troops that the church currently is sponsoring.

    a. How much must the church borrow to implement the project?

    b. Calculate the amount of the equal annual payments required to repay the 12-percent, six-year term loan.

    c. Perform the test for project financial viability.

	Timing	Values
1. Net project cost	Year 0	$18,500
2. Planning period		6 years
3. Cash on hand allocated to the project	Year 0	$3,000
4. Annual appropriation to the project from the church	Years 1-6	$3,000
5. Growth rate of appropriation	Years 1-6	6%
6. Rate of return on investment of surplus cash	Years 1-6	5%
7. Interest rate on borrowed funds	Years 1-6	12%
8. Debt maturity		6 years

5. The scout leaders were disappointed when the Holy Cross Church budget and finance committee informed them that they could not approve the financing plan for the log house (see problem 4). Since the house would be built exclusively with volunteer help and much of the material was being provided at or below cost, the estimate of the net project could not be reduced.

When the scout leaders met with the chairman of the budget and finance committee, they asked him what, if anything, the scouts could do to change the committee's decision. After explaining why the project was not financially viable, the chairman said that if the scout leaders could find a lender who would charge a lower interest rate for the loan, or if the scout troops would be willing to help out with the debt-service charges over the six-year period, the committee might change its position on the project.

a. Calculate the interest rate on borrowed funds that would make the project presented in problem 4 financially viable.

b. If the church could not borrow at a rate below 12 percent, how much money per year would the scout troops need to appropriate to debt service to get the committee to agree to proceed with the project?

c. One of the scout leaders said that the church could earn a higher return on its surplus cash by investing in a money-market mutual fund. The rate available on one such fund is 10 percent. Assuming the other choices are out of the question, will this higher rate of return on surplus cash be sufficient to achieve project financial viability?

19

Managing Financial Distress

This chapter examines an approach to managing financial distress in nonprofit organizations called fiscal triage.[1] *The intent of the triage approach is to cure the underlying cause of the problems that lead to threatened insolvency rather than to treat the immediate symptoms. Triage employs the capital budgeting model, presented in chapters 14 and 18, as the basis for the decision criterion and to develop alternative solutions to financial distress.*

Financial distress in any organization is not difficult to identify or define, but it is never a pleasant experience. Simply stated, financial distress occurs when an organization's cash outflows exceed its inflows for some extended period. When that situation develops, some action is required on the part of management. If it is a temporary event — such as when cash on hand is insufficient to pay the bills that are due, but cash inflows will remedy that situation in a short time — management need only defer payment of the bills until the cash balance is rebuilt to a level that will cover the organization's outstanding obligations.

When the period of financial distress is expected to be longer than one or two weeks, however, deferring payment of bills that are due obviously will not cure the situation. The organization may borrow funds until it can either liquidate assets or increase its fund-raising activities to bring its cash flows back into balance. But debt service — payment of principal and interest — will simply increase total cash outflows when the

---

1. This chapter is based on C. B. Doss, Jr., and R. F. Wacht, *Fiscal Triage for Government* (Atlanta: Georgia State University Business Press, 1989).

indebtedness comes due. Besides, deferring payment—no matter how it is done—does not cure the cause of the cash-flow imbalance; it merely treats the symptom and almost guarantees its return after a time.

When an organization faces either a permanent decline in cash inflows or a permanent increase in operating expenditures in excess of its ability to increase receipts, it faces a *dire scarcity* of funds. To borrow a phrase from the lexicon of municipal government, a condition of dire scarcity signals the start of *cutback management* activities for an organization, in which programs must be either cut back in size or eliminated altogether to bring the cash flow back into balance. An approach to cutback management comprises the focus of this chapter. Its theoretical basis is founded in the process of *medical triage*.

MEDICAL TRIAGE

In popular usage, the word *triage* typically refers to the practice that hospital personnel employ in classifying victims of a catastrophe prior to beginning treatment of their injuries. The victims, whose number outstrips the capacity of the hospital to render adequate medical care to all, are classified into three groups: (1) those who are expected to die regardless of the type of treatment rendered; (2) those who do not require much, if any, treatment to survive; and (3) those who will probably die unless they receive immediate aid at some level. Most of the hospital's resources are focused on the individuals classified in group 3, and the result of the procedure, in theory at least, is minimizing the loss of life by employing the limited medical and hospital resources in the most effective manner.

Medical triage is based on the concept of dire scarcity. In a condition of dire scarcity, the amount of some life-saving resource is insufficient to sustain the lives of all who are in need of that resource. Consequently, those who would likely die even if they use the resource (group 1) are denied access to it, and those who are likely to survive even if the resource is withheld for a time (group 2) will have their access to it delayed for some period. The members of group 3 are given immediate access, since their situations allow optimum utilization of the resource.

TRIAGE AND FINANCIAL DISTRESS

The analogy between rendering medical care to victims of a catastrophe and saving a nonprofit organization from insolvency in a period of financial distress is not so farfetched. If we consider a nonprofit organization as a collection of programs that compete with one another for an organization's scarce financial resources, the triage classification scheme becomes plausible as a management tool. What is needed to implement the fiscal triage process within this context is a means of examining and classifying each program into its proper group. For this purpose we may use the concept of financial viability introduced earlier in this book and quantified in chapters 14 and 18.

Financial Viability

You will recall that a financially viable program is defined as one that *can be implemented or can continue to function over its expected life, using either available financial resources or those acquired specifically for that program.* While a viable program may generate cash surpluses, it may not by definition consume cash in amounts in excess of its initially planned appropriations over time.

A financially nonviable program, if implemented or continued, either will cause or create an absolute shortage of cash within the organization or result in the subsequent involuntary reallocation of resources from other ongoing programs in order to maintain the nonviable program. When resources are reallocated from financially viable programs, those programs frequently become nonviable as a result of the loss of funds. The unfortunate but inevitable result in either case is a diminution of the organization's overall professional effectiveness. That is, the quality of service increases as a result of the addition of a nonviable program, but at the sacrifice of either the quantity or quality of other services provided to the organization's constituencies.

Unfortunately, achieving financial viability does not ensure the overall (professional and financial) success of the organization; it is a necessary condition, but it is not sufficient of itself to guarantee professional goal achievement. Resource allocation decisions in nonprofit organizations must therefore involve two determinations: professional acceptance and financial viability.

Neither the professional objectives nor the financial goal can be given clear priority. Insufficient attention to attainment of the financial goal will clearly reduce the ability of the organization to achieve its professional goals by creating a climate characterized by constant financial crisis. Conversely, overemphasis on financial security will simply result in a malallocation of resources away from the support of the organization's professional pursuits and toward "cashness" or the building of cash reserves for the sake of liquidity. Failure to pursue one or the other of these goal sets will create severe problems for the nonprofit organization, while the vigorous pursuit of both will ensure a unit's ultimate success in both dimensions.

OVERVIEW OF THE FISCAL TRIAGE MODEL

The Fiscal Triage Model is part quantitative and part qualitative. For proper implementation, its quantitative portion requires a person with expertise in technical financial skills, and its qualitative portion requires the presence of individuals possessing expert knowledge of the organization's professional mission.

The triage model is depicted graphically in Exhibit 19–1. The process prescribed by the model is quite simple, but the application is necessarily rather complex because it involves extensive financial and political analyses of each of the organization's major spending programs. The financial model developed in chapter 14 will be reintroduced later in this chapter. First, however, let us briefly examine each of the four major steps that constitute the Fiscal Triage Model.

Classify and Evaluate Programs

The triage process begins by classifying spending programs into three groups using rational (quantitative or financial) criteria. The first classification includes those programs that are considered *healthy* because they are either financially viable or, since their operations must absolutely be continued if the principal mission of the organization is to be sustained, they will always receive full funding while the organization remains in existence.

The second classification, which includes all operable programs, contains those that readily can be salvaged by either allocating relatively small amounts of available resources to them, reducing the scope of each sufficiently to enable them to continue with the resources currently earmarked for their use, or transferring them to another agency or to the private sector. The third group of programs are those that are *dying* either because of a total loss of funding or a reduction in support of such magnitude that the programs cannot continue even as scaled-down versions.

The classification process is based on the objective of financial viability; that is, each of the organization's programs is tested for viability, using the financial model. Those that are viable are classified as *healthy*. Those that provide the basic services but are not viable are also classified as healthy; however, the amount of resources needed to enable each to achieve financial viability is noted for use in the next step of the triage process.

The nonbasic programs that fail the test of viability are classified as either *operable* or *dying*. The placement of a program in one or the other of these two groups is based on the size of the deficit each will produce and the likelihood that the deficit can be financed either with available and forthcoming revenues or from new sources of funds from grants or

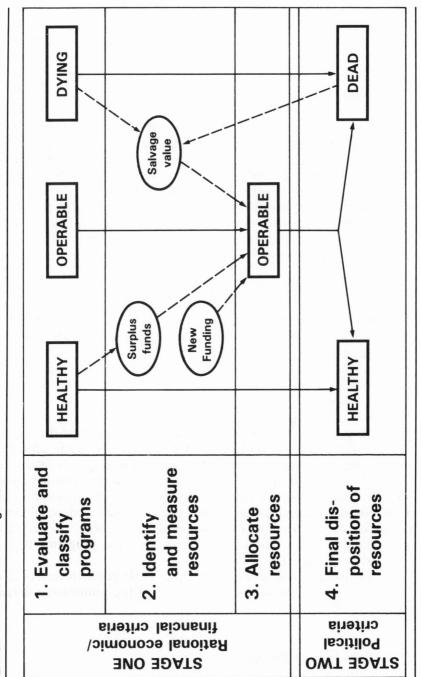

Exhibit 19-1. The Fiscal Triage Model

gifts. In most cases, a program will be classified as dying at this point in the process only if it is obvious that its deficit cannot be eliminated in any way.

Identify and Measure Resources

The tests of financial viability will provide the decision maker with the amount of surplus or deficit each program will generate over the planning period (generally five years or longer). The salvage values or total amounts of resources released from programs classified as dying will also be determined during the preceding classification step in the triage process. That information is used in this step to plan the internal reallocation of resources among programs, to evaluate the success of joint ventures with the private sector, and to form the basis for submitting applications for new sources of revenues from outside sources.

In short, this step involves identifying the alternative sources of funding and preparing and submitting grant applications and funding requests to outside agencies. This information and the results of the search for new funds form the parameters that are used in the next step of the process.

Allocate Resources

The objective in this third step is to determine which of the operable and dying programs identified in step one can be made financially viable using the sources of funding developed in step two. Again, the financial model will provide the tests of financial viability. Those programs that cannot be made to achieve viability, even after being scaled to minimum proportions, will often produce additional salvage values that can be used by those that remain operable. This part of the process will generate alternative sets of operable programs that are financially self-sufficient.

Completion of this step ends the financial officer's involvement in the triage process and begins the involvement of the professional decision makers.

Final Disposition of Resources

The final step involves selecting the set of financially viable, operable programs that produces the highest level of professional goal achievement for the nonprofit organization's clientele. In many cases, the choices will be clear enough to the professional managers, who may have in mind a clear indication of the priorities that must be followed. In some situations, however, the choices are not so easily made because the professional managers may disagree among themselves about the proper ordering of priorities. In such cases, the final selection from among alternative financially viable sets of programs can be made easier if supported by a decision technique capable of dealing with a multiplicity of goals within a budget constraint.

One such technique uniquely suited to solving problems of this nature is goal programming.[2] Goal programming is a linear mathematical programming technique that permits the decision maker to simultaneously consider several relevant organizational goals while seeking a *satisfactory* solution to a resource allocation problem. Goal programming cannot select an optimum solution (that is, prescribe a maximizing or minimizing behavior) because the solution process involves trade-offs among the several goals that the politicians have decided to pursue. Moreover, in defining the problem for application of the technique, the decision makers must determine satisfactory ranges of attainment for each of their goals. This computational procedure selects from among all possible realistic solutions the one (or ones) that best fulfills the decision makers' requirements. Thus the technique leads to satisfactory, rather than optimum or maximum, resource allocation decisions.

THE FINANCIAL MODEL

The model that generates the financial data that drives the first three stages of the Fiscal Triage Model is the model developed in chapter 14. You will recall that the technique enables a financial manager to test an organization's major spending programs for financial viability. The technique compares cash outflows for future construction, equipment purchases, and operating and maintenance costs with cash inflows from any one or a combination of several financing options available to the organization. The financing options include gifts, grants, internal transfers from other programs, and operating revenues from the imposition of user fees.

The financial model employs the time value of money concept in equating the present value of future cash outflows with the present value of future cash inflows from the relevant financing options, both of which are adjusted for the effects of inflation. When the present values

---

2. A full discussion of the goal-programming technique is presented in Chapter 15. A further example of its application in a similar context may be found in Richard F. Wacht and David T. Whitford, "A Goal Programming Model for Capital Investment Analysis in Nonprofit Hospitals," *Financial Management,* 5 (Summer 1976): 37–46.

of the cash inflows and outflows are equal, or the inflows exceed the outflows, the project is financially viable. When the outflows exceed the inflows, the technique clearly indicates both the reason why the project is not viable and the steps needed to correct the condition.

For example, if a project is not financially viable, the financial manager may recommend (based on information produced by the model) reducing the scale of the project or locating an external or internal source of funding in an amount that will cause it to become exactly viable. The model will indicate the maximum size of the project and/or the minimum amount of added funds needed to make the project exactly viable. The same kind of indicators are provided when the program is overfunded; that is, when cash inflows exceed outflows.

In addition to producing an estimate of the program's funding requirements, the approach permits the financial manager to answer "what if" questions. For example, the estimates developed by the sponsor of a new program being considered for implementation may specify operating and maintenance costs at a certain level. The financial manager may ask, "What if these costs are 10 percent higher? How will that affect the program's financing costs?" By changing the operating and maintenance cost estimates to allow for the uncertain trends in, say gasoline prices and utility rates, the financial manager can obtain insights regarding the impact of inflation on project financial viability.

A SIMPLE ILLUSTRATION OF THE TRIAGE MODEL

To conceptualize the way in which the financial model drives the first three steps of the Fiscal Triage Model, let us take a look at a highly simplified illustrative example.

Step One: Evaluate and Classify the Program

Suppose the Laurie Gunn Society, an organization that provides visiting nurses to care for indigent patients in their homes, is facing dire scarcity. It is operating one discretionary program through which it provides sickroom equipment and supplies (such as hospital beds, wheelchairs, bedpans, and so forth) to its clients. Unfortunately, the current funding for the program is completely inadequate. The society also is operating several other programs, including its basic mission of home health care for the indigent, in-service training for its volunteer nurses, training teenagers for hospital volunteer work, and instruction in patient care for the family members of its clients, all of which the society's management has determined to be inviolable so far as service levels are concerned. These basic programs are operating on a combined break-even basis in the current fiscal year out of donations, endowment income, client fees, and other miscellaneous revenues. Management feels that the society will be able to continue to operate these basic programs on a cash break-even basis in the long run.

Exhibit 19–2 presents the cash flows associated with operating the sickroom equipment program over a five-year planning period. As shown in the exhibit, the program requires normal replacement of equipment and other capital items of $15,000 in 1990, $40,000 in 1991, and $8,000 per year thereafter. Operating and maintenance cost are $6,500 per year. Financial support for the program is provided out of a five-year grant from a private foundation, which totaled only $5,000 in 1989, and $9,000 per year thereafter. User fee revenue of $1,000 per year is included in the forecast. Expansion plans and some equipment purchases for the society's other programs have been deferred so that funding could continue for the discretionary program; however, these plans cannot be deferred any longer without jeopardizing the society's basic mission.

Casual inspection of the exhibit reveals that the project easily can be classified in terms of the Fiscal Triage Model as either *dying* or *operable,* but certainly not as a *healthy* program.

Exhibit 19–2 Cash Flows Associated with the Laurie Gunn Discretionary Program

Year	Capital replacement	Operating and maintenance	Total cash outflows	Revenue and grants	Surplus (Deficit)
1990	$15,000	$6,500	$21,500	$ 6,000	($15,500)
1991	40,000	6,500	46,500	10,000	(36,500)
1992	8,000	6,500	14,500	10,000	(4,500)
1993	8,000	6,500	14,500	10,000	(4,500)
1994	8,000	6,500	14,500	10,000	(4.500)

The relevant assumptions required by the financial model are presented in Exhibit 19–3. These assumptions are used within the model to develop estimates of the funding requirements needed to make the program financially viable.

Exhibit 19–3. Planning Assumptions Used by the Laurie Gunn Society

Inflation rates:	
1. Equipment	7.0%
2. Operations & maintenance	5.0%
3. Revenue from rental fees	0.0%
Interest rates:	
1. Return on surplus cash	7.5%
2. Short-term debt	9.0%

Exhibit 19–4 presents the results of the application of the financial model to the discretionary program being examined by the Laurie Gunn

Society, given the program's cash flows and planning estimates provided in Exhibits 19–2 and 19–3, respectively. The information in the exhibit spells out the two options that the society has for making the program exactly financially viable.

Exhibit 19–4. **Results of the Application of the Planning Model to the Laurie Gunn Discretionary Program**

---

1. One-time grant in 1990 in the amount of $71,680.

2. Increase revenue of the five-year grant, 1990–1994:

Year	Revenue or grant funding needed to achieve financial viability	Required increase
1990	$ 17,717	$ 11,717
1991	17,717	7,717
1992	17,717	7,717
1993	17,717	7,717
1994	17,717	7,717

Step Two: Identify and Measure Resources

If neither of the options for achieving financial viability is feasible at this time, and since no surplus funds are available within the society's other programs, the sickroom equipment discretionary program must be classified as *dying,* and the salvage value of the program should be determined. In most cases, the salvage value of the program is the amount by which the expense budget can be reduced below its budgeted revenues by eliminating the program in its entirety, plus the market value of any surplus property that is no longer required because of the demise of the program.

For example, eliminating this program may permit the society to reduce expenses through employee attrition, elimination of equipment repair and replacement costs, and the reduction of rental expense for leased storage space. Capital equipment, including the sickroom equipment and the delivery truck, can be sold or put to use elsewhere by the society, thereby enabling the society's other programs to expand without having to acquire added funding from outside sources.

Step Three: Allocate Resources

The surplus funds released from the now dead program can be used to reduce any indebtedness of the society or to supplement user fees or other types of revenues. Alternatively, they may be used to fund another smaller program that may have been deferred because of a lack of funding.

Let us assume, however, that the second alternative in Exhibit 19–4 is considered feasible by the Laurie Gunn Society's treasurer, Mae Cameron. Through her contacts, she learned of a grant program offered by the federal government for which the sickroom program certainly would qualify. Unfortunately, significant changes in the society's accounting methods, record keeping, and program structure would be needed before it could qualify for the federal program. If the society did qualify and did receive the grant funds, the sickroom equipment program would be classified as *operable.*

Step Four: Final Disposition of Funds

The recommendation of the treasurer to apply for a grant from the federal government requires the society's board of trustees to decide whether they wish to accept the conditions that such a grant will impose on the organization in order to save the program. The members of the Board of Trustees must now operate within the professional arena to determine whether or not the sick-room equipment program should be allowed to die or should be given new life by applying for the grant. They may chose to accept the restrictions that will accompany the acceptance of the grant, or they may simply let the program die after due deliberation. In any event, the Fiscal Triage Model has provided the rational/financial data needed to support the professional decision.

If it decides to kill this discretionary program, and in fact a smaller program is waiting in the wings for funding (for instance, a heretofore unidentified *operable* program is awaiting a funding decision), the board of trustees can allocate the salvage value of the dead program to the unfunded smaller one, subsequent to testing it for financial viability, of course. Whether the smaller program or the sickroom equipment program survives, or whether the salvage value from the dead program is used to supplement some other expenditure category within the organization is a matter primarily of *professional* concern.

While the politics of that decision lie outside the scope of both the financial model and the responsibility of the treasurer or financial officer, it is nevertheless an essential and integral element of the Fiscal Triage Model. As such, it should not be avoided, deferred, or allowed to be made by default. Some insight as to how this type of decision can be addressed by the professional decision makers was provided in the discussion of the goal-programming technique of resource allocation presented in chapter 15.

To more carefully examine the financial aspects of the Fiscal Triage Model, the following section describes a situation in which the Laurie Gunn Society, with its total of five programs, is facing dire scarcity. We will see how the society's treasurer, Mae Cameron, uses a computer-supported version of the Fiscal Triage Model to analyze those programs and produce a set of data for the Board of Trustees to use in its decision-making process.[3]

A CASE STUDY IN FINANCIAL DISTRESS: THE LAURIE GUNN SOCIETY

None of the members of the Laurie Gunn Society's Board of Trustees felt particularly good about the unanimous vote that had just been recorded. But in light of the steady downward trend in the organization's cash reserve position over the past seven months, another reduction in staff—the second in these seven months—seemed to be a solution arrived at through desperation. Margaret Gillis, the chairperson of the board, Lily MacLoed, the society's president, and treasurer Mae Cameron agreed that the reduction in staff was not the best solution, but they felt that the move would give them time to develop a plan that would place the organization on sound financial footing without destroying the effectiveness of the five health care support programs included in its mission.

The programs that comprise the mission of the Laurie Gunn Society include (1) home health care, (2) in-service nurses training, (3) teen training, (4) family training, and (5) the sickroom equipment program. The first two of these five programs were budgeted by line item and fully funded for the next fiscal year. Thanks to a recent commitment by the local Rotary Club to provide a rather generous donation to the organization's endowment fund, the home health care program would provide a surplus of revenues and support over expenses, which surplus could be used to support any of the other programs.

The existence of the other three programs—(3) through (5)—was now threatened by what seemed to the Board as a dire scarcity of resources within the society's budget. Only two of the programs were receiving an appropriation from the endowment fund, but these funds would no longer be made available beyond the remaining commitments for the current fiscal year. All three programs would have to be funded from this point forward with a combination of donated funds, grants, and user fee revenues, or else one or more of them would have to be abandoned.

The Five Laurie Gunn Society Programs

The programs facing extinction had become institutions in the community. Their demise would not go unnoticed or unprotested.

---

3. The computer-assisted version of the financial model used in this illustration is called CBits. It is included in the study guide material that may be purchased from the publisher.

Consequently, Ms. Gillis asked Mae Cameron to undertake a careful analysis of all five programs and formulate her recommendations regarding which could be continued and which could not. Brief descriptions of the programs follow.

Home Health Care for the Indigent. The Home Health Care program was begun in 1938 when the society's founder and a few of her close friends began to visit the sick in the community, bringing food and doing some cooking, cleaning, and running errands to help those who could not afford the cost of home care. As the years went by, the ladies gradually began to organize their efforts, and then in 1947 they established a permanent organization that solicited funds and volunteer nurses to provide such care to the indigent who were ill.

Today, the program is staffed with 52 volunteer nurses and carries a case load of over 350 families per month. Referrals are received from hospitals, doctors, churches, and several charitable organizations in the city and its surrounding areas. The services generally are provided free, but fees sometimes are charged to the patient on an ability-to-pay basis. Most of the financial support for the program comes from current donations and the society's endowment fund. Mae Cameron expects a small surplus in the program's operations next year.

In-service Nurses Training. Home health care requires special training, not so much from the medical perspective as from the human relations point of view. The nurses are given instruction relating to their conduct in the home of indigent patients, how to elicit the cooperation of family members, how to handle special situations, such as alcohol and drug abuse by household members, and, of course, the administrative requirements imposed by the society for the protection of the patients, nurses, and the society itself.

A number of consultants and instructors are employed by the organization to conduct the training programs. Each volunteer nurse is required to attend eight hours of instruction per quarter. Classes are given in the social hall of a local church. All of the expenses are paid for out of the endowment fund.

Teen Hospital Volunteers. The training program for teenage hospital volunteers is a recent addition to the society's mission, having been started four years ago. Most of the recruits come from the families that are enrolled in the home health care program. The training is conducted on Saturday mornings during the school year and at various times during the summer months. The sessions are conducted in the hospitals by hospital employees without cost to the society or the volunteers.

Program expenses include training materials, transportation for the teen volunteers when needed, the uniforms that the teens wear on the job, and special incentives for the participants who excel in the program.

The teen program draws little support from the society's donor constituents; consequently, almost all of the funding must come from unrestricted funds, which now are in short supply. Ms. Cameron feels that this program may be the most difficult to justify continuance.

Family Training. Ms. Gillis began the family training program ten years ago as a result of a decline in nurse volunteers. The program is designed to train family members to give injections and alcohol rubs to the chronically ill, bathe the patients, prepare healthy meals, measure and administer proper doses of medication, and so forth. Having such in-home training allows the home health care program to become much more efficient and effective. Unfortunately, like teen volunteer training, this program does not appear very glamorous to the donors, and it, too, faces a struggle for survival. Its support comes principally from the society's unrestricted funds.

Sickroom Equipment. The sickroom equipment program, described in an earlier section, was begun three years ago when a small nonprofit hospital in a nearby community was forced to close as the result of financial difficulty. Its assets were auctioned off by its creditors, and the Laurie Gunn Society purchased a number of hospital beds and other useful equipment and supplies at attractive prices. It next purchased a delivery truck, thus beginning the program that gives, loans, rents, or sells sickroom equipment and supplies to its home health care clientele.

The program is supported with a small amount of user fees and a grant from a private foundation. The possibility also exists for funding from a federal grant; however, the Board is currently examining the full consequences of obtaining federal government funding. Because of the need to replace so much equipment within the next two years, the program faces a huge deficit without added funding.

APPLICATION OF THE FISCAL TRIAGE MODEL

Mae Cameron approached the analysis of the five programs by applying the Fiscal Triage Model. She used a computer-assisted version of the Triage financial model, called CBits, to perform the calculations called for in the first three steps of the Triage analysis. Printed copies of the financial analyses of the five programs are included in Appendices 19-A, 19-B, and 19-C at the end of this chapter.

Step One: Evaluate and Classify the Programs

The first step taken by Mae Cameron was to evaluate and classify each of the six programs by first discussing the programs with Ms. Gillis and

Lily MacLoed and then subjecting the cash-flow estimates prepared by the supervisors of the programs to the tests of financial viability. Exhibit 19–5 summarizes the data that Mae Cameron used in her analysis.

Exhibit 19-5: **Laurie Gunn Society's Program Financial Profiles**

		Home Health Care	In-Service Nurses Training	Teen Training	Patient Family Training	Sickroom Equipment
1. Capital costs		$0	$510	$0	$0	$79,000
2. Sources of funding						
A. Gifts and grants		YES	NO	YES	YES	YES
B. User revenues		YES	NO	NO	NO	YES
C. Endowment		YES	YES	NO	NO	NO
3. Triage classification		Healthy	Healthy	Operable	Dying	Dying
4. Present value of project surplus (deficit)		$22,872	$63	($9,262)	($48,911)	($64,141)
5. Annual net cash flows, adjusted for inflation:						
Expected year-end surplus	1990	$16,500	$0	$650	$4,200	$4,000
Budget	1991	1,775	0	(2,187)	(12,166)	(19,825)
Projection	1992	1,650	0	(2,389)	(13,031)	(42,861)
Projection	1993	1,585	84	(2,606)	(13,948)	(7,171)
Projection	1994	1,590	0	(2,839)	(14,919)	(8,180)
Projection	1995	1,674	1	(3,089)	(15,950)	(9,254)
		$24,774	$85	($12,460)	($65,814)	($83,291)

Sources of data: Data input forms and cash-flow statements in Appendices A and B.

The results of the tests for financial viability are shown in lines 4 and 5 in Exhibit 19–5. The Home Health Care program and In-service Nurses Training are the only programs of the five that produce a present-value cash surplus (line 4) and require no added outside funding to achieve cash-flow break-even (line 5). Consequently, these two programs clearly can be classified as healthy in triage terminology—that is, they are financially viable over the planning period.

Mae Cameron classified two programs as dying—Patient Family Training and Sickroom Equipment. Line 4 in Exhibit 19–5 shows the size of a one-time cash gift received that was immediately needed to support the operations of the two programs, and the totals in line 5 show the cumulative cash-flow deficits of each of the programs. Clearly, the two dying programs promise to consume significant amounts of resources if they are continued. The remaining program—Teen Training—appears operable, given the surplus from the Home Health Care and the potential salvage values that might be derived from letting the dying programs fail.

Exhibit 19–6 summarizes Ms. Cameron's notes on the five discretionary programs.

Exhibit 19–6. Program Classification Under Triage Analysis

Program	Classification	Comments
Home Health Care	Healthy	Producing annual surplus cash flows
Nurses Training	Healthy	Very close to financial break-even
Teen Training	Operable	Relatively small annual cash-flow deficits
Family Training	Dying	Producing large cash deficits
Sickroom Equipment	Dying	Requires extensive capital investment

---

Ms. Cameron not only examined each program separately, but she also determined the cash-flow impact of the five programs in aggregate if the Board of Trustees decided that it could not eliminate any of them, not even those she classified as dying. Exhibit 19–7 shows what would happen to the society's cash reserve position under this circumstance, assuming that no new outside funding were available. As the exhibit indicates, the Laurie Gunn Society could operate all five programs through 1990 and through most of 1991; however, if continued through 1995, the programs would consume total cash in excess of $157,000.

Exhibit 19-7: Expected End-of-year Cash Balances Without New Program Funding

	1990	1991	1992	1993	1994	1995
Home Health Care	$16,500	$19,884	$23,473	$27,346	$31,603	$36,358
Nurses Training	0	0	0	84	92	102
Teen Training	650	(1,473)	(4,006)	(7,003)	(10,525)	(14,640)
Family Training	4,200	(7,557)	(21,324)	(37,351)	(55,912)	(77,314)
Sick Room Equipment	4,000	(12,435)	(56,508)	(69,119)	(84,114)	(101,570)
Year-end Cash Balance	$25,350	($1,581)	($58,365)	($86,043)	($118,856)	($157,064)

Source of data: Cash flow statements in Appendix B.

Step Two: Identify and Measure Resources

The second step in the Fiscal Triage Model calls for a search for new funds from external and internal sources. After an exhaustive search, Mae Cameron was unable to locate any likely sources of gifts from within the community or grants from federal, state, or charitable sources to apply to the future program deficits. The only other available internal funding source that could be used is the salvage values available from the demise of each of the five society programs.

In her discussions with Lily MacLoed and Ms. Gillis, Mae Cameron developed estimates of the salvage values of both the operable and the dying programs. The officers agreed that any cash generated through these salvage values would be used to either save the operable program, expand one of the two healthy programs, or fund some new program that the officers might like to inaugurate. Exhibit 19–8 lists the yearly cash flows that Ms. Cameron found would be available to apply to other programs. She omitted the Home Health Care and In-service Nurses Training programs, because these programs were central to the society's mission. In fact, the society would have no reason to exist without their continuance.

Exhibit 19-8: **Estimated Program Salvage Values**

	1990	1991	1992	1993	1994	1995
Teen Training	$650	$100	$100	$100	$100	$100
Family Training	4,200	1,200	1,200	1,200	1,200	1,200
Sick Room Equipment	6,500	0	0	0	0	0

The officers were confident that the 1990 expected cash surpluses for each of the programs were accurate estimates. These figures therefore were recorded in the 1990 column of Exhibit 19–8. The salvage values for 1991 through 1995 for Teen Training and Patient Family Training were the donated funds that the officers felt would continue to be received even if the programs were eliminated. These amounted to $100 annually for Teen Training and $1,200 per year for Family Training.

The Sickroom Equipment program was funded by a grant from a private foundation. The chairman of the foundation's grants committee told Mae Cameron that the grant would not be continued if the program were dropped by the Laurie Gunn Society. But he encouraged her to apply for funding if the society wanted to establish a similar program in the future. Since none of the future funding could be salvaged, the total salvage value of the program was $2,500, the current market price of the equipment now held by the society, plus the $4,000 in surplus for the current year, or a total of $6,500.

Step Three: Allocate Resources

Before making her recommendations to the Board of Trustees, Mae Cameron decided to "package" the program cash flows according to her initial classification of the five programs. That is, to the surplus cash flows from the two healthy programs she added the salvage values from

the two dying programs to see if the operable program—Teen
Training—could be made healthy. These cash flows are shown in Exhibit
19–9.

Exhibit 19-9: Cash-Flow Analysis by Program Classification Under Triage

	1990	1991	1992	1993	1994	1995
Healthy programs:						
Home Health Care	$16,500	$1,775	$1,650	$1,585	$1,590	$1,674
Nurses Training	0	0	0	84	0	1
Salvage values:						
Family Training	4,200	1,200	1,200	1,200	1,200	1,200
Sick Room Equipment	6,500	0	0	0	0	0
Total cash available	$27,200	$2,975	$2,850	$2,869	$2,790	$2,875
Operable Program Cash Requirements:						
Teen Training	(650)	2,187	2,389	2,606	2,839	3,089
Cash surplus (deficit)	$27,850	$788	$461	$263	($49)	($214)
Beginning cash balance		27,850	31,284	34,717	38,278	41,865
Interest earned @ 9.5%		2,646	2,972	3,298	3,636	3,977
Ending cash balance	27,850	31,284	34,717	38,278	41,865	45,628

Source of data: Exhibits 19-5 and 19-7.

Although the bottom line in Exhibit 19–9 contains cash deficits for
1994 and 1995, the cash surpluses generated in the earlier years are more
than sufficient to offset those cash drains. Thus, the Teen Training
program can be continued. And because the Laurie Gunn Society likely
will enjoy budget surpluses for the period 1991 through 1993 if it drops
the Family Training and Sickroom Equipment programs at the end of
1990, the officers can examine the society's newly created options. This
examination comprises the final step of the Triage Model.

Step Four: Final Disposition of Funds

The final step in the Triage process requires the professional
management of an organization to decide how the organization will
resolve its financial distress. Based on the data generated by Mae
Cameron, Ms. Gillis and the other officers and trustees of the Laurie
Gunn Society met to consider the several options they had to bring the
society back on a healthy financial basis.

The first option was to expand some of its continuing programs with
the funds identified as salvage values from the dying programs. Second,

the trustees could elect to fund a new program out of expected surpluses. Third, the society could simply operate the Home Health Care, In-service Nurses Training, and the Teen Training program and let the surpluses accumulate in the endowment fund as a cushion against future financial distress. Finally, it may decide to abandon all but its two basic programs and enjoy even larger annual surpluses in its operations. The final option would not add to professional goal achievement, however.

Lily MacLoed recommended to the Board that the society drop the two dying programs and continue the Teen Training. She recommended against expanding the Home Health Care program because the current demand did not warrant expansion. But because of a growing shortage of nurses in the area, she recommended that the society use the new surplus to establish a scholarship fund in the nursing careers, with the graduates of the Teen Training program to be given first consideration.

SUMMARY

The primary purpose of this chapter is to present and illustrate a systematic approach to analyzing the causes of and defining a solution to financial distress in a nonprofit organization. The Triage Model described here enables a team of financial and professional managers to sort an organization's programs (or spending units) in a logical manner based on their individual contributions to either cash surpluses or cash deficits. And based on this program delineation, the team can both strengthen the organization's financial position and provide maximum professional benefit to the organization's clientele, commensurate with its total financial resources.

The case analysis involving the Laurie Gunn Society detailed the steps necessary to logically and systematically sort through a complex resource allocation problem. The case study did not introduce a totally new set of concepts. But it arranged these concepts into a rather straightforward approach to dealing with financial distress on a programmatic basis.

FURTHER READING

This book provided the basis for applying Triage to financial distress in the local and state government contexts:

Doss, C. Bradley, Jr., and Richard F. Wacht. *Fiscal Triage for Government*. Atlanta: Georgia State University Business Press, 1989.

QUESTIONS

1. How is financial distress defined in the context of the nonprofit organization?

2. Define medical triage in terms of the classifications used to sort the victims.

3. List and describe the three classifications used in fiscal triage.

4. Explain how the concept of financial viability is used to classify programs for a nonprofit organization facing dire scarcity.

5. List and briefly describe the four steps in the application of the fiscal triage model.

6. Which of the four steps in the application of the fiscal triage model ends the involvement of the financial officer?

7. Describe the functioning of the financial model used in generating the data necessary for the application of the triage model.

PROBLEM

1. The Cape Breton Public Library was facing a difficult period because of a decline in the local industry that supported the city's economy. In late 1990, while she was preparing the annual budget, the library's director, Jan Swinkles, felt that she had to cut costs in some areas, even if she had to eliminate one or more of the library's three discretionary programs. Financial profiles of the three programs are as follows:

	Bookmobile	Children's Films	Adult Literacy
Equipment replacement:			
1991		$650	
1994	$22,500		
Annual operating costs	6,500	1,460	$25,430
Annual user revenues	0	800	10,500
Annual city appropriation	5,200	0	11,000
Annual gifts	0	0	0
Annual deficits	1,300	660	3,930

The library currently carries a bank balance of $9,453 in a money market account that yields 8.5 percent interest. The balance was available to be spent for any reason. The library does not have an endowment fund and is unable to borrow any money.

As close as she could determine, Jan Swinkles thought the library faced the following inflation and growth rates:

Equipment replacement	12%
Operating costs	8%
Revenue growth:	
City appropriations	5%
User revenue	4%
Donations	0%

Until now, the library had not solicited donations from the community, but Ms. Swinkles felt that now was a good time to start and that she could probably raise $2,000 each year from the library's strongest supporters. The library's general fund budget showed a surplus for the next year (1991) of $1,550, and Ms. Swinkles felt that the surplus could be maintained at that level in the future, including inflationary effects.

Ms. Swinkles felt that if she eliminated the programs, the library could realize the following salvage values:

Bookmobile: Sell the vehicle for $4,500 and retain $1,200 in annual city appropriations.

Children's Films: No salvage value.

Adult Literacy: Retain $2,500 in annual city appropriations.

She ranked the values of the programs qualitatively, giving the highest rank to the Adult Literacy program and the lowest rank to the Children's Films.

a. Test each of the three discretionary programs for financial viability.

b. Classify each of the programs as either operable or dying.

c. Prepare a schedule similar to Exhibit 19–8 with your recommendations under the Triage approach to the library's financial problem.

Appendix 19-A

THE LAURIE GUNN SOCIETY
DATA ENTRY FORMS

DATA ENTRY FORMS

PROGRAM TITLE: HOME HEALTH CARE   Version 1

I. General Information

    A. Current Year: 1990

    B. Final Year of Program Analysis: 1995

II. Equipment Replacement
     Year 0 ....
     Year 1   0
     Year 2   0
     Year 3   0
     Year 4   0
     Year 5   0

III. Operating and Maintenance Expense
      Year 0 ....
      Year 1   65,300
      Year 2   65,300
      Year 3   65,300
      Year 4   65,300
      Year 5   65,300

IV. Revenues
     Year 0 ....
     Year 1   8,750
     Year 2   8,750
     Year 3   8,750
     Year 4   8,750
     Year 5   8,750

DATA ENTRY FORMS

PROGRAM TITLE: HOME HEALTH CARE   Version 1

V. Grants/Gifts

    Initial Year   12,500
    Year 1   15,000
    Year 2   15,000
    Year 3   15,000
    Year 4   15,000
    Year 5   15,000

    Number of Years Funding
    Available under a Multi-year Grant (2-5)   5

VI. Internal Appropriations

Initial Year	4,000
Year 1	43,500
Year 2	43,500
Year 3	43,500
Year 4	43,500
Year 5	43,500

VII. Cash Management

    1. Size of current unencumbered,
nondesignated cash surplus immediately
available to cover temporary cash
deficits for the project: 0

    2. Expected average rate of return
from the investment of cash
surplus over the life of the project
to the nearest one-tenth of one percent
(enter as a decimal): 9.5%

    3. Short-term Borrowing Rate 12.8%

DATA ENTRY FORMS

PROGRAM TITLE: HOME HEALTH CARE   Version 1

VIII. Inflation Rates

    1. Schedule of inflation rates (round to nearest one percent
and enter as a decimal):

Category	Annual Inflation Rate
a. Equipment Replacement	12.0%
c. Operation/Maintenance	6.0%
c. User Fee Revenue	3.0%
d. Internal Appropriations	8.0%

DATA ENTRY FORMS

PROGRAM TITLE: IN-SERVICE NURSES TRAINING Version 1

I. General Information

  A. Current Year: 1990

  B. Final Year of Program Analysis: 1995

II. Equipment Replacement

Year 0	
Year 1	0
Year 2	0
Year 3	510
Year 4	0
Year 5	0

III. Operating and Maintenance Expense
     Year 0   ....
     Year 1   22,800
     Year 2   22,800
     Year 3   22,800
     Year 4   22,800
     Year 5   22,800

IV. Revenues
     Year 0   ....
     Year 1   0
     Year 2   0
     Year 3   0
     Year 4   0
     Year 5   0

DATA ENTRY FORMS

PROGRAM TITLE: IN-SERVICE NURSES TRAINING Version 1

V. Grants/Gifts

        Initial Year   0
        Year 1   0
        Year 2   0
        Year 3   800
        Year 4   0
        Year 5   0

        Number of Years Funding
        Available under a Multi-year Grant (2-5)   5

VI. Internal Appropriations

        Initial Year   0
        Year 1   22,800
        Year 2   22,800
        Year 3   22,800
        Year 4   22,800
        Year 5   22,800

VII. Cash Management
     1. Size of current unencumbered,
         nondesignated cash surplus immediately
         available to cover temporary cash
         deficits for the project: 0

     2. Expected average rate of return
         from the investment of cash
         surplus over the life of the project
         to the nearest one-tenth of one percent
         (enter as a decimal): 9.5%

     3. Short-term Borrowing Rate 12.8%

DATA ENTRY FORMS

PROGRAM TITLE: IN-SERVICE NURSES TRAINING Version 1

VIII. Inflation Rates

      1. Schedule of inflation rates (round to nearest one percent
         and enter as a decimal):

Category	Annual Inflation Rate
a. Equipment Replacement	12.0%
c. Operation/Maintenance	6.0%
c. User Fee Revenue	0.0%
d. Internal Appropriations	6.0%

DATA ENTRY FORMS

PROGRAM TITLE: TEEN TRAINING   Version 1

I. General Information

  A. Current Year: 1990

  B. Final Year of Program Analysis: 1995

II. Equipment Replacement
      Year 0 ....
      Year 1   0
      Year 2   0
      Year 3   0
      Year 4   0
      Year 5   0

III. Operating and Maintenance Expense
      Year 0 ....
      Year 1   2,500
      Year 2   2,500
      Year 3   2,500
      Year 4   2,500
      Year 5   2,500

IV. Revenues
      Year 0 ....
      Year 1   0
      Year 2   0
      Year 3   0
      Year 4   0
      Year 5   0

DATA ENTRY FORMS

PROGRAM TITLE: TEEN TRAINING   Version 1

V. Grants/Gifts

        Initial Year   0
        Year 1   500
        Year 2   500
        Year 3   500
        Year 4   500
        Year 5   500

        Number of Years Funding
        Available under a Multi-year Grant (2-5)   5

VI. Internal Appropriations

        Initial Year   650
        Year 1   0
        Year 2   0
        Year 3   0
        Year 4   0
        Year 5   0

VII. Cash Management
        1. Size of current unencumbered,
            nondesignated cash surplus immediately
            available to cover temporary cash
            deficits for the project: 0

        2. Expected average rate of return
            from the investment of cash
            surplus over the life of the project
            to the nearest one-tenth of one percent
            (enter as a decimal): 9.5%

        3. Short-term Borrowing Rate 12.8%

DATA ENTRY FORMS

PROGRAM TITLE: TEEN TRAINING   Version 1

VIII. Inflation Rates

        1. Schedule of inflation rates (round to nearest one percent
            and enter as a decimal):

                    Category   Annual Inflation Rate
                    ---------   ---------------------
            a. Equipment Replacement 12.0%
            c. Operation/Maintenance 7.5%
            c. User Fee Revenue 0.0%
            d. Internal Appropriations 0.0%

DATA ENTRY FORMS

PROGRAM TITLE: PATIENT FAMILY TRAINING   Version 1

I. General Information

    A. Current Year: 1990

    B. Final Year of Program Analysis: 1995

II. Equipment Replacement
     Year 0 ....
     Year 1   0
     Year 2   0
     Year 3   0
     Year 4   0
     Year 5   0

III. Operating and Maintenance Expense
      Year 0 ....
      Year 1   13,600
      Year 2   13,600
      Year 3   13,600
      Year 4   13,600
      Year 5   13,600

IV. Revenues
     Year 0 ....
     Year 1   0
     Year 2   0
     Year 3   0
     Year 4   0
     Year 5   0

DATA ENTRY FORMS

PROGRAM TITLE: PATIENT FAMILY TRAINING   Version 1

V. Grants/Gifts

     Initial Year   700
     Year 1   2,250
     Year 2   2,250
     Year 3   2,250
     Year 4   2,250
     Year 5   2,250

     Number of Years Funding
     Available under a Multi-year Grant (2-5)   5

VI. Internal Appropriations

     Initial Year   3,500
     Year 1   0
     Year 2   0
     Year 3   0
     Year 4   0
     Year 5   0

VII. Cash Management
  1. Size of current unencumbered,
      nondesignated cash surplus immediately
      available to cover temporary cash
      deficits for the project: 0

  2. Expected average rate of return
      from the investment of cash
      surplus over the life of the project
      to the nearest one-tenth of one percent
      (enter as a decimal): 9.5%

  3. Short-term Borrowing Rate 12.8%

DATA ENTRY FORMS

PROGRAM TITLE: PATIENT FAMILY TRAINING   Version 1

VIII. Inflation Rates

  1. Schedule of inflation rates (round to nearest one percent
      and enter as a decimal):

Category	Annual Inflation Rate
a. Equipment Replacement	12.0%
c. Operation/Maintenance	6.0%
c. User Fee Revenue	0.0%
d. Internal Appropriations	0.0%

DATA ENTRY FORMS

PROGRAM TITLE: SICKROOM EQUIPMENT   Version 1

I. General Information

  A. Current Year: 1990

  B. Final Year of Program Analysis: 1995

II. Equipment Replacement
     Year 0 ....
     Year 1   15,000
     Year 2   40,000
     Year 3   8,000
     Year 4   8,000
     Year 5   8,000

III. Operating and Maintenance Expense
     Year 0 ....
     Year 1   6,500
     Year 2   6,500
     Year 3   6,500
     Year 4   6,500
     Year 5   6,500

IV. Revenues
```
     Year 0   ..............................
     Year 1   ..............................        2,000
     Year 2   ..............................        2,000
     Year 3   ..............................        2,000
     Year 4   ..............................        2,000
     Year 5   ..............................        2,000
```

DATA ENTRY FORMS

PROGRAM TITLE: SICKROOM EQUIPMENT   Version 1

V. Grants/Gifts
```
     Initial Year  ........................        4,000
     Year 1   ..............................       4,000
     Year 2   ..............................       8,000
     Year 3   ..............................       8,000
     Year 4   ..............................       8,000
     Year 5   ..............................       8,000
```

     Number of Years Funding
     Available under a Multi-year Grant (2-5)   5

VI. Internal Appropriations
```
     Initial Year  ........................        0
     Year 1   ..............................        0
     Year 2   ..............................        0
     Year 3   ..............................        0
     Year 4   ..............................        0
     Year 5   ..............................        0
```

VII. Cash Management
      1. Size of current unencumbered,
          nondesignated cash surplus immediately
          available to cover temporary cash
          deficits for the project: 0

      2. Expected average rate of return
          from the investment of cash
          surplus over the life of the project
          to the nearest one-tenth of one percent
          (enter as a decimal): 9.5%

      3. Short-term Borrowing Rate 12.8%

DATA ENTRY FORMS

PROGRAM TITLE: SICKROOM EQUIPMENT   Version 1

VIII. Inflation Rates

1. Schedule of inflation rates (round to nearest one percent
    and enter as a decimal):

Category	Annual Inflation Rate
a. Equipment Replacement	7.0%
c. Operation/Maintenance	5.0%
c. User Fee Revenue	2.5%
d. Internal Appropriations	0.0%

Appendix 19-B

THE LAURIE GUNN SOCIETY
STANDARD REPORT FORMS

HOME HEALTH CARE

The following are the minimum requirements needed to achieve program
financial viability. All amounts shown are in addition to current
funding levels.

1. One-year gift/grant, funds received in 1989.   ($22,872)

2. One-year gift/grant, funds received in 1990.   ($25,045)

3. Zero-year gift/grant, funds received starting
                                    1989 ..   ($5,440)per year

4. Zero-year gift/grant, funds received starting
                                    1990 ..   ($5,957)per year

5. Revenues, no growth ....   ($5,957)per year

6. Revenues, 0 % annual growth: 1990 ..   ($5,640)
                                       1991 ..   ($5,809)
                                       1992 ..   ($5,984)
                                       1993 ..   ($6,163)
                                       1994 ..   ($6,348)

7. Maximum debt supported by the project ......   ($24,902)per year

8. Additional Annual Appropriations,
        0 % annual growth: 1990 ..   ($5,640)
                                       1991 ..   ($6,091)
                                       1992 ..   ($6,579)
                                       1993 ..   ($7,105)
                                       1994 ..   ($7,673)

IN-SERVICE NURSES TRAINING

The following are the minimum requirements needed to achieve program
financial viability. All amounts shown are in addition to current
funding levels.

1. One-year gift/grant, funds received in 1989.   ($63)

2. One-year gift/grant, funds received in 1990.   ($69)

3. Zero-year gift/grant, funds received starting
                                        1989 ..   ($15)per year

4. Zero-year gift/grant, funds received starting
                                        1990 ..   ($17)per year

5. Revenues, no growth ....   ($17)per year

6. Revenues, 0 % annual growth: 1990 ..   ($17)
                                     1991 ..   ($17)
                                     1992 ..   ($17)
                                     1993 ..   ($17)
                                     1994 ..   ($17)

7. Maximum debt supported by the project ......   ($0)per year

8. Additional Annual Appropriations,
        0 % annual growth: 1990 ..   ($17)
                                      1991 ..   ($17)
                                      1992 ..   ($19)
                                      1993 ..   ($20)
                                      1994 ..   ($21)

TEEN TRAINING

The following are the minimum requirements needed to achieve program
financial viability. All amounts shown are in addition to current
funding levels.

1. One-year gift/grant, funds received in 1989. $9,262

2. One-year gift/grant, funds received in 1990. $10,142

3. Zero-year gift/grant, funds received starting
                                        1989 .. $2,203 per year

4. Zero-year gift/grant, funds received starting
                                        1990 .. $2,412 per year

5. Revenues, no growth .... $2,412 per year

6. Revenues, 0 % annual growth: 1990 .. $2,412
                                     1991 .. $2,412
                                     1992 .. $2,412
                                     1993 .. $2,412
                                     1994 .. $2,412

7. Maximum debt supported by the project ......   ($10,222)per year

8. Additional Annual Appropriations,
    0 % annual growth: 1990 .. $2,412
                                      1991 .. $2,412
                                      1992 .. $2,412
                                      1993 .. $2,412
                                      1994 .. $2,412

PATIENT FAMILY TRAINING

The following are the minimum requirements needed to achieve program financial viability. All amounts shown are in addition to current funding levels.

1. One-year gift/grant, funds received in 1989. $48,911

2. One-year gift/grant, funds received in 1990. $53,558

3. Zero-year gift/grant, funds received starting
                                      1989 .. $11,633 per year

4. Zero-year gift/grant, funds received starting
                                      1990 .. $12,738 per year

5. Revenues, no growth .... $12,738 per year

6. Revenues, 0 % annual growth: 1990 .. $12,738
                                      1991 .. $12,738
                                      1992 .. $12,738
                                      1993 .. $12,738
                                      1994 .. $12,738

7. Maximum debt supported by the project ......   ($52,886)per year

8. Additional Annual Appropriations,
    0 % annual growth: 1990 .. $12,738
                                      1991 .. $12,738
                                      1992 .. $12,738
                                      1993 .. $12,738
                                      1994 .. $12,738

SICKROOM EQUIPMENT

The following are the minimum requirements needed to achieve program financial viability. All amounts shown are in addition to current funding levels.

1. One-year gift/grant, funds received in 1989. $64,141

2. One-year gift/grant, funds received in 1990. $70,235

3. Zero-year gift/grant, funds received starting
                                      1989 .. $15,255 per year

4. Zero-year gift/grant, funds received starting
                                      1990 .. $16,705 per year

5. Revenues, no growth .... $16,705 per year

6. Revenues, 0 % annual growth: 1990 .. $15,961
                                       1991 .. $16,360
                                       1992 .. $16,769
                                       1993 .. $17,189
                                       1994 .. $17,618

7. Maximum debt supported by the project ......   ($13,386)per year

8. Additional Annual Appropriations,
     0 % annual growth: 1990 .. $15,961
                                       1991 .. $15,961
                                       1992 .. $15,961
                                       1993 .. $15,961
                                       1994 .. $15,961

Appendix 19-C

THE LAURIE GUNN SOCIETY
CASH-FLOW REPORTS

HOME HEALTH CARE

OPTION: No. 1 One-year Gift/Grant, Funds Received in Current Year

YEAR	INFLATED CASH OUTFLOWS	INFLATED CASH INFLOWS	NEW FUNDING	NET CASH FLOW	BEGINNING CASH BALANCE	INTEREST RECEIVED (PAID)	ENDING CASH BALANCE
1990	$0	$16,500	(22,872)	($6,372)	$0	$0	($6,372)
1991	69,218	70,993	0	1,775	(6,372)	(605)	(5,203)
1992	73,371	75,021	0	1,650	(5,203)	(494)	(4,048)
1993	77,773	79,358	0	1,585	(4,048)	(385)	(2,847)
1994	82,440	84,029	0	1,589	(2,847)	(270)	(1,528)
1995	87,386	89,060	0	1,674	(1,528)	(145)	(0)

Because the short-term borrowing rate is higher than the
rate of return from the investment of cash surplus, the
program will incur an added interest cost of......... $585

IN-SERVICE NURSES TRAINING

OPTION: No. 1 One-year Gift/Grant, Funds Received in Current Year

YEAR	INFLATED CASH OUTFLOWS	INFLATED CASH INFLOWS	NEW FUNDING	NET CASH FLOW	BEGINNING CASH BALANCE	INTEREST RECEIVED (PAID)	ENDING CASH BALANCE
1990	$0	$0	(63)	($63)	$0	$0	($63)
1991	24,168	24,168	0	0	(63)	(6)	(69)
1992	25,618	25,618	0	(0)	(69)	(7)	(76)
1993	27,872	27,955	0	83	(76)	(7)	0
1994	28,784	28,784	0	(0)	0	0	(0)
1995	30,512	30,512	0	0	(0)	(0)	0

Because the short-term borrowing rate is higher than the
rate of return from the investment of cash surplus, the
program will incur an added interest cost of.......... $6

TEEN TRAINING

OPTION: No. 1 One-year Gift/Grant, Funds Received in Current Year

YEAR	INFLATED CASH OUTFLOWS	INFLATED CASH INFLOWS	NEW FUNDING	NET CASH FLOW	BEGINNING CASH BALANCE	INTEREST RECEIVED (PAID)	ENDING CASH BALANCE
1990	$0	$650	9,262	$9,912	$0	$0	$9,912
1991	2,688	500	0	(2,188)	9,912	942	8,666
1992	2,889	500	0	(2,389)	8,666	823	7,100
1993	3,106	500	0	(2,606)	7,100	674	5,169
1994	3,339	500	0	(2,839)	5,169	491	2,821
1995	3,589	500	0	(3,089)	2,821	268	(0)

Because the short-term borrowing rate is higher than the rate of return from the investment of cash surplus, the program will incur an added interest cost of............ $0

PATIENT FAMILY TRAINING

OPTION: No. 1 One-year Gift/Grant, Funds Received in Current Year

YEAR	INFLATED CASH OUTFLOWS	INFLATED CASH INFLOWS	NEW FUNDING	NET CASH * FLOW	BEGINNING CASH BALANCE	INTEREST RECEIVED (PAID)	ENDING CASH BALANCE
1990	$0	$4,200	48,911	$53,111	$0	$0	$53,111
1991	14,416	2,250	0	(12,166)	53,111	5,046	45,991
1992	15,281	2,250	0	(13,031)	45,991	4,369	37,329
1993	16,198	2,250	0	(13,948)	37,329	3,546	26,928
1994	17,170	2,250	0	(14,920)	26,928	2,558	14,566
1995	18,200	2,250	0	(15,950)	14,566	1,384	0

Because the short-term borrowing rate is higher than the
rate of return from the investment of cash surplus, the
program will incur an added interest cost of........ $0

SICKROOM EQUIPMENT

OPTION: No. 1 One-year Gift/Grant, Funds Received in Current Year

YEAR	INFLATED CASH OUTFLOWS	INFLATED CASH INFLOWS	NEW FUNDING	NET CASH FLOW	BEGINNING CASH BALANCE	INTEREST RECEIVED (PAID)	ENDING CASH BALANCE
1990	$0	$4,000	64,141	$68,141	$0	$0	$68,141
1991	22,875	6,050	0	(16,825)	68,141	6,473	57,790
1992	52,962	10,101	0	(42,861)	57,790	5,490	20,419
1993	17,325	10,154	0	(7,171)	20,419	1,940	15,187
1994	18,387	10,208	0	(8,180)	15,187	1,443	8,451
1995	19,516	10,263	0	(9,253)	8,451	803	0

Because the short-term borrowing rate is higher than the rate of return from the investment of cash surplus, the program will incur an added interest cost of.......... $0

Appendix A

Present Value of $1: PVIF = $1/(1 + k)^t$

Period	1%	2%	3%	4%	5%	6%	7%	8%	9%	10%	12%	14%	15%	16%	18%	20%	24%	28%	32%	36%
1	.9901	.9804	.9709	.9615	.9524	.9434	.9346	.9259	.9174	.9091	.8929	.8772	.8696	.8621	.8475	.8333	.8065	.7813	.7576	.7353
2	.9803	.9612	.9426	.9246	.9070	.8900	.8734	.8573	.8417	.8264	.7972	.7695	.7561	.7432	.7182	.6944	.6504	.6104	.5739	.5407
3	.9706	.9423	.9151	.8890	.8638	.8396	.8163	.7938	.7722	.7513	.7118	.6750	.6575	.6407	.6086	.5787	.5245	.4768	.4348	.3975
4	.9610	.9238	.8885	.8548	.8227	.7921	.7629	.7350	.7084	.6830	.6355	.5921	.5718	.5523	.5158	.4823	.4230	.3725	.3294	.2923
5	.9515	.9057	.8626	.8219	.7835	.7473	.7130	.6806	.6499	.6209	.5674	.5194	.4972	.4761	.4371	.4019	.3411	.2910	.2495	.2149
6	.9420	.8880	.8375	.7903	.7462	.7050	.6663	.6302	.5963	.5645	.5066	.4556	.4323	.4104	.3704	.3349	.2751	.2274	.1890	.1580
7	.9327	.8706	.8131	.7599	.7107	.6651	.6227	.5835	.5470	.5132	.4523	.3996	.3759	.3538	.3139	.2791	.2218	.1776	.1432	.1162
8	.9235	.8535	.7894	.7307	.6768	.6274	.5820	.5403	.5019	.4665	.4039	.3506	.3269	.3050	.2660	.2326	.1789	.1388	.1085	.0854
9	.9143	.8368	.7664	.7026	.6446	.5919	.5439	.5002	.4604	.4241	.3606	.3075	.2843	.2630	.2255	.1938	.1443	.1084	.0822	.0628
10	.9053	.8203	.7441	.6756	.6139	.5584	.5083	.4632	.4224	.3855	.3220	.2697	.2472	.2267	.1911	.1615	.1164	.0847	.0623	.0462
11	.8963	.8043	.7224	.6496	.5847	.5268	.4751	.4289	.3875	.3505	.2875	.2366	.2149	.1954	.1619	.1346	.0938	.0662	.0472	.0340
12	.8874	.7885	.7014	.6246	.5568	.4970	.4440	.3971	.3555	.3186	.2567	.2076	.1869	.1685	.1372	.1122	.0757	.0517	.0357	.0250
13	.8787	.7730	.6810	.6006	.5303	.4688	.4150	.3677	.3262	.2897	.2292	.1821	.1625	.1452	.1163	.0935	.0610	.0404	.0271	.0184
14	.8700	.7579	.6611	.5775	.5051	.4423	.3878	.3405	.2992	.2633	.2046	.1597	.1413	.1252	.0985	.0779	.0492	.0316	.0205	.0135
15	.8613	.7430	.6419	.5553	.4810	.4173	.3624	.3152	.2745	.2394	.1827	.1401	.1229	.1079	.0835	.0649	.0397	.0247	.0155	.0099
16	.8528	.7284	.6232	.5339	.4581	.3936	.3387	.2919	.2519	.2176	.1631	.1229	.1069	.0930	.0708	.0541	.0320	.0193	.0118	.0073
17	.8444	.7142	.6050	.5134	.4363	.3714	.3166	.2703	.2311	.1978	.1456	.1078	.0929	.0802	.0600	.0451	.0258	.0150	.0089	.0054
18	.8360	.7002	.5874	.4936	.4155	.3503	.2959	.2502	.2120	.1799	.1300	.0946	.0808	.0691	.0508	.0376	.0208	.0118	.0068	.0039
19	.8277	.6864	.5703	.4746	.3957	.3305	.2765	.2317	.1945	.1635	.1161	.0829	.0703	.0596	.0431	.0313	.0168	.0092	.0051	.0029
20	.8195	.6730	.5537	.4564	.3769	.3118	.2584	.2145	.1784	.1486	.1037	.0728	.0611	.0514	.0365	.0261	.0135	.0072	.0039	.0021
25	.7798	.6095	.4776	.3751	.2953	.2330	.1842	.1460	.1160	.0923	.0588	.0378	.0304	.0245	.0160	.0105	.0046	.0021	.0010	.0005
30	.7419	.5521	.4120	.3083	.2314	.1741	.1314	.0994	.0754	.0573	.0334	.0196	.0151	.0116	.0070	.0042	.0016	.0006	.0002	.0001
40	.6717	.4529	.3066	.2083	.1420	.0972	.0668	.0460	.0318	.0221	.0107	.0053	.0037	.0026	.0013	.0007	.0002	.0001	*	*
50	.6080	.3715	.2281	.1407	.0872	.0543	.0339	.0213	.0134	.0085	.0035	.0014	.0009	.0006	.0003	.0001	*	*	*	*
60	.5504	.3048	.1697	.0951	.0535	.0303	.0173	.0099	.0057	.0033	.0011	.0004	.0002	.0001	*	*	*	*	*	*

*The factor is zero to four decimal places.

Appendix

Appendix B

Present Value of an Annuity of \$1 Per Period for n Period: $\text{PVIFA} = \sum_{t=1}^{n} \dfrac{1}{(1+k)^t}$

$$= \dfrac{1 - \dfrac{1}{(1+k)^n}}{k}$$

Number of payments	1%	2%	3%	4%	5%	6%	7%	8%	9%	10%	12%	14%	15%	16%	18%	20%	24%	28%	32%
1	0.9901	0.9804	0.9709	0.9615	0.9524	0.9434	0.9346	0.9259	0.9174	0.9091	0.8929	0.8772	0.8696	0.8621	0.8475	0.8333	0.8065	0.7813	0.7576
2	1.9704	1.9416	1.9135	1.8861	1.8594	1.8334	1.8080	1.7833	1.7591	1.7355	1.6901	1.6467	1.6257	1.6052	1.5656	1.5278	1.4568	1.3916	1.3315
3	2.9410	2.8839	2.8286	2.7751	2.7232	2.6730	2.6243	2.5771	2.5313	2.4869	2.4018	2.3216	2.2832	2.2459	2.1743	2.1065	1.9813	1.8684	1.7663
4	3.9020	3.8077	3.7171	3.6299	3.5460	3.4651	3.3872	3.3121	3.2397	3.1699	3.0373	2.9137	2.8550	2.7982	2.6901	2.5887	2.4043	2.2410	2.0957
5	4.8534	4.7135	4.5797	4.4518	4.3295	4.2124	4.1002	3.9927	3.8897	3.7908	3.6048	3.4331	3.3522	3.2743	3.1272	2.9906	2.7454	2.5320	2.3452
6	5.7955	5.6014	5.4172	5.2421	5.0757	4.9173	4.7665	4.6229	4.4859	4.3553	4.1114	3.8887	3.7845	3.6847	3.4976	3.3255	3.0205	2.7594	2.5342
7	6.7282	6.4720	6.2303	6.0021	5.7864	5.5824	5.3893	5.2064	5.0330	4.8684	4.5638	4.2883	4.1604	4.0386	3.8115	3.6046	3.2423	2.9370	2.6775
8	7.6517	7.3255	7.0197	6.7327	6.4632	6.2098	5.9713	5.7466	5.5348	5.3349	4.9676	4.6389	4.4873	4.3436	4.0776	3.8372	3.4212	3.0758	2.7860
9	8.5660	8.1622	7.7861	7.4353	7.1078	6.8017	6.5152	6.2469	5.9952	5.7590	5.3282	4.9464	4.7716	4.6065	4.3030	4.0310	3.5655	3.1842	2.8681
10	9.4713	8.9826	8.5302	8.1109	7.7217	7.3601	7.0236	6.7101	6.4177	6.1446	5.6502	5.2161	5.0188	4.8332	4.4941	4.1925	3.6819	3.2689	2.9304
11	10.3676	9.7868	9.2526	8.7605	8.3064	7.8869	7.4987	7.1390	6.8052	6.4951	5.9377	5.4527	5.2337	5.0286	4.6560	4.3271	3.7757	3.3351	2.9776
12	11.2551	10.5753	9.9540	9.3851	8.8633	8.3838	7.9427	7.5361	7.1607	6.8137	6.1944	5.6603	5.4206	5.1971	4.7932	4.4392	3.8514	3.3868	3.0133
13	12.1337	11.3484	10.6350	9.9856	9.3936	8.8527	8.3577	7.9038	7.4869	7.1034	6.4235	5.8424	5.5831	5.3423	4.9095	4.5327	3.9124	3.4272	3.0404
14	13.0037	12.1062	11.2961	10.5631	9.8986	9.2950	8.7455	8.2442	7.7862	7.3667	6.6282	6.0021	5.7245	5.4675	5.0081	4.6106	3.9616	3.4587	3.0609
15	13.8651	12.8493	11.9379	11.1184	10.3797	9.7122	9.1079	8.5595	8.0607	7.6061	6.8109	6.1422	5.8474	5.5755	5.0916	4.6755	4.0013	3.4834	3.0764
16	14.7179	13.5777	12.5611	11.6523	10.8378	10.1059	9.4466	8.8514	8.3126	7.8237	6.9740	6.2651	5.9542	5.6685	5.1624	4.7296	4.0333	3.5026	3.0882
17	15.5623	14.2919	13.1661	12.1657	11.2741	10.4773	9.7632	9.1216	8.5436	8.0216	7.1196	6.3729	6.0472	5.7487	5.2223	4.7746	4.0591	3.5177	3.0971
18	16.3983	14.9920	13.7535	12.6593	11.6896	10.8276	10.0591	9.3719	8.7556	8.2014	7.2497	6.4674	6.1280	5.8178	5.2732	4.8122	4.0799	3.5294	3.1039
19	17.2260	15.6785	14.3238	13.1339	12.0853	11.1581	10.3356	9.6036	8.9501	8.3649	7.3658	6.5504	6.1982	5.8775	5.3162	4.8435	4.0967	3.5386	3.1090
20	18.0456	16.3514	14.8775	13.5903	12.4622	11.4699	10.5940	9.8181	9.1285	8.5136	7.4694	6.6231	6.2593	5.9288	5.3527	4.8696	4.1103	3.5458	3.1129
25	22.0232	19.5235	17.4131	15.6221	14.0939	12.7834	11.6536	10.6748	9.8226	9.0770	7.8431	6.8729	6.4641	6.0971	5.4669	4.9476	4.1474	3.5640	3.1220
30	25.8077	22.3965	19.6004	17.2920	15.3725	13.7648	12.4090	11.2578	10.2737	9.4269	8.0552	7.0027	6.5660	6.1772	5.5168	4.9789	4.1601	3.5693	3.1242
40	32.8347	27.3555	23.1148	19.7928	17.1591	15.0463	13.3317	11.9246	10.7574	9.7791	8.2438	7.1050	6.6418	6.2335	5.5482	4.9966	4.1659	3.5712	3.1250
50	39.1961	31.4236	25.7298	21.4822	18.2559	15.7619	13.8007	12.2335	10.9617	9.9148	8.3045	7.1327	6.6605	6.2463	5.5541	4.9995	4.1666	3.5714	3.1250
60	44.9550	34.7609	27.6756	22.6235	18.9293	16.1614	14.0392	12.3766	11.0480	9.9672	8.3240	7.1401	6.6651	6.2482	5.5553	4.9999	4.1667	3.5714	3.1250

Appendix C

Future Value of $1 at the End of n Periods: $FVIF_{k,n} = (1 = k)_n$

Period	1%	2%	3%	4%	5%	6%	7%	8%	9%	10%	12%	14%	15%	16%	18%	20%	24%	28%	32%	36%
1	1.0100	1.0200	1.0300	1.0400	1.0500	1.0600	1.0700	1.0800	1.0900	1.1000	1.1200	1.1400	1.1500	1.1600	1.1800	1.2000	1.2400	1.2800	1.3200	1.3600
2	1.0201	1.0404	1.0609	1.0816	1.1025	1.1236	1.1449	1.1664	1.1881	1.2100	1.2544	1.2996	1.3225	1.3456	1.3924	1.4400	1.5376	1.6384	1.7424	1.8496
3	1.0303	1.0612	1.0927	1.1249	1.1576	1.1910	1.2250	1.2597	1.2950	1.3310	1.4049	1.4815	1.5209	1.5609	1.6430	1.7280	1.9066	2.0972	2.3000	2.5155
4	1.0406	1.0824	1.1255	1.1699	1.2155	1.2625	1.3108	1.3605	1.4116	1.4641	1.5735	1.6890	1.7490	1.8106	1.9388	2.0736	2.3642	2.6844	3.0360	3.4210
5	1.0510	1.1041	1.1593	1.2167	1.2763	1.3382	1.4026	1.4693	1.5386	1.6105	1.7623	1.9254	2.0114	2.1003	2.2878	2.4883	2.9316	3.4360	4.0075	4.6526
6	1.0615	1.1262	1.1941	1.2653	1.3401	1.4185	1.5007	1.5869	1.6771	1.7716	1.9738	2.1950	2.3131	2.4364	2.6996	2.9860	3.6352	4.3980	5.2899	6.3275
7	1.0721	1.1487	1.2299	1.3159	1.4071	1.5036	1.6058	1.7138	1.8280	1.9487	2.2107	2.5023	2.6600	2.8262	3.1855	3.5832	4.5077	5.6295	6.9826	8.6054
8	1.0829	1.1717	1.2668	1.3686	1.4775	1.5938	1.7182	1.8509	1.9926	2.1436	2.4760	2.8526	3.0590	3.2784	3.7589	4.2998	5.5895	7.2058	9.2170	11.703
9	1.0937	1.1951	1.3048	1.4233	1.5513	1.6895	1.8385	1.9990	2.1719	2.3579	2.7731	3.2519	3.5179	3.8030	4.4355	5.1598	6.9310	9.2234	12.166	15.916
10	1.1046	1.2190	1.3439	1.4802	1.6289	1.7908	1.9672	2.1589	2.3674	2.5937	3.1058	3.7072	4.0456	4.4114	5.2338	6.1917	8.5944	11.805	16.059	21.646
11	1.1157	1.2434	1.3842	1.5395	1.7103	1.8983	2.1049	2.3316	2.5804	2.8531	3.4785	4.2262	4.6524	5.1173	6.1759	7.4301	10.657	15.111	21.198	29.439
12	1.1268	1.2682	1.4258	1.6010	1.7959	2.0122	2.2522	2.5182	2.8127	3.1384	3.9960	4.8179	5.3502	5.9360	7.2876	8.9161	13.214	19.342	27.982	40.037
13	1.1381	1.2936	1.4685	1.6651	1.8856	2.1329	2.4098	2.7196	3.0658	3.4523	4.3635	5.4924	6.1528	6.8858	8.5994	10.699	16.386	24.758	36.937	54.451
14	1.1495	1.3195	1.5126	1.7317	1.9799	2.2609	2.5785	2.9372	3.3417	3.7975	4.8871	6.2613	7.0757	7.9875	10.147	12.839	20.319	31.691	48.756	74.053
15	1.1610	1.3459	1.5580	1.8009	2.0789	2.3966	2.7590	3.1722	3.6425	4.1772	5.4736	7.1379	8.1371	9.2655	11.973	15.407	25.195	40.564	64.358	100.71
16	1.1726	1.3728	1.6047	1.8730	2.1829	2.5404	2.9522	3.4259	3.9703	4.5950	6.1304	8.1372	9.3576	10.748	14.129	18.488	31.242	51.923	84.953	136.96
17	1.1843	1.4002	1.6528	1.9479	2.2920	2.6928	3.1588	3.7000	4.3276	5.0545	6.8660	9.2765	10.761	12.467	16.672	22.186	38.740	66.461	112.13	186.27
18	1.1961	1.4282	1.7024	2.0258	2.4066	2.8543	3.3799	3.9960	4.7171	5.5599	7.6900	10.575	12.375	14.462	19.673	26.623	48.038	85.070	148.02	253.33
19	1.2081	1.4568	1.7535	2.1068	2.5270	3.0256	3.6165	4.3157	5.1417	6.1159	8.6128	12.055	14.231	16.776	23.214	31.948	59.567	108.89	195.39	344.53
20	1.2202	1.4859	1.8061	2.1911	2.6533	3.2071	3.8697	4.6610	5.6044	6.7275	9.6463	13.743	16.366	19.460	27.393	38.337	73.864	139.37	257.91	468.57
21	1.2324	1.5157	1.8603	2.2788	2.7860	3.3996	4.1406	5.0338	6.1088	7.4002	10.803	15.667	18.821	22.574	32.323	46.005	91.591	178.40	340.44	637.26
22	1.2447	1.5460	1.9161	2.3699	2.9253	3.6035	4.4304	5.4365	6.6586	8.1403	12.100	17.861	21.644	26.186	38.142	55.206	113.57	228.35	449.39	866.67
23	1.2572	1.5769	1.9736	2.4647	3.0715	3.8197	4.7405	5.8715	7.2579	8.9543	13.552	20.361	24.891	30.376	45.007	66.247	140.83	292.30	593.19	1178.6
24	1.2697	1.6084	2.0328	2.5633	3.2251	4.0489	5.0724	6.3412	7.9111	9.8497	15.178	23.212	28.625	35.236	53.108	79.496	174.63	374.14	783.02	1602.9
25	1.2824	1.6406	2.0938	2.6658	3.3864	4.2919	5.4274	6.8485	8.6231	10.834	17.000	26.461	32.918	40.874	62.668	95.396	216.54	478.90	1033.5	2180.0
26	1.2953	1.6734	2.1566	2.7725	3.5557	4.5494	5.8074	7.3964	9.3992	11.918	19.040	30.166	37.856	47.414	73.948	114.47	268.51	612.99	1364.3	2964.9
27	1.3082	1.7069	2.2213	2.8834	3.7335	4.8223	6.2139	7.9881	10.245	13.110	21.324	34.389	43.535	55.000	87.259	137.37	332.95	784.63	1800.9	4032.2
28	1.3213	1.7410	2.2879	2.9987	3.9201	5.1117	6.6488	8.6271	11.167	14.421	23.883	39.204	50.065	63.800	102.96	164.84	412.86	1004.3	2377.2	5483.8
29	1.3345	1.7758	2.3566	3.1187	4.1161	5.4184	7.1143	9.3173	12.172	15.863	26.749	44.693	57.575	74.008	121.50	197.81	511.95	1285.5	3137.9	7458.0
30	1.3478	1.8114	2.4273	3.2434	4.3219	5.7435	7.6123	10.062	13.267	17.449	29.959	50.950	66.211	85.849	143.37	237.37	634.81	1645.5	4142.0	10143.
40	1.4889	2.2080	3.2620	4.8010	7.0400	10.285	14.974	21.724	31.409	45.259	93.050	188.88	267.86	378.72	750.37	1469.7	5455.9	19426	66520.	*
50	1.6446	2.6916	4.3839	7.1067	11.467	18.420	29.457	46.901	74.357	117.39	289.00	700.23	1083.6	1670.7	3927.3	9100.4	46890.	*	*	*
60	1.8167	3.2810	5.8916	10.519	18.679	32.987	57.946	101.25	176.03	304.48	897.59	2595.9	4383.9	7370.1	20555	56347.	*	*	*	*

*FVIF > 99,999

Appendix D

Sum of an Annuity of $1 Per Period for n Periods: $\text{FVIFA}_{k,n} = \sum_{t=1}^{n} (1 \times k)^{t-1}$

$$= \frac{(1+k)^n - 1}{k}$$

Number of Periods	1%	2%	3%	4%	5%	6%	7%	8%	9%	10%	12%	14%	15%	16%	18%	20%	24%	28%	32%	36%
1	1.0000	1.0000	1.0000	1.0000	1.0000	1.0000	1.0000	1.0000	1.0000	1.0000	1.0000	1.0000	1.0000	1.0000	1.0000	1.0000	1.0000	1.0000	1.0000	1.0000
2	2.0100	2.0200	2.0300	2.0400	2.0500	2.0600	2.0700	2.0800	2.0900	2.1000	2.1200	2.1400	2.1500	2.1600	2.1800	2.2000	2.2400	2.2800	2.3200	2.3600
3	3.0301	3.0604	3.0909	3.1216	3.1525	3.1836	3.2149	3.2464	3.2781	3.3100	3.3744	3.4396	3.4725	3.5056	3.5724	3.6400	3.7776	3.9184	4.0624	4.2096
4	4.0604	4.1216	4.1836	4.2465	4.3101	4.3746	4.4399	4.5061	4.5731	4.6410	4.7793	4.9211	4.9934	5.0665	5.2154	5.3680	5.6842	6.0156	6.3624	6.7251
5	5.1010	5.2040	5.3091	5.4163	5.5256	5.6371	5.7507	5.8666	5.9847	6.1051	6.3528	6.6101	6.7424	6.8771	7.1542	7.4416	8.0484	8.6999	9.3983	10.146
6	6.1520	6.3081	6.4684	6.6330	6.8019	6.9753	7.1533	7.3359	7.5233	7.7156	8.1152	8.5355	8.7537	8.9775	9.4420	9.9299	10.980	12.135	13.405	14.798
7	7.2135	7.4343	7.6625	7.8983	8.1420	8.3938	8.6540	8.9228	9.2004	9.4872	10.089	10.730	11.066	11.413	12.141	12.915	14.615	16.533	18.695	21.126
8	8.2857	8.5830	8.8923	9.2142	9.5491	9.8975	10.259	10.636	11.028	11.435	12.299	13.232	13.726	14.240	15.327	16.499	19.122	22.163	25.678	29.731
9	9.3685	9.7546	10.159	10.582	11.026	11.491	11.978	12.487	13.021	13.579	14.775	16.085	16.785	17.518	19.086	20.798	24.712	29.369	34.895	41.435
10	10.462	10.949	11.463	12.006	12.577	13.180	13.816	14.486	15.192	15.937	17.548	19.337	20.303	21.321	23.521	25.958	31.643	38.592	47.061	57.351
11	11.566	12.168	12.807	13.486	14.206	14.971	15.783	16.645	17.560	18.531	20.654	23.044	24.349	25.732	28.755	32.150	40.237	50.398	63.121	78.998
12	12.682	13.412	14.192	15.025	15.917	16.869	17.888	18.977	20.140	21.384	24.133	27.270	29.001	30.850	34.931	39.580	50.894	65.510	84.320	108.43
13	13.809	14.680	15.617	16.626	17.713	18.882	20.140	21.495	22.953	24.522	28.029	32.088	34.351	36.786	42.218	48.496	64.109	84.852	112.30	148.47
14	14.947	15.973	17.086	18.291	19.598	21.015	22.550	24.214	26.019	27.975	32.392	37.581	40.504	43.672	50.818	59.195	80.496	109.61	149.23	202.92
15	16.096	17.293	18.598	20.023	21.578	23.276	25.129	27.152	29.360	31.772	37.279	43.842	47.580	51.659	60.965	72.035	100.81	141.30	197.99	276.97
16	17.257	18.639	20.156	21.824	23.657	25.672	27.888	30.324	33.003	35.949	42.753	50.980	55.717	60.925	72.939	87.442	126.01	181.86	262.35	377.69
17	18.430	20.012	21.761	23.697	25.840	28.212	30.840	33.750	36.973	40.544	48.883	59.117	65.075	71.673	87.068	105.93	157.25	233.79	347.30	514.66
18	19.614	21.412	23.414	25.645	28.132	30.905	33.999	37.450	41.301	45.599	55.749	68.394	75.836	84.140	103.74	128.11	195.99	300.25	459.44	700.93
19	20.810	22.840	25.116	27.671	30.539	33.760	37.379	41.446	46.018	51.159	63.439	78.969	88.211	98.603	123.41	154.74	244.03	385.32	607.47	954.27
20	22.019	24.297	26.870	29.778	33.066	36.785	40.995	45.762	51.160	57.275	72.052	91.024	102.44	115.37	146.62	186.68	303.60	494.21	802.86	1298.8
21	23.239	25.783	28.676	31.969	35.719	39.992	44.865	50.422	56.764	64.002	81.698	104.76	118.81	134.84	174.02	225.02	377.46	633.59	1060.7	1767.3
22	24.471	27.299	30.536	34.248	38.505	43.392	49.005	55.456	62.873	71.402	92.502	120.43	137.63	157.41	206.34	271.03	469.05	811.99	1401.2	2404.6
23	25.716	28.845	32.452	36.617	41.430	46.995	53.436	60.893	69.531	79.543	104.60	138.29	159.27	183.60	244.48	326.23	582.62	1040.3	1850.6	3271.3
24	26.973	30.421	34.426	39.082	44.502	50.815	58.176	66.789	76.789	88.497	118.15	158.65	184.16	213.97	289.49	392.48	723.46	1332.6	2443.8	4449.9
25	28.243	32.030	36.459	41.645	47.727	54.864	63.249	73.105	84.700	98.347	133.33	181.87	212.79	249.21	342.60	471.98	898.09	1706.8	3226.8	6052.9

26	29.525	33.670	38.553	44.311	51.113	59.156	68.676	79.954	93.323	109.18	150.33	208.33	245.71	290.08	405.27	567.37	1114.6	2185.7	4260.4	8233.0
27	30.820	35.344	40.709	47.084	54.669	63.705	74.483	87.350	102.72	121.09	169.37	238.49	283.56	337.50	479.22	681.85	1383.1	2798.7	5624.7	11197.9
28	32.129	37.051	42.930	49.967	58.402	68.528	80.697	95.338	112.96	134.20	190.69	272.88	327.10	392.50	566.48	819.22	1716.0	3583.3	7425.6	15230.2
29	33.450	38.792	45.218	52.966	62.322	73.639	87.346	103.96	124.13	148.63	214.58	312.09	377.16	456.30	669.44	984.06	2128.9	4587.6	9802.9	20714.1
30	34.784	40.568	47.575	56.084	66.438	79.058	94.460	113.28	136.30	164.49	241.33	356.78	434.74	530.31	790.94	1181.8	2640.9	5873.2	12940	28172.2
40	48.886	60.402	75.401	95.025	120.79	154.76	199.63	259.05	337.88	442.59	767.09	1342.0	1779.0	2360.7	4163.2	7343.8	22728	69377.	*	*
50	64.463	84.579	112.79	152.66	209.34	290.33	406.52	573.76	815.08	1163.9	2400.0	4994.5	7217.7	10435	21813	45497.	*	*	*	*
60	81.669	114.05	163.05	237.99	353.58	533.12	813.52	1253.2	1944.7	3034.8	7471.6	18535	29219	46057	*	*	*	*	*	*

*FVIFA > 99,999

Glossary

Acceleration clause: A clause in a bond indenture that permits the creditor to demand immediate repayment of the unpaid principal amount if the borrower violates other specified clauses.

Accountability: *See* **Dollar accountability** and **Operational accountability**.

Accounts receivable: Amounts due from debtors arising out of the extension of open account credit, usually in connection with the sale of goods or services to customers.

Accrual accounting: Accounting systems that record business transactions that result from the exchange of cash and financial assets and claims.

ACP: *See* **Average collection period**.

Amortization: The process of liquidating a loan on an installment basis or writing off an intangible asset with periodic charges against revenues.

Annuity: Fixed dollar amounts paid at regular intervals over a specified number of years.

Appropriation budget: *See* **Fixed budget**.

Auditor's opinion: An opinion rendered by an independent auditor regarding the method in which the organization's accounting records have been maintained and the summary financial statements presented. Different types of opinions include: clean opinion, in which no material fault is found; qualified opinion, in which certain areas of the accounting records were untested; and denial, in which material defects in the records were observed that prevent the auditor from rendering a clean opinion.

Average collection period: The ratio of receivables to average daily revenues, or the time required to collect the average account outstanding.

Balance sheet: An accounting statement showing the amounts and nature of an organization's assets, liabilities, and fund balance on a given date.

Balloon payment: The final installment on a loan that, by agreement, is larger than the normal payment and is equal to the unpaid principal plus accumulated interest remaining at maturity.

Bankruptcy: The legal procedure for reorganizing or liquidating an organization that has failed to remain solvent or is in danger of becoming insolvent.

Bond: A long-term debt instrument that is usually marketable.

Bond indenture: The formal written agreement between the issuer of the bond and the bondholders.

Book value: The value of an asset, liability, or fund balance account as listed on a balance sheet. The book value of an asset is its cost less accumulated depreciation or allowances for bad debts, etc. The book value of a liability is its actual liquidating value.

Break-even analysis: A technique for analyzing the relationships among costs, volume, and "profits," where costs are defined in terms of both their fixed and variable components. Also, any similar analysis in which the objective is to determine the level of operation that produces zero profits or cash flows.

Budgets: Planning documents used by an organization, generally prepared and presented in standard accounting formats and emphasizing dollar revenues, expenditures, and costs. *See* **Capital budget, Cash budget, Flexible budget,** and **Fixed budget**.

CAF: *See* **Compound annuity factor**.

Call premium: The difference between the call price of a bond and its face value.

Call price: The price that must be paid to the bondholder by the issuing organization to call the bond prior to its maturity. The call price is the sum of the face value of the bond plus a call premium.

Capital asset: A relatively long-lived asset purchased for purposes other than immediate resale or conversion into cash in the ordinary course of operations.

Capital budget: An accounting document detailing certain information about one or more capital assets scheduled for purchase or construction during the current accounting period.

Capital lease: *See* **Financial lease.**

Capital structure: The sum or the relative proportions of the long-term sources of funds used to finance an organization, including long-term debt, leases, and equity (fund balance).

Capitalization: A method of accounting for fixed assets in which the cost of the asset is recorded on the balance sheet and is subsequently written down by any one of several methods. Also, the process by which the value of leased property is placed on the balance sheet.

Capitalization rate: The interest rate used to calculate the capitalized value of a lease for balance sheet reporting purposes. The capitalization rate is the smaller of the implicit lease cost and the organization's long-term borrowing rate. *See also* **Discount rate.**

Cash basis accounting: Accounting systems that only record transactions that affect cash.

Cash discount: A discount from the total amount of the invoice offered by a supplier to its trade customers for prompt payment of amounts due.

Cash discount: A discount from the total amount of the invoice offered by a supplier to its trade customers for prompt payment of amounts due.d

Cash flow: The sum of the excess of revenues over expenses plus the noncash charges against revenues over a given period.

Certificate of deposit: A document issued by a commercial bank or savings and loan association in evidence of funds placed on deposit for a specified period at a particular rate of interest.

Charitable trust: A collection of financial assets or real property administered by a trustee for charitable purposes.

CIF: *See* **Compound interest factor.**

Clean opinion: *See* **Auditor's opinion.**

Commercial paper: Short-term, unsecured, marketable promissory notes issued by the larger, more creditworthy firms to supply their temporary working capital needs.

Commitment fee: A fee paid to a lender to guarantee the availability of funds under a formal line of credit.

Compensating balances: A required minimum demand deposit balance that must be maintained with a commercial bank as consideration for credit extension and services rendered to the customer by the bank.

Compound annuity factor: The compound sum of one dollar per period paid over a given number of periods at a given rate of interest. The compound annuity factor is calculated using the general formula $[(1-r)^t - 1]/r$, where r is the interest rate and t is the number of periods. It is abbreviated **CAF**.

Compound interest: Interest earned in one period added to the principal amount, on which interest is earned in subsequent periods.

Compound interest factor: The future value of one dollar, compounded over a given number of periods at a given interest rate. The compound interest factor is calculated using the general formula $(1 + r)^t$, where r is the interest rate and t is the number of compounding periods. It is abbreviated **CIF**.

Concentration banking: A method of accelerating funds flows from accounts and pledges receivable by establishing multiple centers for billing and collecting customer or donor payments.

Corporate bonds: Long-term debt instruments issued by a corporation.

Corporation: A legal form of business organization which has as its main characteristics perpetual life and limited liability for its owners or members.

Cost-benefit analysis: A technique used in the professional evaluation of capital expenditures in which the present values of a project's cost and benefits are compared. Project costs and benefits are defined broadly to include both cash flows and utility.

Cost of social capital: The discount rate used in the professional evaluation of capital expenditures. It is the opportunity cost of investing in social programs.

Covenants: Protective clauses included in loan agreements and bond indentures designed to limit the risks of extending credit to the borrower.

Current assets: Cash and other assets that normally will be converted into cash in the ordinary course of business within one accounting period.

Current liabilities: Short-term debt, lease payments, and that portion of long-term debt payable in the current accounting period.

Current ratio: Current assets divided by current liabilities.

Cutback management: The process of eliminating programs or reducing the scope of programs in order to avoid cash-flow deficits in an organization.

Debenture: An unsecured, long-term promissory note backed by the general credit of an organization.

Default risk: The risk a security holder is exposed to as a result of the likelihood of the debtor's becoming bankrupt and the security being in default.

Denial: *See* **Auditor's opinion**.

Depreciation: A noncash expense charged against revenue, used to write off the cost of a fixed asset over its useful life.

Direct lobbying: Attempting to influence legislation by dealing directly with members of legislative bodies or government officials.

Direct placement: The sale of a new bond issue to a single investor through direct negotiation between the issuing organization and the investor.

Discounting: The process of calculating the present value of future cash flows at some predetermined compound interest rate.

Discount rate: The interest rate used in the discounting process, generally defined as either the cost of funds, the investment rate, or the cost of social capital. It is sometimes called the **Capitalization rate**.

Dollar accountability: The basis used in accounting systems of nonprofit organizations to ensure that the money and assets employed by the organization can be fully accounted for.

Economic order quantity: Optimum amount of periodic inventory purchase that will minimize total inventory cost. It is abbreviated **EOQ**.

Endowment fund: A fund used to account for all contributions of cash and other assets on which donors have placed restrictions as to either the use of the asset or the income derived from the investment of the asset.

EOQ: *See* **Economic order quantity**.

Face value: The dollar value shown on the "face" of a bond certificate, indicating the principal amount payable at maturity.

Factor: A financial institution that extends credit to businesses and organizations by purchasing (and subsequently collecting for its own account) accounts and pledges receivable.

Financial lease: A lease arrangement in which the lessee agrees to make a certain number of periodic payments in exchange for the use of an asset. It is also known as a **Capital lease**.

Financial statements: Accounting statements prepared at the end of an accounting period or subperiod, including a balance sheet; a statement of revenues, expenditures, and changes in fund balance; and a statement of changes in financial position.

Financial viability: The status achieved when a capital expenditure or noncapital project is able to operate as initially conceived without consuming more resources than originally were allocated to its support.

Fiscal triage: An approach to managing financial distress in nonprofit organizations.

Fixed assets: Noncash assets, including buildings, equipment, furniture, and so forth, that are not completely converted into cash or used up in one accounting period.

Fixed budget: A system of budgeting in which revenues and expenditures are fixed for the duration of the budget period. It is also called an **Appropriation budget**.

Fixed costs: Costs that do not vary with the level of economic activity within the organization in the short run.

Fixed rate of return: An approach to endowment management that fixes the spending rate out of the endowment and reserves the remaining income for reinvestment purposes.

Flexible budget: A budget system in which revenue and expenditure estimates are recorded for the budget period as guides to operations, but both can be, and are expected to be, changed as a result of changes that are likely to occur in the organization's operations.

Float: The amount of cash in the process of being collected in the bank check clearing system.

Functional discount: A discount offered to different types of customers based on their place in the distribution chain. It is also called a **Trade discount**.

Fund: One of several accounting entities maintained under a fund accounting system, the most common of which are operating fund, unrestricted investment fund, plant fund, and endowment fund.

Fund accounting: A branch of accounting designed for use by nonprofit organizations, governments, and government agencies in which the accounting entity is viewed as a collection of separate "funds."

Fund balance: The difference between the assets and liabilities of a nonprofit organization, as shown in the balance sheet. The equivalent of the equity portion of the balance sheet of a profit-seeking business.

Goal programming: A mathematical programming technique useful for allocating resources among competing alternative uses on the basis of qualitative criteria.

Grass roots lobbying: Attempting to influence legislation by publicly advocating a position or by urging the public to engage in direct lobbying.

Immediate write-off: A method of accounting for fixed assets in which the cost of the asset is recorded and immediately written off against current revenues.

Indenture: *See* **Bond indenture**.

Inflation protection approach: An approach to endowment management in which a fixed rate of reinvestment is used to maintain the purchasing power of the endowment. The remaining income is available to be used for current spending.

Interest: The dollar amount paid by a borrower to a lender for the use of a specified amount of money.

Interest rate: The interest charged on a loan or bond expressed as a percentage of the amount borrowed.

Interest rate risk: The risk of loss of principal a bondholder faces as a consequence of an increase in the market rates of interest.

Inventory: Raw materials, supplies, or finished products held as a buffer against stock-outs.

Inventory turnover: The ratio of cost of goods sold for a period to average or ending inventory.

Investment banker: A financial institution engaged in planning, underwriting, and distributing new investment securities on behalf of the security issuer.

Lease: A financing arrangement in which the lessee gains the use of, but not ownership of, an asset.

Lessee: A party to a leasing agreement who pays for the use of an asset.

Lessor: A party to a leasing agreement who owns the property and receives payment in exchange for letting others use it.

Leverage: The use of assets or liabilities having fixed costs associated with them to produce a greater return on sales or investment than would otherwise be possible.

Line of credit: A short-term borrowing arrangement in which a financial institution agrees to lend up to a specific amount for a specific period (of a year or less) and at a given rate of interest. *See also* **Revolving line of credit**.

Liquidity: That characteristic inherent in an organization's asset structure or cash-flow pattern that provides it with the ability to meet its maturing financial obligations as they come due.

Lockbox system: A technique for accelerating funds flows from accounts or pledges receivable to cash in which local banks are authorized to pick up customer remittances directly from post office boxes, record the payments, and deposit the funds to the organization's account.

Maintenance lease: A lease that requires the lessor to perform all of the maintenance and repair work necessary to keep the property in good working order.

Matching principal of debt financing: The principal that short-term financial needs should be met with short-term funds and that long-term needs should be met with long-term funds.

Money market fund: A mutual fund holding a portfolio of money market securities.

Mortgage: The pledge of real property as security for a loan or bond issue.

Net lease: A lease arrangement in which the lessee assumes all of the risks of ownership, including maintenance, taxes, and losses in the value of the property.

Net present value: The present value of the future cash flows from a capital expenditure less the present value of the costs associated with the expenditure, both discounted at an appropriate rate of interest. It is abbreviated **NPV**.

Net working capital: Current assets minus current liabilities.

Nonprofit organization: A legally constituted, nongovernmental, nonhospital organization that has been granted an exemption from the payment of federal and state income taxes and that actively seeks to contribute to the public welfare as its principal objective.

Nontrading organization: A nonprofit organization that does not sell its products or services to its clientele.

Normative theory: A theory that describes what ought to be done to accomplish a stated objective.

NPV: *See* **Net present value**.

Operating lease: A lease arrangement in which the lessee acquires the use of the property on a period-to-period basis.

Operational accountability: The basis for accounting systems used by for-profit business enterprise in order to measure how well operations are being managed in producing profits for the owners.

PAF: *See* **Present value of an annuity factor**.

Pledges receivable: Amounts pledged by donors during a fund-raising campaign that have not yet been collected by the organization.

Positive theory: A theory that describes the way in which an economic entity behaves.

Present value: Present worth of a future payment or a number of such payments as valued at some appropriate rate of interest or discount. It is abbreviated **PV**.

Present value factor: The present value of one dollar promised at a given future time and discounted at a given interest rate. The present value factor is calculated using the general formula $1/(1 + r)^t$, where r is the interest rate and t is the period. It is abbreviated **PVF**.

Present value of an annuity factor: The present value of one dollar per period promised over a given number of periods and discounted at a given interest rate. The annuity factor is calculated using the general formula $[1 - 1/(1 + r)^t]r$, where r is the interest rate and t is the number of periods. It is abbreviated **PAF**.

Prime rate: The rate of interest that commercial banks charge their best and largest corporate customers for short-term credit.

Private foundation An organization granted a tax-exempt status under Section 501(c)(4) of the Internal Revenue Code of 1954.

Private placement: *See* **Direct placement**.

Program classification: Under fiscal triage, the sorting of programs as *healthy*, *operable*, and *dying*, according to cash-flow criterion.

Pro forma financial statements: Projected financial statements that show the future financial position or the operating results of an organization under a set of certain specified assumptions.

Prudent man rule: A statement of law that requires those who work in a fiduciary capacity to exercise discretion in their affairs equal to that of a prudent man.

Public charity: An organization that has a broad base of financial support from the public and that is operated for charitable purposes.

Public offering: A new bond issue offered for sale to the public.

PV: *See* **Present value**.

PVF: *See* **Present value factor**.

Receivables turnover The ratio of credit sales in a period to the average of year-end accounts or pledges receivable outstanding.

Refunding: Retiring an outstanding bond issue with the proceeds of a new issue.

Reorder point: The level of inventory at which an organization will place another order that will replenish the inventory held.

Repurchase agreement: A short-term purchase of any money market security from a dealer who agrees to repurchase the security at a set price plus interest at a specified later date.

Revolving line of credit: An intermediate-term loan whose principal amount outstanding "revolves" with the credit needs of the borrower.

Risk: The variability of expected future returns, cash flows, profits, sales, etc., brought about by factors beyond the control of the organization or investor.

Risk premium: The difference between the risk-free rate of interest and the stated rate of interest on a loan or investment arising from the riskiness of the borrower or security.

Sale and lease-back: An arrangement in which the original owner of the property sells it to a leasing company for cash and leases it back from the company.

Section 501(c)(3) organization: An organization granted a tax exemption under Section 501(c)(3) of the Internal Revenue Code of 1954. This is the preferred status for nonprofit organizations, since it provides both the organization and its donors and members with the largest tax benefits.

Section 501(c)(4) organization: An organization granted a tax exemption under Section 501(c)(4) of the Internal Revenue Code of 1954. The organizations classified under this section of the code are primarily private foundations.

Securities: Certain types of short-term investment media and most long-term obligations, including common stock and long-term bonds of corporations and municipalities. Marketability is the feature that distinguishes securities from other types of financial assets.

Share value basis: *See* **Unit of account.**

Sister organization: A subsidiary organization formed most often to prevent the loss of the preferred tax-exempt status of the parent organization while it pursues legislative activities generally prohibited to 501(c)(3) organizations.

Sinking fund: The required annual repayment of the principal amount of a bond issue designed to amortize it over a given period.

Stock-out: Running short of inventory.

Subordinated debenture: An unsecured, long-term bond that ranks behind all other secured debts and specified unsecured debts in the event of liquidation of an organization under bankruptcy.

Term loan: A loan of intermediate maturity (over 1 year to 10 years).

TIC: *See* **True interest cost.**

Times interest earned: The ratio of "profits" before interest to interest charges on all outstanding debt.

Total return concept: A concept of endowment income that includes interest, dividends, and capital appreciation within the definition.

Trade credit: Debt arising from purchase and sale of goods or services in commercial transactions. To the seller, it is accounts receivable; to the buyer, accounts payable.

Trade discount: *See* **Functional discount.**

Trading organization: A nonprofit organization that operates as a business in carrying on trade on a more or less continuous basis.

Treasury bill: Discounted promissory note of the United States government ranging in denominations from $10,000 to $1,000,000 with maturities of 180 days or less.

Treasury bond: An interest-bearing bond sold by the United States government.

Triage: *See* Fiscal triage.

True interest cost: A method of comparing the costs of alternative bond issues based on the present value of the debt service costs. It is abbreviated **TIC**.

Underwriting: Process of issuing new securities of a corporation by an investment banker by outright purchase of the securities at a price agreed upon in advance.

Unincorporated association: A legal form of organization created by adopting a set of articles and bylaws.

Unit of account: A method of measuring portfolio investment performance in which the portfolio is divided into shares, and the various claimants to the assets measure all transactions in terms of shares valued at current (market-determined) prices. This method is also called the **Share value basis.**

Unrelated business income: Income earned by a nonprofit organization through activities unrelated to its tax-exempt purpose. Such income earned in excess of $1,000 is taxable at normal corporate income tax rates.

Utility: The underlying value provided by the possession or use of goods or services.

Variable costs: Costs that are expected to vary with the economic activity of an organization in both the short and long run.

Wire transfer: A method of moving cash from one financial institution to another, utilizing the wire transfer facilities of the Federal Reserve System, the nation's central bank.

Working capital: In general, the total current assets of an organization. Often it is used interchangeably with the term **Net working capital**.

Zero-base budgeting: A method of reviewing programs for the purpose of reallocating resources away from nonproductive uses.

Index